BRITISH PROFESSIONAL BOXERS' RECORDS
FIRST EDITION 1993

COMPILED AND EDITED BY BOB MEE

DEDICATION

To those who were knocked out by "Bagel Boy" Nazerman...

*****   *****

Published by Bob Mee
6 The Terrace, The Green, Snitterfield, Warwickshire, CV37 0JD
Copyright, Bob Mee.

Cover Design: Glenn Richards
Produced by Bob Mee, Glenn Richards and Janet Mee.
Cover photos: Lennox Lewis - Sporting Pictures (UK) Ltd.
              Bob Fitzsimmons - Boxing News archives.

Printed and bound in England.

All rights reserved. Except where permitted under the Copyright, Designs and Patents Act, 1988, no part of this publication may be reproduced, stored in a retrieval system or transmitted in any form or by any means, without the prior permission in writing of the publisher, nor be otherwise circulated in any form of binding or cover other than that in which it is published and without a similar condition, including this condition, being imposed on the subsequent publisher.

While every effort has been made to ensure accuracy of the information contained in this book, the publisher cannot accept any legal responsibility for any errors or omissions that may take place. Are you really still reading this ?

ISBN 0 9520807 0 2

Bob Mee, 1993

INTRODUCTION

This book stands for itself: it is exactly what you see. All of the 750 or so British professional boxers who were active in 1992 are here - with a few "extras" thrown in, like Crisanto Espana, the WBA welterweight champion from Venezuela who lives in Ireland and works out of the Barney Eastwood gym, and youngsters Lee Tonks and Kenny Rainford, who are taking their first steps into the pro world in the USA.

The decision to compile the book was made in mid-November 1992. It was put together in six weeks, from the first tentative discussion to the all-night push to make the copy deadline of January 4, and was largely fitted around the "normal" everyday running of our freelance business, not to mention the Christmas and New Year celebrations. We make no secret of the fact that it was a hectic schedule, and while this is no excuse for even a single error to creep in, anyone knowing or suspecting that they have discovered one is very welcome to ring, fax or write. We are also willing to listen to constructive suggestions concerning possible improvements to any future volumes. Between the three of us, we had no previous experience of producing this kind of publication. It's been a mixture of fun, chaos, frustration and worry, but hopefully we have learned something as we have stumbled along and we trust you will find the result worthwhile.

Thanks are due to to those fighters who added to the chaos by either deciding to make comebacks in the second or third week of December after not boxing for the first 50 weeks of the year. And a special word to Tony Booth, who squeezed in a 6-rounder in Belgium on Christmas Day! We got that result via the extraordinarily helpful Dr Peter Stucki of the EBU and Swiss Federation. If any miscreant made himself a few shekels with a Christmas payday in Mali or Madagascar, we hold up our hands: OK, you've beaten us!

It would have been lovely to have done a worldwide book, if only to give more of the exotic names in boxing a mention: I promised myself I'd write about Understanding Allah of the USA and the legendary Abnormal Romeo of New Zealand one day - another ambition fulfilled! But seriously, we have no plans to infringe on the market commanded so brilliantly by Ralph Citro and Pugilato.

We have tried hard to make the book easy to read and use. For the uninitiated, professional records are in bold, amateur summaries in light type. Career totals are of professional records only. The key is simple and now more or less universally used.

- KO = Knockout.
- RSF = Referee stopped fight.
- RTD = Retired.
- DIS = Disqualification
- TDEC = Technical decision
- PTS = Points.

(S) and (M) after some points entries indicate where a decision is either split or majority, rather than unanimous. (A split verdict is a 2-1 vote by 3 judges. A majority is 2-0 with one scoring a draw.) In Britain, of course, this issue doesn't arise as we still use the referee as the solitary scoring official.

Finally, thanks to all those who helped support this venture by taking advertising space. It is genuinely appreciated. A full index of our advertisers is at the end of the book.

Bob Mee, Glenn Richards, Janet Mee.   January 1993.

Ojay ABRAHAMS
Welterweight
Watford, born London 17 December 1964
Vauxhall Motors ABC

1991
Sep 21	Gordon Webster	w rsf 3	Tottenham 10-7
Oct 26	Mick Reid	w rsf 5	Brentwood 10-7
Nov 26	John Corcoran	w pts 6	Bethnal Green 10-8

1992
Jan 21	Dave Andrews	drew 6	Norwich 10-8
Mar 31	Marty Duke	w rsf 2	Norwich 10-10-4
May 19	Michael Smyth	l pts 6	Cardiff 10-7
Jun 16	Ricky Mabbett	w pts 6	Dagenham 10-9
Oct 13	Vince Rose	l rsf 3*	Mayfair 10-9

Fights 8 Won 5 Lost 2 Drawn 1

Kevin ADAMSON
Light-middleweight
Walthamstow born 19 February 1968
Waltham Forest ABC
1989 NE London ABA light-middleweight semi-final (w rsf 2 P Riley, l T Taylor)

1989
Jul 17	Calton Myers	w rsf 1	Stanmore 11-1-4

1990
Dec 4	Darron Griffiths	l rsf 4	Southend 11-4

1991
Nov 12	Danny Shinkwin	w rsf 4*	Milton Keynes 11-2

1992
Apr 30	Wayne Appleton	w rsf 2	Bayswater 11-0

Fights 4 Won 3 Lost 1

Tanveer AHMED
Lightweight
Glasgow
Southpaw
Blantyre ABC & Glasgow Transport ABC
1989 Scottish ABA lightweight semi-final (w rsf 2 F King, w rsf 3 P Halbert, l C Kane)
1990 Scottish ABA lightweight prelim (l H Collins)
1991 Scotland (v En, l rsf 1 P Ramsey; v Ir, l M Winter)
1991 Scottish ABA lightweight final (w rsf 3 M Clegg, w W Leckie, l A McDowall)

1992
Oct 22	John B.Kelly	w pts 6	Glasgow 9-8
Dec 1	Sean Armstrong	l pts 6	Hartlepool 9-9-8

Fights 2 Won 1 Lost 1

Henry AKINWANDE

Heavyweight
Dulwich born 12 October 1965
Lynn ABC

1986 ABA heavyweight final (w D Stewart, w A Denham, w I Joseph, w D Simmonds, w rsf 1 R Flanagan, w L Maxwell, l dis 3 E Cardouza)

1986 England (v Pol, w J Dyla; v Ire, w T de Loughrey)

1987 ABA heavy finalist (w R McKenzie, w rsf 1 T Denham, w A Kerrick, w rtd 1 M Stevens, w G Sanderson, w ko 1 K McCormack, l J Moran)

1987 England (v Sco, w ko 1 D McKay; v Ire, w P Douglas; v Pol, l A Golota; v Cze, l L Husarik)

1988 ABA heavyweight champion (w rsf 1 T Denham, w M Stevens, w D Westover, w S Henry, w rsf 1 R Martin, w H Hylton)

1988 Seoul Olympics heavyweight prelim (l A Vanderlijde, Hol)

1988 England (v Cze, w R Gavenciak; v WGer, w B Teuchert)

1989 ABA heavyweight champion (w J Lewis, w rsf 1 M Lynch, w ko 1 B Auckett, w rsf 2 D Abbott, w rsf 1 C Coughlan, w H Hide)

1989
Oct 4	Carlton Headley	w ko 1	Albert Hall 14-12
Nov 8	Dennis Bailey	w rsf 2	Wembley GH 15-4
Dec 6	Paul Neilson	w rsf 1	Wembley GH 14-13

1990
Jan 10	John Fairbairn	w rsf 1*	Albert Hall 14-10-4
Mar 14	Warren Thompson	w pts 6	Albert Hall 15-1-8
May 9	Mike Robinson	w ko 1	Wembley CC 15-4
Oct 10	Tracy Thomas	w pts 6	Albert Hall 15-4
Dec 12	Francois Yrius	w rsf 1	Albert Hall 15-8

1991
Mar 6	J.B.Williamson	w rsf 2	Wembley 15-8
Jun 6	Ramon Voorn	w pts 8	Barking 15-10
Jun 28	Marshall Tillman	w pts 8	Nice
Oct 9	Gipsy John Fury	w ko 3	Manchester
	(eliminator, British heavyweight title)		
Dec 6	Tim Bullock	w rsf 3	Dusseldorf 15-11-4

1992
Feb 29	Young Joe Louis	w rsf 3	Issy-les-Moulineaux 15-10
Mar 26	Michael Richards	w rsf 2	Telford 16-0
Apr 10	Lumbala Tshibamba	w pts 8	Carquefou
Jun 5	Kimmuel Odum	w dis 6	Marseille 16-0
Jul 18	Steve Garber	w rtd 2	Manchester 15-11
Dec 19	Axel Schulz	drew 12	Berlin 15-0-6
	(vacant European heavyweight title)		

Fights 19 Won 18 Lost 0 Drawn 1

Korso ALEAIN

Light-welterweight
Paddington, born Algiers 18 October 1962

1992
Mar 6	Everald Williams	l ko 6	Battersea 10-3
Apr 30	Erwin Edwards	w pts 6	Bayswater 9-13-12
May 17	Brian Coleman	w rsf 5	Harringay 10-1-8
Sep 26	Paul Ryan	l ko 4	Olympia 10-0

Fights 4 Won 2 Lost 2

Raziq ALI

Welterweight
Bradford born 14 September 1972
Kingston ABC
1992 Yorkshire & Humberside ABA light-welterweight final (w ko 3 J Bretton, l rsf 2 M Barker)

1992
Sep 8	Wayne Panayiotiou	w pts 6	Doncaster 10-12
Oct 5	Sean Baker	l pts 6	Bristol 10-9-12

Fights 2 Won 1 Lost 1

Michael ALLDIS

Bantamweight
Crawley born 25 May 1968
Crawley ABC
1989 Southern ABA flyweight final (l rsf 3 J Armour)
1990 Southern ABA bantamweight champion (w.o., w ko 1 D Simpkin, w rsf 2 B Trainer, l P Lloyd)
1991 ABA bantamweight semi-final (w rtd 2 J Matthews, w D Dainty, w N McCallum, l D Hardie)
1991 England (v Pol, l P Dolinski)
1992 ABA bantamweight final (w M Wright, w C Slatcher, w D Dainty, w A Mulholland, w.o., l P Mullings)

1992
Sep 15	Ceri Farrell	w rsf 3	Crystal Palace 8-9
Nov 10	Kid McAuley	w pts 6	Dagenham 8-10-6
Dec 12	Kid McAuley	w ko 1	Muswell Hill 8-12-12

Fights 3 Won 3

Dean ALLEN

Light-heavyweight
Swansea born 3 August 1967
Bonymaen ABC
1989 Welsh ABA light-heavyweight semi-final (l J Mitchell)

1991
Jan 24	Max McCracken	l pts 6	Brierley Hill 12-6
Apr 24	Paul Hanlon	w pts 6	Port Talbot 13-1
Nov 13	Terry Johnson	w rsf 2*	Liverpool 12-5

1992
Sep 7	Phil Soundy	l rtd 4	Bethnal Green 13-0

Fights 4 Won 2 Lost 2

Mark ALLEN

Light-welterweight
Denaby born Mexborough 11 January 1970
Real name: Mark Hodgson
No amateur experience

1992
Mar 24	Jamie Morris	l pts 6	Wolverhampton 10-2
Jun 4	Blue Butterworth	l rsf 5	Burnley 10-2-8
Nov 10	Bobby Guynan	l rsf 2	Dagenham 9-13
Dec 9	Simon Hamblett	drew 6	Stoke 9-10

Fights 4 Lost 3 Drawn 1

Jimmy ALSTON

Light-middleweight
Preston born 2 February 1967

1991 Northern ABA light-middleweight champion (w P Hennegan, w A Thompson, w R Murray, w M Chicocki, l L Ferrie)

1992 East Lancs & Cheshire ABA light-middleweight champion (w C Walker, w J Whiteside, l D Peters)

1992
Dec 7	Spencer Alton	w pts 6	Manchester 11-1

Fights 1 Won 1

Spencer ALTON

Middleweight
Derby born 4 October 1966

Askam ABC   1987 Midlands ABA middleweight final (w J Fearn, w O Comrie, l rsf 1 G Lewis)

1988
Jun 13	Ian Midwood-Tate	w pts 6	Manchester 11-1-8
Jul 10	Lou Ayres	l pts 6	Eastbourne 11-0
Aug 31	Ian Midwood-Tate	l pts 6	Stoke 11-1
Sep 13	Steve West	l ko 3	Battersea 10-13
Oct 19	Wilbert Halliday	w ko 6	Evesham 10-9
Oct 31	Michael Oliver	w rsf 2	Leicester 10-9
Nov 14	Gary Booth	l rsf 7*	Manchester 11-5
Dec 13	Paul Dolan	w rtd 4*	Glasgow 10-13
Dec 20	Wayne Ellis	l rtd 4*	Swansea 11-3

1989
Jan 27	Neil Patterson	w ko 1	Durham 11-1
Jan 31	Brian Robinson	l pts 6	Reading 11-4
Feb 15	Mark Holden	drew 6	Stoke 11-6
Mar 6	Mark Howell	l pts 8	Manchester 11-3
Mar 21	Ricky Nelson	l pts 6	Cottingham 11-0
Apr 4	Graham Burton	l rsf 3*	Sheffield
May 9	Wayne Ellis	l rsf 3	St Albans 11-7
Jun 20	Peter Vosper	l pts 6	Plymouth 11-7
Jul 6	Ian Strudwick	l pts 8	Chigwell 11-6
Sep 26	Frank Eubanks	w pts 6	Oldham 11-2
Oct 10	Terry Morrill	l pts 6	Hull 10-12
Oct 17	Peter Vosper	drew 8	Plymouth 11-10
Nov 8	Neville Brown	l rsf 4*	Wembley GH 11-9
Dec 20	Mick Morgan	w rsf 5*	Swansea 11-13

1990
Jan 15	Andy Marlow	drew 6	Northampton 11-8
Jan 30	Darren Pilling	l pts 6	Manchester 11-2
Feb 13	Colin Pitters	w pts 6	Wolverhampton 11-5
Feb 26	Antoine Tarver	l pts 4	Crystal Palace 11-10
Mar 22	Richard Carter	l pts 6	Wolverhampton 11-8-8
May 24	Andy Flute	w rsf 1*	Dudley 11-4
Jun 21	Paul Murray	w pts 6	Alfreton 11-4

1991
inactive

1992
Sep 10	David Johnson	l pts 6	Sunderland 11-7
Oct 23	Terry French	l pts 6	Gateshead 11-9
Dec 7	Jimmy Alston	l pts 6	Manchester

Fights 33 Won 10 Lost 20 Drawn 3

Trevor AMBROSE
Welterweight
Leicester born 8 September 1963
Central ABC

1990
Feb 19	Ian Thomas	l rsf 3	Kettering 10-7
Apr 6	Colin Pitters	w pts 6	Telford 10-10
Apr 24	Barry Messam	w rsf 4	Stoke 10-9
May 14	Gordon Blair	l ko 5	Northampton 10-10
Sep 12	Dave Fallone	w ko 3	Battersea 10-7
Oct 23	Dave Lake	w pts 6	Leicester 10-9-4
Nov 14	Eddie King	w rsf 3	Doncaster 10-6
Nov 21	Andreas Panayi	w rsf 5	Solihull 10-9

1991
Feb 14	Adrian Riley	w ko 6	Southampton 10-10
Mar 28	Richard O'Brien	w rsf 1	Alfreton
Apr 25	Gary Logan	l pts 8	Mayfair 10-10
Jul 3	Darren Dyer	l pts 6	Brentwood 10-9
Sep 24	Willie Beattie	l pts 8	Glasgow 10-7

1992
Mar 11	John Davies	l rsf 5	Cardiff 10-7
May 19	Paul Jones	l pts 6	Cardiff 10-9

Fights 15 Won 8 Lost 7

Dean AMORY
Super-featherweight
Birmingham born 2 July 1969
Kingshurst ABC
1989 Birmingham ABA featherweight final (l P Ramsey)
1990 South Midlands ABA featherweight semi-final (l Y Vorajee)
1991 Midlands ABA featherweight champion (w rsf 2 M Harris, w Y Vorajee, w.o., withdrew)
1992 ABA lightweight champion (w dis 3 K Price, w J Gonzales, w D Kehoe, w rsf 1 D Sowden, w J Wilson, w P J Gallagher, w M Gowans, w M Newton)

1992
Oct 21	Brian Hickey	w pts 6	Stoke 9-5

Fights 1 Won 1

Derek AMORY
Featherweight
Birmingham born 12 January 1966
Kingshurst ABC
1984 Midlands ABA bantamweight champion (w P Walters, w M Markie, l M Scholey)
1985 Midlands ABA bantamweight champion (w K Kearney, w M Greenwood, w rsf 3* S Murphy, l G Dainty)
1986 Midlands ABA featherweight final (l rsf 3 C Lynch)

1986
Sep 25	Roy Williams	w ko 2	Wolverhampton 8-12	
Oct 23	Shane Porter	drew 6	Birmingham 9-0	
Nov 3	Mark Bignell	w rsf 1	Edgbaston	
Nov 18	Carl Parry	l pts 6	Swansea 8-12-8	

1987
Jan 26	Tony Heath	w pts 8	Nottingham 8-13	
Mar 10	Mike Whalley	l rsf 2	Manchester 9-0	CTD...

(Derek AMORY ctd)

May 9	Sean Murphy	l rsf 2	Battersea 8-10-12
Sep 30	Lambsy Kayani	drew 8	Solihull 9-2-4
Nov 18	Carl Parry	w pts 8	Solihull 8-13-8
Dec 7	Graham O'Malley	w pts 8	Birmingham
Dec 14	Craig Windsor	l pts 6	Edgbaston 9-1-4
1988			
Jan 20	Lambsy Kayani	w pts 8	Solihull 9-2-8
Feb 24	Tony Heath	w pts 8	Leicester 9-0-4
Jun 17	John Hyland	w rsf 3*	Edgbaston 9-1-8
Sep 28	Colin Lynch	l pts 10	Solihull 9-0
	(vacant Midlands featherweight title)		
Oct 27	Dave George	w pts 8	Birmingham 9-0
Nov 15	Joe Donohoe	l pts 8	NSC 9-2-4
Nov 23	Patrick Kamy	l rsf 2	Solihull 9-2-4
1989			
Jan 25	Russell Davison	l pts 8	Solihull 9-1-4
Mar 1	Henry Armstrong	l pts 8	Stoke 9-1
May 10	Peter English	l pts 8	Solihull 9-2
Oct 4	Mark Holt	l pts 10	Solihull 8-13-8
	(Midlands featherweight title)		
1990			
Apr 30	Peter Judson	w pts 6	Brierley Hill 9-3
Sep 3	Miguel Matthews	w pts 6	Dudley 9-2
Sep 24	Noel Carroll	l pts 8	Manchester 9-2
Oct 8	James Drummond	w pts 8	Cleethorpes 8-13
Oct 15	Jamie McBride	w rtd 4*	Brierley Hill 9-1
Dec 13	Darren Elsdon	l pts 6	Hartlepool 9-4
1991			
Jan 29	Carl Roberts	w pts 4	Stockport 9-2
Mar 18	Joe Donohue	l pts 8	NSC 9-1-8
Jun 17	Kelton McKenzie	l rsf 6	Edgbaston 9-2
Oct 7	Ervine Blake	l pts 6	Birmingham 9-2
1992			
Jan 22	John Williams	l pts 6	Cardiff 9-8
Feb 11	Jimmy Clark	l pts 6	Barking 9-5
May 9	Luis Rolon	l ko 7	Madrid
Oct 28	Barrie Kelley	l pts 6	Cardiff 9-4-8

Fights 36 Won 14 Lost 20 Drawn 2

Francis AMPOFO

Flyweight
Bethnal Green born Kumasi, Ghana 5 June 1967
Lion ABC
1988 NE London ABA flyweight final (l ko 3 D Dent)
1989 London ABA flyweight champion (l R Beard, rplcd Beard, w S Osuji, l J Lyon)

1990			
Jan 31	Neil Parry	w pts 6	Bethnal Green 8-2
Mar 6	Robbie Regan	l pts 6	Bethnal Green 8-3
May 29	Eric George	w rsf 3*	Bethnal Green 8-3
Sep 12	Eric George	w ko 2	Bethnal Green 8-1
1991			
Mar 26	Ricky Beard	w pts 8	Bethnal Green 8-0
Jun 22	Neil Johnston	w rsf 2*	Earls Court 8-2
Sep 3	Robbie Regan	w rsf 11*	Cardiff 7-13-12
	(British flyweight title)		

Dec 17	Robbie Regan (British flyweight title)	l pts 12	Cardiff 7-13-8
1992			
Feb 25	Ricky Beard	w pts 8	Crystal Palace 8-3-12
Jun 16	Shaun Norman	w rsf 4*	Dagenham 8-2
Dec 22	James Drummond (vacant British flyweight title)	w pts 12	Mayfair

Fights 11 Won 9 Lost 2

Colin ANDERSON

Welterweight
Leicester born 7 June 1962

1983			
Sep 30	Wayne Trigg	w pts 4	Leicester
1984			
Feb 14	Peter Bowen	w pts 6	Wolverhampton
Feb 20	Nicky Day	drew 6	Mayfair
Mar 15	Wayne Trigg	l rsf 2	Leicester
Oct 1	Joey Morris	l pts 6	Leicester
1985-91 inactive			
1992			
Dec 2	Chris Mulcahy	l pts 6	Bardon 10-11

Fights 6 Won 2 Lost 3 Drawn 1

David ANDERSON

Lightweight
Glasgow born 23 December 1965
Bellahouston ABC
1983 Scottish ABA bantamweight final (l D Lee)
1984 ABA bantamweight final (w D Leith, w S Murphy, l J Hyland)
1986 ABA featherweight final (w Lawless, w C Kane, w C Lynch, l rsf 3 P Hodkinson)
1987 Scottish ABA lightweight champion (w L Crampsey, w J Milne, w D Robb, l A Hall)
1987 European Championships lightweight (w Kujtin, Yug; w Toikkanen, Fin; l w/o Chuprenski, Bul)
1987 Scotland (v Wal, w rsf 3 L Davies)
1988 Scotland (v Eng, w M Ayers)
1988 ABA featherweight champ (w T Hilton, w S Mann, w D Brown, w A Ewen, w J Irwin, w C McMillan)
1988 Olympic Games featherweight (w D Damigella, Arg; w P Fitzgerald, Ire; l rsf 2 R Tuur, Hol)
1989 Scottish ABA featherweight champion (w rsf 1 H McCutcheon, w I McGirr, w J Stewart, withdrew)
1989 European Championships bronze medal (w B Espensen, Den; w E Tchuprenski, Bul; withdrew)
1990 Commonwealth Games bronze medal (w rsf 3 A Aba, PNG; w P Richardson, Eng; l G Nyakana, Uga)

1990			
Sep 25	Junaid Musah	w rsf 3	Glasgow 9-9
Oct 9	Alan Peacock	w rsf 3*	Glasgow 9-9
Dec 10	Chris Bennett	w rsf 7	Glasgow 9-5
1991			
Feb 11	Steve Pollard	w pts 6	Glasgow 9-5
Apr 15	Tony Foster	w pts 8	Glasgow 9-5-8
Sep 24	Ian Honeywood	w pts 8	Glasgow 9-12-10
Nov 28	Pete Roberts	w rsf 3	Glasgow 9-8
1992			
Sep 11	Kevin Toomey	w pts 8	Glasgow 9-9
Oct 22	Kevin McKenzie	w rtd 3*	Glasgow 9-8

Fights 9 Won 9

Shaun ANDERSON

Bantamweight
Maybole, born Girvan 20 September 1969
Southpaw
Sydney Street ABC
1992 Scotland (v En, l P Lloyd; v Ir, w P Norton)
1992 Scottish ABA bantamweight final (w R Silverstein, l J Murray)

1992
May 29	Tucker Thomas	w rsf 1	Glasgow 8-7
Sep 11	Mark Hargreaves	w pts 6	Glasgow 8-7-8
Dec 10	Graham McGrath	w pts 6	Glasgow 8-8

Fights 3 Won 3

Alfie ANDREWS

Light-middleweight
Birmingham born 29 April 1964
Nechells ABC

1988
Oct 11	Mohammed Ayub Malik	w pts 6	Wolverhampton 10-7
Nov 22	Frank Graham	l rsf 6	Wolverhampton 11-3

1989
Mar 1	Peter Reid	l rsf 2	Stoke 11-4
May 8	Ernie Loveridge	l pts 6	Edgbaston 11-3
Oct 2	Paul Walters	l rsf 5*	Hanley 11-2
Nov 13	Andre Wharton	l pts 6	Brierley Hill 11-2

1990
Feb 5	Andre Wharton	l rsf 4	Brierley Hill 11-2
Jun 4	Dave Whittle	l pts 6	Edgbaston 11-0
Oct 8	Tony Booth	l rsf 3	Cleethorpes 11-0
Nov 13	Wayne Appleton	l rsf 5	Edgbaston 11-1

1991
Apr 15	Scott Newman	l rsf 1	Birmingham 11-2
May 30	Darren Morris	l rsf 3	Birmingham 10-13

1992
May 21	Warren Stephens	w pts 6	Cradley Heath 10-9
Oct 30	Warren Stephens	w pts 6	NEC 11-0

Fights 14 Won 3 Lost 11

Dave ANDREWS

Welterweight
Merthyr born 22 July 1968
Trelewis ABC
Two Welsh junior titles, 2 Gaelic gold medals
1986 Welsh ABA welterweight semi-final (l C Piper)
1987 NABC Class C champion (w P Mulcahy)
1987 Welsh ABA welterweight champion (w M Morrison, l T Morrill)
1987 Wales (v Ir, l B Walsh)
1988 Welsh ABA welterweight final (l J Hudd)

1988
Sep 12	Ian Midwood-Tate	l rtd 4*	Northampton 10-12-4
Dec 5	Robert Dugdale	w pts 6	Northampton 11-0

1989
Jan 16	Graham Burton	l pts 6	Northampton 11-1
Mar 6	Jimmy Thornton	w pts 6	Northampton 10-10
Mar 28	Jim Beckett	l pts 6	Chigwell 10-11

Jun 8	John Davies	l rsf 3	Cardiff 10-10-12
1990			
Feb 26	Rocky Bryan	l rsf 2	Crystal Palace 10-10
Sep 17	Julian Eavis	w pts 6	Cardiff 10-9
Nov 19	Andrew Williams	w rsf 1*	Cardiff 10-7-12
1991			
Mar 5	Brian Cullen	w rsf 1	Cardiff 10-10-12
Apr 11	Robert McCracken	l rtd 4	Willenhall 10-10
Nov 19	Paul Dyer	l pts 6	Norwich 10-8
Dec 17	Mark Atkins	w rsf 3	Cardiff 10-8
1992			
Jan 21	Ojay Abrahams	drew 6	Norwich 10-11
Feb 9	Paul Burke	l pts 6	Bradford 10-7-8
Mar 3	Howard Clarke	l rsf 3*	Cradley Heath 10-10

Fights 16 Won 6 Lost 9 Drawn 1

Dennis ANDRIES

Cruiserweight
Hackney, born Buxton, Guyana 5 November 1953
Colvestone ABC
1978 English ABA light-heavyweight semi-final (w ko 1 E Wilmot, l D Bailey, rplcd Bailey, l V Smith)

1978

May 16	Ray Pearce	w ko 2	Newport
Jun 1	Mark Cumber	w ko 1	Heathrow
Jun 20	Bonny McKenzie	l pts 8	Southend
Sep 18	Ken Jones	w pts 6	WSC
Oct 31	Neville Estaban	w pts 6	Barnsley 12-0-8
Nov 14	Les McAteer	drew 8	Birkenhead
Nov 22	Tom Collins	w pts 8	Southend
Dec 4	Glen McEwan	w rsf 7	Stoke
1979			
Jan 22	Bunny Johnson	l pts 10	Wolverhampton
Jan 30	Tom Collins	w ko 6	Southend
Apr 5	Francis Hand	w rsf 8	Liverpool
Jun 6	Bonny McKenzie	w pts 8	Stoke
Sep 17	Johnny Waldron	w rtd 10*	WSC
	(Southern light-heavyweight title)		
1980			
Feb 27	Bunny Johnson	l pts 15	Stoke
	(British light-heavyweight title)		
Apr 17	Mustapha Wasajja	l pts 8	Copenhagen
Jun 18	Chris Lawson	w rsf 8	Stoke 12-7
1981			
Mar 23	Shaun Chalcraft	w pts 10	WSC
	(Southern light-heavyweight title)		
Sep 16	Liam Coleman	w rsf 6	Stoke
Oct 12	David Pearce	l rsf 7	Bloomsbury
Nov 23	Alek Penarski	w pts 10	Chesterfield
1982			
Mar 15	Tom Collins	l pts 15	Bloomsbury
	(British light-heavyweight title)		
Aug 10	Keith Bristol	w pts 10	Strand
	(Southern light-heavyweight title)		
1983			
Feb 28	Karl Canwell	w ko 4	Strand
	(Southern light-heavyweight title)		

CTD...

(Dennis ANDRIES ctd.)

Date	Opponent	Result	Venue
May 19	Chris Lawson	w ko 4	Porchester Hall
Sep 22	Keith Bristol (Southern light-heavyweight title)	w ko 4	Strand 12-6
1984			
Jan 26	Tom Collins (British light-heavyweight title)	w pts 12	Strand 12-5
Apr 6	Tom Collins (British light-heavyweight title)	w pts 12	Watford 12-7
Oct 10	Devon Bailey (British light-heavyweight title)	w ko 12	Shoreditch 12-4-8
1985			
Mar 23	Jose Seys	w rsf 3	Strand 12-7-12
May 7	Jeff Meachum	w ko 4	New Orleans
May 25	Tim Broady	w rsf 5	Atlantic City
Jun 6	Marcus Dorsey	w ko 3	Lafayette
Dec 11	Alex Blanchard (European light-heavyweight title)	drew 12	Fulham 12-5-12
1986			
Feb 13	Keith Bristol (British light-heavyweight title)	w rsf 6	Longford 12-6-12
Apr 30	J.B. Williamson (WBC light-heavyweight title)	w pts 12 (s)	Edmonton
Sep 10	Tony Sibson (WBC & British light-heavyweight titles)	w rsf 9	Muswell Hill
1987			
Mar 7	Thomas Hearns (WBC light-heavyweight title)	l rsf 10	Detroit 12-5-8
Oct 6	Robert Folley	w pts 10	Phoenix 12-7-8
1988			
Feb 20	Jamie Howe	w pts 10	Detroit 12-5
May 22	Bobby Czyz	w pts 10	Atlantic City 12-7-8
Sep 10	Tony Harrison	w rtd 7	Auburn Hills 12-6
Oct 17	Paul Madison	w rsf 4	Tucson 12-10-8
1989			
Feb 21	Tony Willis (vacant WBC light-heavyweight title)	w rsf 5	Tucson
Jun 24	Jeff Harding (WBC light-heavyweight title)	l rsf 12	Atlantic City 12-7
Oct 26	Art Jimmerson	w pts 10	Atlantic City
1990			
Jan 20	Clarismundo Silva	w rsf 7	Auburn Hills
Jul 28	Jeff Harding (WBC light-heavyweight title)	w ko 7	Melbourne 12-6-4
Oct 10	Sergio Merani (WBC light-heavyweight title)	w rtd 5*	Albert Hall 12-5-4
1991			
Jan 19	Guy Waters (WBC light-heavyweight title)	w pts 12	Adelaide 12-6-12
Sep 11	Jeff Harding (WBC light-heavyweight title)	l pts 12 (m)	Hammersmith 12-7
Nov 15	Ed Neblett	w rsf 4	Tampa 13-7
Dec 11	Paul Madison	w rtd 8	Duluth, Mn 13-9
1992			
Feb 27	Akim Tafer (vacant European cruiserweight title)	l pts 12 (m)	Beausoleil 13-7-12

Fights 53 Won 41 Lost 10 Drawn 2

Derek ANGOL
Cruiserweight
Gravesend born 28 November 1964
Lynn ABC
1983 Young England (v EGer, w rsf 3 Rath; w R Suetovius)
1984 Young England (v USA. w rsf 3 R Hall)
1984 London ABA light-heavyweight champion (w L Gent, w D Simmonds, w B Parkes, l T Wilson)
1985 Young England (v USA, l A Washington)
1985 East Berlin TSC (l dis 3 H Muss, EGer)
1985 London ABA light-heavyweight final (w H Lawson, l rsf 2 J Beckles)
1986 London ABA light-heavyweight final (w rsf 1 A Mohammed, l J Beckles)

1986
Date	Opponent	Result	Venue
Dec 15	Gus Mendes	w rsf 3	NSC 13-0-8

1987
Date	Opponent	Result	Venue
Jan 22	Abner Blackstock	w pts 6	Bethnal Green 13-2
Mar 12	Patrick Collins	w ko 6	NSC 13-6-8
Apr 9	Mick Cordon	w rsf 4	Bethnal Green 13-8
Oct 8	Lennie Howard	w rsf 5	Bethnal Green 13-5-4

1988
Date	Opponent	Result	Venue
Feb 15	Abner Blackstock	w rsf 6	NSC
Mar 14	Alek Penarski	w ko 2	NSC 13-10
Apr 13	Jonjo Greene	w pts 6	Bethnal Green 13-5
May 5	Cordwell Hylton	w rsf 5	Bethnal Green 13-9-12
Oct 17	Roy Smith	w rsf 1	NSC
Dec 19	Jack Johnson	w ko 1	NSC 13-10

1989
Date	Opponent	Result	Venue
Jan 18	Rick Enis	w rsf 3	Albert Hall 13-10
Mar 8	Jamie Howe	w pts 8	Albert Hall 13-9
Mar 29	Teo Arvizu	w rsf 3	Wembley 13-9
Jun 7	Andre Crowder	w rsf 3	Wembley 13-6-8
Oct 4	Raymond Gonzalez	w rsf 2	Albert Hall 13-11-8
Nov 30	Apollo Sweet (Commonwealth cruiserweight title)	w pts 12	Southwark 13-7-8

1990
Date	Opponent	Result	Venue
Feb 8	Eddie Smith	w rsf 2	Southwark 13-13
Mar 14	Andy Straughn (Commonwealth cruiserweight title)	w ko 8	Albert Hall 13-8
Oct 4	Manfred Jassmann	w rsf 8	Bethnal Green 13-9-12

1991
Date	Opponent	Result	Venue
Jan 10	Dan Murphy	w rsf 9	Battersea
Feb 13	Dave Garside (Commonwealth and vacant British cruiserweight titles)	w rsf 2	Wembley CC 13-7-8
Apr 17	Yves Monsieur	w rsf 2	Albert Hall 13-10
May 8	Tee Jay (British and Commonwealth cruiserweight titles)	w rsf 3	Albert Hall
Oct 17	Dave Russell (Commonwealth cruiserweight title)	w rsf 4	Southwark 13-8

1992
Date	Opponent	Result	Venue
May 16	Robert Clevenger	w ko 2	Muswell Hill 13-10-8
Jul 25	Tyrone Booze (vacant WBO cruiserweight title)	l ko 7	Manchester
Oct 22	Akim Tafer (European cruiserweight title)	l rsf 10	Epernay 13-7-12

Fights 28 Won 26 Lost 2

Joel ANI

Welterweight
Hackney born 6 February 1971

1992
Oct 22   Danny Quacoe   w ko 1   Bethnal Green 10-7-14

Fights 1 Won 1

Mark ANTONY

Welterweight
Worksop born 24 January 1968
Real name: Mark Brooks
Worksop ABC

1987
Nov 16	Robbie Bowen	l ko 5	Stratford 10-0

1988
Mar 22	Paul Bowen	l rsf 3*	Wolverhampton 9-8
Nov 14	Phil Lashley	w rsf 2	Stratford 9-6
Nov 21	Paul Chedgzoy	w ko 2	Leicester 9-5-12
Dec 1	Andrew Robinson	w pts 6	Stafford 9-7
Dec 14	Paul Bowen	l pts 6	Evesham 9-11

1989
Feb 2	Shaun Cooper	l ko 3	Wolverhampton 9-9-8
Apr 20	Andrew Brightman	w pts 6	Weston-super-Mare 9-12
May 17	Mark Tibbs	l pts 6	Millwall 9-12
May 29	Michael Close	l pts 6	Liverpool 9-10
Sep 4	Warren Bowers	l pts 6	Cleethorpes 10-0
Oct 4	Karl Taylor	l ko 2	Stafford 9-9
Dec 6	Peter Bowen	l pts 6	Stoke 9-10-8

1990
Feb 13	Peter Bowen	w rsf 1	Wolverhampton 9-10
Mar 7	Stuart Rimmer	w rsf 1	Doncaster 9-9
Mar 21	Nick Hall	l pts 6	Solihull 9-10
Mar 27	Shaun Cogan	l ko 1	Wolverhampton 10-2
May 21	Tony Feliciello	l rtd 2	Cleethorpes 9-10-4
Jun 21	Andrew Robinson	w pts 6	Alfreton 10-0
Oct 30	Billy Schwer	l rsf 2	Wembley 9-10
Dec 3	Nigel Senior	w pts 8	Cleethorpes 9-10
Dec 12	Richard Woolgar	l rsf 5	Basildon 10-1

1991
Mar 5	Jim Moffat	l pts 6	Glasgow 10-2
Mar 12	Wayne Windle	l ko 1	Mansfield 9-13
Nov 12	Shaun Cooper	l ko 1	Wolverhampton 9-12

1992
Jan 20	Jamie Morris	w rsf 5	Coventry 10-2
Feb 11	Billy Robinson	l rsf 5	Wolverhampton 10-2
Mar 11	Simon Hamblett	w ko 1	Stoke
May 11	Patrick Delargy	l pts 6	Coventry 10-1-8
Jun 4	Darren Powell	w ko 2	Burnley 10-3
Nov 23	Darren McInulty	l pts 6	Coventry 10-8
Dec 7	Spencer McCracken	l ko 1	Birmingham 10-8

Fights 32 Won 11 Lost 21

Nick APPIAH

Welterweight
Hayes born 29 November 1968
Lynn ABC & Hanwell ABC
1991 NW London ABA welterweight final (w J Paul, l V Rose)
1992 SE London ABA welterweight semi-final (l A Schembri)

1992
Oct 29   Michael Dick   w pts 6   Hayes 10-7

Fights 1 Won 1

Wayne APPLETON

Light-middleweight
Pontefract, born 9 November 1967
Sharlston ABC
1990 Yorkshire & Humberside ABA light-middleweight prelim (l T Massey)

1990
Nov 13   Alfie Andrews   w rsf 5   Edgbaston 11-0
Nov 26   Stuart Good   w ko 4   Lewisham 10-8
Dec 10   Wayne Timmins   w ko 4   Birmingham 10-10
1991
Mar 15   Andre Wharton   l rsf 7*   Willenhall 11-3
Nov 14   Dave Hindmarsh   w rsf 8   Edinburgh 10-12-8
1992
Apr 30   Kevin Adamson   l rsf 2   Bayswater 10-13-8

Fights 6 Won 4 Lost 2

Lee ARCHER

Light-heavyweight
Dudley, born West Bromwich 3 January 1971
Priory ABC
1991 Birmingham ABA light-heavyweight final (l L Page)

1991
Nov 12   Paul Murray   w pts 6   Wolverhampton 12-6
1992
Mar 24   Darryl Ritchie   w pts 6   Wolverhampton 12-8
Apr 28   Carl Smallwood   l pts 6   Wolverhampton 12-8-8
May 18   Marc Rowley   w pts 6   Bardon 12-7
Oct 5   Paul Murray   w pts 6   Bardon 12-12
Oct 13   Paul Murray   w pts 6   Wolverhampton 12-12
Oct 23   Ian Henry   l rtd 1*   Gateshead 12-7
Nov 24   Zak Chelli   l pts 6   Wolverhampton 12-7

Fights 8 Won 5 Lost 3

John ARMOUR

Bantamweight
Chatham born 26 October 1968
Southpaw
St Mary's ABC
1984 National Schools final (l G Naylor)
1986 Young England (v EGer, l Hinz)
1986 Southern ABA light-flyweight champion
1987 Young England (v EGer, l rsf 1 J Quast)
1987 England (v Ire, l P Buttimer)
1987 Southern ABA light-flyweight champion (w A Derry, l rsf 1 M Reynolds)   CTD

(John ARMOUR ctd)

1988 Southern ABA flyweight champion (w rsf 3 A Smith, w rsf 2 B Trainor, w rsf 3 M Whetton, l J Lyon)
1988 England (v Cze, w l Misco; v WGer, w U Besken; v Ire, l J Lawlor)
1988 Acropolis Cup (l P Wartelle, Fr)   1989 England (v Sco, l A Docherty)
1989 Southern ABA flyweight champion (w rsf 3 M Aldis, w rsf 3 R Williams, l J McLean)
1989 Silver medal, Canada Cup (w J McLean, Sc; l De Leon, DR)
1990 ABA flyweight champion (w A Smith, w R Williams, w M Horobin, w rsf 3 S Rees, w P Ingle)
1990 Gold medal, Canada Cup (w Gonzales, Mx; w Mikaielan, USSR; w.o.)

1990
Sep 24	Lupe Castro	w pts 6	Lewisham 8-3
Oct 31	Juan Camero	w rsf 4	Crystal Palace 8-3

1991
Jan 21	Elijiro Mejia	w rsf 1	Crystal Palace 8-9
Sep 30	Pat Maher	w ko 1	Albert Hall 8-4
Oct 29	Peter Buckley	w pts 6	Albert Hall 8-4-12
Dec 14	Gary Hickman	w rsf 6	Bexleyheath 8-7

1992
Mar 25	Miguel Matthews	w pts 6	Dagenham 8-7
Apr 30	Ndaba Dube	w rsf 12	Albert Hall 8-3-4
	(vacant Commonwealth bantamweight title)		
Oct 17	Mauricio Bernal	w pts 8	Wembley 8-6
Dec 3	Albert Musankabala	w rsf 5	Catford 8-5
	(Commonwealth bantamweight title)		

Fights 10 Won 10

Henry ARMSTRONG

Super-featherweight
Manchester born 10 December 1967
Real name: Kevin Morris/No amateur experience

1987
Dec 9	Sean Hogg	w pts 6	Stoke 9-6

1988
Mar 28	Steve Bowles	w rsf 5	Stoke 9-1
Apr 20	Dean Lynch	l pts 6	Stoke
May 3	Paul Charters	w pts 4	Stoke 9-3
May 16	Dean Dickinson	w pts 6	Manchester 9-3
Aug 9	Dean Dickinson	l rsf 4	St. Helier 9-4
Sep 20	Jimmy Vincent	w pts 6	Stoke 9-4-8
Oct 10	Jimmy Vincent	w pts 6	Manchester 9-9-8
Dec 12	Les Walsh	l dis 3	Manchester 9-2-4

1989
Jan 25	Nigel Senior	w pts 8	Stoke 9-4-8
Mar 1	Derek Amory	w pts 8	Stoke 9-1-8
Apr 15	Keith Wallace	l ko 7	Salisbury 9-0-4
Sep 20	Gary De Roux	w pts 8	Stoke 9-1
Oct 16	Graham O'Malley	w pts 8	Manchester 9-1
Nov 13	Gary Maxwell	w pts 8	Stratford 9-2

1990
Mar 14	Mark Holt	w pts 8	Stoke 9-0
Apr 19	Gary De Roux	l ko 8	Oldham 9-2-4
Dec 12	Colin Lynch	w rsf 3	Stoke 9-1

1991
Apr 12	Ray Newby	w pts 8	Manchester 9-2

1992
Jan 31	Steve Robinson	w pts 6	Manchester 9-0
Mar 2	Jyrki Vierela	drew 6	Helsinki
Sep 15	Dean Lynch	w rsf 5	Liverpool 9-7

Fights 22 Won 16 Lost 5 Drawn 1

Michael ARMSTRONG
Super-featherweight
Manchester born 18 December 1968
Real name: Michael Morris
No amateur experience

1988
Jan 27	John Hales	w rsf 1	Stoke 8-6
Mar 2	Gipsy Johnny	w rsf 2	Stoke 8-6
Apr 20	Kerry Webber	w pts 6	Stoke
May 16	Steve Bowles	w rsf 3	Manchester 8-10
Jun 13	Tony Heath	w pts 6	Manchester 9-2
Aug 9	Gamel Corbett	w dis 6	St.Helier 8-12-8
Sep 20	Darren Weller	w pts 8	Stoke 8-10
Oct 26	Gary King	drew 8	Stoke 9-0-8
Dec 7	Mark Holt	l pts 8	Stoke 9-2

1989
Feb 15	Gerry McBride	w rsf 5	Stoke 9-0
Apr 19	Russell Davison	w pts 8	Stoke 9-1
May 24	Anthony Barela	w pts 8	Hanley 9-0
Sep 4	Steve Pollard	w pts 8	Hull 9-0
Dec 6	Russell Davison	l pts 8	Stoke 9-0

1990
Mar 6	Russell Davison	w pts 10	Stoke 8-9
Sep 18	Modest Napunyi	l ko 9	Stoke 8-13-8
	(Commonwealth featherweight title)		

1991
Oct 14	Barrie Kelley	w ko 4	Manchester 9-0
Dec 7	Mark Holt	w rsf 4*	Manchester

1992
Jan 21	Darren Elsdon	w rsf 1	Stockport 9-3-4
	(eliminator, British super-featherweight title)		
Apr 25	John Doherty	w rsf 7	Manchester 9-2-8
	(British super-featherweight title)		
Jul 25	Karl Taylor	w rsf 3*	Manchester 9-5-4
Oct 13	Neil Haddock	l rsf 6	Bury 9-3-12
	(British super-featherweight title)		

Fights 22 Won 17 Lost 4 Drawn 1

Neil ARMSTRONG
Flyweight
Paisley born Glasgow 19 June 1970
Paisley ABC
1988 Scottish ABA light-flyweight final (l W Docherty)
1989 Scotland (v Wal, w M Coakley)
1990 Scottish ABA flyweight champion (w P Quinn, w A Docherty, l rsf 2 P Ingle)
1990 Scotland (v Eng, l l Sodhi)
1991 Scottish ABA flyweight final (w K Knox, l J McLean)

1992
Jan 31	Mark Robertson	w rsf 6*	Glasgow 8-1
Mar 4	Des Gargano	w pts 6	Glasgow 8-2
Mar 12	Louis Veitch	w pts 6	Glasgow 8-1
Apr 10	Shaun Norman	drew 8	Glasgow 8-2
Sep 11	Louis Veitch	w pts 6	Glasgow 8-1
Dec 10	L.C.Wilson	w pts 6	Glasgow 8-2

Fights 6 Won 5 Drawn 1

Sean ARMSTRONG

Lightweight
Hartlepool born 22 August 1968
Hartlepool Boys Welfare ABC
1991 North-East Division light-welterweight final (l P Richardson)
1992 Northern ABA light-welterweight final (w rsf 2 T George, w M Barker, l rsf 3 D McCarrick)

1992
Oct 5	Shea Neary	l rsf 6	Liverpool 9-12
Dec 1	Tanveer Ahmed	w pts 6	Hartlepool 9-11-8

Fights 2 Won 1 Lost 1

Graham ARNOLD

Heavyweight
Bury St Edmunds born Fulford 29 June 1968
Phoenix ABC
1991 Eastern ABA super-heavyweight final (w rsf 1 D Warrington, wdrw)

1991
Sep 24	John Palmer	w ko 2	Basildon 14-9
Oct 26	Gary Charlton	l rsf 1	Brentwood 14-12

1992
Jan 21	Steve Yorath	l pts 6	Norwich 14-7
Mar 31	Steve Yorath	w pts 6	Norwich 14-10-4
Sep 8	Steve Stewart	l rsf 3*	Norwich 14-12

Fights 5 Won 2 Lost 3

Crawford ASHLEY

Light-heavyweight
Leeds born 20 May 1964
Real name: Gary Crawford
Burmantofts ABC
1979 National Schools champion
1980 Junior ABA champion (w C Woods)
1980 National Schools champion
1981 Junior ABA champion (w.o.)
1984 Northern ABA light-heavyweight final (w P Taylor, l C Edwards)
1985 North-East ABA light-heavyweight semi-final (l rsf 2 B Webb)
1986 Northern ABA light-heavyweight final (w rsf 1 J Purkis, w rsf 1 B Webb, l ko 1 C Edwards)
1987 Yorkshire ABA light-heavyweight final (l ko 2 M Gale)

1987
Mar 26	Steve Ward	w rsf 2	Wimbledon 13-0
Apr 29	Lee Woolis	w rsf 3	Stoke
Sep 14	Glazz Campbell	l pts 8	Bloomsbury 12-8
Oct 7	Joe Frater	w rsf 4	Burnley 12-6-8
Oct 28	Ray Thomas	w rsf 1	Stoke 12-9
Dec 3	Jonjo Greene	w rsf 7	Leeds 12-9

1988
May 4	Johnny Nelson	l pts 8	Solihull 12-12
Nov 15	Richard Bustin	w ko 3	Norwich 12-6
Nov 22	Cordwell Hylton	w ko 3	Basildon 12-10

1989
Jan 24	John Foreman	w rsf 4	Kings Heath 12-5-12
Feb 8	Lavell Stanley	w ko 1	Albert Hall 12-5-8
Mar 28	Blaine Logsdon	l rsf 2	Glasgow 12-8-8
May 10	Serg Fame	w rtd 7*	Solihull 12-8-4

Oct 31	Carl Thompson	w rsf 6	Manchester 12-3
	(vacant Central light-heavyweight title)		
1990			
Jan 24	Brian Schumacher	w rsf 3*	Preston 12-6-12
	(Central light-heavyweight title)		
Apr 25	Dwayne Muniz	w rsf 1	Brighton 12-7-14
Nov 26	John Williams	w rsf 1	NSC 13-0
1991			
Feb 12	Melvin Ricks	w ko 1	Belfast 12-4
Mar 1	Graciano Rocchigiani	l pts 12 (s)	Dusseldorf 12-3-12
	(vacant European light-heavyweight title)		
Jul 25	Roy Skeldon	w rsf 7*	Dudley 12-5
	(vacant British light-heavyweight title)		
1992			
Jan 30	Jimmy Peters	w rsf 1	Southampton 12-4-8
	(British light-heavyweight title)		
Apr 25	Glazz Campbell	w rsf 8	Belfast
	(British light-heavyweight title)		
Sep 23	Yawe Davis	drew 12	Campione d'Italia 12-5-4
	(vacant European light-heavyweight title)		

Fights 23 Won 18 Lost 4 Drawn 1

John ASHTON

Middleweight
Alfreton, born Somercotes 22 June 1961
SAPA ABC & Blackwell ABC
1978 NABC champion (w P Huggins)
1983 Midlands ABA light-heavyweight final (l dis 2 T Wilson)
1984 Midlands ABA middleweight champion (w M Christie, l J Peters)
1985 Midlands ABA light-middleweight champion (w rsf 1 A McFarlane, w rsf 3 J Whitbread, w ko 1 D Barry, w J Smith, l G Phillips)

1986			
Mar 13	Steve Yorath	w ko 3	Alfreton 11-0-8
Mar 25	Newton Barnett	w pts 8	Wandsworth 11-1-8
Apr 12	Denys Cronin	l rsf 5*	Douglas 11-7-8
May 30	Paul Smith	w pts 8	Stoke 11-2
Sep 15	Wim Thijssen	l rsf 5*	Scheidam
Dec 16	Micky Lerwill	w pts 6	Alfreton 11-1
1987			
Feb 17	Johnny Elliot	drew 6	Alfreton 11-0-8
Mar 2	Ian Chantler	l rsf 4*	Birmingham 11-2
Mar 30	Wally Swift	l pts 8	Birmingham 11-0
Oct 20	Wally Swift	w pts 8	Stoke 10-11
1988			
Feb 7	Kid Milo	w pts 10	Stafford 10-13-12
	(vacant Midlands light-middleweight title)		
Apr 12	Derek Wormald	l rsf 4*	Oldham 11-0
	(eliminator, British light-middleweight title)		
1989			
Oct 7	Andrea Magi	l pts 6	Pesaro 12-4
1990			
Jan 24	Kesem Clayton	w pts 10	Solihull 11-6
	(vacant Midlands middleweight title)		
Mar 22	Paul Wesley	w pts 10	Wolverhampton 11-5
	(Midlands middleweight title)		
Jun 21	Franki Moro	w pts 8	Alfreton 11-8-8
			CTD..

(John ASHTON ctd)
1991

Jan 17	Graham Burton	w pts 10	Alfreton 11-8
Mar 28	Tony Burke	w pts 10	Alfreton
	(eliminator, British middleweight title)		
Aug 24	Sumbu Kalambay	l rtd 6	Pesaro 11-5-8
	(vacant European middleweight title)		
Dec 10	Herol Graham	l rsf 6	Sheffield 11-6
	(British middleweight title)		

1992

Mar 26	Marvin O'Brian	w pts 8	Telford 11-12
Oct 1	Richie Woodhall	l pts 12	Telford 11-5-12
	(Commonwealth middleweight title)		

Fights 22 Won 12 Lost 9 Drawn 1

Abel ASINAMALI

Middleweight
Tooting, born California 20 March 1964

1990

Jan 8	Vince Durham	w pts 5	Los Angeles 11-10
Feb 4	Vince Durham	l pts 6	Los Angeles 11-10
Apr 26	Ken Johnson	drew 4	Irvine 11-11
Oct 9	Billy Lewis	l pts 6	San Diego
Oct 16	Jerome Hill	w pts 6	Albuquerque 12-8
Nov 29	Paul Vega	tdraw 1	Irvine 12-4
Dec 6	Erik Brown	l ko 2	Modesto 12-9

1991
inactive

1992

Apr 23	Jason McNeill	w ko 3	Eltham 12-1
Dec 10	Russell Washer	l pts 6	Bethnal Green 11-9

Fights 9 Won 3 Lost 4 Drawn 2

Chris ASTON

Light-welterweight
Huddersfield born 17 August 1961
No amateur experience

1991

Oct 7	Mick Holmes	w rsf 2	Bradford 10-4
Oct 28	Charles Shepherd	l pts 6	Leicester 10-2
Nov 21	Dean Hiscox	w pts 6	Stafford 10-1
Dec 9	Dave Thompson	w pts 6	Bradford 10-0

1992

Jan 21	Rob Stewart	l rsf 4	Stockport 10-0
Feb 28	Mark Legg	l rsf 5	Irvine 9-12
Apr 28	Richard Swallow	l rsf 3*	Solihull 10-0-12

Fights 7 Won 3 Lost 4

Richard ATKINSON

Light-heavyweight
Dewsbury born 25 February 1973
Batley & Dewsbury ABC
1992 Yorkshire & Humberside ABA light-heavyweight final (w A Call, l C Joseph)

1992
Apr 27	Greg Scott-Briggs	w pts 6	Bradford 12-8
Nov 12	Carl Smallwood	l pts 6	Stafford 12-8

Fights 2 Won 1 Lost 1

Michael AYERS

Lightweight
Ealing born 26 January 1965
All Stars ABC
1987 ABA lightweight champ (w rsf 1 E Brown, w dis 3 M Moran, w rsf 1 M Dykes, w R Guynan, w rsf 2 S Gibbons, w rsf 1 K Andrews, w A Hall)
1987 England (v Ire, l M Carruth; v Pol, l D Kosedowski)
1987 Acropolis Cup bronze medal (l Pritsch, WGer)
1988 England (v Sco, l D Anderson)
1988 NW London ABA lightweight semi-final (l rsf 2* E Brown)

1989
May 16	Joe Rafiu King	w rsf 5	Battersea 9-8
Jun 27	Greg Egbuniwe	w rsf 1	Albert Hall 9-10-8
Nov 15	Mille Marcovic	w rsf 2	Catford 9-11
Dec 5	Darren Mount	w rsf 2	Catford 9-10-8

1990
Apr 26	Nick Hall	w ko 3	Battersea 9-10-4

1991
Jun 4	Stuart Rimmer	w ko 1	Bethnal Green 9-11
Jun 22	Wayne Weekes	w rsf 7	Earls Court 9-7-8
	(vacant Southern lightweight title)		
Sep 21	Peter Till	w rsf 5*	Tottenham 9-9
	(eliminator, British lightweight title)		

1992
Jan 28	Jorge Pompe	w pts 8	Hamburg 9-11
Feb 19	Rudi Valentino	w rsf 7	Muswell Hill 9-7-4
	(Southern lightweight title, eliminator British title)		
Jun 27	Sugar Gibiliru	w rsf 6	Quinta Do Lago 9-8
Oct 13	Scott Brouwer	w rsf 4	Mayfair 9-8-8
	(vacant WBC International lightweight title)		

Fights 12 Won 12

Mossa AZWARD

Middleweight
Hackney born 11 August 1962

1992
May 17	Adrian Haughton	l dis 1	Harringay 11-4-8
Oct 5	Paul Vache	l rsf 2	Bristol 11-4

Fights 2 Lost 2

PAT BROGAN

INTERNATIONAL PROMOTER, MANAGER AND MATCHMAKER

Wishes

BRITISH PROFESSIONAL BOXERS' RECORDS

every success
with the first
and future editions

PAT BROGAN
112 CREWE ROAD
HASLINGTON
CREWE
CHESHIRE

Tel: (work) 0270 588873
Tel: (home) 0270 874825
Fax: 0270 874825

Ian BAILLIE

Flyweight
Corby, born London 23 July 1966
Corby Olympic ABC
1987 North Midlands flyweight final (l M Whetton)
1988 North Midlands flyweight final (l M Whetton)
1989 North Midlands flyweight final (w S Norman, l C Robson)
1990 Leics, Rutland & Northants fly final (l rsf 3 S Norman)

1992
Dec 10　　Tiger Singh　　　　　l pts 6　　　Corby 8-2

Fights 1 Lost 1

Mark BAKER

Super-middleweight
Sidcup born 14 July 1969
Orpington ABC & Repton ABC
1988 Southern ABA light-heavy champ (w J Gosling, w J Pennington, w ko 1 W Wood, w E Blake, l M Coore)
1989 Southern ABA light-heavyweight semi-final (w G Hutchins, l G Donaldson)
1990 ABA light-heavy final (w dis 3 G Delaney, w R Fraser, w C Okoh, w P Rogers, w D Hitchings, l rsf 2 J McCluskey)
1990 England (v Ire, w D Curran)
1991 London ABA middleweight champion (w J Matthews, w M Graham, w A King, l E Noi)

1992
Sep 7　　Jason McNeill　　　w rsf 2　　Bethnal Green 12-3-8
Oct 15　　Graham Jenner　　w rtd 4　　Catford 12-4-8
Dec 3　　Adrian Wright　　　w rsf 1　　Catford 12-1-4

Fights 3 Won 3

Sean BAKER

Light-middleweight
Bristol born 21 February 1969
Broad Plain ABC
1992 Western Counties (North) light-middleweight semi-final (l rsf 3 G Catley)

1992
Sep 7　　Delwin Panayiotiou　　w rsf 2　　Southend 10-10
Oct 5　　Raziq Ali　　　　　　　w pts 6　　Bristol 10-10-12
Dec 1　　Wayne Panayiotiou　　w rsf 3　　Bristol 10-11-12

Fights 3 Won 3

Phil BALL

Super-middleweight
Doncaster born 23 May 1968

1992
Nov 24　　Martin Jolley　　　drew 6　　Doncaster 12-2-8

Fights 1 Drawn 1

Tony BANKS
Light-welterweight
Leeds born 20 June 1967
1983 NABC Class A final (l R Rowland)

1986
Nov 13	Kevin Spratt	drew 6	Huddersfield 9-7-8
Nov 24	Tony Connellan	l pts 6	Leicester 9-9-8

1987
Mar 2	Dean Eshelby	drew 6	Huddersfield 9-10

1988
Feb 8	Barry North	w rsf 3*	Nottingham 9-6
Apr 18	Roy Doyle	w rsf 1	Manchester 9-11
Nov 17	Pete Roberts	w pts 6	Stockport

1989
Feb 17	Jim Moffat	w pts 6	Irvine 9-13-4
May 31	Sugar Gibiliru	l ko 5	Manchester
Sep 21	Kid Sumaila	w rsf 1	Harrogate 9-12
Nov 27	Ludovic Proto	l pts 6	Nogent-sur-Marne 9-11

1990
Feb 26	Paul Gadney	l pts 8	Crystal Palace 9-12

1991
inactive

1992
Feb 24	Rob Stewart	drew 6	Bradford 10-1
Dec 4	Charles Baou	l ko 1	Hyeres

Fights 13 Won 5 Lost 5 Drawn 3

Nicky BARDLE
Welterweight
Ware born 30 January 1972
Haileybury ABC
1987 England Schools (v Wal, l rsf 3 J Calzaghe)
1988 National Schools final (l A Mason)
1988 NABC Class A final (l J Calzaghe)
1989 NABC Class B champion (w A Houldey)
1990 NABC Class C final (l S Hall)

1991
Nov 7	Michael Clynch	w rsf 4	Peterborough 9-11

1992
Feb 12	Steve Hearn	w rsf 1*	Watford
Apr 30	James Campbell	l ko 1	Watford 10-6
Sep 17	Brian Coleman	w rsf 4	Watford 10-0-12

Fights 4 Won 3 Lost 1

Jason BARKER
Light-welterweight
Chesterfield born 1 June 1973

1992
Jan 30	Nico Lucas	w pts 6	Southampton 9-13
Feb 12	Roger Hunte	l rtd 4*	Wembley GH 9-11
Apr 29	Dave Lovell	l pts 6	Stoke 10-1
Jun 3	John O. Johnson	l pts 6	Newcastle-under-Lyme 9-13
Jul 7	Patrick Loughran	l pts 6	Bristol 10-1-8
Oct 21	Brian Coleman	l pts 6	Stoke 10-0
Nov 2	Shea Neary	l rsf 3	Liverpool 10-1
Dec 9	John O. Johnson	l pts 8	Stoke 10-2

Fights 8 Won 1 Lost 7

Newton BARNETT

Light-middleweight
Camberwell, born Jamaica 19 October 1959
Fisher ABC

1983
Oct 3	Ian Martin	l pts 6	Eltham 11-1-8
Nov 21	Ian Martin	l pts 6	Eltham
Nov 30	Kevin Webb	l pts 6	NSC 11-1

1984
Feb 6	Cliff Eastwood	w pts 6	Mayfair 11-2-4
Mar 1	Tony Rabbetts	drew 6	Queensway 11-0-12
Mar 14	Danny Sullivan	l pts 6	NSC 11-1
Apr 17	Danny Sullivan	l pts 6	Wimbledon 11-2-8
Sep 17	Rocky McGran	l ko 3	Brighton 11-0
Oct 29	Tony Baker	w pts 6	Lewisham 10-13-4
Nov 20	Karl Barwise	l pts 6	Wimbledon 11-0-12
Nov 30	Karl Barwise	w pts 6	Longford 11-4

1985
Apr 30	Tony Rabbetts	w pts 8	Wimbledon 11-1-4
Sep 2	Seamus Casey	drew 8	Coventry 11-2
Nov 14	Ian Martin	w rsf 8*	Wimbledon 11-0-8
Dec 2	Seamus Casey	drew 8	Dulwich 11-2
Dec 9	Victor Carvalho	w pts 6	Wandsworth

1986
Feb 24	Charlie Watson	l pts 6	Bradford 10-12
Mar 25	John Ashton	l pts 8	Wandsworth 11-0
May 19	Lee Woolis	w pts 8	Nottingham 10-12
Sep 4	Steve Davies	l pts 8	Wimbledon 11-0-12
Oct 3	John Mortensen	l ko 2	Copenhagen 10-13

1987
Nov 16	Paul McCarthy	l pts 8	Southampton 11-7
Dec 14	Gerry Richards	w pts 6	NSC 11-1

1988
Jan 29	Mark Howell	l pts 8	Holborn 11-5
Apr 22	Joao Cabreiro	l pts 6	Lisbon 11-2
May 11	Dave Thomas	l pts 6	Greenwich 11-2
May 25	Leigh Wicks	drew 8	Hastings 11-1-8
Sep 30	Mark Howell	l pts 8	Gillingham 11-2
Oct 26	Ian Strudwick	l pts 6	Albert Hall 11-1
Nov 23	Tony Britton	l pts 8	NSC 11-0-8

1989
Feb 8	Terry Morrill	l pts 6	Albert Hall 11-0-8
Feb 20	Tony Britton	l pts 8	NSC 11-4-8
Mar 1	Winston Wray	l pts 6	Bethnal Green 11-2
Mar 21	R.W.Smith	w rtd 5*	Battersea 11-0-8
Apr 5	Carlton Warren	l pts 8	Albert Hall
May 21	Winston May	l pts 4	Finsbury Park 10-12
Jun 3	Alfonso Redondo	l rsf 3*	Madrid 10-11
Sep 18	Chris Haydon	w pts 8	NSC 10-13-4
Sep 25	Winston May	l pts 6	Crystal Palace 11-0-8
Oct 25	Derek Grainger	l pts 8	Wembley 10-12-8

1990
Mar 14	W.O.Wilson	l rsf 1*	Albert Hall 10-13
Apr 26	Paul Jones	l pts 8	Mayfair 11-0
May 9	Derek Grainger	l rsf 4	Wembley CC 10-12 /CTD..

(Newton BARNETT ctd)

Sep 22	Damien Denny	w rsf 6	Albert Hall 10-11
1991			
Feb 6	Damien Denny	l pts 8	Bethnal Green 10-13
Feb 13	Derek Grainger	l rsf 3	Wembley CC 11-1
Jul 13	Genaro Leon	l ko 2	Fores-les-Eaux
Sep 7	Crisanto Espana	l rtd 4*	Belfast 11-2-8
Oct 31	Robert McCracken	l dis 2	Telford 11-0
1992			
Apr 30	Kevin Lueshing	l pts 6	Albert Hall 11-1-12
Jun 27	Carlo Colarusso	l rtd 6*	Quinta Do Lago 11-1-4

Fights 51 Won 11 Lost 36 Drawn 4

Pat BARRETT

Light-welterweight

Manchester born 27 July 1967
Collyhurst & Moston ABC
1987 East Lancs ABA lightweight prelims (l N Boyd)

1987

May 1	Gary Barron	w rsf 6	Peterborough 9-12-8
May 18	Jim Moffat	w rsf 1*	Glasgow 10-0
Jun 1	Paul Burke	l pts 6	Bradford
Jun 13	Eamonn Payne	w rsf 3	Great Yarmouth 10-1
Jul 1	Iskender Savas	w ko 1	Interlaken
Aug 3	Mike Russell	w pts 6	Stoke 9-10
Oct 20	Michael Howell	w pts 4	Stoke
1988			
Feb 8	Oliver Henry	w rsf 2	Manchester 9-12
Mar 1	Sugar Gibiliru	drew 8	Manchester 9-13
Mar 22	Donnie Parker	w pts 6 (s)	Baltimore
Apr 12	Stanley Jones	w rsf 2	Cardiff 10-4
May 3	Lennie Gloster	w pts 8	Solihull 10-3-8
Jun 8	Dave McCabe	w rsf 2	Glasgow 10-1-8
Oct 10	Dave Haggarty	w rsf 7*	Glasgow 10-8
Nov 1	Jeff Decker	w rsf 5*	Glasgow 10-7
Nov 29	Kevin Plant	w pts 10	Manchester 9-13
	(vacant Central light-welterweight title)		
1989			
Mar 6	Dean Bramhald	w rsf 7	Glasgow 10-4-8
Mar 28	Marc Delfosse	w ko 1	Glasgow 10-4
Apr 11	Sugar Gibiliru	w ko 8	Oldham 10-0
	(Central light-welterweight title)		
May 9	Tony Willis	w ko 9	St Albans 10-0
	(vacant British light-welterweight title)		
Jun 7	John Rafuse	w ko 6	Wembley 10-3
Jun 27	Roberto Trevino	w ko 2	Bellahouston 10-3
Sep 19	Dana Roston	w rsf 4	Millwall 10-4
Oct 24	Robert Harkin	w pts 12	Wolverhampton 9-13-8
	(British light-welterweight title)		
Nov 21	Joey Ferrell	w rsf 6	Glasgow 10-5-8
1990			
Jun 2	Juan Nunez	w rsf 1	Manchester 10-3-8
Aug 24	Efrem Calamati	w rsf 4	Salerno 10-0
	(European light-welterweight title)		

| Oct 4 | Dwayne Swift | w pts 10 | Bethnal Green 10-2-4 |
| Nov 15 | Eduardo Jacques | w rsf 1 | Oldham 10-2-8 |

1991

Jan 16	Jimmy Harrison	w rtd 1	Albert Hall 10-4
Feb 13	Salvatore Nardino (European light-welterweight title)	w ko 6	Wembley CC 10-0
Apr 17	Mark McCreath (European light-welterweight title)	w rsf 6	Albert Hall 10-0
Oct 9	Racheed Lawal (European light-welterweight title)	w rsf 4	Manchester
Dec 19	Mike Johnson	w rsf 2	Oldham 10-4-8

1992

Jul 25	Manning Galloway (WBO welterweight title)	l pts 12	Manchester 10-4-10
Nov 20	Tomas Quinones	w rsf 1	Casino
Dec 19	Sam Gervins	w ko 1	San Severo

Fights 37 Won 34 Lost 2 Drawn 1

Gary BARRON

Light-welterweight
Peterborough born 21 December 1964
Focus ABC
1984 Eastern ABA lightweight final (l rsf C Rance)

1987

| Feb 19 | Tim O'Keefe | w pts 6 | Peterborough 9-9-8 |
| May 1 | Pat Barrett | l rsf 6 | Peterborough 9-11 |

1988

Feb 14	Andrew Pybus	w ko 1	Peterborough 9-10
Feb 23	Kevin Plant	drew 6	Leicester 9-12
Nov 3	James Hunter	w pts 6	Leicester 9-13-8

1989

Feb 14	Tony Feliciello	nd 8	Wolverhampton 9-10
Mar 1	Brian Cullen	l pts 6	Stoke 9-12
Apr 17	Frankie Lake	w ko 4	Birmingham 10-0
Sep 11	Darren Mount	drew 8	Manchester 10-2
Oct 4	Oliver Harrison	w pts 8	Solihull 10-2
Oct 23	Lyn Davies	l ko 2	Nottingham 10-3

1990

| Jan 24 | Guillermo Zuniga | l ko 1 | Trapani 10-2 |
| Dec 14 | Paul Charters | w rsf 3* | Peterborough |

1991

Feb 13	Robert McCracken	l rtd 2	Wembley CC 10-10-8
Apr 19	Tony Swift	drew 8	Peterborough
Nov 14	Paul Charters	l rsf 4*	Gateshead 10-0

1992

Feb 12	Carlos Chase	l rsf 5	Watford 10-0
Mar 25	Donald Stokes	l rsf 2	Dagenham 10-5-8
Apr 30	Mark McCreath	l rsf 5	Mayfair 10-3
Jun 18	Marcel Herbert	w pts 6	Peterborough 10-1
Jul 9	Peter Bradley	l pts 8	Glasgow 10-2
Dec 7	Mark McCreath	l rsf 5*	Mayfair 10-5

Fights 22 Won 7 Lost 11 Drawn 3 No decisions 1

Karl BARWISE

Super-middleweight
Tooting born 19 September 1965
Norwood ABC
1984 Essex ABA middleweight final (l R Turp)

1984

Sep 18	John Hargin	w pts 6	Wimbledon 11-2
Oct 23	Tony Baker	drew 6	Battersea 11-1
Nov 20	Newton Barnett	w pts 6	Wimbledon 11-0-8
Nov 30	Newton Barnett	l pts 6	Longford 11-4
Dec 19	Rocky McGran	w pts 6	Belfast 11-4

1985

Jan 24	Paul Allen	w ko 2	Streatham 11-4
Feb 11	Tony Baker	w pts 8	Dulwich 11-4-8
Feb 26	Mark Mills	l pts 6	Battersea 11-6-4
Apr 1	Dalton Jordan	w pts 8	Dulwich 11-7-8
Apr 30	Alan Baptiste	drew 8	Wimbledon 11-8
Oct 10	Alan Baptiste	w pts 8	Wimbledon 11-7-8
Oct 29	Christophe Tiozzo	l pts 8	Paris
Nov 19	Alan Baptiste	l pts 6	Battersea 11-13

1986

Jan 30	Steve Ward	w pts 6	Wimbledon
Feb 19	Michael Watson	l rsf 3	Albert Hall 11-7-8
Apr 15	Neil Munn	w pts 6	Wimbledon 11-9-4
Apr 22	Sam Storey	l pts 6	Belfast 11-9-8
Sep 1	Dennis O'Brien	w rsf 2	Ealing 11-11
Oct 16	Johnny Graham	l pts 6	Wimbledon 12-0
Oct 29	Nicky Thorne	drew 6	Muswell Hill 11-12

1987-89 inactive

1990

| Sep 5 | Sean Heron | l pts 6 | Brighton 11-12 |
| Sep 22 | Errol Christie | l rtd 7 | Albert Hall 11-8 |

1991

Mar 21	Lester Jacobs	l pts 6	Battersea 12-0
Apr 3	Ali Forbes	l rtd 4*	Bethnal Green 11-11-8
Apr 26	Benji Good	l rsf 3*	Crystal Palace 11-12
May 30	Ray Webb	l pts 8	Mayfair 12-0
Oct 16	Andy Flute	w rsf 8*	Stoke 11-11-8
Oct 22	Tony McCarthy	w pts 6	Battersea 12-0
Nov 13	Sam Storey	l pts 6	Belfast 12-1
Dec 7	Pietro Pellizzaro	l pts 6	Rossano Calabro

1992

May 12	Roland Ericsson	l pts 6	Crystal Palace 12-1-4
Sep 8	Richard Bustin	l pts 6	Norwich 12-0
Sep 15	Lou Gent	l rsf 6*	Crystal Palace 12-1
Dec 4	Neville Brown	l rsf 6	Telford 11-8-8

Fights 34 Won 12 Lost 19 Drawn 3

Mark BATES

Super-featherweight
Stanford-le-Hope born 22 January 1967
Berry Boys ABC

1986
| Dec 15 | Steve Brown | l pts 6 | NSC 9-7-12 |

1987
Feb 16	Geoff Sillitoe	w pts 6	Gloucester 9-7-4
Apr 15	Geoff Sillitoe	w ko 3	Lewisham 9-7
May 27	Mickey Crawford	w pts 6	Lewisham
Jun 25	Mike Russell	l pts 6	Bethnal Green 9-5-8

1988-89 inactive

1990
Jun 20	Elvis Parsley	w ko 1	Basildon 9-4
Jul 10	Steve Robinson	w pts 6	Canvey Island 9-3
Dec 12	Lee Fox	w pts 6	Basildon 9-6-12

1991
Jan 23	Phil Lashley	w rtd 3	Brentwood 9-2-12
May 1	Phil Lashley	w pts 6	Bethnal Green 9-2
Sep 24	Peter Buckley	l rtd 5*	Basildon 9-2

1992
| Feb 19 | Lee Fox | w pts 6 | Muswell Hill 9-7 |

Fights 12 Won 9 Lost 3

Jason BEARD

Light-welterweight
Beckton born 24 April 1967
West Ham ABC, Newham ABC
1992 NE London ABA welterweight semi-final (l A Wilton)

1992
| Dec 3 | Robert Whitehouse | w rsf 3 | Catford 10-3-8 |

Fights 1 Won 1

Ricky BEARD

Flyweight
Dagenham born 1 March 1963
St Monicas ABC, Barking ABC & Eltham ABC
1987 London ABA bantamweight final (w M Chance, l N Dickinson)
1988 NE London ABA bantamweight final (l M Ward)
1989 NE London ABA flyweight champion (w F Ampofo, wthdrw)

1989
May 2	Jed Goodwin	w rsf 1	Chigwell 8-2
Jun 6	Jed Goodwin	w rtd 1	Chigwell 8-0
Sep 19	Eric George	l pts 6	Bethnal Green 8-3-8
Oct 4	Gordon Shaw	l pts 6	Basildon 8-6-8

1990
| Oct 3 | Neil Johnston | drew 6 | Basildon 8-1 |
| Nov 19 | Robbie Regan | l rsf 6 | Cardiff 8-2 |

1991
| Mar 26 | Francis Ampofo | l pts 8 | Bethnal Green 8-1-8 |
| Sep 30 | Micky Cantwell | l pts 8 | Albert Hall 7-13 |

1992
| Feb 25 | Francis Ampofo | l pts 8 | Crystal Palace 8-3 |
| Apr 14 | Naseem Hamed | l ko 2 | Mansfield 8-2 |

Fights 10 Won 2 Lost 7 Drawn 1

Willie BEATTIE

Welterweight
Glasgow born 25 October 1967
East End ABC & Dennistoun ABC
1986 Scottish ABA lightweight final (w M Gowans, l K Salmon)
1988 Scottish ABA welterweight semi-final (w rsf 3 J Forbes, w A Docherty, l P Dolan)
1988 Scotland (v Ire, l W Walsh)

1988
Dec 13	John Mullen	w pts 6	Glasgow 10-2

1989
Mar 6	Calum Rattray	w rsf 3*	Glasgow 10-4-12
Mar 28	Ian Honeywood	w pts 4	Glasgow 10-5-8
May 8	Mick Harkin	w dis 5	Edgbaston 10-6
Jun 12	Ernie Noble	w pts 6	Glasgow 10-4
Jun 27	Calum Rattray	w rsf 2*	Bellahouston 10-4
Oct 12	Quinn Payntor	w pts 8	Glasgow 10-9
Nov 21	Darren Mount	w pts 8	Glasgow 10-6
Dec 18	Dave Worthington	w rtd 4	Glasgow 10-9

1990
Feb 27	Humphrey Harrison	l rsf 2*	Manchester 10-6-4
May 1	Glyn Rhodes	w rsf 5*	Oldham 10-6
May 29	Kevin Plant	w pts 8	Glasgow
Dec 2	Antoine Fernandez	l rsf 4*	Elancourt

1991
Feb 11	Des Robinson	w pts 8	Glasgow 10-8
Sep 24	Trevor Ambrose	w pts 8	Glasgow 10-9-2

1992
Jan 31	Gordon Blair	w rsf 3	Glasgow 10-7
	(vacant Scottish welterweight title)		
Apr 10	Tony Swift	l pts 10	Glasgow 10-6-8
	(eliminator, British welterweight title)		
Nov 7	Godfrey Nyakana	l ko 1	Differdange

Fights 18 Won 14 Lost 4

Chris BECK

Light-heavyweight
Cwmavon born 18 December 1972
Cymmer Afan ABC
1991 Welsh ABA light-heavyweight final (w L Hogan, w rsf 3 S Davies, l L Duncan)
1991 Wales (v Sco, l J McCluskey; v Ir, w dis 3 M Delaney)
1992 Welsh ABA light-heavyweight final (w J David, w I Bishop, l rsf 3 D Hitchings)

1992
Oct 7	Karl Mumford	l pts 6	Barry 12-11-8

Fights 1 Lost 1

John BECKLES

Light-heavyweight
Islington born 1 January 1963
Islington ABC & Fairbairn House ABC
1982 Young England (v Fin, w rsf 1 P Hurme; w dis 2 J Kapola)
1983 London ABA light-heavy finalist (w ko 2 T Akay, w rtd 1* B Parkes, l D Simmons)
1984 London ABA middleweight semi-final (w S Harris, l ko 1 M Watson)
1985 ABA light-heavyweight champion (w rsf 1 T Dixon, w ko 3 I Yorke, w rsf 1 J Skyers, w rsf 3 P Passley, w rsf 2 D Angol, w rsf 2 J Moran, w rsf 2 S Williams, w B Pullen)
1985 Canada Cup silver medal (w J Glynn, l rsf 1 E Marcus)

1985 European Championships bronze medal (w rsf 1 A Manfredini, It; w rsf 2 Tunali, Tur; l M Bott, Gr)
1986 England (v Ire, l dis 1 J O'Sullivan; w R Kane)
1987 ABA light-heavyweight champion (w ko 1 A Hodge, w T Dixon, w E Guthrie, w M Gale, w A Cook, w rsf 2 H Lawson)

1989
Apr 22	Marc Randazzo	t.draw 1	Atlantic City 12-10-4
May 11	Chris Collins	w rsf 2	New York 12-7-8
May 22	Ruben Flores	w rsf 3	Atlantic City 12-8-8
Aug 15	Alfred Cole	l rsf 4	West Orange 12-9

1990-91 inactive

1992
Mar 6	Tony Booth	l rsf 6	Battersea 12-7

Fights 5 Won 2 Lost 2 Drawn 1

Tony BEHAN
Light-heavyweight
Birmingham born 5 March 1967
Austin ABC

1986
Sep 22	W.O.Wilson	l ko 2	NSC 12-0

1987
Mar 18	Paul Hanlon	w pts 4	Stoke 11-12
Apr 6	Jimmy Peters	l pts 4	Southampton 12-3
Aug 3	Darren Hobson	l pts 6	Stoke 12-0
Nov 19	Darren McKenna	l rsf 1	Ilkeston 12-7

1988
Mar 14	Richard Bustin	l rsf 3	Norwich 12-9
Apr 25	Steve Coffey	w rsf 4*	Birmingham 11-10
May 3	Peter Elliott	l pts 6	Stoke 11-10
May 10	Floyd Davidson	w pts 6	Edgbaston 11-11
May 23	John Ellis	drew 6	NSC 11-11
Sep 22	Richard Carter	l pts 6	Wolverhampton 12-0
Oct 17	Ted Cofie	drew 6	Birmingham 12-0

1989
Apr 5	Ian Strudwick	l pts 6	Albert Hall
Apr 19	Peter Elliott	drew 6	Stoke 11-12
May 8	Ian Vokes	w pts 6	Grimsby 12-7-8
May 16	Ian Strudwick	l pts 8	Battersea
Oct 2	Peter Elliott	l pts 10	Hanley 11-10-8
	(vacant Midlands super-middleweight title)		

1990 inactive

1991
Mar 4	Paul Hanlon	w pts 6	Birmingham 12-4
May 13	Nigel Rafferty	l dis 7	Birmingham 12-4
May 23	Joey Peters	l pts 6	Southampton 12-4
Dec 2	Darryl Ritchie	w rsf 1	Birmingham 12-9-8

1992
Jan 20	Gil Lewis	l pts 8	Coventry 12-9

Fights 22 Won 6 Lost 13 Drawn 3

Leo BEIRNE

Bantamweight
Llanelli, born Roscommon, Ireland 2 December 1966
Castlerea ABC

1992
Dec 1	Graham McGrath	l pts 6	Liverpool 8-8

Fights 1 Lost 1

Nigel BENN

Super-middleweight
Ilford born 22 January 1964
West Ham ABC
1985 NE London ABA middleweight semi-final (w W May, l R Douglas)
1986 ABA middleweight champion (w dis 2 W Henry, w rsf 2 R Andre, w R Douglas, w rsf 1 G Finn, w M Edwards, w F Smith, w P Lewis, w rsf 3 J Melfah)

1987
Jan 28	Graeme Ahmed	w rsf 2	Croydon 11-7-12
Mar 4	Kevin Roper	w rsf 1*	Basildon 11-12-8
Apr 22	Bob Nieuwenhuizen	w rsf 1	Albert Hall 11-6-8
May 9	Winston Burnett	w rsf 4	Battersea 12-1-12
Jun 17	Reginald Marks	w rsf 1	Albert Hall 11-8
Jul 1	Leon Morris	w ko 1	Albert Hall 11-9-12
Aug 9	Eddie Smith	w ko 1	Windsor 11-9
Sep 16	Winston Burnett	w rsf 3	Albert Hall 11-10
Oct 13	Russell Barker	w rsf 1	Windsor 11-7
Nov 3	Ronnie Yoe	w rsf 1	Bethnal Green 11-8
Nov 24	Ian Chantler	w ko 1	Wisbech 11-8
Dec 2	Reggie Miller	w ko 7	Albert Hall 11-10

1988
Jan 27	Fermin Chirinos	w ko 2	Bethnal Green 11-10
Feb 7	Byron Prince	w rsf 2	Stafford 11-6
Feb 24	Greg Taylor	w rsf 2*	Aberavon 11-9
Mar 14	Darren Hobson	w ko 1	Norwich 11-7
Apr 20	Abdul Umaru Sanda	w rsf 2	Muswell Hill 11-4
	(vacant Commonwealth middleweight title)		
May 28	Tim Williams	w rsf 2	Albert Hall 11-6-8
Oct 26	Anthony Logan	w ko 2	Albert Hall 11-5-4
	(Commonwealth middleweight title)		
Dec 10	David Noel	w rsf 1	Crystal Palace 11-5-4
	(Commonwealth middleweight title)		

1989
Feb 8	Mike Chilambe	w ko 1	Albert Hall 11-6
	(Commonwealth middleweight title)		
Mar 28	Mbayo Wa Mbayo	w ko 2	Glasgow 11-8
May 21	Michael Watson	l ko 6	Finsbury Park 11-5-12
	(Commonwealth middleweight title)		
Oct 20	Jorge Amparo	w pts 10	Atlantic City 11-8
Dec 1	Jose Quinones	w rsf 1	Las Vegas 11-9

1990
Jan 14	Sanderline Williams	w pts 10 (s)	Atlantic City 11-8-4
Apr 29	Doug DeWitt	w rsf 8	Atlantic City 11-4
	(WBO middleweight title)		
Aug 18	Iran Barkley	w rsf 1	Las Vegas 11-5-8
	(WBO middleweight title)		

Nov 18	Chris Eubank (WBO middleweight title)	l rsf 9	NEC 11-5-12
1991			
Apr 3	Robbie Sims	w rsf 7	Bethnal Green 11-4-8
Jul 3	Kid Milo	w rsf 4*	Brentwood 11-7
Oct 26	Lenzie Morgan	w pts 10	Brentwood 12-0-12
Dec 7	Hector Lescano	w ko 3	Manchester 11-12-8
1992			
Feb 19	Dan Sherry	w rsf 3	Muswell Hill 11-9-2
May 23	Sugarboy Malinga	w pts 10	Birmingham 12-0
Oct 3	Mauro Galvano (WBC super-middleweight title)	w rsf 3*	Marino
Dec 12	Nicky Piper (WBC super-middleweight title)	w rsf 11	Muswell Hill 11-13-10

Fights 37 Won 35 Lost 2

Barry BENNETT

Middleweight
Aylesbury born 13 March 1963
Aylesbury ABC

1987			
Feb 20	Paul Wesley	w pts 6	Maidenhead 11-6
Mar 3	Steve McCarthy	l ko 3	Southend 11-5
Apr 7	Johnny Nanton	l pts 6	Southend 11-5
Apr 29	Gary Finn	l pts 6	Hastings 11-6
1988			
Jan 21	Steve Aquilina	l pts 6	Battersea 11-8
Mar 12	Joao Cabreira	l pts 6	Lisbon 11-2
May 4	Fran Harding	l rsf 1	Wembley 11-1
1989			
Jan 25	Ray Close	l rsf 3	Belfast 11-4
Mar 22	Mickey Duncan	w pts 6	Sheppey 11-5-12
Apr 4	Martin Rosamond	w pts 6	Southend
Apr 26	George Moody	w rsf 4	Battersea 11-3-12
May 4	Stan King	w rsf 5	NSC 11-4
May 22	Chris Richards	w pts 8	NSC 11-4
Sep 14	Tony Collins	l rsf 1	Basildon 11-4-12
1990			
Sep 13	Gary Pemberton	l rsf 4	Watford 11-7
1991			
Nov 28	Mick Mulcahy	w pts 6	Evesham 10-12-8
1992			
Mar 10	Warren Stowe	l pts 6	Bury 11-0-8

Fights 17 Won 7 Lost 10

Mervyn BENNETT

Lightweight
Cardiff born 20 February 1960
Prince of Wales ABC
1978 European Junior featherweight bronze medal
1978 Welsh ABA featherweight champion (w Don George, l ko 2 M O'Brien)
1978 Wales (v Ire, l J Shaw)
1980 Welsh ABA lightweight final (l E Pritchard)
1980 Wales (v WGer, l dis 2 W Schafter; v Den, w F Krogh)

1981
Jan 6	Jeff Smart	w rsf 6	Bethnal Green
Jan 26	Paddy Maguire	w rsf 2	Edgbaston
Apr 7	Philip Morris	w pts 6	Newport
Sep 25	Alex Irvine	w pts 6	Nottingham
Oct 12	Richie Foster	w pts 8	Bloomsbury
Nov 19	Don George (Welsh featherweight title)	l pts 10	Ebbw Vale

1982
Oct 26	Mick Rowley	l pts 8	Newport
Nov 24	Jimmy Duncan	l pts 8	Stoke

1983
Feb 17	Kevin Pritchard	l rsf 5*	Coventry
Apr 18	Keith Foreman	l rsf 6*	Bradford

1984-85 inactive

1986
Feb 17	Dave Smith	w pts 8	NSC 9-7
Apr 10	Dave Pratt	w ko 6	Leicester 9-5
Oct 29	Keith Parry	l rsf 3	Ebbw Vale 9-8-8

1987
Jan 19	John Mullen	w ko 1	Glasgow 9-8-8
Feb 16	Ray Newby	l ko 8	Glasgow 9-8

1988-91 inactive

1992
May 19	Eddie Lloyd	l rsf 5*	Cardiff 9-8-8
Oct 28	Mike Morrison	w pts 8	Cardiff 9-12
Dec 14	Mike Morrison	w pts 6	Cardiff 9-10-8

Fights 18 Won 10 Lost 8

Adey BENTON

Bantamweight
Dewsbury born 26 August 1973
Batley & Dewsbury ABC
1990 Junior ABA champion
1991 Young England (v Ire, l S Cowan)
1992 North-East ABA featherweight final (w J Barker, w J Stovin, l A Temple)

1992
Apr 27	Mark Hargreaves	w pts 6	Bradford 8-10
Oct 29	Vince Feeney	drew 6	Bayswater 8-8-4
Nov 9	Stevie Wood	w pts 6	Bradford 8-6

Fights 3 Won 2 Drawn 1

Ensley BINGHAM

Light-middleweight
Manchester born 27 May 1963
Moss Side ABC & Collyhurst ABC
1983 Northern ABA light-middleweight final (w ko 1 C Sampson, l rsf 2 M Esa)
1986 North-West ABA welterweight final (w T Kershaw, w rtd 1 O Maddix, l K Wall)

1986			
Nov 20	Steve Ward	w ko 4	Bredbury 11-2
1987			
Dec 16	Tony Britland	w ko 1	Manchester 10-8-12
1988			
Feb 23	Franki Moro	w pts 6	Oldham 10-9-8
Mar 1	Kelvin Mortimer	w pts 8	Manchester 10-7
Apr 26	Clinton McKenzie	l pts 8	Bethnal Green 10-9-4
Oct 18	Kostas Petrou	l rsf 7	Oldham 10-10
1989			
Mar 22	Gary Cooper	l pts 8	Reading 11-2
Sep 26	Wally Swift	w pts 10	Oldham 10-13-4
	(eliminator, British light-middleweight title)		
1990			
Mar 28	Bernard Alanis	l rsf 3*	Manchester 11-1-12
Jun 6	Andy Till	w dis 3	Battersea 11-0
	(final eliminator, British light-middleweight title)		
1991			
Mar 19	Wally Swift	l rsf 4	Birmingham 10-13-8
	(vacant British light-middleweight title)		
Nov 29	Russell Washer	w rsf 4	Manchester 11-2
1992			
May 29	Graham Jenner	w ko 5	Manchester 11-4
Jul 18	Gordon Blair	w rsf 2	Manchester 11-0-4
Nov 2	Robert McCracken	l rsf 10	Wolverhampton 10-12-8
	(eliminator, British light-middleweight title)		

Fights 15 Won 9 Lost 6

Dave BINSTEED

Light-middleweight
Liverpool born 16 June 1962
Skelmersdale ABC

1986			
Apr 28	Derek Wormald	l rsf 2	Liverpool 10-11
1987			
Feb 19	Mark Hill	l rsf 2	St Helens 11-1
Mar 25	Keith Scott	l pts 6	Stafford 10-9
1988-90			
inactive			
1991			
May 13	Dave Hall	w rsf 2*	Birmingham 11-4
May 20	Darren McInulty	drew 6	Leicester 11-0
Oct 7	Willie Yeardsley	l pts 6	Liverpool 11-1
Dec 2	Dave Radford	l rsf 6	Liverpool 11-4
1992			
Jan 31	Humphrey Harrison	l ko 1	Manchester 10-13

Fights 8 Won 1 Lost 6 Drawn 1

Gordon BLAIR

Welterweight
Glasgow born 26 February 1969
Gallowgate ABC
1987 Scotland (v Ire, l ko 1 B Walsh)
1988 Scottish ABA welterweight quarter-final (w K Kinnear, l ko 2 A Craig)
1989 Scottish ABA welterweight prelims (l rsf 3 W Collins)

1989
Nov 21	Gavin Fitzpatrick	w rsf 3	Glasgow 10-3
Dec 18	John Ritchie	w pts 4	Glasgow 10-8

1990
Feb 19	Trevor Meikle	w pts 6	Glasgow 10-7
Feb 26	James Conley	w rsf 3	Bradford 10-8
Apr 26	Kid Silvester	l pts 6	Halifax 10-11
May 14	Trevor Ambrose	w ko 5	Northampton 10-9
Sep 25	Calum Rattray	w rsf 3	Glasgow 10-7-4
Oct 22	Seamus Casey	w rsf 3	Glasgow 10-8
Nov 6	Leigh Wicks	l pts 8	Mayfair 10-9
Dec 10	Quinton Payntor	w pts 6	Glasgow 10-13

1991
Jan 25	Danny Quigg	w pts 6	Shotts 11-2
Feb 18	Gary Logan	l ko 1	NSC 10-9-12
Apr 15	Colin Pitters	l pts 6	Glasgow 10-8
May 31	Paul King	w pts 8	Glasgow 10-9
Jun 20	Delroy Waul	w ko 2	Liverpool 10-12
Sep 24	Bozon Haule	w rsf 8	Glasgow 10-10-12
Nov 19	Tony McKenzie	l rsf 5	Norwich 10-6-4

1992
Jan 31	Willie Beattie	l rsf 3	Glasgow 10-6-12
	(vacant Scottish welterweight title)		
Mar 12	Mark Jay	drew 8	Glasgow 10-12
May 29	Ossie Maddix	l pts 6	Manchester 10-12
Jul 18	Ensley Bingham	l rsf 2	Manchester 10-11-8
Oct 27	Howard Clarke	w rsf 4	Cradley Heath 10-12
Nov 24	Errol McDonald	l rsf 5*	Doncaster 10-9

Fights 23 Won 13 Lost 9 Drawn 1

Chris BLAKE

Welterweight
Croydon born 14 May 1962
Sir Philip Game ABC & Fitzroy Lodge ABC
1981 SE London ABA welterweight champion (w K Secular, l J Andrews)
1982 SE London ABA welterweight final (l M Mills)
1983 ABA welterweight semi-final (w ko 3 M Mills, w O Jones, w ko 3 C Phillips, w R Lewis, l T Campbell)
1984 London ABA welterweight final (w A Eka, w B Greenland, l M Hughes)
1984 England (v Sco, w A Laurie; v Ire, l N Reid; v WGer, l A Kunzler)
1984 Great Britain (v Ire, l K Joyce)
1985 London ABA welterweight final (w A Eka, w J Nanton, w R Arthey, l M Patrick)

1985
Oct 16	Gary Champion	w pts 6	Albert Hall 10-3-8
Nov 19	Vince Stewart	w pts 6	Battersea 10-4-4
Dec 4	Lennie Gloster	w pts 6	Albert Hall 10-3
Dec 11	Junaid Musah	w pts 6	Fulham 10-2

1986
Feb 3	Dave Heaver	w rsf 3	Dulwich 10-8

Feb 27	Lennie Gloster	w pts 6	Bethnal Green 10-3-12
Mar 25	Tony Smith	w pts 8	Wandsworth
May 8	Simon Eubanks	w pts 8	Bayswater 10-5
Oct 9	Gary Champion	w rsf 2	Croydon 10-2
Nov 29	Peter Ashcroft	w pts 8	Battersea 10-4

1987

Jan 28	Robert Harkin	w rsf 3	Croydon 10-2
Mar 14	Lennie Gloster	w pts 10	Southwark 10-0
	(Southern light-welterweight title; elim. British title)		
Oct 1	John Senegal	w rsf 4	Croydon 10-2-8
Nov 19	Lloyd Christie	l rsf 1	Battersea 10-0
	(British light-welterweight title)		

1988

Mar 10	Clinton McKenzie	l pts 8	Croydon 10-3-8
Apr 22	Glyn Rhodes	w pts 6	Lisbon 10-4
May 4	Wally Swift	l pts 8	Solihull 11-1
Jun 16	Paul Seddon	w rtd 6*	Croydon 10-7
Oct 5	Mickey Hughes	l rsf 5	Wembley GH
Dec 14	George Collins	l pts 8	Bethnal Green 10-9

1989

Feb 28	Ken Foreman	l rsf 4*	Chigwell
Nov 8	Gary Logan	w pts 8	Wembley GH 10-9
Dec 5	Davey Hughes	w rtd 5*	Catford 10-9-12

1990

Oct 31	Ian John-Lewis	w rsf 5*	Crystal Palace
Dec 15	Daniel Bicchieray	l pts 8	Vichy

1991

Apr 19	Mauro Martelli	l pts 8	Marignane
May 22	Ludovic Proto	l rsf 1	Paris
Nov 20	Derek Grainger	drew 8	Albert Hall 10-12

1992

Apr 25	Oscar Checa	l rsf 1	Belfast 11-0

Fights 29 Won 18 Lost 10 Drawn 1

Everton BLAKE

Light-heavyweight
Luton born 18 November 1963
Lewsey Centre ABC

1985 Home Counties ABA light-heavyweight champion (w rsf 1 K McGrath, l rsf 3 J Moran)
1987 ABA light-heavyweight semi-final (w ko 1 S Moule, w G Wilson, w rsf 2 N Wadman, w rsf 3 J Jones, w D Coyle, l H Lawson)
1988 Home Counties ABA light-heavyweight champion (w rsf 2 A Tant, w N Smith, w G Barker, l M Baker)

1989

Apr 6	Steve Conway	w rsf 3	Stevenage 12-10
May 4	Dave Furneaux	w rsf 3	Mayfair 12-9
Jun 22	Reuben Thurley	w rsf 5	Stevenage 12-12
Nov 13	John Foreman	l pts 6	Brierley Hill 12-11

1990

Apr 6	Dave Owens	w rsf 6	Stevenage 12-9
May 3	Maurice Core	l pts 8	Marble Arch 12-9
Sep 14	Jason Baxter	w pts 6	Telford 12-10
Nov 26	Gipsy Carmen	w pts 6	Bethnal Green 12-11

1991

Feb 22	Maurice Core	l rsf 8	Manchester 12-10
Apr 22	Terry Dixon	w rsf 8	AASC 12-10-4

/CTD...

(Everton BLAKE ctd)

Nov 14	Johnny Graham (Southern cruiserweight title)	w pts 10	Marble Arch 13-0-8
1992			
Oct 29	Gipsy Carmen (Southern cruiserweight title)	w rsf 4*	Hayes 13-7
Nov 26	Johnny Graham (Southern cruiserweight title)	l pts 10	Mayfair 13-0-8

Fights 13 Won 9 Lost 4

Andrew BLOOMER

Bantamweight
Ynysybwl, born Pontypridd 26 September 1964
Ynysybwl ABC, Fleur de Lys ABC
1989 Welsh ABA featherweight prelims (w A Fletcher, wthdrw)
1990 Welsh ABA bantamweight semi-final (l A Ley)
1991 Welsh ABA bantamweight semi-final (w C Samuels, wthdrw)

1991
Jun 30	Leigh Williams	l pts 6	Southwark 8-8
Sep 3	Alan Ley	l pts 6	Cardiff 8-7
Oct 2	Bradley Stone	l pts 6	Barking 8-11
Oct 17	Leigh Williams	l pts 6	Southwark 8-10
Nov 4	Ceri Farrell	l pts 6	Merthyr 8-11
Nov 20	Ceri Farrell	l pts 6	Cardiff 8-11
Nov 28	Chris Morris	l pts 6	Liverpool 8-10
1992			
Feb 24	Alex Docherty	l pts 6	Glasgow 8-8-12
Apr 8	Jacob Smith	l pts 6	Leeds 8-7
Apr 30	Tony Falcone	l pts 6	Mayfair 8-11-8
May 16	Bradley Stone	l pts 6	Muswell Hill 8-11
May 23	Naseem Hamed	l rsf 2	Birmingham 8-8
Oct 5	Tony Falcone	l pts 8	Bristol 9-0
Nov 12	Marcus Duncan	l pts 6	Burnley 8-8

Fights 14 Lost 14

Gareth BODDY

Light-middleweight
Newport born 21 May 1969
Southpaw
St Josephs ABC
1991 Welsh ABA middleweight final (w D Owen, w J McNeill, w A Kearle, l S Thomas)
1992 Welsh ABA middleweight final (w P Watkins, w rsf 3 A Kearle, w C Thomas, l dis 3 C Winstone)

1992
Dec 14	Jerry Mortimer	l pts 6	Cardiff 11-0-3

Fights 1 Lost 1

Tony BOOTH

Light-heavyweight
Sheffield, born Hull 30 January 1970
Hull Boys ABC
1990 Yorkshire & Humberside ABA light-middleweight final (w rsf 3 K Bailey, w P Hepton, l C Manners)

1990
Mar 8	Paul Lynch	l pts 6	Watford 11-2
Apr 11	Mickey Duncan	w pts 6	Dewsbury 10-13
Apr 26	Colin Manners	w pts 6	Halifax 11-2
May 16	Tommy Warde	w pts 6	Hull 11-1-8
Jun 5	Gary Dyson	w pts 6	Liverpool 11-3
Sep 5	Shaun McCrory	l pts 6	Stoke 11-5
Oct 8	Alfie Andrews	w rsf 3	Cleethorpes 11-4

1991
Jan 23	Darron Griffiths	drew 6	Stoke 11-3-8
Feb 6	Shaun McCrory	l pts 6	Liverpool 11-9
Mar 6	Billy Brough	l pts 6	Glasgow 11-11-4
Mar 18	Billy Brough	w pts 6	Glasgow 12-0
Mar 28	Neville Brown	l pts 6	Alfreton
May 17	Glenn Campbell	l rsf 2	Bury 11-13-8
	(Central super-middleweight title)		
Jul 25	Paul Murray	w pts 6	Dudley 12-0
Aug 1	Nick Manners	drew 8	Dewsbury 12-3
Sep 11	Jimmy Peters	l pts 8	Hammersmith 12-8
Oct 28	Eddy Smulders	l rsf 6	Arnhem 12-6-8
Dec 9	Steve Lewsam	l pts 8	Cleethorpes 12-12

1992
Jan 30	Serg Fame	w pts 6	Southampton 12-6-12
Feb 12	Tenko Ernie	w rsf 4	Wembley GH 12-5
Mar 6	John Beckles	w rsf 6	Battersea 12-8
Mar 26	Dave Owens	w pts 6	Hull 12-7
Apr 8	Michael Gale	l pts 8	Leeds 12-9
May 13	Phil Soundy	w pts 6	Albert Hall 12-11
Jun 2	Eddy Smulders	l rsf 1	Rotterdam
Jul 18	Maurice Core	l pts 6	Manchester 12-10
Sep 7	James Cook	l pts 8	Bethnal Green 12-3
Oct 30	Roy Richie	drew 6	Istres
Nov 18	Tony Wilson	drew 8	Solihull 12-7-8
Dec 25	Franco Wanyama	l pts 6	Izegem

Fights 30 Won 12 Lost 14 Drawn 4

Tony BORG

Light-welterweight
Cardiff born 17 December 1964
Roath Youth ABC
1980 National Schools champion (w M Clark)
1980 NABC final (l J McBride)
1981 National Schools champion (w A Mester)
1981 NABC champion (w J Eastwood)
1982 Welsh ABA featherweight champion (w S Bryan, l H Henry)

1983
Mar 21	Kenny Watson	w pts 6	NSC 9-4	
Apr 21	Mick Hoolison	w rsf 2	NSC 8-13	
Jun 14	Eddie Morgan	w pts 6	Newport 9-2	
Nov 29	Steve James	w pts 6	Cardiff 9-3-12	/CTD...

(Tony BORG ctd)

1984
Jan 26	Charlie Coke	l rsf 5	Strand 9-2
Apr 16	Alex Cairney	w ko 2	Glasgow 9-2
Jun 13	Steve James	l pts 8	Aberavon 9-4
Sep 20	Les Walsh	w pts 6	Manchester 9-0
Oct 11	Dave Kenny	l rsf 4	Barnsley 9-3

1985
Jan 16	Gary Nickels	l pts 8	Shoreditch 9-4
Sep 28	Michael Marsden	w pts 6	Newport 9-7-8

1986
May 23	Steve Sims	l pts 10	Newport 9-3-12
	(Welsh super-featherweight title)		
Nov 24	Mark Pearce	l pts 8	Cardiff 9-7

1987
Mar 18	Andrew Furlong	l pts 8	Queensway 9-12
Apr 25	Eamonn McAuley	l rsf 4	Belfast 9-8
Sep 15	Mickey Crawford	w rtd 3*	Kensington 9-8
Oct 19	Ray Newby	w pts 8	Nottingham 9-4-8

1988
Apr 26	Mike Russell	w pts 6	Hove 10-0
May 16	Brian Nickels	w pts 8	NSC 10-1-8
Aug 30	Ian Honeywood	l pts 6	Holborn 9-8
Sep 28	B.F.Williams	w rsf 7	Edmonton 9-13-8

1989-90 inactive

1991
Sep 16	Peter Bradley	l pts 8	AASC 9-12-8
Nov 20	Felix Kelly	w pts 6	Cardiff 9-12-8

1992
Jan 22	Ross Hale	l pts 6	Cardiff 10-2

Fights 24 Won 13 Lost 11

John BOSCO

Light-middleweight
Mitcham, born Uganda 16 July 1967
Real name: John Waigo
1988 Seoul Olympics light-middleweight prelim (l rsf 1 S Sagnon, BFaso)

1991
Dec 5	Tony Kosova	w ko 2	Peterborough 11-2-8

1992
Feb 17	Gilbert Jackson	w pts 6	AASC 11-2-12
Sep 3	Russell Washer	w rsf 2*	Dunstable 11-2-12
Oct 19	Steve Goodwin	w rsf 2*	Mayfair 11-3-8
Dec 7	Griff Jones	w rsf 1	Mayfair 11-0-12

Fights 5 Won 5

Mark BOWEN

Cruiserweight
Millwall born 23 July 1966
West Ham ABC
Southpaw

1990
Apr 24	Pele Lawrence	w ko 5	Eltham 13-4-12
Sep 24	Roger McKenzie	w rsf 1*	AASC 13-3-8
Oct 18	Denzil Browne	l pts 6	Dewsbury 13-4

1991
Feb 21	Denzil Browne	l pts 6	Walsall 13-4
Apr 25	Bruce Scott	w pts 6	Mayfair 13-8
Jun 27	Michael Gale	l pts 8	Leeds 13-3-12

1992
Mar 25	Terry Dixon	l rtd 1	Albert Hall 13-5-12

Fights 7 Won 3 Lost 4

Mark BOWERS

Featherweight
Lock Heath born Fareham 19 October 1970
Pinewood Starr ABC & Fareham ABC
1984 National Schools champion (w R Carter)
1986 National Schools champion (w rsf 2 P Quinn)
1986 Junior ABA Class A champion (w rsf 1 F Peters)
1987 Junior ABA Class B champion (w rsf 1 C Bessey)
1988 NABC Class C champion (w J Reynolds)
1988 European Junior Championships (l rsf 3 K Scheibe, EG)
1990 ABA feather semi-final (w rsf 2 M Smyth, w rsf 1 J Knight, w rsf 1 Y Vorajee, w rsf 2 A Green, l B Carr)
1991 ABA featherweight final (w rsf 1 L Reynolds, w rsf 1 P Cooper, w ko 3 P Bates, w A Jones, w ko 3 I McLeod, l J Irwin)

1992
May 13	Hamid Moulay	w ko 1	Albert Hall 9-0-8
Oct 17	Miguel Matthews	w pts 6	Wembley 9-1-8
Dec 17	Chris Lyons	w ko 2	Wembley GH 9-2

Fights 3 Won 3

Warren BOWERS

Light-welterweight
Grimsby born 14 October 1971
No amateur experience

1989
May 8	Andy Brightman	w rsf 5	Cleethorpes 10-0
Sep 4	Mark Antony	w pts 6	Cleethorpes 10-2

1990
May 14	Barry North	w rsf 4	Cleethorpes 10-3

1991
Mar 2	Andy Kent	l pts 6	Cleethorpes
Nov 25	John Baxter	l rsf 3	Cleethorpes 10-13-8

1992
Jun 4	Peter Reid	l rsf 2	Cleethorpes 10-9

Fights 6 Won 3 Lost 3

Steve BOYLE

Lightweight
Glasgow born 28 November 1962
Southpaw   Scottish National ABC

1983
May 19	Sean Dooney	w rsf 3	Sunderland
Jun 6	Frankie Lake	w rtd 3*	NSC 10-1-4
Jun 13	Mike Mackenzie	w pts 6	Glasgow 10-0
Sep 19	Craig Walsh	w pts 6	Glasgow 9-10
Oct 17	Johnny Grant	w pts 6	Southwark 10-2
Nov 28	Robert Lloyd	l pts 6	Rhyl
Dec 7	Gary Lucas	drew 6	Manchester 9-10

1984
Feb 27	Willy Wilson	w rsf 3*	Nottingham 9-9-8
Mar 26	Rocky Mensah	drew 8	Glasgow 9-12
Jun 11	Dave Haggarty	w rsf 1	Glasgow 9-13
Sep 17	Gary Williams	w ko 2	Glasgow 9-12
Nov 19	Jimmy Bunclark	w rsf 2	Glasgow 9-9-12

1985
Jan 21	Rory Burke	w rsf 3	Glasgow 9-10
Mar 25	Peter Eubanks	w pts 8	Glasgow 9-10-8
Jun 3	Dave Savage	w rsf 7	Glasgow 9-8
	(vacant Scottish lightweight title)		
Sep 16	Junaid Musah	w ko 4	Glasgow 9-11-4
Oct 14	Stanley Jones	w ko 1	Glasgow 9-12

1986
Feb 24	Mickey Baker	w rsf 2	Glasgow 9-8-13
	(eliminator, British lightweight title)		
May 24	Tony Willis	l rsf 9	Manchester 9-9
	(British lightweight title)		
Dec 11	Simon Eubanks	w rsf 6	Livingstone 9-11

1987
Mar 3	Mike Durvan	w pts 10	Livingstone 9-8
Sep 21	Billy Buchanan	w rsf 7	Glasgow 9-8-4
	(Scottish lightweight title; final elim, British title)		
Nov 16	Muhammad Lovelock	w pts 8	Glasgow 9-9-12

1988
Feb 24	Alex Dickson	w ko 2	Glasgow 9-8-8
	(British lightweight title)		
Apr 19	Mark Brannon	w rsf 4*	Glasgow 9-11-10
Nov 1	Joey Jacobs	w ko 8	Glasgow 9-7-12
	(British lightweight title)		

1989
Jan 30	Pedro Gutierrez	w pts 12 (s)	Glasgow 9-8-12
	(WBC International lightweight title)		
Oct 17	Colin Morgan	w rsf 2	Cardiff 9-11
Nov 16	Poli Diaz	l pts 12	Madrid 9-9
	(European lightweight title)		

1990
Feb 14	Mark Fernandez	l rsf 6*	Millwall 9-12

1991
Apr 27	Antonio Renzo	l rtd 7*	Rossano Calabro 9-7-4
	(vacant European lightweight title)		

1992
May 5	Carl Crook	l rsf 7*	Preston 9-8-4
	(British & Commonwealth lightweight titles)		

Fights 32 Won 24 Lost 6 Drawn 2

Robert BRADDOCK

Featherweight
Bolton-on-Dearne, born Mexborough 14 January 1971

1989
Apr 3	Ronnie Stephenson	l ko 4	Manchester 8-10
Oct 13	Dave McNally	l pts 6	Preston 8-6
Oct 24	John Whitelaw	w pts 6	Hull
Oct 30	Peter Buckley	l pts 6	Birmingham 8-12

1990
Jun 28	Peter Buckley	l rsf 5	Birmingham 8-10

1991
Jun 10	Tony Smith	drew 6	Manchester 8-12
Sep 23	Al Garrett	drew 6	Glasgow 9-1-8
Oct 7	Glyn Shepherd	drew 6	Bradford 8-12
Nov 13	Chris Morris	l rsf 5	Liverpool 8-12
Dec 16	Carl Roberts	l pts 6	Manchester 8-12

1992
Apr 28	Chip O'Neill	l pts 6	Houghton-le-Spring 9-0
Jun 1	Alex Docherty	l pts 6	Glasgow 8-10-8
Sep 8	Chris Lyons	w ko 5	Doncaster 9-2
Oct 5	Karl Morling	l pts 6	Northampton 9-2
Nov 9	Chip O'Neill	w rsf 3	Bradford 9-2
Nov 23	Ian McLeod	drew 6	Glasgow 8-13-8
Dec 7	Gary White	l pts 6	Manchester

Fights 17 Won 3 Lost 10 Drawn 4

Nigel BRADLEY

Light-welterweight
Sheffield born 24 February 1968

1987
Dec 14	Lee Amass	l rsf 4	NSC 9-12

1988
Jan 29	John Townsley	l pts 6	Durham 9-8
Mar 23	Darren Darby	w rsf 1*	Sheffield 9-8
Mar 28	Adam Muir	nc 4	Glasgow 9-11
Apr 18	Mark Kelly	l pts 6	Manchester 9-12
Jun 8	Mike Russell	w pts 6	Sheffield 9-12
Sep 8	David Bacon	w rsf 5*	Doncaster 9-11
Oct 26	Dean Dickinson	w pts 6	Sheffield 9-9-12

1989
Feb 23	Chris Mulcahy	w rsf 2	Manchester 9-11
Mar 9	Michael McDermott	w rsf 5	Glasgow 10-0-8
Apr 4	John Mullen	w rsf 6	Sheffield

1990
Oct 8	John Townsley	drew 8	Glasgow 10-2-12
Nov 14	B.F.Williams	w ko 2	Sheffield 10-2-8

1991
Jan 29	Sugar Gibiliru	l pts 8	Stockport 10-0

1992
Feb 11	Dean Hollington	l pts 6	Barking 10-2
Mar 18	Kris McAdam	w ko 2	Glasgow 10-2-12
Apr 14	Dave Whittle	w ko 3	Mansfield 10-2-8
Sep 29	Tony Swift	l pts 8	Stoke 10-5

Fights 18 Won 10 Lost 6 Drawn 1 No Contest 1

Peter BRADLEY

Light-welterweight
Glasgow born 14 November 1963
Holyrood Youth ABC
1981 Scotland (v Eng, l R Ashton)
1983 ABA featherweight champion (w P Downie, w C Lynch, w K Taylor)
1983 Scotland (v Eng, l J Jacobs; v Wal, w S James)
1983 Great Britain (v USA, l rsf 1 J Loving)
1984 Scottish ABA featherweight champion (w D Ingram, l P Moylett)
1984 Scotland (v Eng, l dis 3 K Taylor; v Wal, w T Khan; v Ire, l P Fitzgerald)

1985
Feb 18	Ian Murray	w pts 6	NSC 9-5
Apr 1	Tommy Frankham	l rsf 2	Mayfair 9-6
Jul 1	Willy Wilson	w pts 6	NSC 9-8-12
Sep 23	Gary Flear	w pts 6	NSC 9-9-8
Oct 21	Andrew Mayers	l rtd 6*	NSC 9-9-12
Dec 2	Paul Downie	w pts 8	Glasgow 9-4-8

1986
Feb 10	Edward Lloyd	w pts 8	Glasgow 9-5
Mar 10	Dean Bramhald	w pts 8	Glasgow 9-6
Jun 2	Dean Bramhald	w pts 8	NSC 9-7-8

1987
May 6	Dean Bramhald	w rsf 4	Livingstone 9-5-8
Sep 24	Marvin P. Gray	l pts 8	Glasgow 9-6
Dec 2	Graham Clarke	w pts 8	NSC 9-2

1988
Feb 29	Karl Taylor	w pts 8	Birmingham 9-5
Mar 9	Steve Pollard	w pts 8	Wembley 9-5
Apr 25	Kid Sumaila	w pts 8	Birmingham 9-4-12
Sep 26	Tony Foster	w pts 8	NSC 9-5-8

1989
Jan 17	Steve Pollard	w pts 8	Woodford 9-11
Mar 8	Kid Sumaila	w pts 8	Albert Hall 9-7-8
Apr 10	George Jones	w rsf 4	NSC 9-10
Sep 18	Chubby Martin	w pts 8	NSC 9-8-12
Dec 11	Kid Sumaila	w rsf 3	Mayfair 9-9-4

1990
Feb 18	Alberto Alicia	w rsf 2	NSC 9-12
Mar 27	Rudi Valentino	w pts 8	NSC 9-8-8
Oct 22	Andy Deabreu	w rsf 3*	NSC 9-10

1991
Jan 21	Paul Burke	l pts 10	Glasgow 9-8-4
	(eliminator, British lightweight title)		
Sep 16	Tony Borg	w pts 8	AASC 9-11-8

1992
Mar 30	Alan Peacock	w pts 8	Glasgow 10-1-12
Jul 9	Gary Barron	w pts 8	Glasgow 10-1-8
Sep 4	Soren Sondergaard	l ko 4	Copenhagen
Oct 29	Philip Holliday	l rsf 6	Morula, South Africa 9-11

Fights 30 Won 24 Lost 6

Dean BRAMHALD

Light-welterweight
Doncaster, born Balby 25 May 1963
Elmfield House ABC

1984

Date	Opponent	Result	Venue
Jan 25	Wayne Trigg	l ko 3	Stoke 9-6
Feb 22	Andy Deabreu	l pts 6	Evesham 9-4
Feb 27	Joey Dee	w pts 6	Nottingham 9-6-8
Mar 19	Joey Dee	l pts 6	Bradford 9-6
Mar 27	Neville Fivey	drew 6	Wolverhampton 9-6
Apr 4	Peter Bowen	l pts 6	Evesham 9-7
Apr 12	Andy Deabreu	l pts 6	NSC 9-6
May 9	Wayne Trigg	drew 4	Leicester 9-5
May 21	Doug Munro	l pts 6	Aberdeen 9-10
Jun 11	Glenn Tweedie	l pts 6	Glasgow 9-8
Aug 6	Andy Williams	l pts 6	Aintree 9-9
Sep 21	Clinton Campbell	w pts 6	Alfreton 9-0
Oct 2	John Doherty	l pts 8	Leeds 9-1
Oct 10	Rocky Lawlor	w rsf 5*	Stoke 8-13
Oct 22	John Maloney	drew 6	NSC 9-3-12
Oct 29	Ray Newby	l pts 6	Nottingham 9-6
Nov 19	Dave Adam	l pts 6	Glasgow 9-2-8
Nov 27	Mick Markie	drew 6	Wolverhampton 9-0
Dec 5	Neville Fivey	w pts 6	Stoke 9-5
Dec 16	John Maloney	drew 6	NSC 9-2

1985

Date	Opponent	Result	Venue
Jan 18	Mark Reefer	l rsf 8	Bethnal Green 9-1-8
Feb 21	Stuart Carmichael	drew 6	Stafford 9-3
Mar 1	Craig Windsor	drew 6	Glasgow 9-4
Mar 13	Dave Adam	l pts 8	Stoke 9-2
Mar 25	Michael Marsden	w pts 8	Huddersfield 9-3
Apr 5	Bobby McDermott	l pts 8	Glasgow 9-0
Apr 18	John Doherty	l pts 8	Halifax 9-5-8
Jun 4	Pat Doherty	l ko 6	Streatham 9-1-12
Jul 31	Robert Dickie	l rsf 7	Porthcawl 9-3
Sep 23	Kevin Taylor	l rsf 1*	Bradford 9-3
Oct 21	Kevin Taylor	l pts 6	Bradford 9-4
Nov 21	Russell Jones	l pts 8	Blaenavon 9-9-8
Nov 30	Floyd Havard	l rsf 3*	Cardiff 9-5

1986

Date	Opponent	Result	Venue
Jan 20	Paul Downie	l pts 8	Glasgow 9-8
Feb 6	Stuart Carmichael	w pts 8	Doncaster 9-8-8
Feb 20	Floyd Havard	l pts 6	Halifax 9-7-8
Mar 10	Peter Bradley	l pts 8	Glasgow 9-8
Mar 17	Paul Downie	l ko 5	Glasgow 9-6
Apr 27	Andrew Pybus	w pts 6	Doncaster 9-5
May 20	Eamonn McAuley	l pts 6	Wembley 9-10-8
Jun 2	Peter Bradley	l pts 8	NSC 9-6
Jun 13	Gary Muire	l rsf 7	Gloucester 10-0
Jul 30	Steve James	l pts 8	Ebbw Vale 9-5
Nov 17	Jim Moffat	l pts 6	Glasgow 9-10-8
Nov 25	Joey Joynson	l pts 8	Wolverhampton 9-7
Dec 3	Steve Brown	l pts 6	Stoke 9-9
Dec 15	Rocky Lester	w pts 6	Loughborough 9-8

1987

Date	Opponent	Result	Venue	
Jan 26	Tony Swift	l pts 8	Birmingham 9-11	/CTD..

(Dean BRAMHALD ctd)

Feb 9	Peter Crook	l pts 8	Manchester 9-12-12
Feb 16	Nigel Senior	l pts 8	Glasgow 9-5
Mar 4	Tony Swift	l rsf 5*	Dudley 9-12
Apr 6	Drew Black	l pts 8	Glasgow 9-12
Apr 27	Kevin Spratt	l pts 8	Bradford 9-11
May 6	Peter Bradley	l rsf 4	Livingstone 9-11
Jun 4	David Maw	l pts 6	Sunderland 10-0
Jun 13	Michael Betts	drew 6	Great Yarmouth 10-1
Sep 4	David Maw	l pts 6	Gateshead 10-4-12
Sep 14	John Bennie	w pts 6	Glasgow 9-6
Oct 7	Tony Swift	l pts 8	Stoke 10-0
Oct 19	Peter Till	l pts 8	Birmingham 9-12
Nov 11	Ronnie Shinkwin	w pts 8	Stafford 10-0
Nov 24	Peter Till	l pts 8	Wolverhampton 10-2
Dec 2	Tony Swift	l pts 8	Stoke 10-2
Dec 14	Ronnie Shinkwin	l pts 8	Bedford 10-1
1988			
Jan 20	Davey Robb	l pts 8	Stoke 10-0
Jan 29	Frankie Lake	l pts 8	Torquay
Feb 9	Damien Denny	l pts 4	Stafford 10-2
Feb 24	Dave Lake	w pts 6	Southend 10-2
Mar 9	Mickey Vern	w ko 5	Stoke 10-2
Mar 23	Frankie Lake	drew 8	Evesham 9-13
Apr 13	Davey Robb	w rsf 4*	Wolverhampton 10-1
Apr 25	Nigel Senior	w pts 8	Nottingham 9-10-8
May 16	Ronnie Campbell	l rsf 7*	Wolverhampton 10-6-8
Jun 16	Mark Dinnadge	w pts 8	Croydon 10-3
Sep 26	Dave Croft	drew 4	Bradford 9-12
Oct 6	Ronnie Campbell	w rsf 6	Dudley 10-1-8
Oct 17	David Griffiths	l rsf 5*	NSC 10-2
Nov 17	Tony Feliciello	l pts 8	Weston-super-Mare 9-13-8
Nov 29	Neil Foran	l pts 6	Manchester 10-0-12
Dec 16	Brian Nickels	l pts 6	Brentwood
1989			
Jan 26	George Baigrie	w pts 6	Newcastle 9-12
Feb 14	Steve Hogg	w pts 6	Wolverhampton 10-2
Mar 6	Pat Barrett	l rsf 7	Glasgow 10-2
Apr 3	Brian Cullen	w rsf 3	Manchester 10-1
Apr 19	Calum Rattray	w pts 6	Doncaster 10-2
Apr 26	Michael Driscoll	l rsf 2	Southampton 10-4
May 29	Peter Hart	l rsf 2	Liverpool 10-0
Sep 25	Ian Honeywood	l rtd 4	Crystal Palace 10-2
Oct 25	Oliver Henry	l pts 6	Doncaster 10-3
Nov 28	Shaun Cooper	l ko 2	Wolverhampton 10-1
1990			
Jan 17	Peter Bowen	w pts 6	Stoke 10-0
Jan 24	Paul Bowen	l pts 8	Solihull 10-1
Mar 7	Andrew Robinson	l pts 6	Doncaster 10-1-12
Mar 14	Shaun Cogan	l pts 6	Stoke 10-2
Apr 4	Dave Croft	w pts 6	Stafford 10-2
Apr 26	Seamus O'Sullivan	l pts 6	Battersea 10-0
May 21	Brendan Ryan	drew 6	Cleethorpes 10-1-12
Jun 5	Billy Couzens	l pts 6	Nottingham 10-9
Jun 22	Mark Dinnadge	l pts 6	Gillingham 10-4
Nov 14	James Lawlor	drew 8	Doncaster 10-4
Dec 3	Andy Morgan	drew 8	Cleethorpes 10-1
Dec 10	Colin Sinnott	w pts 6	Bradford 10-4

Dec 17	Sugar Gibiliru	l pts 8	Manchester 10-2
1991			
Jan 17	Riki Burton	l rtd 1*	Alfreton 10-4
Mar 5	Charlie Kane	l rsf 6*	Glasgow 10-1
Apr 10	Ronnie Campbell	w pts 6	Wolverhampton 10-3
Apr 24	Dave Jenkins	l pts 8	Port Talbot 10-1
May 13	Andrew Robinson	l rtd 1*	Birmingham 9-10
Jun 17	Malcolm Melvin	l pts 6	Edgbaston 10-4
Jul 4	Shane Sheridan	l pts 6	Alfreton 10-5
Sep 10	Mark Elliot	l ko 5	Wolverhampton 10-0
Oct 8	Colin Sinnott	l pts 8	Wolverhampton 10-0-8
Oct 21	Colin Sinnott	w pts 6	Cleethorpes 10-2
Nov 20	Rocky Feliciello	l pts 6	Solihull 10-4
Dec 4	Ronnie Shinkwin	w pts 8	Stoke 10-2
1992			
Jan 22	Ray Newby	l pts 8	Solihull 10-2
Jan 30	Ronnie Shinkwin	l pts 6	Southampton 10-2
Feb 11	Ray Newby	l rsf 7	Wolverhampton 10-2
Mar 11	Andreas Panayi	w pts 8	Stoke
Mar 24	Richard Swallow	l pts 8	Wolverhampton 10-2
Apr 6	Richard Swallow	l pts 6	Northampton 10-4
Apr 28	Darren McInulty	l pts 6	Wolverhampton 10-6
May 11	Darren McInulty	l pts 6	Coventry 10-8
Jun 12	Carl Wright	l pts 6	Liverpool 10-2
Sep 15	Mike Morrison	w pts 6	Crystal Palace 9-13
Sep 30	Barrie Kelley	l pts 6	Solihull 9-10
Oct 13	Bernard Paul	drew 6	Mayfair 10-0
Nov 26	Kevin Toomey (Central lightweight title)	w pts 10	Hull 9-8-8
Dec 12	Mark Tibbs	l pts 6	Muswell Hill 9-13-8

Fights 129 Won 29 Lost 86 Drawn 14

Jason BRATTLEY

Light-welterweight
Leeds born 11 November 1970
Market District ABC

1991			
Mar 2	Barry North	w pts 6	Cleethorpes
Mar 25	James Clamp	w rsf 3	Bradford 9-12
May 17	Dave Thompson	drew 6	Bury 10-2
Oct 7	Scott Doyle	l pts 6	Birmingham 10-2
1992			
Mar 30	Dave Thompson	w pts 6	Bradford 10-3
Jun 1	Mike Mulcahy	w pts 6	Manchester 9-12
Jun 8	Kevin McKenzie	l rtd 3*	Bradford 10-0

Fights 7 Won 4 Lost 2 Drawn 1

Steve BRICKNELL

Light-welterweight
Birmingham born 19 February 1970

1991
Oct 1	Billy Robinson	l pts 6	Bedworth 10-3
Oct 21	Ricky North	l pts 6	Cleethorpes 10-2
Nov 28	Dean Carr	l pts 4	Wolverhampton 10-4
Dec 2	Dean Hiscox	l pts 6	Birmingham 10-3

1992
Jan 28	Lee Soar	l pts 6	Piccadilly 10-3

Fights 5 Lost 5

Mark BROOME

Light-welterweight
Grimsby born 1 June 1967
No amateur experience

1985
Sep 30	Dave Hall	w pts 4	Manchester 9-11-12
Nov 19	Barry Bacon	l pts 6	Stafford 9-4
Nov 28	Mark Needham	w pts 6	Ilkeston 9-6

1986
Feb 13	Geoff Calder	l pts 6	Bedworth 9-8
Mar 13	Paul Timmons	l rsf 6	Alfreton 9-7-12
Apr 30	Danny Cooper	l ko 6	Edmonton 9-12

1987-90 inactive

1991
Nov 25	Lee Soar	l pts 6	Cleethorpes 10-3

1992
Jun 4	Darren Henderson	w rsf 3*	Cleethorpes 10-2

Fights 8 Won 3 Lost 5

Dave BROSNAN

Welterweight
Eltham born 2 February 1966
1982 National Schools champion (w P Wright)

1987
Apr 7	Mark Howell	l rsf 6*	Ilford 10-10
Sep 28	Tony Simpson	w ko 1	Dulwich 10-11-4
Oct 12	Brian Butler	w pts 4	Bow 10-9

1988
Jan 21	Shane Traylen	w rtd 2*	Battersea

1989
Dec 6	Graham Burton	l rsf 6	Stoke 11-2-4

1990-91 inactive

1992
Apr 23	Bozon Haule	l rsf 6	Eltham 10-12-4

Fights 6 Won 3 Lost 3

Neville BROWN

Middleweight
Burton born 26 February 1966
Burton Boys ABC
1981 Junior ABA champion (w rsf 3 P Passley)
1981 National Schools champion (w J Bromby)
1982 Junior ABA champion (w rsf 2 L Weir)
1982 National Schools champion (w N Moore)
1982 NABC Class A champion
1983 NABC Class B final (l N Moore)
1985 Young England (v Ire, w rsf 2 C Thornton)
1986 Midlands ABA light-middle champ (w K Thompson, w rsf 3 C Burton, w rsf 2 R Horn, l dis 2 T Velinor)
1986 England (v Pol, w rsf 2 Zmijan; v Ire, w ko 2 K Joyce; w rsf 2 J Reed)
1987 ABA light-middleweight champion (w rsf 3 P Passells, w ko 1 M McAuliffe, w rsf 2 A Smith, w ko 2 C Burton, w rsf 1 T Cox, w S Smith, w ko 1 W Neil, w ko 1 N Pearce, w W May)
1987 European Championships light-middleweight bronze medal (w rsf 3 Salminen, Fin; w rsf 3 S Cirok, Cze; l E Richter, EGer)
1987 England (v Ire, l K Joyce; v Cze, l S Cirok)
1988 ABA light-middleweight semi-final (w rsf 3 S Smith, w rsf 3 D Ashton, w R Woodhall, w rsf 2 S Metherell, w M Shaw, w rsf 1 P D'Santos, w rsf 2 A Velinor, l rsf 1 W Ellis)
1988 England (v WGer, w M Gusnick)
1988 Canada Cup light-middleweight prelim (l D Sherry, Can)
1989 ABA light-middleweight champion (w rsf 2 P Spencer, w ko 1 N Towns, w rsf 1 P Hinch, w rsf 1 S Kenneth, w rsf 2 A Ellison, w rsf 1 C Colarusso)
1989 European Championships light-middleweight (w S Cirok, Cze; l rsf 3 R Obreja, Rum)

1989
Nov 8	Spencer Alton	w rsf 4*	Wembley GH 11-3-12

1990
Jan 10	Colin Ford	w rtd 3	Albert Hall 11-3-4
Mar 27	Jim McDonagh	w rsf 2	NSC 11-8-4
May 9	William Pronzola	w ko 3	Wembley CC 11-1-4
Sep 13	Anthony Campbell	w rsf 2	Watford 11-6-4
Oct 10	Nigel Moore	w ko 1	Albert Hall 11-2
Dec 13	Chris Richards	w rsf 2	Dewsbury 11-3

1991
Jan 17	Seamus Casey	w rsf 4*	Alfreton 11-5-8
Feb 13	Jimmy Thornton	w rsf 1	Wembley CC 11-6-8
Mar 28	Tony Booth	w pts 6	Alfreton 11-3-12
Apr 11	Winston Wray	w rsf 1	Willenhall 11-3
Jul 4	Paul Wesley	l rsf 1	Alfreton 11-3-8
Aug 29	Paul Smith	w rsf 3*	Telford 11-5-8
Oct 3	Paul Wesley	w pts 8	Burton 11-4
Nov 21	Colin Pitters	w rsf 3	Burton 11-2

1992
Mar 26	Paul Murray	w ko 3	Telford 11-7
Oct 1	Ernie Loveridge	w ko 4	Telford 11-7
Nov 2	Horace Fleary	w pts 8	Wolverhampton 11-5-4
Dec 4	Karl Barwise	w rsf 6	Telford 11-6

Fights 19 Won 18 Lost 1

Denzil BROWNE

Cruiserweight
Leeds born 21 January 1969
Burmantofts ABC
1989 Northern ABA heavyweight champion (w ko 1 S Finlayson, w rsf 3 C Bowen-Price, l rsf 3 H Hide)
1990 Northern ABA heavy final (w N Kirkwood, w dis 3 N Whitelam, w ko 2 P Mason, l C Bowen-Price)

1990
Oct 18	Mark Bowen	w pts 6	Dewsbury 13-7	/CTD...

(Denzil BROWNE ctd)

Nov 29	Roger McKenzie	l pts 6	Sunderland 13-6
Dec 13	Gary Railton	w rsf 2	Dewsbury 13-6
1991			
Feb 21	Mark Bowen	w pts 6	Walsall 13-6
Mar 21	Roger McKenzie	w pts 6	Dewsbury 13-11
May 11	Darren McKenna	w pts 6	Leeds 13-11-12
Jun 27	Steve Yorath	w pts 6	Leeds 13-8
Aug 1	Tony Colclough	w rsf 1	Dewsbury 13-10
Oct 9	Roger McKenzie	l pts 6	Manchester
Oct 30	Gus Mendes	w ko 6	Leeds 13-13-12
1992			
Jan 23	Darren McKenna	w pts 6	York 13-11-8
Mar 19	Ian Bulloch	w pts 8	York 13-12
Sep 23	Steve Yorath	w pts 8	Leeds 13-1
Oct 29	Sean O'Phoenix	w rsf 4	Leeds 13-3

Fights 14 Won 12 Lost 2

Frank BRUNO

Heavyweight
Wandsworth born 16 November 1961
Sir Philip Game ABC
1980 London (v Dub, w rsf 2 J Christle)
1980 ABA heavy champ (w rsf 1 G Williamson, w rsf 1 A Elliott, w rsf 1 H Myers, w rsf 2* J Burns, w R Pika)

1982

Mar 17	Lupe Guerra	w ko 1	Albert Hall
Mar 30	Harvey Steichen	w rsf 2	Wembley
Apr 20	Tom Stevenson	w ko 1	Albert Hall
May 4	Ron Gibbs	w rsf 4	Wembley
Jun 1	Tony Moore	w rsf 2	Albert Hall
Sep 14	George Scott	w rsf 1	Wembley
Oct 23	Ali Lukasa	w ko 2	Berlin
Nov 9	Rudi Gauwe	w ko 2	Albert Hall
Nov 23	Georg Butzbach	w rtd 1	Wembley
Dec 7	Gilberto Acuna	w rsf 1	Albert Hall
1983			
Jan 18	Stewart Lithgo	w rtd 4*	Albert Hall
Feb 8	Peter Mulendwa	w ko 3	Albert Hall
Mar 1	Winston Allen	w rsf 2	Albert Hall
Apr 5	Eddie Neilson	w rsf 3*	Albert Hall 15-7-8
May 3	Scott LeDoux	w rsf 3*	Wembley 15-9-8
May 31	Barry Funches	w rsf 5	Albert Hall 15-7
Jul 9	Mike Jameson	w ko 2	Chicago
Sep 27	Bill Sharkey	w ko 1	Wembley 15-8-8
Oct 11	Floyd Cummings	w rsf 7	Albert Hall 15-7
Dec 6	Walter Santemore	w ko 4	Albert Hall 15-9-8
1984			
Mar 13	Juan Figueroa	w ko 1	Wembley 15-10-8
May 13	James Smith	l ko 10	Wembley
Sep 25	Ken Lakusta	w ko 2	Wembley 16-0-8
Nov 6	Jeff Jordan	w rsf 3	Albert Hall 16-2
Nov 27	Phillip Brown	w pts 10	Wembley 16-0-4
1985			
Mar 27	Lucien Rodriguez	w rtd 1	Wembley 15-12-4
Oct 1	Anders Eklund	w ko 4	Wembley 16-0-8
	(European heavyweight title)		
Dec 4	Larry Frazier	w ko 2	Albert Hall 16-3-8

1986			
Mar 4	Gerrie Coetzee (eliminator, WBA heavyweight title)	w rsf 1	Wembley 16-3
Jul 19	Tim Witherspoon (WBA heavyweight title)	l rsf 11	Wembley Stadium 16-3-15
1987			
Mar 24	James Tillis	w rsf 5*	Wembley 16-2-8
Jun 27	Chuck Gardner	w rsf 1	Cannes 16-6
Aug 30	Reggie Gross	w rsf 8	Marbella 16-6
Oct 24	Joe Bugner	w rsf 8	Tottenham 16-6
1988 inactive			
1989			
Feb 25	Mike Tyson (World heavyweight title)	l rsf 5	Las Vegas 16-4
1990 inactive			
1991			
Nov 20	John Emmen	w ko 1	Albert Hall 16-4-12
1992			
Apr 22	Jose Ribalta	w ko 2	Wembley 16-10
Oct 17	Pierre Coetzer (eliminator, IBF heavyweight title)	w rsf 8	Wembley 17-6

Fights 38 Won 35 Lost 3

Del BRYAN

Welterweight
Nottingham born 16 April 1967
Bulwell Red Lion ABC
Southpaw

1986			
Apr 21	Wilbert Halliday	w pts 6	Birmingham 10-4
May 15	Gary Somerville	l pts 6	Dudley 10-7
May 28	Trevor Hopson	w rtd 4*	Catford 10-6
Jun 26	Gary Somerville	l pts 8	Edgbaston 10-5
Sep 26	Gary Cass	w pts 6	Swindon 10-0
Oct 6	Gary Somerville	w pts 8	Birmingham 10-8
Oct 14	Mickey Lerwill	w pts 8	Wolverhampton 10-7
Nov 4	George Collins	l rsf 4	Oldham 10-4
Dec 16	Ray Golding	w pts 6	Alfreton 10-5-4
1987			
Jan 8	Darren Dyer	w pts 6	Bethnal Green 10-6-12
Feb 17	Tommy Shiels	l rsf 2	Alfreton 10-7
Sep 30	Peter Ashcroft	w pts 8	Solihull 10-6
Oct 26	Gary Somerville (vacant Midlands welterweight title)	w rsf 7*	Aston 10-5
Dec 3	Mickey Hughes	w pts 8	Southend 10-7
Dec 15	Lloyd Christie	w pts 8	Bradford 10-4-8
1988			
Feb 24	Gary Jacobs (eliminator, British welterweight title)	l pts 10	Glasgow 10-7
Mar 9	Michael Justin	drew 8	Wembley 10-9
Apr 20	Kelvin Mortimer	w rsf 4*	Stoke
May 4	Gary Somerville	w pts 8	Solihull 10-10
Aug 9	Jimmy Thornton	w pts 6	St Helier
Sep 28	Ossie Maddix	w pts 8	Solihull 10-12 /CTD...

(Del BRYAN ctd)

Dec 12	Michael Justin (Midlands welterweight title)	w rsf 8*	Nottingham 10-6-8
1989			
Mar 22	Lennie Gloster	w pts 8	Solihull 10-5-8
May 10	Crisanto Espana	l pts 8	Albert Hall 10-7-8
Aug 19	Javier Castillejos	w pts 8	Benidorm
Sep 4	Joni Nyman	l pts 8 (s)	Helsinki 10-5
1990			
Jan 30	Simon Eubanks	w pts 6	Battersea 10-12
Feb 16	Arvey Castro	w rsf 1	Bilbao 10-10
Apr 17	Damien Denny (eliminator, British welterweight title)	w pts 10	Millwall 10-7
Sep 30	Phumzile Madikane	l rsf 6	Cape Town 10-5-4
1991			
Jan 16	Kirkland Laing (British welterweight title)	w pts 12	Albert Hall 10-4
Apr 16	Anthony Ivory	w pts 10	Nottingham 10-8-8
Nov 26	Mickey Hughes (British welterweight title)	w rsf 3*	Bethnal Green 10-5
1992			
Feb 20	Gary Jacobs (British welterweight title)	l pts 12	Glasgow 10-5-8
May 12	Darren Dyer	l rsf 10	Crystal Palace 10-7
Sep 29	Chris Peters	w pts 10	Stoke 10-8-8

Fights 36 Won 25 Lost 10 Drawn 1

Denroy BRYAN

Heavyweight
Swindon, born Birmingham 15 November 1959
Park Youth ABC
1980 Western ABA heavyweight final (l rsf 2 H Hylton)
1981 Western ABA heavyweight champion (w rsf 3 K Mills, l R Greenacre)
1982 Western ABA heavyweight champion (w ko 2 A Griffiths, l rsf 1 K Ferdinand)
1983 Western ABA heavyweight final (l dis 1 A Griffiths)

1983			
Sep 16	Michael Armstrong	w rsf 1	Swindon 14-6
Nov 14	Michael Armstrong	w rsf 4	Nantwich
1984			
Feb 22	Glenn McCrory	l pts 6	Albert Hall 14-8
Apr 30	Dave Garside	l pts 8	Mayfair 14-12
1985			
Jan 25	Noel Quarless	l rsf 1	Liverpool 14-9
Apr 22	Ralph Irving	w pts 6	Southwark 14-13-12
May 30	Carl Gaffney	l rsf 1	Halifax 14-10
Sep 12	Ian Priest	w rsf 7	Swindon 14-10
Oct 1	Dave Garside	l rsf 3	Wembley 14-6
Nov 14	Paul Lister	l pts 8	Newcastle 14-10
1986			
Feb 19	Gary Mason	l ko 1	Albert Hall 15-6
1987			
Apr 1	Barry Ellis	drew 8	Southsea 15-6
Oct 12	John Emmen	l pts 8	Den Bosch 15-0
1988			
Feb 9	James Oyebola	l rsf 6	Bethnal Green 15-3
Mar 29	Keith Ferdinand	l rsf 2	Bethnal Green 15-2

May 16	Al Malcolm	l pts 10	Wolverhampton 15-2
	(Midlands heavyweight title)		
Oct 25	Jess Harding	l rsf 4	Brentwood 15-7
Dec 5	David Jules	drew 6	Dudley 16-0
1989			
Jan 18	David Jules	l rsf 2	Stoke 15-7
Oct 23	John Williams	drew 6	NSC 15-0
Nov 10	Barry Ellis	w rsf 3	Battersea 15-7
Dec 5	Adam Fogerty	l rsf 3	Dewsbury 14-9
1990			
Feb 3	Gary McConnell	l rsf 9	Bristol 14-8-8
Mar 6	Manny Burgo	l pts 8	North Shields 14-5
Mar 20	Paul Lister	l pts 8	Hartlepool 14-7
Jun 25	Cesare Di Benedetto	l rsf 5	Avezzano
Nov 29	Adam Fogerty	l rsf 2	Sunderland 15-1
1991			
Nov 12	J.A.Bugner	l pts 4	Milton Keynes 15-0
Dec 11	Joe Egan	w rsf 4*	Dublin 14-10-8
1992			
Jan 31	Maurice Core	l rsf 1	Manchester 14-2
Oct 5	Damien Caesar	l rsf 5	Bristol 15-1
Dec 1	Barry Ellis	w pts 6	Bristol 14-11

Fights 32 Won 7 Lost 22 Drawn 3

Wayne BUCK
Heavyweight
Nottingham born 31 August 1966
Nottingham School of Boxing ABC

1990			
Mar 26	Michael Richards	w ko 1	Nottingham
Apr 30	Chris Hubbert	l ko 4	Nottingham 16-4
1991			
inactive			
1992			
Jun 4	Gary Charlton	w pts 6	Cleethorpes 15-11-12
Sep 8	David Jules	w rsf 3	Doncaster 15-10
Nov 12	Gary Charlton	w pts 8	Stafford 15-5-8

Fights 5 Won 4 Lost 1

Peter BUCKLEY
Featherweight
Birmingham born 9 March 1969
Ladywood ABC
1985 NABC Class A final (l M Tibbs)

1989			
Oct 4	Alan Baldwin	drew 6	Stafford 9-2
Oct 10	Ronnie Stephenson	l pts 6	Wolverhampton 9-0
Oct 30	Robert Braddock	w pts 6	Birmingham 8-13
Nov 14	Neil Leitch	w pts 6	Evesham 9-0
Nov 22	Peter Judson	w pts 6	Stafford 9-1
Dec 11	Stevie Wood	w pts 6	Bradford 8-12
Dec 21	Wayne Taylor	w pts 6	Kings Heath 9-1
1990			
Jan 10	John O'Meara	w pts 6	Albert Hall 8-13-8 /CTD...

(Peter BUCKLEY ctd)

Feb 19	Ian McGirr	l pts 6	Birmingham 8-13
Feb 27	Miguel Matthews	drew 6	Evesham 8-13
Mar 14	Ronnie Stephenson	drew 6	Stoke 8-12-8
Apr 4	Ronnie Stephenson	l pts 8	Stafford 8-13
Apr 23	Ronnie Stephenson	w pts 6	Birmingham 8-13
Apr 30	Chris Clarkson	l pts 8	NSC 8-13
May 17	Johnny Bredahl	l pts 6	Aars
Jun 4	Ronnie Stephenson	w pts 8	Birmingham 8-12
Jun 28	Robert Braddock	w rsf 5	Birmingham 8-12-8
Oct 1	Miguel Matthews	w pts 8	Cleethorpes 8-13-8
Oct 9	Miguel Matthews	l pts 8	Wolverhampton 8-13
Oct 17	Tony Smith	w pts 6	Stoke 8-12
Oct 29	Miguel Matthews	w pts 8	Birmingham 8-10
Nov 21	Drew Docherty	l pts 8	Solihull 8-10-8
Dec 10	Neil Leitch	w pts 8	Birmingham 9-0
1991			
Jan 10	Duke McKenzie	l rsf 5	Battersea
Feb 18	Jamie McBride	l pts 8	Glasgow 9-0-4
Mar 4	Brian Robb	w rsf 7*	Birmingham 9-1-8
Mar 26	Neil Leitch	drew 8	Wolverhampton
May 1	Mark Geraghty	w pts 8	Solihull 9-1-8
Jun 5	Brian Robb	w pts 10	Wolverhampton 9-3-8
	(vacant Midlands super-featherweight title)		
Sep 9	Mike Deveney	l pts 8	Glasgow 9-1-8
Sep 24	Mark Bates	w rtd 5*	Basildon 9-4
Oct 29	John Armour	l pts 6	Albert Hall 8-9
Nov 14	Mike Deveney	l pts 6	Edinburgh 9-0-4
Nov 28	Craig Dermody	l pts 6	Liverpool 8-10
Dec 19	Craig Dermody	l pts 6	Oldham 8-11
1992			
Jan 18	Alan McKay	drew 8	Albert Hall 9-0
Feb 20	Brian Robb	w rsf 10	Telford 9-2-8
	(Midlands super-featherweight title)		
Apr 27	Drew Docherty	l pts 8	Glasgow 8-10-8
May 15	Ruben Condori	l pts 10	Augsburg
May 29	Donnie Hood	l pts 8	Glasgow 8-11
Sep 7	Duke McKenzie	l rtd 3	Bethnal Green 8-12
Nov 12	Naseem Hamed	l pts 6	Liverpool 8-10-8

Fights 42 Won 18 Lost 19 Drawn 5

J.A. BUGNER

Heavyweight
St Ives born 12 August 1970   Sandy ABC
1990 Home Counties ABA super-heavyweight final (l P Eugene)
1991 Home Counties ABA super-heavyweight champion (w S Stewart, w C Parsons, l C Brown)

1991			
Nov 12	Denroy Bryan	w pts 4	Milton Keynes 16-0
1992			
Feb 6	Gary Railton	w ko 3	Peterborough 16-0
Mar 6	John Harewood	w pts 4	Battersea 16-4-8
Apr 22	Gary McCrory	w pts 4	Wembley 15-13
Sep 7	Gary Williams	w pts 4	Bethnal Green 15-12
Oct 17	Steve Gee	w pts 6	Wembley 16-4
Dec 17	Chris Coughlan	w rsf 3	Wembley GH 15-10

Fights 7 Won 7

Ian BULLOCH

Cruiserweight
Bolsover born 25 January 1965
SAPA ABC
1987 Midlands ABA light-heavyweight final (w G Barker, w E Cardouza, l J Foreman)

1987			
Mar 24	Danny Hassan	w rsf 4	Nottingham 12-10-4
Apr 9	Patrick Collins	w pts 6	Weston 13-2-12
Apr 29	Gus Menzies	w pts 6	Stoke 12-13
Jun 9	Steve Osborne	w pts 6	Manchester 13-5-8
Aug 3	Ray Thomas	w pts 8	Stoke 13-0
Oct 6	Sean Daly	w rsf 4*	Manchester 13-8
Nov 10	Gary Railton	w pts 6	Batley 13-8
1988			
Jan 12	Abner Blackstock	w pts 8	Cardiff 13-11
Mar 7	Danny Lawford	w pts 8	Hove 13-10
May 9	Roy Smith (Midlands cruiserweight title)	l pts 10	Nottingham 13-4-8
Nov 15	Noel Magee	drew 10	Hull 13-4
Dec 13	Yawe Davis	l rsf 6*	San Pellegrino
1989			
Jun 3	Dave Garside (eliminator, British cruiserweight title)	w pts 10	Stanley 13-4
Oct 2	Johnny Nelson (British cruiserweight title)	l ko 2	Hanley 13-4-8
1990			
Mar 1	Fabrice Tiozzo	l pts 6	Nice 13-5-8
May 12	Franco Wanyama	l rsf 5	Waasmunster 13-3-8
Sep 18	Gary McCrory	l pts 8	Stoke 13-9-8
1991			
Mar 2	Roy Smith (Midlands cruiserweight title)	l pts 10	Cleethorpes 13-8
Jun 24	Pedro van Raamsdonk	l pts 8	Rotterdam
Oct 13	Przemyslaw Saleta	l rsf 8	Warsaw
1992			
Mar 19	Denzil Browne	l pts 8	York 13-12
Apr 27	Terry Dixon	l rsf 4	AASC 13-9
Oct 26	Art Stacey	w pts 6	Cleethorpes 13-9

Fights 23 Won 11 Lost 11 Drawn 1

Nigel BURDER

Welterweight
Swansea born Gorseinon 7 September 1963
Penyrheol ABC

1991			
Nov 4	Chris Mylan	l ko 3	Merthyr 10-4-8
1992			
Mar 2	Steve Edwards	l rsf 1	Merthyr 9-13
May 11	Dewi Roberts	l ko 3	Llanelli 10-6-8

Fights 3 Lost 3

Paul BURKE

Lightweight
Preston born 2 July 1966
Bamber Bridge ABC

1987
Jan 21	Steve Brown	w ko 4	Stoke 9-12
Jan 30	Paul Marriott	l pts 6	Liverpool 9-13
Mar 2	Brian Murphy	w ko 2	Middlesbrough 9-9
Apr 6	Paul Marriott	w pts 6	Newcastle 9-10
Apr 30	Paul Gadney	w pts 6	Bethnal Green 9-10
Jun 1	Pat Barrett	w pts 6	Bradford
Sep 15	Marvin P. Gray	l rsf 6	Batley 9-12
Nov 18	Rudi Valentino	w pts 6	Bethnal Green 9-12
Dec 15	James Jiora	l pts 4	Bradford 9-11-8

1988
Feb 11	Paul Gadney	drew 8	Gravesend 9-9

1989
Jan 25	Paul Charters	w pts 6	Bethnal Green 9-13
Feb 23	Mark Kelly	l dis 5	Manchester 9-12
Mar 7	Tony Connellan	w rsf 5*	Manchester 9-12
Apr 11	Billy Buchanan	w rsf 4	Oldham 9-12
Oct 21	Aaron Kabi	drew 8	Middlesbrough 9-12-12
Dec 9	Angel Mona	l rsf 3	Toulouse

1990
Apr 27	Tony Richards	l pts 10	Glasgow 9-8-9
	(eliminator, British lightweight title)		
Sep 25	Robert Harkin	w pts 8	Glasgow 9-13

1991
Jan 21	Peter Bradley	w pts 10	Glasgow 9-8-12
	(eliminator, British lightweight title)		
May 31	Art Blackmore	w rsf 3	Manchester 10-1
Sep 20	Tony Richards	w pts 8	Manchester 9-13

1992
Feb 9	Dave Andrews	w pts 6	Bradford 10-3
Apr 28	Paul Charters	w rsf 7	Houghton-le-Spring 9-7-8
	(final eliminator, British lightweight title)		
Sep 28	Marcel Herbert	w pts 6	Manchester 9-12-12
Nov 17	Jean-Baptiste Mendy	l pts 12	Paris
	(European lightweight title)		

Fights 25 Won 16 Lost 7 Drawn 2

Winston BURNETT

Cruiserweight
Cardiff, born Jamaica 4 May 1959
Llandaff ABC

1980
Feb 12	Mike Burton	l pts 4	Wembley
Mar 24	Mike Burton	l pts 4	AASC
May 27	Ron Pearce	l pts 6	Newport 11-9
Oct 20	Pharoah Bish	w pts 6	Birmingham 11-8
Oct 27	Prince Wilmot	w pts 6	AASC 11-9-8
Nov 10	Neville Wilson	w pts 6	Birmingham 11-7-12

1981
Jan 19	John Humphreys	drew 6	Birmingham

Jan 27	Mark Kaylor	l pts 8	Albert Hall
Feb 16	Terry Christle	l pts 6	WSC
Mar 2	Peter Gorny	l pts 6	NSC 11-8-8
Mar 16	Paddy Ryan	w pts 6	AASC
Mar 24	Mick Mills	l pts 8	Sheffield 11-6
Mar 30	Archie Salmon	l pts 8	NSC
Jun 22	Henry Cooper	w pts 8	Glasgow 11-2-8
Sep 21	Billy Lauder	drew 8	Glasgow
Oct 6	Peter Gorny	w pts 8	NSC
Nov 3	Mark Kaylor	l rsf 6*	Albert Hall
Dec 8	Steve Davies	l pts 8	Pembroke

1982

Feb 23	Terry Christle	l pts 7	Belfast
Mar 8	Billy Lauder	l pts 8	Hamilton
Mar 15	Steve Johnson	l rsf 5	Bloomsbury
Jun 22	Andy Straughn	l pts 6	Hornsey
Aug 31	Barry Ahmed	l pts 8	South Shields
Oct 7	Michael Madsen	l pts 6	Copenhagen
Oct 18	Nick Jenkins	l pts 8	Southwark
Nov 23	Cordwell Hylton	l rsf 5	Wolverhampton

1983

Mar 12	Nick Jenkins	l pts 6	Swindon
Mar 15	Jimmy Price	l pts 6	Bloomsbury
Apr 13	Paul Shell	l pts 6	Evesham 11-12
Sep 16	Cliff Curtis	w pts 6	Swindon 11-10
Oct 12	Deano Wallace	l pts 6	Evesham 12-1
Nov 1	Mickey Kidd	l pts 6	Dudley 11-8
Dec 9	Sammy Brennan	l pts 8	Liverpool 12-2
Dec 19	Dave Mowbray	w rsf 4	Bradford 11-12

1984

Jan 30	Sammy Brennan	w pts 8	Manchester 11-11
Feb 25	Paul Tchoue	l rtd 5*	Paris
Apr 2	Mickey Kidd	l pts 8	NSC 11-9
Apr 12	Alex Romeo	w pts 6	NSC 12-3-8
Apr 17	Alex Romeo	w pts 6	NSC 12-5
May 2	Romal Ambrose	l pts 8	Solihull 12-4
May 12	Willie Wright	l pts 8	Hanley 12-2
Jun 4	Chris Devine	l pts 6	NSC 12-7
Jul 7	Stuart Robinson	l pts 6	Birmingham 12-8
Jul 22	Brian Anderson	l pts 8	Sheffield 12-2
Sep 17	Bernie Kavanagh	l pts 8	Bradford 12-11-8
Oct 1	Harry Cowap	l pts 8	Southwark 12-6-8
Oct 22	Chris Devine	l pts 8	NSC 12-8-8
Nov 9	John Mortensen	l pts 6	Copenhagen

1985

Jan 11	Tony Morrison	w pts 6	Cork 12-9
Jan 24	Keith Bristol	l rtd 5*	Streatham 13-2
Feb 28	Tony Wilson	l rsf 5	Wolverhampton 12-11
Apr 17	Nigel Shingles	w pts 6	Bethnal Green 12-4-8
Apr 30	Mike Farghaly	l pts 8	Chorley 12-10
May 11	Patrick Lumumba	l rsf 2	Vasa
Jun 26	Terry Gilbey	w pts 6	Basildon 13-0
Oct 8	Glazz Campbell	l pts 6	Southend 12-10
Oct 14	Barry Ahmed	w pts 6	Glasgow 12-8
Oct 25	Lou Gent	l pts 6	Fulham 12-8
Nov 6	Noel Magee	l pts 8	Nantwich 12-10
Nov 14	Lou Gent	l pts 8	Wimbledon 12-9-8
Dec 11	Noel Magee	l pts 8	Stoke /CTD...

(Winston BURNETT ctd)
1986

Feb 4	Geoff Rymer	w pts 6	Southend 12-2
Mar 5	Noel Magee	l pts 8	Stoke 12-3
Mar 13	Harry Cowap	l pts 8	Fulham 11-13
Mar 25	Serg Fame	l pts 8	Tunbridge Wells 12-4
Apr 1	Tom Collins	l pts 8	Leeds 12-2
Apr 9	John Moody	l pts 8	Albert Hall 11-12
Apr 23	Lee Davis	l pts 8	Basildon 12-2
May 23	Glazz Campbell	l pts 6	Newport 11-13-8
Aug 23	Eddie Smith	l rsf 2	Manchester 11-12
Oct 29	Gary Gething	l pts 6	Ebbw Vale 11-12-8
Nov 11	Bobby Williams	w pts 8	Southampton 11-12
Nov 20	Andy Wright	l pts 8	Wimbledon 12-0
Nov 29	Mickey Ould	l pts 6	Battersea 12-5-8
Dec 11	Steve Williams	l pts 6	Livingstone

1987

Jan 19	Alex Mullen	l pts 6	Glasgow 11-10
Jan 28	Byron Pullen	l pts 6	Croydon 12-6-8
Feb 20	T.P.Jenkins	l pts 8	Maidenhead 12-5
Feb 24	Mike Aubrey	l pts 6	Ilford 12-5
Mar 7	Frank Tate	l rsf 8	Basildon 12-4
Apr 6	Steve McCarthy	l pts 8	Southampton 12-12
Apr 14	Peter Brown	l pts 8	Cumbernauld 12-4
Apr 28	Byron Pullen	l pts 6	Halifax 12-3
May 9	Nigel Benn	l rsf 4	Battersea 12-4
Sep 7	Jason Baxter	l pts 6	Southend 12-0
Sep 16	Nigel Benn	l rsf 3	Albert Hall 12-0
Oct 19	Steve Williams	l pts 6	Glasgow 12-0
Dec 1	Branko Pavlovic	l rsf 1	Bow 12-8

1988

Feb 24	Brian Schumacher	l pts 8	Southend
Mar 7	Chris Eubank	l pts 6	Hove 12-4
Apr 12	Kevin Roper	l pts 6	Cardiff 12-8-8
Apr 21	Lennie Howard	l pts 6	Bethnal Green 12-7
May 5	Terry Duffus	w pts 8	Bayswater 12-6-12
May 18	Adam Cook	l pts 6	Port Talbot 12-5
May 26	Richard Bustin	l pts 6	Albert Hall 12-4
Jun 8	Dave Lawrence	l pts 6	Sheffield
Oct 10	Sean Heron	l pts 8	Glasgow
Oct 26	Errol Christie	l pts 8	Albert Hall 12-7-8
Nov 2	Jimmy Peters	l pts 8	Southwark 12-9

1989
inactive

1990

Nov 14	Carl Williams	l pts 4	Chicago 13-5
Dec 13	Lyle McDowell	l pts 4	Rosemont 13-3

1991

Feb 5	Anthony Wade	l pts 4	Memphis 14-2
Feb 18	Dan Murphy	drew 8	Omaha
Mar 8	Greg Gorrell	l rsf 6*	Wichita
Mar 16	Steve Brewer	w pts 4	Louisville 13-0
Apr 2	Dan Ward	l pts 10	Memphis 13-5
May 23	Dan Murphy	l pts 6	Omaha 13-0
May 24	Tim Morrison	w pts 8	Missouri
Jun 6	Anthony Wade	l pts 6 (s)	Hammond 13-2
Jun 15	Dan Murphy	l pts 6	Louisville 12-12
Jun 18	Anthony Wade	l pts 6	Evansville 13-0

Sep 10	Willie Jake	l pts 6	Indianapolis 12-13
Oct 18	Shawn Clarkson	l pts 6	Elkhart
Nov 12	Shawn Clarkson	l pts 5	South Bend 13-1
1992			
Oct 14	Mark Randazzo	l pts 8 (m)	Rosemount 13-5
Nov 27	Issa Moluh	l pts 8	Geneva

Fights 116 Won 20 Lost 93 Drawn 3

Gary BURRELL

Lightweight
Kirkcaldy born 9 July 1965

1992			
Sep 21	Alan Graham	w pts 6	Glasgow 9-9-8
Nov 9	Alan Graham	w pts 6	Bradford 9-8

Fights 2 Won 2

Graham BURTON

Super-middleweight
Chesterfield born 16 June 1964
Unity Boys ABC
1988 Humberside & Yorkshire ABA light-middleweight final (l rsf 1 P Hepton)

1988			
Oct 10	Frank Mobbs	w rsf 3	Manchester 11-2
Nov 3	Terry French	w rsf 3	Manchester 11-1-8
1989			
Jan 16	Dave Andrews	w pts 6	Northampton 11-2
Apr 4	Spencer Alton	w rsf 3*	Sheffield
Dec 6	Dave Brosnan	w rsf 6	Stoke 11-4-8
1990			
Jan 29	Darren McKenna	w pts 4	Hull 11-5
Apr 23	Steve Davies	w pts 6	Bradford 11-13
Jun 5	Nick Gyaamie	w pts 6	Eltham 11-12
Sep 18	Wayne Timmins	w pts 6	Wolverhampton 11-4
1991			
Jan 17	John Ashton	l pts 10	Alfreton 11-8-8
Mar 12	Peter Gorny	w pts 6	Mansfield 11-11
Jun 13	Michael Gale	l ko 4	Hull 12-2
Nov 12	Paul Busby	l rsf 3*	Wolverhampton 11-10
1992			
Feb 4	Richie Woodhall	l rsf 2	Alfreton 11-3-12
Mar 17	Andy Flute	l pts 8	Wolverhampton 11-10
Oct 13	Richard Carter	drew 8	Wolverhampton 11-13
Nov 24	Nigel Rafferty	l pts 8	Wolverhampton 11-13

Fights 17 Won 10 Lost 6 Drawn 1

Paul BURTON

Super-middleweight
Chesterfield born 26 February 1963
Wicker ABC
1985 North-East ABA welterweight final (w D Curtis, l B Neil)

1986
Feb 11	Paul Boyce	w rsf 1	Wolverhampton 10-6
Apr 17	Trevor Grant	l pts 6	NSC 11-1-8
Sep 15	John Davies	l ko 6	Manchester 10-13-8
Nov 25	Malcolm Davies	w rsf 6*	Wolverhampton 11-0

1987
Feb 17	Frank Graham	w ko 1	Alfreton 11-1-8
Sep 22	Cornelius Carr	l rsf 5	Bethnal Green 10-12
Nov 9	Lee Hartshorn	w pts 6	Leicester 11-5-8
Nov 30	Darren Parker	l rsf 6*	Manchester 11-2

1988
Mar 11	David Heath	w pts 6	Cottingham
Apr 22	Rob Thomas	l rsf 2	Lisbon 11-1
Nov 14	Darren Pilling	w rsf 2*	Manchester 11-5
Dec 1	Mark White	w rsf 4	Gravesend 11-8

1989
Sep 14	Carlo Colarusso	l rsf 5	Basildon 11-6

1990
Mar 21	Sean Heron	l ko 1	Preston 12-0
Nov 27	Andy Flute	w pts 6	Stoke 11-13
Dec 10	Chris Walker	l rsf 4*	Nottingham 11-13

1991
Feb 18	Max McCracken	l rtd 3*	Birmingham 12-0
Apr 15	Dave Radford	w rtd 1*	Birmingham 11-11
Apr 23	Simon McDougall	w pts 8	Evesham 12-2
May 18	Cornelius Carr	l rsf 3	Verbania 11-11-8
Nov 14	Paul Hitch	l ko 2	Gateshead 12-2

1992
Oct 23	Paul Hitch	l rtd 5	Gateshead 12-1-8

Fights 22 Won 10 Lost 12

Riki BURTON

Light-welterweight
Manchester born Jamaica 7 November 1970
Collyhurst & Moston ABC, Manco ABC

1989
Sep 10	Calum Rattray	w rsf 4*	Glasgow 10-2-8
Sep 25	Lee Ahmed	w rsf 4	NEC 10-0
Oct 11	Mike Morrison	w pts 6	Stoke 9-13
Dec 13	Tomas Arguelles	drew 6	Liverpool 10-0

1990
Nov 15	Mike Howell	w ko 5	Oldham 10-3

1991
Jan 17	Dean Bramhald	w rtd 1*	Alfreton 10-4
Jan 31	Mike Morrison	w pts 6	Stockport
May 16	Chris Saunders	w pts 6	Liverpool 10-3-8
Jun 20	James Lawlor	l pts 6	Liverpool 10-2-4
Nov 21	John Smith	w pts 6	Burton 10-4
Dec 19	John Smith	w pts 6	Oldham 10-3-8

1992
Feb 27	Chris Saunders	w pts 10	Liverpool 9-13-8
	(vacant Central light-welterweight title)		
Jul 2	Ray Newby	w pts 6	Middleton 10-2
Sep 24	Rob Stewart	w pts 10	Manchester 9-11-8
	(Central light-welterweight title)		

Fights 14 Won 12 Lost 1 Drawn 1

Rocky BURTON
Heavyweight
Bedworth, born Nuneaton 28 October 1958
Golden Eagle ABC
Real name: Wayne Burton

1977
Oct 18	Tony Bennett	w ko 1	Wolverhampton
Nov 30	Joey Williams	w pts 4	Wolverhampton

1978
Feb 13	Eddie Vierling	l rsf 2	Reading
Mar 6	Joey Williams	l pts 6	Wolverhampton
Oct 31	Reg Squire	l rtd 2*	Wolverhampton 12-9
Nov 27	Manny Gabriel	l pts 6	Kettering

1979
Jan 31	Roy Skeldon	l pts 4	Stoke
Mar 15	Roy Skeldon	l pts 4	Dudley
Mar 21	Emmanuel Lucas	w pts 6	Stoke
Mar 28	Manny Gabriel	l ko 1	Kettering
Jun 6	Emmanuel Lucas	w pts 6	Bedworth
Sep 26	Peter Les Reed	w pts 6	Stoke
Dec 17	John O'Neill	w pts 6	Wolverhampton

1980
Jan 28	George Lewis	w rsf 3	Birmingham
Feb 18	Nigel Savory	w pts 6	Stockport
Mar 18	Gary Jones	w pts 6	Wolverhampton
Mar 27	Stan Carnall	w rsf 4	Bradford
Apr 21	Nigel Savory	w rsf 4	Bradford
Sep 29	Terry O'Connor	l rsf 6	Bradford 15-0
	(vacant Midlands heavyweight title)		
Nov 25	Colin Flute	w rsf 7	Bedworth

1981
Mar 11	Steve Gee	l pts 8	Solihull 15-0
Sep 11	Paddy Finn	l pts 6	Edgbaston
Nov 10	Ricky James	l ko 6	Bedworth
	(Midlands heavyweight title)		

1982
Feb 4	Funso Banjo	l rsf 2	Walthamstow
Sep 20	Frankie Robinson	w pts 6	Wolverhampton
Oct 20	Steve Howard	w ko 1	Strand
Nov 11	Frankie Robinson	w pts 6	Stafford

1983
Feb 17	Ricky James	l ko 3	Coventry
	(Midlands heavyweight title)		
Sep 10	Thomas Classen	l pts 4	Cologne 15-8
Nov 1	Frankie Robinson	w rsf 5	Dudley 15-7

1984
Jan 26	Martin Nee	w rsf 3	Strand 15-0	/CTD...

(Rocky BURTON ctd)

Mar 10	Anaclet Wamba	l rsf 3	St Brieuc
Oct 5	Anders Eklund	l ko 1	Randers
1985			
Feb 4	Al Malcolm	l ko 1	Birmingham
Apr 9	John Westgarth	l ko 1	Darlington
1986-87 inactive			
1988			
Feb 24	Ian Priest	w pts 6	Leicester 16-4-4
Mar 2	Ian Priest	l pts 6	Stoke 16-12
Mar 22	Mick Cordon	w pts 6	Wolverhampton 15-7
Jun 7	Mario Guedes	l pts 6	Cologne 16-4
Oct 28	Denis Truchet	l ko 6	Grenoble
1989			
Feb 7	Michael Murray	l pts 6	Manchester 15-12
Feb 28	Gary McCrory	w pts 6	Middlesbrough
Mar 20	Andy Gerrard	drew 6	Nottingham 15-2
Apr 19	David Jules	w rsf 3	Doncaster 15-1
May 16	Adam Fogerty	l rsf 2	Halifax 15-7
1990			
Mar 19	Sean Hunter	w pts 6	Leicester 16-0
1991 inactive			
1992			
Feb 24	David Jules	l ko 1	Coventry 16-2

Fights 47 Won 22 Lost 24 Drawn 1

Paul BUSBY

Middleweight
Worcester born 20 April 1966
Worcester City ABC

1988 ABA middle semi (w D Simpson, w M Rowley, w A Wright, w J Fearn, w M Wright, w E Noi, l N Piper)
1989 Midlands ABA middleweight champion (w P Christie, w A Wright, w C Cope, l L Woolcock)
1990 Midlands ABA middle champ (w R Golding, w T Broadbridge, w D Ashton, w C Cope, w rsf 2 G Booker, w rsf 2 L Woolcock, l S Johnson)

1990			
Nov 18	Carlos Christie	w pts 6	NEC 11-7
Dec 4	Marty Duke	w pts 6	Bury St Edmunds 11-4
1991			
Jan 23	Tony Wellington	w rsf 2	Brentwood 11-6-12
Feb 27	Paul Murray	w pts 6	Wolverhampton 11-8
Mar 19	Paul Smith	w pts 6	Leicester 11-9
Sep 10	Nigel Rafferty	w rsf 2	Wolverhampton 11-8-8
Nov 12	Graham Burton	w rsf 3*	Wolverhampton 11-8-8
Dec 17	Paul Murray	w ko 3	Cardiff 11-7
1992			
Feb 1	John Kaighin	w pts 4	Birmingham 11-9
May 23	Stinger Mason	w rsf 2	Birmingham 11-8
Nov 14	Paul Wesley	w pts 8	Cardiff 11-8

Fights 11 Won 11

Rick BUSHELL

Lightweight
Herne Bay, born Bridge 1 March 1965
Southpaw
Canterbury ABC
1989 Southern ABA light-welterweight semi-final (w S Bloomfield, w T Turner, wthdrw)

1989
Dec 11	Denzil Goddard	w rsf 2*	Mayfair 9-5-12

1990
Jan 15	Carl Brasier	w ko 1	NSC 9-8
Apr 11	James Jiora	w pts 6	Dewsbury 9-7
Apr 26	Andy Deabreu	l pts 6	Mayfair 9-5
May 21	Vaughan Carnegie	w pts 6	NSC 9-9
Sep 12	Eamonn McAuley	l rsf 4	Battersea 9-5

1991
Jan 10	Mike Morrison	w pts 6	Battersea 9-13
Feb 7	B.F.Williams	w rtd 2	Watford 10-0
Feb 18	Robert Smyth	w pts 6	NSC 9-9-12
Feb 28	Marvin P. Gray	l pts 6	Sunderland 9-9-8
Apr 10	Vaughan Carnegie	w rsf 3	Newport 9-10-12
Apr 18	Felix Kelly	l pts 6	Kensington 9-7
Jun 22	Felix Kelly	w pts 6	Earls Court 9-8
Oct 23	Mark Tibbs	l rsf 4*	Bethnal Green 9-10
Dec 11	Mark Tibbs	l rsf 2*	Basildon 9-11

1992
Mar 2	Jose Tuominen	drew 4	Helsinki
Mar 14	Soren Sondergaard	l ko 3	Copenhagen
May 16	Dean Hollington	l rsf 2	Muswell Hill 9-13-8
Oct 21	Rocky Milton	drew 4	Earls Court 9-10-4
Dec 17	Paul Ryan	l rsf 1	Barking 9-8-12

Fights 20 Won 9 Lost 9 Drawn 2

Richard BUSTIN

Super-middleweight
Norwich born 9 October 1964
Watton ABC

1988
Feb 15	Roger Silsby	l pts 6	Copthorne 12-0
Mar 14	Tony Behan	w rsf 3	Norwich 12-2-8
Apr 5	Steve Conway	w rsf 4	Basildon 12-4
May 26	Winston Burnett	w pts 6	Albert Hall 12-2
Oct 17	Dennis Banton	w rsf 5	NSC 12-1
Nov 15	Crawford Ashley	l ko 3	Norwich 12-1

1989
Feb 7	Alan Baptiste	w pts 6	Southend 12-0
May 15	Alex Romeo	l rsf 2	Northampton 12-3
Oct 3	Alan Baptiste	w pts 6	Southend 12-2
Oct 17	Mick Maw	w ko 2	Cardiff 12-4-8

1990
Mar 14	Paul McCarthy	l rsf 7*	Battersea 11-11-12
	(vacant Southern super-middleweight title)		
Nov 12	Alan Baptiste	w rsf 1	Norwich 12-7

1991
Jan 29	Simon Harris	l rsf 3*	Wisbech 12-7	/CTD..

(Richard BUSTIN ctd)

Apr 18	John Foreman	w pts 8	Kensington 12-6
Jun 11	Gary Ballard	l pts 8	Leicester 12-6
Nov 19	Glazz Campbell	l ko 7	Norwich
	(vacant Southern light-heavyweight title)		
1992			
Jan 31	Bobbi Joe Edwards	l pts 6	Manchester 12-9
Mar 31	Gipsy Carmen	l pts 6	Norwich 12-11-12
Jun 27	Dariusz Michalczewski	l rsf 4	Quinta Do Lago
Sep 8	Karl Barwise	w pts 6	Norwich 12-0

Fights 20 Won 10 Lost 10

Blue BUTTERWORTH
Light-welterweight
Burnley, born London 5 October 1970
Sandygate ABC

1992			
Mar 31	Brian Coleman	w pts 6	Stockport 10-3-4
Jun 4	Mark Allen	w rsf 5	Burnley 10-1-12
Sep 14	Lee Soar	w ko 4	Bradford 10-3
Nov 12	Dave Madden	w rsf 2	Burnley 10-2

Fights 4 Won 4

Michael BYRNE
Welterweight
Birmingham born 16 May 1972

1991			
Sep 16	Dean Carr	l pts 6	Cleethorpes 10-7
Oct 1	Jamie Morris	drew 4	Bedworth 10-4
Oct 16	Jamie Morris	l pts 6	Stoke 10-3-8
Oct 28	Kevin McKillan	l pts 6	Leicester 10-2
Dec 9	Rick North	l rsf 2	Cleethorpes 10-4
1992			
Apr 4	Mick Mulcahy	l rsf 4	Cleethorpes 10-2

Fights 6 Lost 5 Drawn 1

Sean BYRNE
Super-middleweight
Northampton born 20 September 1965
Kingsthorpe ABC

1992			
Apr 6	Martin Jolley	w rsf 6	Northampton 11-8
Apr 28	John Mackenzie	w rsf 6*	Corby 11-10
Oct 5	Russell Washer	w pts 6	Northampton 11-6

Fights 3 Won 3

TOMMY GILMOUR Jnr.
International Boxing Manager & Matchmaker

Team 1993

Flyweight
PAT CLINTON, W.B.O. World Champion
JAMES DRUMMOND   PAUL WEIR

Bantamweight
DREW DOCHERTY, British Champion
RONNIE CARROLL   STEVIE WOODS

Featherweight
JAMIE McBRIDE, Scottish Champion
WILSON DOCHERTY   AL GARRETT   IAN McLEOD   ALEX DOCHERTY

Super-Featherweight
MARK GERAGHTY, Scottish Champion
IAN McGIRR   DAVY McHALE

Lightweight
KRIS McADAM, Scottish Champion
ALAN INGLE   HUGH COLLINS   GARY BURRELL

Light-Welterweight
ALAN PEACOCK   PETER BRADLEY   DREW BLACK

Welterweight
JOHN MULLEN

Middleweight
WILLIE QUINN

Super-Middleweight
SEAN HERON

Light-Heavyweight
JOE McCLUSKEY   STEVIE WILSON

ADMINISTRATIVE OFFICES:
ST. ANDREW'S SPORTING CLUB,
FORTE CREST, BOTHWELL STREET, GLASGOW G2 7EN
Tel—Office: 041-248 5461 & 041-248 2656   Fax 041-221 8986   Telex 77440.
Tel—Home: 041-639 2553

Sporting Club

"The Pursuit of Excellence"

10 Western Road
Romford
Essex
RM1 3JT

Tel: (0708) 730480 (Office)
(0708) 724023 (Gym) Freddie King
Fax: (0708) 723425
Telex: 893334

Damien CAESAR

Heavyweight
Stepney born 2 October 1965
Repton ABC
1988 London ABA super-heavyweight semi-final (w.o., l ko 1 R Callus)
1989 NE London ABA super-heavyweight semi-final (l rsf 2 D Holness)

1991
Apr 22	Larry Peart	w rsf 2	AASC 15-0
May 30	Tony Colclough	w rsf 1	Mayfair 15-4

1992
Feb 17	Steve Stewart	w rsf 5	AASC 15-13
Apr 27	Gary Williams	w rsf 4	AASC 14-7-12
Oct 5	Denroy Bryan	w rsf 5	Bristol 15-6

Fights 5 Won 5

Geoff CALDER

Light-middleweight
Kidderminster born 21 April 1967
Stourport ABC

1985
Nov 6	Wayne Goult	w pts 6	Evesham 10-1-8
Nov 14	Mark Poultney	l pts 6	Dudley 10-0
Dec 4	Rocky Lester	w rsf 3	Stoke 10-0

1986
Jan 27	Gary Somerville	l pts 6	Dudley 10-3
Feb 13	Mark Broome	w pts 6	Bedworth 9-10
Feb 24	Paul Seddon	l pts 6	Dudley 9-13
Mar 12	John Daly	l pts 6	Stoke 9-13
Mar 17	Dean Murray	l ko 1	Birmingham 10-4
Apr 29	Trevor Grant	l rsf 3	NSC
Oct 8	Mike Mackenzie	w rtd 1*	Stoke 10-8
Oct 14	Rory Callaghan	l pts 6	Wolverhampton 10-9
Nov 10	Graeme Griffin	w rsf 5	Birmingham 10-8
Nov 21	Geoff Sharp	l pts 6	Maidenhead 10-11
Dec 3	Wilbert Halliday	drew 6	Stoke 10-8

1987
Feb 19	Steve Hogg	w pts 6	St Helens 10-8
Mar 9	Mark Howell	l pts 6	NSC 10-9
Mar 24	Steve Kiernan	drew 6	Wolverhampton 10-7
Apr 18	Darren Dyer	l rsf 2	Albert Hall 10-8-8
Sep 3	Levi Stephenson	drew 6	NSC 10-12
Sep 30	Keith Scott	w rsf 3*	NSC
Oct 13	Rafaele Feliciello	l pts 8	Wolverhampton 11-0
Dec 15	Tony Collins	l rsf 2	Cardiff 11-4

1988
Feb 24	Tony Collins	l rsf 3	Aberavon 11-1
May 16	Steve West	l rsf 4	NSC 10-9
Oct 19	Paul Murray	nc 5	Evesham 10-12
Oct 31	Peter Sorbey	l rsf 4	Leicester 10-12

1989-91 inactive

1992
Sep 24	Darren Pilling	l rsf 5	Manchester
Oct 27	Andre Wharton	l pts 4	Cradley Heath 10-13-4

Fights 28 Won 7 Lost 17 Drawn 3 No Contests 1

Doug CALDERWOOD

Middleweight
Leeds, born Scotland 28 April 1964
Scarborough Eastfield ABC
1982 Humberside ABA middleweight final (l rsf 1 M Esa)
1983 Humberside ABA middleweight final (l ko 1 B Webb)
1984 North East ABA middleweight final (l G Horne)

1985			
Dec 6	Malcolm Kay	w ko 5	Everton 11-9
1986			
Feb 5	Deano Wallace	w pts 8	Sheffield 11-9
Apr 7	Peter Brown	l pts 6	Manchester 11-8
May 30	Ray Golding	w rsf 1*	Stoke 10-13
Nov 6	Alex Mullen	l pts 8	Glasgow 11-6
Nov 24	Neil Fannon	l pts 6	Middlesbrough 11-7
1987			
Jan 26	Leon Thomas	w ko 1	Leamington 11-6
Mar 2	Ian Bayliss	drew 6	Middlesbrough 11-9
Sep 30	Johnny Elliot	l pts 6	Solihull 11-8-12
1988			
Feb 23	Darren Burford	w pts 6	Bedford 12-3
Nov 2	Ray Webb	l rsf 6	Southwark 11-10
1989-90 inactive			
1991			
May 13	Stinger Mason	w ko 3	Manchester 12-3
Oct 1	Simon McDougall	l rsf 4*	Liverpool 12-3
Dec 12	Paul Hitch	l pts 6	Hartlepool
1992			
Mar 11	Chris Walker	l pts 8	Solihull 12-1

Fights 15 Won 6 Lost 8 Drawn 1

Mike CALDERWOOD

Welterweight
Salford born 17 September 1964

1983			
Feb 14	Peter Flanagan	l pts 6	Manchester
Apr 11	Bobby Welburn	drew 6	Manchester 10-1
Apr 25	Colin Neagle	l pts 6	Liverpool 10-6
May 13	Mohammed Aslam	w rsf 5*	Morley 10-5-8
May 23	Tommy Bennett	l pts 6	Sheffield
Jun 20	Mick Dono	l pts 6	Manchester 10-4
1984			
Apr 9	Tony Kempson	l rsf 5*	Manchester 10-9
Jun 4	Chris Edge	drew 6	Manchester 10-9
Nov 12	George Jones	drew 6	Nantwich
Nov 30	Chris McReedy	l rsf 3	Liverpool 10-0
1985-87 inactive			
1988			
Mar 1	Steve Phillips	l pts 6	Manchester 10-4
Apr 18	Karl Davey	l rsf 5	Manchester 10-6
1989-90 inactive			

1991			
Jun 10	Mick Mulcahy	w pts 6	Manchester 10-5-8
Oct 1	Kevin Toomey	w rsf 2*	Liverpool 10-2
Oct 21	Brian Cullen	l pts 6	Bury 10-3-8
Dec 2	John Smith	drew 8	Liverpool 10-3
1992			
Mar 9	Robert Lloyd	w rsf 1	Manchester 10-1-12
Mar 31	Rob Stewart	l pts 4	Stockport 10-2-4

Fights 18 Won 4 Lost 10 Drawn 4

Albert CALL

Cruiserweight
Grimsby born 17 April 1967
Grimsby ABC
1991 Yorkshire & Humberside ABA light-heavyweight final (w M Brook, l A Walton)
1992 Yorkshire & Humberside ABA light-heavyweight semi-final (l R Atkinson)

1992			
Sep 21	John Pierre	w pts 6	Cleethorpes 13-11
Dec 14	Art Stacey	w pts 6	Cleethorpes 13-6

Fights 2 Won 2

Dave CAMPBELL

Bantamweight
South Shields born 13 December 1968
Simonside ABC & Horsley Hill ABC
1987 North-East Division ABA flyweight semi-final (l S Parry)
1989 North East Division ABA flyweight semi-final (l N Johnson)
1990 North East Division ABA flyweight final (l ko 1 S Parry)
1991 North-East ABA bantamweight final (l ko 3 P Ingle)

1991			
Sep 11	Mark Hargreaves	l rsf 4	Stoke 8-6
Nov 14	Dave Martin	w pts 6	Marble Arch 8-7
Nov 27	Shaun Norman	w pts 6	Marton
1992			
May 18	Glyn Shepherd	w rsf 1	Marton 8-7
Sep 23	Tony Silkstone	l rsf 4	Leeds 8-9

Fights 5 Won 3 Lost 2

Glazz CAMPBELL

Light-heavyweight
Brockley, born Sheffield 9 August 1962
Eckington ABC

1985			
Oct 8	Winston Burnett	w pts 6	Southend 12-9
Oct 30	Lennie Howard	l pts 8	Basildon 12-12-8
1986			
May 23	Winston Burnett	w pts 6	Newport 12-8-8
Sep 25	Serg Fame	w pts 8	Crystal Palace 12-7-8
Nov 3	Blaine Logsdon	l ko 3	Manchester 12-8
1987			
Jan 29	Lou Gent	l pts 6	Wimbledon 12-9-12
Sep 14	Crawford Ashley	w pts 8	Bloomsbury 12-10 /CTD...

(Glazz CAMPBELL ctd)

Dec 3	Mike Aubrey	w pts 8	Southend 12-11-4
1988			
Apr 26	Agamil Yilderin	drew 8	Cologne 12-8
Sep 13	Serg Fame	l pts 10	Battersea 12-5-8
	(vacant Southern light-heavyweight title)		
1989			
Feb 20	Pedro van Raamsdonk	l pts 8	Arnhem 12-8-8
Sep 25	Alek Penarski	w rsf 4	NSC
Oct 23	Derek Myers	l pts 8	NSC 12-11
1990			
Apr 27	Mwehu Beya	drew 8	Pesaro 12-7-8
Jun 2	Cordwell Hylton	l pts 4	Manchester 13-2
Sep 15	Noel Magee	l pts 8	Belfast 12-6
Dec 7	Henry Maske	l pts 8	Berlin
1991			
Apr 12	Maurice Core	l ko 2	Manchester 12-10-8
Jun 29	Christophe Girard	l pts 8	Le Touquet
Aug 24	Mwehu Beya	l pts 6	Pesaro 12-9-12
Oct 2	Tony Wilson	w pts 8	Solihull 12-9-8
Nov 19	Richard Bustin	w ko 7	Norwich 12-6-8
	(vacant Southern light-heavyweight title)		
1992			
Mar 18	Tom Collins	w pts 10	Glasgow 12-7
	(final eliminator, British light-heavyweight title)		
Apr 25	Crawford Ashley	l rsf 8	Belfast
	(British light-heavyweight title)		

Fights 24 Won 9 Lost 13 Drawn 2

Glenn CAMPBELL

Super-middleweight
Bury born 22 April 1970
Bury ABC
1990 East Lancs ABA light-heavyweight final (l C Edwards)

1990			
Apr 19	Ian Vokes	w ko 1	Oldham 12-3-4
May 1	Steve Davies	w rsf 2	Oldham 12-2-12
May 21	Andy Marlow	w rsf 6	Hanley 12-0-8
Jun 11	Stinger Mason	w rtd 5*	Manchester 12-4-12
Sep 26	Tony Kosova	w rsf 2	Manchester 12-3
Oct 22	Simon McDougall	w rsf 4	Manchester 12-6
Nov 26	Sean O'Phoenix	w rsf 4	Bury 11-12
	(vacant Central super-middleweight title)		
1991			
Feb 28	Simon McDougall	w pts 10	Bury 11-13
	(Central super-middleweight title)		
May 17	Tony Booth	w rsf 2	Bury 11-11
	(Central super-middleweight title)		
1992			
Jan 21	Nigel Rafferty	w rsf 6	Stockport 11-11-12
Mar 10	Carlos Christie	drew 8	Bury
May 5	Ian Henry	w rsf 1	Preston 12-2

Fights 12 Won 11 Drawn 1

James CAMPBELL

Welterweight
Birmingham born 12 July 1967
Birmingham City ABC & Aston Villa ABC
1987 Birmingham ABA welterweight prelim (l M Elliot)

1991
Oct 21	Dean Carr	w rsf 5	Cleethorpes 10-9
Nov 26	Julian Eavis	l pts 8	Wolverhampton 10-7

1992
Feb 20	Peter Reid	w pts 6	Telford 10-8
Apr 30	Nick Bardle	w ko 1	Watford 10-6
Sep 17	B.F.Williams	l pts 6	Watford 10-3
Oct 30	Steve Scott	w pts 6	NEC 10-10
Nov 23	James McGee	drew 6	Coventry 10-12
Dec 14	Barry Thorogood	l rsf 4	Cardiff 10-12

Fights 8 Won 4 Lost 3 Drawn 1

Ray "Razza" CAMPBELL

Light-welterweight
Dudley born 29 June 1966

1991
Nov 26	Moses Sentamu	l rsf 2	Wolverhampton 9-13

1992
Mar 11	Jamie Morris	w pts 6	Stoke
Mar 30	Gavin Lane	w pts 6	Coventry 9-13

Fights 3 Won 2 Lost 1

Micky CANTWELL

Flyweight
Eltham born 23 November 1963
Lynn ABC, Fisher ABC & Eltham ABC
1982 London ABA light-flyweight final (w rsf 2 A Dann, w J Walker, l J McBride)
1983 London ABA light-flyweight final (l P Maher)
1984 London ABA light-flyweight champion (w.o., l rsf 3 J Lyon)
1986 Acropolis Cup gold medal
1987 ABA light-flyweight semi-final (w D Dent, w rsf 3 J Simpson, w rsf 2 M Reynolds, l W Docherty)
1988 ABA light-fly champ (w rtd 2 N Persaud, w rsf 1 M Khan, w J Simpson, w M Reynolds, w R Regan)
1988 England (v WGer, w rsf 2 U Krane)
1988 Canada Cup
1989 ABA light-flyweight champion (w rsf 1 L Harris, w N Persaud, w N Tooley, w I Lang)
1989 England (v Sco, l P Weir)
1990 Commonwealth Games (l ko 3 J Juuko, Uga)

1991
Jan 21	Eddie Vallejo	w rsf 4	Crystal Palace 7-12
Mar 26	Mario Alberto Cruz	w pts 6	Bethnal Green 7-12
Sep 30	Ricky Beard	w pts 8	Albert Hall 7-13
Oct 22	Carlos Manrigues	w rsf 5	Bethnal Green 7-10
Dec 14	Shaun Norman	w pts 8	Bexleyheath 7-13

1992
May 16	Louis Veitch	w pts 6	Muswell Hill 8-3-4

Fights 6 Won 6

Gipsy CARMEN

Cruiserweight
Norwich, born Wisbech 23 November 1964
Real name: George Carmen
Southpaw
Parsons Drove ABC

1984
Jan 30	Dave Mowbray	w pts 6	Manchester 12-0
Feb 16	Lennie Howard	l rtd 1*	Basildon 12-7
Apr 3	Gordon Stacey	w pts 6	Lewisham 12-8
Jun 7	Dekka Williams	l pts 6	Dudley
Oct 29	Wes Taylor	w pts 6	Streatham 12-13

1985
Feb 4	Lee White	w pts 6	Lewisham 13-8
Feb 20	Charlie Hostetter	l pts 6	Muswell Hill 13-12
Mar 27	Glenn McCrory	l pts 8	Gateshead 13-2
May 9	Barry Ellis	l pts 8	Acton 14-6-12
Jun 10	Chris Jacobs	drew 6	Cardiff 14-6-8
Sep 2	Barry Ellis	l pts 8	Coventry 14-7
Oct 31	Tee Jay	l pts 6	Wandsworth 14-2

1986
Mar 15	Mick Cordon	w pts 8	Norwich 13-10
Mar 24	Chris Harbourne	w pts 6	NSC 13-12
Sep 10	Tee Jay	l rsf 4*	Norwich 13-5
	(vacant Southern cruiserweight title)		
Nov 20	Lou Gent	l ko 1	Wimbledon 13-8

1987
Jan 11	Patrick Collins	w pts 8	Glasgow 14-0
Jan 19	Johnny Nelson	l pts 6	NSC 13-7-8
Feb 19	Danny Lawford	l pts 6	Peterborough 13-8
Mar 4	Tommy Taylor	l pts 8	Dudley 13-5
Nov 24	Tommy Taylor	w pts 8	Wisbech 13-10

1988
Mar 14	Blaine Logsdon	l rsf 8*	Norwich 13-5
Apr 25	Gerry Storey	l pts 6	Bethnal Green 13-10

1989
Sep 15	Carlton Headley	w pts 6	High Wycombe 13-7

1990
Feb 22	Lou Gent	l pts 10	Battersea 13-5-8
	(Southern cruiserweight title)		
May 7	Eddy Smulders	l rsf 4	Arnhem 12-10
Nov 26	Everton Blake	l pts 6	Bethnal Green 12-13

1991
Oct 22	Tenko Ernie	w pts 6	Battersea 12-12-8

1992
Jan 21	Dave Lawrence	w pts 6	Norwich 13-4
Mar 31	Richard Bustin	w pts 6	Norwich 13-3-8
Oct 29	Everton Blake	l rsf 4*	Hayes 13-1
	(Southern cruiserweight title)		

Fights 31 Won 12 Lost 18 Drawn 1

Ian CARMICHAEL

Heavyweight
Preston born 7 October 1965
Preston & Fulwood ABC
1987 East Lancs & Cheshire ABA heavyweight final (w rsf 1 S Henry, l C Harrison)

1987
Jun 13	Montague Butler	w pts 6	Great Yarmouth
Sep 15	Randy B. Powell	w pts 6	Kensington

1988
Dec 1	Steve Lewsam	l ko 2	Stafford 13-8

1989-91 inactive

1992
Feb 24	Dean Josham	w pts 6	Bradford 14-0

Fights 4 Won 3 Lost 1

Vaughan CARNEGIE

Light-welterweight
Newport born 16 December 1963
St Josephs ABC

1990
Jan 16	David Jenkins	w pts 6	Cardiff 9-13-12
Feb 3	David Jenkins	l pts 6	Bristol
Feb 14	Benny Collins	l pts 6	Millwall 9-13
Feb 20	Mick Moran	w rsf 3	Brentford 9-10
Mar 19	Shaun Cooper	l pts 8	Brierley Hill 9-12
Apr 25	Benny Collins	l pts 6	Millwall 10-4
May 14	Brendan Ryan	w pts 6	Leicester 10-2
May 21	Rick Bushell	l pts 6	NSC
Jun 6	Stuart Good	l pts 6	Battersea 10-7-8

1991
Feb 12	Jason Rowland	l pts 6	Basildon 10-2
Mar 7	Jason Rowland	l ko 2	Basildon 10-0-12
Apr 10	Rick Bushell	l rsf 3	Newport 9-13-8

1992
Dec 14	Lee Taylor	w rsf 2*	Cardiff 10-0-4

Fights 13 Won 4 Lost 9

Cornelius CARR

Middleweight
Middlesbrough born 9 April 1969
Real name: John Carr
1984 Junior ABA semi-final (l G Brooks)
1987 ABA middleweight final (w P Salter, w rsf 3 K Duke, w H Wharton, w P Wright, w rsf 1 N Rodney, w S Heron, l R Douglas)
1987 Sardinia multi-nations bronze medal

1987
Sep 22	Paul Burton	w rsf 5	Bethnal Green 11-1-12
Nov 28	Dave Heaver	w rsf 2	Windsor 11-2-8

1988
Jan 12	Seamus Casey	w rsf 6*	Cardiff 10-13-4
Jan 27	Kesem Clayton	w pts 6	Bethnal Green 10-13 /CTD...

(Cornelius CARR ctd)

Mar 29	Darren Parker	w rsf 1	Bethnal Green 11-1
Apr 12	Franki Moro	w pts 6	Cardiff 11-1
May 10	Andy Catesby	w rsf 5	Tottenham 11-1
Nov 15	Skip Jackson	w ko 1	Norwich 11-3
Dec 20	Kevin Hayde	w pts 6	Swansea
1989			
Mar 22	Bocco George	l rsf 3	Reading 11-4-8
Oct 24	Carlo Colarusso	w rtd 4*	Watford 11-1
1990			
Feb 20	Peter Gorny	w rsf 4	Millwall 11-13
Apr 21	Franki Moro	w pts 8	Sunderland 11-9-8

Sep 12: Boxed 2 exhibitions in Louisiana State Penitentiary:
  James Richards w EXH ko 2 Angola, La
  Eddie Tate w EXH ko 2 Angola, La 11-2

Sep 26	John Malreaux	w ko 1	Metairie, La 11-6
Oct 27	Jerry Nestor	w ko 1	Greenville, Ms 11-0
1991			
Feb 16	Frank Eubanks	w rsf 5	Thornaby 11-9-12
Mar 2	Carlo Colarusso	w pts 8	Darlington 11-7
May 18	Paul Burton	w rsf 3	Verbania 11-11
Sep 7	Marvin O'Brian	w rsf 8	Salemi 11-9-4
1992			
Oct 29	Alan Richards	w pts 8	Bayswater 11-7-8

Fights 20 Won 19 Lost 1

Dean CARR

Welterweight
Doncaster born 29 April 1967

1991			
Apr 29	Mick Reid	l rsf 1	Cleethorpes 10-4
Sep 16	Michael Byrne	w pts 6	Cleethorpes 10-7
Oct 1	Darren McInulty	l pts 6	Bedworth 10-8
Oct 21	James Campbell	l rsf 5	Cleethorpes 10-6
Nov 25	Steve Bricknell	w pts 4	Wolverhampton 10-5
Dec 4	Rob Stewart	l rtd 5	Stoke 10-3
1992			
Nov 19	Billy McDougall	l pts 6	Evesham 10-8
Dec 7	Billy McDougall	l pts 6	Birmingham 10-10

Fights 8 Won 2 Lost 6

Noel CARROLL

Featherweight
Manchester, born Dublin 7 January 1968
Southpaw/ Port Laoise ABC

1989			
Nov 16	Wayne Windle	w pts 6	Manchester 8-10
Nov 30	Des Gargano	w pts 6	Oldham
Dec 7	Kruger Hydes	w rsf 4	Manchester 8-9
1990			
Jan 30	Dave Buxton	w pts 6	Manchester 8-11
Feb 27	Steve Armstrong	w pts 6	Manchester 8-9
Mar 15	Chris Clarkson	l pts 6	Manchester 8-12

Sep 24	Derek Amory	w pts 8	Manchester 9-2
Dec 10	Nigel Senior	l pts 6	Nottingham 9-5
1991			
Jan 29	Neil Leitch	w rsf 4*	Stockport 9-1-8
Feb 21	Peter Judson	l pts 8	Leeds 9-2-8
Mar 18	Ian McGirr	w pts 6	Manchester 9-4
Apr 30	Colin Innes	w pts 4	Stockport 9-0
Jun 10	Mark Loftus	w pts 6	Manchester 8-13
Sep 19	Mick Deveney	w pts 6	Stockport 9-0-4
Nov 18	Graham O'Malley	w pts 6	Manchester 8-13-8
Dec 16	Chris Clarkson	w pts 6	Manchester 9-0
1992			
Feb 3	Barrie Kelley	w pts 8	Manchester 9-5-8
May 5	Kevin Jenkins	w pts 7	Preston 8-7-4

Fights 18 Won 15 Lost 3

Ronnie CARROLL

Bantamweight
Glasgow born 5 November 1963
Argo Youth ABC
1981 Scottish ABA light-flyweight final (l K Grant)
1982 Scottish ABA light-flyweight champion (w J Glencross, l J McBride)
1983 Scotland (v Ire, l G Hawkins)
1983 Scottish ABA flyweight final (l P Clinton)
1984 Scottish ABA flyweight final (l P Clinton)
1986 Scotland (v Eng, w ko 1 P Moylett; v Wal, l T Khan)

1986			
Jul 17	Gipsy Johnny	w pts 6	Blackpool 8-5
Sep 10	Gary McGuinness	w rsf 4	Muswell Hill
Sep 22	Simon Turner	w pts 6	Edgbaston 8-8
Oct 3	Eyup Can	l pts 4	Copenhagen 8-6-8
Nov 17	Shane Porter	w pts 6	Stafford 8-7
Dec 8	Rocky Lawlor	w pts 8	Birmingham 8-7
1987			
Jan 28	Shane Silvester	w pts 8	Dudley
Mar 2	Jamie McBride	w pts 6	Glasgow 8-9
Mar 18	Shane Silvester	w rsf 8	Solihull 8-7
Oct 19	Nigel Crook	drew 8	Glasgow 8-6-8
1988			
Jan 19	Gerry McBride	w pts 8	Kings Heath 8-9
Jun 13	Rocky Lawlor	w pts 8	Glasgow 8-8
Oct 17	Francisco Garcia	w pts 10	Glasgow 8-6
1989			
Feb 14	Billy Hardy (British bantamweight title)	l pts 12	Sunderland 8-4-10
Oct 23	Ray Minus (Commonwealth bantamweight title)	l rsf 11*	Glasgow 8-5-12
1990			
Mar 10	Vincenzo Belcastro (European bantamweight title)	l pts 12	Lamezia Terme
Apr 27	Lee Cargle	w pts 10	Glasgow 8-8
Nov 29	Billy Hardy (British bantamweight title)	l rsf 8	Sunderland 8-5
1991			
Oct 21	Joe Kelly (vacant British bantamweight title)	drew 12	Glasgow 8-6

/CTD..

(Ronnie CARROLL ctd)
1992
Jan 27	Joe Kelly	l pts 12	Glasgow 8-6
	(vacant British bantamweight title)		
May 29	John Green	l pts 10	Manchester 8-6
	(eliminator, British bantamweight title)		

Fights 21 Won 12 Lost 7 Drawn 2

Richard CARTER
Middleweight
Wolverhampton born 3 September 1970
Bilston Golden Gloves ABC
1984 National Schools final (l M Bowers)
1987 Junior ABA champion

1988
Sep 22	Tony Behan	w pts 6	Wolverhampton 11-13
Dec 5	Paul Murray	w pts 6	Dudley 11-6-8
Dec 12	Andy Catesby	w pts 6	Birmingham 11-9

1989
Apr 13	Dean Murray	w pts 6	Wolverhampton 11-10
Oct 24	Graeme Watson	w ko 2	Wolverhampton 11-7

1990
Mar 22	Spencer Alton	w pts 6	Wolverhampton 11-8
Oct 15	Shaun McCrory	w pts 8	Brierley Hill 12-0

1991
Mar 15	Alan Pennington	w ko 6	Willenhall 11-7
Jun 5	Colin Manners	l ko 1	Wolverhampton 11-10
Sep 10	Paul Hanlon	w rsf 3	Wolverhampton 11-10
Dec 5	Paul Murray	w pts 8	Cannock 11-6

1992
Oct 13	Graham Burton	drew 8	Wolverhampton 11-11

Fights 12 Won 10 Lost 1 Drawn 1

Seamus CASEY
Middleweight
Alfreton, born Pinxton 13 January 1960
Real name: Seamus West
South Normanton ABC

1984
Jan 25	Tony Burke	l ko 1	Solihull 11-10-4
Apr 16	Ronnie Fraser	l rsf 3	Nottingham 11-7
Jul 5	Craig Edwards	l pts 6	Prestatyn 11-5
Sep 21	Dave Foley	w pts 6	Alfreton 11-9
Sep 28	Dennis O'Brien	l pts 6	Bath 11-7
Oct 11	Terry Gilbey	l pts 6	Barnsley 11-2
Oct 22	Dave King	w pts 6	South Shields 11-11
Nov 9	Reuben Thurley	w ko 4	Alfreton 11-3
Nov 16	Mark Watts	l pts 6	Leicester 11-2
Nov 26	Terry Gilbey	l rsf 1	Liverpool 11-5

1985
Jan 14	Mark Walker	l pts 6	Manchester 12-0
Jan 24	Tommy Campbell	l pts 8	Manchester 10-8
Feb 11	Paul Smith	w pts 6	Manchester 11-8
Feb 18	Johnny Graham	l pts 6	NSC 11-10

Mar 1	Dennis Sheehan	w pts 6	Mansfield 11-5
Mar 11	Sean O'Phoenix	l pts 6	Manchester 11-7
Mar 20	Sean O'Phoenix	l pts 6	Stoke 11-11
Apr 15	Ronnie Tucker	l pts 6	Manchester 11-8
May 14	Dennis Sheehan	l pts 10	Mansfield 10-10-4
	(Midlands light-middleweight title)		
Jun 5	Gary Stretch	l rsf 2	Albert Hall 10-9-12
Sep 2	Newton Barnett	drew 8	Coventry 11-4
Sep 12	Cliff Curtis	w rsf 7	Swindon 11-3
Sep 23	Danny Quigg	l pts 8	Glasgow
Oct 10	Dave Cox	w pts 6	Alfreton 11-0
Oct 22	Mick Mills	l rsf 3	Hull 10-13-8
Dec 2	Newton Barnett	drew 8	Dulwich 11-2
Dec 9	Steve Ward	l pts 6	Nottingham 11-0
Dec 16	Robert Armstrong	w pts 6	Bradford 11-2

1986

Jan 20	Billy Ahearne	l pts 8	Leicester 11-7
Feb 6	Denys Cronin	l rsf 6	Adwick 11-2
Mar 10	Neil Munn	l pts 8	Cardiff 11-2
Mar 20	Andy Wright	l rsf 4	Wimbledon 11-7
Apr 22	Franki Moro	l pts 8	Carlisle 11-7-4
Apr 29	Johnny Graham	l pts 8	NSC 11-9
May 8	Randy Henderson	l pts 8	Bayswater 11-6
May 19	Joe Lynch	w rsf 2*	Plymouth 11-6
May 28	Andy Wright	l pts 6	Catford 11-10
Sep 15	Gerry Sloof	l pts 6	Scheidam
Sep 23	Derek Wormald	l pts 8	Batley 11-2
Oct 6	David Scere	l pts 6	Leicester 10-13
Oct 21	David Scere	w pts 8	Hull
Oct 29	Peter Elliott	w pts 6	Stoke 11-1
Nov 25	Steve Foster	l pts 8	Manchester 11-2
Dec 15	Mark Watts	drew 6	Loughborough 11-9

1987

Jan 13	Robert Armstrong	l pts 6	Oldham 11-2
Jan 26	Richard Wagstaff	w pts 8	Bradford 11-0
Feb 5	Neil Patterson	l pts 6	Newcastle 11-2
Feb 20	Dennis O'Brien	l pts 8	Maidenhead 11-6
Mar 2	Robby Maxwell	l pts 6	Glasgow 11-0
Mar 24	Ian Chantler	l pts 8	Nottingham 11-2-12
Apr 7	Richard Wagstaff	l pts 8	Batley 11-0
Apr 28	Sean Leighton	drew 8	Manchester 11-10
May 5	Dave Owens	l pts 6	Leeds 11-9
May 12	Jason Baxter	l pts 6	Alfreton 11-8
Jun 23	Terry Magee	l ko 6	Swansea 11-0
	(vacant Irish light-middleweight title)		
Jul 31	Cyril Jackson	l rsf 5*	Wrexham 11-5
Sep 20	Brian Robinson	l pts 6	Bethnal Green 11-4
Sep 28	Sean Leighton	l pts 8	Bradford 11-9-8
Oct 19	Sam Storey	l pts 6	Belfast 11-12
Nov 10	Peter Brown	l pts 8	Batley 11-10-8
Nov 19	Ian Murray	w pts 6	Ilkeston 11-4
Nov 26	Trevor Smith	l ko 4	Fulham 10-12

1988

Jan 12	Cornelius Carr	l rsf 6*	Cardiff 11-5
Feb 15	Leigh Wicks	l pts 6	Copthorne 11-4
Feb 25	R.W.Smith	l rsf 3	Bethnal Green 11-4
Mar 28	Tony Britton	l pts 8	Birmingham 11-6
Jun 13	Jim Kelly	l pts 6	Glasgow 10-12-12 /CTD..

(Seamus CASEY ctd)

Jun 25	Wayne Ellis	l pts 6	Luton 11-4
Sep 12	Shaun Cummins	l ko 3	Northampton 11-2
Oct 17	Jim Kelly	l pts 6	Glasgow 10-12
Nov 1	Brian Robinson	l pts 6	Reading 11-5
Nov 17	Mark Howell	l ko 1	Ilkeston 11-2
Dec 16	Conrad Oscar	l pts 6	Brentwood 11-7

1989

Jan 25	Tony Velinor	l rtd 3*	Basildon 11-4
Feb 22	Mick Murray	drew 6	Doncaster 11-7-8
Mar 1	Nigel Fairbairn	l pts 6	Stoke 11-7
Mar 21	Dave Thomas	l pts 6	Cottingham 11-4
Mar 29	W.O.Wilson	l rsf 5	Wembley 11-4
May 8	Antonio Fernandez	l pts 6	Edgbaston 11-8
May 31	Ossie Maddix	l ko 3	Manchester 11-4
Sep 11	Terry French	w pts 6	Nottingham 11-8
Sep 18	Skip Jackson	w pts 6	Northampton 11-8
Sep 26	Theo Marius	l pts 8	Chigwell 11-7
Oct 5	Val Golding	l pts 6	Stevenage 11-6-8
Oct 17	Carl Harney	l pts 4	Oldham 11-2
Nov 13	Ian Vokes	w rsf 5*	Bradford 11-8
Nov 29	Ray Close	l ko 2	Belfast 11-11

1990

Jun 21	Skip Jackson	w pts 6	Alfreton 11-2
Sep 4	Peter Bowman	w pts 6	Southend 11-3
Sep 14	Chris Richards	l pts 6	Telford 11-0
Oct 8	Billy Brough	w pts 6	Leicester 11-6
Oct 22	Gordon Blair	l rsf 3	Glasgow 11-2
Nov 22	Jimmy Thornton	w pts 6	Ilkeston 11-4
Dec 14	Stefan Wright	l pts 6	Peterborough 11-4

1991

Jan 17	Neville Brown	l rsf 4*	Alfreton 11-6
Feb 21	Richie Woodhall	l rsf 3	Walsall 10-13
Mar 28	Peter Bowman	w pts 6	Alfreton 10-10-4
Apr 11	Martin Rosamond	w pts 6	Willenhall 11-2
May 13	Paul King	w pts 6	Northampton 11-0
Jul 4	Dave Hall	w pts 6	Alfreton 11-0
Sep 11	Clay O'Shea	l pts 6	Hammersmith 11-4
Oct 10	David Johnson	l pts 6	Gateshead 11-4
Oct 17	Tyrone Eastmond	l pts 6	Mossley 11-4
Nov 14	David Johnson	l pts 6	Gateshead 11-6
Nov 28	Ian Vokes	w pts 6	Hull 11-6
Dec 7	Steve Foster	l pts 8	Manchester

1992

Mar 17	Gary Osborne	l rsf 5	Wolverhampton 10-12
	(vacant Midlands light-middleweight title)		
May 28	Mark Jay	l pts 8	Gosforth 11-6
Jul 25	Warren Stowe	l ko 2	Manchester 11-2
Oct 15	Terry Morrill	l pts 6	Hull 11-7
Oct 23	Fran Harding	l pts 6	Liverpool 11-13
Nov 12	Gipsy Johnny Price	l pts 6	Burnley 11-6
Dec 14	Peter Waudby	l pts 6	Cleethorpes 11-4

Fights 113 Won 25 Lost 83 Drawn 5

Fidel CASTRO (Slugger O'Toole)

Super-middleweight
Sheffield, born Nottingham 17 April 1963
Real name: Fidel Castro Smith. Formerly boxed as Slugger O'Toole.
Sneinton ABC
1986 Midlands ABA middleweight champion (w ko 3 G Baker, w D Earle, l N Benn)
1986 England (v Pol, l H Petrych)

1987			
Apr 6	Ian Bayliss	w rsf 5	Newcastle 11-8
Apr 28	Nick Gyaamie	w rsf 2	Manchester 11-11-12
Apr 29	Leigh Wicks	l pts 6	Hastings 11-2
May 11	Steve Foster	w pts 8	Manchester 11-7
Sep 23	Ian Jackson	w pts 6	Stoke 11-10
Nov 11	Denys Cronin	w pts 8	Usk 11-8-8
1988			
Feb 24	Ian Bayliss	w rsf 6	Sheffield 11-5
	(Central middleweight title)		
May 9	Franki Moro	w rsf 2	Nottingham 11-6
May 18	Chris Galloway	w pts 6	Gillingham 11-13
May 23	Sean Heron	w rsf 4	NSC 11-11
Jul 8	Francesco Dell A'quila	l dis 3	San Remo
Nov 19	Paul Tchoue	w rsf 3	Chateau Thierry
1989			
Jan 23	Andre Mongelema	l pts 8	Paris
Jun 22	Denys Cronin	w rsf 7	Stevenage 11-12
1990			
Jan 27	Tom Covington	w pts 8	Sheffield 11-9
Mar 12	Darren McKenna	w pts 6	Hull
May 20	Nigel Fairbairn	w rsf 7	Sheffield 11-12-8
Aug 20	Elvis Parks	w pts 6	Helsinki
Oct 29	Dave Owens	w pts 6	Birmingham 11-12
Nov 24	Johnny Melfah	w rsf 4*	Benalmadena 11-7
1991			
Sep 24	Ian Strudwick	w rsf 6*	Basildon 12-0
	(vacant British super-middleweight title)		
Oct 1	Johnny Melfah	w rsf 7	Sheffield
1992			
Feb 25	Lou Gent	w pts 12	Crystal Palace 11-13-12
	(British super-middleweight title)		
Jul 18	Frank Eubanks	w rtd 6	Manchester 11-13-12
Sep 23	Henry Wharton	l pts 12	Leeds 11-13-8
	(British & Commonwealth super-middleweight titles)		
Dec 16	Vincenzo Nardiello	l pts 12	Ariccia
	(vacant European super-middleweight title)		

Fights 26 Won 21 Lost 5

Sean CAVE

Welterweight
Leicester born 4 May 1967
Belgrave ABC

1987			
Sep 23	Barry Messam	w pts 6	Loughborough 10-5
1988-90			
inactive			/CTD..

(Sean CAVE ctd)
1991
Dec 5   Dave Fallone   l pts 6   Peterborough 10-10
1992
Apr 28 Kevin Mabbutt   l pts 6   Corby 10-12
Jun 18 George Wilson   w pts 6   Peterborough 10-9

Fights 4 Won 2 Lost 2

Ian CHANTLER

Light-middleweight
St Helens born 13 June 1960
Real name: Ian Ashton
Southpaw

1982
Jun 21	Elvis Morton	w rsf 3	Liverpool
Jun 30	Ian Murray	w pts 6	Liverpool
Sep 23	Tony Brown	l pts 8	Liverpool
Oct 5	Tony Brown	w pts 8	Liverpool
Oct 18	Billy Ahearne	w rsf 3*	Blackpool
Dec 6	Lee Hartshorn	l pts 8	Manchester

1983
Jan 20	Robert Armstrong	w rtd 1	Birkenhead
Jan 28	Geoff Pegler	l pts 8	Swansea
Feb 14	Billy Ahearne	w rsf 6	Liverpool 10-9
Mar 4	Danny Garrison	w ko 5	Queensferry
Mar 25	Martin Patrick	l pts 8	Bloomsbury
Apr 29	Paul Mitchell	l pts 8	Liverpool 10-11-8
Oct 17	Gavin Stirrup	l pts 8	Manchester 10-12
Dec 6	Rocky Kelly	l rsf 7	Albert Hall 10-8-12

1984
Apr 6	Jim McIntosh	l dis 3	Edinburgh 10-9-8
Jun 12	Ray Murray	w rsf 2	St Helens 10-10
Nov 12	Franki Moro	l pts 8	Nantwich 10-12
Dec 5	Paul Kelly	w ko 3	Stoke 10-8-8
Dec 14	John Ridgman	l rsf 8	Wembley CC 10-9

1985
Feb 1	Cliff Domville	w pts 8	Warrington 10-9
Apr 1	Mark Mills	l dis 2	Dulwich 10-12
Apr 10	Alistair Laurie	w rsf 8	Leeds 10-7
May 9	John Ridgman	w rsf 8*	Warrington 10-9
May 31	Franki Moro	w pts 8	Liverpool 10-10
Jul 19	Steve Davies	w pts 6	Colwyn Bay 10-8
Sep 12	Steve Watt	l pts 8	Wimbledon 10-8
Oct 3	Wayne Crolla	w rsf 3	Liverpool 10-10
Nov 4	Jim Kelly	w pts 8	Motherwell 10-7
Dec 6	Tony Brown	l rsf 7*	Liverpool 10-3
	(Central welterweight title)		

1986
Jan 27	Charlie Watson	l rsf 4*	Bradford 10-10
Apr 23	Judas Clottey	l pts 8	Stoke 10-12
Sep 25	Sammy Sampson	w pts 8	Preston 11-0-8
Oct 23	Mickey Hughes	l rsf 6	Basildon 11-0-8
Dec 3	Wally Swift	l pts 8	Stoke 11-0

1987
Jan 19	Michael Watson	l rtd 4*	NSC 11-7-4
Mar 2	John Ashton	w rsf 4	Birmingham 11-1
Mar 11	Dean Barclay	w pts 8	Albert Hall 11-2

Mar 24	Seamus Casey	w pts 8	Nottingham 11-4-8
Apr 9	Johnny Williamson	w rsf 4	Bethnal Green 11-1
May 26	Mick Courtney	w rtd 5*	Wembley 11-0-8
Oct 5	Marc Ruocco	l pts 8	Paris 10-12
Nov 8	Romeo Kensmil	w ko 6	Amsterdam
Nov 24	Nigel Benn	l ko 1	Wisbech 11-5
1988			
Feb 8	George Collins	l pts 8	Bethnal Green 11-0
Mar 4	Mbayo Wa Mbayo	l pts 8	Villeurbane
Mar 19	Edip Secovic	l ko 4	Vienna
Apr 28	Ossie Maddix	w rsf 3*	Manchester 10-11
Jul 5	Giovanni Di Marco	l pts 6	Roseto
1989			
Jan 9	Gilbert Dele	l rsf 3	Nogent-sur-Marne 11-0-4
Mar 15	Kesem Clayton	w ko 4	Stoke 11-1
Sep 6	Wayne Ellis	l rsf 4	Port Talbot 10-12
Nov 22	Kesem Clayton	l pts 8	Solihull 11-0
1990			
Jun 2	Steve Foster	drew 4	Manchester 11-5
Sep 12	Tony Velinor	w rsf 4*	Bethnal Green 11-2
Oct 27	Santo Columbo	l pts 8	Rimini
Dec 12	Kevin Hayde	w pts 8	Basildon 11-0
1991			
Jan 23	Shaun Cummins	l pts 10	Brentwood 11-0
May 15	Silvio Branco	l rsf 2	Montichiari 11-5
1992			
Mar 17	Stan King	l ko 3	Mayfair 11-5
Apr 25	Ray Close	l rsf 2*	Belfast 11-6
Nov 26	Richard Okumu	l rsf 2*	Mayfair 11-2

Fights 61 Won 27 Lost 33 Drawn 1

Gary CHARLTON

Heavyweight
Leeds born 6 April 1968
Real name: Gary Wilkes
Market District ABC & World Of Suits ABC
1989 Yorkshire ABA super-heavyweight champion (w.o. then withdrwl)
1990 Yorkshire & Humberside ABA super-heavyweight semi-final (l rsf 1 C Jennings)
1991 Yorkshire & Humberside ABA super-heavyweight final (l ko 2 J Corrigan)

1991			
Oct 10	John Pierre	l pts 6	Gateshead 15-0
Oct 26	Graham Arnold	w rsf 1	Brentwood 14-12
Nov 11	Gary Railton	l pts 6	Bradford 14-12
1992			
Apr 23	Wayne Llewellyn	l rsf 6	Eltham 16-0
Jun 4	Wayne Buck	l pts 6	Cleethorpes 15-10
Oct 7	John Harewood	l pts 6	Sunderland 15-10
Nov 12	Wayne Buck	l pts 8	Stafford 16-10
Dec 17	Kevin McBride	drew 6	Barking 16-7

Fights 8 Won 1 Lost 6 Drawn 1

Paul CHARTERS

Light-welterweight
North Shields, born London 14 September 1964
Benfield ABC
1988 North-East England ABA light-welterweight final (w M Legg, l A Hall)

1988
Mar 10	John Naylor	l pts 6	Croydon 9-8
Apr 11	Jim Moffat	l pts 8	Glasgow 9-9
Apr 22	Tony Foster	w pts 6	Gateshead 9-6-12
May 3	Henry Armstrong	l pts 4	Stoke 9-5
May 16	Shaun Cooper	l pts 6	Wolverhampton 9-7-8
Jun 18	Darren Jackson	w rsf 6	Gateshead 9-10
Jun 29	Steve Griffith	w pts 8	Basildon 9-12-8
Dec 6	Oliver Henry	l ko 1	Southend 9-10

1989
Jan 25	Paul Burke	l pts 6	Bethnal Green 9-11
Feb 28	Chris Bennett	w pts 6	Middlesbrough
Mar 29	B.F.Williams	l pts 6	Bethnal Green 9-10
Sep 14	Nick Hall	l pts 6	Motherwell 9-10-8
Sep 25	Paul Bowen	w pts 8	NEC 9-11-8
Oct 9	Kris McAdam	w pts 6	Glasgow 9-11-4
Oct 23	Dave Pratt	w rtd 3*	Nottingham 9-12
Nov 14	Robert Smyth	w pts 8	Evesham 9-12
Dec 5	James Jiora	w rsf 4	Dewsbury 9-10

1990
| Jan 15 | Tomas Arguelles | l pts 8 | NSC 9-10 |
| Mar 5 | Marvin P. Gray | w pts 10 | Northampton 9-9 |

(vacant Northern lightweight title)

May 15	Brian Cullen	w rsf 5	South Shields 9-12
Jun 5	Paul Gadney	w rsf 1	Eltham 9-12-8
Nov 13	John Smith	w rsf 4*	Hartlepool 9-12-8
Dec 14	Gary Barron	l rsf 3*	Peterborough 10-3

1991
| Feb 21 | Peter Till | w rsf 6 | Walsall 9-8-8 |

(eliminator, British lightweight title)

| May 10 | Kevin Spratt | w rsf 2 | Gateshead 10-1-8 |
| Aug 14 | Antonio Renzo | l ko 11 | Alcamo 9-7 |

(European lightweight title)

| Nov 14 | Gary Barron | w rsf 4* | Gateshead 9-11-8 |

1992
| Mar 3 | John Smith | w pts 8 | Houghton-le-Spring 10-0 |
| Apr 28 | Paul Burke | l rsf 7 | Houghton-le-Spring 9-7-8 |

(final eliminator, British lightweight title)

Sep 10	Steve Pollard	w rtd 5*	Sunderland 9-13
Oct 23	Colin Sinnott	w rtd 4	Gateshead 10-1
Nov 27	Racheed Lawal	l ko 6	Randers 10-0

Fights 32 Won 19 Lost 13

Carlos CHASE

Light-welterweight
Bushey, born Watford 18 August 1966
Real name: Ivan Chase
Bushey ABC
1988 Home Counties ABA light-welterweight semi-final (l rtd 3 P Day)
1989 Home Counties ABA light-welterweight final (w O Blayachi, l R Woolgar)

1989
Sep 28	Tony Gibbs	w pts 6	Battersea 10-2
Dec 12	Carl Brasier	w pts 6	Brentford 9-13

1990
Jan 30	Barry North	w rsf 2	Battersea 10-1
Mar 14	Trevor Meikle	w pts 6	Battersea 10-2-12

1991
Apr 3	Seamus O'Sullivan	w pts 8	Bethnal Green 10-3-8
Jun 1	Marcel Herbert	w pts 6	Bethnal Green 10-3-8
Nov 12	Tony Swift	l pts 6	Milton Keynes 10-4

1992
Feb 12	Gary Barron	w rsf 5	Watford 10-0
Apr 30	Dave Pierre	l rsf 7	Watford 9-13
	(Southern light-welterweight title)		
Sep 17	Felix Kelly	w rsf 2	Watford 10-0

Fights 10 Won 8 Lost 2

Zak CHELLI

Light-heavyweight
Leicester, born Nabeul,Tunisia 2 May 1968
Full name: Zakaria Chelli. Amateur in Tunisia

1992
Nov 24	Lee Archer	w pts 6	Wolverhampton 12-8

Fights 1 Won 1

Mark CHICOCKI

Light-middleweight
Hartlepool
Hartlepool Catholic ABC
1991 Northern ABA light-middleweight final (w K Morrison, w R Aldridge, w D Larkin, l J Alston)
1992 North East Division ABA light-middle semi-final (w rsf 3 M Lumley, w W Neil, l dis 3 J Mett)

1992
Dec 1	Tony Trimble	w pts 6	Hartlepool 11-2-8

Fights 1 Won 1

Carlos CHRISTIE

Super-middleweight
Birmingham born 17 August 1966
Real name: Peter Christie
Handsworth Police ABC & Ladywood ABC
1988 Birmingham ABA light-heavyweight final (l K Mills)
1989 Birmingham ABA middleweight final (w S Richards, l P Busby)
1990 Birmingham ABA light-heavyweight champion (w L Pruden, w/d)

1990
Jun 4	Roger Wilson	l pts 6	Birmingham 12-0
Sep 17	John Kaighin	w pts 6	Cardiff 12-2
Sep 27	Colin Manners	w pts 6	NEC 11-12
Oct 29	Paul Murray	w pts 6	Birmingham 12-2
Nov 18	Paul Busby	l pts 6	NEC 11-12
Nov 27	Nigel Rafferty	w pts 8	Wolverhampton 11-10-8
Dec 6	Nigel Rafferty	w pts 6	Wolverhampton 12-0

1991
Jan 10	Ray Webb	l pts 6	Battersea 12-1
Jan 28	Gil Lewis	w pts 8	Birmingham 12-5
Mar 4	Nigel Rafferty	w pts 8	Birmingham 12-3
Mar 14	Michael Gale	l pts 8	Middleton
May 1	Peter Elliott	w ko 9	Solihull 11-13-8
	(vacant Midlands super-middleweight title)		
May 11	Ray Close	l pts 6	Belfast 11-13-8
Sep 7	Ray Close	l pts 6	Belfast 12-6
Nov 20	Nicky Piper	l ko 6	Cardiff 12-3

1992
Mar 10	Glenn Campbell	drew 8	Bury 12-3-8
Sep 15	Roland Ericsson	w rsf 4	Crystal Palace 12-2

Fights 17 Won 9 Lost 7 Drawn 1

Floyd CHURCHILL

Super-featherweight
Liverool born 19 January 1969
Kirkby ABC

1992
Apr 29	Terry Smith	w rsf 2	Liverpool 9-8
May 14	Jamie Davidson	w rsf 4	Liverpool 9-11
Jun 18	Kevin McKillan	l pts 6	Liverpool 9-12
Sep 26	Richie Wenton	w rsf 2	Olympia 9-4-8
Nov 12	Brian Hickey	w ko 1	Liverpool 9-3-12

Fights 5 Won 4 Lost 1

Cliff CHURCHWARD

Welterweight
Bournemouth, born Weymouth 7 June 1966
Poole ABC

1989
Oct 4	Tony White	l rsf 5	Basildon
Nov 14	Trevor Meikle	l pts 6	Evesham 10-6
Nov 22	Trevor Meikle	l pts 6	Stafford 10-7

Dec 11	Ernie Loveridge	l pts 6	Birmingham 10-9
1990			
Feb 27	Micky Lerwill	l pts 6	Evesham 10-8
Mar 7	Eddie King	l ko 6	Doncaster 10-7
Jun 28	Gary Simkiss	drew 6	Birmingham 10-12
Dec 8	Martin Rosamond	l pts 6	Bristol 10-8
1991			
Jan 23	Ernie Loveridge	l pts 6	Solihull 11-1
Feb 4	Andreas Panayi	l pts 6	Leicester 10-12
May 8	Kevin Sheeran	l pts 6	Millwall 10-7
May 20	James McGee	l pts 6	Leicester
Jun 5	Ernie Loveridge	l pts 8	Wolverhampton 10-8
Jun 17	Eddie King	l pts 6	Edgbaston
1992			
Feb 12	B.F.Williams	l pts 6	Watford 10-6
Apr 30	Danny Shinkwin	w pts 6	Watford
Oct 5	Kevin Mabbutt	l pts 6	Northampton 10-11
Dec 1	Andrew Jervis	l pts 6	Liverpool 10-13
Dec 10	Sean Metherell	l pts 6	Corby 10-10

Fights 19 Won 1 Lost 17 Drawn 1

Jimmy CLARK

Super-featherweight
Tilbury born 27 December 1969
Southpaw
Tilbury ABC
1985 National Schools champion

1988			
Sep 21	Alan Roberts	w ko 1	Basildon 9-0
Oct 25	Gary Hickman	w pts 6	Brentwood 8-11-8
Nov 22	Alan Roberts	w rsf 3	Basildon 9-1
Dec 16	Des Gargano	w pts 6	Brentwood 8-12
1989			
Jan 25	Darren Weller	w rsf 4	Basildon 9-0
Mar 10	Renny Edwards	l pts 6	Brentwood 9-2
May 9	Tony Heath	w pts 6	St Albans 9-4
Sep 14	Marcel Herbert	w pts 4	Basildon 9-2
Oct 24	Miguel Matthews	w pts 6	Watford 9-5
Nov 30	Gary Hickman	w pts 6	Barking 8-13-8
1990			
Oct 10	John Green	w pts 6	Millwall 8-13
1991			
Oct 2	Charlie Coke	w pts 6	Barking 9-1
Dec 11	Miguel Matthews	w pts 6	Basildon 9-2-8
1992			
Feb 11	Derek Amory	w pts 6	Barking 9-5
Apr 2	Chubby Martin	w rsf 6*	Basildon 9-4-8

Fights 15 Won 14 Lost 1

Howard CLARKE

Welterweight
Warley born 23 September 1967
Warley ABC
1988 Birmingham ABA welterweight semi-final (l R Wright)
1989 Birmingham ABA welterweight semi-final (l M Elliot)
1990 Midlands ABA welterweight champion (w R Edwards, w rsf 3 S Handley, w rsf 1 J Scanlon, w ko 1 G Simkiss, l R McCracken [box-off])
1991 South Midlands ABA welterweight final (w M Santini, l J Scanlon)

1991
Oct 15	Chris Mylan	w pts 4	Dudley 10-6-12
Dec 9	Claude Rosse	w rsf 3*	Brierley Hill 10-9

1992
Feb 4	Julian Eavis	w pts 4	Alfreton 10-8-8
Mar 3	Dave Andrews	w rsf 3*	Cradley Heath 10-8
May 21	Richard O'Brien	w ko 1	Cradley Heath 10-3
Sep 29	Paul King	w pts 6	Warley 10-4-8
Oct 27	Gordon Blair	l rsf 4	Cradley Heath 10-7

Fights 7 Won 6 Lost 1

Chris CLARKSON

Featherweight
Hull born 15 December 1967
1983 National Schools champion
1984 National Schools champion (w L McDonald)

1985
Mar 18	Gipsy Johnny	l pts 4	Bradford 8-7
Apr 13	Terry Allen	w pts 4	South Shields 8-9
Apr 30	Terry Allen	w pts 4	Chorley 8-7-8
May 30	Gipsy Johnny	l pts 4	Blackburn
Oct 16	Tony Heath	w pts 4	Leicester 8-3

1986
Feb 13	Glen Dainty	l rsf 4	Longford 8-9-4
Mar 17	Jamie McBride	l pts 4	Glasgow 8-8-8
Nov 3	Gerry McBride	drew 6	Manchester 8-9-8
Nov 13	Gordon Stobie	w rsf 4*	Huddersfield 8-8-8
Dec 1	Nigel Crook	l rsf 6	Nottingham 8-4

1987
Jan 27	Donnie Hood	l pts 6	Glasgow 8-6
Feb 23	Dave Mallaby	w pts 4	Bradford 8-7-8
Mar 2	Dave Mallaby	w ko 3	Nottingham 8-7
Mar 16	Kerry Webber	w pts 6	Glasgow 8-7
Mar 24	Nigel Crook	w pts 6	Cottingham 8-8
Apr 6	Joe Kelly	l pts 8	Glasgow 8-6
Apr 14	Jamie McBride	l pts 6	Cumbernauld 8-8
Apr 28	John Green	l rsf 6	Manchester 8-10
Jun 13	Ronnie Stephenson	w pts 8	Gt Yarmouth 8-8-8
Sep 23	Mitchell King	l pts 6	Loughborough 9-0

1988
Nov 15	Gordon Shaw	w pts 6	Hull 8-10
Nov 29	Des Gargano	l pts 6	Manchester 8-12
Dec 14	Dave George	l pts 6	Evesham 8-13

1989
Feb 16	Johnny Bredahl	l pts 6	Copenhagen
Mar 9	Mark Geraghty	l pts 6	Glasgow 9-1-12

Mar 20	George Bailey	w pts 6	Bradford 8-10
Jul 11	Des Gargano	w pts 6	Batley 9-2
Oct 10	Gerry McBride	w pts 10	Hull 8-5-12
	(vacant Central bantamweight title)		
Nov 23	Drew Docherty	l pts 6	Motherwell 8-9

1990

Mar 15	Noel Carroll	w pts 6	Manchester 9-0
Apr 19	Gerry McBride	w dis 5	Oldham 9-0
	(vacant Central featherweight title)		
Apr 30	Peter Buckley	w pts 8	NSC 9-0-8
Nov 19	James Drummond	w pts 8	Glasgow 8-10

1991

Mar 2	Francisco Arroyo	l rsf 4	Darlington 8-5-8
	(vacant IBF Intercontinental bantamweight title)		
Apr 4	Duke McKenzie	l rsf 5	Watford 8-13-8
Oct 9	Mark Geraghty	l pts 6	Glasgow
Oct 21	Ian McGirr	drew 6	Glasgow 9-0-8
Dec 16	Noel Carroll	l pts 6	Manchester 8-13

1992

Mar 3	Billy Hardy	l rsf 5	Houghton-le-Spring 8-11
Dec 14	David Ramsden	w pts 4	Bradford 8-13

Fights 40 Won 18 Lost 20 Drawn 2

Kesem CLAYTON

Middleweight
Coventry born 19 May 1962
Coachmakers, Massey Ferguson, Triumph ABC
1984 South Midlands ABA light-welterweight semi-final (l P Till)
1985 South Midlands ABA light-welterweight final (l M Elliot)

1986

Oct 6	Rocky Reynolds	w pts 6	Birmingham 10-9
Nov 26	Ian Murray	w pts 6	Wolverhampton 10-5

1987

Jan 21	Cecil Branch	w rsf 4	Stoke 10-8
Mar 4	Ian John-Lewis	w rsf 3*	Dudley 10-9-8
Mar 30	Mark Howell	l pts 6	Birmingham 10-10-8
Apr 8	Kevin Hayde	w pts 6	Evesham 10-10
Jun 12	Mark Howell	l pts 6	Leamington 10-10
Sep 30	Theo Marius	drew 6	NSC 11-2
Oct 12	Andy Catesby	w rsf 3	NSC 11-0
Nov 16	Rafaele Feliciello	w pts 8	Stratford 11-2
Nov 28	Mark Howell	l pts 6	Windsor 11-0

1988

Jan 27	Cornelius Carr	l pts 6	Bethnal Green 11-4
Mar 9	Brian Robinson	w pts 6	Bethnal Green 11-8
Mar 21	Dean Barclay	drew 8	Bethnal Green 11-0
Apr 17	R.W. Smith	w rsf 4	Peterborough 11-0
Oct 6	Kid Milo	l rsf 4	Dudley 11-7
Dec 16	Tony Velinor	w rsf 2	Brentwood 11-1-8

1989

Feb 6	Mel Justin	l pts 8	Nottingham 11-1
Mar 15	Ian Chantler	l ko 4	Stoke 11-0
Jul 15	Michele Mastrodonato	l rsf 2	San Severiano
Oct 4	Shaun Cummins	w rsf 6*	Solihull 11-2
Nov 22	Ian Chantler	w pts 8	Solihull 11-2
Dec 14	Benito Guida	l pts 8	Milan /CTD..

(Kesem CLAYTON ctd)

1990
Jan 24	John Ashton	l pts 10	Solihull 11-2
	(vacant Midlands middleweight title)		
Oct 12	Frederic Seillier	l rsf 1	Toulon

1991
Feb 22	Steve Foster	l ko 6	Manchester 11-3-8
Dec 2	Nigel Rafferty	l pts 8	Birmingham 11-12

1992
Mar 31	Stan King	l rsf 4	Norwich 11-6-12

Fights 28 Won 12 Lost 14 Drawn 2

Justin CLEMENTS

Middleweight
Birmingham born 25 September 1971
Kyrle Hall ABC

1991
Dec 2	Adrian Wright	w pts 6	Birmingham 11-11

1992
Mar 3	Andy Manning	drew 6	Cradley Heath 11-9-4

Fights 2 Won 1 Drawn 1

Pat CLINTON

Flyweight
Croy born 4 April 1964
Croy Miners ABC
Southpaw
1981 Scotland (v Eng, l J Hyland; v Ire, l G Hawkins)
1983 ABA flyweight final (w R Carroll, w rsf 2 S Murphy, l S Nolan)
1983 Scotland (v Eng, w S Nolan; v Wal, w J Marden)
1983 Great Britain (v USA, l S McCrory)
1983 Commonwealth Federation championships gold medal (w S Nolan, sf;)
1984 ABA flyweight champion (w R Carroll, w J Green, w J McBride)
1984 Scotland (v Ire, w S Donnelly, w M Quinn)
1984 Los Angeles Olympics flyweight prelims (w L Makhanya, Swa; l ko 2 R Redzepovski,Yug)
1985 Scotland (v Eng, w M Smith)
1985 ABA flyweight champion (w rsf 3 M Smith, w L Williams)

1985
Oct 10	Gordon Stobie	w pts 6	Alfreton
Nov 11	Tony Rahman	w pts 6	Glasgow

1986
Feb 24	Tony Rahman	w pts 6	Glasgow
Apr 29	Des Gargano	w pts 6	Manchester
Jun 9	George Bailey	w ko 2	Glasgow 8-3-8
Oct 20	Adrian Staples	w ko 2	Glasgow 8-3-8
Nov 17	Gipsy Johnny	w rsf 5	Glasgow 8-1-4

1987
Jan 19	Sean Casey	w ko 6	Glasgow 8-5-8
Feb 16	Des Gargano	w pts 6	Glasgow 8-3
Apr 14	Jose Manuel Diaz	w rsf 8	Cumbernauld 8-1-12
May 19	Miguel Pequeno	w ko 4	Cumbernauld 8-2
Sep 20	Joe Kelly	w rsf 2*	Bethnal Green 7-13-12
	(Scottish flyweight title; final elim, British title)		

1988
Mar 9	Joe Kelly	w pts 12	Bethnal Green 8-0
	(vacant British flyweight title)		

1989			
Feb 16	Eyup Can (vacant European flyweight title)	l pts 12	Copenhagen 7-13
Oct 24	Danny Porter (British flyweight title)	w rsf 5	Watford 8-0
Dec 19	David Afan-Jones (British flyweight title)	w rsf 6	Gorleston 7-13-12
1990			
Aug 4	Salvatore Fanni (vacant European flyweight title)	w pts 12 (s)	Cagliari
1991			
Sep 9	Armando Diaz	w pts 8	Glasgow 8-2
Nov 18	Alberto Cantu	w pts 8	Glasgow 8-2-12
1992			
Mar 18	Isidro Perez (WBO flyweight title)	w pts 12 (s)	Glasgow
Sep 26	Danny Porter (WBO flyweight title)	w pts 12	Glasgow

Fights 21 Won 20 Lost 1

Ray CLOSE
Super-middleweight
Belfast born 20 January 1969
1986 Irish Junior champion (w rsf 1 A Peel, w rsf 3 G O'Halloran)
1987 Irish ABA middleweight champion (w H Byrne, w P Ruth)
1987 Ireland (v Eng, l rsf 1 H Wharton)
1987 World Junior Championships (l W Martinez, Cub)
1988 Irish ABA middleweight champion (w C Thornton, w H Byrne)
1988 Ireland (v Pol, w D Banaski; v USA, w C Santiago, w D Leonardo; v Sco, w rsf 2 S Newnes; v Cub, l ko 3 I Camacho; v Wal, l N Piper; v Can, w J Hope)

1988			
Oct 21	Steve Foster	w rsf 2	Belfast 11-10
Dec 14	Kevin Roper	w pts 4	Liverpool 11-9
1989			
Jan 25	B.K.Bennett	w rsf 3	Belfast 11-9
Mar 8	Andy Wright	w rsf 4	Belfast 11-10
Apr 12	Dennis White	w rsf 2	Belfast 11-12
Sep 19	Gary Pemberton	w pts 6	Belfast 11-9-8
Oct 31	Rocky McGran (vacant Irish super-middleweight title)	w rsf 7	Belfast
Nov 29	Seamus Casey	w ko 2	Belfast 11-9-8
Dec 13	Denys Cronin	l pts 4	Liverpool 11-11-8
1990			
Feb 21	Frank Eubanks	w pts 8	Belfast 11-10
Mar 27	Denys Cronin	w pts 8	Belfast 12-0
May 23	Rocky McGran	w rtd 1*	Belfast
Sep 15	Ray Webb	w pts 8	Belfast 11-10
1991			
May 11	Carlos Christie	w pts 6	Belfast 11-11-8
Sep 7	Carlos Christie	w pts 6	Belfast 11-13
Nov 13	Simon Collins	w pts 6	Belfast 12-1-8
Dec 11	Terry Magee (Irish super-middleweight title)	w rsf 7	Dublin 11-13-8
1992			
Apr 25	Ian Chantler	w rsf 2*	Belfast 11-10
Jul 3	Franck Nicotra (European super-middleweight title)	l rsf 8	Pontault-Combault 11-12-4 /CTD..

(Ray CLOSE ctd)
Dec 18   Jean-Roger Tsidjo   w pts 8   Clermont Ferrand

Fights 20 Won 18 Lost 2

Judas CLOTTEY
Welterweight
Liverpool, born Accra 24 August 1958

1980
Date	Opponent	Result	Venue
Nov 2	Eddie Kotei	w ko 5	Accra
Dec 26	Ran Coco	w rsf 4	Accra

1981
Date	Opponent	Result	Venue
May 2	Dan Patterson	w rsf 5	Accra
May 30	Franki Moro	w pts 10	Accra
Aug 28	Hunter Clay	w dis 4	Lagos

1982
Date	Opponent	Result	Venue
Jun 30	P.J.Davitt	w pts 8	Liverpool 10-6-8
Sep 4	John Assibri	w ko 1	Accra
Nov 6	Bernard Daryi	w rsf 2	Accra
Dec 9	Johnny Andrews	drew 6	Bloomsbury 10-9

1983
Date	Opponent	Result	Venue
Feb 3	Rocky Kelly	w pts 8	Bloomsbury 10-5
Feb 21	Tony Willis	l rsf 5*	Edgbaston 10-5
Jun 10	Fighting Romanus (vacant African welterweight title)	w pts 12	Lagos
Dec 7	Sylvester Mittee	w rsf 3*	Bloosmbury 10-9-8

1984
Date	Opponent	Result	Venue
Jan 28	Sylvester Mittee	l rsf 2	Stoke
Feb 22	Chris Pyatt	l pts 8	Albert Hall 10-8-4
Mar 21	Dean Scarfe	w pts 6	Bloomsbury 10-10
May 2	Rafaele Feliciello	l pts 8	Solihull
Dec 12	Armstrong Azizi	w ko 3	Accra

1985
Date	Opponent	Result	Venue
Jan 10	Rocky Mussa	w ko 5	Accra
Mar 20	Lloyd Christie	w rsf 5*	Solihull
Apr 27	Chris Kazuma (African welterweight title)	w ko 5	Lusaka
Nov 20	Terry Brooks	w pts 8	Solihull

1986
Date	Opponent	Result	Venue
Jan 16	Sammy Sampson	w ko 5	Preston
Apr 23	Ian Chantler	w pts 8	Stoke 10-11
Jun 27	Charles Nwokolo (African welterweight title)	l pts 12	Lagos
Nov 3	Marc Ruocco	w pts 8	Paris

1987
Date	Opponent	Result	Venue
Feb 6	Said Skouma	w dis 5	Antibes
Apr 6	Brian Janssen (vacant Commonwealth welterweight title)	l pts 12 (s)	Brisbane 10-6-8
May 18	Marc Ruocco	l pts 8	La Seyne-sur-Mer

1988
Date	Opponent	Result	Venue
Feb 23	Derek Wormald	l pts 10	Oldham 10-12
Apr 18	Aaron Davis	l pts 8 (m)	Paris 10-9-12
Jun 1	Nino La Rocca	l ko 6	Compiegne
Oct 1	Alain Cuvillier	l pts 8	St Quentin
Oct 29	Paolo Pesci	drew 8	San Giuseppe Vesuviano
Nov 29	Alessandro Duran	l pts 8	San Pellegrino Terme

1989

Mar 8	Crisanto Espana	l rsf 2	Belfast 10-10
May 28	Musonga Chinongu	drew 10	Lusaka 10-6-8
Sep 2	Troy Waters	l pts 12	Brisbane 10-12-12
	(Commonwealth light-middleweight title)		
Nov 11	Romolo Casamonica	w pts 8	Rimini 10-10
Dec 9	Silvio Branco	drew 8	Teramo
1990			
Feb 10	Frederic Seillier	l ko 4	Hyeres
Dec 15	Genaro Leon	drew 8	Monte Carlo
1991			
Feb 22	Ossie Maddix	l pts 8	Manchester 10-10
Mar 7	Jorge Castro	l pts 8 (s)	Madrid
May 22	Julio Cesar Vasquez	l ko 1	Paris
Oct 12	Stefano Pompilio	drew 6	Monte Carlo
Dec 6	Oleg Chalajev	drew 8	Dusseldorf 10-10-8
1992			
Mar 12	Ekoli Mahenge Zulu	l rsf 5	Pesaro
May 9	Juan Medina Padilla	l pts 8 (s)	Madrid 10-12
Sep 29	Eamonn Loughran	l pts 8	Hamburg

Fights 50 Won 22 Lost 21 Drawn 7

Michael CLYNCH

Lightweight
Peterborough born London 22 June 1970
Focus ABC
1988 Eastern ABA bantamweight champion (w D Adams, w P Georgiou, l M Tierney)
1990 Eastern ABA lightweight semi-final (l rsf 2 S Garner)
1991 Eastern ABA lightweight champion (w M Green, l rsf 1 P Ramsey)

1991			
Oct 8	Gary Peynado	w ko 2	Wolverhampton 10-0
Nov 7	Nick Bardle	l rsf 4	Peterborough 9-11-8
1992			
Feb 6	Brian Hickey	w dis 5	Peterborough 9-10
Mar 25	Paul Ryan	l rsf 4	Dagenham 9-12-4
Apr 28	G.G.Goddard	w rtd 4*	Corby 9-7

Fights 5 Won 3 Lost 2

Shaun COGAN

Light-welterweight
Birmingham born 7 August 1967
Small Heath ABC
1987 Irish Junior light-welterweight champion (w rsf 2 R Carson)
1988 Irish ABA light welter prelim (l A Floody)

1989			
Sep 25	Peter Bowen	w rsf 1	NEC 9-12
Oct 24	Gary Quigley	w rsf 2	Wolverhampton 10-0
Dec 6	George Jones	w pts 6	Stoke 9-12-8
1990			
Mar 14	Dean Bramhald	w pts 6	Stoke 10-0-8
Mar 27	Mark Antony	w ko 1	Wolverhampton 10-3
Apr 23	Mike Morrison	w pts 8	Birmingham 10-2-8
1991			
Feb 21	Tony Britland	w pts 6	Walsall 10-1-8 /CTD..

(Shaun COGAN ctd)

Mar 19	Rocky Lawlor	w rsf 2	Birmingham 9-12-8
Jul 25	Dave Thompson	w ko 1	Dudley 10-0
Dec 5	Steve Pollard	w pts 6	Telford 9-12
1992			
Nov 27	Soren Sondergaard	l pts 6	Randers 10-0

Fights 11 Won 10 Lost 1

Carlo COLARUSSO

Light-middleweight
Llanelli born 11 February 1970
Trostre ABC
1985 Welsh Junior champion
1986 Welsh Youth champion
1987 Welsh Youth champion
1988 Welsh Youth champion
1988 Wales (v Sco, w rsf 2 C Millard)
1989 ABA light-middleweight finalist (w rsf 2 C Piper, w M Turner, w rsf 1 C Harney, l rsf 1 N Brown)

1989

Sep 14	Paul Burton	w rsf 5	Basildon 11-4
Oct 11	Lindon Scarlett	l pts 8	Stoke 11-0
Oct 24	Cornelius Carr	l rtd 4*	Watford 11-1
Nov 22	Lindon Scarlett	l pts 8	Solihull 10-13-8
1990			
Mar 1	Kevin Hayde	w rtd 3	Cardiff 11-1
Mar 14	Kevin Plant	w pts 8	Stoke 10-10
Mar 21	Sammy Sampson	w rsf 3	Preston 11-2
Apr 6	Ray Webb	w pts 6	Telford 11-1
Nov 19	Gary Pemberton	w rsf 3	Cardiff 11-0-8
Nov 29	Nigel Moore	l pts 6	Bayswater 11-0-8
1991			
Jan 24	Gary Pemberton	w rsf 8	Gorseinon 11-0
	(vacant Welsh light-middleweight title)		
Mar 2	Cornelius Carr	l pts 8	Darlington 11-4-8
1992			
May 11	Russell Washer	w rsf 5	Llanelli 10-12-8
	(Welsh light-middleweight title)		
Jun 27	Newton Barnett	w rtd 6*	Quinta Do Lago 11-1-12
Oct 28	Lloyd Honeyghan	l rsf 6*	Albert Hall 11-0-8

Fights 15 Won 9 Lost 6

Tony COLCLOUGH

Heavyweight
Birmingham, born 9 May 1960

1991

Apr 15	Steve Yorath	l pts 6	Wolverhampton 14-7-8
May 30	Damien Caesar	l rsf 1	Mayfair 14-6
Aug 1	Denzil Browne	l rsf 1	Leeds 13-9
Oct 7	Karl Guest	drew 6	Birmingham 12-8
Oct 15	Jason McNeill	w pts 6	Dudley 12-7
Dec 2	Karl Guest	w rsf 2	Birmingham 12-8
1992			
Mar 3	Greg Scott-Briggs	l rsf 2*	Cradley Heath 12-10

May 21	Mark Hale	drew 6	Cradley Heath 12-4
Jun 1	Mark Hale	w pts 6	NEC 12-3-8
Nov 27	Mark Hulstrom	l ko 2	Randers 15-3

Fights 10 Won 3 Lost 5 Drawn 2

Brian COLEMAN

Light-welterweight
Birmingham born 27 July 1969
Birmingham City ABC

1991
Nov 21	Jamie Morris	drew 6	Stafford 10-3
Dec 11	Craig Hartwell	drew 6	Leicester 10-7

1992
Jan 22	John O. Johnson	l pts 6	Stoke 10-3
Feb 20	Davey Robb	l pts 6	Telford 10-4-4
Mar 31	Blue Butterworth	l pts 6	Stockport 10-2
May 17	Korso Aleain	l rsf 5	Harringay 10-2
Sep 17	Nicky Bardle	l rsf 4	Watford 10-2
Oct 21	Jason Barker	w pts 6	Stoke 10-2
Dec 10	Rocky Milton	drew 4	Bethnal Green 10-1

Fights 9 Won 1 Lost 5 Drawn 3

Eddie COLLINS

Super-middleweight
Peterborough born London 13 October 1968
Tate & Lyle ABC

1987
May 26	Terry Vosper	l rsf 3	Plymouth 11-0
Sep 10	Dave Kettlewell	w pts 6	Peterborough 10-10
Oct 13	Kevin Thompson	l ko 1	Wolverhampton 10-10
Nov 18	Andy Catesby	w pts 6	Peterborough 11-2
Nov 26	Peter Crook	l pts 6	Horwich 10-9
Dec 15	James Conley	l pts 4	Bradford 10-13

1988
Feb 14	Andy Catesby	w rsf 1*	Peterborough
Feb 24	Nick Riozzi	l pts 6	Leicester 11-0
Mar 7	Humphrey Harrison	l rsf 2	Manchester 10-6
Apr 17	Steve Winstanley	w pts 6	Peterborough 10-12
Jul 10	Jim McDonagh	l pts 8	Eastbourne 11-3
Sep 8	Mickey Murray	l rsf 2	Doncaster 11-3-4
Oct 10	Paul Dolan	l pts 6	Glasgow
Dec 12	James Conley	l rsf 2	Bradford 11-0

1989
Mar 6	Dave Maxwell	l pts 6	Leicester 11-7
Dec 4	Carl Watson	w pts 6	Cleethorpes 11-3

1990
Feb 19	Matt Sturgess	l pts 6	Nottingham 11-4
Mar 8	Gary Dyson	w pts 6	Peterborough 11-0-8
Mar 19	Matt Sturgess	drew 6	Leicester 11-2
Apr 5	Gary Dyson	l pts 6	Liverpool
Oct 22	John Kilshaw	w pts 6	Peterborough
Nov 12	Terry French	l pts 6	Bradford 12-2
Dec 14	Ian Henry	l pts 6	Peterborough 12-4 /CTD..

(Eddie COLLINS ctd)
1991
Apr 19	Dave Lawrence	l pts 6	Peterborough 12-4
May 10	Terry French	l pts 6	Gateshead 12-3
1992			
Sep 8	Earl Ling	l pts 6	Norwich 11-13

Fights 26 Won 7 Lost 18 Drawn 1

Simon COLLINS
Super-middleweight
Merthyr Tydfil born 16 February 1967

1985
Oct 1	Tony Stevens	w pts 6	NSC 11-2-8
Oct 14	Malcolm Davies	w pts 6	Birmingham 11-2
Dec 4	Malcolm Melvin	w pts 6	Stoke 11-2
1986			
Apr 21	Paul Smith	drew 6	Birmingham 11-6
Apr 29	Deano Wallace	l pts 6	NSC 11-2
Jul 19	Michael Watson	l ko 1	Wembley 11-9-14
Oct 23	W.O.Wilson	l pts 8	Birmingham 11-8-12
1987			
Jun 3	Andy Wright	drew 6	Southwark 11-9-12
1988			
Nov 24	Paul McCarthy	drew 8	Southampton 11-13
Dec 1	Tony Collins	l pts 8	Edmonton 11-9
Dec 20	Paul McCarthy	l dis 3	Swansea 12-2-8
1989			
Jan 31	Chris Eubank	l rsf 4	Bethnal Green 12-0
Mar 1	Darryl Ritchie	w rsf 1	Cardiff 12-6
Mar 13	Dennis Banton	w rsf 5	NSC 12-7-8
Apr 17	Nigel Fairbairn	l pts 8	Birmingham 11-10
Jul 8	Willie Monroe	nd 5	Paris 11-13-12
Aug 19	Antoine Tarver	w rsf 3	Cardiff 12-0-8
Oct 5	Kid Milo	l pts 8	Stevenage 11-12
Nov 9	Frank Grant	l rtd 6*	Cardiff 11-9
1990			
Feb 2	Roland Ericsson	l pts 8	Geneva
Mar 27	Sam Storey	l rsf 7	Belfast
Apr 26	Steve Johnson	l pts 6	Merthyr
1991			
May 11	Noel Magee	l pts 8	Belfast 12-3-12
Nov 13	Ray Close	l pts 6	Belfast 11-13
1992			
Jul 14	Lou Gent	l rsf 5	Mayfair

Fights 25 Won 6 Lost 15 Drawn 3 No Decisions 1

Steve COLLINS

Middleweight
Dublin born 21 July 1964
St Saviours ABC
1983 Irish junior light-heavyweight champion (w M Crawford)
1984 Irish senior light-heavyweight final (w P Lawlor, l N Magee)
1985 Irish senior middleweight final (w rsf 1 M Stewart, w H Byrne, l S Storey)
1985 Dublin (v Lon, l dis 3 H Lawson)
1985 Ireland (v Sc, w rsf 2 J McIntyre; v En, w D McCarthy)
1986 Ireland (v Hun, w Z Fuezesy)
1986 Irish senior middleweight champion (w J Keenan, w H Byrne)

1986
Oct 24	Julio Mercado	w rsf 3	Lowell 11-7
Nov 26	Mike Bonislawski	w pts 4	Dorchester 11-9
Dec 20	Richard Holloway	w rsf 2	Dorchester 11-8

1987
Oct 10	Jimmy Holmes	w rsf 1	Attleboro 11-8
Oct 20	Harold Souther	w pts 8	Lowell
Nov 20	Mike Williams	w pts 6	Atlantic City 11-8
Dec 9	Benny Sims	w pts 8	Atlantic City 11-8

1988
Mar 18	Sam Storey (Irish middleweight title)	w pts 10	Boston
May 26	Lester Yarborough	w pts 10	Boston 11-8
Jul 30	Mike Dale	w pts 8	Brockton 11-6
Oct 22	Muhammad Shabbaz	w rsf 4	Salem
Dec 10	Jesse Lanton	w pts 10	Salem 11-8

1989
Feb 7	Paul McPeek	w rsf 9*	Atlantic City 11-7
May 9	Kevin Watts (USBA middleweight title)	w pts 12	Atlantic City 11-6
Jul 26	Tony Thornton (USBA middleweight title)	w pts 12 (m)	Atlantic City 11-5
Nov 21	Roberto Rosiles	w rsf 9	Las Vegas 11-8

1990
Feb 3	Mike McCallum (WBA middleweight title)	l pts 12	Boston 11-6
Aug 16	Fermin Chirino	w rsf 6	Boston 11-9
Nov 24	Eddie Hall	w pts 10	Boston 11-8

1991
May 11	Kenny Snow	w rsf 3	Belfast 11-8
May 25	Jean-Noel Camara	w ko 3	Brest
Dec 11	Dan Morgan	w rsf 3	Dublin 11-12

1992
Apr 22	Reggie Johnson (vacant WBA middleweight title)	l pts 12 (m)	East Rutherford
Oct 22	Sumbu Kalambay (European middleweight title)	l pts 12 (m)	Verbania

Fights 24 Won 21 Lost 3

Tom COLLINS
Light-heavyweight
Leeds, born Curacao 1 July 1955
Real name: Elton Collins
Market District ABC

1977
Jan 17	Ginger McIntyre	w rsf 2	Birmingham
May 16	Mick Dolan	w pts 6	Manchester
Jun 1	Johnny Cox	w ko 3	Dudley
Nov 23	George Gray	w rsf 3	Stoke

1978
Jan 19	Clint Jones	w rsf 3	Wimbledon
Mar 21	Joe Jackson	w pts 8	Luton 12-8
May 9	Harald Skog	l pts 8	Oslo
Jul 17	Karl Canwell	l rsf 6	WSC
Nov 22	Dennis Andries	l pts 8	Southend
Nov 28	Carlton Benoit	w ko 1	Sheffield

1979
Jan 30	Dennis Andries	l ko 6	Southend
Oct 22	Danny Lawford	w rsf 7	Nottingham
Nov 28	Eddie Smith	w pts 8	Solihull

1980
Feb 25	Greg Evans	w rsf 1	Bradford
Apr 15	Chris Lawson	w rsf 4	Blackpool
Dec 4	Mustapha Wasajja	l pts 8	Randers

1981
Mar 9	Karl Canwell	w pts 10	Bradford
	(eliminator, British light-heavyweight title)		

1982
Mar 15	Dennis Andries	w pts 15	Bloomsbury
	(vacant British light-heavyweight title)		
May 26	Trevor Cattouse	w ko 4	Leeds
	(British light-heavyweight title)		
Oct 7	John Odhiambo	l rsf 5	Copenhagen

1983
Mar 9	Antonio Harris	w rsf 6	Solihull
	(British light-heavyweight title)		
Apr 9	Alex Sua	w pts 12 (m)	Auckland 12-5-12
	(eliminator, Commonwealth light-heavyweight title)		
Dec 16	Leslie Stewart	l pts 10	Port of Spain

1984
Jan 26	Dennis Andries	l pts 12	Strand 12-5
	(British light-heavyweight title)		
Apr 6	Dennis Andries	l pts 12	Watford 12-4-4
	(British light-heavyweight title)		
Sep 21	Alek Penarski	l pts 8	Alfreton 12-9-8

1985
Jan 24	Jonjo Greene	w rsf 7*	Manchester 12-9
Mar 30	Chisanda Mutti	l pts 10	Dortmund 12-10-8
Apr 18	Andy Straughn	l ko 1	Halifax 12-9
Oct 14	Harry Cowap	w ko 4	Southwark 12-9
Nov 29	Ralf Rocchigiani	l pts 8	Frankfurt
Dec 20	Pierre Kabassu	drew 8	Forbach

1986
Apr 1	Winston Burnett	w pts 8	Leeds 12-9
Apr 19	Yawe Davis	w ko 3	San Remo
Nov 26	Alex Blanchard	l pts 10	Arnhem

1987
Mar 11	John Moody	w rsf 10	Albert Hall 12-5-8
	(vacant British light-heavyweight title)		
Nov 11	Alex Blanchard	w ko 2	Usk 12-5
	(European light-heavyweight title)		

1988
May 11	Mark Kaylor	w ko 9	Wembley GH
	(European light-heavyweight title)		
Sep 7	Pedro van Raamsdonk	l rsf 7*	Reading 12-6
	(European light-heavyweight title)		

1989
Mar 22	Tony Wilson	w rsf 2	Reading 12-6-8
	(British light-heavyweight title)		
Oct 24	Jeff Harding	l rtd 2	Brisbane 12-3-12
	(WBC light-heavyweight title)		

1990
Aug 11	Eric Nicoletta	w ko 9	Le Cap D'Agde
	(European light-heavyweight title)		
Oct 18	Pierre-Frank Winterstein	l pts 10 (m)	Paris
Dec 21	Christophe Girard	w ko 2	Romorantin
	(European light-heavyweight title)		

1991
May 11	Leeonzer Barber	l rtd 6	Leeds 12-6-8
	(vacant WBO light-heavyweight title)		
Dec 6	Henry Maske	l rsf 8*	Dusseldorf 12-6-4

1992
Mar 18	Glazz Campbell	l pts 10	Glasgow 12-7
	(eliminator, British light-heavyweight title)		
Nov 21	Joseph Chingangu	l ko 2	Johannesburg

Fights 48 Won 26 Lost 21 Drawn 1

Tony COLLINS

Light-middleweight
Yateley born London 11 May 1970
Pinewood Starr ABC
1983 National Schools champion
1984 National Schools champion (w M Oliver)
1985 Junior ABA champion
1985 National Schools champion
1986 Junior ABA champion (w J Allen)
1986 NABC Class A champion (w rsf 3 S Grant)
1987 NABC Class B champion (w R Day)

1987
Jul 1	Terry Vosper	w rsf 1*	Albert Hall 10-9
Sep 16	Willie McDonald	w rsf 1	Albert Hall 10-10-8
Oct 13	Bernard Matthews	w pts 4	Windsor 10-8-8
Nov 28	Kevin Hayde	w pts 4	Windsor 10-12
Dec 15	Geoff Calder	w rsf 2	Cardiff 11-3

1988
Jan 27	Robert Armstrong	w ko 1	Bethnal Green 11-2
Feb 24	Geoff Calder	w rsf 3	Port Talbot 11-3-8
Mar 29	Rob Thomas	w pts 4	Bethnal Green 11-3
Apr 12	Rocky Reynolds	w pts 4	Cardiff 11-1
Apr 20	Steve Foster	w pts 4	Muswell Hill 11-2-8
May 10	Ollie Hutchinson	w rsf 1	Tottenham 11-2 /CTD..

(Tony COLLINS ctd)

May 26	Chris Richards	w rsf 3	Albert Hall 11-0-8
Jun 25	Franki Moro	w pts 6	Luton 11-2-8
Nov 1	Jose Becerra De Lima	w rsf 6	Reading
Dec 1	Simon Collins	w pts 6	Edmonton 11-0
Dec 20	Russell Mitchell	l ko 3	Swansea 10-12
1989			
Jan 31	Willie Montana	w rsf 4	Reading 11-3
May 17	Don Johnson	w pts 8	Millwall 11-2-8
Sep 14	Barry Bennett	w rsf 1	Basildon 11-2-12
Oct 11	Gary Pemberton	w ko 1	Millwall 11-2-8
Nov 15	Antonio Guerra	w ko 3	Reading 11-2
Dec 19	Roger Silsby	w ko 5	Gorleston 11-2-8
1990			
Feb 20	Joe Hernandez	w ko 1	Millwall 11-0-8
May 26	Hugo Marinangeli	w pts 12 (m)	Reading 10-13-12
	(vacant WBC International light-middleweight title)		
Oct 10	Ricardo Nunez	w pts 12 (s)	Millwall 10-13-8
	(WBC International light-middleweight title)		
1991			
May 8	Ricardo Nunez	w pts 12 (s)	Millwall 10-12-8
	(WBC International light-middleweight title)		
Jul 3	Wally Swift	l pts 12	Reading 10-13
	(British light-middleweight title)		
Oct 29	Paul Wesley	drew 8	Albert Hall 11-2
1992			
Jun 18	Russell Washer	w rsf 2*	Peterborough 11-1
Oct 22	Curtis Summit	l rsf 7	Bethnal Green 10-12-8
	(vacant WBC International light-middleweight title)		
Dec 10	Andy Till	l rsf 3	Bethnal Green
	(British light-middleweight title)		

Fights 31 Won 26 Lost 4 Drawn 1

Danny CONNELLY

Super-featherweight
Glasgow born 14 May 1971
Sidney Street ABC
1990 Scottish ABA light champ (w ko 1 J Jamieson, w H Collins, w R Ewing, w M Gowans, l B Schwer)
1990 Scotland (v USA, l K Childrey; v Ire, l B Geraghty)

1990			
Dec 10	Tommy Smith	w pts 6	Glasgow 9-5
1991			
May 31	Miguel Matthews	w pts 8	Glasgow 9-4
1992			
May 29	Lee Fox	w pts 6	Glasgow 9-5

Fights 3 Won 3

Eddie COOK

Featherweight
Larkhall born 30 November 1967
Larkhall ABC
1982 Scottish Youth champion (w C Hollinson)
1986 Scottish ABA bantamweight final (w Brand, l G Brooks)
1987 Scottish ABA bantamweight semi-final (w C Byrne, l J Mullen)
1988 Scottish ABA bantamweight semi-final (w C Glencross, l A Lees)

1989
May 17	Joe Mullen	l pts 8	Glasgow 8-10-8
Sep 14	Steve Walker	w pts 6	Motherwell 9-1-8
Nov 4	Steve Walker	l pts 4	Eastbourne 9-2
Nov 23	Ian McGirr	l pts 6	Motherwell 9-2

1990
Feb 23	Dave Buxton	w rtd 1*	Irvine 8-13
Mar 19	Jamie McBride	w pts 6	Glasgow 9-2-8
Mar 26	Ian McGirr	w pts 6	Glasgow 9-3-8
May 22	Dave Buxton	l pts 6	Thornaby 9-2
Jun 4	Neil Leitch	w pts 8	Glasgow 9-1-12
Nov 19	Ian McGirr	w pts 6	Glasgow 9-5

1991
Mar 1	Ian McGirr	w pts 6	Irvine 9-1
Apr 15	Darren Elsdon	drew 6	Glasgow 9-1
Oct 24	Des Gargano	w rsf 5	Glasgow 8-13

1992
Jan 21	Des Gargano	w pts 6	Glasgow 8-13
Feb 20	Miguel Matthews	w pts 6	Glasgow 9-0
Apr 8	Tony Silkstone	l pts 8	Leeds 8-13

Fights 16 Won 10 Lost 5 Drawn 1

James COOK

Super-middleweight
Peckham born Jamaica 17 May 1959
East Lane ABC
1977 SE London ABA middleweight final (l rsf 2 H Thompson)
1981 London ABA middleweight final (w rsf 2 D Smith, w T Godfrey, l J Graham)
1982 London ABA middleweight final (w rsf 3 S Edwards, w S Middleton, w T Godfrey, l J Graham)

1982
Oct 20	Mick Courtney	w pts 6	Strand
Nov 1	Gary Gething	w rsf 2	NSC

1983
Jan 19	Paul Shell	w pts 8	Solihull
Feb 3	Jimmy Price	l pts 6	Bloomsbury
Mar 9	Willie Wright	w pts 8	Solihull
Apr 14	Dudley McKenzie	w pts 8	Basildon 11-5
May 16	Eddie Smith	w rsf 6	Manchester 11-5
Nov 23	Vince Gajny	w rtd 6*	Solihull

1984
Jun 5	T.P.Jenkins	w rsf 9	Albert Hall 11-4-12
	(vacant Southern middleweight title)		
Sep 25	Jimmy Price	l ko 2	Wembley 11-5-4
	(eliminator, British middleweight title)		

1985
May 4	Conrad Oscar	w pts 10	Queensway 11-4-8 /CTD..

(James COOK ctd)

Oct 2	Tony Burke	l ko 2	Solihull 11-6
	(Southern middleweight title)		
1986			
Mar 1	Graciano Rocchigiani	l pts 8	Cologne
Mar 26	Jan Lefeber	l ko 3	Amsterdam 11-8
May 20	Michael Watson	w pts 8	Wembley 11-9-4
1987			
Feb 13	Mbayo Wa Mbayo	l pts 8	Villeurbanne
Oct 2	Willie Wilson	w ko 6	Perugia
Oct 26	Tarmo Uusivirta	l pts 10	Jyvaskyla
1988			
Apr 5	Cliff Curtis	w rsf 4	Basildon 11-13-4
Jun 8	Herol Graham	l rsf 5	Sheffield 11-5-8
	(vacant British middleweight title)		
1989			
Jan 31	Errol Christie	w rsf 5	Bethnal Green 11-8-8
Sep 28	Brian Schumacher	w rsf 5	Battersea 11-10-8
	(final eliminator, British super-middleweight title)		
1990			
Oct 30	Sam Storey	w rsf 10	Belfast 11-11
	(British super-middleweight title)		
1991			
Mar 10	Pierre-Frank Winterstein	w ko 12	Paris 11-13-4
	(vacant European super-middleweight title)		
Jun 1	Mark Kaylor	w rtd 6	Bethnal Green 11-12
	(European super-middleweight title)		
Oct 22	Tarmo Uusivirta	w rtd 7	Battersea 11-12
	(European super-middleweight title)		
1992			
Apr 3	Franck Nicotra	l ko 1	Vitrolles
	(European super-middleweight title)		
Sep 7	Tony Booth	w pts 8	Bethnal Green 12-1-8
Oct 17	Terry Magee	w rsf 5	Wembley 12-3-8

Fights 29 Won 20 Lost 9

John J. COOKE

Super-middleweight
Coventry born 22 January 1966
Christ The King ABC & Coventry Colliery ABC
1989 Warwickshire ABA middleweight final (l G Lewis)
1990 Warwickshire ABA light-heavyweight champion (w M Moran, l A Wright)
1991 Warwickshire ABA light-heavyweight final (w rsf 1 C Smallwood, l N Simpson)
1992 Warwickshire ABA light-heavyweight final (l N Simpson)

1992			
Oct 5	Paul Hanlon	w rsf 1	Bardon 12-3
Nov 23	Paul Murray	w ko 1	Coventry 12-3
Dec 2	Nigel Rafferty	w pts 6	Bardon 12-8

Fights 3 Won 3

Maurice CORE

Light-heavyweight
Manchester born 22 June 1965
Moss Side ABC. Real name: Maurice Coore.
1985 Northern ABA middleweight champion (w I Bayliss, w P Harding, w rsf 2 J Lockwood, l ko 1 J Melfah)
1987 East Lancs ABA middleweight semi-final (l E Noi)
1988 ABA light-heavyweight finalist (w rtd 2 D Charles, w S McDougall, w dis 3 K Price, w M Gale, w M Baker, l H Lawson)
1989 North-West ABA light-heavyweight final (w rsf 1 D Margiotta, w rtd 1 S McGrath, l P Wright)

1990
Jan 15	Dennis Banton	w pts 6	NSC 12-4
May 3	Everton Blake	w pts 8	Marble Arch 12-8-8
May 22	Nicky Piper	drew 6	St Albans 12-11

1991
Feb 22	Everton Blake	w rsf 8	Manchester 12-9-12
Apr 12	Glazz Campbell	w ko 2	Manchester 12-11-8
May 31	Rodney Brown	w rsf 6	Manchester 12-8-12
Nov 29	Steve Osborne	w pts 6	Manchester 12-12

1992
Jan 31	Denroy Bryan	w rsf 1	Manchester 12-13
Apr 5	Willie Ball	w rsf 3	Bradford 12-9
Jul 18	Tony Booth	w pts 6	Manchester 12-9-8
Sep 28	Noel Magee	w rsf 9	Manchester 12-6-4
	(vacant British light-heavyweight title)		

Fights 11 Won 10 Drawn 1

John CORCORAN

Welterweight
Alfreton, born Chesterfield 16 December 1967
South Normanton ABC
1985 North Midlands ABA light-welterweight champion (w rtd 2 J Fitzpatrick, w T Richards, wthdrw)
1988 Derbyshire ABA welterweight final (l C Harrison)

1988
Feb 29	Barry Messam	w rsf 3	Birmingham 10-9
Apr 17	Eddie Collins	l pts 6	Peterborough 10-10
Nov 23	Tony Britland	drew 8	Solihull 10-8

1989
Jan 25	Tony Britland	w pts 8	Solihull 10-10-8
Mar 20	James Conley	w rsf 5	Bradford 10-9
May 8	Barry Messam	w ko 5	Leicester 10-7
May 16	Ian Midwood-Tate	w pts 6	Halifax 10-6
Sep 25	Delroy Matthews	w rsf 5	Crystal Palace 10-7

1990
Feb 20	Mickey Lloyd	l rsf 2	Brentford 10-6

1991
Mar 13	Ernie Loveridge	l rsf 4	Stoke 10-8
Oct 3	Tony Britland	l rsf 5*	Burton 10-9
Nov 26	Ojay Abrahams	l pts 6	Bethnal Green 10-9

1992
Jan 22	Dave Hall	w pts 8	Stoke 10-11
Mar 11	Dave Hall	w pts 8	Stoke
Mar 19	Charlie Moore	l pts 6	York 10-8
Apr 29	Steve Goodwin	l pts 8	Stoke 10-12-8

Fights 16 Won 8 Lost 7 Drawn 1

Chris COUGHLAN

Heavyweight
Swansea born 21 May 1963
Gwent ABC
1989 Welsh ABA heavyweight champion (w M Trotman, w H Hartt, l rsf 1 H Akinwande)

1989
Oct 3	Ahcene Chemali	l rsf 1*	Southend 14-4
Dec 3	John Foreman	l rsf 2	Birmingham 13-6

1990
Mar 10	Mark Langley	w pts 6	Bristol 13-13
Mar 28	Phil Soundy	l pts 6	Bethnal Green 13-5-12
Jun 5	Trevor Barry	l pts 6	Liverpool 13-4
Sep 17	Steve Yorath	l pts 6	Cardiff 13-1
Nov 6	Art Stacey	l rsf 4*	Southend
Dec 8	Gary McConnell	l pts 6	Bristol 14-0

1991
Jan 16	Phil Soundy	l pts 8	Albert Hall
Feb 15	Niels H. Madsen	l rsf 3	Randers
Nov 4	Nick Howard	w ko 3	Merthyr 13-11
Dec 11	Ray Kane	l pts 6	Dublin 13-9-12

1992
Jan 18	Wayne Llewellyn	l rsf 3	Albert Hall 14-0
Dec 17	J.A. Bugner	l rsf 3	Wembley GH 15-0

Fights 14 Won 2 Lost 12

Lee CROCKER

Middleweight
Swansea born 9 January 1969
Gwent ABC
Southpaw

1991
Jan 31	Colin Manners	l pts 6	Stockport 11-5
Feb 12	Paul Evans	w rsf 2	Cardiff 11-11
Apr 4	Johnny Pinnock	w rsf 5	Watford 11-0
Jun 30	Andrew Furlong	drew 6	Southwark 11-1-8
Sep 30	Fran Harding	l rsf 3	Albert Hall 11-4

1992
Mar 11	Russell Washer	w pts 6	Cardiff 11-7
Apr 30	Winston May	w rsf 2	Bayswater 11-3
Sep 23	Nick Manners	l ko 1	Leeds 11-8
Dec 17	Jamie Robinson	l rtd 2	Barking 11-2

Fights 9 Won 4 Lost 4 Drawn 1

Con CRONIN

Lightweight
Watford born London 27 August 1962
Islington ABC

1984
May 1	Steve Cooke	drew 6	Maidstone
May 9	Nicky Day	drew 6	Mayfair 10-0-12
Sep 17	Mark Simpson	l rsf 6	Brighton 9-10
Nov 1	Micky Hall	l pts 6	Basildon 9-11-8

1985
Mar 1	Steve Friel	l rsf 3*	Longford 10-5

May 4	Nicky Day	drew 6	Queensway 10-0
May 25	Kenny Watson	w pts 6	Longford 10-0
Jul 22	Gary King	drew 6	Longford 9-11-8
Nov 7	Nicky Day	l pts 6	Tottenham 10-2-8

1986-87 inactive

1988

Apr 25	Wayne Goult	w ko 3	Bethnal Green 9-12
May 26	Steve Taggart	w pts 6	Bethnal Green 10-0-4
Jun 14	Shaun Cooper	l pts 6	Dudley

1989-91 inactive

1992

Sep 17	Jason Lepre	w pts 6	Watford 9-9
Nov 2	Gareth Jordan	l ko 2	Wolverhampton 9-6-8

Fights 14 Won 4 Lost 6 Drawn 4

Carl CROOK

Lightweight
Chorley, born Bolton 10 November 1963
Army & Chorley ABC
1979 National Schools champion
1980 NABC champion (w D Tovey)
1982 Combined Services ABA lightweight champion (w M Kirk, w S Snagg, w G Mitchell, l J McDonnell)
1983 Combined Services ABA lightweight champion (w S Snagg, w D Taunton, l K Willis)
1984 ABA lightweight finalist (w ko 1 D Robb, w N Meloscia, w K Parry, l A Dickson)
1984 England (v Ire, w T Tobin)
1985 ABA lightweight finalist (w rsf 3 R Davison, w M Gallagher, w rsf 3 P Gettins, w N Haddock, w rsf 2 J Bennie, l rsf 2* E McAuley)

1985

Dec 16	George Jones	w pts 6	Bradford 9-8

1986

Jan 27	Russell Jones	w rsf 4	Bradford 9-6
Mar 24	Doug Munro	w ko 2	Bradford 9-9
Apr 17	Muhammad Lovelock	w ko 6	Bradford 9-9
May 20	George Jones	w rsf 1	Horwich 9-8
Sep 22	Sugar Gibiliru	w pts 6	Bradford 9-7
Nov 4	Brian Roche (vacant Central lightweight title)	drew 10	Oldham 9-8-4
Dec 15	Sugar Gibiliru	w pts 8	Bradford 9-11

1987

Jan 27	Dean Marsden	w rsf 1	Manchester 9-10
Feb 23	Muhammad Lovelock (vacant Central lightweight title)	w pts 10	Bradford 9-9
Apr 28	George Baigrie	w pts 8	Manchester 9-11-12
Jun 9	Tony Richards	w pts 8	Manchester 9-9
Sep 20	Joey Jacobs (Central lightweight title)	l pts 10	Oldham 9-7-8
Oct 7	Marvin P. Gray	w pts 8	Burnley 9-11
Nov 28	Marvin P. Gray	w pts 8	Horwich 9-10-8

1988

Apr 26	Keith Parry (eliminator, British lightweight title)	w pts 10	Bradford 9-8-12
Oct 25	Patrick Kamy	w pts 8	Hartlepool 9-9

1989

Feb 14	Steve Topliss	w rtd 5*	Manchester 9-9-12
Apr 14	Ned Simmons	w rsf 8	Manchester 9-11 /CTD..

(Carl CROOK ctd)

May 31	Steve Pollard	w rsf 4*	Manchester 9-9
Oct 13	Mohammed Ouhmad	w pts 8	Preston 9-11
1990			
Jan 24	Joel Dulys	w rsf 2	Preston 9-12
Mar 21	Najib Daho	w pts 12	Preston 9-8
	(Commonwealth lightweight title)		
Nov 14	Tony Richards	w pts 12	Sheffield 9-9
	(Commonwealth and vacant British lightweight titles)		
Dec 19	Ian Honeywood	w rsf 4	Preston 9-8
	(British and Commonwealth lightweight titles)		
1991			
Apr 24	Najib Daho	w rsf 10	Preston 9-8-8
	(British and Commonwealth lightweight titles)		
Jun 22	Brian Roche	w ko 10	Earls Court 9-8-12
	(British and Commonwealth lightweight titles)		
Dec 7	Antonio Renzo	l rsf 6	Rossano Calabro 9-9
	(European lightweight title)		
1992			
May 5	Steve Boyle	w rsf 7*	Preston 9-8-8
	(British & Commonwealth lightweight titles)		
Oct 28	Billy Schwer	l rtd 9	Albert Hall 9-8-8
	(British & Commonwealth lightweight titles)		

Fights 30 Won 26 Lost 3 Drawn 1

Phil CULLEN

Lightweight
Swansea born 4 February 1972

1992
Mar 25	Roger Hunte	l rsf 3	Albert Hall 9-8-8

Fights 1 Lost 1

Shaun CUMMINS

Light-middleweight
Leicester born 8 February 1968
Belgrave ABC

1986
Sep 29	Michael Justin	w pts 6	Loughborough 10-13
Nov 24	Gary Pemberton	w rsf 6*	Cardiff 10-12
1987			
Feb 9	Rob Thomas	w pts 8	Cardiff 11-4
Sep 23	Chris Richards	w pts 6	Loughborough 11-0
1988			
Mar 7	Antonio Fernandez	w pts 6	Northampton 11-1
Sep 12	Seamus Casey	w ko 3	Northampton 11-4-8
Oct 24	Frank Grant	l rtd 7*	Northampton 11-5
1989			
Mar 1	Gary Pemberton	w ko 2	Cardiff 11-0
Apr 5	Efren Olivo	w rsf 1	Albert Hall 11-0
Oct 4	Kesem Clayton	l rsf 6*	Solihull 10-12

1990
Jan 31	Tony Velinor	w pts 8	Bethnal Green 11-2
Feb 20	Brian Robinson	w rsf 5	Millwall 11-3
Apr 26	Wally Swift	l pts 10	Merthyr 10-12
	(vacant Midlands light-middleweight title)		
Sep 18	Paul Wesley	w rsf 1	Wolverhampton 11-3-8
Oct 31	Terry Morrill	w rsf 1	Crystal Palace 10-13-12

1991
Jan 23	Ian Chantler	w pts 10	Brentwood 10-13-12
Mar 19	Martin Smith	drew 8	Leicester 11-2
Nov 7	Jason Rowe	w rsf 2	Peterborough 11-1-8
Dec 5	Winston May	w rsf 2	Peterborough 11-1

1992
Jun 18	Leroy Owens	w rsf 2	Peterborough 11-2
Sep 26	John Kaighin	w rtd 4	Olympia 11-6
Nov 28	Steve Foster	w pts 12	Manchester 10-13-12
	(vacant WBA Pentacontinental title)		

Fights 22 Won 18 Lost 3 Drawn 1

GUS ROBINSON

GEORGE BOWES

GUS ROBINSON
Promotions

PROMOTING & MANAGING
NORTH-EAST FIGHTERS
GYM & VENUE - HARTLEPOOL
BOROUGH HALL

CONTACT GUS ROBINSON
ON
(0429) 234221 - OFFICE
(0429) 869822 - OFFICE FAX
(091) 587 0336 - HOME

Derrick DANIEL

Light-welterweight
Leyton, born 3 April 1963
Leyton ABC
1985 NE London ABA light-welterweight final (w M Barrett, l D Dyer)

1990
Mar 6	John Marshall	w rsf 5	Bethnal Green 10-3-4
May 9	Gavin Fitzpatrick	w rsf 1	Albert Hall 10-2
Sep 12	Ross Hale	l pts 6	Bethnal Green 10-7

1991
Mar 26	Mick O'Donnell	drew 6	Bethnal Green 10-1

1992
May 11	Carl Hook	w pts 6	Piccadilly 10-0
Jun 16	Carl Hook	l rsf 2	Dagenham 10-1

Fights 6 Won 3 Lost 2 Drawn 1

Hugh DAVEY

Welterweight
Wallsend born 27 January 1966

1992
Mar 30	Wayne Shepherd	w pts 6	Bradford 10-9
Apr 28	Benji Joseph	w rsf 4*	Houghton-le-Spring 10-9-8
Sep 10	Darren McInulty	w pts 6	Sunderland 10-8
Sep 21	Rick North	drew 6	Cleethorpes 10-10
Oct 23	Richard O'Brien	w pts 6	Gateshead 10-9

Fights 5 Won 4 Drawn 1

Jamie DAVIDSON

Light-welterweight
Liverpool born 1 April 1970
Real name: David Prescott
Southpaw
Greenall St Helens ABC
1990 West Lancs & Cheshire ABA light-welterweight semi-final (l G Beadman)

1991
Nov 18	Ty Zubair	w pts 6	Manchester 9-12

1992
Feb 10	Kevin McKillan	w pts 6	Liverpool 9-12
Mar 11	Kevin McKillan	drew 6	Stoke
Apr 28	Micky Hall	w pts 6	Houghton-le-Spring 9-13-8
May 14	Floyd Churchill	l rsf 4	Liverpool 9-13

Fights 5 Won 3 Lost 1 Drawn 1

John DAVIES

Welterweight
Ammanford, born Swansea 10 September 1964
Blaenau ABC
1978 National Schools champion
1979 National Schools champion
1980 National Schools champion (w A Velinor)
1981 National Schools final (l A Velinor)
1982 NABC Class C champion (w rsf 3 A Boukriss)

1982
Oct 13	Dalton Jordan	w ko 4	Evesham 10-9
Nov 1	Rafaele Feliciello	l pts 6	Liverpool 11-1-8
Nov 10	Bert Myrie	w rsf 1*	Evesham
Nov 23	Clifton Wallace	w pts 6	Wolverhampton
Dec 1	Ian Murray	drew 6	Stafford 11-2
Dec 6	Ian Murray	w rsf 5*	Edgbaston 10-9

1983-85 inactive

1986
Sep 15	Paul Burton	w ko 6	Manchester
Oct 10	Peter Reid	w rsf 2	Gloucester 10-12

1987
Feb 16	Johnny Stone	w pts 6	Gloucester 11-0
Apr 15	Franki Moro	w rtd 3*	Carmarthen 10-6-8

1988 inactive

1989
Mar 22	John Smith	w pts 8	Solihull 10-6
Jun 8	Dave Andrews	w rsf 3	Cardiff 10-11
Nov 13	Linda Nondzaba	w pts 10	Cape Town 10-6

1990
Apr 26	Kelvin Mortimer	w rsf 2	Merthyr 10-7
	(vacant Welsh welterweight title)		
Nov 18	Phumzile Madikane	w ko 10	Cape Town

1991
Oct 15	Andy Till	l pts 12 (s)	Dudley 10-13-8
	(vacant WBC International light-middleweight title)		

1992
Mar 11	Trevor Ambrose	w rsf 5	Cardiff 10-12

Fights 17 Won 14 Lost 2 Drawn 1

John DAVISON

Featherweight
Newcastle born 30 September 1958
Grainger Park ABC, West Denton ABC
Southpaw
1984 North-East England ABA featherweight final (l M Hanif)
1985 England (v Ire, w R Nash)
1985 East German Multi-Nations (l Kim-dsi Jon, NKor)
1985 ABA featherweight final (w rsf 1 P Hodkinson, w ko 1 C Lynch, w rsf 2 J Leys, l F Havard, splt)
1985 European championships featherweight (l rsf 1 K-D Kirschstein, EGer)
1986 World championships featherweight (l R Breitbarth, EGer)
1986 England (v Sco, w D Hood)
1986 Northern ABA featherweight final (w rsf 2 A Steadman,l P Hodkinson)
1987 ABA bantamweight semi-final (w rsf 3 F Foster, w rsf 2 R Wenton, w rsf 2* M Tierney, l M Deveney)
1987 England (v Sco, w rsf 1 M Deveney)
1988 England (v Sco, w M Deveney)
1988 Northern ABA bantamweight champion (w M Gibbons, w rsf 2 R Wenton, l K Howlett)

1988			
Sep 22	Des Gargano	w pts 8	Newcastle 8-12
Sep 29	Des Gargano	w pts 8	Sunderland 8-13-8
Oct 10	Gary Maxwell	w rsf 1	Nottingham 8-13
Nov 22	James Hunter	w pts 6	Middlesbrough 9-7
Dec 12	Gary Maxwell	l pts 8	Nottingham 9-1
1989			
Feb 14	Nigel Senior	w rsf 8	Sunderland 8-13-12
Sep 11	Colin Lynch	w rsf 2	Nottingham 8-13
Oct 23	Andre Seymour	w pts 8	Glasgow 9-1-4
Dec 6	Karl Taylor	w pts 8	Leicester 9-2
1990			
Feb 19	Bruce Flippens	w rsf 6	Glasgow 9-1-8
Mar 20	Srikoon Narachawat	w ko 5	Hartlepool 8-12-12
	(WBC International featherweight title)		
May 15	Bangsaen Yodmuaydang	w rsf 5	South Shields 8-13-8
	(WBC International featherweight title)		
Nov 13	Jae-hyun Hwang	w rsf 5	Hartlepool 8-12
	(WBC International featherweight title)		
1991			
May 24	Fabrice Benichou	l pts 12	Brest
	(vacant European featherweight title)		
Aug 9	Richard Savage	w rsf 6*	Juan-les-Pins
Oct 22	Sakda Sorpakdee	w pts 12 (s)	Hartlepool 8-9-4
	(WBC International super-bantamweight title)		
1992			
May 29	Fabrice Benichou	l pts 12 (m)	Amneville
	(European featherweight title)		
Sep 10	Tim Driscoll	w ko 7	Sunderland 8-13
	(vacant British featherweight title)		

Fights 18 Won 15 Lost 3

Russell DAVISON

Featherweight
Salford born 2 October 1961
Salford ABC
1985 East Lancs & Cheshire ABA lightweight final (l rsf 3 C Crook)

1986			
May 22	Nigel Crook	l pts 6	Horwich 9-1
Jun 9	Gary Maxwell	l pts 6	Manchester 9-2
Sep 25	Nigel Crook	l pts 6	Preston 9-1-12
Oct 14	David Hughes	w pts 6	Manchester 9-3-8
Nov 25	Carl Gaynor	w pts 6	Manchester 9-2
Dec 10	Davey Hughes	w pts 8	Stoke 9-2
1987			
Jan 27	Nigel Senior	drew 8	Manchester 9-3-8
Mar 4	Tim Driscoll	l pts 8	Stoke 9-3
Mar 31	Stuart Carmichael	w pts 6	Oldham
May 26	Kevin Taylor	l pts 10	Oldham 9-0
	(Central super-featherweight title)		
Oct 6	Gary Maxwell	l pts 8	Manchester 9-1-8
Dec 16	Mike Whalley	w pts 8	Manchester 9-0-8
1988			
Mar 16	Gary De Roux	l pts 8	Solihull 9-2
May 3	Rocky Lawlor	l pts 8	Stoke 9-1
Nov 29	Mike Whalley	l rsf 7	Manchester 8-13-12
	(vacant Central featherweight title)		/CTD..

(Russell DAVISON ctd)

1989
Jan 25	Derek Amory	w pts 8	Solihull 9-2-8
Apr 19	Michael Armstrong	l pts 8	Stoke 9-2
Dec 6	Michael Armstrong	w pts 8	Stoke 9-2-4
Dec 23	Kevin Kelley	l pts 8	Hoogvliet 9-0-4

1990
Mar 6	Michael Armstrong	l pts 10	Stoke 9-0
Sep 26	Steve Robinson	l pts 8	Manchester 9-1-12
Nov 19	Peter Judson	w pts 8	Manchester 9-3
Dec 17	Dave Buxton	w pts 8	Manchester 9-1-8

1991
Jan 29	Peter Judson (vacant Central featherweight title)	w pts 10	Stockport 9-0
Mar 5	Colin McMillan	l pts 6	Millwall 9-3
Apr 24	Steve Robinson	l rtd 6	Preston 9-4
Sep 9	Jimmy Owens (Central featherweight title)	w pts 10	Liverpool 8-13

1992
Feb 29	Moussa Sangare	l rsf 5	Gravelines
Oct 13	Craig Dermody (Central featherweight title)	l pts 10	Bury 9-0

Fights 29 Won 11 Lost 17 Drawn 1

Mark DAWSON

Light-middleweight
Burton born 26 February 1971
Real name: Mark Lee
Burton Boys ABC
1991 Staffordshire ABA light-middleweight final (w J Steel, w A Peach, l A Williams)
1992 Midlands ABA light-middleweight champion (w L White, w A McFarlane, w S Goodwin, withdrew, ill)

1992
Jun 3	Ricky North	w pts 6	Newcastle-under-Lyme 10-5
Sep 9	Jimmy Vincent	w pts 6	Stoke 10-8
Sep 29	Steve Goodwin	l rsf 1*	Stoke 10-12
Oct 28	Steve McNess	w rsf 2*	Albert Hall 10-13-8
Dec 7	Steve Goodwin	w pts 6	Mayfair 11-1

Fights 5 Won 4 Lost 1

Gary DELANEY

Light-heavyweight
West Ham born 12 August 1970
West Ham ABC
1986 NABC Class A champion
1987 Junior ABA Class B champion
1988 NABC Class C champion
1988 Young England (v WGer, w M Fronwerk)
1989 London ABA light-heavy champ (w N Mirza, w D Weaver, w ko 1 V Clarke, w T Dixon, l P Wright)
1990 NE London ABA light-heavyweight final (w dis 3 B Scott, l dis 3 M Baker)
1991 NE London ABA light-heavyweight final (nc M Wright - both dsq in 3rd rnd)

1991
Oct 2	Gus Mendes	w rsf 1	Barking 12-10
Oct 23	Joe Frater	w rsf 1	Bethnal Green 12-11
Nov 13	John Kaighin	w pts 6	Bethnal Green 12-7-8
Dec 11	Randy Powell	w rsf 1	Basildon 12-10

1992			
Feb 11	Simon Harris	drew 8	Barking 12-7
May 12	John Williams	w pts 6	Crystal Palace 13-0
Jun 16	Nigel Rafferty	w ko 5	Dagenham 12-12
Sep 15	Gil Lewis	w rsf 2	Crystal Palace 12-8-12
Oct 6	Simon McDougall	w pts 8	Antwerp
Nov 10	John Oxenham	w ko 5	Dagenham 12-6-8
Dec 12	Simon McDougall	w pts 8	Muswell Hill 12-7

Fights 11 Won 10 Drawn 1

Patrick DELARGY

Light-welterweight
Coventry, born Hoddesdon 9 October 1968
Full name: Owen Patrick Delargy
Talbot ABC
1984 NABC Class A finalist (l L McDonald)

1989			
Feb 14	Peter Bowen	w rtd 1*	Wolverhampton 9-12
Feb 20	Erwin Edwards	w pts 6	Birmingham 9-9
Mar 15	Dave Croft	l rsf 3*	Stoke 9-8
Jun 28	Dave Pierre	l rtd 2*	Kenilworth 9-12
1990			
Dec 5	Dave Jenkins	l rsf 4	Stafford 9-10
1991			
Sep 24	Bernard Paul	l rsf 5	Basildon 10-2
1992			
May 11	Mark Antony	w pts 6	Coventry 10-0

Fights 7 Won 3 Lost 4

Carlos DEMONIKOS

Lightweight
Doncaster born 13 May 1966

1992			
Oct 19	Marco Fattore	l rtd 4	Mayfair 9-7-8

Fights 1 Lost 1

Damien DENNY

Light-middleweight
Lisburn born 20 April 1966
Holy Trinity ABC, Belfast
1983 Irish Junior final (l ko 3 B Joyce)
1983 Young Ireland (v Wal, w S Jones)
1985 Ireland (v US, l D Rolon; v Sc, w J Pender; w Wal, w K Parry)
1985 European Championships (l U Junger, WG)
1985 Irish ABA light-welterweight champion (w rsf 2 B Walsh)
1986 Ireland (v En, w rsf 3 K Wall)
1986 Irish ABA welterweight champion (w rsf 3 E Considine, w B Walsh)
1986 Commonwealth Games welterweight bronze medal (w M Mulchlis, Sin; l D Dyer, En)
1986 World Championships welter quarter-final (w A Madura, Bra; w S Mercado, Equ; l C Duvergel, Cub)
1987 Irish ABA welterweight final (w J Webb, l B Walsh)

/CTD..

(Damien DENNY ctd)
1987
Jul 1	Manny Romain	w ko 1	Albert Hall 10-8
Aug 9	Joe Lynch	w rsf 1	Windsor 10-11-4
Sep 16	Billy Cairns	w pts 8	Albert Hall 10-7-8
Oct 13	Chris Richards	w pts 6	Windsor 10-8

1988
Jan 27	Simon Lee	w ko 7	Bethnal Green 10-8
Feb 9	Dean Bramhald	w pts 4	Stafford 10-7
Mar 9	Jimmy Thornton	w pts 8	Bethnal Green 10-11
Jun 25	Martin Smith	nc 5	Luton 10-9-8
Nov 15	Tommy McCallum	w rsf 2	Norwich 10-13
Dec 1	Kelvin Mortimer	w rsf 1	Edmonton 10-9-8

1989
Mar 28	Mickey Lloyd	w rsf 4	Bethnal Green
Apr 11	Winston May	w rsf 3	Port Talbot 10-13
Sep 19	Mark Holden	w rsf 2	Millwall 10-8

1990
| Apr 17 | Del Bryan | l pts 10 | Millwall 10-6-8 |

(eliminator, British welterweight title)

| Jul 6 | Parrish Johnson | w rsf 4 | Brentwood 10-12-12 |
| Sep 22 | Newton Barnett | l rsf 6 | Albert Hall 10-12 |

1991
| Feb 6 | Newton Barnett | w pts 8 | Bethnal Green 11-0 |
| Apr 9 | Jason Rowe | l ko 7 | Mayfair 11-1 |

1992
| Dec 1 | Bozon Haule | w pts 6 | Bristol 10-12-12 |

Fights 19 Won 15 Lost 3 No Contests 1

Craig DERMODY

Featherweight
Manchester born 11 September 1970
Collyhurst and Moston ABC
1988 NABC Class C champion
1988 Young England (v Ita, w N Sciarotta)
1989 North-West ABA flyweight final (l J Lyon)

1991
Jan 31	Karl Morling	w rsf 5	Stockport 8-7
Mar 14	Kelton McKenzie	w rsf 3	Middleton 8-9
Apr 16	Miguel Matthews	w pts 6	Nottingham 8-9
May 16	Andrew Robinson	w pts 6	Liverpool 8-9-4
Jun 20	Gary Hickman	w rsf 2	Liverpool 8-8-4
Aug 1	James Hunter	w rsf 2*	Dewsbury 8-9
Nov 21	Miguel Matthews	w pts 6	Burton 8-9
Nov 28	Peter Buckley	w pts 6	Liverpool 8-12
Dec 19	Peter Buckley	w pts 6	Oldham 8-9-4

1992
Feb 27	Miguel Matthews	w pts 6	Liverpool 8-10
Jul 2	Alan Smith	w rsf 3	Middleton 8-11-4
Oct 13	Russell Davison	w pts 10	Bury 8-11-12

(Central featherweight title)

Fights 12 Won 12

Mike DEVENEY

Featherweight
Paisley, born Elderslie 14 December 1965
Paisley ABC
1987 Scotland (v Eng, l rsf 1 J Davison; v Wal, w rsf 2 J Pardoe)
1987 ABA bantamweight finalist (w D McCrindle, w S Taylor, w J Mullen, w J Davison, l J Sillitoe)
1987 European championships bantamweight (l rsf 3 I Hristov, Bul)
1988 Scottish ABA bantamweight champion (w G Ferry, w J Drummond, w A Lees, l rsf 3* K Howlett)
1988 Scotland (v Eng, l J Davison)
1988 Olympic Games bantamweight (l A Machaze, Moz)
1989 Scottish ABA bantamweight final (w D Hardie, l rsf 2 W Docherty)
1989 Scotland (v Wal, w J Williams; v EGer, l M Beyer)
1990 Scottish ABA featherweight semi-final (w A Garrity, l G Hughes)
1990 Commonwealth Games featherweight (l I Tembo, Zam)

1991			
Feb 18	John George	w pts 6	Glasgow 9-1
Mar 18	Francisco Ventura	w pts 6	NSC 9-0
Apr 22	Neil Leitch	w pts 6	Glasgow 9-0-8
Sep 9	Peter Buckley	w pts 8	Glasgow 9-2
Sep 19	Noel Carroll	l pts 6	Stockport 9-0
Nov 14	Peter Buckley	w pts 6	Edinburgh 9-0-12
1992			
Jan 28	Graham O'Malley	l rsf 1	Piccadilly 9-3
Feb 28	Gary Hickman	w pts 6	Irvine 8-12
Sep 14	David Ramsden	l pts 6	Bradford 9-0
Oct 7	Mark Hargreaves	l rsf 7	Glasgow 8-12
Dec 7	Carl Roberts	w pts 6	Manchester 9-2

Fights 11 Won 7 Lost 4

Eunan DEVENNEY

Featherweight
Bushey Heath, born Donegal 2 February 1968
Twan Towns ABC, Donegal

1991			
Sep 4	Alan Smith	w ko 1	Bethnal Green 9-2
Sep 26	Kevin Lowe	l ko 2	Dunstable 9-2
Nov 28	Greg Upton	l pts 6	Evesham 9-1
1992			
Mar 30	David Ramsden	l rsf 2	Bradford 9-2

Fights 4 Won 1 Lost 3

Norman DHALIE

Featherweight
Birmingham born 24 March 1971
Kyrle Hall ABC

1992			
Apr 6	Karl Morling	l pts 6	Northampton 9-1
Apr 27	Wilson Docherty	l rsf 2	Glasgow 9-2-4
Jul 2	John White	l rsf 5	Middleton 8-13
Sep 29	Gary Marston	drew 6	Stoke 9-3
Oct 7	Jacob Smith	w pts 6	Sunderland 8-11
Dec 3	Bradley Stone	l ko 4	Catford 8-12

Fights 6 Won 1 Lost 4 Drawn 1

Harry DHAMI

Welterweight
Gravesend born 17 April 1972

1992
Oct 29   Johnny Pinnock   w pts 6   Hayes 10-9

Fights 1 Won 1

Michael DICK

Welterweight
Aylesbury born 29 October 1964
Aylesbury ABC
1989 Home Counties ABA light-middleweight prelim (l G Stevens)
1991 Home Counties ABA light-middleweight final (l L Pugh)
1992 Home Counties ABA welterweight semi-final (l rsf 2* A Chase)

1992
Oct 29   Nick Appiah   l pts 6   Hayes 10-9

Fights 1 Lost 1

Clive DIXON

Light-middleweight
Dulwich, born 11 May 1965
Hollington ABC
1988 SE London ABA welterweight semi-final (l ko 1 K Lueshing)
1989 SE London ABA welterweight final (w rsf 2 M Clarke, l l rsf 3 K Lueshing)
1991 SE London ABA light-middleweight champion (w.o., l M Scott)

1991
May 22   Benny Collins   w pts 6   Millwall 10-6
Sep 4   Kevin Sheeran   l rsf 4*   Bethnal Green 11-2
1992
Mar 1   Tracy Jocelyn   l pts 6   St Leonard's On Sea 11-2

Fights 3 Won 1 Lost 2

Terry DIXON

Cruiserweight
West Ham born 29 July 1966
All Stars ABC & Middle Row ABC
1987 NW London ABA light-heavyweight champion (w ko 1 M Witter, w M Akay, l J Beckles)
1988 ABA light-heavyweight semi-final (w ko 1 M Witter, w rsf 1 R Webb, w R Carless, l H Lawson)
1989 London ABA light-heavyweight final (w rsf 1 P Hardy, l G Delaney)

1989
Sep 21   Dave Mowbray   w rsf 2   Southampton 12-10-8
Nov 30   Brendan Dempsey   w rsf 8   Barking 12-10-8
1990
Mar 8   Cordwell Hylton   w pts 8   Watford 12-12
Apr 6   Prince Rodney   w rsf 7   Stevenage 12-10
Oct 23   Dennis Bailey   w pts 6   Leicester 13-8
1991
Mar 7   Carl Thompson   l pts 8   Basildon 13-5-8
Apr 22   Everton Blake   l rsf 8   AASC 12-11
1992
Mar 25   Mark Bowen   w rtd 1   Albert Hall 13-6
Apr 27   Ian Bulloch   w rsf 4   AASC 13-7-8
Oct 17   Darren McKenna   l rsf 3   Wembley 13-8-8

Fights 10 Won 7 Lost 3

Alex DOCHERTY

Bantamweight
Craigneuk born 5 June 1972
Blantyre ABC
1989 World Junior Championships (l T Bedir, Tur)
1990 Scottish ABA flyweight final (w K Knox, w R Grant, l N Armstrong)
1990 European Junior Championships (l D de Gregorio, It)
1990 Scotland (v Eng, l M Jones)
1991 Scotland (v Eng, l rsf 1 N McCallum)
1991 Scottish ABA featherweight semi-final (w B Wardrop, l B Carr)

1992
Feb 24	Andrew Bloomer	w pts 6	Glasgow 8-8-8
Jun 1	Robert Braddock	w pts 6	Glasgow 8-8-8
Sep 19	Kid McAuley	w pts 6	Glasgow 8-10-8

Fights 3 Won 3

Drew DOCHERTY

Bantamweight
Condorrat, born Glasgow 29 November 1965
Croy Miners ABC
1984 Scottish ABA light-flyweight champion (w E Rennie, l J Lyon)
1985 Scottish ABA light-flyweight champion (l M Epton)
1985 European Championships, Budapest (l R Isaszegi, Hun)
1986 ABA flyweight finalist (w J McLean, w D Shankland, w M Fairman, l J Lyon)
1986 Scotland (v Wal, w ko 3 P Dix)
1986 Commonwealth Games flyweight quarter-final (l Beaupre, Can)
1987 Scotland (v Eng, w K Robson)
1987 Scottish ABA flyweight champion (w w J Stewart, w B Carr, l J Lyon)
1987 European Championships, Turin (l Johansen, Den)
1988 ABA flyweight finalist (w dis 2 J Coyle, w B Carr, w M Clarke, l J Lyon)
1988 Scotland (v Eng, w D McNally, v Ire, w W McCullough; dr C Notarantonio)
1989 Scottish ABA flyweight finalist (w rsf 3 J Murray, l J McLean)
1989 Scotland (v Eng, w J Armour)
1989 European Championships, Athens (l N Aliuta, Rum)

1989
Sep 14	Gordon Shaw	w pts 6	Motherwell 8-6-8
Nov 23	Chris Clarkson	w pts 6	Motherwell 8-8-8

1990
May 9	Rocky Lawlor	drew 8	Solihull 8-8
Oct 3	Steve Robinson	w pts 8	Solihull 8-9
Nov 21	Peter Buckley	w pts 8	Solihull 8-9

1991
Nov 14	Stevie Wood	w rsf 1	Edinburgh 8-6-4

1992
Jan 27	Neil Parry	w rsf 4	Glasgow 8-8
Apr 27	Peter Buckley	w pts 8	Glasgow 8-10
Jun 1	Joe Kelly	w rsf 5	Glasgow 8-5-12
	(British bantamweight title)		

Fights 9 Won 8 Drawn 1

Wilson DOCHERTY

Featherweight
Condorrat born 15 April 1968
Croy Miners ABC
1986 Scottish ABA light-flyweight champion (w Byrne, w P Weir, l rsf 3 M Epton)
1986 Scotland (v Eng, l rsf 2 M Epton; v Wal, w R Regan)
1986 Commonwealth Games light-flyweight bronze medal (l rsf 2 M Epton)
1986 European Junior Championships light-flyweight (l Sijevski, Yug)
1987 ABA light-flyweight finalist (w D Grant, w M Cantwell, l M Epton)
1987 Scotland (v Eng, l M Epton; v Wal, w R Regan)
1988 Scottish ABA light-flyweight champion (w rsf 1 M McLaughlin, w N Armstrong, withdrew)
1988 Scotland (v Ire, w rsf 1 G Griffen)
1989 Scottish ABA bantam champ (w rsf 2 G Ferrie, w rtd 2 G Hughes, w J Drummond, w rsf 2 M Deveney, wthdrw)
1989 Scotland (v Eng, l N McCallum; v Wal, w M Coakley; v EGer, l A Tews)
1989 European Championships bantamweight (l S Todorov, Bul)
1990 Commonwealth Games bantamweight (l E Younan, Aus)
1990 Scottish ABA bantamweight champion (w ko 1 T McDonald, w rsf 1 D Hardie, l rsf 3 P Lloyd)
1990 Scotland (v Wal, w rsf 1 A Ley; v USA, l G Jorrin)
1991 Scottish ABA bantamweight final (w rsf 1 J Smith, l D Hardie)
1991 Scotland (v Eng, w P Lloyd; v Ire, l J Lawlor)
1991 European Championships (w V Tutuk, Tur; l J Manyanja, Swe)

1992
Apr 27	Norman Dhalie	w rsf 2	Glasgow 9-1
Jul 9	Graham McGrath	w rsf 4	Glasgow 8-10

Fights 2 Won 2

John DOHERTY

Super-featherweight
Bradford, born 12 July 1962
Real name: Patrick Doherty
Bradford YMCA ABC

1982
May 26	Taffy Mills	l rsf 1	Leeds
Oct 7	John Lodge	w rsf 4	Morley
Oct 18	Carl Gaynor	w pts 6	Blackpool
Nov 18	Stuart Carmichael	w pts 6	Coventry

1983
Jan 24	Stuart Carmichael	w pts 6	Bradford
Feb 17	Stuart Carmichael	w pts 6	Coventry
Mar 9	John Mwaimu	w rsf 2	Stoke 9-0
Mar 21	Muhammad Lovelock	w pts 6	Bradford 9-0
May 9	Les Walsh	w pts 6	Manchester 9-1
May 19	Ray Plant	drew 8	Sunderland
Jun 13	Steve Enright	drew 6	Doncaster 8-12
Sep 27	Anthony Brown	l pts 6	Stoke 9-5
Oct 15	Stuart Shaw	w pts 8	Coventry 9-1-4
Oct 27	Brett Styles	w pts 8	Ebbw Vale 8-13
Nov 14	Stuart Carmichael	l rsf 7*	Nantwich

1984
Feb 9	Les Walsh	drew 6	Manchester 8-13
Mar 13	Joey Wainwright	w pts 8	Hull 9-0
Apr 16	Les Walsh	w pts 6	Stoke 9-3
Jun 6	Gary Nickels	w pts 8	NSC 9-1-8
Oct 2	Dean Bramhald	w pts 8	Leeds 9-2
Oct 24	Clinton Campbell	w pts 8	Stoke 9-2
Dec 17	Steve Pollard	w pts 10	Bradford 8-13
	(Central featherweight title)		

1985			
Feb 18	Muhammad Lovelock	w pts 8	Bradford 9-3
Apr 18	Dean Bramhald	w pts 8	Halifax
Oct 3	Dave Pratt	w rsf 6	Bradford 8-13-8
Nov 27	Clyde Ruan	w pts 10	Bradford 9-2
	(eliminator, British super-featherweight title)		
1986			
Jan 16	Pat Doherty	w pts 12	Preston 9-3
	(vacant British super-featherweight title)		
Apr 17	Pat Cowdell	l rsf 6	Bradford 9-2
	(British super-featherweight title)		
Oct 20	Stuart Carmichael	w pts 8	Bradford 9-3-8
1987			
Feb 10	Dave Savage	w pts 10	Batley 9-3-8
	(eliminator, British super-featherweight title)		
Jun 2	Kevin Pritchard	w pts 12	Bradford 9-3-8
	(final eliminator, British super-featherweight title)		
1988			
Nov 7	Les Walsh	w pts 8	Bradford 9-2
1989			
Mar 17	Racheed Lawal	l ko 4	Braedstrup 9-2-4
	(European super-featherweight title)		
Sep 6	Floyd Havard	w rtd 11*	Port Talbot 9-1
	(British super-featherweight title)		
1990			
Feb 6	Joey Jacobs	l pts 12	Oldham 9-3
	(British super-featherweight title)		
May 22	Sean Murphy	l ko 3	St Albans 8-13
	(vacant British featherweight title)		
1991			
Apr 22	Frankie Foster	w pts 10	Glasgow 9-3-8
	(eliminator, British super-featherweight title)		
Sep 19	Sugar Gibiliru	w pts 12	Stockport 9-4
	(British super-featherweight title)		
1992			
Apr 25	Michael Armstrong	l rsf 7	Manchester 9-2-8
	(British super-featherweight title)		

Fights 39 Won 28 Lost 8 Drawn 3

Paul DONAGHEY

Featherweight
Islington, born Derry 22 August 1969

1991			
Jun 4	Phil Lashley	w ko 1	Bethnal Green 9-2
Jul 3	Paul Forrest	l ko 2	Brentwood 9-0-8
1992			
Feb 11	Chris Francis	w ko 2	Barking 9-6

Fights 3 Won 2 Lost 1

Darrit DOUGLAS

Super-middleweight
Hove born 13 January 1971
1992 Southern ABA middleweight champion (w rsf 1 L Morris, w ko 2 W Sutherland, l rsf 2 R Golding)

1992
Oct 27	Cyril Jackson	w rsf 3	Leicester 11-13
Dec 22	John Kaighin	l pts 6	Mayfair 12-2

Fights 2 Won 1 Lost 1

Barry DOWNES

Light-heavyweight
Northampton born 27 September 1966
No amateur experience

1989
Sep 18	Hugh Fury	l rsf 1	Northampton 12-1-8

1990
Dec 12	Ian Vokes	w pts 6	Leicester 12-8

1991
Feb 18	Ian Vokes	l pts 6	Derby 12-8
Feb 27	Lee Prudden	l pts 6	Wolverhampton 12-7

1992
Oct 5	Paul McCarthy	l pts 6	Northampton 12-10
Dec 14	Ian Vokes	w pts 6	Northampton 12-10

Fights 6 Won 2 Lost 4

Scott DOYLE

Light-welterweight
Birmingham born 14 June 1968
Kyrle Hall ABC
1987 Midlands ABA feather champ (w E Blake, w K Kearney, w S Hamblett, w P Clifton, l D Simmons)
1988 Birmingham ABA featherweight final (l M Holt)

1991
Mar 15	Chris Cooper	w rsf 1	Willenhall 9-12
Apr 11	Barry North	w pts 6	Willenhall 9-12
Jun 17	Tony Doyle	w pts 6	Birmingham 10-0
Oct 7	Jason Brattley	w pts 6	Birmingham 10-0
Nov 21	Shane Sheridan	w pts 6	Ilkeston
Dec 9	Peter Till	l ko 3	Brierley Hill 10-0

1992
Feb 3	Ricky Sackfield	l pts 6	Manchester 10-3
Mar 3	Richard O'Brien	w pts 4	Cradley Heath 10-4
May 14	Joey Moffat	l rsf 8*	Liverpool 10-1

Fights 9 Won 6 Lost 3

Tony DOYLE

Lightweight
Sheffield, born Rotherham 26 December 1962
Real name: Tony Dodson
Doublemasters ABC
1984 North-East ABA featherweight semi-final (w.o. then withdrew!)

1990
Mar 27	Martin Evans	w rsf 3	Leicester 9-4
Apr 6	Stewart Fisher-Mack	l rsf 5	Telford 9-0

May 16	Des Gargano	l pts 6	Hull
Sep 10	Finn McCool	w pts 6	Northampton 9-10
Oct 1	Finn McCool	w pts 6	Cleethorpes 9-8
Nov 19	Mark Geraghty	l pts 8	Glasgow 9-7-12
Dec 10	Peter Campbell	l pts 6	Nottingham

1991

Jan 23	Richie Joyce	l ko 6	Stoke 9-10
Mar 13	Bobby Beckles	l pts 6	Stoke 9-9
Apr 12	Roy Doyle	drew 6	Manchester 9-10
Apr 23	Barry North	w pts 6	Evesham 9-12
Jun 17	Scott Doyle	l pts 6	Edgbaston 9-13
Oct 17	Paul Hughes	l pts 6	Mossley 9-13
Nov 21	Brian Hickey	w pts 6	Ilkeston
Dec 5	Davey Robb	l pts 6	Telford 9-12

1992

Feb 10	Joey Moffatt	l rsf 3	Liverpool 9-9
Apr 4	Andy Kent	w rsf 5	Cleethorpes 9-9
Oct 15	Tony Foster	l pts 8	Hull 9-12

Fights 18 Won 6 Lost 11 Lost 1

Michael DRISCOLL

Light-welterweight
Portsmouth born 18 May 1969
Parade ABC
1985 NABC Class A champion (w J Green)
1985 National Schools champion
1987 NABC Class C finalist (l M Ramsey)
1987 Young England (v WGer, w D Meyer, l dis 2 W Hett; v Ire, w N Gough; v Sco, w rsf 2 M Strachan; v EGer, l ko 1 M Berger)
1988 Southern ABA lightweight champion (w rtd 1 T Turner, w rsf 2 M Atkin, l rsf 3* M Ramsey)

1988

Jun 16	Dave Pierre	l pts 6	Croydon 9-11-8
Jul 10	David Bacon	w pts 6	Eastbourne
Aug 30	Mike Russell	w ko 2	Holborn 10-3
Sep 15	Ricky Maxwell	drew 6	High Wycombe 10-2-8
Oct 26	Mick O'Donnell	w rsf 2	Albert Hall 10-2
Dec 1	Neil Haddock	drew 6	Gravesend 9-11

1989

Feb 2	Dave Croft	w rsf 2	Croydon 10-0
Apr 26	Dean Bramhald	w rsf 2	Southampton 10-0-8
Oct 31	Steve Foran	drew 6	Manchester 9-13-8

1990

Feb 22	B.F.Williams	w ko 2	Battersea 9-13-12
Mar 6	Billy Couzens	w rsf 2	Bethnal Green 9-13-12
Nov 26	Wayne Windle	w rsf 3*	Bethnal Green 10-1

1991

May 2	Andy Morgan	w pts 6	Bayswater 9-12
Jun 22	Steve Foran	w rsf 4*	Earls Court 10-0

1992

Feb 1	Peter Till	w rsf 3	Birmingham
Apr 25	Allan Hall	l pts 6	Manchester 9-12-8
Oct 27	Marvin P. Gray	w pts 8	Leicester 10-2
Dec 12	Bernard Paul	w rsf 2*	Muswell Hill 10-2

Fights 18 Won 13 Lost 2 Drawn 3

Tim DRISCOLL

Featherweight
Bermondsey born 15 May 1964
Fisher ABC
1982 NABC champion (w J Malloy)
1982 Young England (v Fin, w rsf 3 M Rantala)
1983 London ABA featherweight final (w S Eubanks, w M Hull, l T Graham)
1984 SE London ABA featherweight champion (w T Reid, l H Henry)
1986 SE London ABA featherweight champion (w J Dobson, w E Edwards, l C McMillan)

1986
Sep 8	Andy Pybus	w rsf 4	Dulwich 9-1-12
Oct 13	Nigel Lawrence	w pts 6	Dulwich 9-0-8
Nov 17	Mike Russell	w pts 6	Dulwich 9-1
Dec 15	Gary De Roux	w pts 6	Eltham 9-1-4

1987
Mar 4	Russell Davison	w pts 8	Stoke 9-4-8
Dec 1	Kid Sumaila	w pts 8	Bow 9-0-8
Dec 14	Shane Silvester	w rsf 2	Bedford 9-0-8

1988
Jan 21	Patrick Kamy	w pts 8	Battersea 9-1-8
Mar 10	Johnny B. Good	w pts 10	Croydon 8-13
	(vacant Southern featherweight title; elim, British featherweight title)		
Jun 6	Russell Jones	l pts 8	Northampton 9-2

1989
Feb 2	Johnny B. Good	l pts 10	Croydon 9-0
	(Southern featherweight title)		
Oct 24	Alan McKay	w pts 6	Bethnal Green 9-0

1990
Jan 31	Graham O'Malley	w pts 8	Bethnal Green 9-1
Apr 14	Rocky Lawlor	w pts 6	Albert Hall
May 29	Johnny B. Good	l pts 10	Bethnal Green 8-13-13
	(Southern featherweight title)		
Sep 12	Steve Robinson	w pts 8	Bethnal Green 9-2

1991
Feb 6	Des Gargano	w pts 6	Bethnal Green 9-2
Apr 18	Aldrich Johnson	w pts 8	Kensington 9-2
Jun 22	Ruben Aguirre	w pts 8	Earls Court 9-2
Nov 7	Maurizio Stecca	l rtd 9	Campione d'Italia 8-13-12
	(WBO featherweight title)		

1992
Sep 10	John Davison	l ko 7	Sunderland 9-0
	(vacant British featherweight title)		

Fights 21 Won 16 Lost 5

James DRUMMOND

Flyweight
Kilmarnock born 11 February 1969
North West ABC
Gaelic Youth champion (w ko 1 J Hunter)
1986 Scotland (v Wal, w rsf 2 S Ward)
1986 Scottish ABA flyweight semi-final
1986 European Junior Championships (l J Kanninen, Fin)
1988 Scottish ABA bantamweight semi-final (w I McGirr, l M Deveney)
1988 Scotland (v Ire, l J Lowey; w D O'Neill)
1989 Scottish ABA bantamweight semi-final (w C Baird, l W Docherty)

1989
Sep 10	Tony Smith	w rsf 1	Glasgow 8-7-12
Oct 9	Kruger Hydes	w rsf 3	Glasgow 8-6-12

1990
Jan 22	Kevin Jenkins	l pts 6	Glasgow 8-8
Mar 6	Kevin Jenkins	w rsf 5	Glasgow 8-8-8
Mar 19	Neil Parry	w rsf 4	Glasgow 8-8
Oct 8	Derek Amory	l pts 8	Cleethorpes 8-10
Nov 19	Chris Clarkson	l pts 8	Glasgow 8-7

1991
Mar 18	Stewart Fisher-Mack	w rsf 8	NSC 8-5
May 7	Des Gargano	w pts 8	Glasgow 8-6
Jun 1	Mercurio Ciamitaro	drew 6	Ragusa
Nov 16	Salvatore Fanni (European flyweight title)	l pts 12	Omegna

1992
May 19	Robbie Regan (British flyweight title)	l rsf 9	Cardiff 7-13
Dec 22	Francis Ampofo (vacant British flyweight title)	l pts 12	Mayfair

Fights 13 Won 6 Lost 6 Drawn 1

John DUCKWORTH

Light-middleweight
Burnley born 25 May 1971

1992
Apr 4	Warren Stephens	w rsf 5	Cleethorpes 11-0
Apr 13	Steve Goodwin	l pts 6	Manchester 11-0
Jun 4	Phil Foxon	w rsf 4*	Burnley 11-1-4
Oct 5	David Maj	drew 6	Manchester 10-10
Oct 29	Tony Massey	w rtd 4*	Leeds 11-0

Fights 5 Won 3 Lost 1 Drawn 1

Terry DUFFUS

Light-heavyweight
Gloucester born 18 September 1960

1988
Feb 29	Maurice Thomas	w rsf 1	Bradford 12-8	
Mar 21	Dave Lawrence	drew 4	Bethnal Green 12-0	
May 5	Winston Burnett	l pts 8	Bayswater 12-10	
May 12	Michael Madsen	l pts 4	Copenhagen	
Nov 15	David Haycock	w ko 6	Chigwell 12-13	
Dec 19	Dave Lawrence	l pts 6	NSC 12-12	/CTD..

(Terry DUFFUS ctd)

1989
Jan 17	Kevin Roper	l rsf 2	Woodford 13-1
Mar 22	Andy Balfe	w pts 6	Gloucester 12-8-12
Apr 26	Paul McCarthy	l pts 8	Southampton 12-10-8
May 8	Brendan Dempsey	l rsf 1	NSC 13-0

1990
Feb 26	Mark Spencer	w rsf 3	Crystal Palace 12-12
Oct 10	Jimmy Peters	l rsf 2	Albert Hall 12-9

1991
Jan 31	Nick Manners	l rsf 1	Stockport 12-7
Mar 7	Phil Soundy	l rsf 2	Basildon 13-9-4
Sep 12	Keith Inglis	l ko 5	Battersea 12-7-12

1992
Mar 25	Joey Peters	l rsf 1	Albert Hall 12-10

Fights 16 Won 4 Lost 11 Drawn 1

Marty DUKE
Light-middleweight
Great Yarmouth born 19 June 1967
Kingfisher ABC

1988
May 16	Wayne Timmins	l pts 6	Wolverhampton 10-10
Sep 6	Tony Cloak	w pts 6	Southend 11-4
Sep 26	Tony Cloak	l rsf 2*	Bedford 11-12
Oct 27	Matthew Jones	l pts 6	Birmingham 11-2
Dec 6	Peter Mundy	w pts 6	Southend 11-5

1989
Jan 25	Tony Hodge	w rsf 2	Basildon 12-0
Feb 7	Dennis White	l pts 6	Southend 11-6
Apr 4	Tony Cloak	w rsf 5	Southend
Apr 27	Steve West	l rsf 1	Southwark 11-6
Oct 3	Colin Ford	l pts 6	Southend 11-10
Oct 23	Andy Catesby	w pts 6	NSC 11-7
Dec 19	Mike Jay	drew 6	Gorleston 11-8

1990
Feb 8	Dean Lake	l rsf 4*	Southwark 11-9
Mar 14	Ahmet Canbakis	l rsf 6	Battersea 11-11
Nov 12	Chris Haydon	w pts 6	Norwich 11-7
Dec 4	Paul Busby	l pts 6	Bury St Edmunds 11-7

1991
Jan 29	Paul Smith	l pts 6	Wisbech 11-3
Apr 15	James McGee	w pts 6	Leicester 10-13
May 8	Martin Rosamond	drew 6	Millwall 10-12
May 16	Danny Shinkwin	l pts 6	Battersea 10-13
May 30	Richie Woodhall	l rsf 4*	Birmingham 11-0
Jul 4	Robert McCracken	l rsf 1	Alfreton 10-11-8
Sep 3	Eamonn Loughran	l pts 6	Cardiff 10-6-4
Sep 26	Adrian Riley	l pts 6	Dunstable 10-8
Nov 5	Tony McKenzie	l rsf 7	Leicester 10-8

1992
Mar 31	Ojay Abrahams	l rsf 2	Norwich 10-10-4
Sep 8	Ricky Mabbett	drew 6	Norwich 10-8
Nov 14	Vince Rose	l pts 6	Cardiff 10-11-8

Fights 28 Won 7 Lost 18 Drawn 3

Marcus DUNCAN

Bantamweight
Lancaster born 1974

1992
Nov 12　　　Andrew Bloomer　　　w pts 6　　　Burnley 8-9

Fights 1 Won 1

Mickey DUNCAN

Light-middleweight
Newcastle born 24 August 1969
Somervyl & Longbenton ABC

1988			
Sep 29	Skip Jackson	l rsf 3	Sunderland 10-13
1989			
Mar 13	Richard Thompson	w pts 6	NSC 11-3
Mar 22	Barry Bennett	l pts 6	Sheppey 11-7
May 19	John Tipping	w pts 6	Gateshead 11-7
Jun 5	Paul Abercromby	l rsf 2	Glasgow 11-4-8
Oct 12	Steve West	l rsf 5	Southwark 11-7
1990			
Mar 6	Paul King	l pts 6	North Shields 11-0
Apr 11	Tony Booth	l pts 6	Dewsbury 11-2
May 16	Chris Richards	w pts 6	Hull
Jun 11	Tommy Warde	w pts 6	Manchester 10-12
Oct 15	Andre Wharton	l pts 6	Brierley Hill 11-0
Nov 26	Rob Pitters	drew 6	Bury 10-8
Dec 13	Richard O'Brien	w pts 6	Hartlepool 10-9-8
1991			
Feb 18	Tommy Milligan	l pts 6	Glasgow 10-8
Mar 6	Danny Quigg	l pts 6	Glasgow 10-12-4
Mar 18	Allan Grainger	w pts 6	Glasgow 10-12
May 10	Rob Pitters	l rsf 3	Gateshead 11-1
Sep 23	Danny Quigg	drew 6	Glasgow 10-13-8
Oct 7	Tyrone Eastmond	l rsf 5	Bradford 11-2
Nov 18	Allan Grainger	w pts 6	Glasgow 11-1-4
Nov 25	Willie Yeardsley	w pts 6	Liverpool 11-0-8
Dec 12	David Johnson	l pts 6	Hartlepool
1992			
Jan 20	Mark Jay	l pts 6	Bradford 11-2
Feb 20	Leigh Wicks	w pts 8	Glasgow 10-11-12
Mar 6	Oleg Chalajev	w pts 8	Berlin
May 13	Lloyd Honeyghan	l rsf 2	Albert Hall 11-0-8
Jun 27	Reiner Gies	l ko 7	Halle
Oct 15	Gary Logan	l pts 8	Catford 10-10

Fights 27 Won 10 Lost 16 Drawn 1

Stuart DUNN

Light-middleweight
Leicester born 19 January 1970
Braunstone ABC
1990 Leics. Rutland & Northants light-middleweight final (w ko 3 M Williams, l N Hutcheon)
1991 North Midlands ABA light-middleweight final (w N Hutcheon, l G Rooksby)

1991
Oct 15	Spencer McCracken	drew 6	Dudley 11-3-8
Dec 9	Wayne Panayiotiou	w ko 4	Brierley Hill 11-1

1992
Jan 23	Charlie Moore	l rsf 3	York 10-13-8
Oct 27	Andy Peach	w rsf 3	Leicester 11-2

Fights 4 Won 2 Lost 1 Drawn 1

Terry DUNSTAN

Cruiserweight
Hackney born 21 October 1968
St Monicas ABC
1989 NE London ABA heavyweight semi-final (l rsf 2 M Lynch)
1991 NE London ABA heavyweight final (l dis 3 P Lawson)
1992 London ABA heavyweight final (w rsf 2 S Lukacs, w.o., l C Henry)

1992
Nov 12	Steve Osborne	w pts 6	Bayswater 13-8-8
Nov 26	Steve Yorath	w pts 8	Mayfair 13-8-4

Fights 2 Won 2

Darren DYER

Welterweight
Islington born 31 July 1966
Colvestone ABC & St Monica's ABC
1980 National Schools champion (w rsf 1 J Kerr)
1982 National Schools champion (w J Marples)
1985 London ABA light-welterweight final (w D Farquhar, w ko 2 L Collins, w D Daniels, w rsf 1 M Spillane, l I Mustapha)
1986 ABA welterweight champion (w rsf 1 T Jones, w rsf 1 R Arthey, w rsf 2 J Nanton, w rsf 3 P Wilson, w rsf 1 K Wall, w rsf 3 C Piper, w rsf 3 M Elliot)
1986 Commonwealth Games welter gold medal (w rsf 1 C Piper, w rsf 2 D Obah, w D Denny, w rsf 1* J McAllister)

1986
Nov 20	Trevor Grant	w rsf 2	Bethnal Green 10-6

1987
Jan 8	Del Bryan	l pts 6	Bethnal Green 10-8-4
Feb 26	Ian Murray	w ko 3	Bethnal Green 10-9-4
Apr 18	Geoff Calder	w rsf 2	Albert Hall 10-8-8
Sep 7	Kelvin Mortimer	l rsf 1	NSC 10-8-4

1988
Feb 25	Donald Gwinn	w ko 1	Bethnal Green 10-10
Apr 13	Kent Acuff	w ko 2	Bethnal Green 10-9
May 16	Thomas Garcia	w rsf 2*	NSC 10-11-8
Nov 2	Harlein Holden	w rsf 2	Southwark 10-8-8
Dec 7	Jean-Marc Phenieux	w rsf 3	NSC 10-8

1989
Jan 12	Anthony Joe Travers	w rsf 6	Southwark 10-8-8
Mar 29	Mario Coronado	w ko 1	Wembley 10-7
Oct 4	Efraim Brown	w rsf 4	Albert Hall 10-8

1990
Jan 11	Fernando Segura	w ko 2	Dewsbury 10-7
Mar 14	Jorge Maysonet	l rsf 2	Albert Hall 10-10

1991
Jul 3	Trevor Ambrose	w pts 6	Brentwood 10-9
Oct 26	Kelvin Mortimer	w rsf 2*	Brentwood 10-7
Nov 26	Robert Wright	w rsf 3	Bethnal Green 10-8

1992
Feb 19	Ian John-Lewis	w rsf 2	Muswell Hill 10-5-12
May 12	Del Bryan	w rsf 10	Crystal Palace 10-6
Nov 10	Chris Peters	w rsf 9*	Dagenham

Fights 21 Won 18 Lost 3

NATIONAL PROMOTIONS
INTERNATIONAL BOXING MATCHMAKER AND MANAGER

MICKEY DUFF

OFFICE:	National House	TELEPHONES:	071 734 1041
	60/66 Wardour Street		071 437 5956
	London	HOME:	071 723 9629
	W1V 3HP	FAX:	071 437 4005
	England		

HEAVYWEIGHT
FRANK BRUNO - Former undefeated European Heavyweight Champion.
HENRY AKINWANDE - London. 2 times British ABA Heavyweight Champion - Undefeated in 18 contests. No. 1 contender for British & European Heavyweight titles.

CRUISERWEIGHT
DENZIL BROWNE - Leeds.

LIGHT HEAVYWEIGHT
MICHAEL GALE - Leeds. Central Area Champion. Undefeated in 18 contests.
BRUCE SCOTT - London.

SUPER MIDDLEWEIGHT
HENRY WHARTON - York. British & Commonwealth Champ. Undefeated in 16 contests - rated WBC No.1, WBO No.2, IBF no.8.
JAMES COOK - Former European Champion, rated No. 9 by WBA.
NICK MANNERS - Leeds.
MARK BAKER - Sidcup.

MIDDLEWEIGHT
HEROL GRAHAM - Sheffield. Former British & European Middleweight Champion & former British Commonwealth & European Light Middle Champion.
RITCHIE WOODHALL - Telford. Commonwealth Middleweight Champion - former Olympic bronze medallist. Undefeated in 11 contests.

LIGHT MIDDLEWEIGHT
LLOYD HONEYGHAN - Bermondsey - former Undisputed World Welterweight Champion - undefeated as a light middleweight.
NEVILLE BROWN - Burton - three time ABA Champion. 19 contests 18 wins 13 KOs 1 defeat (since reversed).
ROBERT McCRACKEN - Birmingham - former World Amateur silver medallist - 13 contests 13 wins 12 KOs
CHARLES MOORE - Darlington - undefeated in 5 contests.
DAVID LARKIN - Leeds.

WELTERWEIGHT
GARY JACOBS - British Welterweight Champ, former WBC International & Commonwealth Champ.
GARY LOGAN - Croydon - top prospect 21-1.
PHILIP EPTON - Doncaster - ex ABA International.
STEVE McNESS - Bethnal Green.
LINDON SCARLETT - Birmingham.

LIGHT WELTERWEIGHT
ANDY HOLLIGAN - Liverpool - British & Commonwealth Champion - undefeated in 20 contests.
MARK McCREATH - Lincoln.
MARK ELLIOT - Telford.

LIGHTWEIGHT
BILLY SCHWER - Luton - British & Commonwealth Champ. Undefeated in 18 contests.
GARETH JORDAN - Monmouth.

SUPER BANTAMWEIGHT
DUKE McKENZIE - Croydon - WBO Super Bantamweight Champ & former WBO Bantamweight & IBF Flyweight Champion of the World.

BANTAMWEIGHT
JOHNNY ARMOUR - Chatham - Bantamweight Commonwealth Champ - undefeated in 10 contests.
TONY SILKSTONE - Leeds - undefeated in 12 contests.

FLYWEIGHT
MICKEY CANTWELL - Bermondsey - undefeated in 6 contests.

Tyrone EASTMOND

Light-middleweight
Oldham, born Barbados 26 September 1960

1991
Mar 25	Benji Joseph	l pts 6	Bradford 10-13-8
Apr 15	Jim Kirk	w rsf 4	Glasgow 11-3
May 17	Tommy Warde	w rsf 4	Bury 11-6
Jun 10	David Johnson	l pts 6	Manchester 11-5-8
Oct 7	Mickey Duncan	w rsf 5	Bradford 11-2
Oct 17	Seamus Casey	w pts 6	Mossley 11-3
Nov 11	Ian Midwood-Tate	w rsf 2*	Bradford 11-1-8
Dec 16	Mark Jay	w pts 6	Manchester 11-1

1992
Mar 9	David Radford	drew 6	Manchester 11-2

Fights 9 Won 6 Lost 2 Drawn 1

Julian EAVIS

Welterweight
Yeovil born Bourton 3 December 1965
Blackmore Vale ABC
1987 Western ABA welterweight final (w P Withard, w N Purcell, l rsf 3 D Miller)
1988 Western ABA welterweight semi-final (w N Purcell, w M Shepherd, l rsf 2 M Nardiello)

1988
Oct 12	Noel Rafferty	w pts 6	Stoke 10-7
Oct 17	Steve Taggart	w pts 6	Birmingham 10-3
Nov 17	G.W.Gully	w pts 6	Weston-super-Mare 10-8
Dec 7	Adrian Din	l pts 6	Stoke 10-8
Dec 14	G.W.Gully	l pts 6	Evesham 10-7

1989
Jan 30	Frank Harrington	w pts 6	Leicester 10-6
Feb 6	G.W.Gully	l rsf 4	Nottingham 10-4-8
Mar 15	Steve Taggart	w pts 6	Stoke 10-4
Mar 21	Steve Hogg	w pts 6	Wolverhampton 10-7
Apr 15	Andy Tonks	w pts 6	Salisbury 10-12
May 9	Mark Purcell	l rsf 5	Plymouth 10-5-12
	(Western welterweight title)		
Sep 25	Wayne Timmins	l pts 6	NEC 10-9
Oct 4	Barry Messam	w pts 8	Stafford 10-7
Oct 10	Robert Wright	l pts 8	Wolverhampton 10-7
Oct 30	Wayne Timmins	l pts 8	Birmingham 10-6
Nov 14	Bobby McGowan	w pts 6	Evesham 10-9
Nov 22	Ronnie Campbell	w pts 8	Solihull 10-11
Dec 6	Lindon Scarlett	l pts 8	Stoke 10-9

1990
Jan 10	Gary Logan	l pts 8	Albert Hall 10-9-8
Jan 24	Kevin Plant	l pts 6	Solihull 10-7-8
Feb 6	Tony Connellan	l pts 6	Oldham 10-7
Feb 13	Kevin Thompson	l pts 8	Wolverhampton 10-8
Feb 27	Ernie Loveridge	l pts 6	Evesham 10-9-8
Mar 7	Kevin Plant	l pts 8	Doncaster 10-10
Mar 22	Wayne Timmins	l pts 8	Wolverhampton 10-7
Apr 26	Leigh Wicks	drew 8	Mayfair 10-9
May 24	Gary Osborne	l pts 6	Dudley 10-9
Jun 4	Paul Wesley	l pts 8	Birmingham 10-10
Sep 17	Dave Andrews	l pts 6	Cardiff 10-7 /CTD..

(Julian EAVIS ctd.)

Oct 1	Kevin Plant	l pts 8	Cleethorpes 10-8
Oct 9	Ronnie Campbell	drew 6	Wolverhampton 10-3
Oct 17	Paul Wesley	l pts 6	Stoke 10-10
Oct 30	Mickey Lloyd	l pts 8	Wembley 10-9
Nov 14	Glyn Rhodes	l rsf 5*	Sheffield 10-7
Dec 12	Barry Messam	l pts 6	Leicester 10-9
Dec 19	Carl Wright	l pts 6	Preston 10-7-8
1991			
Jan 16	Gary Logan	l rsf 5	Albert Hall 10-10
Mar 5	Eamonn Loughran	l pts 6	Cardiff 10-10
Mar 20	Kevin Plant	l pts 6	Solihull 10-8-4
Apr 10	Ernie Loveridge	drew 8	Wolverhampton 10-8
May 1	Humphrey Harrison	l pts 6	Solihull 10-10
May 28	Darren Liney	l pts 6	Cardiff 10-11
Jun 5	Wayne Timmins	l pts 6	Wolverhampton 10-7
Jun 11	James McGee	l pts 6	Leicester 10-12
Jul 3	Benny Collins	l pts 6	Reading 10-8
Sep 3	Michael Smyth	l pts 6	Cardiff 10-9-8
Oct 1	Lee Ferrie	l pts 6	Bedworth 10-11
Oct 22	Kevin Lueshing	l rsf 2	Bethnal Green 10-8
Nov 26	James Campbell	w pts 8	Wolverhampton 10-9
Dec 4	Peter Reid	w pts 6	Stoke 10-9
Dec 11	James McGee	drew 6	Leicester 11-0
Dec 17	Michael Smyth	l pts 6	Cardiff 10-9
1992			
Jan 15	Robert Wright	l pts 8	Stoke 10-12
Feb 4	Howard Clarke	l pts 4	Alfreton 10-10
Feb 11	Jamie Robinson	l pts 6	Barking 10-13
Feb 24	Lee Ferrie	l pts 8	Coventry 10-12
Mar 11	Rob Pitters	l pts 6	Solihull 10-12
May 11	James McGee	l rsf 3*	Coventry 11-0
Jul 7	Ross Hale	l rsf 8	Bristol 10-4-12
	(vacant Western welterweight title)		
Oct 5	James McGee	w pts 6	Bardon 11-0
Nov 28	Warren Stowe	l rsf 6	Manchester 10-10

Fights 61 Won 13 Lost 44 Drawn 4

Bobbi Joe EDWARDS

Light-heavyweight
Manchester, born Jamaica 25 December 1957
Real name: Clive Edwards
Manco ABC & Moss Side ABC
1983 ABA light-heavy finalist (w dis 3 V Aley, w D Cross, w P McNamee, w ko 2 M Pearson, l T Wilson)
1983 England (v EGer, l J Demmler)
1984 ABA light-heavy final (w ko 2 G Sanderson, w S Stenson, w G Crawford, w rsf 2 M Lee, w E Miles, l T Wilson)
1984 England (v WGer, l M Bott)
1985 Northern ABA light-heavy champ (w rsf 2 R Saunders, w I Carter, w D Roberts, w rsf 1 J Fairbairn, l dis 3 M Lee)
1987 Northern ABA light-heavyweight final (w L Richards, w D Roberts, l M Gale)
1990 ABA light-heavy semi-final (w rsf 1 G Stevens, w G Campbell, w rsf 3 D Roberts, w I Meredith, w G Donaldson, l J McCluskey)

1990			
Oct 9	Doug McKay	w rsf 1	Glasgow 13-1
Nov 26	Keith Inglis	w rsf 1	NSC 13-2
1991			
Feb 22	Cordwell Hylton	l rtd 6*	Manchester 13-3-8

Nov 29	Dave Brown	w rsf 4	Manchester 12-8-8
1992			
Jan 31	Richard Bustin	w pts 6	Manchester 12-9-8
May 29	John Foreman	l rsf 4*	Manchester 12-10
Oct 29	Michael Gale	l pts 10	Leeds 12-6-8
	(Central light-heavyweight title)		

Fights 7 Won 4 Lost 3

Erwin EDWARDS

Light-welterweight
Camberwell born Barbados 31 October 1966
Southpaw   Lynn ABC
1985 Young England (v EGer, l S Freed)
1985 SE London ABA featherweight final (l J Good)
1986 SE London ABA featherweight semi-final (l T Driscoll)

1988

Sep 26	Mark Jackson	w pts 6	Bedford 9-10
Oct 26	Brian Cullen	l pts 6	Stoke 9-10
Nov 15	Tony Whitehouse	w pts 6	NSC 9-12
Nov 29	Danny Ellis	l pts 6	Battersea 9-10

1989

Feb 7	Muhammad Shaffique	l pts 6	Southend 9-12
Feb 20	Patrick Delargy	l pts 6	Birmingham 9-8
Feb 28	Terry Collins	l pts 6	Chigwell 9-8

1990-91 inactive

1992

Apr 7	B.F.Williams	l pts 6	Southend 10-0-8
Apr 30	Korso Aleain	l pts 6	Bayswater 10-0
Jul 7	George Wilson	w rsf 4	Bristol 10-0-4
Sep 7	George Wilson	w rsf 3*	Southend 10-0-8

Fights 11 Won 4 Lost 7

Renny EDWARDS

Lightweight
Haverfordwest born 10 February 1968
1986 Welsh ABA featherweight semi-final
1987 Welsh ABA bantamweight semi-final (w rsf 3 M Cutujar, l dis 2 S Boyce)
1987 Wales (v Sc, w rsf 1 I McGirr; v Bav, w ko 1 P Jahn)
1988 Welsh ABA feather champ (w rsf 1 P Simmons, w rsf 2 A Calpin, w ko 1 M Lyons, l C McMillan)

1988

Dec 7	Des Gargano	w pts 6	Port Talbot 8-12

1989

Feb 6	Dave George	l pts 8	Swansea 9-0-8
Mar 10	Jimmy Clark	w pts 6	Brentwood 9-2
Aug 19	Ian Johnson	w pts 6	Cardiff 9-1
Nov 10	Greg Egbuniwe	w rsf 4	Battersea 9-1-12

1990 inactive

1991

Aug 29	Brian Robb	l pts 6	Telford 9-3
Oct 30	Tony Silkstone	l pts 6	Leeds 9-1

1992

Dec 15	George Naylor	w rtd 5	Liverpool 9-9

Fights 8 Won 5 Lost 3

Steve EDWARDS

Lightweight
Haverfordwest born 18 July 1970
Pennar ABC
1989 Welsh ABA lightweight prelim (l J Matthews)

1992
Mar 2   Nigel Burder   w rsf 1   Merthyr 9-12-8

Fights 1 Won 1

Greg EGBUNIWE

Lightweight
Bethnal Green, born 12 October 1964
St Monicas ABC & Broad Street ABC
1985 NE London ABA lightweight final (w rtd 2 D Staples, l M O'Brien)
1986 London ABA lightweight champion (w rsf 1 A Mesher, w rsf 2 R McLean, w rsf 3 T Dwyer, l S Snagg)
1988 NE London ABA lightweight semi-final (w rtd 1 S Somerville, l B Guynan)

1989
Jun 27   Michael Ayers   l rsf 1   Albert Hall 9-10-8
Sep 28   Eamonn McAuley   l pts 6   Battersea 9-5-8
Oct 5   Robert Smythe   l ko 4   Stevenage 9-8-8
Nov 10   Renny Edwards   l rsf 4   Battersea 9-6
1990
Jan 29   Jimmy Owens   l pts 6   Hull 9-5-8
Feb 22   John Baker   l ko 1   Battersea 9-8
1991
Oct 24   Ross Hale   l rsf 4   Bayswater 10-0
1992
Feb 12   Shaun Shinkwin   w dis 1   Watford 9-9
Apr 7   Alex Sterling   w rsf 4   Southend 9-10-8
Apr 30   Carl Tilley   w pts 6   Albert Hall 9-11-12
May 16   Paul Ryan   l rsf 4   Muswell Hill 9-11

Fights 11 Won 3 Lost 8

Tony EKUBIA

Light-welterweight
Manchester, born Nigeria 6 March 1960
Moss Side ABC
1985 East Lancs ABA light-welterweight prelims (w N Berry, l P Hampson)

1986
Nov 18   Dean Eshelby   l pts 6   Adwick 9-12
Dec 2   Danny Cooper   w rsf 4   Southend 10-1
1987
Jan 13   Paul McKenzie   w ko 3   Oldham 10-2
Mar 18   Simon Eubanks   w pts 8   Solihull 10-3-4
Apr 13   Tommy Farrell   w rsf 5   Manchester 9-12-8
May 12   Jimmy Thornton   w pts 6   Alfreton 10-3-4
Sep 28   Mike Russell   w rsf 3   Manchester 9-12
Nov 17   Mike Mackenzie   w ko 2   Manchester 10-3
Dec 3   Richard Wagstaff   w rsf 2   Leeds 10-4-8
          (vacant Central welterweight title)

1988			
Feb 23	Lennie Gloster	w rtd 6	Oldham 9-13
Apr 12	Jimmy Thornton	w rsf 5	Oldham 10-5
Oct 18	Mark Kelly	w rsf 7	Oldham 9-8-12
	(vacant Central lightweight title)		
1989			
Apr 14	Humphrey Harrison	w rsf 5	Manchester
	(Central welterweight title)		
Sep 26	Steve Larrimore	w pts 12	Oldham 9-13
	(Commonwealth light-welterweight title)		
1990			
Mar 28	Victorio Belcher	l rsf 8	Manchester 10-1-12
Sep 26	Alex Dickson	w ko 11	Manchester 10-0
	(Commonwealth & vacant British light-welterweight titles)		
Nov 19	David Chibuye	w rsf 5	Cardiff 9-13
	(Commonwealth light-welterweight title)		
1991			
Jan 29	Juma Kutondo	w rtd 6	Stockport 9-13-12
	(Commonwealth light-welterweight title)		
Jun 20	Andy Holligan	l pts 12	Liverpool 9-12
	(British & Commonwealth light-welterweight title)		
1992			
Mar 10	Eamonn Loughran	w dis 5	Bury 10-6-8
	(eliminator, British welterweight title)		
Mar 31	Verdell Smith	w rsf 2	Stockport 10-4
Sep 15	Andy Holligan	l ko 7	Liverpool 9-13-4
	(British & Commonwealth light-welterweight titles)		

Fights 22 Won 18 Lost 4

Mark ELLIOT

Light-welterweight

Telford born 2 February 1966

GKN Sankey ABC

1984 Birmingham ABA light-welterweight champion (w R Campbell, l P Till)

1985 ABA light-welterweight final (w K Clayton, w ko 3 P Till, w A Richards, w J Evans, w T Harmey, w D Miller, w J Samuels, l I Mustapha)

1986 4th place at TSC Multi-nations, Berlin (w ko 2 Nagashima, Jap; w Constantin, Rum; l Ostrovsky, USSR; l J-L Hernandez, Cub)

1986 ABA welterweight final (w J Hemmings, w L Ferrie, w L Bazeley, w rsf 1 R Lewis, w D Miller, w J McAllister, l ko 3 D Dyer)

1986 England (v Pol, w Czernij; v Ire, w G Joyce, l G Joyce)

1987 European Championships, Turin (w G Joyce, Ire; w S Kolethras, Gre; l Abadjiev, Bul)

1988 ABA welterweight champion (w H Clarke, w R Edwards, w S Jenkinson, w ko 2 G Barker, w G McCreesh, w dis 2 R Wileman, w J Jones)

1988 Seoul Olympics light-welterweight (w T Ruiz, Spa; l rsf 1* L Proto, Fra)

1988 England (v WGer, w F Ruf; v Ire, w J Lowe)

1989 England (v Sco, w rsf 1 A Grainger)

1989 World Championships (l G Johnson, Can)

1991			
Sep 10	Dean Bramhald	w ko 5	Wolverhampton 10-2
Nov 12	John Smith	w pts 6	Wolverhampton 10-3-8
Dec 5	Mick Mulcahy	w rsf 2	Cannock 10-2
1992			
Mar 17	Andy Morgan	w pts 6	Wolverhampton 10-3

Fights 4 Won 4

Barry ELLIS

Heavyweight
Burnt Oak, born Islington 25 October 1957
All Stars ABC Full name: Barrington Ellis.
1983 NW London ABA heavyweight champion (w.o., l ko 1 W Greenwood)

1983
Sep 22	Mark Cleverly	w pts 6	Strand 14-7
Oct 3	Alan Douglas	w pts 6	Eltham 14-6-4
Dec 12	Phil Simpson	w ko 3	Bedworth 14-2

1984
Feb 6	Glenn McCrory	l rsf 1	Mayfair 14-11
Mar 1	Michael Armstrong	w pts 6	Queensway 14-7
Apr 17	Bob Young	drew 8	Wimbledon 15-0
Sep 18	Bob Young	w ko 1	Wimbledon 14-7-8
Oct 29	Dave Garside	l ko 8	Streatham 14-9

1985
Feb 11	Derek Williams	l rsf 2	Dulwich 15-0
May 9	Gipsy Carmen	w pts 8	Acton 14-7
Jul 22	Ron Ellis	l rsf 3	Longford 15-0
Sep 2	Gipsy Carmen	w pts 8	Coventry 14-9
Dec 9	Jess Harding	l pts 8	Wandsworth 15-3

1986
Mar 1	Mike Simuwelu	l rsf 4	Cologne
Oct 1	Daniel T. Moul	w pts 6	Lewisham 15-2

1987
Jan 11	Ivan Joseph	l pts 8	Ealing 14-12
Feb 5	Paul Lister	l pts 8	Newcastle 15-0
Feb 18	Glenn McCrory	l pts 8	Fulham 14-11
Mar 2	Patrick Collins	w pts 6	Longford 15-6
Apr 1	Denroy Bryan	drew 8	Southsea 15-10
May 17	Siza Makhathini	l pts 8	Durban
Nov 16	Ramon Voorn	w ko 1	Arnhem 16-7

1988
Jan 20	Jess Harding	l rsf 2	Hornsey 15-6
Mar 14	John Emmen	l rsf 4*	Arnhem 15-3
Apr 25	Chris Jacobs	l pts 8	Bethnal Green 15-0
May 23	Ivan Joseph	l rsf 5	NSC 15-4

1989
May 10	Michael Murray	l rsf 3	Solihull 15-7
Nov 10	Denroy Bryan	l rsf 3	Battersea 15-12-12

1990
Mar 10	Gary McConnell	w rsf 4	Bristol 15-10
Jun 2	Biagio Chianese	l rsf 3	Rome
Sep 15	Gary McConnell	l pts 8	Bristol 15-7
Dec 7	Axel Schulz	l pts 6	Berlin

1991
inactive

1992
May 1	Mario Guedes	l rsf 6	Aachen
Dec 1	Denroy Bryan	l pts 6	Bristol 15-2

Fights 34 Won 11 Lost 21 Drawn 2

Wayne ELLIS

Middleweight
Cardiff born 18 July 1968
Cardiff YMCA
1987 NABC Class C champion (w rsf 1* J Robinson)
1987 Welsh ABA light-middleweight champion (w G Thomas, w T Feal, w C Winstone, withdrew)
1987 Wales (v Ire, w K Joyce)
1988 ABA light-middleweight champion (w rsf 1 W Panayiotou, w rsf 1 N Pearce, w rsf 1 N Brown, w W Neil)

1988
Jun 25	Seamus Casey	w pts 6	Luton 11-4
Sep 7	Kevin Hayde	w pts 6	Reading 11-3-8
Nov 1	Dennis White	w ko 2	Reading 11-4
Dec 20	Spencer Alton	w rtd 4*	Swansea 11-5-8

1989
Apr 11	Mark Howell	w pts 6	Port Talbot 11-7
May 9	Spencer Alton	w rsf 3	St Albans 11-5-8
Sep 6	Ian Chantler	w rsf 4	Port Talbot 11-5

1990
Feb 14	Lindon Scarlett	drew 6	Millwall 11-2
May 22	Paul Jones	w pts 6	St Albans 11-5-12
Oct 10	Frank Eubanks	w pts 6	Millwall 11-9-8

1991
Mar 5	Johnny Melfah	w rsf 2*	Cardiff 11-9
Sep 3	Colin Manners	l rsf 1	Cardiff 11-7-12

1992
Feb 11	Alan Richards (vacant Welsh middleweight title)	w pts 10	Cardiff 11-6
Jul 14	Mike Phillips (Welsh middleweight title)	w rsf 7	Mayfair 11-6

Fights 14 Won 12 Lost 1 Drawn 1

Darren ELSDON

Super-featherweight
Hartlepool born 16 February 1971
Belle Vue ABC, United Services ABC, Hartlepool Catholic ABC
1987 NABC Class A final (l T Mullen)
1988 NABC Class B champion (w T French)
1989 North-East ABA lightweight champion (w ko 2 C Innes, w rsf 1 I Walker, l ko 3 I Foster)

1990
Nov 13	Peter Campbell	w pts 4	Hartlepool 9-4-8
Dec 13	Derek Amory	w pts 6	Hartlepool 9-1

1991
Apr 6	Harry Escott	w rsf 3*	Darlington 9-2-8
Apr 15	Eddie Cook	drew 4	Glasgow 9-3
Oct 22	Frankie Foster (Northern super-featherweight title)	w rsf 7	Hartlepool 9-3
Dec 12	Ian McGirr	w ko 4	Hartlepool 9-5

1992
Jan 21	Michael Armstrong (eliminator, British super-featherweight title)	l rsf 1	Stockport 9-2
Sep 10	Frankie Foster (Northern super-featherweight title)	l pts 10	Sunderland 9-3-8

Fights 8 Won 5 Lost 2 Drawn 1

Phil EPTON

Welterweight
Doncaster born 14 June 1968
Hatfield Main ABC, Doncaster PWAC ABC
1987 Yorkshire ABA welterweight semi-final (w rtd 3 M Miles, l J Nicholson)
1988 Humberside & Yorkshire ABA light-middle final (w rsf 1 G Burton, l rsf 1 A Penn)
1989 Northern ABA light-middleweight final (w C Manners, w rsf 2 G Kirby, l C Harney)
1990 Humberside & Yorkshire ABA light-middleweight semi-final (l T Booth)

1990
Oct 18	Mark Jay	w pts 6	Dewsbury 10-6
Nov 15	Paul King	l pts 6	Oldham 10-5

1991
Feb 7	Pat Durkin	w pts 6	Watford 11-0
Mar 21	Paul King	l pts 6	Dewsbury 10-10
Jun 13	Willie Yeardsley	w rsf 3*	Hull 10-10

1992
Jan 23	Carl Hook	w pts 6	York 10-5-4
Mar 19	Ricky Mabbett	l rsf 3	York 10-6
Sep 23	Jimmy Vincent	l rsf 6*	Leeds 10-10

Fights 8 Won 4 Lost 4

Roland ERICSSON

Super-middleweight
Sweden, based London. Born Gothenburg 15 February 1962
1985 Swedish amateur light-heavyweight champion

1987
Oct 9	Dragan Komazec	w ko 1	Aosta
Oct 26	Tommy Beckett	w rsf 1	Jyvaskyla

1988
Feb 7	Derek Myers	w pts 6	Laukka
Feb 13	Russell Barker	w pts 6	Helsingor
Sep 11	Sid Conteh	w pts 6	Laukka

1989
Feb 16	Alan Baptiste	w rsf 5	Battersea 12-12
Apr 26	Abdul Umaru Sanda	w rsf 5	Battersea 12-4
Jun 22	Cliff Curtis	w ko 4	Stevenage

1990
Feb 2	Simon Collins	w pts 8	Geneva
Feb 22	Sean Stringfellow	w rsf 4	Wandsworth 12-1
Jun 6	Cliff Curtis	w rtd 2*	Battersea 12-1-12
Nov 24	Thomas Covington	w rsf 6	Benalmadena 11-11

1991
Mar 20	Mark Kaylor	l rsf 4*	Battersea 12-0
May 16	Johnny Melfah	l rsf 4*	Battersea 12-3-8
Oct 22	Frank Eubanks	l rtd 3	Battersea 11-13-8
Dec 13	Marian Rudi	w rsf 3	Minden

1992
Feb 25	Peter Vosper	w rsf 6	Crystal Palace 11-12
Apr 4	Jan Franek	w rsf 5	Minden
May 12	Karl Barwise	w pts 6	Crystal Palace 12-4-8
Sep 15	Carlos Christie	l rsf 4	Crystal Palace 12-2
Nov 27	Terry Magee	w pts 8	Randers 12-3

Fights 21 Won 17 KOs 11 Lost 4

Tenko ERNIE

Light-heavyweight
Fulham born 25 February 1963
Real name: Ernie Tenkorang
No amateur experience

1988
Apr 21	Randy B. Powell	w rsf 1	Bethnal Green 12-10
Apr 26	Kevin McGrath	w pts 6	Bethnal Green 12-8
May 11	Billy Sim	l rsf 6	Wembley 12-10
Oct 31	Dave Muhammed	l pts 6	Bedford 13-2-12
Nov 22	John Moody	l ko 5	Basildon

1989
Apr 4	Calvin Hart	w rsf 3	Southend
May 4	Carl Thompson	l ko 4	Mayfair 13-0

1990
inactive

1991
Apr 26	Dave Lawrence	w rsf 3	Crystal Palace 12-11
Oct 22	Gipsy Carmen	l pts 6	Battersea 12-9

1992
Feb 12	Tony Booth	l rsf 4	Wembley GH 12-4

Fights 10 Won 4 Lost 6

Harry ESCOTT

Super-featherweight
Sunderland, born West Germany 17 October 1969
Horsley Hill ABC
1985 NABC Class A Champion (w rsf 2 P Reynolds)

1987
Feb 26	Kenny Walsh	w rsf 4	Hartlepool 9-5-8
Apr 6	Alvin Finch	w pts 4	Newcastle 9-6
Apr 23	Alvin Finch	w pts 4	Newcastle 9-5
Apr 30	Craig Windsor	w rsf 3*	Washington 9-6
May 22	Adrian Staples	w rsf 1	Peterlee 9-4
Jun 4	Barry Bacon	w rsf 2	Sunderland 9-4-12
Sep 4	Kevin Plant	l rsf 2	Gateshead 9-5-8

1988
Jan 26	Michael Howell	w rsf 4	Hartlepool 9-6-8
Mar 17	Ian Honeywood	w rsf 4	Sunderland 9-7-4
Apr 25	Les Walsh	w pts 8	Bradford 9-4
May 23	Tony Foster	l rsf 6*	Bradford
Sep 22	Dave Kettlewell	w pts 6	Newcastle 9-10
Nov 14	John Townsley	w pts 8	Glasgow 9-6-12

1989
Jan 30	Tony Dore	drew 8	Glasgow
Feb 14	Kevin Pritchard	w rsf 3*	Sunderland 9-6-4
Mar 13	Joe Rafiu King	w pts 8	Glasgow 9-4-4
Apr 11	Muhammad Lovelock	w pts 6	Oldham 9-9
Jun 5	Gary Maxwell	w pts 8	Glasgow 9-5-12
Sep 11	Gary Maxwell	w pts 8	Nottingham 9-2
Oct 19	Rudi Valentino	w rtd 4*	Manchester 9-6
Dec 7	Joey Jacobs	w pts 6	Manchester 9-4

1990
Jan 24	Tomas Arguelles	w pts 6	Sunderland 9-5
May 15	Kevin Pritchard	l pts 8	South Shields 9-5-8 /CTD...

(Harry ESCOTT ctd.)

Nov 13	Brian Roche	l rsf 3	Hartlepool 9-6-8
1991			
Mar 2	Steve Walker	drew 6	Darlington 9-3-4
Apr 6	Darren Elsdon	l rsf 3*	Darlington 9-3-8
Jul 6	Jackie Gunguluza	l ko 6	Diano Marino
Sep 20	Steve Walker	drew 6	Manchester 9-4
1992			
Feb 4	Neil Smith	w pts 8	Alfreton 9-3-8
Mar 17	Floyd Havard	l rsf 7	Mayfair 9-6
May 27	Wilson Rodriguez	l pts 10	Cologne
Oct 7	Dominic McGuigan	w rtd 5	Sunderland 9-7
Oct 30	Eugene Speed	l pts 8	Istres
Dec 1	Neil Haddock	l pts 10	Liverpool 9-4-8

Fights 34 Won 21 Lost 10 Drawn 3

Crisanto ESPANA
Welterweight
Venezuela born 25 October 1964
Based Belfast. Lives Bangor, Co. Down.

1984			
Mar 30	Elias Gonzalez	w ko 1	Venezuela
Jul 13	Jose Campos	w ko 3	Venezuela
Oct 10	Morgan Medina	w ko 1	Venezuela
1985			
Sep 7	Edgar Rodrigues	w ko 3	Venezuela
1986			
inactive			
1987			
Feb 21	Rolando Ruiz	w ko 1	Panama City
1988			
Oct 21	Dave Pierre	w pts 6	Belfast 10-4
Dec 7	Simon Eubanks	w rsf 1	Belfast 10-6
Dec 14	Gary Pemberton	w rsf 1	Liverpool 10-9
1989			
Jan 25	Billy Buchanan	w rsf 3	Belfast 10-2-8
Feb 20	Mike Essett	w rsf 2	NSC 10-10
Mar 8	Judas Clottey	w rsf 2	Belfast 10-10
Apr 12	Antonio Campbell	w rsf 2	Belfast 10-8
May 10	Del Bryan	w pts 8	Albert Hall 10-7-4
Oct 31	Carlos Zambrano	w rsf 2*	Belfast
Nov 29	Mario Moreno	w dis 1	Belfast 10-8-8
Dec 13	Lloyd Christie	w rtd 3*	Liverpool 10-9
1990			
Feb 21	Delfino Marin	w rsf 6	Belfast 10-7-8
Mar 28	Jorge Hernandez	w rsf 1	Manchester 10-8
May 23	Francisco Bobadilla	w ko 4	Belfast 10-6-8
Sep 15	Felix Dubray	w ko 3	Belfast 10-6-8
Oct 30	Luis Mora	w rsf 7	Belfast 10-5-4
1991			
Feb 12	Luis Santana	w pts 12	Belfast 10-6-8
	(vacant WBC International welterweight title)		
May 30	Larry McCall	w rsf 4	Madrid
Sep 7	Newton Barnett	w rtd 4*	Belfast 10-9-8
Nov 13	Hector Hugo Vilte	w rsf 7	Belfast 10-6-12
	(WBC International welterweight title)		

1992

Jun 13	Kevin Whaley-El	w rsf 1	Bilbao 10-12-8
Jul 3	David Taylor	w rsf 7	Pontault-Combault 10-6-12
Oct 31	Meldrick Taylor (WBA welterweight title)	w rsf 8	Earls Court 10-7

Fights 28 Won 28

Chris EUBANK
Super-middleweight
Brighton, born Dulwich 8 August 1966

1985

Oct 3	Tim Brown	w pts 4	Atlantic City 11-0-4
Nov 7	Kenny Cannida	w pts 4	Atlantic City 11-0

1986

Jan 8	Mike Bragwell	w pts 4	Atlantic City
Feb 25	Eric Holland	w pts 4	Atlantic City

1987

Mar 25	James Canty	w pts 4	Atlantic City

1988

Feb 15	Darren Parker	w rsf 1	Copthorne 11-2
Mar 7	Winston Burnett	w pts 6	Hove 11-9
Apr 26	Michael Justin	w rsf 5	Hove 11-4-8
May 4	Greg George	w rsf 5*	Wembley GH 11-4
May 18	Steve Aquilina	w rsf 4	Portsmouth

1989

Jan 31	Simon Collins	w rsf 4	Bethnal Green 11-2
Feb 8	Anthony Logan	w pts 8	Albert Hall 11-9
Mar 1	Franki Moro	w pts 8	Bethnal Green 11-10
May 26	Randy Smith	w pts 10	Bethnal Green 11-10
Jun 28	Les Wisniewski	w rsf 2	Brentwood 11-7
Oct 4	Ron Malek	w rsf 5	Basildon 11-8
Oct 24	Jean-Noel Camara	w rsf 2	Bethnal Green 11-9
Nov 5	Johnny Melfah	w ko 4	Albert Hall 11-9-8
Dec 20	Jose Da Silva	w rtd 6	Liverpool 11-7

1990

Jan 16	Denys Cronin	w rsf 3	Cardiff 11-13-8
Mar 6	Hugo Corti (WBC International middleweight title)	w rsf 8*	Bethnal Green 11-6
Apr 25	Eduardo Contreras (WBC International middleweight title)	w pts 12	Brighton 11-5-14
Sep 5	Kid Milo (WBC International middleweight title)	w rsf 8*	Brighton 11-6
Sep 22	Renaldo Dos Santos	w ko 1	Albert Hall 11-9
Nov 18	Nigel Benn (WBO middleweight title)	w rsf 9	NEC 11-5-8

1991

Feb 23	Dan Sherry (WBO middleweight title)	w tdec (s) 10	Brighton 11-6
Apr 18	Gary Stretch (WBO middleweight title)	w rsf 6	Olympia 11-6
Jun 22	Michael Watson (WBO middleweight title)	w pts 12 (m)	Earls Court 11-6
Sep 21	Michael Watson (vacant WBO super-middleweight title)	w rsf 12	Tottenham 11-13

/CTD..

(Chris EUBANK ctd.)
1992
Feb 1	Sugarboy Malinga (WBO super-middleweight title)	w pts 12 (s)	Birmingham 12-0
Apr 25	John Jarvis (WBO super-middleweight title)	w ko 3	Manchester 12-0
Jun 27	Ron Essett (WBO super-middleweight title)	w pts 12	Quinta Do Lago 12-0
Sep 19	Tony Thornton (WBO super-middleweight title)	w pts 12	Glasgow 12-0
Nov 28	Juan Carlos Gimenez (WBO super-middleweight title)	w pts 12	Manchester 12-0

Fights 34 Won 34

Frank EUBANKS

Super-middleweight
Manchester born 25 June 1967
Moss Side ABC
1985 East Lancs & Cheshire ABA middleweight prelim (l I Bayliss)
1988 East Lancs & Cheshire ABA middleweight final (l E Noi)

1989
Sep 26	Spencer Alton	l pts 6	Oldham 11-7-12
Nov 4	Antoine Tarver	l pts 4	Eastbourne 11-10
Nov 10	Calton Myers	w rsf 5	Battersea 11-9
Nov 30	Steve West	w rsf 3	Southwark 11-9-8

1990
Feb 21	Ray Close	l pts 8	Belfast 11-12-8
Sep 7	Alan Pennington	w rsf 2	Liverpool 11-10-8
Oct 10	Wayne Ellis	l pts 6	Millwall 11-10
Oct 24	Roger Wilson	w pts 6	Stoke 11-7
Nov 27	Franki Moro	w rsf 6	Liverpool
Dec 12	Adrian Wright	w pts 6	Stoke 11-10

1991
Feb 16	Cornelius Carr	l rsf 5	Thornaby 11-9-12
Apr 12	Peter Vosper	w rsf 1	Manchester 11-12-8
Jun 24	Marvin O'Brian	w pts 6	Liverpool 11-4
Oct 22	Roland Ericsson	w rtd 3	Battersea 12-1

1992
Jan 22	Nicky Piper (eliminator, British super-middleweight title)	l pts 10	Cardiff 11-13-8
Jul 18	Fidel Castro	l rtd 6	Manchester 12-0-8

Fights 16 Won 9 Lost 7

Simon EUBANKS

Welterweight
Brighton, born Manchester 23 March 1962
Peckham ABC
1983 SE London ABA featherweight final (l T Driscoll)

1984
Nov 29	Michael Justin	w rsf 5	Digbeth

1985
Mar 25	Steve Griffith	w pts 8	Glasgow 10-1
May 8	Ken Foreman	l pts 8	Solihull 10-1-12
Jun 8	Gary Muire	w pts 6	Shepherds Bush 10-1-4
Oct 2	Rafaele Feliciello	w pts 8	Solihull 10-1

1986
Jan 22	Ken Foreman	l dis 1	Solihull 10-3
Feb 6	Dave Griffiths	l rsf 2	Adwick 10-1-8
Mar 17	Tony McKenzie	l rsf 4	Solihull 10-5
May 8	Chris Blake	l pts 8	Bayswater 10-4-8
Oct 1	Andrew Mayers	l rsf 6*	Solihull 10-1
Nov 17	Sugar Gibiliru	w pts 8	Dulwich 10-3
Dec 11	Steve Boyle	l rsf 6	Livingstone 9-13-12

1987
Mar 18	Tony Ekubia	l pts 8	Solihull 10-4-8

1988
Jun 12	Hugo Hernandez	l rsf 1	Rome
Dec 7	Crisanto Espana	l rsf 1	Belfast 10-8

1989
Jan 30	Alex Dickson	l pts 8	Glasgow 10-4
Mar 16	Derek Grainger	l rsf 6	Southwark 10-10
Apr 27	Michael Oliver	w pts 6	Mayfair 10-8-4
Oct 4	Gary Logan	l pts 6	Albert Hall 10-7
Dec 12	Mickey Lloyd	l pts 8	Brentford 10-8-12

1990
Jan 30	Del Bryan	l pts 6	Battersea 10-12-12
Sep 12	Trevor Smith	w rsf 8	Battersea 10-10

1991
Jan 29	Glyn Rhodes	l rsf 3	Wisbech 10-9
May 16	Andy Holligan	l ko 2	Liverpool 10-8-8
Oct 1	Paul Jones	l ko 6	Sheffield 10-10-8

1992
Jan 18	Kevin Lueshing	l ko 4	Albert Hall 10-10

Fights 26 Won 7 Lost 19

Dennie Mancini

International Boxing Agent, Manager, Matchmaker and Second.
Official British Representative for Mr. Henk Ruhling, Holland.

**16 ROSEDEW ROAD, HAMMERSMITH
LONDON W6 9ET**
TELEPHONES: (081) 748 8790 (Home) : (081) 748 2571 (Home Answer Service)
(071) 437 1526 (Office) : (081) 746 3005 (Fax).

Over 31 years' experience of handling boxers at all levels including:
**WORLD CHAMPION (Agent) : EUROPEAN (Manager) : BRITISH CHAMPIONS (Manager)
COMMONWEALTH (Manager) : IRELAND (Manager) : 24 Area Champions.**

BOXING IS MY BUSINESS - ALL ENQUIRIES DEALT WITH PROMPTLY.

ANGLO/SWEDISH PROMOTIONS

INTERNATIONAL PROMOTERS, MANAGERS, MATCHMAKERS & AGENTS

KURT SJOLIN	GREG STEENE	BENNY ROSEN
UK Office:		**Swedish Office:**
11 Whitcomb Street		Box 6003, Gothenburg
London WC2H 7HA		Sweden 40060

**Tel: 071-839 4532   Fax: (London) 071-839 4367
Fax: (Gothenburg) 010-46312561-69**

Boxers managed by Greg Steene:

Lou Gent	Super-middleweight, Former Southern Area Cruiserweight Champion.
Roland Ericsson	Super-middleweight
Andy Wright	Former undefeated Southern Area Super-middleweight Champion
Tony McCarthy	Super-middleweight
Stan King	Middleweight
Conrad Oscar	Middleweight
Georgy Wilson	Light-welterweight
Matt Mason	Lightweight

Also UK representative for Horace Fleary - German International Super-middleweight Champ.
TRAINERS: Trevor Cattouse, Casley McCallum, Peter Cann, Dave Payne

Any boxer who wants top management

Tony FALCONE

Featherweight
Chippenham born 15 October 1966
Malmesbury ABC
1988 Western ABA featherweight final (w rsf 2 J Blackwood, l A Jones)
1989 Western ABA featherweight final (l dis 1 P Hardcastle)
1990 Western ABA featherweight semi-final (l A McNally)

1990
Oct 22	Karl Morling	l pts 6	NSC 8-13
Nov 21	Barrie Kelley	l pts 6	Chippenham 9-1-8

1991
Feb 18	Barrie Kelley	w rsf 6*	NSC 9-1-8
Feb 28	Paul Wynn	w pts 6	Sunderland 9-2
Mar 21	Tony Silkstone	l pts 6	Dewsbury 8-13-12
Apr 22	Alan Smith	l rsf 5*	AASC 9-0-12
May 30	Alan Smith	w pts 6	Mayfair 9-1
Dec 11	Dennis Adams	w rtd 4*	Basildon 9-3

1992
Apr 30	Andrew Bloomer	w pts 6	Mayfair 8-13-8
Jul 7	Miguel Matthews	w pts 6	Bristol 9-0-8
Oct 5	Andrew Bloomer	w pts 8	Bristol 9-0-4

Fights 11 Won 7 Lost 4

Serg FAME

Light-heavyweight
Paddington, born 22 February 1962
Real name: Serg Theophane
Four Feathers ABC

1985
Mar 1	David Furneaux	w rsf 5	Longford 12-8
Mar 23	Greg George	l pts 6	Strand 12-3
Apr 26	Thomas G. Lawrence	w pts 6	Longford 12-7
May 25	Thomas G. Lawrence	w rsf 4	Longford 12-7
Oct 25	Lee Davis	w rsf 3	Fulham 12-4-4
Nov 22	Terry Gilbey	w ko 4	Longford 12-4
Dec 11	Lou Gent	w rsf 2*	Fulham 12-6

1986
Mar 20	Lou Gent	w ko 2	Wimbledon
Mar 25	Winston Burnett	w pts 8	Tunbridge Wells 12-7
Sep 25	Glazz Campbell	l pts 8	Crystal Palace 12-7
Nov 17	Noel Magee	l pts 8	Dulwich 12-4

1987
Mar 2	Mamdoo N'Didye	w pts 8	Lewisham 12-7
May 6	Ray Thomas	w pts 6	Solihull 12-6
Nov 16	Pedro van Raamsdonk	l pts 8	Arnhem 12-5-8

1988
Sep 13	Glazz Campbell	w pts 10	Battersea 12-4
	(vacant Southern light-heavyweight title)		
Nov 24	Steve McCarthy	l pts 10	Southampton 12-4
	(Southern light-heavyweight title)		

1989
Apr 8	Nelson Alex Alves	l ko 2	Berlin 12-7-12
May 10	Crawford Ashley	l rtd 7*	Solihull 12-4-8

1990
Jan 30	Johnny Graham	w rsf 1	Battersea 12-5-8
	(vacant Southern light-heavyweight title)		

/CTD...

(Serg FAME ctd.)

Jun 6	Derek Myers	w pts 10	Battersea 12-6
	(Southern light-heavyweight title)		
Oct 25	Steve McCarthy	l pts 12	Battersea 12-7
	(vacant British light-heavyweight title)		
1991			
Feb 14	Jimmy Peters	l rsf 4	Southampton 12-6
	(Southern light-heavyweight title)		
1992			
Jan 30	Tony Booth	l pts 6	Southampton 12-7-4

Fights 23 Won 13 Lost 10

Joe FANNIN
Lightweight
Birmingham born 18 May 1970

1992			
Oct 5	Craig Murray	w rsf 1	Manchester 9-5
Oct 27	Richard Woolgar	l pts 6	Leicester 9-8

Fights 2 Won 1 Lost 1

Ceri FARRELL
Bantamweight
Swansea born 27 October 1967
City ABC

1990			
May 14	Kruga Hydes	l pts 6	Cleethorpes 8-4
Jun 6	Con McMullan	l rsf 5	Battersea 8-5
Oct 3	Tim Yeates	l pts 6	Basildon 8-7
Dec 5	Paul Dever	w rsf 2	Stafford 8-5
Dec 12	Tim Yeates	l pts 6	Basildon 8-7
Dec 19	Mercurio Ciaramitaro	drew 6	Rimini 8-5-8
1991			
Jan 24	Kevin Jenkins	l pts 6	Gorseinon 8-7
Feb 7	Mark Tierney	l pts 6	Watford 8-3-8
Mar 6	Mark Tierney	l pts 6	Wembley 8-4
Apr 25	Mark Loftus	l rsf 3	Basildon 8-6
Nov 4	Andrew Bloomer	w pts 6	Merthyr 8-9-8
Nov 20	Andrew Bloomer	w pts 6	Cardiff 8-10
Nov 29	John Green	l rtd 4	Manchester 8-9
1992			
Jan 8	Miguel Matthews	l pts 6	Burton-on-Trent 8-12
Jan 22	Alan Ley	l pts 6	Cardiff 8-11
Feb 9	Peter Judson	l pts 6	Bradford 8-11
Sep 15	Michael Alldis	l rsf 3	Crystal Palace 8-9

Fights 17 Won 3 Lost 13 Drawn 1

Lee FARRELL

Welterweight
Pontypool, born Cardiff 3 July 1967
Pontnewynydd ABC

1988
| Nov 23 | Brian Robinson | l rsf 1 | Bethnal Green 10-12 |

1989
| Feb 20 | Louie Antuna | l ko 4 | Glasgow 10-7 |

1990
| Dec 8 | Dean Cooper | l pts 6 | Bristol 10-12 |

1991
Jan 28	Colin Pitters	l pts 6	Birmingham 10-11
Feb 12	Mick Betts	l rsf 1	Wolverhampton
May 15	Mark Verikios	l rsf 5*	Swansea 10-10

1992
| Mar 2 | Jerry Mortimer | l pts 6 | Merthyr 11-0 |
| May 16 | Santo Serio | l rsf 2 | Muswell Hill 10-12 |

Fights 8 Lost 8

Marco FATTORE

Super-featherweight
Watford born 17 October 1968
Bushey ABC
1991 Home Counties ABA featherweight final (l S Dunne)
1992 Home Counties ABA lightweight semi-final (l J Wilson)

1992
Sep 3	Jason White	w rsf 1*	Dunstable 9-4-12
Oct 19	Carlos Demonikos	w rtd 4	Mayfair 9-5
Dec 7	Steve Patton	w rsf 6*	Mayfair 9-4-8

Fights 3 Won 3

Vince FEENEY

Bantamweight
London, born Sligo
Real name: John Feeney
Inner City ABC, Dublin & Sealink, Dublin
1990 Irish Junior flyweight champion (w.o.)
1991 Young Ireland (v Eng, w C. Slatcher)
1992 Irish Intermediate bantamweight final (l rsf 2 F Slane)

1992
| Oct 29 | Adey Benton | drew 6 | Bayswater |

Fights 1 Drawn 1

Antonio FERNANDEZ

Middleweight
Birmingham born 3 January 1965
Real name: Antonio Golding
Kingshurst ABC

1987
Mar 10	David Heath	w rsf 5	Manchester
Apr 29	Darren Hobson	l pts 6	Stoke 11-2
Nov 18	Tony White	w pts 6	Solihull 11-1-8

1988
Jan 19	Malcolm Melvin	w rsf 4*	Kings Heath 11-2
Mar 7	Shaun Cummins	l pts 6	Northampton 11-1
Oct 10	Chris Richards	w pts 6	Edgbaston 11-1
Nov 23	Chris Richards	w pts 8	Solihull 11-2

1989
Jan 24	Paul Murray	w pts 6	Kings Heath 11-2-4
May 8	Seamus Casey	w pts 6	Edgbaston 11-6-8
Nov 13	Cyril Jackson	w pts 8	Brierley Hill 11-7-8
Dec 3	Steve Foster	l pts 8	Birmingham 11-6

1990
Mar 6	Paul Jones	l pts 8	Stoke 11-5
Apr 30	Alan Baptiste	w pts 6	Brierley Hill 11-7
Jun 4	Chris Richards	w pts 8	Edgbaston 11-5
Nov 13	Chris Walker	w pts 6	Edgbaston 11-7

1991
Jan 24	Franki Moro	w pts 6	Brierley Hill 11-6-4
Oct 7	Paul Murray	w rsf 7	Birmingham 11-7
Dec 9	Paul McCarthy	w pts 8	Brierley Hill 11-10

1992
Mar 3	Paul Wesley (vacant Midlands middleweight title)	w pts 10	Cradley Heath 11-5-12
Oct 28	Darron Griffiths (eliminator, British middleweight title)	l pts 10	Cardiff 11-3-8

Fights 20 Won 15 Lost 5

Rocky FERRARI

Super-featherweight
Glasgow born 27 October 1972
Real name: Robert Ewing
Gallowgate ABC
Gaelic Games gold medal
1990 Scottish ABA lightweight semi-final (w rsf 1 C Anderson, w ko 1 D Docherty, l D Connolly)
1990 European Junior Championships (l Dollinger, WGer)

1991
Jan 25	James Hunter	w ko 1	Shotts 9-6
Feb 11	Sol Francis	w rsf 5	Glasgow 9-5
Mar 5	Chris Saunders	w pts 4	Glasgow 9-5

1992
Sep 11	Mick Mulcahy	w pts 6	Glasgow 9-7

Fights 4 Won 4

Lee FERRIE
Light-middleweight
Coventry born 10 July 1964
Coventry Boys & Triumph ABC
1984 Warwickshire ABA light-middleweight final (l P Boyden)
1985 Midlands ABA welterweight final (w rsf 1 J Hemming, w A Docherty, l E McDonald)
1986 South Midlands ABA welterweight final (l M Elliot)
1987 South Midlands ABA light-middleweight semi-final (l rsf 2* A Smith)
1991 ABA light-middleweight final (w rsf 1 E Wilkinson, w ko 1 G Rooksby, w rsf 1 A Ewan, w S Kenneth, w J Alston, w rsf 1 S Morrison, l T Taylor)

1991
Oct 1	Julian Eavis	w pts 6	Bedworth 11-0
Nov 5	Trevor Meikle	w pts 6	Leicester 10-13
Dec 11	Noel Henry	w rsf 5	Leicester 11-3

1992
Jan 20	Martin Rosamond	w rsf 2	Coventry 11-5
Feb 24	Julian Eavis	w pts 8	Coventry 11-0
Mar 25	Mick Reid	w rsf 3	Hinckley 11-3

Fights 6 Won 6

Darren FIFIELD
Flyweight
Abingdon born 9 October 1969
Abingdon Town ABC & Henley ABC
1986 Junior ABA champion
1988 NABC Class C final (l C Dermody)
1989 Home Counties ABA light-flyweight champion (w A Derry, l M Reynolds)
1990 Home Counties ABA light-flyweight final (l A Derry)
1991 England (v Sc, l K Knox)
1991 ABA light-flyweight semi-final (w rtd 2 A Derry, w L Harris, l A Mooney)
1992 ABA light-flyweight champion (w K Hassell, w L Harris, w rsf 3 L Woodcock)

1992
Oct 22	Glyn Shepherd	drew 4	Bethnal Green 8-3
Dec 10	Anthony Hanna	w rsf 6	Bethnal Green 8-2

Fights 2 Won 1 Drawn 1

Crain FISHER
Light-middleweight
Rochdale born 28 February 1966
Middleton & Rochdale ABC
1988 East Lancs & Cheshire welterweight semi-final (l rsf 2 C Smith)
1990 East Lancs & Cheshire light-middleweight semi-final (l ko 2 M Gormley)

1990
Oct 22	Richard O'Brien	w ko 3	Manchester 10-10

1991
Feb 28	Rob Pitters	l rsf 6	Bury 10-12
Oct 21	James McGee	w rsf 4	Bury 10-12

1992
Apr 13	Trevor Meikle	w pts 6	Manchester 10-11
May 5	Frank Harrington	w rsf 4	Preston 10-12-8
Oct 13	Robert Riley	l pts 4	Bury 10-12

Fights 6 Won 4 Lost 2

Simon FISHER
Welterweight
Coventry born 12 December 1965
RAF, Standard Triumph ABC

1992
| Sep 21 | Peter Waudby | l rsf 2 | Cleethorpes 10-8 |
| Nov 23 | Warren Stephens | l pts 6 | Coventry 10-9-8 |

Fights 2 Lost 2

Horace FLEARY
Middleweight
Huddersfield, born Jamaica 22 April 1961
Southpaw

1987
Jul 4	Salvador Yanez	l rsf 3	Helmstedt
Oct 17	Harald Schulte	w pts 6	Gifhorn
Oct 31	Niyazi Aytekin	l pts 6	Paderborn
Nov 23	Mourad Louati	l rsf 3	L'Aja

1988
Jan 9	Yurder Demircan	l rsf 4*	Helmstedt
Mar 14	Henk van den Tak	l pts 6	Arnhem
May 12	Mike Wissenbach	w pts 6	Berlin
Jun 29	Silvio Mieckley	drew 4	Hamburg
Jul 2	Zelkjo Seslek	w rsf 4*	Helmstedt
Sep 16	Jose Varela	l pts 8	Berlin
Oct 28	Zeljko Seslek	w rsf 5	Braunschweig
Nov 8	Ferdinand Pachler	l pts 8	Vienna
Nov 12	Josef Kossmann	w pts 8	Oberkassel
Nov 16	Mike Wissenbach	l pts 6	Berlin

1989
Feb 25	Paddy Pipa	l pts 8	Hamburg 11-4
Sep 16	Josef Rajc	w ko 1	Wiener Neustadt
Sep 30	Owen Reece	l pts 6	Hamburg 10-12
Oct 13	Frederic Seillier	l ko 1	Sete
Nov 10	Jean-Paul Roux	l dis 8	St Quentin
Nov 27	Franck Nicotra	l dis 6	Nogent 11-5
Dec 1	Andy Marks	l pts 8	Berlin 11-6
Dec 9	Hamedidi Maimoun	l rsf 3	Grande Synthe

1990
| Oct 12 | Joseph Kossmann | w ko 8 | Gelsenkirchen |

1991
Jan 4	Andreas Schweiger	w ko 9	Supplingen
Mar 20	Paul Wesley	w rsf 5*	Solihull 11-4-8
Apr 4	Jurgen Broszett	w ko 2	Bielfeld
Jun 22	Said Skouma	l pts 8	Paris
Sep 13	Nelson Alex Alves	l ko 7	Dusseldorf 11-3

(German International super-middleweight title)

| Nov 20 | Kevin Sheeran | l rsf 2 | Cardiff 11-0 |

1992
| Jan 10 | Teddy Jensen | w ko 2 | Aachen |
| Feb 28 | Thomas Mateoi | w rsf 2 | Supplingen |

(German International light-middleweight title)

| Apr 4 | Jan Mazgut | w rsf 4 | Minden |

May 1	Trpmir Jandrek	w rsf 2	Aachen
May 12	Adrian Strachan	l pts 6	Crystal Palace 11-2
Oct 1	Robert McCracken	l pts 8	Telford
Nov 2	Neville Brown	l pts 8	Wolverhampton 11-5-8
Nov 27	Miroslav Strbak	w pts 6	Suhl
Dec 4	Richie Woodhall	l pts 8	Telford 11-8

Fights 38 Won 15 Lost 22 Drawn 1

Andy FLUTE
Middleweight
Coseley born Wolverhampton 5 March 1970
Tipton ABC & Wednesfield ABC
1987 Young England (v WGer, l J Fronbeck)
1988 Young England (v WGer, w rtd 2 T Bochert)
1989 Staffordshire ABA middleweight final (l A Wright)

1989
| May 24 | Stinger Mason | w pts 6 | Hanley 11-11 |
| Oct 24 | Paul Murray | w rsf 3 | Wolverhampton 11-11 |

1990
Mar 22	David Maxwell	w rsf 5*	Wolverhampton 11-9
May 24	Spencer Alton	l rsf 1*	Dudley 11-9-8
Sep 18	Tony Hodge	w rsf 2	Wolverhampton 12-0
Oct 24	Nigel Rafferty	w ko 6	Dudley 11-7-8
Nov 27	Paul Burton	l pts 6	Stoke 11-13

1991
Mar 13	Robert Peel	w pts 6	Stoke 11-12
Apr 10	Russell Washer	w pts 6	Wolverhampton 11-9
May 14	Alan Richards	w pts 8	Dudley 11-10-8
Oct 16	Karl Barwise	l rsf 8*	Stoke 11-11
Dec 5	Richard Okumu	drew 8	Cannock 11-7

1992
| Mar 17 | Graham Burton | w pts 8 | Wolverhampton 11-9 |
| Apr 28 | Paul Smith | w rsf 5 | Wolverhampton 11-8 |

Fights 14 Won 10 Lost 3 Drawn 1

Steve FORAN
Light-welterweight
Liverpool born 19 October 1967
Rotunda ABC
1981 National Schools champion (w R Woodhall, w P Richards)
1982 National Schools champion (w M Moran)
1983 Junior ABA semi-final (l M Moran)
1983 National Schools champion
1983 England Schools (v Wal, w ko 1 L Davies)
1984 National Schools champion (w R Woodhall, w L Shaw)
1984 Junior ABA champion (w rsf N Featherbee, w rsf 2 M Dunican)
1985 NABC Class C champion (w R Adams)
1985 Young England, Multi-Nations, East Germany (l Pal, Rum)
1985 World Junior Championships (w J Dydak, Pol; w rsf 2 K Toshihiko, Jap; l R Castillo, Cub)
1985 Young England (v YUSA, l rtd 1 D Rolon)
1985 England (v Ire, w P Murphy)
1986 West Lancs ABA light-welterweight final (l T Langton)
1988 Northern ABA welterweight final (w P Carroll, w C Teasdale, w rsf 1 P Hampson, l J Nicholson)

1988
| Nov 29 | John Mullen | drew 6 | Manchester 10-2-4 |
| Dec 16 | Dean Dickinson | w pts 6 | Brentwood 10-0 /CTD.. |

(Steve FORAN ctd)

1989
May 2	Danny Ellis	w rsf 3	Chigwell 10-6
Jun 6	Jim Talbot	l pts 8	Chigwell 10-4
Jun 28	Dave Lake	w rsf 2	Brentwood 10-2
Sep 26	Dave Maw	w pts 8	Chigwell 10-4
Oct 31	Michael Driscoll	drew 6	Manchester 10-1-12

1990
Mar 21	Mike Morrison	w pts 6	Preston 10-2
Jun 5	Glyn Rhodes	drew 6	Nottingham 10-8-4
Oct 17	Darren Mount	w rsf 6*	Bethnal Green 10-6

1991
Apr 24	Wayne Windle	w ko 3	Preston 10-1
Jun 22	Michael Driscoll	l rsf 4*	Earls Court 10-2

1992
Oct 23	Robert Whitehouse	w rsf 2	Liverpool 10-5
Nov 20	Kevin McKillan	w pts 6	Liverpool 10-0

Fights 14 Won 9 Lost 2 Drawn 3

Ali FORBES
Super-middleweight
Sydenham born 7 March 1961
Peckham ABC

1989
Feb 16	David Haycock	w rsf 4	Battersea 12-4-8

1990
Jun 22	Andy Marlow	w rtd 3*	Gillingham 12-0
Sep 26	Peter Vosper	w pts 6	AASC 12-1

1991
Feb 6	Adrian Wright	w pts 6	Battersea 11-12
Apr 3	Karl Barwise	w rtd 4*	Bethnal Green 11-13-8
May 16	Quinton Paynter	drew 6	Battersea 11-13
Jun 1	Paul McCarthy	w ko 2	Bethnal Green 12-4-8

1992
Mar 11	Ian Strudwick	l pts 10	Solihull 11-13
	(Southern super-middleweight title)		
Oct 29	Nick Manners	w rsf 3	Leeds 12-2

Fights 9 Won 7 Lost 1 Drawn 1

Simon FORD
Lightweight
Shrewsbury born 8 February 1971
No amateur experience

1992
Sep 3	Shea Neary	l rsf 1	Liverpool 9-12

Fights 1 Lost 1

Hugh FORDE

Super-featherweight
Birmingham born 7 May 1964
Southpaw
Sheldon Heath ABC
1986 South Midlands ABA lightweight final (l R Joyce)

1986
May 13	Little Currie	w pts 6	Digbeth
Jun 26	Carl Cleasby	w rsf 3*	Edgbaston 9-5
Sep 22	Carl Gaynor	w pts 6	Edgbaston 9-2-8
Oct 25	Tony Graham	w pts 6	Stevenage 9-6
Nov 3	John Bennie	w rsf 3	Edgbaston 9-3-12
Dec 8	Darren Connellan	w pts 6	Edgbaston 9-3

1987
Jan 21	Craig Walsh	w pts 8	Solihull 9-7
Apr 7	Gary Maxwell	w pts 8	West Bromwich 9-5
Apr 24	Lambsy Kayani	w pts 8	Evesham 9-4-8
Dec 14	Patrick Kamy	w pts 8	Edgbaston 9-3-8

1988
Jan 19	Billy Cawley	w pts 8	Kings Heath 9-6
Apr 5	Rudi Valentino	w rsf 2	Aston 9-5-12
Jun 17	Gary Maxwell	w rsf 2	Edgbaston 9-2
	(vacant Midlands super-featherweight title)		
Oct 10	Wayne Weekes	w rsf 7	Edgbaston 9-6-8
Nov 28	Brian Cullen	w rtd 4*	Edgbaston 9-7

1989
May 8	Paul Bowen	w rsf 4	Edgbaston 9-6
Oct 31	Brian Roche	w rsf 2	Manchester 9-3-8
	(eliminator, British super-featherweight title)		

1990
Feb 14	Harold Warren	w pts 8	Brentwood 9-5
Apr 25	Delfino Perez	w rsf 2	Brighton 9-6
Sep 18	Joey Jacobs	w rsf 11	Wolverhampton 9-4
	(British super-featherweight title)		
Oct 24	Kevin Pritchard	l ko 4	Dudley 9-3-8
	(British super-featherweight title)		

1991
Feb 27	Tony Pep	l rsf 9	Wolverhampton 9-5
May 14	Richie Joyce	w rtd 5	Dudley 9-11-4
Sep 10	Thunder Ayeh	w pts 12	Wolverhampton 9-4
	(Commonwealth super-featherweight title)		
Nov 12	Paul Harvey	l rsf 3	Wolverhampton 9-4
	(Commonwealth super-featherweight title)		

1992
Nov 2	Karl Taylor	w pts 6	Wolverhampton 9-13-8

Fights 26 Won 23 Lost 3

John FOREMAN

Light-heavyweight
Birmingham born 6 November 1967
Birmingham City ABC
1984 Junior ABA champion (w A Lovell)
1987 NABC Class C champion (w G Parsons)
1987 Midlands ABA light-heavyweight champion (w S Brown, w I Bulloch, l J Jones)

1987
Oct 26	Randy B. Powell	w rsf 1	Aston 12-7-8
Nov 18	Dave Owens	l rsf 5	Solihull 12-9

1988
Mar 16	Jon Fairbairn	w pts 6	Solihull 12-8-8
Apr 5	David Jono	w ko 1	Aston 12-12
Apr 11	Byron Pullen	w pts 6	Northampton 12-9
Jun 17	Gus Mendes	w rsf 5	Edgbaston 12-1
Nov 28	Dave Owens	w ko 1	Edgbaston 12-9-4

1989
Jan 24	Crawford Ashley	l rsf 4	Kings Heath 12-7-12
Nov 13	Everton Blake	w pts 6	Brierley Hill 12-10
Dec 3	Chris Coughlan	w rsf 2	Birmingham 12-10

1990
Mar 19	Abner Blackstock	w pts 8	Brierley Hill 13-0
Jun 4	Brian Schumacher	w rsf 4	Edgbaston 12-10
Sep 3	Roy Skeldon	l rtd 6*	Dudley 12-6-4

(Midlands light-heavyweight title, eliminator British title)

1991
Apr 18	Richard Bustin	l pts 8	Olympia 12-6
Jun 22	Gil Lewis	drew 6	Earls Court 12-9
Dec 16	Steve McCarthy	l pts 8	Southampton 12-7-4

1992
Jan 26	Fabrice Tiozzo	l rsf 6	Saint-Ouen 13-2
May 29	Bobbi Joe Edwards	w rsf 4*	Manchester 12-7
Oct 6	Eddy Smulders	l rsf 4*	Antwerp

Fights 19 Won 11 Lost 7 Drawn 1

Jason FORES

Light-middleweight
Worksop born 27 November 1970

1989
Jan 26	Seamus Sheridan	l rsf 1	Newcastle 10-12

1990-91 inactive

1992
Dec 9	Andy Peach	l pts 6	Stoke 11-2

Fights 2 Lost 2

Paul FORREST

Featherweight
Middlesbrough born 31 October 1969

1990
Nov 19	Darren Weller	w pts 6	Cardiff
Dec 19	Miguel Matthews	w pts 6	Preston

1991			
Jul 3	Paul Donaghey	w ko 2	Brentwood 9-1
Oct 1	Colin Lynch	l pts 6	Sheffield 9-1-8
Dec 10	Colin Lynch	w pts 6	Sheffield 9-1-8
1992			
Jan 28	Joan Lupu	l rsf 4*	Hamburg

Fights 6 Won 4 Lost 2

Frankie FOSTER

Super-featherweight
Newcastle born 25 May 1968
Somervyl & Longbenton ABC, West Denton ABC
1987 North-East England ABA bantamweight final (l rsf 3 J Davison)
1988 North-East England ABA lightweight final (w R Gamblin, l K McKenzie)

1988			
Sep 22	Mick Mulcahy	w pts 6	Newcastle 9-6
Sep 29	Paul Chedgzoy	w pts 6	Sunderland 9-6
Nov 7	Pete Roberts	w pts 6	Bradford 9-8
Dec 1	Peter English	l pts 8	Manchester 9-4
1989			
Jan 26	James Jiora	w pts 6	Newcastle 9-5
Mar 9	John Townsley	w pts 8	Glasgow 9-7
Apr 3	Jose Tuominen	l pts 4 (s)	Helsinki 9-4
Apr 24	Jim Moffat	l pts 8	Glasgow 9-8
Jun 21	Paul Gadney	l pts 6	Eltham 9-7
Oct 2	Sean White	drew 6	Bradford
Oct 11	Lester James	w pts 6	Stoke 9-4-8
Oct 21	Chad Broussard	l pts 6	Middlesbrough 9-5
Nov 13	Steve Winstanley	l pts 6	Bradford 9-3-8
1990			
Jan 24	Kid Sumaila	w pts 6	Sunderland 9-10-8
Feb 5	Muhammad Shaffique	l pts 6	Brierley Hill 9-4-8
Mar 20	Dominic McGuigan	drew 6	Hartlepool 9-6
Apr 26	Les Walsh	w pts 8	Manchester 9-4
Jun 4	Stuart Rimmer	w pts 6	Glasgow 9-8-4
Oct 18	Nigel Senior	w ko 2	Hartlepool 9-4
	(vacant Northern super-featherweight title)		
Nov 19	Sugar Gibiliru	drew 8	Manchester 9-6
1991			
Apr 22	John Doherty	l pts 10	Glasgow 9-2-9
	(eliminator, British super-featherweight title)		
Aug 14	Gianni Di Napoli	l pts 8	Alcamo
Oct 22	Darren Elsdon	l rsf 7	Hartlepool 9-4
	(Northern super-featherweight title)		
1992			
Mar 31	Sugar Gibiliru	l pts 8	Stockport 9-5-12
Sep 10	Darren Elsdon	w pts 10	Sunderland 9-4
	(Northern super-featherweight title)		

Fights 25 Won 11 Lost 11 Drawn 3

Steve FOSTER

Light-middleweight
Salford born 28 December 1960
Manchester YMCA ABC

1981
Feb 9	Pat McCarthy	w rsf 3	Manchester
Mar 16	Dave Dunn	l pts 6	Manchester
Mar 26	John Lindo	l rsf 1	Newcastle

1982-84 inactive

1985
Nov 25	Malcolm Melvin	drew 6	Ilkeston 11-2-8

1986
Mar 6	Taffy Morris	l pts 6	Manchester 11-2
Apr 17	Martin Kielty	w rsf 3	Wolverhampton 11-5
Nov 25	Seamus Casey	w pts 8	Manchester 11-2

1987
Apr 28	Cyril Jackson	w rsf 7*	Manchester 11-5
May 11	Fidel Castro	l pts 8	Manchester 11-6-12
Oct 19	Cyril Jackson	w rtd 3*	Manchester 10-13
Dec 14	Sean Leighton	l pts 8	Bradford 11-6

1988
Jan 27	Sam Storey	l rsf 4	Belfast 11-10
Apr 20	Tony Collins	l pts 4	Muswell Hill 11-7
Oct 21	Ray Close	l rsf 2	Belfast
Dec 14	Fran Harding	l pts 6	Liverpool 11-8

1989
Mar 1	Dario Deabreu	w rsf 2	Cardiff 11-8
Mar 6	Steve Aquilina	w pts 6	Manchester 11-8
Dec 3	Antonio Fernandez	w pts 6	Birmingham 11-9

1990
Feb 6	Sean O'Phoenix	w rsf 4*	Oldham 11-9-8
Mar 14	Andy Till	l rtd 5	Battersea 11-10-12
Jun 2	Ian Chantler	drew 4	Manchester 11-8

1991
Feb 22	Kesem Clayton	w ko 6	Manchester 11-5
Sep 20	Colin Pitters	w rtd 5	Manchester 11-2-4
Dec 7	Seamus Casey	w pts 8	Manchester

1992
Mar 10	Mike Phillips	w rsf 4*	Bury 11-3
Apr 25	Mark Jay	w rsf 7	Manchester 11-3
Nov 28	Shaun Cummins	l pts 12 (s)	Manchester 10-12-12

(vacant WBA Pentacontinental light-middleweight title)

Fights 27 Won 14 Lost 11 Drawn 2

Tony FOSTER

Super-featherweight
Hull born 9 July 1964
Southpaw
Hull Fish Trades ABC

1987
Sep 4	Paul Kennedy	l pts 6	Gateshead
Sep 18	Ian Hosten	l pts 6	Gravesend
Sep 28	Steve Winstanley	l pts 6	Bradford 9-5-8
Oct 6	Roy Doyle	l pts 6	Manchester 9-6

Nov 3	Darren Darby	l pts 6	Cottingham 9-5
Nov 25	Kevin McCoy	w rsf 4	Cottingham 9-8
Dec 2	Alan Roberts	w rsf 5	NSC 9-7
Dec 11	Mitchell King	drew 8	Coalville 9-1
1988			
Jan 11	Paul Chedgzoy	w pts 6	Manchester 9-6
Jan 25	Johnny Walker	l pts 6	Glasgow 9-7-12
Feb 1	Sean Hogg	w pts 6	Manchester 9-5-8
Feb 11	Lee Amass	l rsf 6*	Gravesend 9-7
Mar 28	Darrell Pettit	w pts 6	Bradford 9-4
Apr 22	Paul Charters	l pts 6	Gateshead 9-5-12
May 9	Gary Maxwell	l pts 6	Nottingham
May 17	Warren Slaney	w pts 6	Leicester 9-7
May 23	Harry Escott	w rsf 6*	Bradford 9-7
Sep 26	Peter Bradley	l pts 8	NSC 9-5-8
Oct 17	John Townsley	l pts 8	Glasgow 9-9
Nov 15	Steve Pollard	w rsf 3*	Hull 9-6
Dec 12	Mark Kelly	w pts 6	Nottingham 9-8
1989			
Feb 8	Paul Gadney	w pts 6	Albert Hall 9-9-12
Apr 3	Jari Gronroos	w pts 4	Helsinki 9-4
Apr 15	Paul Moylett	w pts 6	Salisbury 9-9-8
Jun 27	Ian Honeywood	l pts 6	Albert Hall 9-10-8
Oct 10	Steve Pollard	w rsf 3*	Hull 9-5-8
Nov 16	Sugar Gibiliru	w pts 8	Manchester 9-7
Nov 30	Joey Jacobs	l ko 4	Middleton 9-7
1990			
Jan 30	Sugar Gibiliru	l pts 10	Manchester 9-8
	(vacant Central lightweight title)		
Apr 21	Marvin P. Gray	drew 6	Sunderland 9-13
May 22	Marvin P. Gray	l pts 6	Thornaby 9-12
Jun 15	Marcel Herbert	l rsf 4	Telford 9-6
1991			
Feb 15	Jimmi Bredahl	l pts 6	Randers
Mar 5	Floyd Havard	l pts 8	Millwall 9-9
Apr 15	David Anderson	l pts 8	Glasgow 9-8
May 12	Alain Simoes	w pts 8	Voiron
Sep 11	Billy Schwer	l pts 8	Hammersmith 9-8
Nov 21	Giovanni Parisi	l rsf 6	Perugia 9-9-4
1992			
Jan 31	Angel Mona	l pts 8	Esch
Mar 30	Ian Honeywood	l rsf 4*	Eltham 9-12
Jun 13	Pierre Lorcy	l pts 8	Levallois
Oct 19	Tony Doyle	w pts 8	Hull 9-9
Oct 31	Dingaan Thobela	l pts 8	Earls Court 9-12-12

Fights 43 Won 16 Lost 25 Drawn 2

Lee FOX
Super-featherweight
Chesterfield born 20 January 1970
Chesterfield ABC

1989			
Nov 13	Steve Armstrong	w pts 6	Manchester 9-2-8
Dec 6	Steve Armstrong	w pts 6	Stoke 9-2
1990			
Feb 5	Neil Leitch	l pts 6	Brierley Hill 9-3-8 /CTD..

(Lee FOX ctd.)

Apr 25	Bernard McComiskey	l rtd 3*	Brighton 9-2
Jun 15	Chris Cooper	w pts 6	Telford 9-0
Sep 5	Nico Lucas	drew 6	Brighton 9-4
Oct 3	Nico Lucas	l rtd 2*	Basildon 9-2
Nov 26	Bobby Guynan	w pts 6	Bethnal Green 9-4
Dec 12	Mark Bates	l pts 6	Basildon 9-2-10
1991			
Feb 6	Bobby Guynan	l pts 6	Bethnal Green 9-4
Mar 12	Charlie Coke	w pts 6	Mansfield 9-4-8
Mar 26	Bobby Guynan	w rtd 3*	Bethnal Green 9-8
Jun 11	Neil Smith	l pts 6	Leicester 9-4
Aug 15	Felix Garcia Losada	l ko 3	Marbella
1992			
Jan 21	Richard Woolgar	l pts 6	Norwich 9-5
Feb 19	Mark Bates	l pts 6	Muswell Hill 9-6
Feb 27	Wayne Rigby	w pts 6	Liverpool 9-4
Apr 14	Dean Lynch	l pts 6	Mansfield 9-4
Apr 29	Andrew Robinson	w pts 6	Stoke 9-5-8
May 29	Danny Connelly	l pts 6	Glasgow
Oct 19	Dave McHale	l rsf 3	Glasgow 9-4

Fights 21 Won 8 Lost 12 Drawn 1

Phil FOXON
Light-middleweight
Louth born 12 August 1971

1992			
Mar 19	Tony Massey	l rsf 1	York 11-3
Jun 4	John Duckworth	l rsf 4*	Burnley 11-2

Fights 2 Lost 2

Chris FRANCIS
Super-featherweight
Stepney born 23 October 1968

1991			
Oct 2	Richard Dimmock	w pts 6	Barking 9-5
1992			
Feb 11	Paul Donaghey	l ko 2	Barking 9-7

Fights 2 Won 1 Lost 1

Joe FRATER
Light-heavyweight
Grimsby, born Jamaica 30 April 1961
Grimsby ABC

1980			
Feb 6	Nigel Savory	l rsf 3	Liverpool
Mar 31	John Stone	w rsf 1	Cleethorpes
Apr 14	Paul Heatley	w rsf 5	Manchester
May 12	Chuck Hirschmann	drew 4	Manchester
Jun 16	Joe Dean	w pts 6	Manchester

Sep 9	Nigel Savory	l ko 6	Sheffield
Oct 8	Steve Fox	w pts 4	Stoke
Nov 5	Willie Wright	w pts 6	Evesham
Dec 8	Steve Fenton	l pts 6	Nottingham
1981			
Feb 12	Paul Heatley	w pts 6	Bolton
Mar 30	Steve Fenton	l rsf 1	Cleethorpes
Sep 21	Chris Thorne	w pts 6	Nottingham
Nov 11	Steve Babbs	l pts 6	Evesham
1982			
Feb 1	P.T. Grant	w pts 8	Newcastle
May 10	Devon Bailey	l ko 2	Copthorne
Jun 7	Jonjo Greene	l pts 6	Sheffield
Jun 21	Geoff Rymer	w pts 8	Hull
Sep 4	Andy Straughn	l rsf 3	Bloomsbury
1983-86 inactive			
1987			
Mar 2	Ray Thomas	l pts 6	Birmingham 12-8-8
Oct 7	Crawford Ashley	l rsf 4	Burnley 12-8
Nov 9	Mark Watts	l pts 6	Leicester 12-8
1988			
Mar 22	Darren Jones	l pts 6	Wolverhampton 12-4
Sep 22	Wayne Hawkins	l pts 6	Wolverhampton 12-10
Oct 27	Dave Lawrence	w pts 6	Birmingham 12-9
Nov 10	Wayne Hawkins	l rsf 3	Wolverhampton 12-10-8
1989			
May 8	Decka Williams	l rsf 5	Cleethorpes 13-2
Sep 4	Nigel Rafferty	w pts 6	Cleethorpes 12-6
Dec 4	Tony Lawrence	w pts 6	Cleethorpes 12-8-8
1990			
May 14	Dave Owens	l pts 6	Cleethorpes 12-9
Oct 8	Alan Baptiste	drew 6	Cleethorpes 12-9
Dec 11	Tony Lawrence	w pts 6	Evesham 12-9
1991			
Mar 2	Nicky Vardy	w rsf 1	Cleethorpes
Apr 23	Dave Owens	l pts 6	Evesham 12-9
Oct 23	Gary Delaney	l rsf 1	Bethnal Green 12-13
1992			
Jun 4	Greg Scott-Briggs	w pts 6	Cleethorpes 12-8
Oct 26	Dave Owens	l pts 6	Cleethorpes 12-10

Fights 36 Won 15 Lost 19 Drawn 2

Terry FRENCH
Super-middleweight
Gateshead born 15 January 1967
Swalwell ABC

1988			
Oct 10	Adrian Din	l pts 6	Nottingham 11-1
Nov 3	Graham Burton	l rsf 3	Manchester 11-2
Dec 7	Anthony Lawrence	w pts 6	Stoke 11-4
1989			
Mar 13	Paul Abercromby	w rsf 4	Glasgow 11-3-8
Apr 11	Paul Hendrick	l pts 6	Oldham 11-4
Apr 19	Mickey Murray	w pts 6	Doncaster 11-9
Jun 12	Max Wallace	l pts 6	Battersea 11-12
Sep 11	Seamus Casey	l pts 6	Nottingham 11-10 /CTD..

(Terry FRENCH ctd.)

Oct 2	Hugh Fury	w pts 6	Bradford 11-9
Oct 10	Darren Pilling	l pts 6	Sunderland 11-7
Oct 23	Chris Walker	w pts 6	Nottingham 11-11
Nov 14	David Maxwell	w pts 6	Evesham 11-12
Dec 11	Tony Lawrence	l pts 6	Bradford 12-0
1990			
Jan 22	George Ferrie	l pts 6	Glasgow 11-11
Feb 26	Trevor Barry	w rtd 4*	Bradford 12-3
Mar 20	Steve Davies	w pts 6	Hartlepool 12-2
Apr 9	Sean O'Phoenix	drew 8	Manchester 12-0
Apr 21	Dave Scott	w ko 3	Sunderland 12-3-4
May 15	Simon McDougall	l pts 4	South Shields 12-2
Nov 12	Eddie Collins	w pts 6	Bradford 12-3
Dec 13	Steve Davies	w pts 10	Hartlepool 12-1
	(vacant Northern light-heavyweight title)		
1991			
Apr 3	Sean O'Phoenix	l pts 8	Manchester 12-3
May 10	Eddie Collins	w pts 6	Gateshead 12-3
Oct 10	Simon McDougall	w pts 6	Gateshead 12-6
Nov 14	Quinton Paynter	l ko 6	Gateshead 12-1
1992			
Mar 3	Dave Owens	l ko 1	Houghton-le-Spring 12-7
Oct 23	Spencer Alton	w pts 6	Gateshead 11-11

Fights 27 Won 14 Lost 12 Drawn 1

Andrew FURLONG

Light-middleweight
Hammersmith born 29 July 1967
Heathbrook ABC
Southpaw

1985			
Nov 14	Robert Southey	w pts 6	Wimbledon 9-10
Nov 22	Tony Richards	w pts 6	Longford 9-9-12
1986			
Jan 10	Bill Smith	w pts 6	Fulham 9-12
Jan 30	Marvin P. Gray	w pts 6	Wimbledon 9-10
Feb 27	Barry Bacon	w rsf 6*	Wimbledon 9-9
Apr 15	Willy Wilson	w pts 8	Wimbledon 9-8-4
May 28	Joey Dee	w rsf 2	Catford 9-7
Sep 4	Les Remikie	w pts 8	Wimbledon 9-9-12
Oct 22	Gary Muire	l rsf 2	Greenwich 9-10
Nov 20	Chubby Martin	drew 8	Wimbledon 9-12
1987			
Jan 11	Chubby Martin	w pts 8	Ealing 9-9
Jan 22	Brian Nickels	l pts 8	Bethnal Green 9-7-8
Mar 2	Mark Dinnadge	drew 8	Lewisham 9-11
Mar 18	Tony Borg	w pts 8	Queensway 9-11
Apr 1	Frankie Lake	w pts 8	Southsea 9-10-8
Apr 30	Andrew Prescod	w pts 8	Bethnal Green 9-10-8
May 27	Wayne Weekes	l rsf 1	Lewisham 9-8-8
Sep 25	Oliver Henry	w rtd 5*	Tooting 10-1
Dec 7	Eamonn McAuley	w rtd 3*	Belfast 9-9-8
1988			
Jan 18	Ian Honeywood	l pts 8	NSC 9-11-8
Mar 8	Neil Haddock	w pts 6	Holborn 9-12-12
Sep 19	Tony Richards	l rsf 7	NSC 10-5

Nov 14	Joni Nyman	l rsf 2	Helsinki 10-6
1989			
May 16	Ian John-Lewis	w rsf 3*	Battersea 10-4-4
Jun 12	Rocky Kelly	l rsf 5	Battersea 10-5-4
Oct 11	Brian Robinson	l pts 6	Millwall 11-0
1990			
inactive			
1991			
May 2	Delroy Waul	l rsf 5	Northampton 10-13
Jun 30	Lee Crocker	drew 6	Southwark 11-2-8
1992			
Feb 12	Gary Pemberton	w pts 6	Wembley GH 11-2
Mar 25	Clay O'Shea	drew 6	Albert Hall 11-1-8
May 13	Clay O'Shea	drew 6	Albert Hall 11-1-8
Jun 16	Mickey Hughes	l ko 1	Dagenham 11-0-6
Oct 2	Patrick Vungbo	l rsf 8	Waregem

Fights 33 Won 17 Lost 11 Drawn 5

Hugh FURY
Super-middleweight
Haslingden, born Colchester 23 May 1964

1988			
Dec 1	Paul Hendrick	l rsf 3	Manchester 11-7
1989			
Apr 24	Ian Vokes	w pts 6	Bradford 12-1
Jun 3	Shaun McCrory	l pts 6	Stanley 12-4-12
Jun 20	Darren Jones	l rtd 4*	Doncaster 12-3
Sep 19	Barry Downes	w rsf 1	Northampton 12-3
Oct 2	Terry French	l pts 6	Bradford 12-1
1990			
inactive			
1991			
Oct 17	Wilf McGee	drew 6	Mossley 11-10
Nov 20	Matt Mowatt	l pts 6	Solihull 11-7
Dec 9	Matt Mowatt	w rsf 5*	Bradford 11-7
1992			
Jan 27	Willie Quinn	l rsf 3	Glasgow 11-8-8

Fights 10 Won 3 Lost 6 Drawn 1

NATIONAL PROMOTIONS
INTERNATIONAL BOXING MATCHMAKER AND MANAGER

TERRY LAWLESS

OFFICE:	National House	TELEPHONES:	071 734 1041
	60/66 Wardour Street		071 437 5956
	London	FAX:	071 437 4005
	W1V 3HP	HOME:	0708 476061
	England	FAX:	0708 437757

HEAVYWEIGHT

DAMIAN CAESAR — London - Undefeated in 5 contests

CRUISERWEIGHT

DEREK ANGOL — Commonwealth Champion 26 - 2
PHIL SOUNDY — Benfleet
TERRY DIXON — Harlesdon

LIGHT HEAVYWEIGHT

JOEY PETERS — Southampton - Undefeated in 9 contests

SUPER MIDDLEWEIGHT

MARK BAKER — Sidcup - Undefeated in 3 contests

WELTERWEIGHT

ROY ROWLAND — West Ham - 20 wins 2 losses
STEVE McNESS — Bethnal Green - Former amateur star

LIGHT WELTERWEIGHT

JASON ROWLAND — West Ham - Unbeaten in 9 contests

FEATHERWEIGHT

MARK BOWERS — Southampton - Unbeaten in 2 contests

BANTAMWEIGHT

BRADLEY STONE — Canning Town - Unbeaten in 14 contests

Carl GAFFNEY

Heavyweight
Leeds born 15 April 1964
Market District ABC

1984
May 12	Steve Abadom	w rsf 3	Stoke 16-6-8
Oct 2	Theo Josephs	w pts 6	Leeds 16-3

1985
Jan 23	Alfonso Forbes	l ko 1	Solihull 15-12
Mar 25	Dave Madden	w rsf 1	Huddersfield 15-11
May 30	Denroy Bryan	w rsf 1	Halifax 15-10
Nov 21	Al Malcolm	w pts 8	Huddersfield 15-7-8

1986
Jan 16	Joe Threlfall	l ko 3	Preston 15-11
Feb 20	Chris Devine	w rsf 8	Halifax 15-10
Oct 24	Damien Marignan	l pts 8	Pointe-a-Pitre
Dec 1	Mike Simuwelu	l rsf 7	Arnhem 15-13-8

1987
inactive

1988
Dec 14	Keith Ferdinand	w pts 8	Bethnal Green 16-7

1989
Jun 14	Rodolfo Marin	l rsf 2	Madrid 16-0
Oct 25	Andrei Oreshkin	l rsf 1	Wembley 16-7-8

1990
inactive

1991
May 2	Sean Hunter	w pts 6	Bayswater 16-4
Sep 19	Michael Murray	l rsf 8	Stockport 16-4
	(vacant Central heavyweight title)		

1992
Feb 9	Steve Garber	w pts 6	Bradford 16-13

Fights 16 Won 9 Lost 7

Michael GALE

Light-heavyweight
Leeds, born Cardiff 28 October 1967
Compton Arms ABC & White Rose ABC
1986 NABC Class C champion (w rsf 2 M Wheatcroft)
1987 Northern ABA light-heavyweight champion (w ko 2 G Crawford, w C Edwards, l J Beckles)
1987 England (v Ire, w J O'Sullivan; v Pol, w H Petrich)
1988 Northern ABA light-heavyweight final (w rsf 2 J Oxenham, w J Hunter, l M Coore)
1988 England (v Sco, w rtd 2 J Garvey; v Cze, l M Franek; v WGer, w rtd 3 M Keusgen)
1989 Northern ABA light-heavyweight final (w J Denham, w rsf 1 I Meredith, l P Wright)
1989 Cologne multi-nations (w A Kojoularov, Bul; l J Quintana, Cub)

1989
Sep 21	Dave Lawrence	w rtd 4	Harrogate 12-9
Nov 13	Coco Collins	w ko 1	Manchester 12-13
Dec 5	Randy B. Powell	w rsf 1	Dewsbury 12-6

1990
Jan 11	Cliff Curtis	w rsf 2*	Dewsbury 12-9
Jan 24	Andy Marlow	w rsf 2	Sunderland 12-9
Mar 3	Peter Vosper	w rsf 2	Wembley 12-10
Apr 11	Teo Arvizu	w pts 6	Dewsbury 12-9
Oct 18	Mick Queally	w rsf 5*	Dewsbury 12-10-8
Nov 15	Steve Osborne	w pts 6	Oldham 13-2 /CTD..

(Michael GALE ctd.)

1991
Mar 14	Carlos Christie	w pts 8	Middleton 13-0
Mar 21	David Haycock	w rsf 2	Dewsbury 13-1
May 9	Steve Osborne	w rsf 2	Leeds 12-12-12
Jun 13	Graham Burton	w ko 4	Hull 12-6
Jun 27	Mark Bowen	w pts 8	Leeds 13-0
Oct 30	Denys Cronin	drew 8	Leeds 12-10

1992
Jan 23	John Kaighin	w pts 8	York 12-8
Apr 8	Tony Booth	w pts 8	Leeds 12-9-8
Oct 29	Bobbi Joe Edwards	w pts 10	Leeds 12-5-12

(vacant Central light-heavyweight title)

Fights 18 Won 17 Drawn 1

Patrick GALLAGHER

Lightweight
Islington, born Co. Offaly, Ireland 23 July 1971
Angel ABC
1987 Junior ABA champion
1988 Junior ABA champion
1989 Young England (v Nor, w rsf 2 R Ervik)
1990 Young England (v Hun, l A Tulkan)
1990 ABA lightweight champion (w rsf 2 N King, w rsf 1 S Bardoville, w rsf 3 M Dykes, w I Smith, l M Harley, rplcd Harley, w rsf 1 P Campbell, w M Newton, w B Schwer)
1990 England (v Sc, w rsf 1 M Gowans)
1991 ABA lightweight final (w ko 1 S Frailing, w I Smith, w rsf 3 M Harley, w S Cole, w A McDowall, wthdrw.)

1992
Dec 22	Karl Taylor	w rsf 3*	Mayfair 9-10

Fights 1 Won 1

Paul GAMBLE

Middleweight
Norwich born 31 March 1964
Norwich Lads ABC & Broadside Oasis ABC
1982 Eastern ABA light-middle champ (w rsf 2 D Duthrie, w B Barnes, w rsf 3 A Ashgar, wthdrw)

1984
Dec 3	Rex Weaver	w rsf 2	Manchester 11-8

1985
Jan 31	John Hargin	w rsf 2	Basildon 11-7
Feb 26	Dave Scott	w pts 6	Bethnal Green 11-8
Apr 1	Johnny Graham	l pts 6	Mayfair 11-8-8
Apr 18	Alan Baptiste	l pts 6	NSC 11-8
Sep 7	Neil Munn	l pts 6	Douglas 11-12
Nov 6	Mickey Kidd	w pts 6	Evesham 11-10

1986
Feb 3	Alan Baptiste	l ko 8	Dulwich 11-11
Mar 15	Cliff Curtis	w pts 6	Norwich 12-2
Sep 10	Dennis Hogan	w rsf 5*	Norwich 12-2

1987-91 inactive

1992
Sep 8	Gilbert Jackson	l rsf 1*	Norwich 11-5

Fights 11 Won 6 Lost 5

Steve GARBER

Heavyweight
Bradford born 20 June 1962
Bradford YMCA ABC

1985
Apr 22	Mick Cordon	drew 6	Bradford 15-2
May 30	Mick Cordon	l pts 6	Blackburn 14-9
Jul 2	Joe Threlfall	w rsf 2	Preston
Oct 3	Dave Shelton	w pts 4	Bradford 15-1
Nov 27	Mick Cordon	w pts 6	Bradford 15-7

1986
Feb 6	Mick Cordon	l pts 6	Adwick 15-6-8
Apr 27	Mick Cordon	l pts 6	Doncaster
May 22	Sean Daly	w pts 6	Horwich 15-3
Sep 18	Gary McConnell	l pts 6	Weston 16-1-8
Sep 25	Carl Timbrell	w pts 6	Wolverhampton 16-0
Oct 20	Dave Madden	w pts 4	Bradford 15-9
Dec 1	Tony Hallett	w pts 6	Nottingham 15-10

1987
Feb 24	Gary McConnell	l ko 1	Ilford 15-6
Oct 7	Gipsy John Fury	l pts 6	Burnley 16-1

1988
Jan 18	Mick Cordon	w pts 6	Bradford 16-0
Feb 11	John Love	l ko 1	Gravesend 16-0-8
Mar 21	Ted Shaw	w ko 4	Leicester
Apr 20	Manny Burgo	l pts 6	Gravesend 16-0
May 23	Ted Shaw	w ko 3	Bradford 16-0
Sep 26	Gifford Shillingford	w rsf 4	Bradford 16-0
Oct 25	Paul Lister	l pts 6	Hartlepool 15-10
Nov 17	Michael Murray	l pts 6	Stockport

1989
Jan 18	Peter Nyman	w pts 6	Albert Hall 16-3
May 19	Joe Threlfall	w rsf 3	Gateshead 15-12
Oct 10	Lennox Lewis	l ko 1	Hull 16-0

1990
Mar 20	Chris Hubbert	w rsf 1	Hartlepool 15-10
May 5	Knud Blin	l pts 6	Hamburg
Nov 12	David Jules	w rsf 6*	Bradford 16-0
Nov 30	Steve Gee	w pts 6	Birmingham 16-0

1991
Mar 19	Al Malcolm	w rsf 5	Birmingham 16-0
Apr 30	Michael Murray	l ko 1	Stockport 16-0
May 31	Axel Schultz	l ko 5	Berlin 16-5-8
Oct 10	Paul Lister	l pts 8	Gateshead 16-0

1992
Feb 9	Carl Gaffney	l pts 6	Bradford 15-8-8
Apr 5	David Jules	w rsf 4	Bradford 16-0
May 8	Alex Miroschnichenko	l ko 1	Waregem 15-8-12
Jul 18	Henry Akinwande	l rtd 2	Manchester 16-0

Fights 37 Won 18 Lost 18 Drawn 1

Des GARGANO

Bantamweight
Manchester, born Brighton 20 December 1960
Real name: Des Southern
Boarshaw ABC
1984 East Lancs ABA bantamweight champion (w A Finch, l rsf 2 J Hyland)

1985
Jan 25	Sugar Gibiliru	l pts 4	Liverpool 8-13
Mar 18	Sugar Gibiliru	l pts 6	Liverpool 8-13-8
Apr 24	Glen McLaggon	l pts 6	Stoke 8-10
Jun 3	Anthony Wakefield	drew 6	Manchester 9-0
Jun 17	Anthony Wakefield	w pts 6	Manchester 8-10-8
Oct 3	Anthony Brown	l pts 6	Liverpool 8-12
Oct 13	Gary Maxwell	l pts 6	Sheffield 8-12-8
Dec 9	Robert Newbiggin	w pts 6	Nottingham 9-0
Dec 16	Gipsy Johnny	w pts 6	Bradford 8-10

1986
Feb 24	Kevin Taylor	w pts 6	Bradford 8-12
Apr 1	Carl Cleasby	l pts 6	Leeds 8-13
Apr 7	Gerry McBride	w pts 6	Manchester
Apr 29	Pat Clinton	l pts 6	Manchester 8-7
Sep 23	David Ingram	l pts 6	Batley 8-7
Nov 24	Andrew Steadman	l pts 6	Leicester 8-11
Dec 3	Sean Murphy	l pts 6	Muswell Hill 8-9
Dec 15	Tony Heath	l pts 8	Loughborough 8-11

1987
Jan 30	Nigel Crook	l pts 6	Liverpool 8-10
Feb 16	Pat Clinton	l pts 6	Glasgow 8-10
Apr 13	Jimmy Lee	w pts 6	Manchester 8-12-8
May 26	John Green	l pts 6	Oldham 8-9
Oct 19	John Green	l pts 6	Manchester 8-8
Oct 28	Paul Thornton	w rsf 6	Stoke 8-10-8
Nov 9	Tony Heath	l pts 6	Leicester 8-12-4

1988
Jan 26	Graham O'Malley	l pts 4	Hartlepool 8-10
Mar 23	Lambsy Kayani	l pts 6	Sheffield 9-0
Mar 29	Graham O'Malley	l pts 8	Middlesbrough 8-7
Apr 25	Ronnie Stephenson	w pts 8	Bradford 8-11
Jun 6	Darrell Pettit	w pts 6	Manchester 9-0
Jun 13	Joe Mullen	l pts 6	Glasgow 8-9
Sep 5	Wull Strike	drew 6	Glasgow 8-10
Sep 22	John Davison	l pts 8	Newcastle 8-8
Sep 29	John Davison	l pts 8	Sunderland 8-10-8
Oct 10	Shane Silvester	l pts 8	Edgbaston 8-6-8
Oct 18	Peter English	l pts 4	Manchester 8-12
Oct 28	Eyup Can	l pts 6	Copenhagen
Nov 21	Ronnie Stephenson	w pts 6	Leicester 8-10
Nov 29	Chris Clarkson	w pts 6	Manchester
Dec 7	Renny Edwards	l pts 6	Port Talbot 8-7
Dec 16	Jimmy Clark	l pts 6	Brentwood 8-9-8

1989
Feb 14	Nigel Crook	l pts 10	Manchester
	(eliminator, Central bantamweight title)		
Mar 17	Jimmi Bredahl	l pts 6	Braedstrup
Apr 17	Mark Priestley	w pts 8	Middleton 8-12
May 10	Mark Goult	l pts 8	Solihull 8-13-8
May 17	Mark Geraghty	l pts 8	Glasgow 8-11-8

Date	Opponent	Result	Venue
Jun 12	Neil Parry	w pts 6	Manchester 8-8
Jul 11	Chris Clarkson	l pts 6	Batley 8-12
Sep 4	Ronnie Stephenson	w pts 6	Hull 8-9-8
Sep 11	Paul Dever	w rsf 1	Manchester 8-9
Sep 20	Miguel Matthews	w pts 6	Stoke 8-12
Oct 5	Wayne Windle	w pts 6	Middleton 8-11
Oct 16	Wayne Windle	l pts 6	Manchester 8-13
Oct 31	Dave McNally	l pts 6	Manchester
Nov 10	Kruga Hydes	l pts 6	Liverpool 8-8
Nov 20	Dave Buxton	l pts 6	Leicester 8-8
Nov 30	Noel Carroll	l pts 6	Middleton
Dec 11	Joe Kelly	l pts 6	Mayfair 8-10
1990			
Feb 14	Danny Porter	l pts 6	Brentwood 8-12
Mar 6	Bradley Stone	l pts 6	Bethnal Green 8-11
Mar 17	John Lowey	l rsf 6	Belfast 8-10-8
Apr 24	Jamie Morris	w pts 4	Stoke 9-1-8
May 9	Terry Collins	l pts 6	Albert Hall 9-5
May 16	Tony Doyle	w pts 6	Hull
Jun 11	Steve Armstrong	w pts 6	Manchester 8-7
Sep 5	John George	l pts 6	Stoke 8-11-12
Oct 1	Tony Smith	w pts 6	Cleethorpes 8-9-8
Oct 9	Brian Robb	l pts 6	Wolverhampton 8-8
Oct 22	John George	l pts 6	Cleethorpes 8-9
Nov 26	Tony Smith	w pts 8	Bury 8-7
Dec 3	Tony Smith	w pts 6	Cleethorpes 8-8
Dec 11	Stuart Fisher-mack	w pts 8	Evesham 8-7-8
1991			
Jan 16	Tony Smith	w pts 6	Stoke 8-8
Feb 6	Tim Driscoll	l pts 6	Bethnal Green 8-12
Feb 28	Carl Roberts	w pts 6	Bury 8-9
May 7	James Drummond	l pts 8	Glasgow 8-9-4
May 16	Jimmy Owens	l rsf 2*	Liverpool 8-12
Aug 19	Petteri Rissanen	l pts 4	Helsinki
Oct 2	Eric George	l pts 6	Solihull 8-8
Oct 24	Eddie Cook	l rsf 5	Glasgow 8-9
Nov 29	Harald Geier	l dis 8	Lansenkirken-Frohsdorf
1992			
Jan 31	Eddie Cook	l pts 6	Glasgow 8-9
Feb 24	Colin Lynch	l pts 6	Coventry 8-13
Mar 4	Neil Armstrong	l pts 6	Glasgow 8-9
Mar 11	Dennis Oakes	l pts 6	Stoke
Apr 27	David Ramsden	l pts 6	Bradford 8-11
Jun 1	Mark Hargreaves	l pts 6	Manchester 8-10-8
Jun 8	David Ramsden	l pts 6	Bradford 8-8-8
Oct 7	Naseem Hamed	l rsf 4	Sunderland 8-8
Nov 20	Paul Lloyd	l pts 4	Liverpool 8-8-8

Fights 89 Won 26 Lost 61 Drawn 2

Al GARRETT

Featherweight
Glasgow born 21 December 1966
Real name: Al Garrity
Partick ABC, Croy Miners ABC
1989 Scottish ABA featherweight prelim (l M McCutcheon)
1990 Scottish ABA featherweight quarter-final (l M Deveney)

1991
Sep 23	Robert Braddock	drew 6	Glasgow 9-2
Dec 9	Chris Jickells	l rsf 2	Bradford 9-2

1992
Nov 18	Colin Innes	drew 6	Solihull 9-1-4

Fights 3 Lost 1 Drawn 2

Dermot GASCOIGNE

Heavyweight
Bexleyheath
Finchley ABC, Metropolitan Police ABC
1991 SW London ABA super-heavyweight champion (w.o., l H Senior)
1992 NW London ABA super-heavyweight final (l D Holness)

1992
Dec 17	John Harewood	w rsf 5	Barking 15-7-8

Fights 1 Won 1

Steve GEE

Heavyweight
Birmingham, born Bradford 1 April 1961
Real name: Steve Egege
Nechells ABC

1980
Apr 15	Mike Creasy	w rsf 5	Blackpool
Apr 29	Don Charles	w rsf 2	AASC 13-13-8
May 14	Colin Flute	w pts 6	Stoke 14-2
Sep 22	Colin Flute	w pts 6	Birmingham 14-10
Oct 19	Jim Burns	w rsf 3	Birmingham 13-9
Oct 30	Derek Simpkin	drew 6	Wolverhampton 13-10
Nov 10	Bob Hennessey	l pts 8	Birmingham 13-10

1981
Jan 19	Martin Nee	l rsf 5	Wimbledon
Mar 11	Rocky Burton	w pts 8	Solihull 14-2-8
Mar 25	Ian Scotting	w pts 8	Doncaster
Apr 28	Theo Josephs	w pts 8	Leeds
Sep 11	Jim Burns	l pts 8	Edgbaston
Oct 5	Hughroy Currie	l pts 6	Birmingham
Nov 8	Joe Christle	l pts 6	Navan

1982
Jan 12	Martin Herdman	w pts 6	Bethnal Green
Feb 18	Noel Quarless	l pts 6	Liverpool
Mar 9	Martin Nee	w pts 8	Hornsey
Mar 30	Rudi Pika	l pts 8	Wembley
Apr 22	Joe Christle	w rsf 6	Liverpool
Jun 22	Tommy Kiely	w rsf 7	Hornsey
Sep 7	Stan McDermott	l pts 8	Hornsey

Oct 16	Mel Christle	w rsf 6*	Killarney
Nov 2	Martin Nee	w rtd 5*	Hornsey
Nov 14	Joe Christle	drew 6	Navan
Nov 22	Billy Aird	l pts 8	Lewisham
Dec 7	Theo Josephs	w pts 8	Southend
1983			
Apr 14	Winston Allen	w pts 8	Basildon
Jun 14	Mike Perkins	l pts 8 (s)	Atlantic City
Sep 3	Pierre Coetzer	l pts 8	Johannesburg
Dec 17	Anders Eklund	l rsf 5*	Mariehamn
1984			
Jan 28	Daniel Falconi	l pts 6	Marsala
1985			
May 1	Al Syben	l pts 8	Brussels
Jul 1	Rudi Pika	l pts 8	NSC 15-5
Nov 5	Gary Mason	l rsf 5*	Wembley 15-10-4
Dec 4	Gary Mason	l rsf 5*	Albert Hall 15-11-8
1986			
Jan 30	Derek Williams	l pts 6	Wimbledon 16-0
Apr 30	Andy Straughn	l pts 8	Edmonton 14-10
May 23	Andy Gerrard	l pts 8	Newport 15-2
Oct 16	Paul Lister	l pts 8	Newcastle 15-0
Nov 29	Keith Ferdinand	l pts 6	Battersea 15-3-8
Dec 16	Ian Priest	l pts 6	Alfreton 15-4
1987			
Feb 22	Derek Williams	l pts 6	Wembley GH 15-2
1988-89			
inactive			
1990			
Nov 30	Steve Garber	l pts 6	Birmingham 15-1-12
1991			
Jan 23	Manny Burgo	l pts 6	Brentwood 16-0
Mar 13	Michael Richards	l pts 6	Stoke 15-4
Apr 6	Corrie Sanders	l rsf 5	Darlington 15-11
May 30	Al Malcolm	drew 6	Birmingham 15-12
Jul 12	Garing Lane	l pts 8	Cannes
Sep 13	Axel Schulz	l ko 2	Dusseldorf 16-5
Nov 15	Massimo Migliaccio	l pts 6	Omegna 16-6-12
Dec 7	Michael Murray	l rsf 7	Manchester 15-13-4
1992			
Oct 17	J.A. Bugner	l pts 6	Wembley 15-6
Nov 27	Brian Nielsen	l pts 6	Randers 16-3

Fights 53 Won 16 Lost 34 Drawn 3

Lou GENT

Super-middleweight
Streatham, born 21 April 1965
Mitcham ABC & New Addington ABC
1981 Junior ABA final (l G McCrory)
1984 SE London ABA light-heavyweight final (l D Angol)

1984			
Sep 18	Wes Taylor	w pts 6	Wimbledon 12-9
1985			
Feb 5	Harry Andrews	w pts 6	Battersea 12-8
Feb 26	Lee White	w pts 6	Battersea 12-10
Mar 23	Simon Harris	l pts 6	Strand /CTD..

(Lou GENT ctd.)

Apr 30	Tee Jay	drew 6	Wimbledon 12-9
Sep 12	Harry Andrews	w rsf 2	Wimbledon 12-9
Oct 25	Winston Burnett	w pts 6	Fulham 12-7-8
Nov 14	Winston Burnett	w pts 8	Wimbledon 12-8
Dec 11	Serg Fame	l rsf 2*	Fulham 12-7
1986			
Feb 27	John Williams	w rsf 4	Wimbledon 12-9-12
Mar 20	Serg Fame	l ko 2	Wimbledon 12-6-12
Jun 16	Blaine Logsdon	w pts 8	Manchester 12-10
Sep 4	Chris Devine	w rsf 6	Wimbledon 12-11-8
Oct 16	Jerry Reed	w rsf 7	Wimbledon 12-12-12
Nov 20	Gipsy Carmen	w ko 1	Wimbledon 12-12
1987			
Jan 29	Glazz Campbell	w pts 6	Wimbledon 12-9-12
Mar 26	Danny Lawford	l rsf 7	Wimbledon 12-11-12
1988			
Mar 18	Abner Blackstock	w rsf 5	Battersea 13-3
Apr 20	Glenn McCrory	l rtd 8*	Gateshead 13-1-8
	(British and Commonwealth cruiserweight titles)		
1989			
Feb 16	Lennie Howard	w rsf 2	Battersea 13-3-4
	(vacant Southern cruiserweight title)		
Apr 26	Ezeke Cyril Minnus	w dis 3	Battersea 13-6
1990			
Feb 22	Gipsy Carmen	w pts 10	Battersea 13-4
	(Southern cruiserweight title)		
Mar 28	Johnny Nelson	l rsf 4	Bethnal Green 13-2-14
	(British cruiserweight title)		
Oct 18	Jose Seys	w pts 8	Battersea 12-4-8
1991			
Mar 20	Derek Myers	w rsf 7	Battersea 12-3
	(eliminator, British light-heavyweight title)		
May 16	Gus Mendes	w ko 8	Battersea 12-3
Oct 30	Henry Wharton	drew 12	Leeds 11-11-12
	(Commonwealth super-middleweight title)		
1992			
Feb 25	Fidel Castro	l pts 12	Crystal Palace 12-0
	(British super-middleweight title)		
May 12	Johnny Melfah	l rsf 3*	Crystal Palace 12-0-12
Jul 14	Simon Collins	w rsf 5	Mayfair 12-1-12
Sep 15	Karl Barwise	w rsf 6*	Crystal Palace 12-1

Fights 31 Won 21 Lost 8 Drawn 2

Mark GERAGHTY

Super-featherweight
Glasgow, born Paisley 25 August 1965
Argo ABC, Northampton ABC
1987 Scottish ABA lightweight prelims (w A Cameron, l M Logan)
1988 Scottish ABA lightweight semi-final (w J Keatings, l dis 3 M Gowans)

1988			
Nov 14	Mark Priestley	w pts 6	Glasgow 8-13
1989			
Jan 27	Gordon Stobie	w pts 6	Durham 8-12-8
Feb 14	Gary Hickman	l pts 6	Sunderland 8-12-12
Mar 9	Chris Clarkson	w pts 6	Glasgow 9-1-8
Mar 20	Ian Johnson	l pts 6	Nottingham 9-1-8

Apr 24	Sean Hogg	w pts 6	Glasgow 9-4-4
May 17	Des Gargano	w pts 8	Glasgow 8-12
Jun 9	Jimmi Bredahl	l pts 6	Aarhus
Oct 2	Steve Winstanley	l pts 6	Bradford 9-2
Nov 20	Gordon Shaw	w rsf 3*	Glasgow 8-11-8

1990

Jan 22	Neil Leitch	w pts 8	Glasgow 9-2
Mar 19	Joe Donahoe	l rsf 3*	Glasgow 9-2
Sep 17	Peter Judson	l pts 8	Glasgow 9-5-8
Oct 8	Peter Judson	w pts 8	Glasgow 9-6-8
Nov 19	Tony Doyle	w pts 8	Glasgow 9-7
Nov 27	Muhammad Shaffique	l pts 8	Glasgow 9-5

1991

| Mar 6 | Neil Leitch | w pts 10 | Glasgow 9-3-8 |

(vacant Scottish super-featherweight title)

May 1	Peter Buckley	l pts 8	Solihull 9-1-8
Jun 3	Neil Leitch	l pts 8	Glasgow
Sep 23	Neil Leitch	w pts 10	Glasgow 9-2-12

(Scottish super-featherweight title)

| Oct 9 | Chris Clarkson | w pts 6 | Glasgow |
| Nov 20 | Tony Feliciello | l rsf 4 | Solihull 9-3-8 |

1992

Feb 24	Colin Innes	w pts 8	Glasgow 9-6
Mar 18	Barrie Kelley	w pts 8	Glasgow 9-6-8
Sep 19	Micky Hall	w pts 6	Glasgow 9-6-8
Oct 19	Kevin Lowe	w pts 8	Glasgow 9-5-8
Nov 28	Alan Levene	l pts 6	Manchester 9-6

Fights 27 Won 16 Lost 11

Tony GIBBS

Welterweight
East Ham, born 20 January 1964

1987

| Oct 8 | Barry Messam | w pts 6 | Bethnal Green 10-6 |

1988

Feb 25	Mike Russell	l pts 6	Bethnal Green 10-4
Mar 8	Dave Lake	w pts 6	Holborn 10-7
Apr 13	Dave Lake	w rsf 1	Gravesend 10-6-8
May 5	Mark Pearce	l rsf 4	Bethnal Green 10-0
Nov 2	Gary Logan	l pts 6	Southwark 10-7
Nov 15	Tony Britland	drew 6	NSC 10-7-8
Nov 30	Derek Grainger	l ko 3	Southwark 10-9

1989

Mar 13	Dennis Sullivan	w pts 6	NSC 10-8-8
Apr 6	Davey Hughes	l pts 6	Cardiff 10-7
Sep 15	B.F.Williams	l pts 6	High Wycombe 10-2-8
Sep 28	Carlos Chase	l pts 6	Battersea 10-3-12
Oct 12	Leigh Wicks	l ko 2	Southwark 10-4-8
Nov 30	Ross Hale	l pts 6	Marble Arch 10-0

1990

Apr 5	Andy Robins	w pts 6	Southend 10-2
Jun 5	Tim Harmey	l pts 6	Eltham
Oct 18	Felix Kelly	drew 6	Battersea 10-8
Nov 16	Lindon Scarlett	l pts 6	Telford 10-5

1991

| May 8 | Robert McCracken | l ko 1 | Albert Hall 10-12-8   /CTD.. |

(Tony GIBBS ctd.)

Nov 20 1992	Robert Wright	l rtd 2	Solihull 10-9-8
Apr 2	Dean Hollington	l ko 1	Basildon 10-4

Fights 21 Won 5 Lost 14 Drawn 2

Sugar GIBILIRU
Light-welterweight
Liverpool born 13 July 1966
Real name: Dramani Gibiliru
Myrtle ABC

1984
Nov 30	Steve Benny	l pts 4	Liverpool 9-4

1985
Jan 25	Des Gargano	w pts 4	Liverpool 9-2
Feb 4	Martin Power	w rtd 3*	Liverpool 9-2
Mar 18	Des Gargano	w pts 6	Liverpool 9-3
Mar 29	Craig Windsor	l pts 6	Liverpool 9-2
Apr 17	Carl Gaynor	l pts 6	Nantwich 9-2
Apr 29	Carl Gaynor	l pts 6	Liverpool 9-3
Oct 7	Martin Power	w rsf 4	Liverpool 9-2
Nov 11	Nigel Senior	w rsf 5	Liverpool 9-2
Dec 6	Anthony Brown	l pts 8	Liverpool 9-4

1986
Jan 22	Floyd Havard	l pts 6	Muswell Hill 9-7
Mar 4	Brian Roche	l pts 8	Manchester 9-11
Apr 7	Muhammad Lovelock	drew 8	Manchester 9-9-12
May 24	Floyd Havard	l pts 8	Manchester 9-10
Jun 16	Brian Roche	l pts 8	Manchester 9-11-8
Sep 22	Carl Crook	l pts 6	Bradford 9-9
Oct 14	Muhammad Lovelock	drew 8	Manchester 9-9-8
Nov 17	Simon Eubanks	l pts 8	Dulwich 10-0
Nov 20	Joey Jacobs	l pts 8	Bredbury 9-12
Dec 15	Carl Crook	l pts 8	Bradford 9-12

1987
Jan 13	Edward Lloyd	l pts 8	Oldham 9-11
Apr 24	Dean Binch	w ko 3	Everton 9-8
Jun 15	Muhammad Lovelock	l pts 8	Manchester 9-11
Sep 20	Ray Taylor	l pts 6	Oldham 10-0
Nov 16	Robert Harkin	drew 8	Glasgow 10-2
Dec 5	Glyn Rhodes	l pts 8	Doncaster 10-2

1988
Mar 1	Pat Barrett	drew 8	Manchester 10-1
Apr 13	Peter Till	l pts 8	Wolverhampton 9-12-8
Apr 28	Mark Kelly	drew 6	Manchester 9-12
Sep 10	Jean-Charles Meuret	l pts 8	Geneva
Sep 28	Glyn Rhodes	drew 8	Solihull 10-1
Dec 1	Mark Kelly	l pts 6	Manchester 9-12
Dec 14	Andy Holligan	l pts 8	Liverpool 10-5

1989
Jan 25	Ray Taylor	l pts 6	Solihull 10-6
Apr 11	Pat Barrett	l ko 8	Oldham 9-13-8
	(Central light-welterweight title)		
May 31	Tony Banks	w ko 5	Manchester 9-10
Jun 21	Rudi Valentino	l pts 6	Eltham 9-10
Sep 19	Nigel Wenton	l pts 8	Belfast 9-8-4
Nov 16	Tony Foster	l pts 8	Manchester 9-7

1990			
Jan 30	Tony Foster	w pts 10	Manchester 9-7-8
	(vacant Central lightweight title)		
Mar 7	Peter Gabbitus	w rtd 6	Doncaster 9-3-8
	(vacant Central super-featherweight title)		
May 1	Mark Reefer	l rsf 5	Oldham 9-4
	(Commonwealth super-featherweight title)		
Sep 7	Kris McAdam	w pts 8	Liverpool 9-12
Nov 19	Frankie Foster	drew 8	Manchester 9-6
Dec 17	Dean Bramhald	w pts 8	Manchester 10-0
1991			
Jan 29	Nigel Bradley	w pts 8	Stockport 9-13
Apr 30	Robert Dickie	w rsf 9	Stockport 9-3-12
	(British super-featherweight title)		
Sep 19	John Doherty	l pts 12	Stockport 9-4
	(British super-featherweight title)		
Dec 7	Paul Harvey	l pts 12	Manchester 9-2-8
	(Commonwealth super-featherweight title)		
1992			
Mar 31	Frankie Foster	w pts 8	Stockport 9-6-8
Jun 27	Michael Ayers	l rsf 6	Quinta Do Lago 9-10
Dec 1	Ross Hale	l ko 1	Bristol 9-13-12

Fights 52 Won 14 Lost 31 Drawn 7

Barry GLANISTER

Lightweight
East Grinstead, born Warrington 27 April 1964
Southpaw

1991			
May 16	Bobby Beckles	l rsf 1	Battersea 9-12
Oct 24	Moses Sentamu	l pts 6	Bayswater 9-12
Nov 13	Kevin McKillam	l pts 6	Liverpool 9-10
1992			
Jan 21	Danny Kett	l ko 1	Norwich 10-0

Fights 4 Lost 4

G.G.GODDARD

Super-featherweight
Alfreton, born Swaziland 6 April 1966
Real name: Godfrey Goddard
No amateur experience

1990			
Nov 22	Shaun Hickey	w rtd 4*	Ilkeston 9-5
1991			
Jan 17	Paul Chedgzoy	w rsf 3*	Alfreton 9-7
May 13	Finn McCool	l pts 6	Northampton 9-10
May 20	Finn McCool	w pts 6	Bradford 9-7
Oct 23	Chubby Martin	l pts 8	Stoke 9-10
1992			
Feb 4	Kevin Toomey	l pts 6	Alfreton 9-8
Mar 11	Micky Hall	drew 6	Solihull 9-7
Apr 28	Michael Clynch	l rtd 4	Corby 9-5
Jul 9	Davey McHale	l rtd 4	Glasgow 9-5-12
Nov 18	Ian McGirr	l pts 6	Solihull 9-5

Fights 10 Won 3 Lost 6 Drawn 1

Val GOLDING

Middleweight
Croydon born 9 May 1964
Real name: Valentine Golding
St Monicas ABC & Fitzroy Lodge ABC
1987 SE London ABA middleweight champion (w ko 1 D Ould, w rsf 1 D Gaywood, l rsf 1 R Douglas)
1988 NE London ABA middleweight final (w ko 3 D White, w rtd 2 J Robinson, l ko 1 S Butler)
1989 NE London ABA middleweight champion (w rsf 3 R Andre, w rsf 1 C O'Reilly, l ko 2 J Woods)

1989
Jul 17	Robert Harron	w rsf 2	Stanmore 11-6-12
Oct 5	Seamus Casey	w pts 6	Stevenage 11-6
Dec 12	Neil Munn	w rsf 2	Brentford 11-8

1990
Apr 14	Ian Strudwick	l pts 6	Albert Hall 11-6-6
Sep 22	Franki Moro	w rsf 6	Albert Hall 11-9
Oct 15	Tod Nadon	l rsf 6	Lewisham 11-10

1991
Sep 4	Russell Washer	w rtd 5	Bethnal Green 11-7-8
Oct 29	Graham Jenner	w rsf 3	Albert Hall 11-8-8

1992
Jan 18	Quinton Paynter	l rsf 7	Albert Hall 11-7
Sep 26	Kevin Sheeran	l rsf 1	Olympia 11-3

Fights 10 Won 6 Lost 4

Zak GOLDMAN

Light-heavyweight
Doncaster, born Alnwick 19 July 1964
Real name: Robert Timothy Goldman
Tom Hill Youth ABC
Southpaw

1992
Dec 7	Paul Hanlon	l pts 6	Birmingham 12-8
Dec 15	Kenley Price	l rtd 2	Liverpool 13-3

Fights 2 Lost 2

Steve GOODWIN

Light-middleweight
Derby born 7 February 1966
Merlin Youth ABC
1992 Midlands ABA light-middleweight final (w rtd 2* K Gibbons, w C Harrison, w C Williams, l M Lee)

1992
Apr 13	John Duckworth	w pts 6	Manchester 11-2
Apr 29	John Corcoran	w pts 8	Stoke 10-10
Sep 3	Steve McNess	l pts 6	Dunstable 10-11
Sep 29	Mark Dawson	w rsf 1*	Stoke
Oct 19	John Bosco	l rsf 2*	Mayfair 11-2
Dec 7	Mark Dawson	l pts 6	Mayfair 11-0

Fights 6 Won 3 Lost 3

Alan GRAHAM
Lightweight
Newcastle born 7 October 1973
Grainger Park ABC
1991 North-East Division ABA featherweight final (l S Hurcombe)
1992 North-East Division ABA lightweight semi-final (l A Green)

1992
Sep 21	Gary Burrell	l pts 6	Glasgow 9-6-8
Nov 9	Gary Burrell	l pts 6	Bradford 9-6
Dec 10	Terry Smith	w pts 6	Corby 9-6

Fights 3 Won 1 Lost 2

Herol GRAHAM
Middleweight
Sheffield, born Nottingham 13 September 1959
Southpaw
Radford ABC
1973 National Schools champion
1974 National Schools final (l D Hubbick)
1975 National Schools champion (w S Lee)
1975 NABC Class A final (l T Goodwin)
1976 National Schools champion (w K Moses)
1976 NABC Class B champion (w K Sherwood)
1976 Junior ABA champion (w A Worthington)
1977 NABC Class C final (l M Courtney)
1977 Young England (vWGer, w rsf 3 G Bachl, w rsf 3 H Kunstler; v EGer, w rtd 1 V Schmidt)
1977 Midlands ABA middleweight champion (w rsf 3 G Slater, w Forbes, l J Harrington)
1978 England (v WGer, w H Sixt)
1978 Gold medal, Dutch multi-nations (w D Skaro, Yug)
1978 ABA middleweight champion (w J Claxton, w J Humphreys, w rsf 2 E Ellis, w J Harrington, w L James, w R Mogford, w D Parkes)

1978
Nov 28	Vivian Waite	w pts 6	Sheffield
Dec 4	Curtis Marsh	w rtd 1	Southend

1979
Jan 22	Jimmy Roberts	w rsf 2	Bradford
Feb 12	Dave Southwell	w pts 8	Reading
Feb 28	Dave Southwell	w pts 8	Stoke
Mar 27	George Walker	w pts 8	Southend
Apr 27	Mac Nicholson	w pts 8	Newcastle
May 16	Greg George	w pts 8	Sheffield
Sep 26	Lloyd James	w pts 8	Sheffield
Oct 27	Billy Ahearne	w rsf 3	Barnsley
Nov 27	Errol McKenzie	w pts 8	Sheffield

1980
Feb 12	Glen McEwan	w pts 8	Sheffield
Apr 22	George Danahar	w pts 8	Sheffield
Sep 9	Joey Mack	w pts 8	Sheffield 11-2
Oct 30	Larry Mayes	w rsf 4	Liverpool 11-0-8

1981
Jan 22	Lancelot Innis	w pts 10	Liverpool
Mar 24	Pat Thomas (British light-middleweight title)	w pts 15	Sheffield 10-13-12
Jun 17	Prince Rodney	w rsf 1	Sheffield 11-4-12
Nov 25	Kenny Bristol (Commonwealth light-middleweight title)	w pts 15	Sheffield

1982
Feb 24	Chris Christian (British & Commonwealth light-middleweight titles)	w rsf 9	Sheffield /CTD..

(Herol GRAHAM ctd.)

Apr 22	Fred Coransen	w pts 10	Liverpool
Sep 30	Hunter Clay	w pts 15	Lagos
	(Commonwealth light-middleweight title)		
1983			
Mar 15	Tony Nelson	w rtd 5*	Wembley
May 23	Clemente Tshinza	w ko 2	Sheffield
	(vacant European light-middleweight title)		
Oct 11	Carlos Betancourt	w ko 1	Albert Hall 11-3-12
Dec 9	Germain LeMaitre	w rsf 8*	St Nazaire 10-13-8
	(European light-middleweight title)		
1984			
Jul 22	Lindell Holmes	w rsf 5*	Sheffield
Sep 25	Irvin Hines	w ko 2	Wembley 11-7-8
Oct 16	Jose Seys	w rsf 6	Albert Hall 12-2
Nov 26	Liam Coleman	w rsf 3	Sheffield 11-12-12
1985			
Mar 6	Jose Rosemain	w ko 5	Albert Hall 11-9
Apr 25	Jimmy Price	w ko 1	Shoreditch
	(vacant British middleweight title)		
Oct 16	Roberto Ruiz	w rsf 2*	Albert Hall
Dec 3	Sanderline Williams	w pts 10	Belfast 11-8-8
1986			
Feb 5	Ayub Kalule	w rsf 10	Sheffield 11-5-4
	(European middleweight title)		
Jun 23	Ernie Rabotte	w rsf 1	Las Vegas 11-6-12
Nov 4	Mark Kaylor	w rtd 8*	Wembley 11-4-15
	(European middleweight title)		
1987			
Jan 17	Charlie Boston	w rtd 7	Belfast 11-7-8
May 26	Sumbu Kalambay	l pts 12	Wembley 11-5
	(European middleweight title)		
Dec 5	Ricky Stackhouse	w rsf 8	Doncaster 11-6
1988			
Jun 8	James Cook	w rsf 5	Sheffield 11-6
	(vacant British middleweight title)		
Nov 23	Johnny Melfah	w rsf 5	Bethnal Green 11-6
	(British middleweight title)		
1989			
May 10	Mike McCallum	l pts 12 (s)	Albert Hall
	(vacant WBA middleweight title)		
Oct 25	Rod Douglas	w rsf 9	Wembley 11-6
	(British middleweight title)		
1990			
Apr 11	Ismael Negron	w ko 3	Dewsbury 11-5
Nov 24	Julian Jackson	l ko 4	Benalmadena 11-6
	(vacant WBC middleweight title)		
1991			
Dec 10	John Ashton	w rsf 6	Sheffield 11-6
	(British middleweight title)		
1992			
Mar 12	Sumbu Kalambay	l pts 12	Pesaro 11-5-8
	(European middleweight title)		
Sep 23	Frank Grant	l rsf 9	Leeds 11-5-12
	(British middleweight title)		

Fights 49 Won 44 Lost 5

Johnny GRAHAM

Cruiserweight
Paddington born 12 April 1962
St Pancras ABC
1981 NABC Class C final (l E Christie)
1981 London ABA middleweight champion (w D Sullivan, w G Hobbs, w J Cook, l S Johnson)
1981 Young England (v YDen, w K Christensen)
1982 London ABA middleweight champion (w T Forbes, w T Jenkins, w J Cook, l rsf 1* A Thomas)
1983 England (v Swe, w P Olsson)
1984 England (v Sco, w A McCulloch)

1985
Feb 18	Seamus Casey	w pts 6	NSC 11-9
Apr 1	Paul Gamble	w pts 6	Mayfair 11-11-8
Jun 16	Alan Baptiste	w pts 6	Bethnal Green 11-10
Nov 28	Mickey Kidd	w pts 8	Bethnal Green 11-9-12

1986
Jan 23	Bobby Williams	w pts 8	Bethnal Green 11-11
Apr 29	Seamus Casey	w pts 8	NSC 11-10-4
Oct 16	Karl Barwise	w pts 6	Wimbledon 12-1
Dec 15	Alan Baptiste	w pts 8	NSC 11-11

1987
Mar 12	Ray Thomas	w pts 8	NSC 12-4
Apr 9	Ray Thomas	w pts 8	Bethnal Green 12-2
Oct 26	Alan Baptiste	w pts 8	NSC 12-5
Dec 2	Dennis Banton	w pts 8	NSC 12-7

1988
Mar 24	Chris Galloway	w rsf 6*	Bethnal Green 12-7-4
Apr 21	Derek Myers	drew 8	Bethnal Green 12-8
Nov 15	Abner Blackstock	l pts 8	Chigwell 12-13-4
Dec 12	Peter Brown	w rsf 7	Manchester 12-6-8

1989
inactive

1990
Jan 30	Serg Fame (Southern light-heavyweight title)	l rsf 1	Battersea 12-6

1991
Apr 25	Mike Aubrey (vacant Southern cruiserweight title)	w pts 10	Basildon 13-7-8
Nov 14	Everton Blake (Southern cruiserweight title)	l pts 10	Marble Arch 13-7

1992
Nov 26	Everton Blake (Southern cruiserweight title)	w pts 10	Mayfair 13-5-12

Fights 20 Won 16 Lost 3 Drawn 1

Allan GRAINGER

Light-middleweight
Glasgow born 28 May 1968
Clydeview ABC
1987 Young Scotland (v En, l rsf 1 C Wright)
1988 Scotland (v Ire, l J McCormack)
1989 Scotland (v En, l rsf 1 M Elliot)
1989 Scottish ABA welterweight quarter-final (l G Quigley)

1991
Mar 18	Mickey Duncan	l pts 6	Glasgow 10-12
Sep 9	Willie Yeardsley	w pts 6	Glasgow 11-0
Oct 24	Jim Conley	w pts 6	Glasgow 10-12
Nov 18	Mickey Duncan	l pts 6	Glasgow 11-1

1992
Feb 24	Calum Rattray	w rtd 5	Glasgow 10-12-4
Mar 4	Steve Scott	w pts 6	Glasgow 10-11-12
Oct 19	Tony Trimble	w pts 6	Glasgow 11-2

Fights 7 Won 5 Lost 2

Derek GRAINGER

Welterweight
Bethnal Green born 15 May 1967
Poplar ABC
1985 Young England (v WGer, l rsf 1 J Schroler, l M Ritter)
1986 NABC Class C final (l S Cooper)
1986 Young England (v WGer, w rtd 2 C Schordie)
1987 NE London ABA light-welterweight final (l W Couzens)

1988
Jan 28	Jim Beckett	w pts 6	Bethnal Green 10-8
Feb 25	Richard Thompson	w rsf 3	Bethnal Green 10-8-8
Mar 24	Glyn Mitchell	w rsf 5	Bethnal Green 10-8-12
May 5	Frank Mobbs	w rsf 2	Bethnal Green 10-8-8
Oct 5	Gerry Beard	w pts 4	Wembley GH
Nov 2	Gary Dyson	w rsf 4	Southwark 10-9-8
Nov 30	Tony Gibbs	w ko 3	Southwark 10-11

1989
Mar 16	Simon Eubanks	w rsf 6	Southwark 10-10
May 10	Ronnie Campbell	w rsf 3	Albert Hall 10-10
Oct 12	Barry Messam	w ko 1	Southwark 10-10-12
Oct 25	Newton Barnett	w pts 8	Wembley 10-12-8
Dec 6	G.W.Gully	w rsf 3	Wembley GH 10-11-8

1990
Mar 3	Jerry Smith	w rsf 6	Wembley 10-11-12
Mar 14	Ray Taylor	w ko 2	Albert Hall 10-13-8
May 9	Newton Barnett	w rsf 4	Wembley CC 10-12
Oct 30	Kevin Plant	w rsf 4	Wembley 10-11-4
Dec 12	Chris Peters	w pts 8	Albert Hall 10-11-8

1991
Feb 13	Newton Barnett	w rsf 3	Wembley CC 10-10-8
Apr 17	Humphrey Harrison	l rsf 7	Albert Hall 10-10
Nov 20	Chris Blake	drew 8	Albert Hall 10-11

1992
Dec 17	Bozon Haule	w rsf 5	Barking 10-8

Fights 21 Won 19 Lost 1 Drawn 1

Frank GRANT

Middleweight
Bradford born 22 May 1965
Southpaw
No amateur experience

1986
Oct 20	Lincoln Pennant	l rsf 1	Bradford 11-10

1987
Jun 1	Steve Ward	w rsf 3	Bradford 11-10
Sep 10	Tony Lawrence	w rsf 3	Peterborough 11-8-8
Oct 16	Mick Maw	w pts 6	Gateshead 11-9

1988
Feb 29	Steve Coffey	w rsf 3*	Bradford 11-9
Mar 11	Gerry Richards	w rsf 3	Cottingham
Mar 28	Dave Thomas	w pts 6	Bradford
Oct 24	Shaun Cummins	w rtd 7*	Northampton 11-7-8
Dec 12	Franki Moro	w ko 6	Bradford 11-6

1989
Jan 16	Mark Howell	w rsf 1	Bradford 11-6
Feb 20	Franki Moro	l pts 6	Bradford 11-6
Apr 24	Peter Sorbey	w rsf 1	Bradford 11-6
May 22	Neil Munn	w rsf 3	Bradford 11-6-8
Nov 9	Simon Collins	w rtd 6*	Cardiff 11-7
Dec 11	Steve Aquilina	w rsf 4*	Bradford 11-9

1990
Mar 21	Kid Milo	l pts 10	Solihull 11-10

(eliminator, British super-middleweight title)

1991
Apr 12	Alan Richards	w rsf 5	Manchester 11-11-8
May 31	Tim Dendy	w pts 8	Manchester 11-10
Sep 20	Conrad Oscar	w ko 2	Manchester 11-7-8
Nov 29	Winston Wray	w rsf 3	Manchester 11-6

1992
Feb 9	Willie Ball	w pts 6	Bradford 11-10
Apr 5	Sammy Matos	w ko 1	Bradford 11-10-8
Sep 23	Herol Graham	w rsf 9	Leeds 11-6

(British middleweight title)

Fights 23 Won 20 Lost 3

Marvin P. GRAY

Light-welterweight
Stanley, born Flint Hill 14 December 1965
Real name: Paul Gray
Consett ABC
Southpaw

1985
Mar 27	Kris McAdam	l rsf 3	Gateshead 9-8
Apr 30	Paul Dawson	l pts 6	Wimbledon 9-9-8
Jun 4	Nicky Day	l pts 6	Streatham 9-11
Jun 26	Micky Hull	l pts 8	Basildon 9-9
Sep 3	Anthony Wakefield	w rsf 4	Gateshead 9-1
Sep 10	Chubby Martin	w pts 6	Southend 9-5
Oct 8	Willie McDonald	w pts 6	Preston
Oct 31	Mike Whalley	drew 8	Manchester 9-4
Nov 21	Pat Loftus	l pts 6	Hartlepool 9-4 /CTD..

(Marvin P. GRAY ctd.)
1986

Jan 30	Andrew Furlong	l pts 6	Wimbledon 9-13
Mar 19	Tony Richards	l pts 6	Solihull 9-11
Apr 1	Keith Parry	l rsf 4	Leeds 9-9
May 8	Doug Munro	w pts 8	Newcastle 9-12-8
May 20	Dean Marsden	l rsf 2	Huddersfield 9-11-8
Sep 22	Paul Timmons	w pts 6	Edgbaston 9-5
Oct 16	Willy Wilson	w pts 8	Newcastle 9-7
Nov 13	Ernie Noble	w pts 6	Huddersfield 9-10
Nov 29	Floyd Havard	l rsf 2	Battersea 9-5-8

1987

Mar 2	Willy Wilson	w pts 8	Middlesbrough 9-10
Mar 18	Mark Pearce	w pts 8	Solihull 9-10
Apr 30	Rudi Valentino	l pts 6	Washington 9-10
May 28	Carl Gaynor	w pts 6	Jarrow 9-9
Jun 2	Kevin Spratt	l pts 8	Bradford 9-12
Sep 15	Paul Burke	w rsf 6	Batley 9-10
Sep 24	Peter Bradley	w pts 8	Glasgow 9-9
Oct 7	Carl Crook	l pts 8	Burnley 9-9
Nov 10	James Jiora	w pts 8	Batley 9-11
Nov 26	Carl Crook	l pts 8	Horwich 9-13
Dec 15	Kevin Spratt	l rsf 6	Bradford 9-10

1988

Jan 26	Jeff Decker	l pts 10	Hartlepool 9-11

(vacant Northern light-welterweight title)

Feb 24	Glyn Rhodes	l rsf 1*	Sheffield 9-12

1989

Nov 29	Chris McReedy	w pts 6	Middlesbrough

1990

Mar 5	Paul Charters	l pts 10	Northampton 9-9

(vacant Northern lightweight title)

Apr 21	Tony Foster	drew 6	Sunderland 9-12
May 22	Tony Foster	w pts 6	Thornaby 9-12-8
Aug 10	Guillermo Mosquera	l pts 6	Montecalvo Irpino 9-12-8
Sep 24	Ian Honeywood	l pts 8	Lewisham 9-12
Oct 15	Allan Hall	l rsf 2	Lewisham 10-0
Nov 29	James Jiora	w pts 8	Marton 10-3

1991

Feb 28	Rick Bushell	w pts 6	Sunderland 10-1-8
Mar 10	Alain Simoes	l pts 8	Paris 10-1
May 15	Giovanni Parisi	l rsf 6	Montichiari 9-11-8
Nov 25	Andreas Panayi	l pts 8	Liverpool 10-1

1992

Feb 6	Dave Pierre	l rsf 7	Peterborough 10-2
Oct 27	Michael Driscoll	l pts 8	Leicester 10-0

Fights 45 Won 17 Lost 26 Drawn 2

John GREEN

Bantamweight
Manchester born 5 June 1965
Ardwick Lads ABC & Collyhurst ABC
1982 Junior ABA final (l M Herring)
1983 NABC Class C champion (w Y Mustafa)
1983 Young England (v EGer, l A Zuelow; v USA, w J Gruber)
1984 ABA flyweight semi-final (w rsf 1 R Brindle, w rsf 1 P Lally, w J Craig, w R Bond, l P Clinton)
1985 ABA flyweight semi-final (w S Hulme, w rsf 3 S Mangan, w L Williams, withdrew injured)
1986 TSC Berlin tournament (l R Breitbarth, EGer)
1986 ABA bantamweight final (w S Hulme, w rsf 1 S Mangan, w T Dixon, w rsf 1 T Abbott, w G Brooks, l rsf 2 S Murphy)

1987
Mar 31	Albert Parr	w pts 6	Oldham
Apr 28	Chris Clarkson	w rsf 6	Manchester 8-8
May 26	Des Gargano	w pts 6	Oldham 8-7
Oct 19	Des Gargano	w pts 6	Manchester 8-5
Nov 17	Nigel Crook	w pts 6	Manchester 8-8-8
Dec 16	Gerry McBride	w pts 10	Manchester 8-4-12
	(Central bantamweight title)		

1988
Jan 20	Dave George	w pts 8	Solihull 8-7-8

1989
inactive

1990
Mar 13	Gary De Roux	l rsf 2	Bristol 8-9-12
Oct 10	Jimmy Clark	l pts 6	Millwall 8-12-8

1991
Feb 22	Colin Lynch	w pts 6	Manchester 8-10-8
Apr 12	Sylvester Osuji	w rsf 1	Manchester 8-9-8
May 31	Roland Gomez	w rsf 5	Manchester 8-6-8
Sep 20	Tony Rahman	w rsf 3	Manchester 8-9
Nov 29	Ceri Farrell	w rtd 4	Manchester 8-7-8

1992
Jan 31	Miguel Matthews	drew 6	Manchester 8-10
Feb 9	Steve Young	drew 6	Bradford 8-10
May 29	Ronnie Carroll	w pts 10	Manchester 8-5-8
	(eliminator, British bantamweight title)		

Fights 17 Won 13 Lost 2 Drawn 2

Wayne GREEN

Welterweight
Bristol born 1955
Royal Navy
1974 Navy (v WCos, w R Dorrington)
1975 Combined Services ABA welterweight champion (w J Whiting, l M Jones)
1976 Combined Services ABA light-welterweight champion (w R Dorrington, l rsf 2 R Beaumont)
1977 England (v Rum, l C Hajnal)
1978 Combined Services ABA light-welterweight champion (w rsf 3 B Stephens, w C Sanigar, l D Williams)
1978 England (v Sc, w J McAllister; v Fr, l M Keddari; v WG, l W Schaeffer; v Dn, w J Jorgensen)
1979 Royal Navy ABA welterweight champion (w M Lescott, withdrew)
1980 ABA light-welter semi-final (w rsf 2* M Brooks, w K Brooking, w rsf 3 D Horgan, l rsf 2 J McAllister)
1980 England (v Sc, l rsf 1* S McLeod; v Kn, w ko 2 D Omulu)
1980 ABA Centenary light-welterweight final (w ko 1 R Anderson, Cn; l T Willis)
1981 Combined Services ABA light-welter champion (w rsf 3 B Conchie, w ko 1 R Hutchinson, l T Willis)
1982 Combined Services ABA light-welterweight champion (w P Kearney, w R Hutchinson, l ko 3 C McIntosh)
1983 ABA light-welterweight semi-final (w rsf 3 R Butler, w M Oliver, w ko 1 M Ballard, l ko 1 D Griffiths)

1991
Jan 11	Freddy Demeulenaere	l rsf 7*	Waregem	/CTD..

(Wayne GREEN ctd.)

Apr 12	Aziz Arbia	l rsf 2*	Montpellier
Apr 19	Daniel Bicchieray	l rsf 5	Marignane
Sep 19	Philippe Bafounta	l rsf 3	Paris
1992			
Apr 4	Roland Leclerq	l pts 8	Sin-le-Noble

Fights 5 Lost 5

Darron GRIFFITHS

Middleweight
Porth, born Pontypridd 11 February 1972
Rhondda ABC
Southpaw
1990 ABA middleweight finalist (w dis 3 J Robinson, w S Thomas, w rsf 2 A Kearle, w J Robinson, l S Wilson)
1990 Wales (v Cze, v Nor)

1990			
Nov 26	Colin Ford	drew 6	NSC 11-4
Dec 4	Kevin Adamson	w rsf 4	Southend 11-1
1991			
Jan 23	Tony Booth	drew 6	Stoke 11-0-8
Mar 6	Barry Messam	w pts 6	Croydon 11-2
Apr 10	John Kaighin	w pts 6	Newport 11-3
Apr 25	Michael Graham	w rsf 2	Mayfair 11-5
May 2	Calton Myers	w rtd 5	Bayswater 11-6
Oct 21	John Ogiste	w pts 6	AASC 11-9
Dec 11	Adrian Wright	w pts 6	Stoke 11-6-8
1992			
Jan 22	Richard Okumu	w pts 8	Solihull 11-9
Feb 17	John Ogiste	w rsf 5	AASC 11-10
Apr 29	Colin Manners	drew 8	Solihull 11-5
Sep 30	Colin Manners	w pts 10	Solihull 11-5-12
	(eliminator, British middleweight title)		
Oct 28	Antonio Fernandez	w pts 10	Cardiff 11-4-12
	(eliminator, British middleweight title)		

Fights 14 Won 11 Drawn 3

Bobby GUYNAN

Super-featherweight
East Ham, born Plaistow 4 July 1967
Repton ABC
1987 London ABA lightweight final (w S Somerville, w J Tossell, l M Ayers)
1988 NE London ABA lightweight final (w G Egbuniwe, l rsf 2 P Harvey)
1990 NE London ABA featherweight final (l D Adams)

1990			
Oct 17	John O'Meara	w rtd 2*	Bethnal Green 9-3
Nov 26	Lee Fox	l pts 6	Bethnal Green 9-3-8
1991			
Feb 6	Lee Fox	w pts 6	Bethnal Green 9-5
Mar 26	Lee Fox	l rtd 3*	Bethnal Green 9-1-8
1992			
Nov 10	Mark Allen	w rsf 2	Dagenham 9-11

Fights 5 Won 3 Lost 2

THE LONSDALE INTERNATIONAL SPORTING CLUB

Join a Club that is Serving your Interests Worldwide.

The Lonsdale International Sporting Club is open for membership to all sports enthusiasts at an annual enrolment fee of £40.

Every member will receive a bi-monthly newsletter featuring free competitions with prizes, and will benefit from books and videos at reduced prices, exchange and sale of fight programmes, photographs and other memorabilia, plus organised travel and functions worldwide.

The Lonsdale International Sporting Club has set itself aims and objectives to improve the quality of sport for the sporting enthusiast:

1. To serve the ethic of sport worldwide.
2. To bring sporting enthusiasts together at selected sporting events globally.
3. To sustain and promote the names of Lonsdale and Queensberry in this the second century of gloved boxing by seeking sponsorship of the Lonsdale Belts.
4. To support individual charitable causes with particular emphasis on charities helping ex-sports participants.
5. To aid and assist the development of sports at grass roots level.
6. To arrange events to honour the great sporting personalities.
7. To seek the encouragement of sport at governmental level.

All members receive: Membership Card, Lapel Badge and Club Tie or Cravat. You may consider enrolling a friend or a relation as a gift.

For more information call Steve Millington on our information hotline number

0204 373332

For postal applications write to Mr Steve Millington, Club Administrator. The Lonsdale International Sporting club, 21 Beak Street, London W1R 3LB.

We invite you to join the worldwide association for sports enthusiasts, The Lonsdale International Sporting Club. Serving the ethic of Sport throughout the world.

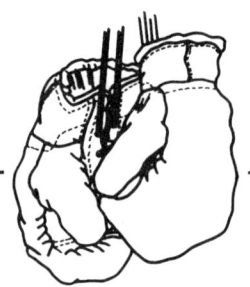

Ringcraft

BOXING SERVICES & RING HIRE SPECIALISTS

THE COUNTRY'S LEADING SUPPLIERS OF BOXING RINGS TO ALL MAJOR PROMOTIONS IN GREAT BRITAIN AND EUROPE.

....

WE CAN SUPPLY CORNER PADS,
RING CANVASSES, ROUND CARDS, M.C., WHIP,
HOUSE SECONDS,
RING GIRLS, etc.

....

TRAINING CAMPS EQUIPPED
GYM RINGS REVAMPED

....

CONTACT MIKE GOODALL
FOR ALL YOUR REQUIREMENTS
TELEPHONE: Day (0386) 47701
Evenings (0386) 442118
Mobile No. (0860) 455608

'RINGCRAFT', GIBBS LANE, OFFENHAM, EVESHAM WR11 5RR

Neil HADDOCK
Super-featherweight
Llanelli, born Newport 22 June 1964
Trostre ABC & Army   Southpaw
1983 Welsh ABA featherweight champion (w A Williams, l rtd 2 G Rogers)
1985 Combined Services lightweight champion (w D Robb, w A Hagger, l C Crook)
1986 Welsh ABA lightweight champion (w A Feliciello, withdrew)
1986 Commonwealth Games silver medal (w B Mphande, Mal; l rsf 1 A Dar, Can)

1987
Feb 16	Mark Purcell	l pts 6	Gloucester 9-10
Mar 19	Rudi Valentino	l pts 6	Bethnal Green 9-7
Apr 1	Gary Cass	w pts 6	Southsea 9-10
Apr 30	Carl Merrett	w pts 6	Newport 9-12
May 26	Joey Jacobs	l pts 8	Oldham 9-8
Oct 1	Lee Amass	w rsf 4	Croydon 9-10-8
Dec 8	Mike Russell	w pts 8	Plymouth 9-11

1988
Feb 17	B.F.Williams	l pts 8	Bethnal Green 9-10
Feb 24	Peter Till	l pts 8	Port Talbot 9-10-8
Mar 8	Andrew Furlong	l pts 6	Holborn 9-12
Mar 29	Richard Adams	w pts 6	Bethnal Green 9-9
Apr 11	Mike Durvan	l rsf 4	NSC 9-9-12
Dec 1	Michael Driscoll	drew 6	Gravesend 9-7

1989
Mar 22	Lee Amass	w rsf 5	Sheppey 9-10

1990
Sep 18	Ditau Molefyane	l rtd 5	Wolverhampton 9-3
Oct 18	Mark Ramsey	w rsf 5	Birmingham 9-2
Nov 19	Steve Robinson	l rsf 9*	Cardiff 9-2-8
	(final eliminator, Welsh super-featherweight title)		

1991
Nov 20	Barrie Kelley	w pts 6	Cardiff 9-5
Dec 17	Andy Deabreu	w rsf 3*	Cardiff 9-2-8

1992
May 11	Steve Robinson	w pts 10	Llanelli 9-3-8
	(vacant Welsh super-featherweight title)		
Oct 13	Michael Armstrong	w rsf 6	Bury 9-4
	(British super-featherweight title)		
Dec 1	Harry Escott	w pts 10	Liverpool 9-7

Fights 22 Won 12 Lost 9 Drawn 1

Mark HALE
Super-middleweight
Bedworth born 13 October 1969
Bedworth Ex-Service ABC

1991
Oct 7	Andy Manning	l pts 6	Liverpool 11-12
Nov 7	Marc Rowley	w pts 6	Peterborough 11-11-8

1992
Jan 15	Paul Murray	w pts 6	Stoke 11-13
Mar 25	Marc Rowley	w pts 6	Hinckley 11-11-8
May 11	Martin Jolley	l pts 6	Coventry 12-1
May 21	Tony Colclough	drew 6	Cradley Heath 12-1-8
Jun 1	Tony Colclough	l pts 6	NEC 11-12
Oct 5	Martin Jolley	l rsf 4	Bardon 12-2

Fights 8 Won 3 Lost 4 Drawn 1

Ross HALE

Light-welterweight
Bristol born 28 February 1967
National Smelting ABC & Kingswood Summit ABC
1985 Western ABA lightweight final (w T Rymell, w rsf 2 R Berry, l A Hagger)
1987 Western ABA light-welterweight final (w dis 3 R Berry, w H Morgan, l M Delves)
1988 Western ABA light-welterweight final (l M Delves)
1989 Western ABA light-welterweight champion (w ko 2 P Gage, w D Hassan, l A Hall)
Southpaw

1989
Nov 16	David Jenkins	w pts 6	Weston 10-1-12
Nov 30	Tony Gibbs	w pts 6	Marble Arch 10-2-8
Dec 12	Chris McReedy	w rsf 4	Brentford 10-1

1990
Mar 13	Davey Hughes	w rsf 4	Bristol 10-0-8
Apr 30	Andy Robins	w rsf 4	Bristol 10-4-4
Sep 12	Derrick Daniel	w pts 6	Bethnal Green 10-2
Nov 21	Mark Kelly	w pts 8	Chippenham 10-1
Nov 29	Chris Saunders	w pts 6	Bayswater 10-2

1991
Oct 24	Greg Egbuniwe	w rsf 4	Bayswater 10-2

1992
Jan 22	Tony Borg	w pts 6	Cardiff 10-1-8
Apr 30	Jason Matthews	w rsf 3	Bayswater 10-3
May 12	John Smith	w ko 1	Crystal Palace 10-1-12
Jul 7	Julian Eavis	w rsf 8	Bristol 10-2-4
	(vacant Western welterweight title)		
Oct 5	Malcolm Melvin	w pts 10	Bristol 9-12-4
	(eliminator, British light-welterweight title)		
Dec 1	Sugar Gibiliru	w ko 1	Bristol 10-0

Fights 15 Won 15

Allan HALL

Light-welterweight
Darlington born 16 November 1969
Darlington ABC & Shildon ABC
1985 National Schools champion (w G Delaney)
1985 Junior ABA final
1986 National Schools champion (w M Brooks)
1987 ABA lightweight final (w H Escott, w P Gettins, w I Foster, w rsf 2 R Ali, w P Hampson, w A Hagger, w D Anderson, l M Ayers)
1987 Young England (v YWGer, w ko 2 C Dokter; v YSco, w S Reid; v YEGer, w C Rennefort)
1988 ABA light-welter champion (w P Charters, w G Rhodes, w rsf 2 N Foran, w M Delves, w M Smyth, w J Talbot)
1988 Acropolis Cup, Athens (l M Calderella, It)
1988 England (v Cze, w R Koller; v Ire, l M Carruth)
1988 Gold medal in Finland multi-nations (w Kallorine, Fin; w Bossako, Bul; w dis Kelp, USA)
1989 England (v Sco, w J Pender)
1989 ABA light-welterweight champion (w ko 1 A Lee, w rsf 1 T Carolan, w rsf 3 M Legg, w rsf 1 C Saunders, w D McCarrick, w R Hale, w M Smythe, w R McCracken)

1989
Oct 10	Saturnin Cabanas	w rsf 2	Hull 9-11
Dec 8	John Smith	w rsf 2	Doncaster 10-3

1990
Feb 22	Muhammad Lovelock	w rsf 1	Hull 9-13
Apr 21	Darren Mount	w pts 6	Sunderland 10-0
May 9	George Jones	w rsf 1	Albert Hall 10-0-8

May 22	Mohamed Ouhmad	w pts 6	Thornaby 9-13-8
Oct 15	Marvin P. Gray	w rsf 2	Lewisham 9-12-8
Oct 31	Gino De Leon	w rsf 1	Crystal Palace 10-1
1991			
Mar 2	Steve Pollard	w pts 6	Darlington 10-0
Apr 6	Alan Peacock	w pts 6	Darlington
Jun 11	Abram Gumede	w pts 8	Leicester 10-2
1992			
Apr 25	Michael Driscoll	w pts 6	Manchester 10-0
Jun 27	Russell Mosley	w pts 6 (m)	San Diego
Jul 11	Steve Barreras	l rsf 5	Las Vegas
Sep 17	Dave Pierre	w pts 10	Watford 9-13-4
	(eliminator, British light-welterweight title)		

Fights 15 Won 14 Lost 1

Dave HALL

Light-middleweight
Birmingham born 25 July 1964

1991			
Apr 15	John Baxter	w ko 3	Leicester
May 13	Dave Binsteed	l rsf 2*	Birmingham 11-4
Jul 4	Seamus Casey	l pts 6	Alfreton 11-0
Sep 16	Marc Rowley	w pts 6	Cleethorpes 11-6
Oct 8	Marc Rowley	w pts 6	Wolverhampton 11-9
Oct 29	Kevin Sheeran	l rsf 1	Albert Hall 11-5
1992			
Jan 22	John Corcoran	l pts 8	Stoke 11-1-8
Mar 11	John Corcoran	l pts 8	Stoke
Apr 29	Matthew Jones	l rsf 2*	Solihull 11-6

Fights 9 Won 3 Lost 6

Micky HALL

Lightweight
Ludworth, County Durham born 23 April 1967
Horden & Peterlee ABC

1992			
Mar 3	Mick Holmes	w rsf 2	Houghton-le-Spring 9-9
Mar 11	G.G.Goddard	drew 6	Solihull 9-8
Apr 28	Jamie Davison	l pts 6	Houghton-le-Spring 9-9-8
Sep 19	Mark Geraghty	l pts 6	Glasgow 9-8
Oct 12	Leo Turner	w rsf 5	Bradford 9-8
Nov 18	Alan Ingle	w rtd 3*	Solihull 9-11

Fights 6 Won 3 Lost 2 Drawn 1

Simon HAMBLETT

Lightweight
Walsall Wood born 10 October 1966
Walsall Wood Police ABC
1987 South Midlands ABA featherweight final (w F Smith, l S Doyle)
1988 Staffordshire ABA lightweight final (l rsf 1 L James)
1989 Staffordshire ABA lightweight champion (w P Gwilt, withdrew)
1991 Staffordshire ABA light-welterweight final (l M Richards)

1992
Feb 24	Jamie Morris	drew 6	Coventry 10-0
Mar 11	Mark Antony	l ko 1	Stoke 10-0
Dec 9	Mark Allen	drew 6	Stoke 9-8

Fights 3 Lost 1 Drawn 2

Naseem HAMED

Bantamweight
Sheffield, born 12 February 1974
Southpaw
St Thomas's ABC & Unity ABC
1987 National Schools champion (w M Wright)
1989 National Schools champion (w S Dann)
1989 Junior ABA semi-final (l D Pithie)
1989 England Schools (won v Wales twice and USA)
1990 NABC Class A champion (w rsf 2 R Izzard)
1990 National Schools champion (w rsf 1 D Williams)
1990 Junior ABA champion (w M Wright)
1990 England "Youth" (v US Junior Olympic team, w D Acevedo)
1990 Junior ABA champion (w M Wright) ** ABA changed system, 2 Junior ABAs fell in 1 yr.

1992
Apr 14	Ricky Beard	w ko 2	Mansfield 8-2
Apr 25	Shaun Norman	w rsf 2	Manchester 8-2
May 23	Andrew Bloomer	w rsf 2	Birmingham 8-2
Jul 14	Miguel Matthews	w rsf 3	Mayfair 8-7-8
Oct 7	Des Gargano	w rsf 4	Sunderland 8-9
Nov 12	Peter Buckley	w pts 6	Liverpool 8-7-8

Fights 6 Won 6

Paul HANLON

Super-middleweight
Birmingham born 25 May 1962
Newtown ABC

1986
Nov 18	Kevin Roper	l rtd 5*	Swansea 11-10-8

1987
Mar 18	Tony Behan	l pts 4	Stoke 11-11

1988-89 inactive

1990
Jun 28	Dave Radford	l rsf 2	Birmingham 11-2
Sep 18	Gary Osborne	l rtd 2	Wolverhampton 11-5
Oct 17	Mike Betts	l rtd 2	Stoke 11-10

1991
Mar 4	Tony Behan	l pts 6	Birmingham 12-3
Mar 18	Willie James	w ko 1	Derby 12-7

Apr 10	Lee Prudden	l pts 6	Wolverhampton 12-0
Apr 24	Dean Allen	l pts 6	Port Talbot 12-6
May 13	Lee Prudden	l pts 6	Birmingham 11-12
May 23	Lee Prudden	w pts 6	Southampton 12-4
Jun 10	Jason Frize	w rsf 2	Manchester 12-7
Sep 10	Richard Carter	l rsf 3	Wolverhampton 11-12
1992			
Jan 22	Lee Prudden	w rsf 4*	Stoke 12-9
Feb 20	Glen Payton	l pts 6	Telford 11-12
Apr 27	Joey Peters	l ko 2	AASC 12-10
Sep 21	Tim Robinson	w pts 6	Cleethorpes 12-2
Oct 5	John J. Cooke	l ko 1	Bardon 12-9
Nov 24	Chris Nurse	w pts 6	Wolverhampton 12-2
Dec 7	Zak Goldman	w pts 6	Birmingham 12-4

Fights 20 Won 7 Lost 13

Anthony HANNA
Flyweight
Birmingham born 22 September 1974
Priory Park ABC

1992			
Nov 19	Nick Tooley	l pts 6	Evesham 8-0
Dec 10	Darren Fifield	l rsf 6	Bethnal Green 8-0

Fights 2 Lost 2

Dave HARDIE
Bantamweight
Glasgow born 10 February 1971
Gallowgate ABC
1989 Scottish ABA bantamweight quarter-final (l M Deveney)
1990 Scottish ABA bantamweight final (w rsf 2 G Barnes, l rsf 1 W Docherty)
1991 ABA bantamweight champion (w J Sanderson, w R Grant, w W Docherty, w M Alldis, w M Gibbons)
1991 Scotland (v Wal, w R Vowles)
1991 Canada Cup silver medal

1991			
Nov 28	Miguel Matthews	w pts 6	Glasgow 8-9
1992			
Feb 20	Shaun Norman	w pts 6	Glasgow 8-7-4

Fights 2 Won 2

Fran HARDING
Middleweight
Liverpool born 5 September 1966
South Liverpool ABC & Liverpool Golden Gloves ABC
1980 National Schools champion (w J Warren)
1981 National Schools champion (w J Warren)
1982 National Schools final (l B Robinson)
1982 Junior ABA champion (w T Kilgallon)
1983 Junior ABA semi-final (l M Graham)
1984 Young England (v YEGer, w H Rettig; l W Schmidt; v YUSA, l M Triplett)
1984 NABC Class C champion (w D Abbott)
1984 Northern ABA welter champ (w ko 1 S Gough, w D Sumner, w B Whelan, l ko 1 M Hughes)
1984 European Juniors bronze medal (w L Smith, WGer; w L Alhonen, Swe; l rsf 3 K Doinov, Bul)
1985 West Lancs & Cheshire ABA champion (w T Dowling, l ko 3 T Kershaw)
1986 Northern ABA light-middleweight final (w D Robinson, l rsf 2* G Phillips)
1987 Northern ABA light-middleweight final (w P Swift, w ko 1 S Strong, l W Neil)
/CTD..

(Fran HARDING ctd)

1987
Jul 27	Johnny Taupau	w pts 6	Sydney

1988
May 4	Barry Bennett	w rsf 1	Wembley GH 11-6-8
Dec 14	Steve Foster	w pts 6	Liverpool 11-9

1989
inactive

1990
May 4	Quinton Paynter	w pts 6	Liverpool 11-2

1991
Sep 30	Lee Crocker	w rsf 3	Albert Hall 11-7

1992
Sep 25	Terry Magee	w pts 6	Liverpool 12-0
Oct 23	Seamus Casey	w pts 6	Liverpool 11-13
Nov 20	Marvin O'Brian	w rsf 4	Liverpool 11-11

Fights 8 Won 8

Billy HARDY

Bantamweight
Sunderland born 15 September 1964
Hylton Castle ABC
1980 National Schools final (l J Groves)
1981 Junior ABA champion (w J Good)
1982 Northern ABA bantamweight final (w T Austin, w rsf 2 C O'Neill, w D Patterson, l R Gilbody)
1982 Young England (v Ire, l P Fitzgerald)
1982 England (v Fin, l J Eskelinen)
1983 Young England (v WGer, w M Niessen)
1983 Northern ABA bantamweight final (l rsf 2 J Hyland)

1983
Nov 21	Kevin Downer	w pts 6	Eltham 8-6
Dec 3	Brett Styles	w pts 6	Marylebone 8-6-12

1984
Jan 27	Keith Ward	w pts 6	Longford 8-7
Feb 13	Johnny Mack	w rsf 5	Eltham 8-9-12
Mar 1	Graham Clarke	w pts 8	Queensway 8-6-4
Mar 27	Glen McLaggon	w pts 6	Battersea 8-6
Apr 6	Graham Clarke	w rsf 7*	Watford 8-8
Apr 25	Anthony Brown	w rsf 5	Muswell Hill 8-6-8
Jun 4	Roy Webb	l pts 6	NSC
Sep 6	Les Walsh	w pts 8	Gateshead 8-8
Oct 10	Jorge Prentas	l rsf 5	Shoreditch 8-7-8

1985
Feb 12	Ivor Jones	w pts 8	Albert Hall 8-4-8
Apr 17	Ivor Jones	w pts 10	Bethnal Green 8-5-12
Jun 8	Valerio Nati	l rsf 4	Florence 8-7-4
Oct 10	Keith Wallace	w rsf 7	Alfreton 8-4-8
	(final eliminator, British bantamweight title)		

1986
Jun 2	Rocky Lawlor	w pts 8	NSC 8-7-8

1987
Feb 19	Ray Gilbody	w rsf 3	St Helens 8-4-8
	(British bantamweight title)		
Apr 23	Rocky Lawlor	w rsf 7*	Newcastle
Jun 4	Brian Holmes	w pts 10	Sunderland

1988
Mar 17	John Hyland	w ko 2	Sunderland 8-5
	(British bantamweight title)		

May 11	Luis Ramos	w rsf 2	Wembley GH 8-6-12
Sep 29	Jose Gallegos	w rsf 4	Sunderland 8-7
Nov 2	Vincenzo Belcastro (European bantamweight title)	l pts 12 (m)	Paola 8-5
1989			
Feb 14	Ronnie Carroll (British bantamweight title)	w pts 12	Sunderland 8-4-10
Mar 28	Jose Soto	w pts 8	Wembley 8-7-8
Jun 28	Vincenzo Belcastro (European bantamweight title)	drew 12	Pavia 8-6
Oct 10	Brian Holmes (British bantamweight title)	w ko 1	Sunderland 8-6
1990			
Jan 24	Orlando Canizales (IBF bantamweight title)	l pts 12 (s)	Sunderland 8-5-2
May 22	Miguel Pequeno	w rsf 4	Thornaby
Nov 29	Ronnie Carroll (British bantamweight title)	w rsf 8	Sunderland 8-5-10
1991			
Feb 28	Francisco Ortiz	w rsf 7	Sunderland
May 4	Orlando Canizales (IBF bantamweight title)	l rsf 8	Laredo 8-6
1992			
Mar 3	Chris Clarkson	w rsf 5	Houghton-le-Spring 8-10-6
Oct 7	Ricky Rayner (vacant Commonwealth featherweight title)	w rsf 10	Sunderland 8-13-8

Fights 34 Won 27 Lost 6 Drawn 1

John HAREWOOD

Heavyweight
Middlesbrough, born Ipswich 23 February 1964
Real name: Walter Harewood
Horsley Hill ABC, Fatfield & Washington ABC
1987 North-East Division ABA super-heavyweight final (w M Hallett, l ko 1 G McCrory)
1988 Northern ABA super-heavyweight champion (w dis 1 G Shillingforth, w P Williams, l ko 1 S Woollaston)
1989 ABA super-heavyweight finalist (w rsf 2 A Williams, w ko 1 P Dickinson, w rsf 1 D Crawford, l P Passley)
1990 Northern ABA super-heavyweight champion (w rsf 1 D Ellrington, w rsf 1 S Bristow, l rsf 1 D Abbott)

1990			
Nov 29	Carlton Headley	w rsf 5	Marton 19-0-8
1991			
Apr 6	Paddy Reilly	l rsf 2	Darlington 17-12
Aug 1	Paddy Reilly	l ko 1	Dewsbury 17-4
1992			
Mar 6	J.A. Bugner	l pts 4	Battersea 17-6
May 27	Freddy Soentgen	l pts 6 (m)	Cologne
Oct 7	Gary Charlton	w pts 6	Sunderland 17-5
Oct 30	Clement Salles	w rsf 4	Istres 17-8-8
Dec 17	Dermot Gascoigne	l rsf 5	Barking 17-5

Fights 8 Won 3 Lost 5

Mark HARGREAVES
Featherweight
Burnley born 13 September 1970
Lancashire Constabulary ABC

1991			
Sep 11	Dave Campbell	w rsf 4	Stoke 8-8
Oct 23	Dave Martin	w pts 6	Stoke 8-9
1992			
Feb 10	Dennis Oakes	l rsf 3	Liverpool 8-9
Mar 30	Ronnie Stephenson	l pts 6	Coventry 8-13
Apr 27	Adey Benton	l pts 6	Bradford 8-10
Jun 1	Des Gargano	w pts 6	Manchester 8-11-8
Sep 11	Shaun Anderson	l pts 6	Glasgow 8-9
Oct 7	Mike Deveney	w rsf 7	Glasgow 8-11-12
Oct 14	Yusuf Vorajee	w rsf 4	Stoke 9-2
Nov 19	Greg Upton	w rsf 3	Evesham 9-1
Nov 28	John White	l pts 4	Manchester 8-12-8

Fights 11 Won 6 Lost 5

Carl HARNEY
Middleweight
Manchester born 24 June 1967
Moss Side ABC
1988 East Lancs & Cheshire light-middleweight final (w w rsf 2 C Scaife, l E Donnelly)
1989 ABA light-middle semi-final (w C Scaife, w ko 1 S Strong, w C Hepton, w P Wilson, l rsf 1 C Colarusso)

1989			
Oct 17	Seamus Casey	w pts 4	Oldham 11-6
1990			
Oct 18	Michael Clarke	w pts 6	Battersea 11-10
1991			
Feb 22	Mike Phillips	l rsf 5*	Manchester 11-8
May 31	Marvin O'Brian	l rsf 5	Manchester 11-9
1992			
May 29	Matthew Jones	w rsf 6	Manchester 11-9
Jul 18	John Kaighin	w pts 6	Manchester 11-11

Fights 6 Won 4 Lost 2

Danny HARPER
Welterweight
Barnsley born 18 October 1967
Grimethorpe ABC
1988 Yorkshire & Humberside ABA welterweight final (w rsf 3 A Massey, l ko 3 J Nicholson)
1992 Yorkshire & Humberside ABA welterweight semi-final (l rsf 3 J Herridge)

1992			
Sep 14	Steve Scott	drew 6	Bradford 10-11
Nov 12	Frank Harrington	w pts 6	Burnley 10-7

Fights 2 Won 1 Drawn 1

Frank HARRINGTON

Welterweight
Lancaster, born Glasgow 1 October 1961
Lancaster Lads ABC

1986			
Apr 21	Michael Betts	w rsf 3*	Bradford 10-4
May 12	Steve Harwood	w ko 4	Manchester 10-4
May 19	Eamonn Payne	l rsf 3	Bradford 10-4
Sep 29	Rocky Lester	w pts 6	Loughborough 10-1
1987			
Feb 26	Brian Wareing	l ko 2	Hartlepool 10-8-8
Jun 13	Wayne Goult	w pts 6	Great Yarmouth 10-5
Oct 7	Joe Janny	w rsf 3	Burnley 10-6
Nov 26	Tony Connellan	l pts 6	Horwich 10-4-8
Dec 16	John Reid	l pts 6	Manchester 10-5
1988			
Jan 18	Pat Durkin	w pts 4	Bradford 10-4
Jan 29	Mike Mackenzie	w pts 6	Durham 10-8
Feb 9	David Binns	w rsf 2*	Bradford 10-4-12
Mar 10	Owen Smith	w rsf 1	Glasgow 10-8
Sep 26	Gerry Beard	l rtd 7*	Leicester 10-8
1989			
Jan 30	Julian Eavis	l pts 6	Leicester 10-8
Feb 14	Dave Kettlewell	w pts 6	Sunderland 10-8-8
1990			
May 21	Trevor Meikle	l rsf 5*	Hanley 10-9
1991			
Apr 23	Steve McGovern	l pts 6	Evesham
1992			
May 5	Crain Fisher	l rsf 4	Preston 10-13-12
Nov 12	Danny Harper	l pts 6	Burnley 10-7

Fights 20 Won 10 Lost 10

Peter HARRIS

Featherweight
Swansea born 23 August 1962
Gwent ABC
1981 ABA featherweight semi-final (l S James; replaced James, l rtd 1 P Hanlon)

1983			
Feb 28	Dave Pratt	l pts 6	Birmingham
Apr 25	Jim Harvey	drew 6	Aberdeen 9-0
May 27	Brett Styles	w pts 8	Swansea 8-12-12
Jun 20	Danny Knaggs	w pts 6	NSC 8-12-8
Dec 19	Kevin Howard	w pts 8	Swansea 8-11-8
1984			
Feb 6	Ivor Jones	drew 8	Bethnal Green 8-5-12
Mar 22	Johnny Dorey	w rsf 6	Bethnal Green 8-9
Jun 13	Keith Wallace	w pts 10	Port Talbot 8-6
Sep 28	Ray Minus Jnr	l pts 10	Nassau
Nov 21	John Farrell	l pts 8	Solihull
1985			
Mar 20	Kid Sumaila	w pts 8	Solihull 8-12
May 9	John Feeney	l pts 10	Warrington
Nov 9	Antoine Montero	l pts 8 (s)	Grenoble 8-9 /CTD..

(Peter HARRIS ctd.)

1986
Mar 26	Steve Pollard	w rsf 3*	Swansea 9-0-8
Apr 22	Roy Webb	w rtd 8*	Belfast 8-8
Nov 18	Kelvin Smart	w pts 10	Swansea 8-13-8
	(vacant Welsh featherweight title)		

1987
Apr 30	Albert Parr	w rsf 3	Newport 9-1
Sep 30	John Farrell	w pts 12	Solihull 8-12-8
	(final eliminator, British featherweight title)		
Dec 15	Roy Williams	w rsf 2	Cardiff 9-1-8

1988
Feb 24	Kevin Taylor	w pts 12	Port Talbot 8-13
	(vacant British featherweight title)		
May 18	Paul Hodkinson	l rsf 12	Port Talbot 9-0
	(British featherweight title)		

1989
Sep 6	Paul Hodkinson	l rsf 9*	Port Talbot 8-12
	(British & European featherweight titles)		

1990
inactive

1991
Apr 24	Colin Lynch	w pts 8	Port Talbot 9-1
Jul 18	Steve Robinson	l pts 10	Cardiff 8-12-12
	(Welsh featherweight title)		

1992
Jun 5	Stephane Haccoun	l pts 8	Marseille
Dec 22	Paul Harvey	l pts 8	Mayfair 9-0

Fights 26 Won 14 Lost 10 Drawn 2

Simon HARRIS
Light-heavyweight
Hanwell born Isleworth 26 December 1961
Hanwell ABC
1980 NW London ABA middleweight final (l C Oscar)
1984 NW London ABA light-heavyweight final (l J Beckles)

1984
Sep 28	Dougie Isles	w rsf 2	Longford 12-6-8
Oct 23	Ronnie Fraser	w rsf 6	Battersea 12-0
Nov 20	Harry Andrews	w rsf 2	Wimbledon 12-0
Nov 30	Gordon Stacey	w ko 2	Longford 12-4

1985
Feb 5	Sean O'Phoenix	w pts 6	Battersea 11-12
Mar 23	Lou Gent	w pts 6	Strand
May 4	Geoff Rymer	w pts 6	Queensferry 12-6
Sep 20	Dave Owens	l pts 6	Longford 12-1-8

1986
Nov 10	John Williams	w pts 6	Longford 12-9
Nov 21	Lee Davis	w rsf 3	Maidenhead 12-8
Dec 3	Tony Wilson	l rtd 6*	Muswell Hill 12-7

1987
inactive

1988
Nov 29	Alan Baptiste	w rsf 4	Battersea 12-7

1989-90
inactive

1991			
Jan 29	Richard Bustin	w rsf 3*	Wisbech 12-8
Jul 3	Nicky Piper	l rsf 1	Reading 12-9-8
1992			
Feb 11	Gary Delaney	drew 8	Barking 12-7-8

Fights 15 Won 11 Lost 3 Drawn 1

Humphrey HARRISON

Welterweight
Manchester, born Jamaica 25 September 1958
No amateur experience

1987			
Oct 5	Steve Hogg	w rsf 1	Manchester 10-0
1988			
Jan 11	Paul Jones	w pts 8	Manchester 10-4
Feb 7	Eddie Collins	w rsf 2	Manchester 10-2
Mar 29	Dave Hindmarsh	w rsf 3	Middlesbrough 10-4
Jun 6	Davey Hughes	w pts 8	Manchester 10-5
Oct 11	Phil Walters	w rsf 1	Wolverhampton 10-1-8
1989			
Apr 14	Tony Ekubia	l rsf 5	Manchester 10-4-4
	(Central welterweight title)		
Jun 12	Tony Swift	l pts 8	Manchester 10-4
Oct 4	Tony Richards	w rsf 7	Solihull 10-3
Nov 10	Tony Brown	w pts 6	Liverpool 10-7
1990			
Feb 27	Willie Beattie	w rsf 2*	Manchester 10-7
1991			
Apr 18	Derek Grainger	w rsf 7	Albert Hall 10-10
May 1	Julian Eavis	w pts 6	Solihull 10-7
1992			
Jan 31	Dave Binsteed	w ko 1	Manchester 10-10
Mar 25	Roy Rowland	l ko 7	Dagenham 10-9-8

Fights 15 Won 12 Lost 3

Craig HARTWELL

Welterweight
Rugby born 24 August 1968
Venture ABC

1991			
Dec 11	Brian Coleman	drew 6	Leicester 10-8
1992			
Mar 25	Benji Joseph	l pts 6	Hinckley 10-8
May 18	Dean Hiscox	l pts 6	Bardon 10-7

Fights 3 Lost 2 Drawn 1

Paul HARVEY

Featherweight
Ilford, born 10 November 1964
Barking ABC
1983 NE London ABA featherweight champion (w.o., l D Butcher)
1987 NE London ABA lightweight final (w ko 2 L Abrahams, l R Guynan)
1988 NE London ABA lightweight champion (w rsf 2 M Tibbs, w rsf 2 R Guynan, l S Nolan)
1989 NE London ABA lightweight final (l J Rowland)

1989
Oct 4	Steve Walker	drew 6	Basildon 9-1

1990
Jan 16	Darren Weller	w rsf 6*	Cardiff 9-3
Mar 6	James Milne	w pts 6	Bethnal Green 9-2
Apr 3	James Hunter	w ko 2	Canvey Island 9-2
Apr 23	Marvin Stone	w pts 6	Crystal Palace 9-3
Jun 20	Brian Robb	w pts 6	Basildon 9-4
Oct 24	Brian Robb	w rsf 2	Dudley 9-2-8
Dec 12	Miguel Matthews	w pts 6	Basildon

1991
Apr 9	Alan McKay	w rsf 4	Mayfair 9-2
Apr 24	Peter Gabbitus	w rsf 5	Preston 9-4
Oct 26	Colin Lynch	w rsf 1	Brentwood 9-1
Nov 12	Hugh Forde	w rsf 3	Wolverhampton 9-3
	(Commonwealth super-featherweight title)		
Dec 7	Sugar Gibiliru	w pts 12	Manchester 9-3-4
	(Commonwealth super-featherweight title)		

1992
Feb 11	Tony Pep	l pts 12	Cardiff 9-3
	(Commonwealth super-featherweight title)		
Jun 2	Regilio Tuur	l ko 5	Rotterdam 9-4
Oct 13	Brian Robb	w rtd 2	Mayfair 9-1-14
Dec 22	Peter Harris	w pts 8	Mayfair 9-2

Fights 16 Won 13 Lost 2 Drawn 1

Adrian HAUGHTON

Light-middleweight
Paddington born 16 October 1965
Southpaw
All Stars ABC
1990 North West London ABA light-middle final (w J Pinnock, l F Finn)
1991 North West London ABA light-middle semi-final (l ko 1 M Scott)

1992
Apr 7	Nigel Kitching	w rsf 5	Southend 11-2
May 17	Mossa Azward	w dis 1	Harringay 11-3-8

Fights 2 Won 2

Bozon HAULE

Welterweight
Woolwich. Born Manda, Tanzania, 4 January 1957

1987
Oct 3	Niyazi Aytekin	drew 6	Stukenbrock
Oct 31	Eric Taton	w pts 6	Paderborn

1988
Jan 9	Klaus Hein	w rsf 3	Helmstedt

Jan 16	Charles Small	w pts 6	Lubeck
Feb 19	Senturk Ozdemir	w rtd 5	Berlin
Mar 5	Konrad Mittermeier	w rsf 3	Karlsruhe
Mar 19	Antonio Nunez Diaz	w rtd 4	Hamm
Apr 23	Michel Simeon	w pts 8	Korbach
Jun 29	Tony Bawa	w rsf 7	Hamburg
Oct 15	Pascal Lorcy	w rsf 7*	St Nazaire
1989			
Feb 17	Ferdinand Pachler	l pts 10	Vienna
Apr 3	Joni Nyman	w ko 1	Helsinki
1990			
Dec 19	Tim Burgess	l pts 12	Glasgow
1991			
May 11	Oscar Checa	l rsf 1	Belfast
Sep 24	Gordon Blair	l rsf 5	Glasgow
1992			
Sep 17	Danny Shinkwin	drew 6	Watford 10-9
Oct 19	Leigh Wicks	l pts 8	Mayfair 10-10
Dec 17	Derek Grainger	l rsf 5	Barking 10-8-8

Fights 18 Won 10 KOs 7 Lost 6 Drawn 2

Floyd HAVARD

Super-featherweight
Swansea born 16 October 1965
Southpaw
Penyrheol ABC
1980 National Schools champion (w T Dwyer)
1980 Welsh Schools (v Eng, l P Hodkinson)
1981 National Schools final (l C Woolnough)
1982 Welsh Youth champion (w P Doherty)
1982 National School champion (w T O'Keefe)
1984 Wales (v Sco, w J Bennie)
1984 Welsh ABA featherweight champion (w M Rees, l K Taylor)
1985 Wales (v Ire, w P Fitzgerald)
1985 ABA featherweight champion (w rtd 1 S Webber, w C McMillan, w J Davison)

1985			
Nov 30	Dean Bramhald	w rsf 3*	Cardiff 9-2
1986			
Jan 22	Sugar Gibiliru	w pts 6	Muswell Hill 9-3-12
Feb 20	Dean Bramhald	w pts 6	Halifax 9-5
Mar 10	Russell Jones	w pts 8	Cardiff 9-7-8
Apr 28	Tony McLaggon	w ko 2	Cardiff 9-4
May 24	Sugar Gibiliru	w pts 8	Manchester 9-5
Sep 20	George Jones	w rsf 3	Hemel Hempstead 9-7
Oct 25	Joe Duffy	w rsf 3	Stevenage 9-1-8
Nov 29	Marvin P. Gray	w rsf 2	Battersea 9-5-8
1987			
Mar 14	Nigel Senior	w rsf 5	Southwark 9-4-12
Apr 14	Ray Newby	w rsf 7	Cumbernauld 9-5-8
Apr 28	Hector Clottey	w rsf 5*	Leeds
May 19	Kid Sumaila	w rtd 2	Cumbernauld 9-4
Sep 22	Mohammed Loukil	w rsf 4*	Bethnal Green 9-7-12
Nov 11	Cedric Powell	w pts 8	Usk 9-7-8
1988			
Jan 12	Mario Salazar	w rsf 2*	Cardiff 9-3-4
Feb 24	Richard Fowler	w rsf 1	Port Talbot 9-5 /CTD..

(Floyd HAVARD ctd.)

Apr 20	Benji Marques	w pts 8	Muswell Hill 9-3
May 18	Pat Cowdell	w rsf 8	Port Talbot 9-3
	(British super-featherweight title)		
Nov 15	John Kalbhenn	w pts 10	Norwich 9-6
1989			
Apr 11	Idabeth Rojas	w pts 10	Port Talbot 9-7
Sep 6	John Doherty	l rtd 11*	Port Talbot 9-3
	(British super-featherweight title)		
1990			
inactive			
1991			
Mar 5	Tony Foster	w pts 8	Millwall 9-7-8
Oct 29	Thunder Ayeh	w rtd 6	Cardiff 9-6
Dec 17	Patrick Kamy	w dis 5	Cardiff 9-8
1992			
Mar 17	Harry Escott	w rsf 7	Mayfair 9-5-8

Fights 26 Won 25 Lost 1

Steve HEARN
Lightweight
Marlow, born Luton 2 December 1966
Previously fought as Steve Leftwich

1989			
May 12	Opponent Unknown	lost	Australia
Dec 6	Brian Burley	l rsf 5	Australia
1990			
Nov 26	Felix Kelly	l rsf 3	Bethnal Green 9-12
1991			
Feb 6	Trevor Royal	drew 6	Battersea 9-12
May 1	Richard Dimmock	w pts 6	Bethnal Green 9-13-8
Nov 26	Paul Knights	l rsf 4*	Bethnal Green
1992			
Feb 12	Nick Bardle	l rsf 1*	Watford
Oct 29	Shaun Shinkwin	l pts 6	Hayes 9-12

Fights 8 Won 1 Lost 6 Drawn 1

Darren HENDERSON
Lightweight
Leeds born 22 March 1966
No amateur experience

1990			
Nov 29	John Patterson	l pts 6	Sunderland 9-6
1991			
inactive			
1992			
Jun 4	Mark Broome	l rsf 3*	Cleethorpes 9-11

Fights 2 Lost 2

Ian HENRY

Light-heavyweight
Gateshead, born 8 May 1967
Swalwell ABC
1990 North East Division ABA light-heavyweight final (l l Meredith)

1990
Apr 26	Willie James	w rsf 3	Manchester 12-0
May 15	Mark Whitehouse	w rsf 4	South Shields 12-0-8
Sep 24	Paul Hendrick	l pts 6	Manchester 12-2
Nov 19	Shaun McCrory	w pts 6	Manchester 12-1-8
Dec 14	Eddie Collins	w pts 6	Peterborough 12-3

1991
Jan 21	Shaun McCrory	w pts 6	Glasgow 11-13
Jan 28	Simon McDougall	l pts 8	Bradford 12-2
Mar 18	Ian Vokes	w rsf 2	Manchester 12-2
Mar 25	Dave Lawrence	w pts 6	Bradford 12-4
May 10	Simon McDougall	w pts 6	Gateshead 12-3
Oct 10	Chris Walker	w pts 4	Gateshead 12-2
Nov 14	Dave Owens	w pts 8	Gateshead 12-7
Nov 27	John Oxenham	w pts 6	Marton

1992
Mar 11	Simon McDougall	w pts 8	Solihull 12-7
May 5	Glenn Campbell	l rsf 1	Preston 12-6-4
Oct 23	Lee Archer	w rtd 1*	Gateshead 12-9

Fights 16 Won 13 Lost 3

Marcel HERBERT

Light-welterweight
Newport born 3 June 1965
Roath Youth ABC

1989
Aug 19	Steve Robinson	w pts 6	Cardiff 9-3
Sep 6	Miguel Matthews	w pts 6	Port Talbot 9-3
Sep 14	Jimmy Clark	l pts 4	Basildon 9-6
Sep 25	Mike Close	w pts 6	Leicester
Oct 11	Colin McMillan	l pts 6	Millwall 9-3
Nov 13	Jari Gronroos	w rsf 6	Helsinki 9-7-8
Dec 1	Frank De Winter	w pts 6	Thienen

1990
Feb 27	Tony Feliciello	w ko 4	Evesham 9-8
Apr 6	Dean Hollington	l pts 6	Stevenage 10-1
Jun 15	Tony Foster	w rsf 4	Telford 9-7
Dec 15	Jean-Pierre Scigliano	drew 8	Vichy 9-11

1991
Apr 10	Rudi Valentino	l rsf 3	Newport 9-8-12
	(eliminator, British lightweight title)		
Jun 1	Carlos Chase	l pts 6	Bethnal Green 10-4-12
Nov 20	Billy Schwer	l pts 8	Albert Hall 9-11-12

1992
Jun 18	Gary Barron	l pts 6	Peterborough 9-12
Sep 28	Paul Burke	l pts 6	Manchester 9-13

Fights 16 Won 7 Lost 8 Drawn 1

Brian HICKEY

Lightweight
Sheffield born 24 January 1973
Southpaw

1991
Nov 21	Tony Doyle	l pts 6	Ilkeston

1992
Feb 6	Michael Clynch	l dis 5	Peterborough 10-3
Oct 21	Dean Amory	l pts 6	Stoke 9-10
Nov 12	Floyd Churchill	l ko 1	Liverpool 9-7

Fights 4 Lost 4

Gary HICKMAN

Featherweight
Sunderland born 9 April 1970
Sunderland ABC
1987 NABC Class B final (l M Jones)
1988 North-East Division ABA bantamweight final (l dis 3 K Robson)

1988
Jun 6	Darren Weller	l pts 4	Northampton 8-11
Oct 17	Brian Connal	w rsf 2	Glasgow 8-10
Oct 28	Jimmy Clark	l pts 6	Bethnal Green 8-10
Dec 13	Joe Mullen	l pts 4	Glasgow 8-9

1989
Feb 14	Mark Geraghty	w pts 6	Sunderland 9-0-12
Oct 30	Phil Lashley	w rsf 4	NSC 9-1
Nov 30	Jimmy Clark	l pts 6	Barking 9-0
Dec 18	Tommy Graham	w rtd 3*	Glasgow 9-0

1990
Feb 26	Marvin Stone	l rsf 5	Crystal Palace 8-11-8
May 3	Alan McKay	l pts 8	Marble Arch 8-10
May 29	Bradley Stone	drew 6	Bethnal Green 8-11

1991
Jun 20	Craig Dermody	l rsf 2	Liverpool 8-11
Dec 14	John Armour	l rsf 6	Bexleyheath 8-10

1992
Feb 28	Mick Deveney	l pts 6	Irvine 8-12

Fights 14 Won 4 Lost 9 Drawn 1

Herbie HIDE

Heavyweight
Norwich born Nigeria 27 August 1971
Norwich Lads ABC
1989 ABA heavyweight finalist (w M Brown, w rsf 1 N Smith, w rsf 3 D Browne, l H Akinwande)

1989
Oct 24	Lee Williams	w ko 2	Bethnal Green 13-6
Nov 5	Gary McCrory	w rtd 1*	Albert Hall 13-11-4
Dec 19	Steve Osborne	w rsf 6	Bethnal Green

1990
Jun 27	Alek Penarski	w rsf 3	Albert Hall 13-7-4
Sep 5	Steve Lewsam	w rsf 4	Brighton 13-12
Sep 26	Jonjo Greene	w rsf 1	Manchester 13-12
Oct 17	Gus Mendes	w rsf 2	Bethnal Green 13-13

Nov 18	Steve Lewsam	w rsf 1	NEC 13-10-8
1991			
Jan 29	Lennie Howard	w rsf 1	Wisbech 13-8
Apr 9	David Jules	w rsf 1	Mayfair 14-0
May 14	John Westgarth	w rtd 4	Dudley 14-8
Jul 3	Michael Richards	w rsf 3	Brentwood 14-3
Oct 15	Eddie Gonzales	w ko 2	Hamburg
Oct 29	Chris Jacobs	w rsf 1	Cardiff 14-11-8
1992			
Jan 21	Conroy Nelson	w rsf 2	Norwich 14-10
	(vacant WBC International heavyweight title)		
Mar 3	Percell Davis	w ko 1	Amsterdam 14-8
Sep 8	Jean Chanet	w rsf 7*	Norwich 14-12
Oct 6	Craig Petersen	w rsf 7	Antwerp
	(WBC International heavyweight title)		
Dec 12	James Pritchard	w rsf 2	Muswell Hill 14-12

Fights 19 Won 19

Tim HILL
Super-featherweight
North Shields born 23 January 1974

1992			
Nov 9	Fred Reeves	w ko 4	Bradford 9-6

Fights 1 Won 1

Dean HISCOX
Welterweight
Dudley born 15 January 1969
Dudley ABC

1988			
Oct 6	Dave Croft	w pts 6	Dudley 9-9
1989-90			
inactive			
1991			
May 14	Eddie King	l pts 6	Dudley 10-4
Jun 5	Eddie King	l pts 6	Wolverhampton 10-7
Nov 21	Chris Aston	l pts 6	Stafford 10-2
Dec 2	Steve Bricknell	w pts 6	Birmingham 10-4
1992			
Mar 17	Mark Legg	l pts 6	Wolverhampton 10-3
May 18	Craig Hartwell	w pts 6	Bardon 10-3
Oct 13	Rob Stevenson	w pts 6	Wolverhampton 10-7
Nov 12	Peter Reid	l pts 6	Stafford 10-10
Dec 2	Darren McInulty	drew 6	Bardon 10-10

Fights 10 Won 4 Lost 5 Drawn 1

Gary HISCOX

Light-welterweight
Dudley born 25 May 1970
Southpaw
Dudley ABC

1992
Oct 14	Alan Ingle	l pts 6	Stoke 9-13
Nov 12	Shane Sheridan	w pts 6	Stafford 10-2

Fights 2 Won 1 Lost 1

Paul HITCH

Super-middleweight
Wingate, born Hartlepool 7 May 1968
Horden & Peterlee ABC
1988 North-East Division ABA light-middleweight final (w ko 1 S McDowell, l rsf 2 W Neil)
1989 North East ABA middleweight final (w S Bellfield, w S McMahon, w rsf 3 K Duke, l rsf 2 H Wharton)
1990 Northern ABA middleweight final (w S Bellfield, w A Exley, w N Manners, l ko 2 E Noi)
1991 Northern ABA middleweight final (w rsf 2 M Pluves, w rsf 1 T Robinson, l E Noi)

1991
May 10	Tony Kosova	w rtd 1	Gateshead 11-12
May 13	Terry Johnson	w pts 6	Middlesbrough 12-1
Jun 17	Max McCracken	w pts 6	Edgbaston 12-0
Oct 22	Chris Walker	w pts 6	Hartlepool 11-13-12
Nov 14	Paul Burton	w ko 2	Gateshead 12-0
Dec 12	Doug Calderwood	w pts 6	Hartlepool

1992
Mar 3	Simon McDougall	w pts 6	Houghton-le-Spring 11-13
Apr 28	Chris Walker	l rsf 2	Houghton-le-Spring 12-1
Sep 10	Griff Jones	w rsf 2	Sunderland 11-13
Oct 23	Paul Burton	w rtd 5	Gateshead 12-2

Fights 10 Won 9 Lost 1

Mick HOBAN

Light-welterweight
Burnley born 25 July 1967
Collyhurst & Moston ABC

1989
Apr 19	Steve Booth	l pts 6	Doncaster 9-12

1990-91 inactive

1992
Oct 13	Danny Kett	w pts 6	Bury 10-3
Dec 7	Lee Soar	w pts 6	Manchester 10-2-8

Fights 3 Won 2 Lost 1

Paul HODKINSON

Featherweight
Liverpool born 14 September 1965
Kirkby ABC
1980 England Schools (v Wal, w F Havard)
1981 National Schools champion (w R Taylor)
1981 Junior ABA final (l S Conyard)
1982 Junior ABA champion (w rsf 3* D Middleton)
1982 National Schools champion (w D Bishop)
1983 Young England (v EGer, w Zulow)
1984 West Lancs ABA bantamweight final (l J Hyland)
1985 Northern ABA featherweight final (w rsf 3 F Ratcliffe, w ko 2 J Gallagher, w rsf 1 D Oakes, w rsf 3 P English, l rsf 1 J Davison)
1985 Acropolis Cup silver medal (w Di Napoli, It; w rsf 2 Moreno, Sp; l Achik, Mor)
1985 England (v Hun, w tdec G Kinces - Hodkinson cut but ahead on points)
1986 ABA featherweight champion (w P English, w J Davison, w C McMillan, w T Khan, w rsf 3 D Anderson)
1986 England (v Sco, w rsf 1 A Ingle)

1986
Jul 19	Mark Champney	w ko 2	Wembley 9-1
Sep 17	Phil Lashley	w rsf 2	Albert Hall 9-2
Sep 29	Les Remikie	w rtd 4*	NSC 9-5
Oct 29	Craig Windsor	w ko 2	Belfast 9-3-12

1987
Jan 17	Steve Sims	w ko 5	Belfast 9-1-8
Feb 26	Kamel Djadda	w rsf 4*	Bethnal Green 9-3
Apr 25	Russell Jones	w rsf 6	Belfast 9-2-12
Jul 31	Tomas Arguelles	drew 6	Panama City
Oct 19	Tomas Arguelles	w ko 6	Belfast
Dec 7	Marcus Smith	w rsf 7	Belfast 9-0-12

1988
Jan 27	Richie Foster	w rsf 3	Belfast 9-0-8
May 18	Peter Harris (British featherweight title)	w rsf 12	Port Talbot 9-0
Dec 14	Kevin Taylor (British featherweight title)	w rsf 2	Liverpool 9-0

1989
Jan 18	Johnny Carter	w ko 1	Albert Hall 9-3-8
Apr 12	Raymond Armand (vacant European featherweight title)	w rsf 2	Belfast 9-0
Sep 6	Peter Harris (British and European featherweight title)	w rsf 9*	Port Talbot 9-0
Dec 13	Farid Benredjeb (European featherweight title)	w rsf 8	Liverpool 8-13-12

1990
Mar 28	Eduardo Montoya	w rsf 3	Manchester 8-13-12
Jun 2	Marcos Villasana (vacant WBC featherweight title)	l rsf 8	Manchester 8-13-8
Oct 30	Guy Bellehigue (European featherweight title)	w rsf 3	Wembley 8-13-12

1991
Nov 13	Marcos Villasana (WBC featherweight title)	w pts 12	Belfast 8-13-12

1992
Apr 25	Steve Cruz (WBC featherweight title)	w rsf 3	Belfast 8-13-12
Sep 12	Fabrice Benichou (WBC featherweight title)	w rsf 10*	Blagnac

Fights 23 Won 21 Lost 1 Drawn 1

Andy HOLLIGAN

Light-welterweight
Liverpool born 6 June 1967
Rotunda ABC
1987 ABA light-welterweight champion (w ko 1 G Hughes, w ko 1 C Teasdale, w ko 3 J Daly, w C Smith,
w M Stones, w B Kearney, w ko 1 D Jenkins, w R Bryan)
1987 Acropolis Cup bronze medal (w rsf 2 Zanker, WGer; l S Kolethras, Gre)

1987
Oct 19	Glyn Rhodes	w pts 6	Belfast 9-13-8
Dec 7	Jimmy Thornton	w rtd 2*	Belfast 10-4-4

1988
Jan 27	Andy Morgan	w rsf 5	Belfast 10-1-12
Mar 26	Tony Richards	w rsf 2	Belfast
Jun 8	David Maw	w rsf 1	Sheffield 10-3
Oct 19	Lennie Gloster	w pts 6	Belfast 10-2-12
Dec 14	Sugar Gibiliru	w pts 8	Liverpool 10-2

1989
Mar 16	Jeff Decker	w rsf 5	Southwark 10-4
Sep 19	Billy Buchanan	w rsf 4	Belfast 10-0-10
Oct 25	Tony Adams	w rsf 5	Wembley 10-1-8

1990
Sep 26	Mike Durvan	w ko 1	AASC 10-1-8
Oct 30	Eric Corroyez	w rtd 2*	Wembley 10-2

1991
Apr 17	Pat Ireland	w rsf 1	Albert Hall 10-3-12
May 16	Simon Eubanks	w ko 2	Liverpool 10-3
Jun 20	Tony Ekubia	w pts 12	Liverpool 9-13
	(British & Commonwealth light-welterweight titles)		
Nov 28	Steve Larrimore	w rsf 8	Liverpool 9-13-12
	(Commonwealth light-welterweight title)		

1992
Feb 27	Tony McKenzie	w rsf 3	Liverpool 9-13-15
	(British & Commonwealth light-welterweight titles)		
Sep 15	Tony Ekubia	w ko 7	Liverpool 9-13
	(British & Commonwealth light-welterweight titles)		
Oct 7	Dwayne Swift	w pts 10	Sunderland 10-2
Nov 12	Mark Smith	w pts 10	Liverpool 10-1-8

Fights 20 Won 20

Dean HOLLINGTON

Light-welterweight
West Ham born 25 February 1969
Repton ABC
1982 National Schools final (l T Lamont)
1983 National Schools champion
1984 Junior ABA champion (w L Woolcock)
1985 Junior ABA champion
1986 NABC Class B final (l C Wright)
1988 NABC Class C champion (w C Donovan)
1989 NE London ABA light-welter semi-final (l rsf 1 E Diedrick)

1990
Feb 20	David Jenkins	w pts 4	Millwall 9-12-8
Apr 6	Marcel Herbert	w pts 6	Stevenage 9-12
Sep 25	Andre Marcel Cleak	w rsf 5	Millwall 10-2

1991
Feb 12	Andy Robins	w rsf 4	Basildon

Mar 7	David Jenkins	w pts 6	Basildon 10-2-8
Apr 17	James Lawlor	w pts 6	Albert Hall 10-2
Oct 23	John Smith	w pts 6	Bethnal Green 10-2-8
Nov 13	James Lawlor	w pts 6	Bethnal Green 10-3
1992			
Feb 11	Nigel Bradley	w pts 6	Barking 10-4
Apr 2	Tony Gibbs	w ko 1	Basildon 10-3-8
May 16	Rick Bushell	w rsf 2	Albert Hall 10-1-12

Fights 11 Won 11

Mick HOLMES

Light-welterweight
Barnsley born Burnley 15 May 1971

1991			
Oct 7	Chris Aston	l rsf 2	Bradford 10-1
1992			
Mar 3	Micky Hall	l rsf 2	Houghton-le-Spring 10-0
Oct 7	Alan Ingle	l rsf 5	Glasgow 10-1

Fights 3 Lost 3

Mark HOLT

Featherweight
Birmingham born 7 March 1967
Southpaw
Nechells ABC
1987 Birmingham ABA lightweight semi-final (l ko 1 L James)
1988 Midlands ABA featherweight champion (w K Williams, w S Doyle, w K Kearney, l M Smyth)

1988			
Nov 18	Alan McKay	l pts 6	NSC 8-13
Nov 22	Michael Close	w ko 2	Wolverhampton 9-1
Dec 7	Michael Armstrong	w pts 8	Stoke 9-3-8
1989			
Mar 22	Kid Sumaila	w pts 6	Solihull 9-3-8
May 10	Colin Lynch	w rsf 7	Solihull 9-0
	(Midlands featherweight title)		
Oct 4	Derek Amory	w pts 10	Solihull 8-12
	(Midlands featherweight title)		
Dec 9	Moussa Sangeree	l rtd 6	Grande-Synthe
1990			
Mar 14	Henry Armstrong	l pts 8	Stoke 9-0
May 3	Jimmi Bredahl	l pts 8	Greve
Oct 3	Rocky Lawlor	w rsf 4*	Solihull 8-11-12
	(Midlands featherweight title)		
Nov 12	Colin McMillan	l pts 8	Norwich 9-2
1991			
Mar 19	Steve Walker	l pts 8	Birmingham 9-2-8
Oct 15	Billy Barton	w pts 8	Dudley 9-2-12
Dec 7	Michael Armstrong	l rsf 4*	Manchester
1992			
Feb 28	Wilson Rodriguez	l rsf 3	Madrid

Fights 15 Won 7 Lost 8

Lloyd HONEYGHAN

Light-middleweight
Bermondsey, born Jamaica 22 April 1960
Downside ABC & Fisher ABC
1977 NABC Class B champion (w D McGarry)
1978 NABC Class C final (l J Frost)
1978 SE London ABA welterweight final (l J Donovan)
1978 Young England (v EGer, l T Rubel)
1979 London ABA welterweight champion (w ko 3 C Phillips, w D Bergonzi, w L Morgan, l J Frost)
1980 England (v Sco, w T McCallum)
1980 SE London ABA welterweight final (l G Roomes)

1980
Dec 8	Mike Sullivan	w pts 6	Albert Hall 10-4-4

1981
Jan 20	Dai Davies	w rsf 5	Bethnal Green
Feb 10	Dave Sullivan	w pts 6	Bethnal Green
Nov 16	Dave Finigan	w rsf 1	AASC
Nov 24	Alan Cooper	w rsf 4	Wembley

1982
Jan 25	Dave Finigan	w ko 2	AASC
Feb 9	Granville Allen	w rsf 5	Albert Hall
Mar 2	Tommy McCallum	w pts 6	Albert Hall
Mar 15	Derek McKenzie	w rsf 6	AASC
Mar 23	Dave Sullivan	w rsf 3	Bethnal Green
May 18	Kostas Petrou	w pts 8	Bethnal Green
Sep 22	Ian Murray	w rsf 3*	WSC
Nov 22	Frank McCord	w ko 1	AASC

1983
Jan 18	Lloyd Hibbert	w pts 10	Albert Hall
	(eliminator, British welterweight title)		
Mar 1	Sid Smith	w ko 5	Albert Hall
	(eliminator, British welterweight title; Southern welterweight title)		
Apr 5	Cliff Gilpin	w pts 12	Albert Hall 10-6-12
	(vacant British welterweight title)		
Jul 9	Kevin Austin	w rsf 10	Chicago
Oct 24	Harold Brazier	w pts 10	Mayfair 10-7-8
Dec 6	Cliff Gilpin	w pts 12	Albert Hall 10-4-4
	(British welterweight title)		

1984
Jun 5	Roberto Mendez	w pts 8	Albert Hall 10-8-8

1985
Jan 5	Gianfranco Rosi	w ko 3	Perugia 10-5-4
	(European welterweight title)		
Feb 12	R.W.Smith	w rtd 6*	Albert Hall
Mar 6	Roger Stafford	w rsf 9	Albert Hall 10-6
Aug 30	Danny Paul	w pts 10	Atlantic City 10-8-4
Oct 1	Ralph Twinning	w rsf 4	Wembley 10-7
Nov 27	Sylvester Mittee	w rsf 8*	Muswell Hill 10-5-12
	(British, Commonwealth & European welterweight titles)		

1986
May 20	Horace Shufford	w rsf 8	Wembley 10-6
	(final eliminator, WBC welterweight title)		
Sep 27	Don Curry	w rsf 6	Atlantic City
	(World welterweight title)		

1987
Feb 22	Johnny Bumphus	w rsf 2	Wembley GH 10-6-6
	(IBF welterweight title)		
Apr 18	Maurice Blocker	w pts 12	Albert Hall 10-7
	(WBC, IBF welterweight titles)		

Aug 30	Gene Hatcher (WBC welterweight title)	w rsf 1	Marbella
Oct 28	Jorge Vaca (WBC welterweight title)	l tdec 8 (s)	Wembley 10-6-9
1988			
Mar 29	Jorge Vaca (WBC welterweight title)	w ko 3	Wembley 10-6-8
Jul 29	Young-kil Chung (WBC welterweight title)	w rsf 5	Atlantic City 10-7
1989			
Feb 4	Marlon Starling (WBC welterweight title)	l rsf 9	Las Vegas 10-6-8
Aug 25	Delfino Marin	w pts 10	Miami 10-9-8
1990			
Mar 3	Mark Breland (WBA welterweight title)	l rsf 3	Wembley
1991			
Jan 10	Mario Olmedo	w rsf 4*	Battersea 11-1-8
Feb 12	John Welters	w rsf 1	Basildon 11-0-8
May 8	Darryl Anthony	w ko 2	Albert Hall 11-1
1992			
Apr 22	Alfredo Ramirez	w pts 8	Wembley 11-1-8
May 13	Mickey Duncan	w rsf 2	Albert Hall 11-4
Oct 28	Carlo Colarusso	w rsf 6*	Albert Hall 11-2

Fights 43 Won 40 Lost 3

Ian HONEYWOOD

Lightweight
Swanley, born Newmarket 20 July 1964
Cambridge Police ABC
1984 Eastern ABA featherweight champion (w rsf 1 A Gouge, w J Doran, w C Lynch, l K Taylor)
1986 Eastern ABA lightweight champion (l L Amass)

1986			
Oct 22	Wayne Weekes	w pts 6	Greenwich 9-7
Nov 10	Andrew Pybus	w rtd 2*	Birmingham 9-7
Nov 17	Lee West	l pts 6	Dulwich 9-7
Nov 28	Nigel Senior	l rsf 5	Peterborough 9-6-8
1987			
May 1	Bill Smith	w pts 6	Peterborough 9-7
May 26	Jess Rundan	w rtd 3*	Plymouth 9-7
Sep 10	Gary Maxwell	drew 6	Peterborough 9-8
Sep 25	Doug Munro	l rsf 5*	Westcliff
1988			
Jan 18	Andrew Furlong	w pts 8	Mayfair 9-11-8
Mar 17	Harry Escott	l rsf 4	Sunderland 9-8-12
Apr 19	Jim Moffat	l pts 8	Glasgow 9-12
May 9	Ray Newby	l rsf 1	Nottingham 9-10
Aug 30	Tony Borg	w pts 6	Holborn 9-12-8
Oct 31	Brian Nickels	l pts 6	Bedford 9-11
Dec 1	Kid Sumaila	w pts 4	Gravesend 9-11
1989			
Jan 18	Nigel Wenton	l rsf 3*	Albert Hall 9-7-8
Feb 18	Sonny Long	w pts 8	Budapest 9-5
Mar 28	Willie Beattie	l pts 4	Glasgow 10-3
Apr 24	Nigel Senior	w pts 4	Nottingham 9-9
May 21	Wayne Weekes (vacant Southern lightweight title)	w rsf 4*	Finsbury Park 9-9

/CTD..

(Ian HONEYWOOD ctd.)

Jun 27	Tony Foster	w pts 6	Albert Hall 9-9
Sep 25	Dean Bramhald	w rtd 4	Crystal Palace 10-2
Dec 18	Johnny Kalbhenn	l pts 8 (m)	Kitchener 9-10-8
1990			
Apr 23	Paul Gadney	w pts 10	Crystal Palace 9-9
	(Southern lightweight title)		
Jun 22	Martin Cruz	w rtd 3*	Gillingham 9-9-4
Sep 24	Marvin P. Gray	w pts 8	Lewisham 9-13-8
Dec 19	Carl Crook	l rsf 4	Preston 9-8
	(British & Commonwealth lightweight titles)		
1991			
Mar 10	Pierre Lorcy	l ko 5	Paris 9-12-12
Sep 24	Dave Anderson	l pts 8	Glasgow 9-12-14
Nov 13	Steve Walker	w pts 6	Bethnal Green 9-11-8
1992			
Jan 18	Steve Pollard	w pts 6	Albert Hall 9-12
Mar 30	Tony Foster	w rsf 4*	Eltham 9-13-12
Apr 30	Sean Murphy	l rsf 1	Albert Hall 9-8-8

Fights 33 Won 18 Lost 14 Drawn 1

Donnie HOOD

Bantamweight
Glasgow born 3 June 1963
Holyrood ABC
1984 Scotland (v Ire, l P Sutcliffe)
1985 Scottish ABA bantamweight champion (w G Brooks, w M Deveney, w D Ingram, l S Murphy)
1985 Scotland (v Wal, l D Lynch; v Ire, l R Nash)
1985 European Championships bantamweight (l R Nistor, Rum)
1986 Scotland (v Eng, l J Davison; v Wal, w D Lynch)
1986 Scottish ABA bantamweight semi-final (w G Shaw, w ko 1 G Gill, l G Brooks)

1986			
Sep 22	Stewart Fisher-Mack	w pts 6	Glasgow 8-9-8
Sep 29	Keith Ward	w pts 6	Glasgow 8-9-8
Dec 8	Jamie McBride	drew 8	Glasgow 8-6
Dec 22	Keith Ward	l pts 8	Glasgow 8-8
1987			
Jan 27	Chris Clarkson	w pts 6	Glasgow 8-7
Feb 9	Danny Porter	w rsf 4	Glasgow 8-5
Feb 24	Danny Lee	w pts 8	Glasgow 8-8
Sep 7	Kid Sumaila	w pts 8	Glasgow 8-9
Sep 15	David Ingram	l pts 8	Batley 8-8
Oct 26	Jimmy Lee	w pts 8	Glasgow 8-9
Nov 25	Brian Holmes	w pts 10	Bellahouston 8-5-12
	(vacant Scottish bantamweight title)		
1988			
Mar 28	Nigel Crook	w ko 2	Glasgow 8-8
May 12	Eyup Can	l pts 8	Copenhagen
Jun 14	Fransie Badenhorst	l rsf 7	Durban
Sep 5	Gerry McBride	w rtd 7	Glasgow 8-9-8
Oct 24	Graham O'Malley	w rsf 9*	Hartlepool 8-4
	(eliminator, British bantamweight title)		
1989			
Mar 6	Francisco Garcia	w rsf 6	Glasgow 8-5-8
Mar 28	John Vasquez	w rtd 5	Glasgow 8-8
Jun 27	Ray Minus jnr	l rsf 6	Bellahouston 8-5
	(Commonwealth bantamweight title)		

1990			
Jan 22	Dean Lynch	w pts 8	Glasgow 8-5
Mar 26	Keith Wallace	w rtd 8	Glasgow 8-6
	(eliminator, British bantamweight title)		
Oct 9	Samuel Duran	w pts 12 (s)	Glasgow 8-5-12
	(WBC International bantamweight title)		
Dec 10	David Moreno	w rsf 4	Glasgow 8-8-8
1991			
Jan 25	Dave Buxton	w rsf 5	Shotts
Mar 5	Virgilio Openio	w pts 12 (s)	Glasgow 8-5-14
	(WBC International bantamweight title)		
May 31	Willie Richardson	w pts 8	Glasgow 8-10
Sep 24	Rocky Commey	w pts 12	Glasgow 8-6
	(WBC International bantamweight title)		
Oct 24	Vinnie Ponzio	w pts 8	Glasgow
1992			
Mar 14	Johnny Bredahl	l rsf 7	Copenhagen
	(vacant European bantamweight title)		
May 29	Peter Buckley	w pts 8	Glasgow 8-8-12

Fights 30 Won 23 Lost 6 Drawn 1

Carl HOOK

Light-welterweight
Swansea born 21 November 1969
RAOB ABC
1990 Welsh ABA light-welterweight final (w ko 3 P Hallett, w W Ousley, l rsf 2 C Smith)
1991 Welsh ABA light-welterweight final (w M Bowley, w T Khan, l J Matthews)
1991 Wales (v Sco, w rsf 1 C Wright)

1991			
Jul 18	Jason Matthews	l pts 6	Cardiff 9-13
Jul 25	Wayne Taylor	w pts 6	Dudley 9-12
Sep 16	Nico Lucas	w pts 6	AASC 9-10
Sep 26	Ronnie Shinkwin	l pts 8	Dunstable 10-0
Oct 24	John O. Johnson	w pts 6	Dunstable 9-12
Oct 31	Davey Robb	l pts 4	Telford 10-0
Dec 5	Mark Ramsey	l rsf 4	Telford 10-0
1992			
Jan 23	Phil Epton	l pts 6	York 10-3-12
Feb 11	Jason Matthews	l pts 6	Cardiff 10-2
May 11	Derrick Daniel	l pts 6	Piccadilly 10-0
Jun 16	Derrick Daniel	w rsf 2	Dagenham 10-0-4
Nov 14	Eddie Lloyd	l pts 6	Cardiff 9-7-4

Fights 12 Won 4 Lost 8

Ron HOPLEY

Welterweight
Ripon born 3 April 1969

1991			
Nov 27	William Beatton	w rsf 2	Marton
1992			
Jan 23	Rick North	w pts 6	York 10-10
Apr 8	Steve Howden	l pts 6	Leeds 10-7

Fights 3 Won 2 Lost 1

Steve HOWDEN
Light-welterweight
Sheffield born 4 June 1969

1992
Apr 8	Ron Hopley	w pts 6	Leeds 10-2
Jun 1	Kevin McKillan	l rsf 2	Manchester 9-12
Jul 7	Mike Morrison	l ko 3	Bristol
Oct 1	Jimmy Reynolds	l rtd 2	Telford 10-0

Fights 4 Won 1 Lost 3

Mickey HUGHES
Light-middleweight
St Pancras born 13 June 1962
St Pancras ABC
1978 Junior ABA champion (w J Moran)
1979 Junior ABA champion
1979 NABC champion
1984 ABA welter champ (w R Callaghan, w ko 2 O Jones, w C Blake, w ko 1 F Harding, w H Mullen, w rsf 3 R Thomas)
1984 Los Angeles Olympics welterweight (w P Rasaminamana, Mad; l G Obreja, Rum)

1985
Oct 1	Steve Tempro	w pts 6	Wembley 10-8-4
Oct 16	Manny Romain	w rsf 2	Albert Hall 10-9-4

1986
May 29	Junaid Musah	w rsf 4	Bethnal Green 10-8-8
Sep 22	Cliff Domville	w rsf 4	NSC 11-0
Oct 23	Ian Chantler	w rsf 6	Basildon 10-12-4
Nov 20	Manny Romain	w ko 4	Bethnal Green 10-11

1987
Jan 22	Simon Paul	w rsf 2	Bethnal Green 10-9
Feb 22	Mike Essett	w rsf 5	Wembley GH 10-7-8
Mar 19	Andy O'Rawe	w rsf 2	Bethnal Green 10-9
Apr 9	Kelvin Mortimer	w rsf 6	Bethnal Green 10-8
Sep 25	Kelvin Mortimer	w pts 8	Westcliff 10-8-4
Oct 24	David Taylor	l pts 8	Tottenham 10-8
Dec 3	Del Bryan	l pts 8	Southend 10-8

1988
Mar 14	Paul Murray	w rsf 4	NSC 10-11
Oct 5	Chris Blake	w rsf 5	Wembley GH
Nov 30	Jeff Decker	w rsf 3	Southwark 10-11

1989
Feb 2	Lennie Gloster	w rsf 6	Southwark 10-6
Sep 28	Trevor Smith	l rsf 6	Battersea 10-6-8
	(Southern welterweight title)		

1990
Mar 6	Josif Rajc	w ko 2	Bethnal Green 10-9
Mar 20	Robert Wright	w rsf 7	Norwich 10-9
Jun 5	Parrish Johnson	w ko 3	Nottingham 10-8-12
Jul 10	Winston Wray	w rsf 5	Canvey Island 10-10
Sep 12	Nick Meloscia	w ko 1	Bethnal Green 10-9
Oct 17	Gary Jacobs	w ko 8	Bethnal Green 10-8-4

1991
Feb 6	Ian John-Lewis	w rsf 9*	Bethnal Green 10-6
Jun 4	Donovan Boucher	l pts 12	Bethnal Green 10-6-12
	(Commonwealth welterweight title)		

Nov 26	Delroy Bryan (British welterweight title)	l rsf 3*	Bethnal Green 10-7
1992			
Jun 16	Andy Furlong	w ko 1	Dagenham 11-0-6
Sep 15	Craig Trotter (vacant Commonwealth light-middleweight title)	w pts 12	Crystal Palace 11-0

Fights 29 Won 24 Lost 5

Paul HUGHES

Light-welterweight
Manchester born 1 December 1966

1991			
Oct 9	Geoff Lawson	w rtd 1*	Middlesbrough 10-0
Oct 17	Tony Doyle	w pts 6	Mossley 9-12
Nov 13	Joey Moffatt	l rtd 4	Liverpool 9-12
1992			
Jun 1	Ty Zubair	w pts 6	Manchester 9-12

Fights 4 Won 3 Lost 1

Roger HUNTE

Lightweight
Leyton born 28 October 1971

1992			
Feb 12	Jason Barker	w rtd 4*	Wembley GH 9-9-8
Mar 25	Phil Cullen	w rsf 3	Albert Hall 9-8

Fights 2 Won 2

Cordwell HYLTON

Cruiserweight
Walsall, born Jamaica 20 September 1958
Bloxwich ABC
1979 Midlands ABA light-heavyweight final (w ko 2 S Calvert, l R Christie)
1980 North Midlands ABA light-heavyweight final (l R Smith)

1980			
Sep 22	Nigel Savory	w pts 6	Wolverhampton 12-5
Oct 30	Steve Fenton	w ko 2	Wolverhampton 12-3
Dec 1	Liam Coleman	l pts 6	Wolverhampton 12-8
1981			
Feb 2	Steve Fenton	w pts 6	Nottingham
Feb 10	John O'Neill	w rsf 6	Wolverhampton
Mar 16	Chris Lawson	l rsf 5	AASC 12-8
Apr 13	Rupert Christie	w rsf 5	Wolverhampton 12-5
May 11	Trevor Cattouse	l pts 8	AASC 12-8
Oct 5	Antonio Harris	w pts 8	Birmingham
Nov 30	Ben Lawlor	w rsf 2	Birmingham
1982			
Jan 23	Chisanda Mutti	l rsf 3	Berlin
Feb 16	Mama Mohammed	l pts 8	Birmingham
Mar 10	Devon Bailey	l rsf 2	Birmingham
May 24	Clive Beardsley	w rsf 4	Nottingham
Sep 20	Keith Bristol	nc 5	Wolverhampton
Oct 5	Alex Tompkins	w pts 8	NSC
Nov 23	Winston Burnett	w rsf 5	Wolverhampton
Dec 13	Steve Babbs	l ko 1	Wolverhampton /CTD..

(Cordwell HYLTON ctd.)

1983

Feb 15	Alek Penarski	w rsf 4	Wolverhampton
Feb 23	Devon Bailey	l rsf 6	Mayfair
Mar 28	Gordon Stacey	w rsf 1	Birmingham 12-7
Apr 25	Alex Tompkins	w pts 8	Southwark 12-6
May 19	Richard Caramanolis	l ko 4	Paris
Dec 3	Andrew Straughn	l pts 8	Marylebone 12-12

1984

Jan 25	Romal Ambrose	w rsf 3*	Solihull 12-4
Jun 7	Roy Skeldon	l ko 7	Dudley 12-9
Dec 1	Louis Pergaud	l dis 6	Dusseldorf

1985

Feb 23	Chris Reid	l ko 3	Belfast 12-10
Mar 25	Harry Andrews	w pts 6	Wolverhampton 12-9
Jun 5	Tony Wilson	l ko 5	Albert Hall 12-9

1986

inactive

1987

Oct 12	Ivan Joseph	l ko 6	Bow 13-3-8

1988

Feb 24	Johnny Nelson	l rsf 1	Sheffield 13-7
Mar 29	Eric Cardouza	w ko 5	Wembley 13-7
May 5	Derek Angol	l rsf 5	Bethnal Green 13-9
Sep 19	Mike Aubrey	l pts 6	NSC 13-6
Nov 22	Crawford Ashley	l ko 3	Basildon 13-3

1989

Feb 2	Branko Pavlovic	w rsf 2	Croydon 13-3
Mar 21	Abner Blackstock	w ko 2	Wolverhampton 13-4
Apr 15	Alfredo Cacciatore	l dis 6	Vasto 13-6
May 21	Brendan Dempsey	w pts 8	Finsbury Park 13-4
Aug 12	Paul Muyodi	l rsf 4*	San Sepoicro
Dec 16	Lajos Eros	l rsf 5	Cesena

1990

Jan 17	Mick Cordon	w pts 8	Stoke 14-0
Feb 8	Jimmy Peters	w rsf 4*	Southwark 13-9
Mar 8	Terry Dixon	l pts 8	Watford 13-8
Apr 25	Tee Jay	l rsf 1	Millwall 13-12
Jun 2	Glazz Campbell	w pts 4	Manchester 13-9
Oct 30	Henry Maske	l rsf 3	Wembley 13-4

1991

Feb 12	Steve Lewsam	w rsf 8	Wolverhampton 13-12
Feb 22	Bobbi Joe Edwards	w rtd 6*	Manchester 14-0
Mar 20	Roy Smith	w rsf 7	Solihull 13-8
	(Midlands cruiserweight title)		
May 17	Niels H. Madsen	l rsf 2	Copenhagen
Jun 22	Norbert Ekassi	l ko 5	Paris
Sep 16	Steve Lewsam	l pts 10	Cleethorpes
	(Midlands cruiserweight title)		
Nov 28	Tony Wilson	l pts 8	Wolverhampton 13-0

1992

Feb 21	Markus Bott	l pts 8	Hamburg
Mar 6	Yuri Razumov	drew 6	Berlin
Mar 27	Jean-Marie Emebe	w rsf 3	Criel
Oct 22	Kemec Saleta	l rsf 4	Bethnal Green 13-9-8

Fights 59 Won 26 Lost 31 Drawn 1 No Contests 1

Vance IDIENS

Heavyweight
Cannock, born Great Wyrley 9 June 1962
Bloxwich ABC

1989
Oct 24	Mick Cordon	w pts 6	Wolverhampton 15-5
Nov 28	Ted Shaw	w ko 1	Wolverhampton 15-4
Dec 6	Mick Cordon	w pts 6	Stoke 15-0

1990
Feb 19	David Jules	w pts 6	Birmingham 15-3
Mar 22	Mick Cordon	w pts 6	Wolverhampton 15-5
May 24	Michael Richards	l rsf 5	Dudley 15-9
Jun 28	Paul Neilson	w pts 8	Birmingham 16-1
Sep 27	Paul Neilson	w pts 8	NEC 15-7-8
Nov 14	Paul Neilson	l rsf 2	Doncaster 15-2

1991
Dec 5	David Jules	w rsf 4*	Cannock 15-7

1992
Mar 6	Mario Schiesser	l rsf 1	Berlin
Dec 9	David Jules	w pts 8	Stoke 15-3

Fights 12 Won 9 Lost 3

Alan INGLE

Light-welterweight
Dunbar, born Haddington 31 August 1968
Haddington ABC
1986 Scotland (v En, l rsf 1 P Hodkinson)
1987 Scottish ABA light-welterweight prelim (l rsf 1 T Larmour)
1991 Scottish ABA welterweight quarter-final (w J Stirling, l T Dingwall)
1992 Scottish ABA welterweight final (w dis 3 T Jolly, w rsf 2 T Gonsalves, l A Craig)

1992
Sep 21	Kevin McKenzie	l pts 6	Glasgow 10-1-8
Oct 7	Mark Holmes	w rsf 5	Glasgow 10-0-8
Oct 14	Gary Hiscox	w pts 6	Stoke 10-0-12
Nov 18	Micky Hall	l rtd 3*	Solihull 9-11-4

Fights 4 Won 2 Lost 2

Colin INNES

Featherweight
Newcastle born 24 July 1964
Benfield ABC
1989 North East & Humberside ABA lightweight prelim (l ko 2 D Elsdon)

1990
Sep 10	Lee Christian	w rsf 5	Northampton 9-2
Sep 24	Steve Armstrong	w pts 6	Manchester 9-0
Oct 8	Ervine Blake	l pts 6	Bradford 9-2
Oct 22	Steve Armstrong	w rsf 6	Manchester 9-4
Nov 26	Carl Roberts	l rsf 3	Bury 9-1

1991
Feb 11	Steve Armstrong	w pts 6	Manchester 9-3
Feb 18	Ian McGirr	l pts 6	Glasgow 9-5
Mar 2	Tommy Smith	w pts 6	Darlington 9-2-8
Mar 28	Darrell Pettit	w rtd 3*	Alfreton 9-4 /CTD..

(Colin INNES ctd.)

Apr 30	Noel Carroll	l pts 4	Stockport 9-3
Sep 19	Carl Roberts	l pts 4	Stockport 9-4
Dec 12	Tommy Smith	l pts 6	Hartlepool
1992			
Feb 24	Mark Geraghty	l pts 8	Glasgow 9-6
Mar 30	Chris Jickells	l rsf 3	Bradford 9-4
May 28	Tommy Smith	l pts 6	Gosforth 9-5-8
Oct 5	Wayne Rigby	l pts 6	Manchester 9-4
Nov 18	Al Garrett	drew 6	Solihull 9-3

Fights 17 Won 6 Lost 10 Drawn 1

John IRWIN

Featherweight
Denaby born 31 May 1969
Tom Hill Youth ABC
1987 Young England (v WG, w rsf 3 T Reindl)
1988 ABA featherweight semi-final (w D Ramsden, w rsf 2 P Cooper, w S Gunning, l D Anderson)
1988 England (v Cze, w M Pecha; v WG, w T Seiler; v Ire, w J Kilroy)
1989 England (v Sco, w R Ewen; v Pol, w G Jablonski; v Ire, w rsf 1 R Nash)
1989 North East Counties ABA featherweight final (l P Richardson)
1990 Commonwealth Games featherweight gold medal (w S Samuel, CkIs; w M Strange, Cn; w dis 3 J Nicholson, Aus; w H Ally, Tan)
1990 England (v Sco, w I McLeod; v Ire, w R Nash)
1991 ABA featherweight champion (w rsf 2 C Jickells, w rsf 2 S Hurcombe, w J Mellor, w M Ward, w P Samuels, w M Bowers)
1991 England (v Sco, w rsf 2 S Taylor; v Den, w B Lamina)
1991 World Championships featherweight (w M Yamoto, Jp; l P Griffin, Ire)
1992 Olympic Qualifying tournament, France (l B Carr, Sc)

1992			
Sep 8	Kid McAuley	w pts 6	Doncaster 9-2
Sep 30	Miguel Matthews	w pts 6	Solihull 9-2
Nov 24	Colin Lynch	w rsf 4	Doncaster 9-2-4

Fights 3 Won 3

Pat Cowdell Boxing Camp

Subsidiary of Pat Cowdell Promotions Ltd

129a Moat Road, Oldbury/Warley,
West Midlands B68 8EE
Tel: 021 552 8082

MALCOLM MELVIN	Midlands Light-Welterweight Champion	6 x 3 8 x 3 10 x 3
JUSTIN CLEMENTS	Super-middleweight	6 x 2 8 x 2
ALAN GANDY	Super-middleweight	6 x 2 8 x 2
ALFIE ANDREWS	Middleweight	6 x 2 8 x 2
ANDRE WHARTON	Middleweight	8 x 2 6 x 3
ERNIE LOCK	Welterweight	6 x 2
HOWARD CLARKE	Welterweight	6 x 3 8 x 3
SPENCER McCRACKEN	Welterweight	8 x 2 6 x 3
DEREK AMORY	9st to 9st 4lb	8 x 2 6 x 3 8 x 3
GRAHAM McGRATH	Bantamweight	6 x 2 8 x 2 4 x 3

129a Moat Road, Oldbury/Warley.
West Midlands B68 8EE
Tel: 021 552 8082

SPORT ART
"SIMPLY THE BEST"
FOR BOXING LIMITED EDITION ART PRINTS & ORIGINALS

From the nation's leading Fight Artists, **DOREEN & BRIAN MEADOWS**. Recognised worldwide for their Boxing studies

MANY WORLD CHAMPIONS PAST & PRESENT ARE THE PROUD OWNERS OF THEIR WORK

Send £1 for brochure

TEL: 0942 58572 (24 HRS)
FAX: 0942 53747 (24 HRS)

4 Balmoral Drive, Hindley, Wigan, Lancs. WN2 3HS

Cyril JACKSON

Super-middleweight
Wrexham born 19 September 1962
Mold ABC

1985
Sep 12	George Gray	w rsf 4	Blaenavon 11-12
Oct 15	John Hadleigh	w pts 6	Leeds 12-0
Nov 6	Joey Saunders	w rsf 3	Nantwich
Dec 11	John McGlynn	l ko 1	Stoke 11-8

1986
Jan 16	Dean Scarfe	l rsf 3	Fulham 11-6

1987
Apr 28	Steve Foster	l rsf 7*	Manchester 11-12
Jul 31	Seamus Casey	w rsf 5*	Wrexham
Oct 19	Steve Foster	l rtd 3*	Manchester 11-2

1988
Dec 7	Rocky Reynolds	w rtd 6*	Port Talbot 11-7

1989
Sep 28	Cliff Curtis	w rtd 3*	Cardiff 11-10
Nov 13	Antonio Fernandez	l pts 8	Brierley Hill 11-9

1990
Feb 3	Ahmet Canbakis	w pts 6	Bristol 11-12

1991
inactive

1992
Oct 27	Darrit Douglas	l rsf 3	Leicester 12-0

Fights 13 Won 7 Lost 6

Gilbert JACKSON

Light-middleweight
Battersea, born Ghana 21 August 1970
Real name: Gilbert Amponsan

1992
Feb 17	John Bosco	l pts 6	AASC 11-4-8
Mar 6	Tony Wellington	w ko 2	Battersea 11-5
Apr 22	Russell Washer	w pts 6	Wembley 11-1
Sep 8	Paul Gamble	w rsf 1*	Norwich 11-4

Fights 4 Won 3 Lost 1

Gary JACOBS

Welterweight
Glasgow born 10 December 1965
Govan ABC
Southpaw

1985
May 20	John Conlan	w pts 6	Glasgow 10-11-8	
Jun 3	Nigel Burke	w pts 6	Glasgow 10-3-12	
Aug 12	Mike Mackenzie	w pts 6	Glasgow 10-5	
Oct 7	Albert Buchanan	w pts 6	Glasgow 10-8	
Nov 11	Tyrell Wilson	w ko 5	Glasgow 10-3-12	
Dec 2	Dave Heaver	w pts 6	Glasgow 10-10	/CTD..

(Gary JACOBS ctd.)

1986
Feb 10	Courtney Phillips	w rsf 5	Glasgow 10-10
Mar 10	Alistair Laurie	w pts 8	Glasgow 10-9
Apr 14	Billy Cairns	w pts 8	Glasgow 10-5
	(eliminator, Scottish welterweight title)		
Jun 24	Dave Douglas	l pts 10	Glasgow 10-6-8
	(vacant Scottish welterweight title)		
Sep 15	Jeff Decker	w rsf 3	Glasgow 10-8
Oct 20	Kelvin Mortimer	w rsf 5*	Glasgow 10-8-12

1987
Jan 27	Dave Douglas	w pts 10	Glasgow 10-5-8
	(Scottish welterweight title)		
Feb 24	Gary Williams	w ko 7	Glasgow 10-6-8
Apr 6	Robert Armstrong	w rtd 5*	Glasgow 10-9
May 19	Gary Williams	w rsf 3	Cumbernauld 10-8
Jun 8	Tommy McCallum	w rsf 5	Glasgow 10-6
	(Scottish welterweight title)		
Nov 26	Jeff Decker	w pts 8	Fulham 10-5

1988
Feb 24	Del Bryan	w pts 10	Glasgow 10-6-8
	(eliminator, British welterweight title)		
Apr 19	Wilf Gentzen	w pts 12	Glasgow 10-7
	(Commonwealth welterweight title)		
Jun 6	Juan Alonzo Villa	w rsf 5	Mayfair 10-9
Sep 16	Javier Suazo	w ko 10	Las Vegas 10-7
	(vacant WBC International welterweight title)		
Nov 29	Richard Rova	w ko 4	Albert Hall 10-7
	(Commonwealth welterweight title)		

1989
Feb 14	Rocky Kelly	w rsf 7*	Battersea 10-7
	(WBC International & Commonwealth welterweight titles)		
Apr 5	George Collins	w pts 12	Albert Hall 10-7
	(WBC International & Commonwealth welterweight titles)		
Jun 27	Rollin Williams	w rsf 1	Albert Hall 10-9
Aug 27	James "Buddy" McGirt	l pts 10	New York 10-6
Nov 23	Donovan Boucher	l pts 12	Motherwell 10-7
	(Commonwealth welterweight title)		

1990
Apr 26	Pascal Lorcy	w rsf 2*	Battersea 10-9
May 9	Mike Durvan	w ko 1	Albert Hall 10-9
Oct 17	Mickey Hughes	l ko 8	Bethnal Green 10-8-4

1991
Mar 5	Kenny Louis	w ko 2	Glasgow 10-9
Nov 20	Peter Eubanks	w pts 8	Albert Hall 10-8-8

1992
Feb 20	Del Bryan	w pts 12	Glasgow 10-6-4
	(British welterweight title)		
Mar 25	Tommy Small	w rsf 2	Albert Hall 10-9-8
Apr 22	Cirillo Nino	w pts 10	Wembley 10-8-8
Jul 9	Robert Wright	w rsf 6	Glasgow 10-6-12
	(British welterweight title)		
Oct 16	Ludovic Proto	l pts 12	Paris 10-5-8
	(vacant European welterweight title)		

Fights 38 Won 33 Lost 5

Mark JAY

Light-middleweight
Newcastle born 4 April 1969
Real name: Mark Jackson
Somervyl & Longbenton ABC

1988
Sep 29	Tony Farrell	w pts 6	Sunderland 10-8-8
Nov 22	Dave Whittle	w pts 6	Middlesbrough 10-11-8

1989
Apr 5	Louis Walsh	l pts 6	Halifax 11-0
May 19	Mick Mulcahy	w pts 6	Gateshead 11-1-8
Sep 25	Calton Myers	w pts 6	NSC 10-10
Oct 21	Ian Thomas	l rsf 5*	Middlesbrough 10-9-8

1990
Apr 24	Ernie Loveridge	l pts 6	Stoke 10-8
May 30	Trevor Meikle	drew 6	Stoke 10-11
Jun 15	Trevor Meikle	l rsf 5*	Telford 10-9
Oct 18	Phil Epton	l pts 6	Dewsbury 10-8-8
Nov 19	John Mullen	drew 6	Glasgow 10-9-8
Nov 29	Barry Messam	l rsf 5*	Sunderland 10-12

1991
Oct 9	Willie Quinn	w pts 6	Glasgow 11-3-8
Dec 16	Tyrone Eastmond	l pts 6	Manchester 11-2-8

1992
Jan 20	Mickey Duncan	w pts 6	Bradford 11-3
Feb 24	David Radford	w pts 6	Bradford 11-4
Mar 3	David Johnson	l pts 6	Houghton-le-Spring 11-6
Mar 12	Gordon Blair	drew 8	Glasgow 10-11
Apr 2	Jamie Robinson	l pts 6	Basildon 11-3
Apr 25	Steve Foster	l rsf 7	Manchester 11-4
May 28	Seamus Casey	w pts 8	Gosforth 11-5
Sep 24	Derek Wormald	l rsf 5	Manchester 11-3
Dec 1	Neil Patterson	w pts 6	Hartlepool 11-2-8
Dec 17	Clay O'Shea	l ko 1	Wembley GH 11-2

Fights 24 Won 9 Lost 12 Drawn 3

Kevin JENKINS

Flyweight
Ammanford born Glanamman 9 December 1970
Towy ABC
1988 Welsh ABA flyweight champion (w A Ley, l rtd 1 J Lyon)
1988 Wales (v Ire, l P Buttimer; v Sco, l G Ferry)

1989
Dec 21	Neil Parry	w pts 6	Kings Heath 8-6-8

1990
Jan 22	James Drummond	w pts 6	Glasgow 8-7
Feb 3	Kruga Hydes	drew 6	Bristol 8-3-12
Mar 6	James Drummond	l rsf 5	Glasgow 8-6-8
Sep 13	Mark Tierney	l pts 6	Watford
Oct 1	Antti Juntumaa	l pts 4	Helsinki 8-2-12
Oct 10	Mark Tierney	l pts 6	Albert Hall 8-2
Oct 17	Tim Yeates	l pts 6	Bethnal Green 8-6

1991
Jan 24	Ceri Farrell	w pts 6	Gorseinon 8-1-4
Feb 12	Robbie Regan	l pts 10	Cardiff 7-13-4
	(vacant Welsh flyweight title)		

/CTD..

(Kevin JENKINS ctd.)
Mar 19	Danny Porter	l rsf 7	Leicester 8-0-8
Oct 9	Stevie Wood	drew 8	Glasgow 8-3
Nov 19	Danny Porter	l rsf 2*	Norwich 8-3-8
1992			
Mar 18	Joe Kelly	l pts 8	Glasgow 8-7-8
May 5	Noel Carroll	l pts 7	Preston 8-3-12

Fights 15 Won 3 Lost 10 Drawn 2

Graham JENNER
Super-middleweight
Hastings born 13 May 1962
HYPA ABC
1981 Southern ABA light-middleweight champion (l E Henderson)

1985			
Oct 10	Gary Tomlinson	l pts 6	Wimbledon 11-10-8
Nov 14	George Mack	w pts 6	Wimbledon 11-11-8
Dec 5	Jason Baxter	l pts 6	Birmingham
1986			
Jan 21	Tony Stevens	w pts 6	Tunbridge Wells 11-10-12
Mar 25	Dave Furneaux	w pts 6	Tunbridge Wells 11-10
Apr 8	Darryl Ritchie	w rsf 3	Southend 11-9
Sep 16	Tommy Becket	w ko 2	Southend 11-9
Sep 25	Andy Till	l pts 6	Crystal Palace 11-8
1987-90 inactive			
1991			
Oct 29	Val Golding	l rsf 3	Albert Hall 11-11-8
1992			
Jan 8	Paul McCarthy	w pts 6	Burton-on-Trent 12-7
Mar 1	Paul McCarthy	w pts 8	St Leonards-on-Sea 12-0
May 29	Ensley Bingham	l ko 5	Manchester 11-10
Oct 15	Mark Baker	l rtd 4	Catford 12-4
Nov 12	John Kaighin	l rsf 5*	Bayswater 12-4

Fights 14 Won 7 Lost 7

Andrew JERVIS
Light-middleweight
Liverpool born 28 June 1969
St Teresas ABC

1992			
Oct 5	Ricky North	w pts 6	Liverpool 10-12
Nov 2	Sean Martin	w ko 2	Liverpool 10-13
Dec 1	Cliff Churchward	w pts 6	Liverpool 11-0-8

Fights 3 Won 3

Chris JICKELLS

Featherweight
Brigg, born Scunthorpe 26 March 1971
Riddings ABC
1991 Yorkshire & Humberside ABA featherweight final (l rsf 2 J Irwin)

1991
Nov 18	Tony Smith	w rsf 4	Manchester
Dec 9	Al Garrett	w rsf 2	Bradford 9-2

1992
Jan 15	Ronnie Stephenson	l pts 6	Stoke 9-0
Mar 30	Colin Innes	w rsf 3	Bradford
Apr 29	Kevin Middleton	w rsf 6	Solihull 9-0-8
Jun 1	Dave McHale	l rsf 4	Glasgow 9-1-8
Oct 12	Ian McGirr	w rsf 3	Bradford 9-2

Fights 7 Won 5 Lost 2

James JIORA

Lightweight
Otley, born Nigeria 6 April 1968
Real name: James Iwenjiora
Leeds ABC & St Patricks ABC
1985 Anglo-Scottish select v New Jersey (w B Mojica)
1987 Yorkshire ABA lightweight champion (w D Mount, w M Smith, l D Maw)

1987
Jun 2	Paul Kennedy	w rsf 6	Bradford 9-11
Sep 15	Ian Murray	w rsf 2	Batley 9-11-8
Nov 2	Michael Howell	w rsf 3	Bradford 10-0
Nov 10	Marvin P. Gray	l pts 8	Batley 9-12
Nov 30	John Townsley	w pts 8	Nottingham 9-9
Dec 15	Paul Burke	w pts 4	Bradford 9-12

1988
Mar 8	Rudi Valentino	l pts 6	Batley 9-6

1989
Jan 26	Frankie Foster	l pts 6	Newcastle 9-8
Feb 20	Peter Bowen	l pts 6	Birmingham 9-11
Mar 20	Dean Dickinson	w pts 6	Bradford
Mar 31	Chris Bennett	l pts 6	Scarborough 9-8
Jul 11	Craig Walsh	l pts 8	Batley 9-11-8
Dec 5	Paul Charters	l rsf 4	Dewsbury 9-8

1990
Jan 11	Kid Sumaila	w pts 4	Dewsbury 9-12
Feb 26	Brendan Ryan	w pts 6	Bradford 9-9
Apr 11	Rick Bushell	l pts 6	Dewsbury 9-8
Nov 29	Marvin P. Gray	l pts 8	Marton 10-5

1991
Jun 13	David Thompson	drew 6	Hull 10-1-12
Aug 1	Chris Saunders	l pts 6	Dewsbury 10-0
Oct 9	John O.Johnson	l pts 6	Manchester
Oct 21	Charlie Kane	l pts 6	Glasgow 10-2-4

1992
Mar 2	Carl Tilley	l pts 6	Marton 9-11
Mar 12	Allan McDowall	l ko 2	Glasgow 9-12

Fights 23 Won 8 Lost 14 Drawn 1

Tracy JOCELYN

Light-middleweight
Stafford born 15 July 1963
Southpaw
Stafford ABC
1982 South Midlands ABA welterweight final (l rtd 3 T Marren)

1990
Nov 27	Danny Walker	l pts 6	Wolverhampton 11-8
Dec 10	Danny Walker	w pts 6	Birmingham 11-10

1991
Nov 19	Adrian Strachan	l pts 6	Norwich 11-1-8

1992
Mar 1	Clive Dixon	w pts 6	St Leonard's on Sea 11-4
Mar 25	Kevin Lueshing	l rsf 3	Dagenham 11-2
Apr 30	Kevin Sheeran	l rsf 3	Albert Hall 11-1-4

Fights 6 Won 2 Lost 4

Ian JOHN-LEWIS

Welterweight
Gillingham born 28 November 1962
St Mary's ABC, Chatham
1985 Southern ABA welterweight champion (w dis 3 J Laundon, l rsf 3* S Kyriakides)
1986 Southern ABA welterweight final (l S Smith)

1987
Mar 4	Kesem Clayton	l rsf 3*	Dudley 10-9
Apr 9	Ray Golding	l pts 6	Weston-super-Mare 10-9
Apr 27	Willie McDonald	w ko 1	Glasgow 10-8-8
Jun 8	Dave Heaver	w rsf 5	Glasgow 10-8
Jun 25	Roy Callaghan	w pts 6	Bethnal Green 10-8
Sep 18	Tony Britland	w pts 6	Gravesend 10-7
Nov 4	Nick Meloscia	w dis 5	Gravesend 10-7
Dec 9	Johnny Nanton	w pts 6	Greenwich 10-7-8

1988
Apr 13	Jim Beckett	w ko 3	Gravesend 10-10
May 18	Tony Baker	w rsf 8	Gillingham 10-10
Sep 30	Paul Seddon	w rsf 4	Gillingham 10-8-8

1989
Jan 24	Trevor Smith	l rsf 8	Battersea 10-5-8
	(vacant Southern welterweight title)		
May 16	Andrew Furlong	l rsf 3*	Battersea 10-6-8
Nov 15	Ray Taylor	w pts 8	Catford 10-9

1990
Apr 23	Chris Haydon	w rsf 1*	Crystal Palace 10-12
Jun 22	Martin Garza	w rsf 1	Gillingham 10-10
Sep 24	Alejandro Barbosa	w rsf 2	Lewisham 10-9-8
Oct 31	Chris Blake	l rsf 5*	Crystal Palace 10-8-12

1991
Feb 6	Mickey Hughes	l rsf 9*	Bethnal Green 10-6

1992
Feb 19	Darren Dyer	l rsf 2	Muswell Hill 10-5-12

Fights 20 Won 13 Lost 7

David JOHNSON

Middleweight
Sunderland, born Boldon 10 August 1972
Boldon ABC
1988 NABC Class A final (l M Scott)
1989 Junior ABA champion (w B Conway)
1990 Young England (v Sco, l W Quinn)

1991
May 13	Rocky Tyrell	w pts 6	Manchester 11-8
May 20	Griff Jones	w pts 6	Bradford 11-7
Jun 10	Tyrone Eastmond	w pts 6	Manchester 11-6
Oct 10	Seamus Casey	w pts 6	Gateshead 11-6
Nov 14	Seamus Casey	w pts 6	Gateshead 11-6
Nov 25	Mike Phillips	l pts 6	Liverpool 11-4
Dec 12	Micky Duncan	w pts 6	Hartlepool

1992
Mar 3	Mark Jay	w pts 6	Houghton-le-Spring 11-5
Apr 28	Shaun McCrory	drew 6	Houghton-le-Spring 11-10-8
Sep 10	Spencer Alton	w pts 6	Sunderland 11-8
Oct 23	Griff Jones	w pts 6	Gateshead 11-6

Fights 11 Won 9 Lost 1 Drawn 1

John O. JOHNSON

Light-welterweight
Nottingham born 2 November 1969
Real name: Paul Johnson
Southpaw
Radford Boys ABC
1991 Midlands ABA light-welter champion (w D Wood, w K Marshall, w S Mabbutt, w A Maynard, l G Smith)

1991
Aug 29	Seth Jones	w dis 1	Telford 10-3
Oct 9	James Jiora	w pts 6	Manchester
Oct 24	Carl Hook	l pts 6	Dunstable 10-1
Oct 31	Darren Morris	w pts 6	Telford 10-5
Nov 26	Bernard Paul	l pts 6	Bethnal Green 10-5

1992
Jan 22	Brian Coleman	w pts 6	Stoke 9-13
Jan 30	Chris Saunders	w pts 6	Southampton 10-0-12
Feb 20	Alan Peacock	w pts 6	Glasgow 10-2
Mar 9	Ricky Sackfield	w pts 6	Manchester 10-1-12
Mar 26	Davey Robb	l pts 6	Telford 10-0
Jun 3	Jason Barker	w pts 6	Newcastle-under-Lyme 10-1
Sep 9	Chris Saunders	drew 6	Stoke 10-3
Dec 9	Jason Barker	w pts 8	Stoke 10-1

Fights 13 Won 9 Lost 3 Drawn 1

Julian JOHNSON

Light-heavyweight
Swansea born 4 October 1967

1991
Nov 20	Nigel Rafferty	drew 6	Cardiff 12-9-8

1992
Jan 22	Paul McCarthy	drew 6	Cardiff 12-1 /CTD..

(Julian JOHNSON ctd.)

Mar 1	John Uphill	w ko 3	St Leonard's On Sea 12-7
Mar 11	Nicky Wadman	l pts 6	Cardiff 12-10
May 11	Andy Manning	l pts 6	Llanelli 12-9-8
Nov 26	Eddie Knight	w rsf 2*	Mayfair 12-8

Fights 6 Won 2 Lost 2 Drawn 2

Martin JOLLEY

Super-middleweight
Alfreton, born Chesterfield 22 November 1967
Southpaw

1992

Mar 10	Gipsy Johnny Price	w rsf 3	Bury 12-3
Apr 6	Sean Byrne	l rsf 6	Northampton 12-0
May 11	Mark Hale	w pts 6	Coventry 12-2
Sep 8	Brian McGloin	w pts 6	Doncaster 12-1
Oct 5	Mark Hale	w rsf 4	Bardon 12-2
Oct 14	Carl Smallwood	w pts 6	Stoke 12-4
Nov 2	Bobby Mack	l pts 6	Wolverhampton 12-4
Nov 24	Phil Ball	drew 6	Doncaster 12-1

Fights 8 Won 5 Lost 2 Drawn 1

Barry JONES

Featherweight
Cardiff born 3 May 1974
Highfield ABC
1992 Welsh ABA featherweight champion (w rsf 2 A Fletcher, w rsf 3 D Jay, w P Samuels, l A Temple)
1992 European Junior Championships featherweight silver medal (w M Eraslem, Tur; w P Soltys, Pol; w A Styve, Nor; l M Silantiev, CIS)

1992

Oct 28	Conn McMullan	w pts 6	Cardiff 9-0
Dec 14	Miguel Matthews	w pts 6	Cardiff 9-1-8

Fights 2 Won 2

Griff JONES

Light-middleweight
Leeds born 26 July 1970
Real name: Kenny Griffin
Market District ABC
Formerly boxed as Kenny Tyson

1991

Jan 21	David Radford	w pts 6	Leeds 11-9
Feb 28	Jon Stocks	l pts 6	Sunderland 11-10
May 20	David Johnson	l pts 6	Bradford 11-6
Jun 1	Gary Booker	l pts 6	Bethnal Green 11-5
Nov 5	Chad Strong	w pts 6	Leicester 11-5
Dec 7	Warren Stowe	l rsf 6	Manchester

1992

Sep 10	Paul Hitch	l rsf 2	Sunderland 11-8
Oct 15	Tim Robinson	w rsf 3*	Hull 11-8
Oct 23	David Johnson	l pts 6	Gateshead 11-2
Dec 7	John Bosco	l rsf 1	Mayfair 11-3

Fights 10 Won 3 Lost 7

Matthew JONES
Middleweight
Cradley Heath, born Bloxwich 20 January 1968
Dudley ABC

1988			
Oct 6	Keith Scott	w pts 6	Dudley 10-13
Oct 12	Keith Scott	w rsf 2	Stoke 11-2
Oct 27	Marty Duke	w pts 6	Birmingham 11-4
1989			
Feb 28	Robert Armstrong	w rsf 4*	Dudley 11-0
1990			
Oct 18	Martin Rosamond	l pts 6	Birmingham 11-4
Nov 16	Adrian Din	w pts 6	Telford 11-2
Nov 30	Calton Myers	w rsf 5	Birmingham 11-5-4
1991			
inactive			
1992			
Apr 29	Dave Hall	w rsf 2*	Solihull 11-4
May 29	Carl Harney	l rsf 6	Manchester 11-6

Fights 9 Won 7 Lost 2

Paul JONES
Light-middleweight
Sheffield born 19 November 1966
Unity ABC

1986			
Dec 8	Paul Gillings	w pts 6	Liverpool 10-2
1987			
Oct 28	Pat Durkin	w pts 4	Sheffield 10-3
Nov 10	David Binns	l pts 6	Batley 10-5
1988			
Jan 11	Humphrey Harrison	l pts 8	Manchester 10-3-8
Sep 27	George Sponagle	drew 8	Halifax, Nova Scotia
Dec 7	Jimmy Thornton	w pts 6	Stoke 11-0
1989			
Jan 23	Donovan Boucher	l dis 6	Toronto 10-8
Mar 13	Dale Moreland	w pts 6	Toronto 10-5
Mar 30	Benoit Boudreau	w pts 10	Moncton 10-1
Apr 19	Anthony Collier	w ko 3	Toronto 10-4
Jun 6	George Sponagle	l pts 8	Halifax, NS 10-10
Sep 6	John Ford	w pts 6	Mississauga 11-5
Nov 13	Ian Midwood-Tate	w rsf 4	Manchester 11-1-8
Dec 8	Antoine Tarver	l pts 4	Doncaster 11-1
1990			
Mar 6	Antonio Fernandez	w pts 8	Stoke 11-0
Mar 22	Darren Pilling	w rtd 7	Gateshead 11-2
Apr 26	Newton Barnett	w pts 8	Mayfair 11-2
May 20	Jim Beckett	w ko 1	Sheffield 11-1
May 24	Wayne Ellis	l pts 6	St Albans 11-2-8
Nov 14	Jason Rowe	w pts 10	Sheffield 10-13-8
	(Central light-middleweight title)		
1991			
Mar 12	Tony Velinor	w pts 8	Mansfield 11-1
Aug 15	Hugo Marinangeli	l ko 2	Marbella /CTD..

(Paul JONES ctd.)

Oct 1	Simon Eubanks	w ko 6	Sheffield 10-7-8
1992			
Mar 14	Paul Lynch	w rsf 3	Mansfield 11-0
May 19	Trevor Ambrose	w pts 6	Cardiff 11-2
Jun 2	Patrick Vungbo	w pts 10	Rotterdam
Sep 19	Ernie Loveridge	w pts 6	Glasgow 11-1-8
Nov 24	Paul Wesley	l rsf 2	Doncaster 11-0

Fights 28 Won 19 Lost 8 Drawn 1

Seth JONES
Light-welterweight
Dyffryn, born St Asaph 9 February 1968
Dyffryn ABC

1991			
Aug 29	John O. Johnson	l dis 1	Telford 10-3
Sep 19	Ricky Sackfield	l rsf 1*	Stockport 10-1-8
Nov 20	Jess Rundan	w ko 4	Cardiff 10-2
Dec 9	Spencer McCracken	l rsf 2	Brierley Hill 10-3
1992			
Feb 19	Paul Knights	l rsf 5	Muswell Hill 10-3
Mar 31	Danny Kett	w ko 1	Norwich 10-2
Jun 16	Paul Knights	l pts 6	Dagenham 10-3-12
Sep 26	Dave Lovell	l rsf 4	Olympia 10-7
Dec 1	Kevin McKenzie	w rsf 3*	Hartlepool 10-1-8

Fights 9 Won 3 Lost 6

Gareth JORDAN
Super-featherweight
Monmouth born 19 December 1971
Pontypool ABC
1991 Welsh ABA lightweight final (w rsf 3 R Jones, w C Heysham, l J Cody)

1992			
Nov 2	Con Cronin	w ko 2	Wolverhampton 9-7-8
Dec 4	Jason White	w rsf 2	Telford 9-7

Fights 2 Won 2

Benji JOSEPH
Light-middleweight
Warrington, born Ipswich 28 March 1969

1991			
Feb 4	Richard Okumu	l pts 6	Leicester 11-0
Mar 5	Tommy Warde	l pts 6	Leicester 11-3
Mar 25	Tyrone Eastmond	w pts 6	Bradford 10-11
Jun 24	Dave Maj	l rsf 4	Liverpool 11-4
Oct 7	Wayne Shepherd	l pts 6	Bradford 10-10
Nov 18	Mick Mulcahy	w pts 6	Manchester
1992			
Jan 20	Willie Yeardsley	l pts 6	Bradford 10-10
Feb 9	Willie Yeardsley	l rsf 4*	Peterborough 10-13
Mar 25	Craig Hartwell	w pts 6	Hinckley 11-1
Apr 28	Hughie Davey	l rsf 4*	Houghton-le-Spring 11-0

Fights 10 Won 3 Lost 7

Dean JOSHAM
Heavyweight
Louth born 3 July 1971

1992
Feb 24   Ian Carmichael   l pts 6   Bradford 14-8

Fights 1 Lost 1

Peter JUDSON
Super-featherweight
Keighley born 14 January 1970
Keighley ABC
1988 North-East ABA bantamweight final (walkover, then withdrew!)

1989
Apr 24   Darrell Pettit   drew 6   Bradford 9-2
Jul 11   Neil Leitch   w pts 6   Batley 9-4
Sep 18   Phil Lashley   w pts 6   NSC 9-1-8
Oct 2   Steve Wood   l pts 6   Bradford 8-13
Nov 22   Peter Buckley   l pts 6   Stafford 9-0
1990
Feb 19   Phil Lashley   w ko 6   Nottingham 9-7
Mar 8   Wayne Goult   l pts 6   Peterborough 9-8
Mar 19   Andrew Robinson   w pts 6   Cleethorpes 9-5
Mar 26   Wayne Marston   w pts 6   Nottingham
Apr 30   Derek Amory   l pts 6   Brierley Hill 9-4
May 9   Brian Robb   w pts 6   Solihull 9-3-8
Jun 4   Jamie McBride   l pts 8   Glasgow 9-3
Sep 17   Mark Geraghty   w pts 8   Glasgow 9-6-8
Sep 26   Carl Roberts   w pts 6   Manchester 9-3-8
Oct 8   Mark Geraghty   l pts 8   Glasgow 9-6-8
Nov 19   Russell Davison   l pts 8   Manchester 9-3
Nov 27   Rocky Lawlor   w pts 8   Wolverhampton 9-3
1991
Jan 29   Russell Davison   l pts 10   Stockport 8-12
           (vacant Central featherweight title)
Feb 21   Noel Carroll   w pts 8   Leeds 9-1-8
Mar 20   Colin Lynch   w rtd 5*   Solihull 9-1
May 1   Jimmy Owens   l pts 6   Liverpool 9-2
May 28   Scott Durham   w pts 6   Cardiff 9-2
Sep 24   Ian McGirr   l pts 6   Glasgow 9-5
Nov 11   Miguel Matthews   w pts 6   Stratford 8-12
Nov 18   Jamie McBride   drew 6   Glasgow 9-3-8
1992
Feb 9   Ceri Farrell   w pts 6   Bradford 8-12
Apr 5   Barrie Kelley   w pts 6   Bradford 9-4
Nov 14   J.T.Williams   drew 6   Cardiff 9-7

Fights 28 Won 15 Lost 10 Drawn 3

David JULES

Heavyweight
Doncaster born 11 July 1965
Tom Hill Youth ABC

1987
Jun 12	Carl Timbrell	w ko 5	Leamington 16-0
Oct 7	Carl Timbrell	l rsf 3*	Stoke 15-10

1988
Mar 17	Peter Fury	w rtd 2	Sunderland 16-9
Mar 21	Jess Harding	l rsf 2	Bethnal Green
Sep 29	Gary McCrory	l pts 6	Sunderland 16-10
Nov 22	Gary McCrory	l pts 6	Middlesbrough 16-10
Dec 5	Denroy Bryan	drew 6	Dudley 16-8

1989
Jan 18	Denroy Bryan	w rsf 2	Stoke 16-8
Feb 22	Tony Hallett	w rsf 1	Doncaster
Apr 19	Rocky Burton	l rsf 3	Doncaster 17-1
Nov 11	Jimmy Di Stolfo	w rtd 1	Rimini 16-8
Dec 1	Biagio Chianese	l rsf 2	Milan 16-4

1990
Feb 19	Vance Idiens	l pts 6	Birmingham 16-0
May 7	Ramon Voorn	l rsf 3	Arnhem 15-10-8
Nov 12	Steve Garber	l rsf 6*	Bradford 15-12

1991
Apr 9	Herbie Hide	l rsf 1	Mayfair 15-7
Dec 5	Vance Idiens	l rsf 4*	Cannock 15-10

1992
Feb 24	Rocky Burton	w ko 1	Coventry 15-12
Apr 5	Steve Garber	l rsf 4	Bradford 15-7
Sep 8	Wayne Buck	l rsf 3	Doncaster 16-4

Fights 20 Won 6 Lost 13 Drawn 1

John KAIGHIN
Super-middleweight
Swansea, born Brecknock 26 August 1967

1990
Sep 17	Carlos Christie	l pts 6	Cardiff
Sep 24	Jim Woolley	l pts 6	Lewisham 12-0
Oct 15	Max McCracken	l pts 6	Brierley Hill 11-9-4
Oct 22	Stefan Wright	l pts 6	Peterborough 11-3
Nov 15	Tony Wellington	w pts 6	Oldham 11-8
Dec 13	Nick Manners	l ko 3	Dewsbury

1991
Jan 24	Robert Peel	l pts 6	Gorseinon 11-11-8
Feb 12	Robert Peel	w pts 6	Cardiff 11-9
Mar 15	Max McCracken	drew 6	Willenhall 12-0-8
Apr 10	Darron Griffiths	l pts 6	Newport 11-5-8
Apr 24	Paul Murray	w pts 6	Port Talbot 12-1
May 8	Benji Good	w rsf 3	Albert Hall 11-9
May 15	Robert Peel	l pts 8	Swansea 11-7
Jun 6	Peter Vosper	drew 6	Barking
Jun 30	John Ogiste	l pts 6	Southwark 11-8-8
Aug 29	Adrian Wright	w pts 6	Telford 11-12-8
Sep 9	Terry Johnson	w rtd 2*	Liverpool 11-7
Sep 11	Lester Jacobs	l rsf 2	Hammersmith 11-7
Oct 22	Andy Wright	drew 6	Battersea 12-4
Nov 13	Gary Delaney	l pts 6	Bethnal Green 12-2
Nov 20	Keith Inglis	w rsf 1	Albert Hall 12-8

1992
Jan 23	Michael Gale	l pts 8	York 12-3
Feb 1	Paul Busby	l pts 4	Birmingham 11-9
Feb 25	Andy Wright	l pts 6	Crystal Palace 12-4
Mar 6	Lester Jacobs	l rsf 1	Battersea 11-11
Apr 27	Bruce Scott	l ko 4	AASC 12-3
Jul 18	Carl Harney	l pts 6	Manchester
Sep 15	Paul Wright	l dis 5	Liverpool 11-11
Sep 26	Shaun Cummins	l rtd 4	Olympia 11-6
Oct 28	Joey Peters	drew 6	Albert Hall 12-6
Nov 12	Graham Jenner	w rsf 5*	Bayswater 12-3-8
Dec 1	Peter Vosper	w rsf 4	Bristol 12-4
Dec 22	Darrit Douglas	w pts 6	Mayfair 12-2

Fights 33 Won 10 Lost 19 Drawn 4

Charlie KANE
Light-welterweight
Clydebank, born Glasgow 2 July 1968
Southpaw
Antonine ABC
1986 Scottish ABA featherweight final (w J Leys, l D Anderson)
1986 Commonwealth Games featherweight prelim (l rsf 2 C Carlton, Ire)
1986 European Junior Championships featherweight (w Skobodzian, Pol; l Cheklat, Fra)
1986 Scotland (v Wal, w M White)
1987 Scottish ABA featherweight champion (w D McHale, w B Connell, l P English)
1987 Scotland (v Eng, w C McMillan; v Wal, w rsf 2 H Jones)
1987 Young Scotland (v Eng, w T Mock)
1987 European Championships (l Ness, Nor)
1988 ABA lightweight champion (w A McDowell, w dis 2 L Crampsie, w rsf 1 M Gowans, w S Nolan, w M Ramsey)
1988 Olympic Games lightweight (w A Taroreh, Indon; w P Hongram, Tha; l G Cramme, Swe) /CTD...

Charlie KANE (ctd)
1989 Scottish ABA lightweight champion (w J McLeod, w T Ahmed, w M Delaney, withdrew)
1989 Scotland (v Wal, w M Smyth; v EGer, w D Drumm)
1990 Commonwealth Games light-welterweight gold medal (w rsf 2 M Rahman, Brunei; w M James, Nig; w S Scriggins, Aus; w N Odore, Ken)
1991 Scotland (v Eng, w P Richardson)

1991
Mar 5	Dean Bramhald	w rsf 6*	Glasgow 10-2
Oct 21	James Jiora	w pts 6	Glasgow 10-2
1992			
Feb 24	Karl Taylor	w pts 8	Glasgow 10-3
Dec 10	Mick Mulcahy	w rsf 2	Glasgow 10-2

Fights 4 Won 4

Barrie KELLEY
Featherweight
Llanelli born 14 February 1972
1990 European Junior Championships featherweight (l J Lorcy, Fra)

1990
Oct 16	Ervine Blake	w pts 6	Evesham 9-2-8
Nov 21	Tony Falcone	w pts 6	Chippenham 9-0
Nov 29	John O'Meara	w rsf 5*	Bayswater 9-1-4
1991			
Jan 24	Martin Evans	w pts 6	Gorseinon 9-2-8
Feb 18	Tony Falcone	l rsf 6*	NSC 9-2
Mar 26	Dennis Adams	w pts 6	Bethnal Green 9-5-8
Jul 18	Robert Smyth	drew 6	Cardiff 9-3-8
Sep 16	Dominic McGuigan	drew 6	AASC 9-5-8
Oct 14	Michael Armstrong	l ko 4	Manchester 9-3
Nov 20	Neil Haddock	l pts 6	Cardiff 9-3-8
1992			
Feb 3	Noel Carroll	l pts 8	Manchester 9-5
Mar 18	Mark Geraghty	l pts 8	Glasgow 9-4-4
Apr 5	Peter Judson	l pts 6	Bradford 9-3
Sep 30	Dean Bramhald	w pts 6	Solihull 9-8-8
Oct 28	Derek Amory	w pts 6	Cardiff 9-3-8

Fights 15 Won 7 Lost 6 Drawn 2

Felix KELLY
Lightweight
Hammersmith, born Sligo 6 June 1965
Four Feathers ABC
1989 North West London ABA light-welter final (w ko 1 M Bryan, l ko 3 R Edwards)
1990 North West London ABA light-welter semi-final (w rsf 3 J Stuart, l G McCabe)

1990
Oct 18	Tony Gibbs	drew 6	Battersea 9-8-8
Nov 26	Steve Hearn	w rsf 3	Bethnal Green 9-9
Dec 4	Frankie Ventura	w pts 6	Southend 9-8
1991			
Feb 6	Wayne Windle	w pts 6	Bethnal Green 9-11
Feb 18	Trevor Royal	w rsf 4	Windsor 9-9-12
Mar 26	Chris Saunders	w pts 6	Bethnal Green 9-10-8
Apr 18	Rick Bushell	w pts 6	Olympia 9-7

Jun 22	Rick Bushell	l pts 6	Earls Court 9-9-8
Sep 26	Billy Schwer	l rsf 2	Dunstable 9-9
Nov 20	Tony Borg	l pts 6	Cardiff 9-10
1992			
Mar 25	Mark Tibbs	drew 8	Dagenham 9-11
Sep 17	Carlos Chase	l rsf 2	Watford 9-11-12
Nov 7	Didier Hughes	w pts 6	Differdange 10-0

Fights 13 Won 7 Lost 4 Drawn 2

Joe KELLY

Bantamweight
Glasgow born 18 May 1964
Holyrood ABC
1981 Scotland (v Ire, w G Duddy)
1982 ABA flyweight champion (w D Lee, w J Hyland, w J Dawson)
1982 Commonwealth Games flyweight silver medal (w G Duddy, Ire; w G Richards, Aus; l M Mutua, Ken)
1983 Scotland (v Ire, w rsf 3 A O'Neill; v Eng, w J Hyland; v Wal, w rsf 2 B Barton)
1984 Scotland (v Eng, w rtd 2 J Knight; v Wal, w J Mardon; v Ire, w G Hawkins, w P Sutcliffe)
1984 Great Britain (v Ire, w rsf 2 R Nash)

1985			
Jan 28	Bobby McDermott	l rsf 3	Glasgow 8-4
Dec 2	Gordon Stobie	w pts 6	Glasgow 8-1
1986			
Feb 24	Gordon Stobie	w pts 6	Glasgow 8-4
Apr 21	Kelvin Smart	drew 8	Glasgow 8-3-12
Jun 9	Kevin Downer	w rsf 6	Glasgow 8-3
Jun 24	Albert Parr	w pts 6	Glasgow 8-3
Oct 20	Dave McAuley	l ko 9	Glasgow 7-13-14
	(vacant British flyweight title)		
Dec 22	Jamie McBride	w rsf 5	Glasgow 8-4
1987			
Jan 11	Gipsy Johnny	w rsf 3	Glasgow 8-2
Apr 6	Chris Clarkson	w pts 8	Glasgow 8-3-8
Apr 13	Nigel Crook	w pts 8	Glasgow 8-2-12
May 6	Ronnie Stephenson	w pts 8	Livingstone 8-2-4
May 18	Gerry McBride	w pts 8	Glasgow 8-4
Sep 20	Pat Clinton	l rsf 2*	Bethnal Green 8-0
	(vacant Scottish flyweight title; final eliminator, British title)		
1988			
Feb 8	Kid Sumaila	w pts 8	Glasgow 8-5
Mar 9	Pat Clinton	l pts 12	Bethnal Green 8-0
	(vacant British flyweight title)		
1989			
Jan 31	Graham O'Malley	w pts 8	Glasgow 8-6
Mar 28	Marvin Stone	w rsf 4*	Glasgow 8-7-4
Dec 11	Des Gargano	w pts 6	Mayfair 8-9-8
1990			
Feb 18	Reggie Brown	w rsf 8	Richmond, VA. 7-13
	(IBF Intercontinental flyweight title)		
Oct 9	David Afan-Jones	w rsf 5	Glasgow 8-2
1991			
Feb 23	Salvatore Fanni	l rsf 2	Cagliari 7-13-4
	(vacant European flyweight title)		
May 28	Robbie Regan	l pts 12	Cardiff 8-0
	(vacant British flyweight title)		
Oct 21	Ronnie Carroll	drew 12	Glasgow 8-4
	(vacant British bantamweight title)		/CTD..

(Joe KELLY ctd)
1992
Jan 27	Ronnie Carroll	w pts 12	Glasgow 8-6
	(vacant British bantamweight title)		
Mar 18	Kevin Jenkins	w pts 8	Glasgow 8-8-4
Jun 1	Drew Docherty	l rsf 5	Glasgow
	(British bantamweight title)		

Fights 27 Won 18 Lost 7 Drawn 2

John B. KELLY
Lightweight
West Hartlepool born 12 June 1970
Hartlepool Boys Welfare ABC
1992 North-East Division ABA lightweight prelim (l A Green)

1992
Oct 22	Tanveer Ahmed	l pts 6	Glasgow 9-9
Nov 2	Kevin Lowe	w pts 6	Liverpool 9-7
Dec 1	Wayne Rigby	w pts 6	Hartlepool 9-8

Fights 3 Won 2 Lost 1

Mark KELLY
Light-welterweight
Denaby born 15 July 1968
Tom Hill Youth ABC

1987
Oct 19	Rocky Lester	w ko 4	Nottingham 9-8
Nov 2	Roy Doyle	w pts 6	Manchester 9-10
Nov 25	Darren Darby	w pts 6	Cottingham 9-10

1988
Jan 11	Oliver Harrison	l rsf 1	Manchester 9-12
Mar 21	Warren Slaney	w rsf 1	Leicester
Apr 18	Nigel Bradley	w pts 6	Manchester 9-11
Apr 26	Sugar Gibiliru	drew 6	Manchester 9-11-12
May 10	George Jones	drew 8	Edgbaston 9-7
Jun 13	Brian Cullen	w pts 8	Manchester 9-11-12
Sep 26	George Baigrie	w pts 8	Bradford 9-12
Oct 18	Tony Ekubia	l rsf 7	Oldham 9-8
	(vacant Central lightweight title)		
Dec 1	Sugar Gibiliru	w pts 6	Manchester 9-11-12
Dec 12	Tony Foster	l pts 6	Nottingham

1989
Jan 24	John Smith	w pts 8	Kings Heath 10-5
Feb 7	Phil Nurse	l pts 8	Manchester 9-11
Feb 23	Paul Burke	w dis 5	Stockport 10-0
Mar 6	Tony Richards	l pts 8	Leicester 9-13
Apr 3	Jan Nyholm	l ko 1	Helsinki 10-1

1990
Jan 24	Kevin Spratt	l rsf 9	Solihull 10-0
	(Central light-welterweight title)		
Apr 10	Brendan Ryan	w pts 6	Doncaster 10-0-4
May 14	Chris Mulcahy	w pts 8	Cleethorpes 10-5

Oct 22	John Ritchie	l rsf 4*	Glasgow 10-5
Nov 21	Ross Hale	l pts 8	Chippenham 10-4
1991			
Jun 6	Roy Rowland	l rsf 4	Barking 10-8
Nov 25	Trevor Meikle	l pts 8	Cleethorpes 10-7-8
Dec 11	Andreas Panayi	drew 8	Stoke 10-5
1992			
May 21	Malcolm Melvin	l pts 8	Cradley Heath 10-11
Jun 1	Darren Morris	l pts 8	NEC 10-8
Dec 15	Andreas Panayi	l pts 8	Liverpool 10-10-8

Fights 29 Won 12 Lost 14 Drawn 3

Paul KELLY
Featherweight
Denaby Main, born Mexborough 18 May 1968
Real name: Paul Nettleship
Mexborough Athletic ABC

1992
May 21	Graham McGrath	l rsf 2	Cradley Heath 8-11
Oct 13	Chris Lyons	l pts 6	Wolverhampton 8-13
Oct 30	Chris Lyons	l ko 1	NEC 8-10

Fights 3 Lost 3

Andy KENT
Lightweight
Gainsborough, born Scunthorpe 10 February 1963
Army

1989
Mar 6	Andy Sweeney	w pts 6	Northampton 9-12
May 15	Brendan Ryan	l pts 6	Northampton 9-9
May 22	Brendan Ryan	l pts 6	Peterborough 9-9
Nov 6	Geoff Ward	w ko 2	Northampton 9-12
1990			
Apr 30	Malcolm Melvin	l rsf 5	Brierley Hill 9-12
Dec 12	Kevin Toomey	drew 6	Leicester 9-10
1991			
Feb 18	Kevin Toomey	w rsf 5	Derby 9-10
Mar 2	Warren Bowers	w pts 6	Cleethorpes
May 2	Peter Campbell	w pts 6	Northampton 9-9
1992			
Apr 4	Tony Doyle	l rsf 5	Cleethorpes 9-4

Fights 10 Won 5 Lost 4 Drawn 1

Lyndon KERSHAW
Flyweight
Halifax born 17 September 1972

1992
| Oct 19 | Steve Wood | w pts 6 | Glasgow 8-4 |
| Dec 14 | Louis Veitch | drew 6 | Bradford 8-0 |

Fights 2 Won 1 Drawn 1

Danny KETT
Light-welterweight
Norwich born 8 October 1970
Norwich Lads ABC
1991 Eastern ABA light-welterweight final (w rsf 3 J Ramirez, w ko 1 J Cobb, l ko 2 G Smith)

1992
Jan 21	Barry Glanister	w ko 1	Norwich 9-11
Mar 31	Seth Jones	l ko 1	Norwich 10-2-8
Oct 13	Mick Hoban	l pts 6	Bury 10-3

Fights 3 Won 1 Lost 2

Eddie KING
Welterweight
Doncaster born 21 February 1966
Doncaster Plant ABC
1983 NABC Class B final (l ko 2 S Butler)

1986
Mar 15	Michael Betts	w rsf 4*	Norwich 10-8
Apr 1	Steve Harwood	l rsf 1	Leeds 10-8
Oct 14	G.W.Gully	l ko 5	Wolverhampton 10-0
Nov 20	David Bacon	w pts 6	Ilkeston 10-2
Dec 1	Jeff Armitage	l rsf 1	Manchester 10-0

1987
Oct 7	Cecil Branch	w pts 6	Stoke 10-4
Oct 13	Cecil Branch	w rsf 4	Wolverhampton 10-2
Nov 9	Frankie Lake	l ko 3	Birmingham 10-0

1988
Mar 22	Andrew Pybus	l rsf 1	Wolverhampton 10-1

1989
Oct 25	Steve Taggart	w rsf 4	Doncaster 10-4

1990
Mar 7	Cliff Churchward	w ko 6	Doncaster 10-7
Mar 19	Dave Croft	l pts 6	Cleethorpes 10-4-8
Mar 27	Ernie Loveridge	l pts 6	Wolverhampton 10-6
Apr 4	Micky Lerwill	l pts 6	Stafford 10-7
Apr 25	Mark Tibbs	l ko 1	Millwall 10-2
Nov 14	Trevor Ambrose	l rsf 3	Doncaster 10-6
Dec 17	David Thompson	l pts 6	Manchester 10-1-8

1991
Jan 16	Gerald Flood	w rsf 3	Stoke 10-4
Jan 29	Gordon Webster	w pts 6	Wisbech 10-7
Feb 12	Andreas Panayi	l ko 2	Wolverhampton 10-6
Apr 29	Gerald Flood	w rsf 4	Cleethorpes 10-4
May 14	Dean Hiscox	w pts 6	Dudley 10-4
Jun 5	Dean Hiscox	w pts 6	Wolverhampton 10-8
Jun 17	Cliff Churchward	w pts 6	Edgbaston 10-6
Sep 16	Rick North	l rsf 5*	Cleethorpes 10-2
Oct 16	Noel Henry	l ko 2	Stoke 10-6-8
Dec 5	Shaun Cooper	l rsf 3	Cannock 10-4

1992
Feb 11	Chris Saunders	l rsf 4	Wolverhampton 10-4
Mar 11	Darren McInulty	l rsf 1	Stoke

Fights 29 Won 12 Lost 17

Paul KING

Welterweight
Newcastle born 3 June 1965
Somervyl & Long Benton ABC
1984 North East Division lightweight final (l T Kelly)

1987
Sep 4	Willie McDonald	w pts 6	Gateshead 10-3
Nov 3	Mick Mason	l pts 6	Sunderland 10-5
Nov 24	Mick Mason	l pts 6	Middlesbrough 10-12

1988
inactive

1989
Jan 31	Jim Larmour	w rtd 4	Glasgow 9-13

1990
Feb 27	Ian Thomas	w pts 6	Middlesbrough 10-10
Mar 6	Mickey Duncan	w pts 6	North Shields 10-12
Nov 15	Phil Epton	w pts 6	Oldham 10-8-8

1991
Feb 28	Dave Kettlewell	w ko 1	Sunderland
Mar 21	Phil Epton	w pts 6	Dewsbury 10-8
May 13	Seamus Casey	l pts 6	Northampton 10-12
May 31	Gordon Blair	l pts 8	Glasgow 10-13
Oct 9	Delroy Waul	l rsf 6	Manchester

1992
Sep 29	Howard Clarke	l pts 6	Stoke 10-6-8

Fights 13 Won 7 Lost 6

Stan KING

Middleweight
Forest Hill, born Jamaica 25 April 1964
Real name: Stan Hibbert
St Monicas ABC

1987
Nov 5	Steve West	w pts 6	Bethnal Green
Nov 18	Max Wallace	w pts 6	Holborn 10-13

1988
Jan 18	Chris Richards	l ko 5	NSC 11-0
Mar 12	Rob Thomas	l pts 6	Lisbon 11-0
Mar 29	Brian Robinson	l pts 6	Bethnal Green 11-1
Oct 5	Rocky Reynolds	l pts 6	Southend
Oct 21	Eamonn Loughran	l pts 6	Belfast 10-11
Nov 14	Hannu Vuorinen	l ko 5	Helsinki 10-12

1989
May 8	Barry Bennett	l rsf 5	NSC 11-3
Nov 30	John Ogiste	drew 6	Marble Arch 11-8

1990
Feb 2	Bernard Bonzon	l pts 6	Geneva
Mar 14	Max Wallace	w pts 6	Battersea 11-5-12
Apr 24	Jimmy Farrell	w rsf 2	Eltham 11-7-4
May 8	David Brown	w pts 6	Eltham 11-9
Jun 16	Miroslav Perunovic	l pts 8	Titograd
Oct 18	Errol Christie	drew 8	Battersea 11-4
Nov 29	Ian Strudwick	w rsf 2*	Bayswater 11-6-8

1991
Apr 3	Ian Strudwick	l rsf 8*	Bethnal Green 11-4-8 /CTD..

(Stan KING ctd.)

Jun 24	Gilbert Hallie	l pts 8 (s)	Rotterdam 11-8-8
1992			
Mar 17	Ian Chantler	w ko 3	Mayfair 11-7-8
Mar 31	Kesem Clayton	w rsf 4	Norwich 11-9
May 11	Tony Velinor	w rsf 3	Piccadilly 11-5
Jul 14	Colin Manners	l pts 8	Mayfair 11-6-12

Fights 23 Won 9 Lost 12 Drawn 2

Nigel KITCHING
Light-middleweight
Bethnal Green born Tidworth 23 December 1965

1992

Apr 7	Adrian Haughton	l rsf 5	Southend 11-1-8

Fights 1 Lost 1

Eddie KNIGHT
Light-heavyweight
Ashford born 4 October 1966
Ashford ABC
1990 Southern ABA heavyweight semi-final (w S Black, withdrew)
1991 Southern ABA heavyweight final (w S Welch, withdrew)

1992

Oct 5	Shaun McCrory	l pts 6	Bristol 12-8-8
Oct 29	Adrian Wright	l pts 6	Bayswater 12-8
Nov 26	Julian Johnson	l rsf 2*	Mayfair 12-7-8

Fights 3 Lost 3

Paul KNIGHTS
Light-welterweight
Redhill born 5 February 1971

1991			
Nov 26	Steve Hearn	w rsf 4*	Bethnal Green 10-0
1992			
Feb 19	Seth Jones	w rsf 5	Muswell Hill 9-13
Jun 16	Seth Jones	w pts 6	Dagenham 10-2
Nov 10	Alex Moffat	w ko 3	Dagenham 10-2

Fights 4 Won 4

Dave LAKE

Light-welterweight
Herne Bay, born London 31 January 1964
Real name: David Noonan
Herne Bay ABC

1987
Nov 4	Lee West	l rsf 6	Gravesend 10-1

1988
Feb 11	Mark Pellat	w rsf 4	Gravesend 10-1-12
Feb 24	Dean Bramhald	l pts 6	Southend 10-2
Mar 8	Tony Gibbs	l pts 6	Holborn 10-7
Apr 13	Tony Gibbs	l rsf 1	Gravesend 10-8
Sep 6	Shane Tonks	w pts 6	Southend 10-0
Sep 26	Steve Taggart	w pts 6	NSC 10-0
Oct 4	Shane Tonks	w rsf 4	Southend
Oct 24	Carl Brazier	w rsf 1*	Windsor
Nov 14	Jan Nyholm	l pts 4	Helsinki 10-1

1989
Apr 6	Ian Hosten	w pts 6	Stevenage 10-2
May 9	Paul Day	l rsf 6	St Albans 10-0
Jun 28	Steve Foran	l rsf 1	Brentwood 10-2

1990
Oct 23	Trevor Ambrose	l pts 6	Leicester 10-3

1991
Mar 5	Benny Collins	l rsf 4	Millwall 10-4

1992
Oct 7	Michael Smyth	l ko 2	Barry 10-11

Fights 16 Won 6 Lost 10

Gavin LANE

Light-welterweight
Paignton, born Rainham, Kent 14 July 1971
Real name: Gavin Keeble
Paignton ABC

1991
Nov 28	Dewi Roberts	w pts 6	Evesham 9-12-8

1992
Mar 30	Razza Campbell	l pts 6	Coventry 10-0

Fights 2 Won 1 Lost 1

David LARKIN

Light-middleweight
Leeds
Bentley Miners ABC
1991 North-East ABA light-middleweight final (w B Dunn, w ko 2 S Cassidy, l M Chicocki)
1992 Yorkshire & Humberside ABA light-middleweight prelim (l C Manterfield)

1992
Oct 29	Rick North	w pts 6	Leeds 11-3-8

Fights 1 Won 1

Phil LASHLEY
Featherweight
Birmingham born 1 May 1965
Birmingham City ABC

1986
Apr 27	Ronnie Stephenson	l pts 4	Doncaster 8-12
May 30	Dave Beech	l pts 6	Stoke 8-9
Sep 10	Gipsy Johnny	w rsf 1*	Stoke 8-10
Sep 17	Paul Hodkinson	l rsf 2	Albert Hall 9-2
Nov 10	Roy Williams	w ko 2	Birmingham 9-0
Nov 18	Dean Lynch	l pts 6	Swansea 9-1
Dec 8	Frank Monkhouse	l rsf 4*	Birmingham 8-12-8

1987
Jan 28	Shane Porter	l rsf 1	Dudley 9-0
Mar 3	John Carlin	l rsf 6	Livingstone 9-0
Mar 24	John Carlin	w rsf 1	Wolverhampton 9-1-8
Apr 8	Gary King	l ko 1	Evesham 8-13
Oct 13	Mick Greenwood	l pts 6	Wolverhampton 9-0
Nov 9	Ronnie Stephenson	drew 4	Birmingham 9-0
Nov 24	Mark Goult	l ko 1	Wisbech 9-2-8

1988
Feb 14	Steve Pike	l ko 1	Peterborough 9-0
Mar 21	Dean Lynch	l pts 6	Bethnal Green 9-8
Apr 13	Paul Bowen	w rsf 1	Wolverhampton 9-8
Apr 20	Chris Cooper	w pts 6	Torquay
May 23	Roy Williams	w rsf 2	NSC 9-4
Sep 8	Ronnie Stephenson	w pts 6	Doncaster 8-10
Sep 29	Peter Gabbitus	l ko 2	Stafford 9-4
Nov 14	Mark Antony	l rsf 2	Stratford 9-7

1989
Feb 2	Lester James	l pts 4	Wolverhampton 9-1-8
Feb 28	Lester James	l pts 6	Wolverhampton 9-2
Mar 15	Andrew Robinson	l pts 6	Stoke 9-0
Apr 17	Lester James	l rsf 5	Birmingham 9-3
Jun 28	Jamie Morris	l rsf 1	Kenilworth 9-2
Sep 18	Peter Judson	l pts 6	NSC 9-2
Oct 4	Craig Garbutt	l pts 6	Stafford 9-6
Oct 16	Neil Leitch	l pts 6	Manchester 9-1
Oct 30	Gary Hickman	l rsf 4	NSC 9-1
Nov 28	Neil Leitch	l pts 6	Wolverhampton 9-6
Dec 4	Neil Leitch	l pts 6	Cleethorpes 9-5
Dec 12	John O'Meara	l ko 3	Brentford 9-1

1990
Feb 8	Jason Primera	l pts 6	Southwark 9-7
Feb 19	Peter Judson	l ko 6	Nottingham 9-1-8
Mar 19	Neil Leitch	l pts 6	Cleethorpes 9-4
Mar 27	Ronnie Stephenson	w pts 6	Wolverhampton 9-3
May 21	Ronnie Stephenson	l pts 6	Cleethorpes 9-3
Jun 4	Elvis Parsley	l rsf 3	Birmingham 9-3-8

1991
Jan 23	Mark Bates	l rtd 3	Brentwood 9-6
Mar 4	Dave Annis	w ko 2	Birmingham 9-3
May 1	Mark Bates	l pts 6	Bethnal Green 9-4
Jun 4	Paul Donaghey	l ko 1	Bethnal Green 8-13
Oct 21	Ronnie Stephenson	l pts 6	Cleethorpes 9-3

Nov 21	Ronnie Stephenson	l pts 6	Stafford 9-4
1992			
Mar 30	Jamie McBride	l rsf 1	Glasgow 9-4
Oct 5	Chip O'Neill	l pts 6	Manchester 9-2

Fights 48 Won 9 Lost 38 Drawn 1

James LAWLOR

Welterweight
Birmingham born 1 March 1961
Birmingham City ABC
1983 Midlands ABA light-welterweight final (w E Considine, l dis 3 A Richards)

1988			
Jun 17	Michael Oliver	drew 6	Edgbaston 10-0
Oct 10	Michael Oliver	l rsf 4	Edgbaston 10-4
Nov 28	B.F.Williams	w pts 6	Edgbaston 10-2
1989			
inactive			
1990			
Jun 21	Richard O'Brien	drew 6	Alfreton 10-0
Oct 3	Trevor Meikle	w pts 6	Solihull 10-4
Oct 9	Stuart Rimmer	l ko 2	Wolverhampton 10-0
Nov 14	Dean Bramhald	drew 8	Doncaster 10-0
Nov 21	Trevor Meikle	w pts 6	Solihull 10-2
Dec 6	Ronnie Campbell	drew 8	Wolverhampton 10-2
1991			
Mar 5	Mark Pearce	w pts 6	Cardiff
Apr 17	Dean Hollington	l pts 6	Albert Hall 10-2
Jun 20	Richard Burton	w pts 6	Liverpool 10-3
Sep 7	Abram Gumede	l pts 6	Belfast 10-6-8
Nov 13	Dean Hollington	l pts 6	Bethnal Green 10-3
Dec 5	Ernie Loveridge	l pts 8	Cannock 10-10
1992			
Feb 20	Wayne Timmins	l pts 6	Telford 10-9
Oct 21	Ricky North	l pts 6	Stoke 10-8
Nov 12	Carl Wright	l rsf 3	Liverpool 10-3-8

Fights 18 Won 5 Lost 9 Drawn 4

Dave LAWRENCE

Cruiserweight
Norwich, born Thetford 14 October 1963
Watton ABC
1987 Eastern ABA light-heavyweight semi-final (l J Jones)

1988			
Mar 21	Terry Duffus	drew 4	Bethnal Green 12-10
Apr 12	Ian Nelson	l rsf 3	Southend 13-3
Jun 8	Winston Burnett	w pts 6	Sheffield 13-0
Sep 26	Andrew Braveo	w rsf 3	Bedford 12-11
Oct 4	Steve Aquilina	l pts 6	Southend
Oct 27	Joe Frater	l pts 6	Birmingham 12-10
Dec 6	Derek Myers	drew 6	Southend 13-1
Dec 19	Terry Duffus	w pts 6	NSC 13-1-8
1989			
Jan 17	Randy B.Powell	w rsf 5	Woodford 13-1
Jan 27	Yurder Demircan	l pts 6	Berlin /CTD..

(Dave LAWRENCE ctd.)

Feb 16	Steve Lewsam	l pts 6	Stafford 13-2
Mar 7	Abner Blackstock	l rsf 1*	Wisbech 13-5
Apr 10	Brendan Dempsey	w pts 6	NSC 12-12-4
Apr 27	Brendan Dempsey	l ko 1	Southwark 12-13
Aug 14	Eddy Smulders	l rsf 2	Zandvoort
Sep 21	Michael Gale	l rtd 4	Harrogate 12-12
Nov 16	Steve Osborne	l pts 6	Ilkeston 13-0
Nov 30	Paul McCarthy	l pts 6	Southwark 12-12
Dec 21	Tony Wilson	l rtd 6	Kings Heath 12-10

1990
Feb 5	Steve Osborne	l pts 8	NSC 13-0

1991
Mar 25	Ian Henry	l pts 6	Bradford 12-9
Apr 19	Eddie Collins	w pts 6	Peterborough 12-6
Apr 26	Tenko Ernie	l rsf 3	Crystal Palace 12-7
Nov 19	Paul McCarthy	drew 6	Norwich 13-0

1992
Jan 21	Gipsy Carmen	l pts 6	Norwich 13-1-8

Fights 25 Won 6 Lost 16 Drawn 3

Mark LEGG

Light-welterweight
South Shields born 25 March 1970
Simonside ABC
1989 North-East England ABA light-welter final (w M Guy, l rsf 3 A Hall)
1990 North-East England ABA light-welter prelim (l B Wright)

1992
Feb 28	Chris Aston	w rsf 5	Irvine 9-12
Mar 17	Dean Hiscox	w pts 6	Wolverhampton 10-1
May 18	Charles Shepherd	l pts 6	Marton 9-11
Sep 24	Ricky Sackfield	w pts 6	Manchester 10-3

Fights 4 Won 3 Lost 1

Jason LEPRE

Super-featherweight
Portsmouth born 11 July 1969
Parade ABC

1989
Apr 26	Alan Roberts	w rtd 1*	Southampton 9-7
May 9	Hugh Ruse	w pts 6	Southend 9-0
Sep 21	Darren Weller	l rsf 3	Southampton 9-4
Oct 30	Steve Walker	l ko 2	NSC 9-4-4

1990
inactive

1991
May 23	Miguel Matthews	w pts 6	Southampton 9-5-12
Dec 16	Mark Loftus	w pts 6	Southampton 9-5-4

1992
Jan 22	Kevin Simons	w pts 6	Cardiff 9-8
Sep 17	Con Cronin	l pts 6	Watford 9-9
Oct 29	Jason White	l pts 6	Hayes 9-8

Fights 9 Won 5 Lost 4

Micky LERWILL
Welterweight
Telford born 6 April 1965
Wrekin School of Boxing ABC

1983
Jun 23	Mickey Bird	w rsf 5*	Wolverhampton 10-1
Sep 27	Mick Harkin	drew 6	Birmingham 9-13
Oct 10	Graeme Griffin	l pts 6	Birmingham 10-0

1984
Jan 18	Rocky Mensah	l pts 6	Stoke 9-13
Jan 30	Hugh Kelly	l pts 6	Glasgow 10-1
Sep 12	Jaswant Singh Ark	l pts 6	Stoke 10-4

1985
Feb 28	Mark Sperin	w pts 6	Wolverhampton 10-5
Mar 26	Steve Craggs	w rsf 3	Chorley
Apr 25	Dave Heaver	w rsf 5	Wolverhampton 10-7
Aug 29	Mauro Martelli	l pts 6	Geneva
Oct 15	Kid Milo	l pts 6	Wolverhampton 10-8
Nov 19	Lennie Gloster	l pts 8	Stafford 10-4

1986
Jan 27	Lennie Gloster	w pts 6	Dudley 10-7
Mar 25	Steve Tempro	w pts 6	Wolverhampton 10-2
Apr 17	Gary Somerville	drew 6	Wolverhampton 10-7
Oct 14	Del Bryan	l pts 8	Wolverhampton 10-8
Dec 16	John Ashton	l pts 6	Alfreton 11-0

1987-89 inactive

1990
Feb 27	Cliff Churchward	w pts 6	Evesham 10-9
Mar 14	Ernie Loveridge	l pts 6	Stoke 10-9
Apr 4	Eddie King	w pts 6	Stafford 10-8
May 24	Ernie Loveridge	drew 6	Dudley 10-8
Sep 14	Trevor Meikle	drew 8	Telford 10-8

1991
Apr 10	Gary Osborne	l pts 10	Wolverhampton 10-7
	(vacant Midlands welterweight title)		
Aug 29	John McGlynn	l pts 6	Telford 10-10
Nov 12	Ernie Loveridge	l pts 6	Wolverhampton 10-10
Dec 5	Trevor Meikle	w pts 6	Telford 10-9

1992
Dec 4	Kevin Thompson	l pts 6	Telford 10-9

Fights 27 Won 9 Lost 14 Drawn 4

Alan LEVENE
Lightweight
Liverpool born 26 February 1968
Everton Red Triangle ABC & Liverpool Golden Gloves ABC
1984 NABC Class A final (l M Ward)
1985 NABC Class B champion
1986 NABC Class C champion
1986 European Junior Championships (l C Serio, Ita)
1987 West Lancs & Cheshire ABA featherweight champion (w M Foley, w rsf 1 D Donnelly, l rsf 3 P English)
1987 England (v Cze, l I Pecha)
1988 Northern ABA featherweight final (w rtd 2 S Mangan, w C Breakwell, l J Irwin)
1988 Acropolis Cup silver medal (w J Fernandez, Por; l rsf 1 R Tuur, Hol)
1988 England (v WGer, l rsf 1 G Kaestner)

/CTD..

(Alan LEVENE ctd.)
1989
Oct 13	Mike Chapman	w pts 6	Preston 9-6
Dec 20	Finn McCool	w rsf 2	Liverpool 9-9

1990
Jan 24	Steve Winstanley	drew 6	Preston 9-7
Oct 17	Sugar Free Sommerville	drew 6	Bethnal Green 9-8

1991
inactive

1992
May 5	Steve Winstanley	w rsf 2	Preston 9-8
Nov 28	Mark Geraghty	w pts 6	Manchester 9-6-4

Fights 6 Won 4 Drawn 2

Steve LEVENE
Light-middleweight
Birmingham born 23 September 1969
Birmingham City ABC
1992 Birmingham ABA light-middleweight final (l L White)

1992
Oct 27	Steve Scott	l rsf 1	Cradley Heath 11-0
Dec 7	Warren Stephens	w ko 2	Birmingham 11-0

Fights 2 Won 1 Lost 1

Gil LEWIS
Light-heavyweight
Coventry born 29 July 1965
Willenhall ABC
1987 Midlands ABA middleweight champion (w rsf 1 M Duffy, w rsf 1 S Aquilina, w rsf 1* S Alton, w R Harley, w rsf 2 D McBarnett, l rsf 1 R Douglas)
1988 Midlands ABA light-heavyweight final (w rsf 2 D Leddington, w K Mills, l rsf 2* G Barker)
1989 South Midlands ABA middleweight semi-final (w J Cooke, l A Wright)

1989
Nov 22	Gus Mendes	w rsf 2	Solihull 12-8

1990
Jan 17	Nigel Rafferty	w pts 6	Stoke 12-4
Mar 21	Lee Woolis	w pts 6	Solihull 12-8-8
May 24	Coco Collins	w pts 6	Dudley 12-8-8
Jun 21	Jimmy Ellis	w pts 6	Alfreton 12-7-8
Dec 6	Dave Owens	w ko 2	Wolverhampton 12-8

1991
Jan 28	Carlos Christie	l pts 8	Birmingham 12-5-8
Feb 27	Alan Baptiste	w rsf 1	Wolverhampton 12-4
Jun 22	John Foreman	drew 6	Earls Court 12-8-8
Oct 1	Lee Prudden	drew 8	Bedworth 12-6
Nov 21	Art Stacey	w rsf 4	Stafford 12-11

1992
Jan 20	Tony Behan	w pts 8	Coventry 12-7
Feb 1	Ginger Tshabalala	l rsf 4*	Birmingham
Sep 15	Gary Delaney	l rsf 2	Crystal Palace 12-7-4

Fights 14 Won 9 Lost 3 Drawn 2

Lennox LEWIS

Heavyweight
Crayford, born West Ham 2 September 1965
Full name: Lennox Claudius Lewis
1982 Gold medal at Stockholm multi-nations
1983 World Junior super-heavyweight champion
1984 Olympic Games super-heavyweight quarter-final (w rsf 3 M Yousof, Pak; l T Biggs, USA)
1984 Canada (v USA, w C Payne; v GB, w ko 3 B Wells)
1985 World Cup super-heavyweight silver medal (w rtd 1 J Diaz, l V Jakovlev, USSR)
1986 Commonwealth Games super-heavyweight gold medallist (w rsf 2 J Oyebola, Eng; w rsf 2 A Evans, Wal)
1986 Fourth place at TSC Berlin multi-nations (l ko 3 V Abadshyan, USSR)
1987 Gold at French multi-nations
1987 Pan-American Games super-heavyweight silver medal (w ko 2 C Barcelete, Bra; l J Gonzalez, Cub)
1987 North-American Championships super-heavyweight gold medal (w J Gonzalez, Cub)
1987 World Cup super-heavyweight (l U Kaden, EGer)
1988 Olympic Games super-heavyweight gold medal (w ko 2 Odera, Ken; w ko 1 U Kaden, EGer; w rsf 2 R Bowe, USA)

1989
Jun 27	Al Malcolm	w ko 2	Albert Hall 16-7
Jul 21	Bruce Johnson	w rsf 2	Atlantic City 16-1
Sep 25	Andy Gerrard	w rsf 4	Crystal Palace 16-10-8
Oct 10	Steve Garber	w ko 1	Hull 16-8
Nov 5	Melvin Epps	w dis 2	Albert Hall 16-6-12
Dec 18	Greg Gorrell	w rsf 5	Kitchener, Ontario 16-4

1990
Jan 31	Noel Quarless	w rsf 2	Bethnal Green 16-1
Mar 22	Calvin Jones	w ko 1	Gateshead 16-9-4
Apr 14	Mike Simuwelu	w ko 1	Albert Hall 16-9-8
May 9	Jorge Dascola	w ko 1	Albert Hall 16-8-8
May 20	Dan Murphy	w rsf 6	Sheffield 16-6-8
Jun 27	Ossie Ocasio	w pts 8	Albert Hall 16-0
Jul 11	Mike Acey	w rsf 2	Mississauga 16-4
Oct 31	Jean-Maurice Chanet	w rsf 6*	Crystal Palace 16-0-8
	(European heavyweight title)		

1991
Mar 6	Gary Mason	w rsf 7*	Wembley 16-3
	(British & European heavyweight titles)		
Jul 12	Mike Weaver	w ko 6	Lake Tahoe
Sep 30	Glenn McCrory	w ko 2	Albert Hall 16-7
	(British & European heavyweight titles)		
Nov 21	Tyrell Biggs	w rsf 3	Atlanta 16-6-8

1992
Feb 1	Levi Billups	w pts 10	Las Vegas 16-1
Apr 30	Derek Williams	w rsf 3	Albert Hall 16-6-8
	(British, Commonwealth & European heavyweight titles)		
Aug 11	Mike Dixon	w rsf 4	Atlantic City 16-9
Oct 31	Razor Ruddock	w ko 2	Earls Court 16-3-8
	(final eliminator, WBC heavyweight title)		

Dec: Awarded WBC heavyweight title.

Fights 22 Won 22

Steve LEWSAM

Cruiserweight
Grimsby, born Cleethorpes 8 September 1960
Grimsby ABC

1982
Nov 22	Winston Wray	w pts 4	Liverpool

1983
Nov 7	Wes Taylor	w pts 6	Birmingham
Nov 22	Jerry Golden	l rsf 5	Manchester

1984-87 inactive

1988
Oct 27	Paul Sheldon	w pts 6	Birmingham 13-7
Dec 1	Ian Carmichael	w ko 2	Stafford 13-7
Dec 7	Chris Little	w rsf 1	Stoke 13-9

1989
Feb 16	Dave Lawrence	w pts 6	Stafford 13-5
May 8	Abner Blackstock	drew 8	Cleethorpes 13-9
Sep 4	Mick Cordon	w pts 8	Cleethorpes 13-10
Dec 4	Abner Blackstock	w pts 8	Cleethorpes 13-8

1990
Mar 19	Dennis Bailey	drew 8	Cleethorpes 13-9
May 21	Dennis Bailey	w pts 8	Cleethorpes 13-8
Sep 5	Herbie Hide	l rsf 4	Brighton 13-10
Nov 18	Herbie Hide	l rsf 1	NEC 13-11

1991
Feb 12	Cordwell Hylton	l rsf 8	Wolverhampton 13-7
Apr 29	David Muhammad	l pts 8	Cleethorpes 13-8
Sep 16	Cordwell Hylton (Midlands cruiserweight title)	w pts 10	Cleethorpes
Dec 9	Tony Booth	w pts 8	Cleethorpes 13-6

1992
Jun 4	Carl Thompson (vacant British cruiserweight title)	l rsf 8	Cleethorpes
Oct 26	Tom Collins	drew 8	Cleethorpes 13-6-8
Dec 1	Eddy Smulders	l ko 4	Rotterdam 13-5

Fights 21 Won 11 Lost 7 Drawn 3

Alan LEY

Bantamweight
Newport born 29 December 1968
St Josephs ABC, Crindau Harlequins ABC, Maindee ABC
1987 Welsh ABA flyweight champion (w P Dicks, l ko 2 J McLean)
1988 Welsh ABA flyweight final (l K Jenkins)
1990 Welsh ABA bantamweight final (w A Bloomer, l rsf 3 S Jones)
1991 Welsh ABA flyweight semi-final (l N Swain)
Southpaw

1991
Sep 3	Andrew Bloomer	w pts 6	Cardiff 8-3-8

1992
Jan 22	Ceri Farrell	w pts 6	Cardiff 8-6
Feb 17	Leigh Williams	w pts 6	AASC 8-4
Oct 19	Shaun Norman	w pts 6	Mayfair 8-4

Fights 4 Won 4

Earl LING

Super-middleweight
Norwich born 9 March 1972

1992
Sep 8   Eddie Collins   w pts 6   Norwich 12-0

Fights 1 Won 1

Wayne LLEWELLYN

Heavyweight
Deptford, born Greenwich 20 April 1970
Southpaw

1992
Date	Opponent	Result	Venue
Jan 18	Chris Coughlan	w rsf 3	Albert Hall 14-2
Mar 30	Steve Stewart	w rsf 4	Eltham 14-10-12
Apr 23	Gary Charlton	w rsf 6	Eltham 14-7
Dec 10	Gary McCrory	w rsf 2	Glasgow 15-0

Fights 4 Won 4

Edward LLOYD

Super-featherweight
Rhyl born St Asaph 23 April 1963
Rhyl Star ABC
1979 NABC champion
1982 Wales (v Swe, l S Odhiambo)

1983
Date	Opponent	Result	Venue
Feb 7	Stan Atherton	w pts 6	Liverpool
Feb 14	Sammy Rodgers	w rsf 4	Manchester 9-11
Feb 21	Paul Cook	l rsf 1	WSC
Apr 27	Bobby Welburn	w pts 6	Rhyl 9-9
May 9	Jimmy Thornton	l rsf 1*	Manchester 9-9
Sep 16	Jim Paton	l pts 6	Rhyl 9-3-12
Nov 28	John Murphy	l pts 8	Rhyl 9-7

1984
Date	Opponent	Result	Venue
Feb 6	Paul Keers	w pts 6	Liverpool 9-12
Mar 6	Gary Felvus	l pts 8	Stoke 9-8
Jun 12	Mickey Brooks	l rsf 6*	St Helens 9-7
Aug 6	Henry Arnold	w rsf 6	Aintree 9-5
Oct 15	Steve Griffith	l rtd 4*	Liverpool 9-10
Dec 5	Jaswant Singh Ark	w rsf 2	Stoke 9-8

1985
Date	Opponent	Result	Venue
Feb 1	Andrew Williams	drew 6	Warrington 9-9
Mar 29	Billy Laidman	w rsf 2*	Liverpool 9-9
Apr 10	Brian Roche	l rsf 7	Leeds 9-8
May 20	Gary Flear	l pts 8	Nottingham 9-9
Jul 19	Stanley Jones	drew 10	Colwyn Bay 9-5
	(vacant Welsh lightweight title)		

1986
Date	Opponent	Result	Venue
Feb 10	Peter Bradley	l pts 8	Glasgow 9-6-4
Mar 6	Najib Daho	l pts 8	Manchester 9-4
Nov 24	Keith Parry	l pts 8	Cardiff 9-7

1987
Date	Opponent	Result	Venue
Jan 13	Sugar Gibiliru	w pts 8	Oldham 9-4-8
Feb 9	Craig Windsor	w rtd 1*	Cardiff 9-3-8 /CTD..

(Edward LLOYD ctd.)

Feb 24	Alonzo Lopez	w rtd 1	Marbella
Oct 31	Abdeselan Azowogue	w pts 6	Marbella 9-7
Nov 30	Gary Maxwell	l pts 8	Nottingham 9-5
1988			
Feb 1	Colin Lynch	l rtd 4*	Northampton 9-2
1989-91 inactive			
1992			
Feb 11	Dewi Roberts	w rsf 1*	Cardiff 9-7
May 19	Mervyn Bennett	w rsf 5*	Cardiff 9-6-12
Oct 7	Steve Robinson	l rtd 8	Barry 9-3-8
Nov 14	Carl Hook	w pts 6	Cardiff 9-5-8

Fights 31 Won 14 Lost 15 Drawn 2

Paul LLOYD

Bantamweight
Ellesmere Port born 7 December 1968
Vauxhall Motors ABC
1988 West Lancs/Cheshire ABA bantamweight semi-final (l P Wright)
1989 Northern ABA bantamweight final (w rsf 3 P Wright, w ko 3 J Gilbertson, w rsf 1 J White, l rsf 1 M Gibbons)
1990 ABA bantamweight champion (w M Gibbons, w M Alldis, w rsf 3 W Docherty, w rsf 2 P Mullings)
1991 West Lancs/Cheshire ABA bantamweight champion (w.o. l rsf 2 J White)
1991 England (v Sco, l W Docherty; v Den, l D Pedersen)
1991 European Championships bantamweight (l V Antonov, USSR)
1992 England (v Sco, w S Anderson)
1992 Olympic Qualifying Tournament bantamweight (w S Anderson, Sco; l rtd 1 D Berg, Ger; l R Ciba, Pol)

1992			
Sep 25	Graham McGrath	w rsf 3	Liverpool 8-11
Oct 23	Kid McAuley	w pts 4	Liverpool 8-11-8
Nov 20	Des Gargano	w pts 4	Liverpool 8-9
Dec 15	Glyn Shepherd	w rsf 1	Liverpool 8-9

Fights 4 Won 4

Robert LLOYD

Light-welterweight
Rhyl, born Prestatyn 4 August 1960
Rhyl ABC
1980 Wales (v WGer, l M Kopzog)

1983			
Feb 17	Bobby McGowan	w rsf 1	Morley
Mar 4	Ron Atherton	w ko 1	Queensferry
Mar 22	Mo Hussein	l pts 6	Bethnal Green
Apr 27	Dave Heaver	drew 6	Rhyl 10-6
May 9	Terry Welch	w pts 6	Manchester 10-5
May 25	Kevin Sheehan	w rsf 5	Rhyl 10-4
Nov 9	Glyn Rhodes	l pts 8	Sheffield 9-12
Nov 28	Steve Boyle	w pts 6	Rhyl 10-2
1984			
Jan 28	Mick Harkin	l pts 6	Hanley 10-2
Feb 6	George Schofield	drew 8	Liverpool 10-3
Mar 6	Lee Roy	l pts 6	Stoke
1985-86 inactive			

1987			
Jul 31	Steve Hogg	l pts 6	Wrexham 10-1
1988-91 inactive			
1992			
Mar 9	Mike Calderwood	l rsf 1	Manchester 10-2-8
Oct 22	Allan McDowall	l rtd 4	Glasgow 9-13

Fights 14 Won 5 Lost 7 Drawn 2

Steve LOFTUS

Light-heavyweight
Stoke born 10 October 1971
Abbey Holton ABC
1991 Staffordshire ABA light-heavyweight final (l rtd 2 D Ashton)

1992			
Sep 29	Bobby Mack	l pts 6	Stoke 12-6
Oct 21	Paul Murray	w pts 6	Stoke 12-9
Dec 9	Lee Prudden	l pts 6	Stoke 12-7

Fights 3 Won 1 Lost 2

Gary LOGAN

Welterweight
Brixton born Lambeth 10 October 1968
Fitzroy Lodge ABC & Repton ABC
1984 Junior ABA final (w W Jones, l F Storey)

1988 ABA welterweight champion (w ko 1 B Perry, w rsf 1 T Chatten, w O Jones, w ko 2 J Hemmings, w ko 1 K Lueshing, l ko 1 M McCreath)

1988			
Oct 5	Gary Muire	w rtd 3*	Wembley GH 10-7-8
Nov 2	Tony Gibbs	w pts 6	Southwark 10-7
Dec 7	Pat Dunne	w pts 6	NSC 10-8-4
1989			
Jan 12	Mike Russell	w ko 1	Southwark 10-9-12
Feb 20	Dave Griffiths	w rsf 5	NSC 10-7-8
Mar 29	Ronnie Campbell	w pts 6	Wembley 10-10-8
May 10	Tony Britland	w ko 1	Albert Hall
Jun 7	Davey Hughes	w ko 1	Wembley 10-8
Aug 24	Mike English	w rsf 2	Tampa 10-9-12
Oct 4	Simon Eubanks	w pts 6	Albert Hall 10-8
Oct 12	Jimmy Thornton	w pts 6	Southwark 10-9-4
Nov 8	Chris Blake	l pts 8	Wembley GH
1990			
Jan 10	Julian Eavis	w pts 8	Albert Hall 10-10
Mar 3	Anthony Travers	w ko 5	Wembley 10-9
May 9	Joseph Alexander	w pts 8	Wembley 10-6-8
Sep 13	Manuel Rojas	w pts 8	Watford 10-7-8
1991			
Jan 16	Julian Eavis	w rsf 5	Albert Hall 10-10-8
Feb 18	Gordon Blair	w ko 1	NSC 10-8
Apr 24	Trevor Ambrose	w pts 8	Mayfair 10-10-8
Oct 17	Des Robinson	w pts 8	Southwark 10-8-8
1992			
Oct 15	Mickey Duncan	w pts 8	Catford 10-8-4
Dec 17	Roy Rowland	w rsf 4*	Wembley GH 10-5-12
	(vacant Southern welterweight title)		

Fights 22 Won 21 Lost 1

Eamonn LOUGHRAN

Welterweight
Ballymena born 5 June 1970
All Saints ABC, Ballymena
1987 Young Ireland (v Eng, l dis 2 D Ashton)
1987 Ireland (v Wal, w rsf 1 S James)
1987 World Junior Championships silver medal (w dis 3 T Robinson, USA; w rsf 1* A Garcia, Cub; w A Duffin, Can; ; L Mihai, Rum)

1987
Dec 7	Adam Muir	w dis 4	Belfast 10-2-8

1988
Jun 8	Tony Britland	w rsf 1	Sheffield 10-9
Jun 25	Antonio Campbell	drew 4	Panama City
Oct 21	Steve King	w pts 6	Belfast 10-10

1989
Sep 19	Ricky Nelson	w rsf 3	Belfast 10-11
Oct 31	Mark Pearce	w pts 6	Belfast
Nov 29	Ronnie Campbell	w rsf 1	Belfast 10-9-8

1990
Nov 24	Parrish Johnson	w rsf 2	Benalmadena 10-9
Dec 12	Mike Morrison	w pts 6	Basildon 10-7-4

1991
Feb 12	Nick Meloscia	w ko 1	Cardiff 10-11-8
Mar 5	Julian Eavis	w pts 6	Cardiff 10-10-12
Mar 26	Stan Cunningham	w rsf 2	Bethnal Green 10-12
Apr 24	Kevin Plant	w rtd 1*	Preston 10-10
May 28	Terry Morrill	w ko 1	Cardiff 10-10
Sep 3	Marty Duke	w pts 6	Cardiff 10-10-12
Sep 21	Glyn Rhodes	w pts 8	Tottenham 10-10
Oct 15	Juan Carlos Ortiz	w pts 8	Hamburg

1992
Mar 10	Tony Ekubia	l dis 5	Bury
	(eliminator, British welterweight title)		
May 19	Kelvin Mortimer	w rsf 1	Cardiff 10-8
Sep 29	Judas Clottey	w pts 8	Hamburg
Nov 24	Donovan Boucher	w rsf 3	Doncaster 10-6
	(Commonwealth welterweight title)		
Dec 8	Desbon Seaton	w rsf 2	Hamburg 10-8

Fights 22 Won 20 Lost 1 Drawn 1

Patrick LOUGHRAN

Light-welterweight
Ballymena born 15 September 1972
All Saints ABC
1990 Irish Junior lightweight champion (w G Rehill)

1991
Sep 11	Kevin Lowe	w pts 6	Stoke 9-9
Dec 11	Keith Hardman	w pts 6	Stoke 10-0

1992
Mar 11	Ricky North	w pts 6	Stoke
Jul 7	Jason Barker	w pts 6	Bristol 10-0-4

Fights 4 Won 4

Dave LOVELL

Light-welterweight
Birmingham born 15 April 1962
Nechells ABC

1992
Mar 25	Billy Robinson	l pts 6	Hinckley 10-2
Apr 29	Jason Barker	w pts 6	Stoke 10-3
Sep 26	Seth Jones	w rsf 4	Olympia 10-6
Oct 27	Spencer McCracken	l pts 4	Cradley Heath 10-3-8
Nov 18	Alan Peacock	l pts 6	Solihull 10-2-8

Fights 5 Won 2 Lost 3

Ernie LOVERIDGE

Light-middleweight
Stourport born Bromsgrove 7 July 1970
Kidderminster ABC

1989
Feb 6	Ricky Nelson	l rsf 6	Nottingham 11-7
Apr 17	Martin Robinson	l pts 4	Birmingham 11-0
May 8	Alfie Andrews	w pts 6	Edgbaston 11-1-8
Jun 5	Alan Richards	l pts 6	Birmingham 11-0
Jun 19	Ian Thomas	drew 6	Manchester 10-10
Jun 28	Barry Messam	l pts 6	Kenilworth 10-12
Oct 10	Matt Sturges	w rsf 1	Wolverhampton 11-0
Oct 25	Darren Mount	l pts 6	Stoke 10-11
Dec 11	Cliff Churchward	w pts 6	Birmingham 10-8

1990
Feb 27	Julian Eavis	w pts 6	Evesham 10-9
Mar 14	Micky Lerwill	w pts 6	Stoke 10-8
Mar 27	Eddie King	w pts 6	Wolverhampton 10-8
Apr 24	Mark Jay	w pts 6	Stoke 10-9
May 24	Micky Lerwill	drew 6	Dudley 10-8
Sep 18	Ronnie Campbell	w pts 6	Wolverhampton 10-7
Oct 24	Trevor Meikle	w pts 6	Dudley 10-8

1991
Jan 23	Cliff Churchward	w pts 6	Solihull 11-0-8
Feb 27	Ronnie Campbell	w pts 8	Wolverhampton 10-7
Mar 13	John Corcoran	w rsf 4	Stoke 10-10
Apr 10	Julian Eavis	drew 8	Wolverhampton 10-11
May 14	Paul Murray	w pts 8	Dudley 10-8-8
Jun 5	Cliff Churchward	w pts 8	Wolverhampton 10-10
Sep 10	Gary Osborne (Midlands welterweight title)	w rsf 1	Wolverhampton 10-6
Nov 12	Micky Lerwill	w pts 6	Wolverhampton 10-9-8
Dec 5	James Lawlor	w pts 8	Cannock 10-7

1992
Feb 1	Michael Oliver	w pts 8	Birmingham 10-12
Sep 19	Paul Jones	l pts 6	Glasgow 11-3
Oct 1	Neville Brown	l ko 4	Telford 11-1

Fights 28 Won 18 Lost 7 Drawn 3

Kevin LOWE
Lightweight
Sheffield born 24 August 1964
Richmond ABC

1991
Sep 11	Patrick Loughran	l pts 6	Stoke 9-8
Sep 26	Eunan Devenney	w ko 2	Dunstable 9-2
Oct 14	Carl Roberts	l pts 6	Manchester 9-3
Oct 22	Tommy Smith	l rsf 4*	Hartlepool 9-4
Nov 28	Joey Moffatt	l pts 6	Liverpool 9-10
Dec 10	Richard Woolgar	l pts 6	Sheffield 9-7-8

1992
Feb 27	Joey Moffatt	l pts 6	Liverpool 9-10
Mar 30	Davey McHale	l rsf 5	Glasgow 9-8-8
Apr 30	Dominic McGuigan	l rsf 6	Mayfair 9-8
Oct 19	Mark Geraghty	l pts 8	Glasgow 9-6
Nov 2	John B. Kelly	l pts 6	Liverpool 9-7-8
Nov 12	Dominic McGuigan	l rsf 2	Liverpool 9-8-8

Fights 12 Won 1 Lost 11

Nicky LUCAS
Light-welterweight
Waltham Cross, born Epping 17 February 1969
Newham ABC

1988
May 11	Joe Duffy	w rsf 6	Greenwich 9-1
Jul 10	Darren Weller	w rsf 4	Eastbourne 9-1

1989
Feb 28	Kid Sumaila	l pts 6	Chigwell 9-8
Apr 6	Steve Robinson	w pts 6	Cardiff 9-3
May 9	Jamie Hinds	w rsf 2	Plymouth 9-3-8
May 26	Alan McKay	l pts 6	Bethnal Green 9-3
Jun 28	Ian Johnson	l pts 8	Brentwood 9-2

1990
Jan 24	J.B. Chadwick	l pts 6	Preston
May 22	Brian Robb	l pts 6	Canvey Island 9-2
Jun 20	Darren Weller	w pts 6	Basildon 9-4
Sep 5	Lee Fox	drew 6	Brighton 9-5
Oct 3	Lee Fox	w rtd 2*	Basildon 9-2

1991
Apr 25	Charlie Coke	w pts 6	Mayfair 9-7-8
May 8	Frankie Ventura	drew 6	Albert Hall 9-3
Jun 6	Martin Evans	w pts 6	Barking 9-9
Jun 30	David Thompson	l pts 6	Southwark 9-12
Sep 16	Carl Hook	l pts 6	AASC 9-11-8
Oct 24	Mark O'Callaghan	l pts 6	Dunstable 9-13-8

1992
Jan 30	Jason Barker	l pts 6	Southampton 10-1

Fights 19 Won 8 Lost 9 Drawn 2

Kevin LUESHING

Light-middleweight
Beckenham born 17 April 1968
South Norwood & Victory ABC
1983 National Schools semi-final
1987 SE London ABA welterweight champion (w D Brosnan, w J Talbot, withdrew)
1988 London ABA welterweight final (w ko 1 C Dixon, w rsf 1 C Hayden, w ko 1 F Finn, l ko 1 G Logan)
1989 London ABA welter champ (w rsf 1 P Harley, w rsf 3 C Dixon, w F Finn, w M Bryan, l rsf 2 J Jones)
1990 SE London ABA welterweight final (w rsf 2 M Clarke, l rsf 1 A Carew)
1991 SE London ABA welterweight final (l M Joyce)

1991
Sep 30	John McGlynn	w rsf 2	Albert Hall 10-10
Oct 23	Julian Eavis	w rsf 2	Bethnal Green 10-9-8
Dec 14	Trevor Meikle	w ko 3	Bexleyheath 10-10

1992
Jan 18	Simon Eubanks	w ko 4	Albert Hall 10-9-8
Mar 25	Tracy Jocelyn	w rsf 3	Dagenham 10-10-12
Apr 30	Newton Barnett	w pts 6	Albert Hall 11-1-12

Fights 6 Won 6

Colin LYNCH

Featherweight
Coventry born 9 November 1961
Massey Ferguson ABC, Coachmakers ABC & Trimuph ABC
1980 NABC Class C final (l T Pearson)
1983 ABA featherweight semi-final (w rsf 1 T Hayward, w rsf 1 M Markie, w ko 3 S Frost, w rsf 3 M Scholey, w rsf 3 S Gill, l P Bradley)
1983 England (v EGer, l F Rauschning)
1983 Great Britain/Canada (v USA, l rsf 1 A Minsker)
1984 Midlands ABA featherweight champion (w rsf 1 J Dicken, w rsf 3 G Maxwell, l I Honeywood)
1985 Midlands ABA featherweight champion (w ko 2 M Hind, w S Porter, l ko 1 J Davison)
1986 ABA featherweight semi-final (w rsf 1 S Gibbons, w rsf 3 D Amory, w rsf 2 J McGowan, w ko 2 R Woolley, l D Anderson)

1987
Jan 26	John Devine	w rsf 1	Leamington 9-2
Mar 18	Shane Porter	l rsf 3	Stoke 8-12-12
	(vacant Midlands featherweight title)		
Jun 12	Stuart Carmichael	w rsf 6	Leamington 9-0
Sep 10	Gary De Roux	l rsf 3	Peterborough 9-2-8
Nov 18	Karl Taylor	l rsf 4	Solihull 9-1

1988
Feb 1	Eddie Lloyd	w rtd 4*	Northampton 9-2
Mar 22	George Jones	w ko 7	Wolverhampton 9-2
Apr 25	Steve Pollard	l pts 8	Birmingham 9-3
Sep 28	Derek Amory	w pts 10	Solihull 8-13-4
	(vacant Midlands featherweight title)		
Nov 23	Dean Lynch	w pts 8	Solihull 9-3

1989
Jan 25	John Naylor	w ko 1	Solihull 9-3
Mar 25	Freddy Cruz	l pts 8	Naples
May 10	Mark Holt	l rsf 7	Solihull 9-0
	(Midlands featherweight title)		
Sep 11	John Davison	l rsf 2	Nottingham 8-10-8
Dec 20	Robert Dickie	l rsf 1	Swansea 9-2-8

1990
Feb 21	Regilio Tuur	l rsf 3	Rotterdam
Dec 12	Henry Armstrong	l rsf 3	Stoke 9-1 /CTD

(Colin LYNCH ctd.)

1991

Feb 22	John Green	l pts 6	Manchester 9-0-8
Mar 20	Peter Judson	l rtd 5*	Solihull 9-2-12
Apr 24	Peter Harris	l pts 8	Port Talbot 9-2
May 28	Steve Robinson	l rsf 6	Cardiff 9-0-12
Oct 1	Paul Forrest	w pts 6	Sheffield 9-2
Oct 26	Paul Harvey	l rsf 1	Brentwood 9-3
Dec 10	Paul Forrest	l pts 6	Sheffield 9-1-8

1992

Jan 22	Kelton McKenzie	l rsf 5	Solihull 9-1-8
Feb 24	Des Gargano	w pts 6	Coventry 9-2
Apr 2	Bradley Stone	l rsf 3	Basildon
Sep 3	Dennis Oakes	l rsf 1	Liverpool
Nov 24	John Irwin	l rsf 4	Doncaster 9-2-8

Fights 29 Won 9 Lost 20

Dean LYNCH

Featherweight
Swansea born 21 November 1964
Clase ABC
1982 Welsh Youth final (l R Allen)
1985 ABA bantamweight final (w P Canty, w P Stephens, l rsf 3 S Murphy)
1985 Wales (v Sco, w D Hood; v Aus, w dis 2 R Bello)
1985 Oslo Multi-nations (w dis 3 C Andersson, Swe)
1986 Wales (v Sco, l D Hood)

1986

Sep 18	Billy Barton	l pts 6	Weston-super-Mare 8-13-8
Oct 6	Paddy Maguire	w pts 6	Birmingham 8-10
Nov 18	Phil Lashley	w pts 6	Swansea 8-11-4

1987
inactive

1988

Mar 1	Gary King	l pts 6	Southend 8-12
Mar 21	Phil Lashley	w pts 6	Bethnal Green 8-13
Apr 9	John Knight	l pts 6	Bristol 9-3
Apr 20	Henry Armstrong	w pts 6	Stoke
May 16	Raymond Armand	l pts 8	Hyeres, France
Nov 23	Colin Lynch	l pts 8	Solihull 9-2-8

1989

Apr 12	James Hunter	l rsf 4	Swansea 9-3
	(vacant Welsh super-featherweight title)		
May 12	Valerio Nati	l rsf 6	Codi 9-0

1990

Jan 22	Donnie Hood	l pts 8	Glasgow 8-13
Feb 19	Regilio Tuur	l pts 6	Arnhem 9-6-8
Mar 10	Freddy Cruz	l rsf 4	Lamezia Terme

1991
inactive

1992

Apr 14	Lee Fox	w pts 6	Mansfield 9-2-8
Sep 15	Henry Armstrong	l rsf 5	Liverpool 9-3
Dec 14	Karl Morling	w rsf 4	Northampton 8-11

Fights 17 Won 6 Lost 11

Paul LYNCH
Light-middleweight
Swansea born 27 December 1966
RAOB ABC
1982 Welsh Youth champion

1989
Oct 23	Darren Burford	w pts 6	NSC 11-1-8
Nov 16	Robert Harron	w pts 6	Weston 11-0
Dec 20	Peter Reid	w rsf 4	Swansea 11-1-4

1990
Mar 8	Tony Booth	w pts 6	Watford 11-1
Dec 4	Ernie Noble	w rsf 3	Southend 11-0

1991
Feb 12	Roy Rowland	w rtd 4*	Basildon 11-0
Oct 1	Peter Manfredo	l pts 8	Providence 11-2

1992
Feb 12	Robert McCracken	l rsf 4*	Wembley GH 10-13-8
Apr 14	Paul Jones	l rsf 3	Mansfield 11-0

Fights 9 Won 6 Lost 3

Chris LYONS

Featherweight
Birmingham born 2 September 1972

1991
Dec 2	Ronnie Stephenson	l pts 6	Birmingham 9-1
Dec 9	Ronnie Stephenson	l pts 6	Cleethorpes 9-0

1992
Jan 22	Dennis Oakes	l rsf 3	Stoke 8-13
May 17	Dave Martin	drew 6	Harringay 8-9
Sep 8	Robert Braddock	l ko 5	Doncaster 9-0
Oct 13	Paul Kelly	w pts 6	Wolverhampton 8-13
Oct 30	Paul Kelly	w ko 1	NEC 8-10

Fights 7 Won 2 Lost 4 Drawn 1

Ricky MABBETT

Welterweight
Leicester born 27 November 1971
Belgrave ABC

1992

Mar 19	Phil Epton	w rsf 3	York 10-2-8
Jun 16	Ojay Abrahams	l pts 6	Dagenham 10-9
Sep 8	Marty Duke	drew 6	Norwich 10-9
Oct 27	Steve McGovern	drew 6	Leicester 10-9

Fights 4 Won 1 Lost 1 Drawn 2

Kevin MABBUTT

Light-middleweight
Northampton born 23 February 1969
Kingsthorpe ABC
1991 Midlands ABA middleweight final (w C Williams, w I Moore, w A Kerr, l rsf 3 R Goulding)

1992

Apr 6	Peter Reid	l pts 6	Northampton 10-13
Apr 28	Sean Cave	w pts 6	Corby 10-13
Oct 5	Cliff Churchward	w pts 6	Northampton 10-12
Dec 14	Billy McDougall	w rtd 4*	Northampton 10-10

Fights 4 Won 4 Lost 1

Bobby MACK

Light-heavyweight
Birmingham born 12 April 1968
Ladywood ABC
Real name: Robert McKenzie

1992

Sep 29	Steve Loftus	w pts 6	Stoke 12-7
Nov 2	Martin Jolley	w pts 6	Wolverhampton 12-4
Dec 3	Joey Peters	l pts 6	Catford 12-11

Fights 3 Won 2 Lost 1

John MACKENZIE

Middleweight
Corby, born Paisley 8 February 1972
Corby Olympic ABC
1990 Three Counties ABA light-heavyweight final (l K Morton)
1991 Three Counties ABA light-heavyweight final (l K Morton, replaced Morton, l O Mintus)

1991

Dec 5	Tony Wellington	w pts 6	Peterborough 11-10

1992

Feb 6	Paul Murray	w pts 6	Peterborough 11-10
Mar 30	Willie Quinn	l rsf 4*	Glasgow 11-7-8
Apr 29	Sean Byrne	l rsf 6*	Corby 11-9

Fights 4 Won 2 Lost 2

Dave MADDEN

Light-welterweight
Birmingham born 18 June 1967
Birmingham City ABC, Kyrle Hall ABC
1989 Birmingham ABA light-welterweight final (w T Dixon, l rtd 1 R McCracken)
1990 Birmingham ABA light-welterweight champion (w P Found, l rsf 3 P Nightingale)

1992
Nov 12	Blue Butterworth	l rsf 2	Burnley 10-2

Fights 1 Lost 1

Ossie MADDIX

Welterweight
Manchester, born London 10 September 1964
Moss Side ABC
1985 East Lancs ABA welterweight semi-final (w D Sumner, l T Kershaw)
1986 East Lancs ABA welterweight semi-final (l rtd 1 E Bingham)

1987
Mar 31	Robert Riley	w rsf 2	Oldham
Apr 27	Owen Smith	w rsf 2	Glasgow 10-8
Jun 9	Tony Britland	w pts 6	Manchester 10-8
Sep 28	Terry Vosper	w ko 3	Manchester 10-10
Oct 19	Tony Britland	w pts 6	Manchester 10-5
Nov 24	Neil Patterson	w rsf 6	Middlesbrough 10-12

1988
Feb 1	Franki Moro	w pts 8	Manchester 10-9
Mar 28	Wally Swift	w pts 8	Stoke 10-11-8
Apr 28	Ian Chantler	l rsf 3*	Manchester 10-10
Sep 28	Del Bryan	l pts 8	Solihull 10-10-4

1989
May 31	Seamus Casey	w ko 3	Manchester 10-9
Oct 17	Kevin Hayde	w pts 8	Oldham 11-2-8

1990
Feb 6	Ray Taylor	w pts 10	Oldham 10-6
	(vacant Central welterweight title)		

1991
Feb 22	Judas Clottey	w pts 8	Manchester 10-10
Nov 29	Kelvin Mortimer	w pts 6	Manchester 10-8

1992
Feb 9	Michael Oliver	w rtd 3	Bradford 10-8
May 29	Gordon Blair	w pts 6	Manchester 10-12

Fights 17 Won 15 Lost 2

Noel MAGEE

Light-heavyweight
Belfast born 16 December 1965
Sacred Heart ABC, Belfast
1984 Irish ABA light-heavyweight champion (w S Collins)
1984 Ireland (v Pol, l rsf 2 S Lakomiec; v Eng, l rsf 2 J Moran)
1985 Ireland (v Wal, w rtd 2 A Blackstock)

1985
May 22	Nigel Prickett	w ko 1	Stoke 12-3-8
Sep 12	Dave Furneaux	w rsf 3	Swindon 12-7
Oct 28	Eddie Chatterton	w rsf 1	Stoke 12-5

| Nov 6 | Winston Burnett | w pts 8 | Nantwich 12-5 |
| Dec 11 | Winston Burnett | w pts 8 | Stoke 12-5 |

1986

Jan 23	Blaine Logsdon	w pts 8	Stoke 12-3
Feb 20	Barry Ahmed	w pts 8	Newcastle 12-4
Mar 5	Winston Burnett	w pts 8	Stoke 12-5
Apr 23	Barry Ahmed	w rsf 7	Stoke 12-5
May 30	Geoff Rymer	w ko 1	Stoke 12-5
Oct 13	Jimmy Ellis	w pts 8	Dulwich 12-7
Nov 17	Serg Fame	w pts 8	Dulwich 12-7

1987

Feb 24	Lennie Howard	w rsf 1	Ilford 12-7-8
Aug 3	Jimmy Ellis	w rsf 6	Stoke 12-6
Oct 20	Johnny Held	l pts 8	Stoke 12-8

1988

Feb 13	Rufino Angulo	drew 8	Paris 12-6
May 3	Mike Brothers	w ko 6	Stoke 12-1
Nov 15	Ian Bulloch	drew 10	Hull 12-8

1989

Feb 15	Yves Monsieur	l rsf 5*	Stoke 12-2
Oct 2	Paul McCarthy	w ko 2	Hanley 12-0-8
Nov 29	Sam Storey	l rsf 9	Belfast 11-9
	(British super-middleweight title)		

1990

| Sep 15 | Glazz Campbell | w pts 8 | Belfast 12-9-8 |
| Oct 30 | Johnny Melfah | w pts 6 | Belfast 12-3-8 |

1991

Feb 12	Roger McKenzie	w pts 6	Belfast 12-9
May 11	Simon Collins	w pts 8	Belfast 12-6
Nov 13	Frank Minton	w rsf 3*	Belfast 12-7
Dec 11	Tony Wilson	w rsf 3	Dublin 12-7-8

1992

Apr 25	Roger McKenzie	w pts 8	Belfast 12-9-4
Sep 28	Maurice Core	l rsf 9	Manchester 12-6-4
	(vacant British light-heavyweight title)		

Fights 29 Won 23 Lost 4 Drawn 2

Terry MAGEE

Super-middleweight
Ammanford, born Belfast 1 November 1964
Sacred Heart ABC, Belfast

1982

| Nov 29 | Robbie Turner | w pts 6 | Brighton |
| Dec 8 | Tony Baker | w pts 6 | NSC |

1983

Feb 7	Alex Romeo	l pts 6	NSC
Feb 21	Tony Burke	l pts 6	NSC
Sep 16	David Scere	w pts 6	Rhyl 11-1
Nov 28	Winston Wray	w pts 6	Rhyl 11-2

1984

Feb 6	Craig Edwards	w rsf 3	Liverpool 11-8
Mar 6	Lou Johnson	w rsf 2	Stoke 11-6
May 12	Cornelius Chisholm	w rtd 3	Stoke 11-2
Sep 12	Phil O'Hare	w pts 8	Stoke 11-2
Oct 24	Nick Riozzi	w rsf 5	Stoke 11-0
Dec 5	Harry Watson	w rsf 3	Stoke 11-2 /CTD

(Terry MAGEE ctd.)

1985
Mar 20	Gary Tomlinson	drew 8	Stoke 11-0
Apr 18	Gary Pearce	w pts 8	Nantwich 10-13-8
Sep 25	Franki Moro	w pts 10	Stoke 10-13
Dec 11	Gerry Sloof	w rsf 6	Stoke 10-13

1986
May 7	Gary Stretch	l rsf 7	Albert Hall 11-1-12

1987
Jun 23	Seamus Casey	w ko 6	Swansea 10-13-8
	(vacant Irish light-middleweight title)		
Nov 1	Charles Oosthuizen	l rsf 8	Johannesburg 11-0

1988
Mar 26	Chris Richards	w pts 8	Belfast
Jun 14	Tony Britton	w pts 6	Birmingham 11-3
Sep 28	Wally Swift	w pts 8	Solihull 11-3-8
Dec 7	Kevin Hayde	w pts 8	Port Talbot 11-2

1989
Apr 12	Tony Britton	w pts 8	Swansea
Nov 16	Jimmy Gourad	w pts 8	Weston 11-2-8

1990
Mar 26	Gilbert Dele	l rtd 3	Paris
	(European light-middleweight title)		

1991
Jun 1	Andy Till	l rsf 4*	Bethnal Green 11-2-4
Dec 11	Ray Close	l rsf 7	Dublin 11-11-4
	(Irish super-middleweight title)		

1992
Sep 25	Fran Harding	l pts 6	Liverpool 11-13
Oct 17	James Cook	l rsf 5	Wembley 12-1
Nov 27	Roland Ericsson	l pts 8	Randers 12-7

Fights 31 Won 20 Lost 10 Drawn 1

Pat MAHER

Featherweight
Hackney, born Sunderland 24 November 1964
Colvestone ABC
1980 National Schools champion (w K Kenmare)
1983 NABC Class C champion (w P Lally)
1983 Young England (v YEGer, l dis 2 R Breitbarth; l Schreier)
1983 London ABA light-flyweight champion (w M Cantwell, l D Porter)

1987
May 7	David Afan-Jones	w pts 6	Bayswater 8-5

1988
May 5	Roy Deeble	l rtd 4*	Bayswater 8-5-8

1989-90 inactive

1991
Sep 30	John Armour	l ko 1	Albert Hall 8-9

1992
Apr 7	Kevin Middleton	l ko 4	Southend 8-13

Fights 4 Won 1 Lost 3

Dave MAJ

Welterweight
Liverpool born 21 November 1964
Real name: Dave Majekodunmi

1991
Jun 24	Benji Joseph	w rsf 4	Liverpool 10-1
Sep 9	Mark Verikios	l pts 6	Liverpool 10-6
Oct 14	David Maw	l pts 6	Manchester 10-7
Dec 16	Wayne Shepherd	drew 6	Manchester 10-5

1992
Feb 3	Wayne Shepherd	w pts 6	Manchester 10-9-12
Mar 9	Willie Yeardsley	w rsf 1	Manchester 10-7-12
Apr 13	Peter Reid	w ko 1	Manchester 10-9-8
May 14	Andreas Panayi	l ko 6	Liverpool 10-7
Oct 5	John Duckworth	drew 6	Manchester 10-8
Nov 12	Mark Verikios	l pts 6	Liverpool 10-4-12

Fights 10 Won 4 Lost 4 Drawn 2

Mohammed MALIK

Light-middleweight
Burnley, born Pakistan 12 June 1965
Full name: Mohammed Ayub Malik

1988
Oct 11	Alfie Andrews	l pts 6	Wolverhampton 10-4

1989-91 inactive

1992
Dec 14	Tim Robinson	l rsf 3	Cleethorpes 11-0

Fights 2 Lost 2

Colin MANNERS

Light-middleweight
Leeds born 4 July 1962
St Patricks ABC
1989 Yorkshire ABA light-middleweight final (l C Hepton)
1990 North-East ABA light-middleweight final (w ko 1 T Massey, w T Booth, l W Neil)

1990
Apr 26	Tony Booth	l pts 6	Halifax 11-2
Sep 27	Carlos Christie	l pts 6	NEC 11-10
Oct 18	Calton Myers	w ko 2	Dewsbury 11-4
Oct 25	Colin Ford	l pts 6	Bayswater 11-6
Dec 12	Tony Kosova	w pts 6	Leicester 11-3

1991
Jan 31	Lee Crocker	w pts 6	Stockport 11-2-12
Feb 18	John Ogiste	l pts 6	NSC 11-4
Mar 14	John Ogiste	l pts 8	Leeds
May 1	Darren Parker	w ko 2	Solihull 11-7
Jun 5	Richard Carter	w ko 1	Wolverhampton 11-7-8
Sep 3	Wayne Ellis	w rsf 1	Cardiff 11-5-4

1992
Apr 29	Darron Griffiths	drew 8	Solihull 11-5-8
May 14	Stan King	w pts 8	Mayfair 11-6
Sep 30	Darron Griffiths	l pts 10	Solihull 11-3

(eliminator, British middleweight title)

Fights 14 Won 7 Lost 6 Drawn 1

Nick MANNERS

Light-heavyweight
Leeds born 23 November 1966
Unity Boys ABC
1990 Yorkshire ABA middleweight champion (w T Robinson, w C Joseph, l P Hitch)

1990

Oct 18	Paul Murray	w pts 6	Dewsbury 12-4
Dec 13	John Kaighin	w ko 3	Dewsbury

1991

Jan 31	Terry Duffus	w rsf 1	Stockport 12-4
Mar 21	Marvin O'Brian	w ko 2	Dewsbury 11-13
May 9	Peter Gorny	w rsf 1	Leeds 12-2-12
Jun 27	Peter Vosper	w rsf 1	Leeds 12-0
Aug 1	Tony Booth	drew 8	Dewsbury 12-2
Oct 30	Kevin Morton	l pts 8	Leeds 12-3-8

1992

Sep 23	Lee Crocker	w ko 1	Leeds 12-1-8
Oct 29	Ali Forbes	l rsf 3	Leeds 12-4

Fights 10 Won 7 Lost 2 Drawn 1

Andy MANNING

Light-heavyweight
Sheffield born 1 June 1970
Parsons Cross ABC
1991 Yorkshire & Humberside ABA middleweight final (l T Robinson)

1991

Oct 7	Mark Hale	w pts 6	Liverpool 11-8
Nov 4	Steve Thomas	l pts 6	Merthyr 11-10
Dec 2	Marc Rowley	w pts 6	Liverpool 12-3

1992

Mar 3	Justin Clements	drew 6	Cradley Heath 12-4-8
Mar 18	Willie Quinn	l pts 6	Glasgow 11-12
Apr 29	Adrian Wright	w pts 6	Stoke 11-13
May 11	Julian Johnson	w pts 6	Llanelli 12-9-12
May 18	John Oxenham	l pts 6	Marton 12-7

Fights 8 Won 4 Lost 3 Drawn 1

Gary MARSTON

Featherweight
Stoke, born Bridgewater, Somerset, 11 December 1966
Butt Lane & Queensberry ABC
1988 Staffordshire ABA featherweight final (w ko 3 N Wooley, l rsf 1 E Parsley)
1991 Staffordshire ABA lightweight champion (w rsf 1 M Abbott, withdrew)
1992 Staffordshire ABA featherweight champion (w.o. then failed to make the weight!)

1992

Sep 29	Norman Dhalie	drew 6	Stoke 9-0

Fights 1 Drawn 1

Chubby MARTIN

Super-featherweight
Islington, born Cardiff 8 August 1964
Real name: Raphael Martin
Llandaff ABC
1980 NABC Class A final (l C Cartledge)

1984
| Dec 4 | Mark Champney | w ko 4 | Southend 9-4 |

1985
Mar 7	Chris Pegg	w pts 6	Nottingham 9-3-8
Apr 18	Ernie Noble	w rsf 2	Halifax 9-7
Jun 4	Steve Cleak	drew 6	Southend 9-8
Sep 10	Marvin P. Gray	l pts 6	Southend 9-4
Oct 3	Stuart Shaw	w rtd 7*	Nottingham 9-8-8
Oct 14	Russell Jones	l rsf 7	Cardiff 9-4

1986
Jan 21	Renard Ashton	w pts 6	Tunbridge Wells 9-10
Mar 25	Paul Huggins	l rsf 7	Tunbridge Wells 9-7
Nov 20	Andrew Furlong	drew 8	Wimbledon 9-11

1987
Jan 11	Andrew Furlong	l pts 8	Ealing 9-10
Feb 22	Brian Nickels	l rsf 5*	Wembley GH 9-10-4
Sep 14	Paul Gadney	l pts 8	Crystal Palace 9-8
Nov 4	Michael McDermott	w pts 6	Gravesend 9-7
Dec 9	B.F.Williams	drew 8	Greenwich 9-7-4

1988
Mar 4	David Thio	l ko 4	Villeurbanne
Apr 20	Mike Russell	w pts 6	Muswell Hill 9-3
May 18	Rudi Valentino	w rsf 5	Lewisham 9-11
Jun 3	Senturk Ozdemir	l pts 6	Berlin
Aug 30	John Bennie	drew 8	Holborn 9-11
Nov 14	Jose Tuominen	l pts 4	Helsinki 9-5-8

1989
| May 6 | Roberto Lauretta | l rsf 1 | Syracusa 9-9 |
| Sep 18 | Peter Bradley | l pts 8 | NSC 9-9-4 |

1990
inactive

1991
Mar 6	Billy Schwer	l rsf 3*	Wembley 9-8-8
Oct 23	G.G. Goddard	w pts 8	Stoke 9-9-12
Nov 14	Alex Sterling	w rsf 5	Marble Arch 9-9-8

1992
| Apr 2 | Jimmy Clark | l rsf 6* | Basildon 9-6 |

Fights 27 Won 10 Lost 13 Drawn 4

Dave MARTIN

Bantamweight
Islington born Cardiff 11 May 1967

1991
| Oct 23 | Mark Hargreaves | l pts 6 | Stoke 8-7-12 |
| Nov 14 | Dave Campbell | l pts 6 | Marble Arch 8-8-4 |

1992
| May 17 | Chris Lyons | drew 6 | Harringay 8-8-8 |

Fights 3 Lost 2 Drawn 1

Dean MARTIN
Lightweight
Birmingham born 28 November 1967

1992
Oct 30   George Naylor   l pts 6   NEC 9-10

Fights 1 Lost 1

Sean MARTIN
Light-middleweight
Scunthorpe born 1 April 1971

1992
Nov 2   Andrew Jervis   l ko 2   Liverpool 11-0

Fights 1 Lost 1

Stinger MASON
Super-middleweight
Sheffield born 27 February 1964
Real name: Paul Mason
Unity ABC

1989
Apr 19   Sean Stringfellow   w pts 6   Sheffield 11-12
May 24   Andy Flute   l pts 6   Hanley 11-4
Nov 16   Tony Lawrence   drew 4   Ilkeston 12-0
1990
Jan 27   Ian Vokes   w pts 6   Sheffield 11-13-8
Mar 28   Cliff Curtis   w pts 6   Bethnal Green 12-1-2
May 21   Tony Hodge   w ko 2   Sheffield 12-2-8
Jun 11   Glenn Campbell   l rtd 5*   Manchester 12-2
Nov 12   Adrian Wright   l rsf 4   Stratford 11-12
1991
Mar 13   Mike Phillips   drew 6   Stoke 11-8
May 13   Doug Calderwood   l ko 3   Manchester 12-1
Oct 23   Roger Wilson   drew 6   Stoke 12-0
Nov 11   Russell Washer   w pts 4   Stratford 11-9
1992
May 23   Paul Busby   l rsf 2   Birmingham 11-8
Sep 28   Quinton Paynter   l ko 1   Manchester 11-11

Fights 14 Won 5 Lost 6 Drawn 3

Tony MASSEY
Light-middleweight
Leeds born 24 January 1968
St Patricks ABC
1988 Yorkshire & Humberside ABA welterweight semi-final (l rsf 3 D Harper)
1990 Yorkshire & Humberside ABA light-middleweight semi-final (w W Appleton, l ko 1 C Manners)

1992
Mar 19   Phil Foxon   w rsf 1   York 11-3
Sep 28   Alan Williams   w rsf 3*   Manchester 11-3
Oct 29   John Duckworth   l rtd 4*   Leeds 11-2

Fights 3 Won 2 Lost 1

Jason MATTHEWS

Light-welterweight
Bargoed born Caerphilly 26 June 1969
Aberbargoed ABC
1989 ABA lightweight final (w S Edwards, w J Evans, w S Cook, w A Khan, w M Culpepper, l M Ramsey)
1989 Wales (v Sco, l D Anderson; w rsf 3 M Gowans)
1990 Commonwealth Games lightweight (l R Wahab, Nig)
1990 Wales (v Sco, w J Pender; v Ire, l B Geraghty)
1991 ABA light-welter champion (w rsf 2 L Thomas, w dis 3 M Stillman, w C Hook, w A Stone, w G Smith)
1991 Wales (v Sco, w rsf 1 J Pender; w rsf 3 S McGhee)

1991
Jul 18	Carl Hook	w pts 6	Cardiff 9-11-12
Oct 29	Robert Peel	w rsf 6*	Cardiff 10-2
Nov 21	Chris Saunders	w rsf 4*	Burton 10-2

1992
Feb 11	Carl Hook	w pts 6	Cardiff 10-0
Apr 30	Ross Hale	l rsf 3	Bayswater 10-3-8

Fights 5 Won 4 Lost 1

Miguel MATTHEWS

Featherweight
Ystalyfera born Glanamman 22 December 1965
Real name: Nicholas Matthews
Blaenant ABC

1988
Sep 21	Terry Collins	l pts 6	Basildon 9-2
Sep 28	Eugene Maloney	drew 6	Edmonton 9-0
Oct 25	Hugh Ruse	l pts 6	Pontardawe 9-3-8
Nov 15	Tony Bernard	w rsf 2	Chigwell 9-0
Dec 14	Richie Wenton	l ko 2	Liverpool 8-10

1989
Feb 14	Brian Robb	w rsf 2*	Wolverhampton 8-12
Mar 6	Mick Markie	l pts 8	Northampton 8-12
Mar 21	Ronnie Stephenson	drew 8	Wolverhampton 8-11
Apr 11	Hugh Ruse	w pts 6	Port Talbot 9-3-8
Jun 5	Lester James	drew 6	Birmingham 9-2
Jun 12	Colin McMillan	l rsf 3	Battersea 8-13-8
Sep 6	Marcel Herbert	l pts 6	Port Talbot 9-1
Sep 20	Des Gargano	l pts 6	Stoke 9-0
Sep 28	Steve Walker	l pts 6	Cardiff 9-1-8
Oct 17	Alan Roberts	w pts 6	Cardiff 9-3
Oct 24	Jimmy Clark	l pts 6	Watford 9-2-8
Nov 6	Mick Markie	drew 8	Northampton 9-1-8
Dec 3	Johnny Bredahl	l pts 6	Copenhagen

1990
Feb 19	Mick Markie	l pts 8	Kettering 9-2
Feb 27	Peter Buckley	drew 6	Evesham 9-0
Mar 21	Rocky Lawlor	l pts 8	Solihull 8-9
Sep 3	Derek Amory	l pts 6	Dudley 9-3
Oct 1	Peter Buckley	l pts 8	Cleethorpes 9-0-8
Oct 9	Peter Buckley	w pts 8	Wolverhampton 8-13-8
Oct 29	Peter Buckley	l pts 8	Birmingham 8-13
Nov 21	Jason Primera	l pts 8	Solihull 9-4
Dec 12	Paul Harvey	l pts 6	Basildon
Dec 19	Paul Forrest	l pts 6	Preston

1991
Mar 7	Bradley Stone	l rsf 4	Basildon 9-0 /CTD..

(Miguel MATTHEWS ctd.)

Apr 4	Mark Tierney	l pts 6	Watford 8-9
Apr 16	Craig Dermody	l pts 6	Nottingham 8-9
Apr 25	Bradley Stone	l pts 6	Basildon 9-0
May 23	Jason Lepre	l pts 6	Southampton 9-0
May 31	Danny Connolly	l pts 8	Glasgow 9-4
Jun 13	Tony Silkstone	l pts 6	Hull 9-4
Jun 24	Jimmy Owens	l pts 6	Liverpool 9-0
Sep 9	Moussa Sangare	l rsf 5	Forges-les-Eaux
Oct 9	Mark Loftus	drew 6	Manchester
Oct 24	Kevin Middleton	l pts 6	Dunstable 9-3
Oct 31	Brian Robb	drew 6	Telford 9-2
Nov 11	Peter Judson	l pts 6	Stratford 9-3
Nov 21	Craig Dermody	l pts 6	Burton 8-12
Nov 28	Dave Hardie	l pts 6	Glasgow 9-0
Dec 11	Jimmy Clark	l pts 6	Basildon 9-2
1992			
Jan 8	Ceri Farrell	w pts 6	Burton-on-Trent 9-1
Jan 31	John Green	drew 6	Manchester 8-13-8
Feb 20	Eddie Cook	l pts 6	Glasgow 9-0-8
Feb 27	Craig Dermody	l pts 6	Liverpool 8-13
Mar 25	John Armour	l pts 6	Dagenham 8-13
Jun 1	Danny Porter	l pts 6	Glasgow 8-6
Jul 7	Tony Falcone	l pts 6	Bristol 8-13
Jul 14	Naseem Hamed	l rsf 3	Mayfair 8-10
Sep 30	John Irwin	l pts 6	Solihull 9-0
Oct 17	Mark Bowers	l pts 6	Wembley 9-1-8
Nov 24	Kid McAuley	l pts 6	Doncaster 9-1-8
Dec 14	Barry Jones	l pts 6	Cardiff 8-13-8

Fights 56 Won 6 Lost 42 Drawn 8

Winston MAY

Light-middleweight
West Ham born 21 November 1962
Southpaw
Fairbairn House ABC
1985 NE London ABA light-middleweight prelims (l N Benn)
1986 NE London ABA light-middleweight semi-final (w C Marquis, l S Butler)
1987 ABA light-middle final (w D Kiely, w S Hibbert, w C Marquis, w R Thompson, w K Wishart, w A Ellison, l A Walker, replaced Walker & l N Brown)
1987 England (v Pol, l D Michalczewski)
1988 London ABA light-middle champ (w K Adamson, w T Taylor, w R Arthey, w P Wilson, w R Atkinson, l W Neil)
1988 England (v Sco, w A Docherty)

1988			
Nov 29	Pat Dunne	w pts 6	Battersea 11-0-4
Dec 10	Mark Howell	w pts 6	Crystal Palace 11-0-8
1989			
Jan 31	Sammy Sampson	w rsf 4*	Bethnal Green
Feb 16	Martin Smith	drew 6	Battersea 10-12
Apr 11	Damien Denny	l rsf 3	Port Talbot 11-0
May 21	Newton Barnett	w pts 4	Finsbury Park 10-11
Sep 25	Newton Barnett	w pts 6	Crystal Palace 11-2
1990			
Feb 26	Alan Richards	l pts 6	Crystal Palace 11-1
Apr 17	Paul Wesley	drew 8	Millwall 11-5
May 3	Johnny Miller	w pts 6	Marble Arch 10-13
Nov 6	Brian Robinson	l rsf 4*	Mayfair 10-12

1991
Dec 5   Shaun Cummins   l rsf 2   Peterborough 11-1
1992
Apr 30   Lee Crocker   l rsf 2   Bayswater 11-0

Fights 13 Won 6 Lost 5 Drawn 2

Trevor MEIKLE
Welterweight
Scunthorpe born 29 January 1967
Riddings ABC
1986 Humberside ABA light-middleweight final (l M Murray)
Southpaw

1989
May 16	Louis Walsh	drew 6	Halifax 10-9
Jun 12	Chris Mulcahy	l pts 6	Manchester 10-3
Jun 19	Anthony Lawrence	l pts 6	Manchester 10-8
Jul 11	Chris Mulcahy	l pts 6	Batley 10-9
Oct 16	Steve Hardman	drew 6	Manchester 10-4
Oct 23	Mick Mulcahy	w pts 6	Cleethorpes
Nov 6	Ian Thomas	w pts 6	Northampton 10-6
Nov 14	Cliff Churchward	w pts 6	Evesham 10-6
Nov 22	Cliff Churchward	w pts 6	Stafford 10-6
Dec 11	Barry Messam	l ko 5	Nottingham 10-1

1990
Feb 5	Malcolm Melvin	l pts 6	Brierley Hill 10-4
Feb 19	Gordon Blair	l pts 6	Glasgow 10-5-12
Feb 27	Dave Whittle	drew 8	Middlesbrough 10-7
Mar 14	Carlos Chase	l pts 6	Battersea 10-5
Mar 27	Barry Messam	w pts 6	Leicester 10-6
Apr 30	G.W.Gully	l pts 6	Brierley Hill 10-7
May 21	Frank Harrington	w rsf 5*	Hanley 10-10
May 30	Mark Jay	drew 6	Stoke 10-10
Jun 15	Mark Jay	w rsf 5*	Telford 10-10
Sep 14	Micky Lerwill	drew 8	Telford 10-7
Oct 3	James Lawlor	l pts 6	Solihull 10-4
Oct 9	Pat Durkin	w dis 3	Liverpool 10-10
Oct 24	Ernie Loveridge	l pts 6	Dudley 10-8
Nov 6	Stuart Good	l pts 6	Southend
Nov 21	James Lawlor	l pts 6	Solihull 10-5
Nov 29	Dave Whittle	l pts 6	Marton 10-11
Dec 10	Kevin Spratt	l pts 6	Bradford 10-6

1991
Feb 11	Steve Hardman	l pts 6	Manchester 10-9
Feb 21	Colin Sinnott	w pts 6	Leeds 10-7
Feb 27	Andreas Panayi	w pts 6	Wolverhampton 10-8
Apr 3	Mick Mulcahy	w pts 6	Manchester 10-8
Apr 10	Wayne Timmins	l pts 6	Wolverhampton 10-7
Apr 22	Nick Cope	w rsf 2	Glasgow 10-6-8
May 1	Tommy Milligan	l pts 6	Liverpool 10-7
May 9	Todd Riggs	l pts 6	Leeds 10-7-12
Jun 3	Tommy Milligan	l pts 6	Glasgow 10-6-8
Jun 10	Chris Mulcahy	drew 6	Manchester 10-5
Aug 14	Efrem Calamati	l rsf 4	Alcamo
Sep 23	Alan Peacock	w pts 6	Glasgow 10-7-10
Oct 1	James McGee	w pts 6	Bedworth 10-10
Nov 5	Lee Ferrie	l pts 6	Leicester 10-13 /CTD..

(Trevor MEIKLE ctd.)

Nov 25	Mark Kelly	w pts 8	Cleethorpes 10-9
Dec 5	Micky Lerwill	l pts 6	Telford 10-9
Dec 14	Kevin Lueshing	l ko 3	Bexleyheath 10-9-8
1992			
Jan 28	Alan Peacock	l pts 8	Piccadilly 10-8
Feb 29	Andre Kimbu	l rtd 5	Gravelines
Apr 13	Crain Fisher	l pts 6	Manchester 10-11
Apr 30	B.F.Williams	l pts 6	Watford
Sep 14	Kevin Spratt	w rsf 4	Bradford 10-5
Oct 23	Andreas Panayi	l pts 6	Liverpool 10-10
Nov 26	Willie Yeardsley	w pts 6	Hull 10-10

Fights 51 Won 17 Lost 28 Drawn 6

Johnny MELFAH

Super-middleweight
Gloucester born 14 December 1960
Brockworth Viking ABC & Gloucester ABC
1981 Western ABA welterweight champion (w rsf 1 S McTierney, l T Marsh)
1982 Western ABA welter champ (w rsf 2 I Baldwin, w rsf 2 C Boyce, w T Burt, w ko 1 M Lescott, l R McKenley)
1983 ABA light-middle final (w R Thomas, w T Burt, w R Rossi, w dis 3 W Walters, w T Price, l R Douglas)
1984 England (v WGer, l N Nieroba)
1984 Western ABA light-middleweight final (l S Pigott)
1985 ABA middleweight semi-final (w rsf 3 M Graham, w ko 2 D McCarthy, w dis 3 A Chambers, w rsf 1 M Core, l D Cronin)
1986 ABA middleweight final (w rsf 3 M Graham, w I Strudwick, w M Khan, w rsf 2 G Ferrie, l rsf 3 N Benn)

1986			
Sep 8	Winston Wray	l rsf 3*	Dulwich 11-6-8
Oct 13	Andy Sumner	w ko 3	Dulwich 11-2-8
Nov 17	Graeme Ahmed	w pts 6	Dulwich 11-4
Dec 15	Mark Mills	w ko 5	Eltham 11-4-8
1987			
May 7	Alan Baptiste	w ko 1	Bayswater 11-6-8
Sep 30	Cliff Gilpin	w pts 8	Solihull 11-5-8
Oct 12	Tony Burke	w rsf 2	Bow 11-9
1988			
Jan 21	Carl Penn	w ko 1	Battersea 11-6
Mar 18	Reggie Miller	w rtd 5*	Battersea 11-6-4
Nov 23	Herol Graham	l rsf 5	Bethnal Green 11-4-8
	(British middleweight title)		
1989			
Feb 8	Eric Mastapha Cole	w rtd 5	Albert Hall 11-9
Mar 22	Winston Wray	w rsf 6	Gloucester 11-7-12
Jun 27	Kid Milo	l ko 7	Albert Hall 11-8
Nov 5	Chris Eubank	l ko 4	Albert Hall 11-10
1990			
Oct 30	Noel Magee	l pts 6	Belfast 12-0-8
Nov 24	Fidel Castro	l rsf 4*	Benalmadena 11-7
1991			
Feb 23	Sean Heron	w pts 8	Brighton 12-2
Mar 5	Wayne Ellis	l rsf 2*	Cardiff 11-10-8
May 16	Roland Ericsson	w rsf 4*	Battersea 11-13-8
Sep 7	Sam Storey	l pts 8	Belfast 12-0
Oct 1	Fidel Castro	l rsf 7	Sheffield
1992			
May 12	Lou Gent	w rsf 3*	Crystal Palace 11-12-4

Jul 25	Nicky Piper	l rsf 5*	Manchester 11-12-4
(eliminator, British super-middleweight title)			

Fights 23 Won 13 Lost 10

Malcolm MELVIN
Light-welterweight
Birmingham born 5 February 1967
Birmingham City ABC

1985
Nov 28	Steve Foster	drew 6	Ilkeston 11-3
Dec 4	Simon Collins	l pts 6	Stoke 11-0

1986
Mar 24	Rocky McGran	l pts 6	NSC 11-6
Apr 10	Lincoln Pennant	w pts 6	Leicester 11-1
Apr 21	Malcolm Davies	w pts 6	Birmingham 11-0
May 7	Julian Monville	w pts 6	Solihull 11-2

1987
inactive

1988
Jan 19	Antonio Fernandez	l rsf 4*	Kings Heath 11-3
Mar 7	John Ellis	l pts 6	NSC 11-7-8

1989
Dec 3	David Jenkins	w pts 6	Birmingham 10-1

1990
Feb 5	Trevor Meikle	w pts 6	Brierley Hill 10-0
Feb 22	Chris Saunders	l pts 4	Hull 10-1-8
Mar 19	Barry North	w pts 6	Brierley Hill 9-9-12
Apr 30	Andy Kent	w rsf 5	Brierley Hill 9-10-12
Jun 4	Brendan Ryan	l rsf 7	Edgbaston 10-0
Sep 3	David Jenkins	w pts 8	Dudley 10-0
Oct 13	Brendan Ryan	w pts 10	Edgbaston 9-13-8
(vacant Midlands light-welterweight title)			

1991
Mar 18	Carl Brasier	w pts 6	NSC 10-3
Jun 17	Dean Bramhald	w pts 6	Edgbaston 10-5

1992
May 21	Mark Kelly	w pts 8	Cradley Heath 10-8
Oct 5	Ross Hale	l pts 10	Bristol 9-13-8
(eliminator, British light-welterweight title)			
Nov 17	Tusikoleta Nkalankete	drew 8	Paris

Fights 21 Won 12 Lost 7 Drawn 2

Sean METHERELL
Welterweight
Kettering born 29 March 1966
Keystone ABC
1988 Midlands ABA light-middleweight final (l rsf 2 N Brown)
1992 Midlands ABA welterweight final (w P Bench, w G Lowe, l rsf 3 M Santini)

1992
Dec 10	Cliff Churchward	w pts 6	Corby 10-8

Fights 1 Won 1

Kevin MIDDLETON

Featherweight
Downham born Deptford 23 May 1968
Eltham ABC
1989 SE London ABA lightweight final (w A Cooper, l T Franklin)
1990 London ABA featherweight champion (w rsf 2 T Rossiter, w dis 2 C McMullen, w dis 3 S McNamara, l rsf 1 K Hodkinson)
1991 SE London ABA featherweight semi-final (l rsf 3 M Brown)

1991
Oct 24	Miguel Matthews	w pts 6	Dunstable 9-3-8

1992
Apr 7	Pat Maher	w ko 4	Southend 9-0
Apr 29	Chris Jickells	l rsf 6	Solihull 9-1
Oct 15	Bradley Stone	l pts 6	Catford 9-2
Dec 4	Brian Robb	w rsf 1	Telford 9-1-4

Fights 5 Won 3 Lost 2

Rocky MILTON

Light-welterweight
Streatham born 5 May 1965
Real name: Alkis Alkiviadov
No amateur experience

1984
Oct 24	Kenny Watson	l pts 6	Mayfair 9-11-4

1985
Jan 24	John Wilder	w rtd 3	Streatham 9-11-4
Feb 4	John Faulkner	l pts 6	Lewisham 9-11
Apr 30	Kenny Watson	w pts 6	Wimbledon 9-10
Nov 28	Brian Nickels	l ko 4	Bethnal Green 9-8

1986
Sep 4	Kevin Spratt	drew 6	Wimbledon 9-8-8

1987
Nov 19	Lee West	l pts 6	Battersea 9-7-8

1988
May 10	Peter Hart	l rsf 1	Tottenham 9-10-8
Dec 6	Shane Tonks	w pts 6	Southend 10-0

1989
inactive

1990
Apr 5	David Jenkins	l pts 6	Southend 10-7
Sep 25	Ray Newby	w pts 6	Millwall 10-0
Nov 12	Darren Morris	w pts 6	Norwich 10-10

1991
May 8	Steve McGovern	l pts 6	Millwall 10-7-8

1992
Jan 8	Darren Morris	l pts 6	Burton-on-Trent 10-9-8
Oct 31	Rick Bushell	drew 4	Earls Court 9-12-12
Dec 10	Brian Coleman	drew 4	Bethnal Green 10-0

Fights 16 Won 5 Lost 8 Drawn 3

Alex MOFFAT
Light-welterweight
Doncaster born 11 November 1965

1992
Nov 10	Paul Knights	l ko 3	Dagenham 10-2
Dec 9	Shane Sheridan	l pts 6	Stoke 10-2

Fights 2 Lost 2

Joey MOFFAT
Light-welterweight
Liverpool born 14 February 1964
Kirkby ABC

1990
Mar 10	David Jenkins	l pts 6	Bristol 9-13-8

1991
Nov 13	Paul Hughes	w rtd 4	Liverpool 9-12
Nov 28	Kevin Lowe	w pts 6	Liverpool 9-10-4

1992
Feb 10	Tony Doyle	w rsf 3	Liverpool 9-9
Feb 27	Kevin Lowe	w pts 6	Liverpool 9-12
Apr 29	Pete Roberts	w rsf 3	Liverpool 9-12
May 14	Scott Doyle	w rsf 8*	Liverpool 9-11
Sep 15	Carl Tilley	w pts 6	Liverpool 9-10

Fights 8 Won 7 Lost 1

Charlie MOORE
Light-middleweight
Darlington born 20 November 1971
Darlington ABC
1985 National Schools champion
1987 National Schools champion
1987 Junior ABA champion
1988 National Schools champion
1990 North East Division ABA welterweight champion (w J McAllister, w dis 3 D Johnson, w rsf 3 M Johnson, l rtd 2 P Waudby)
1991 North East Division ABA welter quarter-final (l J Pearse)

1991
Dec 5	Jim Conley	w ko 2	Peterborough 11-3-8
Dec 19	Robert Riley	w pts 6	Oldham 10-10

1992
Jan 23	Stuart Dunn	w rsf 3	York 10-13
Mar 19	John Corcoran	w pts 6	York 10-13-8
Apr 8	Steve Thomas	w rsf 3	Leeds 10-12

Fights 5 Won 5

Andy MORGAN

Light-welterweight
Port Talbot, born Neath 20 February 1963
Afan Lido ABC
1987 Welsh ABA light-welterweight semi-final (w C Stevens, w S James, l D Jenkins)

1987
Jun 22	Jon Dicken	w ko 1	Stafford 10-0
Oct 5	Gerry Courtney	w pts 6	NSC 10-1-8
Nov 24	Davey Robb	w pts 6	Wolverhampton 10-0

1988
Jan 27	Andy Holligan	l rsf 5	Belfast 10-2-8
Sep 28	David Postane	l pts 6	Edmonton 10-3-12
Oct 25	Mark Purcell	l rtd 4*	Pontardawe 10-3-8
Dec 5	Tony Whitehouse	w rsf 2	Dudley 10-1

1989
Feb 6	Michael Howell	w pts 8	Swansea 10-3
Mar 29	Seamus O'Sullivan	l pts 6	Bethnal Green 10-4-8
May 9	Oliver Henry	w rsf 5	Southend 10-2

1990
Sep 27	Stuart Rimmer	l pts 6	NEC 9-11
Dec 3	Dean Bramhald	drew 8	Cleethorpes 10-1

1991
Feb 12	Stuart Rimmer	w pts 8	Wolverhampton 9-12
Mar 26	John Smith	w rsf 4*	Wolverhampton
Apr 24	John Smith	w pts 6	Port Talbot 10-2-8
May 2	Michael Driscoll	l pts 6	Bayswater 10-2

1992
Mar 17	Mark Elliot	l pts 6	Wolverhampton 10-4

Fights 17 Won 9 Lost 7 Drawn 1

Karl MORLING

Featherweight
Northampton, born Douglas, Isle of Man 26 December 1970
Kingsley Park ABC
1989 Leics, Rutland & Northants ABA lightweight final (l C Kerr)
1990 NABC Class C champion
1990 Young England (v Sco, w J Twycross)

1990
Oct 15	Lee Christian	w rsf 2	Kettering 8-9
Oct 22	Tony Falcone	w pts 6	NSC 8-12

1991
Jan 31	Craig Dermody	l rsf 5	Stockport 8-12
May 2	Sol Francis	w rsf 3	Northampton 8-13
May 13	Paul Wynn	w rsf 2	Northampton 9-0

1992
Apr 6	Norman Dhalie	w pts 6	Northampton 8-11
Oct 5	Robert Braddock	w pts 6	Northampton 8-13
Dec 14	Dean Lynch	l rsf 4	Northampton 8-11

Fights 8 Won 6 Lost 2

Terry MORRILL

Light-middleweight
Hull born 2 February 1965
Humberside Police ABC
1983 North-East ABA light-welterweight semi-final
1985 North-East ABA light-middleweight semi-final (l L Caley)
1986 North-East ABA welterweight champion (w rsf 1 K Knaggs, w G Rhodes, w M McCreath, l rsf 3 K Wall)
1987 ABA welterweight finalist (w J Nicholson, w J Reid, w D Miller, w D Andrews, l M Elliot)
1987 England (v Ire, w W Walsh; v Pol, w B Dudak)
1988 England (v Sco, w rtd 3 L Antuna)
1988 Humberside ABA semi-final (l rsf 2* J Nicholson)

1988
Dec 10	Chris Richards	w pts 6	Crystal Palace

1989
Feb 8	Newton Barnett	w pts 6	Albert Hall 11-0
Mar 28	Skip Jackson	l rsf 5*	Glasgow 11-4
Jun 27	Mark Howell	w pts 6	Albert Hall 11-0-8
Oct 10	Spencer Alton	w pts 6	Hull 10-13
Nov 15	Davey Hughes	drew 4	Catford
Dec 8	Tony Baker	w pts 6	Doncaster 10-9

1990
Feb 22	Mark Holden	w rsf 7	Hull 10-12-12
	(Central light-middleweight title)		
Apr 10	Ernie Noble	w rsf 7	Doncaster 11-1-8
May 21	Jason Rowe	l ko 6	Sheffield 10-12
	(Central light-middleweight title)		
Oct 31	Shaun Cummins	l rsf 1	Crystal Palace 10-11-4

1991
Mar 14	Delroy Waul	drew 8	Middleton 10-13
May 28	Eamonn Loughran	l ko 1	Cardiff 10-10

1992
Oct 15	Seamus Casey	w pts 6	Hull 11-7

Fights 14 Won 8 Lost 4 Drawn 2

Chris MORRIS

Featherweight
Liverpool born 28 December 1970
Croxteth ABC
1991 West Lancs & Cheshire ABA light-welterweight semi-final (l D Owings)

1991
Nov 13	Robert Braddock	w rsf 5	Liverpool 9-2
Nov 28	Andrew Bloomer	w pts 6	Liverpool 9-2-8

1992
Feb 10	Hamid Moulay	w ko 1	Liverpool 9-0-8
Apr 29	Greg Upton	l rsf 2	Liverpool 9-0

Fights 4 Won 3 Lost 1

Darren MORRIS

Light-middleweight
Birmingham born 26 May 1966

1990
Sep 3	Joel Forbes	drew 6	Dudley 10-7	
Sep 12	Keith Hardman	w pts 6	Stoke 10-4	
Oct 3	Mike Betts	l pts 6	Solihull 10-9	/CTD...

(Darren MORRIS ctd.)

Oct 29	Neil Porter	w pts 6	Birmingham 10-6
Nov 12	Rocky Milton	l pts 6	Norwich 10-8
Nov 27	Neil Porter	l pts 6	Stoke 10-10
Dec 6	Gary Osborne	l pts 8	Wolverhampton 10-10
1991			
Feb 21	Richard O'Brien	l pts 6	Walsall 10-7
Mar 5	Mick Mulcahy	w pts 6	Leicester 10-8
Apr 11	Tony Britland	l pts 6	Willenhall 10-10
Apr 24	Andreas Panayi	drew 6	Stoke 10-8
May 30	Alfie Andrews	w rsf 3	Birmingham 10-9
Jul 4	Barry Messam	l pts 6	Alfreton 10-11-12
Oct 23	Andreas Panayi	l pts 6	Stoke 10-6
Oct 31	John O. Johnson	l pts 6	Telford 10-6
Dec 2	Chris Mylan	l pts 8	Birmingham 10-7
1992			
Jan 8	Rocky Milton	w pts 6	Burton-on-Trent 10-10
Mar 17	Wayne Timmins	drew 6	Wolverhampton 10-13
Mar 25	James McGee	drew 6	Hinckley 11-2
Apr 30	Leigh Wicks	drew 6	Mayfair 10-10
Jun 1	Mark Kelly	w pts 8	NEC 10-8
Sep 28	Des Robinson	l pts 6	Manchester 10-10
Oct 28	Roy Rowland	l rsf 2*	Albert Hall 10-10

Fights 23 Won 6 Lost 12 Drawn 5

Jamie MORRIS

Light-welterweight
Nuneaton born 15 February 1970
Nuneaton ABC

1989			
Jun 28	Phil Lashley	w rsf 1	Kenilworth 9-4
Sep 5	Carl Brasier	l rsf 3	Southend 9-8
Oct 10	Andrew Robinson	l pts 6	Wolverhampton 9-3
Dec 6	Wayne Taylor	l rsf 5	Leicester 9-4
1990			
Jan 17	Lee Ahmed	l pts 6	Stoke 9-5
Feb 5	Lee Ahmed	w pts 6	Leicester 9-3
Feb 27	Lee Ahmed	w pts 6	Evesham 9-6
Mar 26	George Bailey	w pts 6	Bradford 9-2
Apr 6	Richard Dimmock	l pts 6	Leicester 9-10-8
Apr 24	Des Gargano	l pts 4	Stoke 9-2
Apr 30	Neil Leitch	l pts 6	Nottingham 9-5
May 14	Tony Heath	l pts 6	Leicester 9-11
1991			
Oct 1	Michael Byrne	drew 4	Bedworth 9-12
Oct 16	Michael Byrne	w pts 6	Stoke 10-2
Nov 11	Mitchell Barney	drew 6	Stratford 10-0
Nov 21	Brian Coleman	drew 6	Stafford 10-0
Dec 4	Sugar Boy Wright	l pts 6	Stoke 9-12
1992			
Jan 20	Mark Antony	l rsf 5	Coventry 9-13
Feb 24	Simon Hamblett	drew 6	Coventry 10-0
Mar 11	Razza Campbell	l pts 6	Stoke
Mar 24	Mark Allen	w pts 6	Wolverhampton 10-3

Fights 21 Won 6 Lost 11 Drawn 4

Jason MORRIS
Bantamweight
Birmingham born 28 May 1972

1992
Sep 28	Jacob Smith	l pts 6	Manchester 8-7-8

Fights 1 Lost 1

Mike MORRISON
Lightweight
Pembroke born Prestatyn 24 February 1963
Pembroke ABC
1986 Wales (v Sco, l T Milligan)
1987 Welsh ABA welterweight final (w rsf 3 M Burrows, w S Lewis, l D Andrews)
1987 Wales (v Bav, l H Zanker)

1989
Sep 14	Paul Day	l pts 6	Basildon 10-3
Sep 21	Steve McGovern	l pts 6	Southampton 10-3
Sep 28	Mark Atkins	w pts 6	Cardiff 10-4
Oct 11	Richard Burton	l pts 6	Stoke 10-0
Nov 15	Jason Rowland	l pts 6	Reading 10-1
Nov 30	Mo Hussein	l pts 8	Barking 10-1
Dec 20	Nigel Dobson	l pts 6	Liverpool 10-1

1990
Jan 16	B.F.Williams	l pts 6	Cardiff 10-1
Jan 24	Carl Wright	l pts 6	Preston 10-1
Mar 1	Russell Jones	l pts 6	Cardiff 9-12
Mar 13	Nick Meloscia	l pts 6	Bristol 9-10
Mar 21	Steve Foran	l pts 6	Preston 10-1
Apr 10	Chris Saunders	l pts 6	Doncaster 10-0
Apr 23	Shaun Cogan	l pts 8	Birmingham 10-2
Apr 30	Shaun Cooper	l pts 6	Brierley Hill 9-12
May 22	Jason Rowland	l pts 6	St Albans 10-1-8
Sep 5	Tim Harmey	l pts 6	Brighton 10-4
Sep 12	Jimmy Harrison	l pts 6	Battersea 9-12-8
Sep 25	Mark Tibbs	l pts 6	Millwall 9-12-8
Oct 3	Nick Hall	l pts 8	Solihull 10-1-8
Oct 10	Benny Collins	l pts 6	Millwall 10-1
Dec 12	Eamonn Loughran	l pts 6	Basildon 10-3-8

1991
Jan 10	Rick Bushell	l pts 6	Battersea 9-12
Jan 24	Andy Williams	l pts 8	Gorseinon 10-4
Jan 31	Riki Burton	l pts 6	Stockport 10-1
Mar 6	Mark Tibbs	l rsf 4*	Wembley 9-8-8
May 2	Richard Swallow	l pts 6	Northampton 10-2
May 23	Martin Rosamond	l pts 6	Southampton 10-4
Jul 18	Michael Smyth	l rsf 2	Cardiff 10-5

1992
Jul 7	Steve Howden	w ko 3	Bristol 9-10
Sep 15	Dean Bramhald	l pts 6	Crystal Palace 9-12
Oct 28	Mervyn Bennett	l pts 6	Cardiff 9-11-8
Dec 14	Mervyn Bennett	l pts 6	Cardiff 9-11

Fights 33 Won 2 Lost 31

Jerry MORTIMER

Middleweight
Clapham, born Mauritius 22 February 1962
Lynn ABC
1991 SE London ABA middleweight semi-final (w rsf 3 M Psaltis, l ko 1 M Graham)

1991
Oct 21	Steve Thomas	l pts 6	AASC 11-8-8

1992
Feb 12	Darren Murphy	w pts 6	Watford
Mar 2	Lee Farrell	w pts 6	Merthyr 11-5
Apr 28	Stefan Wright	l rsf 4	Corby 11-9
Sep 7	Robert Whitehouse	w rsf 3	Southend 11-4
Oct 15	Russell Washer	w rsf 5*	Catford
Dec 14	Gareth Boddy	w pts 6	Cardiff 11-3-8

Fights 7 Won 5 Lost 2

Kelvin MORTIMER

Welterweight
Trebanog born 20 May 1966
Rhondda Valley ABC

1986
Jul 30	Tyrell Wilson	w rsf 2	Ebbw Vale
Sep 10	John Conlan	w pts 6	Stoke 10-2
Sep 29	Alistair Laurie	w ko 3	Glasgow 10-7
Oct 20	Gary Jacobs	l rsf 5*	Glasgow 10-7
Nov 24	Kevin Hayde	drew 6	Cardiff 10-0
Dec 8	Ronnie Campbell	w ko 5	Edgbaston 10-3
Dec 22	Dave McCabe	l pts 8	Glasgow 10-3

1987
Jan 8	Jimmy Harrison	w rsf 3	Bethnal Green 10-7
Jan 20	David Griffiths	l rsf 5	Newport 10-4
Feb 18	Trevor Smith	l pts 8	Fulham 10-4-8
Mar 9	Ken Foreman	w ko 3	NSC 10-6-12
Mar 24	Jimmy Thornton	l pts 6	Nottingham 10-4
Apr 9	Mickey Hughes	l rsf 6	Bethnal Green 10-7
Jul 1	Tommy Shiels	l rsf 3	Albert Hall 10-7
Sep 7	Darren Dyer	w rsf 1	NSC 10-5-8
Sep 25	Mickey Hughes	l pts 8	Westcliff 10-7-8
Nov 3	Tony McKenzie	l rsf 3	Bethnal Green 10-6
Dec 16	Bobby McKenley	w rsf 2	Manchester 10-8

1988
Jan 18	Mark Purcell	l rsf 1*	Cardiff 10-4
Mar 1	Ensley Bingham	l pts 8	Manchester 10-3
Apr 20	Del Bryan	l rsf 4*	Stoke
Jun 17	Kostas Petrou	l pts 8	Edgbaston 10-8
Sep 7	Roy Rowland	l pts 6	Reading
Oct 10	Tony Willis	l rsf 4	Edgbaston 10-5-8
Dec 1	Damien Denny	l rsf 1	Edmonton 10-9

1989
Nov 13	Hannu Vuorinen	l rtd 6	Helsinki 10-10-8

1990
Apr 26	John Davies	l rsf 2	Merthyr 10-6-8
	(vacant Welsh welterweight title)		

1991
Sep 3	Rocky Feliciello	w rsf 2	Cardiff 10-8

Oct 26	Darren Dyer	l rsf 2*	Brentwood 10-7
Nov 29	Ossie Maddix	l pts 6	Manchester 10-7
1992			
Jan 22	Lindon Scarlett	l rsf 1	Solihull 10-7
May 19	Eamonn Loughran	l rsf 1	Cardiff

Fights 32 Won 9 Lost 22 Drawn 1

Kevin MORTON

Super-middleweight
Leicester born 17 April 1969
Belgrave ABC
1989 North Midlands ABA middleweight final (w.o. then l C Cope)
1990 Midlands ABA light-heavyweight final (w ko 3 P Randall, w J Mackenzie, w rsf 1 S Pemberton, l rsf 1 A Wright)
1991 Three Counties ABA light-heavyweight prelim (w J Mackenzie, withdrew)

1991
Feb 6	Dennis Afflick	w pts 6	Liverpool 12-5
Feb 28	Steve Davies	w rsf 3	Bury 12-0
Apr 4	John Uphill	w ko 1	Watford 12-1
May 2	Alan Baptiste	w rsf 2	Northampton 12-0
Oct 30	Nick Manners	w pts 8	Leeds 12-0
1992			
Jun 3	Mark Paine	w pts 6	Newcastle-under-Lyme 12-4
Sep 9	Adrian Wright	w pts 6	Stoke 12-0

Fights 7 Won 7

Hamid MOULAY

Featherweight
Leeds, born Algiers 27 November 1962

1992
| Feb 10 | Chris Morris | l ko 1 | Liverpool 9-2 |
| May 13 | Mark Bowers | l ko 1 | Albert Hall 9-1 |

Fights 2 Lost 2

Matt MOWATT

Middleweight
Sheffield born 8 March 1967

1990
Oct 22	Adrian Din	l pts 6	Cleethorpes 11-12
Oct 29	Mike Phillips	l pts 6	Birmingham 11-5
Nov 27	Paul Walters	l pts 6	Stoke 11-8
Dec 11	Russell Washer	l rsf 6	Evesham 11-7
1991			
Jan 23	Mike Phillips	l rsf 6	Stoke 11-5
Sep 30	Joe Kilshaw	drew 6	Liverpool 11-7
Oct 21	Warren Stowe	l rsf 3	Bury 11-7
Nov 20	Hugh Fury	w pts 6	Solihull 11-8
Nov 28	Rob Stevenson	w pts 6	Hull 11-5
Dec 9	Hugh Fury	l rsf 5*	Bradford 11-6 /CTD...

(Matt MOWATT ctd.)
1992
Feb 24   Willie Yeardsley   l pts 6   Bradford 11-4

Fights 11 Won 2 Lost 8 Drawn 1

Dave MUHAMMED
Cruiserweight
Eastbourne born Ghana 2 March 1960
Real name: Dawuda Muhammed
Indigo ABC, Accra. Named on 1976 Olympic Games draw, but Ghana withdrew.

1988
Sep 13   Thomas Henry   w rsf 3   Battersea 13-5-4
Oct 31   Tenko Ernie   w pts 6   Bedford 13-5-8
1989
Feb 16   Magne Havnaa   l rsf 6   Copenhagen
Mar 22   Mike Aubrey   w rsf 5   Sheppey 13-6-12
Apr 22   Anaclet Wamba   l ko 4   Plerin
Aug 11   Luigi Gaudiano   l ko 6   Montorio al Vomano
Nov 28   Andy Straughn   w pts 8   Battersea 13-6-8
1990
inactive
1991
Apr 29   Steve Lewsam   w pts 8   Cleethorpes 13-8
Oct 12   Axel Schulz   l pts 8   Halle
1992
Mar 27   Norbert Ekassi   l rsf 3   Criel

Fights 10 Won 5 Lost 5

Chris MULCAHY
Welterweight
Rochdale born 18 June 1963
Middleton & Rochdale ABC

1988
Oct 11   Robbie Bowen   w pts 6   Wolverhampton 10-2
Oct 25   Dave Croft   w pts 6   Cottingham 10-5
Nov 3   Pat Durkin   w rsf 2   Manchester
Nov 21   Ian Midwood-Tate   l ko 1   Leicester 10-6
1989
Feb 23   Nigel Bradley   l rsf 2   Manchester 10-2
Apr 17   Dave Kettlewell   w pts 6   Middleton 10-4
Apr 24   Kevin Toomey   w pts 6   Bradford 10-7
May 19   Dave Whittle   w pts 6   Gateshead 10-6
May 29   Martin Ogilvie   l pts 6   Dundee 10-6
Jun 12   Trevor Meikle   w pts 6   Manchester 10-4
Jul 11   Trevor Meikle   w pts 6   Batley 10-5
Oct 3   Banco Bell   w rsf 1   Cottingham 10-2
Oct 23   Karl Ince   l ko 5   Cleethorpes 10-4
Nov 20   Ian Thomas   w pts 6   Leicester 10-2
1990
May 14   Mark Kelly   l pts 8   Cleethorpes 10-6
Jun 11   Alan Peacock   l rsf 3   Manchester 10-7
1991
Mar 5   Pat Durkin   w pts 6   Leicester 10-12
Apr 3   Willie Yeardsley   l pts 6   Manchester 10-12-8

Jun 10	Trevor Meikle	drew 6	Manchester 11-1
Oct 2	Robert Wright	l rsf 1	Solihull 10-12
Nov 21	Richard O'Brien	l rsf 2	Ilkeston
1992			
Jan 20	Darren McInulty	l pts 6	Coventry 10-10
Feb 11	James McGee	l pts 6	Wolverhampton 10-12
Apr 4	Rob Stevenson	w pts 8	Cleethorpes 10-10
Jun 1	Rob Stevenson	w pts 6	Manchester 10-9
Sep 3	John Smith	drew 6	Liverpool
Oct 15	Peter Waudby	l rsf 4	Hull 10-11
Nov 24	Richard Swallow	l pts 6	Wolverhampton 10-6
Dec 2	Colin Anderson	w pts 6	Bardon 10-12

Fights 29 Won 14 Lost 13 Drawn 2

Mick MULCAHY
Light-welterweight
Rochdale born 9 May 1966
Bacup Lads ABC

1988			
Jun 6	Nick Langley	w rsf 3	Manchester 9-9
Sep 5	Johnny Walker	w pts 4	Glasgow 9-8
Sep 22	Frankie Foster	l pts 6	Newcastle 9-6
Oct 2	Neil Leggett	drew 6	Peterborough 9-5
Oct 25	Wayne Windle	w pts 6	Cottingham 9-8
Nov 3	Peter English	l rsf 4	Manchester 9-6
Dec 12	Steve Taggart	l pts 6	Birmingham 9-10
1989			
Jan 25	Mark Tibbs	l ko 1	Bethnal Green 9-9
Feb 23	Sean Conn	w ko 1	Manchester 9-10
Mar 13	Dean Dickinson	w pts 6	Leicester
Apr 17	Neil Leitch	w rsf 2	Middleton 9-8
May 19	Mark Jay	l pts 6	Gateshead 10-8-8
May 29	George Kerr	l pts 6	Dundee
Jun 12	Muhammad Shaffique	l rsf 2	Manchester 9-13
Sep 11	Dave Croft	w pts 4	Manchester 10-3
Sep 19	Billy Couzens	l pts 6	Bethnal Green 10-2
Oct 3	Kevin Toomey	w ko 5	Cottingham 10-2
Oct 13	Carl Wright	l pts 6	Preston 10-2
Oct 23	Trevor Meikle	l pts 6	Cleethorpes 10-2
Oct 31	Carl Wright	l pts 6	Manchester 10-5
Nov 10	Chris McReedy	l pts 6	Liverpool 10-6
Nov 20	Brendan Ryan	l pts 6	Leicester 10-3
Dec 4	Brian Cullen	l pts 8	Manchester 10-3
Dec 19	Errol McDonald	l rsf 3	Bethnal Green
1990			
Apr 24	Brian Cullen	l pts 8	Stoke 10-0-8
Oct 22	Wayne Windle	l pts 4	Cleethorpes 10-4
Nov 12	Richie Joyce	l rsf 6	Stratford
Dec 12	Neil Porter	drew 6	Stoke 10-7
1991			
Jan 24	Robert McCracken	l rsf 1	Brierley Hill 10-10
Mar 5	Darren Morris	l pts 6	Leicester 10-6
Apr 3	Trevor Meikle	l pts 6	Manchester 10-10
Apr 15	Andreas Panayi	l rsf 2	Leicester 10-5
Jun 10	Mike Calderwood	l pts 6	Manchester 10-10
Nov 18	Benji Joseph	l pts 6	Manchester /CTD..2

(Mick MULCAHY ctd.)

Nov 28	Barry Bennett	l pts 6	Evesham 10-10
Dec 5	Mark Elliot	l rsf 2	Cannock 10-4
1992			
Mar 17	Bernard Paul	l pts 6	Mayfair
Apr 4	Michael Byrne	w rsf 4	Cleethorpes 10-0
Jun 1	Jason Brattley	l pts 6	Manchester 10-2
Sep 11	Rocky Ferrari	l pts 6	Glasgow 9-12
Sep 25	Carl Wright	l pts 8	Liverpool 10-3-8
Dec 10	Charlie Kane	l rsf 2	Glasgow 10-2

Fights 42 Won 9 Lost 31 Drawn 2

Karl MUMFORD

Light-heavyweight
Hengoed born 26 February 1963
Fleur De Lys ABC
1991 Welsh ABA heavyweight champion (w G Davies, w rsf 2 J Davies, w T Redman, l rtd 2 D Roberts)
1992 Welsh ABA heavyweight semi-final (l dis 3 H Hartt)

1992

Oct 7	Chris Beck	w pts 6	Barry 12-12-8
Nov 14	Darryl Ritchie	w pts 6	Cardiff 12-9

Fights 2 Won 2

Darren MURPHY

Light-middleweight
Burnt Oak, born Edgware 9 May 1970
Burnt Oak ABC, Northolt ABC
1984 National Schools semi-final (l P Mullings)
1984 England Schools (v Nor, w M Andersen)

1990

Oct 25	Mike Russell	w pts 6	Battersea 11-1-12
Nov 26	Delroy Matthews	l rsf 2	Lewisham 11-0
1991			
Feb 6	Ian Brough	w rsf 1	Battersea 11-2
Feb 18	Clayon Stewart	w pts 6	Windsor 11-3
Jun 1	Johnny Pinnock	w pts 6	Bethnal Green 11-3-12
1992			
Feb 12	Jerry Mortimer	l pts 6	Watford

Fights 6 Won 4 Lost 2

Sean MURPHY

Super-featherweight
St Albans born 1 December 1964
St Albans ABC & London Colney ABC
1983 ABA flyweight semi-final (w P Bunce, w rsf 1* R Bond, w dis 2 D Pope, l rsf 2 P Clinton)
1983 Young England (v EGer, l Schlosser, w rsf 1 Gittner)
1984 Great Britain (v Ire, w rsf 1 C Carlton)
1984 England (v Can, w rtd 3 D Paul; v Ire, l R Nash; v WGer, l B Maczuga)
1984 ABA bantamweight semi-final (w ko 1 S Fishermac, w ko 1 S Pike, w dis 3 M Scholey, w G McGuinness, l D Anderson)
1985 England (v Sco, w rsf 2* B Holmes; v Hun, w T Botos; v EGer, l K-D Kirschstein)
1985 ABA bantamweight champion (w S Fishermac, l rsf 3* D Amory, replaced G Dainty, w rsf 1 D Ingram, w D Hood, w rsf 3 D Lynch)

/Sean MURPHY ctd.

1985 Acropolis Cup gold medal (w B Maczuga, WGer; w Cattai, Ita; w rsf 1 Pascual)
1985 Canada multi-nations gold medal (w D Sebilleagu, w F Mallais)
1986 ABA bantamweight champion (w B Robb, w J Sillitoe, w rsf 2 S Ward, w rsf 2 J Green)
1986 Commonwealth Games gold medal (w rsf 1 P Kunene, Swa; w G Brooks, Aus; w rsf 3 R Nash, Ire)

1986
Sep 20	Albert Parr	w pts 6	Hemel Hempstead
Oct 9	Gordon Stobie	w ko 5	Croydon 8-8
Oct 25	Simon Turner	w pts 6	Stevenage
Dec 3	Des Gargano	w pts 6	Muswell Hill 8-7-8

1987
Jan 28	Keith Ward	w rtd 4*	Croydon 8-9
Apr 22	Kelvin Smart	w ko 3	Albert Hall 8-5-8
May 9	Derek Amory	w rsf 2	Battersea 8-10
Jul 1	Ray Minus jnr.	l rsf 5	Albert Hall 8-5-4
	(Commonwealth bantamweight title)		
Aug 9	Ronnie Stephenson	w rsf 1	Windsor 8-11-12
Sep 16	David Cornbread Williams	w ko 1	Albert Hall 8-8-12

1988
Nov 15	Craig Windsor	w rsf 1	Norwich 9-1
Dec 1	Rocky Lawlor	w rsf 2	Edmonton 9-0

1989
Jan 31	Kid Sumaila	w rtd 2*	Reading 9-1
Mar 7	Mike Whalley	w pts 10	Wisbech 9-0
	(final eliminator, British featherweight title)		
May 9	Jesus Muniz	w pts 8	St Albans 9-2
Sep 19	Les Fabri	w pts 8	Millwall 9-0-12
Oct 24	Gerardo Castillo	w rsf 1*	Watford 9-3

1990
Mar 8	Mario Lozano	w pts 8	Watford 9-1-8
May 22	John Doherty	w ko 3	St Albans 8-12-8
	(vacant British featherweight title)		
Sep 25	Johnny B. Good	w ko 2	Millwall 8-13-4
	(British featherweight title)		

1991
Mar 5	Gary DeRoux	l ko 5	Millwall 8-12-12
	(British featherweight title)		
May 22	Jose Ines Alvarado	w pts 8	Millwall 9-3-8
Oct 29	Colin McMillan	l pts 12	Albert Hall 8-12-12
	(British featherweight title)		

1992
Apr 30	Ian Honeywood	w rsf 1	Albert Hall 9-8-12

Fights 24 Won 21 Lost 3

Craig MURRAY
Super-featherweight
Rochdale born 23 January 1971

1992
Jun 1	Tony Smith	w rsf 2	Manchester 9-6-8
Oct 5	Joe Fannin	l rsf 1	Manchester 9-5

Fights 2 Won 1 Lost 1

Michael MURRAY

Heavyweight
Manchester, born Preston 3 September 1964
No amateur experience

1988
Feb 23	Gipsy John Fury	l pts 6	Oldham 15-10
Apr 28	Ian Nelson	w rsf 6	Manchester 14-9
Nov 17	Steve Garber	w pts 6	Stockport

1989
Feb 7	Rocky Burton	w pts 6	Manchester 15-5
May 10	Barry Ellis	w rsf 3	Solihull 15-5
Sep 9	Noel Quarless	l pts 8	Liverpool 16-2
Oct 17	John Westgarth	w rtd 4	Oldham 16-0

1990
Feb 6	Al Malcolm	w rsf 5	Oldham 15-7-8
Jun 2	Gipsy John Fury	l rtd 6*	Manchester 16-8

1991
Apr 30	Steve Garber	w ko 1	Stockport 16-12
Sep 19	Carl Gaffney	w rsf 8	Stockport 17-1
	(vacant Central heavyweight title)		
Oct 22	Markus Bott	w rsf 7	Hamburg
Dec 7	Steve Gee	w rsf 7	Manchester 16-2

1992
Apr 14	Paddy Reilly	l rsf 8	Mansfield 16-0
Nov 28	Rocky Sekorski	w pts 8	Manchester 16-0

Fights 15 Won 11 Lost 4

Paul MURRAY

Super-middleweight
Birmingham born 8 January 1961
Sheldon Heath ABC
1980 South Midlands ABA welterweight final (l E Byrne)

1980
Sep 4	Gerry White	w pts 6	Morecambe 10-7
Sep 11	Graeme Ahmed	l pts 6	Hartlepool 10-8
Sep 29	Richard Wilson	l pts 6	Bedworth 10-7
Oct 8	Carl North	w ko 2	Stoke 10-6
Oct 14	Steve McLeod	w pts 6	Wolverhampton 10-2
Oct 20	Steve Davies	drew 6	Birmingham 10-9
Oct 30	John Wiggins	w pts 6	Wolverhampton
Nov 7	Archie Salmon	l pts 6	Cambuslang 10-6
Nov 18	John Wiggins	l pts 6	Shrewsbury 10-2
Nov 26	Mike Clemow	l pts 8	Stoke
Dec 8	John Wiggins	l pts 6	Nottingham 10-6

1981
Jan 26	Errol Dennis	w pts 6	Edgbaston
Mar 16	Dennis Sheehan	drew 6	Nottingham 10-7
Apr 15	Nigel Thomas	drew 8	Evesham 10-7
May 28	Martin McGough	l pts 6	Edgbaston 10-7
Jul 9	Roger Guest	l ko 8	Dudley
Sep 21	Gary Buckle	drew 6	Wolverhampton
Oct 7	Kostas Petrou	w rsf 5*	Solihull
Oct 13	Gary Buckle	l pts 6	Wolverhampton
Nov 24	Nick Riozzi	w pts 6	Wolverhampton

1982

Date	Opponent	Result	Venue
Jan 25	Martin McGough	l rsf 4	Wolverhampton
Feb 21	Gary Buckle	w pts 8	Nottingham
Mar 10	Ron Pearce	l pts 8	Solihull
Mar 23	Errol Dennis	l pts 6	Wolverhampton
Mar 29	Tony Brown	l pts 6	Liverpool
Apr 7	Dennis Sheehan	w pts 6	Evesham
Apr 28	Lee Roy	w rsf 4	Stoke
May 17	Paul Costigan	l pts 8	Manchester
May 24	Dennis Sheehan	drew 6	Nottingham
Jun 7	Kostas Petrou	l pts 6	Edgbaston
Sep 13	Paul Costigan	w pts 6	Manchester
Oct 18	Kostas Petrou	l rsf 5	Edgbaston

1983

Date	Opponent	Result	Venue
Feb 15	Bert Myrie	l pts 6	Wolverhampton
Feb 21	Steve Tempro	l dis 3	Edgbaston
Mar 1	Chris Pyatt	l rtd 2*	Albert Hall
May 17	T.P.Jenkins	l pts 6	Bethnal Green 11-8
Jun 23	Wayne Hawkins	l pts 6	Wolverhampton
Sep 19	Bert Myrie	w pts 8	Nottingham 11-7-8
Oct 26	Steve Henty	l pts 6	Stoke
Nov 14	Kid Sadler	l pts 8	Manchester
Dec 14	Johnny Andrews	l pts 6	Stoke

1984

Date	Opponent	Result	Venue
Mar 19	Wayne Barker	l pts 8	Manchester 11-2
Mar 27	Rocky Kelly	l rtd 5	Battersea 11-0
Oct 8	Gavin Stirrup	l pts 6	Manchester 11-4

1985-86 inactive

1987

Date	Opponent	Result	Venue
Jan 22	Chris Walker	l pts 4	Bethnal Green 12-0
Feb 10	Chris Walker	w pts 4	Wolverhampton 11-9
Feb 16	Chris Galloway	w pts 6	NSC 11-11-8
Feb 24	Nicky Thorne	l pts 6	Battersea 11-10
Aug 3	Peter Elliott	l pts 6	Stoke 11-8
Sep 7	Johnny Miller	l rtd 4*	NSC 10-13-4

1988

Date	Opponent	Result	Venue
Jan 25	Paul Wesley	l pts 8	Birmingham 11-8
Feb 29	Paul Wesley	drew 8	Birmingham 11-7
Mar 14	Mickey Hughes	l rsf 4	NSC 11-2
Oct 19	Geoff Calder	nc 5	Evesham 11-0
Oct 26	Franki Moro	l pts 6	Stoke 11-3
Dec 5	Richard Carter	l pts 6	Dudley 11-3

1989

Date	Opponent	Result	Venue
Jan 24	Antonio Fernandez	l pts 6	Kings Heath 10-13
Oct 24	Andy Flute	l rsf 3	Wolverhampton 12-0

1990

Date	Opponent	Result	Venue
Jun 21	Spencer Alton	l pts 6	Alfreton 11-7-8
Sep 13	Nigel Rafferty	l pts 6	Watford 12-0
Sep 27	Nigel Rafferty	drew 6	NEC 12-1
Oct 9	Nigel Rafferty	l pts 6	Wolverhampton 11-13
Oct 18	Nick Manners	l pts 6	Dewsbury 12-0
Oct 29	Carlos Christie	l pts 6	Birmingham
Dec 6	Wayne Hawkins	l pts 6	Wolverhampton 12-10

1991

Date	Opponent	Result	Venue
Jan 28	Lee Prudden	l pts 6	Birmingham 12-4
Feb 6	Paul Walters	drew 6	Liverpool 12-0
Feb 27	Paul Busby	l pts 6	Wolverhampton 11-6 /CTD..

(Paul MURRAY ctd.)

Mar 13	Lee Prudden	drew 6	Stoke 11-10
Apr 24	John Kaighin	l pts 6	Port Talbot 12-6
May 14	Ernie Loveridge	l pts 8	Dudley 11-4
May 30	Robert McCracken	l rsf 2	Birmingham 11-2
Jul 25	Tony Booth	l pts 6	Dudley 11-12
Oct 7	Antonio Fernandez	l rsf 7	Birmingham 11-8
Nov 12	Lee Archer	l pts 6	Wolverhampton 12-4
Dec 5	Richard Carter	l pts 8	Cannock 11-8
Dec 17	Paul Busby	l ko 3	Cardiff 11-10
1992			
Jan 15	Mark Hale	l pts 6	Stoke 11-7
Feb 6	John Mackenzie	l pts 6	Peterborough 11-8
Feb 19	Jim Woolley	w ko 4	Muswell Hill 11-10-12
Mar 26	Neville Brown	l ko 3	Telford 11-6
Oct 5	Lee Archer	l pts 6	Bardon 12-10
Oct 13	Lee Archer	l pts 6	Wolverhampton 12-10
Oct 21	Steve Loftus	l pts 6	Stoke 12-10
Nov 23	John J. Cooke	l ko 1	Coventry 12-3-8

Fights 85 Won 15 Lost 60 Drawn 9 No contests 1

Joe Frater Snr.
Boxing Promotions

4/6 Legsby Avenue, Grimsby, South Humberside DN32 0NP Tel: (0472) 343194

Always looking around for new talent

Always looking to promote more entertaining shows

GARDINER & HAYDE

DAI GARDINER
(Manager)
13, Hengoed Hall Drive,
Cefn Hengoed,
Hengoed,
Mid Glamorgan
(0433 812971)

Dragon Boxing Promotions

KEVIN HAYDE
(Promoter)
17, Whittaker Road,
Tremorfa,
Cardiff
CF2 2RD

0222 227606
0222 497850
Fax: 0222 224947

PRODUCING CHAMPIONS

Katherine Morrison

LICENCED PROMOTER BRITISH BOXING BOARD OF CONTROL

Telephone Office: 041 554 4099
041 554 8704, 041 554 8895
Fax: 041 551 8258
Car: 0860 581582

Morrison's Gym
85 Sydney Street
Glasgow G31 2ND

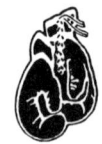

PROMOTING REGULAR SHOWS
MANAGERS & MATCHMAKERS
SEND YOUR LISTS TO ABOVE ADDRESS.

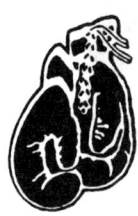

Alex Morrison's Gym

Scotland's only full-time professional gymnasium.

Boxers available:

DONNIE HOOD	-	Bantamweight
DAVE ANDERSON	-	Super featherweight
CHARLIE KANE	-	Light welterweight
WILLIE BEATTIE	-	Welterweight
GORDON BLAIR	-	Welterweight
NEIL ARMSTRONG	-	Flyweight
SHAUN ANDERSON	-	Bantamweight
TANVEER AHMED	-	Lightweight
ALLAN McDOWALL	-	Lightweight
DANNY CONNELLY	-	Lightweight
EDDIE COOK	-	Featherweight

Kris McADAM

Light-welterweight
Glasgow born 1 January 1964
Newarthill ABC

1984
Oct 15	Bobby Welburn	drew 6	Glasgow 9-10

1985
Feb 25	Denzil Goddard	w rsf 1	Glasgow
Mar 27	Marvin P. Gray	w rsf 3	Gateshead 9-13
May 10	Dave Smith	l pts 6	Glasgow 9-10
Sep 16	Russell Jones	l pts 6	Glasgow 9-5-4

1989
Oct 9	Paul Charters	l pts 6	Glasgow 9-12
Nov 29	Chris Bennett	l ko 3	Middlesbrough

1990
Feb 19	Martin Reilly	w pts 6	Glasgow 10-0-8
Mar 19	Martin Reilly	w rsf 8	Glasgow 10-0
Mar 26	Jim Moffat	w pts 8	Glasgow 9-12
Sep 7	Sugar Gibiliru	l pts 8	Liverpool 9-11
Oct 22	Jim Moffat	w rsf 5*	Glasgow 9-8-4

1991
Jan 21	John Smith	w pts 6	Glasgow 10-0
Apr 22	Brian Roche	l rsf 2	Glasgow 9-8-9
	(eliminator, British lightweight title)		
Nov 18	Colin Sinnott	w pts 6	Glasgow 9-13-4

1992
Jan 27	Peter Roberts	w ko 2	Glasgow 10-0-8
Mar 18	Nigel Bradley	l ko 2	Glasgow 10-0

Fights 17 Won 9 Lost 7 Drawn 1

Dave McAULEY

Flyweight
Larne born 15 June 1961
St Agnes ABC
1979 Irish ABA light-flyweight final (l S McDermott)
1980 Irish ABA flyweight champion (w J Carson)
1980 Ireland (v USA, w M Perez)
1980 European Junior Championships flyweight (l rsf 3 J Varadi, Hun)
1981 Irish ABA flyweight final (l H Russell)

1983
Oct 5	John Mwaimu	drew 6	Belfast 8-6
Nov 16	Dave Smith	w ko 1	Belfast

1984
Jan 25	Ian Colbeck	w pts 6	Belfast 8-5-8
Feb 27	Kenny Walsh	drew 6	Birmingham 8-6
Sep 17	Roy Williams	w pts 6	Brighton 8-9-8
Oct 13	John Mwaimu	w pts 6	Belfast 8-9
Nov 13	Dave George	w rsf 6	Belfast 8-6-12
Dec 19	Graham Clarke	w rsf 4	Belfast 8-6-8

1985
Feb 23	Johnny Mack	w rsf 1	Belfast 8-6
Jun 8	Bobby McDermott	w rsf 10	Shepherds Bush 7-13-12
	(eliminator, British flyweight title)		

1986
Feb 15	Kelvin Smart	w dis 6	Dublin 8-4-8	/CTD..

(Dave McAULEY ctd.)

Apr 22	Charlie Brown	w rsf 1	Belfast 7-12-8
	(final eliminator, British flyweight title)		
Oct 20	Joe Kelly	w ko 9	Glasgow 7-12-8
	(vacant British flyweight title)		
1987			
Apr 25	Fidel Bassa	l rsf 13	Belfast 7-13-12
	(WBA flyweight title)		
Dec 7	Roy Thompson	w pts 10	Belfast 8-1
1988			
Mar 26	Fidel Bassa	l pts 12	Belfast 8-0
	(WBA flyweight title)		
1989			
Jun 7	Duke McKenzie	w pts 12	Wembley 8-0
	(IBF flyweight title)		
Nov 8	Dodie Penalosa	w pts 12 (s)	Wembley GH
	(IBF flyweight title)		
1990			
Mar 17	Louis Curtis	w pts 12	Belfast 8-0
	(IBF flyweight title)		
Sep 15	Rodolfo Blanco	w pts 12	Belfast 8-0
	(IBF flyweight title)		
1991			
May 11	Pedro Feliciano	w pts 12	Belfast
	(IBF flyweight title)		
Sep 7	Jacob Matlala	w ko 10	Belfast 7-13
	(IBF flyweight title)		
1992			
Jan 13	Rodolfo Blanco	l pts 12	Bilbao 8-0
	(IBF flyweight title)		

Fights 23 Won 18 Lost 3 Drawn 2

Kid McAULEY

Featherweight
Doncaster born Liverpool 6 June 1968
Real name: Colin McAuley
RAF
1988 Combined Services ABA flyweight final (l J McLean)
1989 Combined Services ABA flyweight final (l ko 3 J McLean)
1990 Combined Services ABA featherweight final (l A Lesbirel)
1991 Combined Services ABA featherweight final (w V Manley, l T Rajcoomar)
1992 Combined Services ABA featherweight champion (w J Basford, l ko 3 K Hodkinson)

1992			
Sep 8	John Irwin	l pts 6	Doncaster 9-2
Sep 19	Alex Docherty	l pts 6	Glasgow 8-13
Sep 30	Yusuf Vorajee	w pts 6	Solihull 9-2
Oct 13	John White	l pts 4	Bury 9-0
Oct 23	Paul Lloyd	l pts 4	Liverpool 9-0
Nov 10	Michael Alldis	l pts 6	Dagenham 8-13
Nov 24	Miguel Matthews	w pts 6	Doncaster 9-2-8
Dec 12	Michael Alldis	l ko 1	Muswell Hill 8-12-12

Fights 8 Won 2 Lost 6

Mark McBIANE

Light-heavyweight
Skegness, born Leamington 6 April 1970
Leamington Spa ABC

1991
Nov 28	Jason McNeill	l pts 6	Evesham 12-2

1992
Feb 4	Greg Scott-Briggs	l pts 6	Alfreton 12-8
Apr 23	Nick Wadman	l rsf 1	Eltham 12-10
Jun 8	Simon McDougall	l pts 6	Bradford 12-6

Fights 4 Lost 4

Jamie McBRIDE

Featherweight
Glasgow born 21 October 1963
Babcock Power ABC

1985
Sep 15	Terry Allen	w pts 6	Glasgow 8-8

1986
Mar 10	Ronnie Stephenson	w pts 4	Glasgow 8-12-8
Mar 17	Chris Clarkson	w pts 4	Glasgow 8-7-12
Apr 21	Gipsy Johnny	w pts 6	Glasgow 8-8
Jun 2	Joe Duffy	l pts 6	Glasgow 8-12-4
Dec 8	Donnie Hood	drew 8	Glasgow 8-8
Dec 22	Joe Kelly	l rsf 5	Glasgow 8-4

1987
Mar 2	Ronnie Carroll	l pts 6	Glasgow 8-10-8
Apr 14	Chris Clarkson	w pts 6	Cumbernauld
May 19	Stuart Carmichael	w pts 6	Cumbernauld 8-11
Jun 8	Billy Barton	l pts 6	Glasgow
Dec 5	Roy Webb	l rsf 4	Doncaster 8-8

1988
inactive

1989
Feb 17	Marvin Stone	l pts 6	Irvine 9-0

1990
Mar 19	Eddie Cook	l pts 6	Glasgow 9-1-12
Apr 27	Paul Chedgzoy	w pts 6	Glasgow 9-1-8
May 3	Johnny Bredahl	l rtd 5	Greve
Jun 4	Peter Judson	w pts 8	Glasgow 9-3
Sep 17	Neil Leitch	w rtd 6	Glasgow 8-13-8
	(vacant Scottish featherweight title)		
Oct 15	Derek Amory	l rtd 4*	Brierley Hill 9-3-8

1991
Feb 18	Peter Buckley	w pts 8	Glasgow 9-0-8
Nov 18	Peter Judson	drew 6	Glasgow 9-2

1992
Mar 30	Phil Lashley	w rsf 1	Glasgow 9-4

Fights 22 Won 11 Lost 9 Drawn 2

Kevin McBRIDE

Heavyweight
Clones born 1972
1990 Irish Junior heavyweight champion (w ko 1 M Aspell)
1991 Irish Intermediate super-heavyweight final (l rsf 2 G McComish)
1992 Irish ABA super-heavyweight champion (w W Clyde, w C Robinson)
1992 Barcelona Olympics super-heavyweight prelim (l P Hrisnak)

1992
Dec 17	Gary Charlton	drew 6	Barking 15-7-8

Fights 1 Drawn 1

Paul McCARTHY

Light-heavyweight
Southampton, born London 24 March 1961
Forest Edge ABC
1986 Southern ABA middleweight champion (w rsf S Kavanagh, w K Cattermole)

1987
Jan 29	Eddie Brooks	l pts 6	Wimbledon 11-4
Mar 3	Jim Beckett	w ko 1	Southend 10-13
Apr 6	Gary Pemberton	l rsf 4	Southampton 11-4
May 26	Neil Simpson	w rsf 1	Plymouth 11-9
Sep 25	Spencer Cummings	w ko 3	Tooting 11-5
Nov 16	Newton Barnett	w pts 8	Southampton 11-7-8
Dec 9	Rocky Boukriss	w ko 1	Greenwich 11-9
Dec 14	Andy Wright	l ko 3	NSC 11-9-8

1988
Mar 14	Mark Howell	w rsf 2*	NSC 11-8
Apr 21	Steve Aquilina	w pts 6	Bethnal Green 12-0
May 18	Joe McKenzie	w rsf 3	Portsmouth 11-11
Aug 31	Denys Cronin	l rsf 4	Stoke 12-4-8
Nov 24	Simon Collins	drew 8	Southampton 12-6-8
Dec 20	Simon Collins	w dis 3	Swansea 11-10-8

1989
Jan 25	Brendan Dempsey	w pts 6	Southampton 12-7
Mar 2	Cliff Curtis	w rtd 7*	Southampton 12-6-8
Apr 4	Chris Galloway	w rsf 3	Southend
Apr 26	Terry Duffus	w pts 8	Southampton 12-7-12
May 9	Derek Myers	l pts 6	Southend 12-6
Oct 2	Noel Magee	l ko 2	Hanley 12-1-8
Nov 30	Dave Lawrence	w pts 6	Southwark 12-4

1990
Mar 14	Richard Bustin	w rsf 7*	Battersea 11-13-8
	(vacant Southern super-middleweight title)		
May 26	Keith Halliwell	w rsf 3*	Reading 12-3
Oct 15	Derek Myers	l pts 8	Lewisham 12-2
Oct 23	Nicky Piper	l rsf 3	Leicester 12-6

1991
Feb 8	Fabrice Tiozzo	l ko 2	Villeurbanne
Mar 20	Andy Wright	l ko 5	Battersea 12-0
	(Southern super-middleweight title)		
May 16	Lester Jacobs	l pts 6	Battersea 12-0
Jun 1	Ali Forbes	l ko 2	Bethnal Green 12-9
Nov 19	Dave Lawrence	drew 6	Norwich 12-11
Dec 9	Antonio Fernandez	l pts 8	Brierley Hill 12-0
Dec 16	Peter Vosper	w pts 6	Southampton 12-5

1992
Jan 8	Graham Jenner	l pts 6	Burton-on-Trent 12-12
Jan 22	Julian Johnson	drew 6	Cardiff 12-1
Mar 1	Graham Jenner	l pts 8	St Leonard's On Sea 12-4
Mar 11	Jason McNeill	l pts 6	Cardiff 12-7
Apr 30	Hussain Shah	l rtd 4*	Albert Hall 13-0
Oct 5	Barry Downes	w pts 6	Northampton 12-12
Dec 10	Stefan Wright	l pts 6	Corby 12-10

Fights 39 Won 18 Lost 18 Drawn 3

Steve McCARTHY
Light-heavyweight
Southampton, born London 30 July 1962
Camberley ABC
Southpaw
1985 Southern ABA middleweight final (l J Smith)

1987
Feb 5	Russell Burnett	w ko 1	Southampton 11-8
Mar 3	Barry Bennett	w ko 3	Southend 11-8
Apr 6	Winston Burnett	w pts 8	Southampton 12-7-8
Oct 6	Jason Baxter	drew 6	Southend 11-12
Nov 16	Paul Wesley	w ko 8	Southampton 11-10-8

1988
Feb 3	Andy Wright	w rsf 4	Wembley GH 12-2
May 18	Mike Aubrey	w rsf 4	Portsmouth 12-5
Nov 24	Serg Fame	w pts 10	Southampton 12-5
	(Southern light-heavyweight title)		

1989
Mar 2	Yves Monsieur	w pts 8	Southampton 12-6-8
Apr 26	John Held	w pts 8	Southampton 12-6-12
Sep 21	Tony Wilson	l rtd 3*	Southampton 12-6-12
	(eliminator, British light-heavyweight title)		

1990
Oct 25	Serg Fame	w pts 12	Battersea 12-7
	(vacant British light-heavyweight title)		

1991
Dec 16	John Foreman	w pts 8	Southampton 12-7-4

1992
Apr 4	Henry Maske	l dis 9	Dusseldorf
Sep 29	Dariusz Michalczewski	l dis 3	Hamburg

Fights 15 Won 11 Lost 3 Drawn 1

Tony McCARTHY
Middleweight
Crayford born 10 April 1968
BOAR & Army champion. Based Germany.

1991
Sep 16	Erich Ecker	w rsf 2	Hamburg 11-4-8
Oct 22	Karl Barwise	l pts 6	Battersea 11-6
Nov 29	Jan Franek	l ko 3	Lansenkirken-Frohsdorf

1992
Feb 25	Mike Russell	w pts 6	Crystal Palace 11-5
Apr 4	Tritmir Jandrek	w pts 6	Minden

Fights 5 Won 3 Lost 2

Joe McCLUSKEY

Light-heavyweight
Croy born 13 March 1970
Croy Miners ABC
1987 Young Scotland (v Eng, w C Johnson)
1988 Scotland (v Ire, l D Galvin)
1989 Scotland (v Eng, l M Edwards)
1989 Scottish ABA middleweight final (w rsf 3 R McTaggart, w rsf 2 S Newns, l rsf 1 S Wilson)
1990 ABA light-heavyweight champion (w A Caulfield, w rtd 3 W Scott, w C Edwards, w rsf 2 M Baker)
1990 Scotland (v Wal, w rsf 1 J Mitchell; v Eng, l M Wright)
1991 Scotland (v Wal, w C Beck; v Ire, l M Delaney)
1991 World Championships light-heavyweight (l B Chong Guang, China)
1992 Scotland (v Ire, l rsf 1 M Delaney)

1992
Apr 27	John Oxenham	w pts 4	Glasgow 12-7-8
Jul 9	Lee Prudden	w pts 6	Glasgow 12-4-6

Fights 2 Won 2

Robert McCRACKEN

Light-middleweight
Birmingham born 31 May 1968
Birmingham City ABC
1988 Midlands ABA light-welterweight champion (w rsf 3 T Dixon, w S Cooper, w rsf 3 R Joyce, w rsf 3 I Kemp, l P Day)
1988 England (v Cze, w rsf 2 V Kucera; v Ire, w S Furlong)
1989 ABA light-welterweight finalist (w S Cogan, w rtd 1 D Madden, w rsf 1 W Pardoe, w C Harrison, w ko 1 M Atkin, w T Turner, w rsf 1 M White, l A Hall)
1989 England (v Sco, w ko 1 P Munro; v Pol, w J Olenkniczak; v Ire, w J Lowe)
1990 Commonwealth Games (w F Barr, Bah; l G Johnson, Can)
1990 English ABA welterweight semi-final (w H Clarke, w rsf 1 K Rayment, w dis 2 G McCreesh, l A Carew)
1990 World Cup silver medal, Dublin (w E Magee, Ire; w E Linton, USA; w ko 2 M Lowe, WGer; l rtd 2* J Hernandez, Cub)

1991
Jan 24	Mick Mulcahy	w rsf 1	Brierley Hill 10-7-12
Feb 13	Gary Barron	w rtd 2	Wembley CC 10-8
Mar 6	Tony Britland	w rsf 2	Wembley 10-9
Apr 11	Dave Andrews	w rtd 4	Willenhall 10-10-4
May 8	Tony Gibbs	w ko 1	Albert Hall 10-8-4
May 30	Paul Murray	w rsf 2	Birmingham 10-9
Jul 4	Marty Duke	w rsf 1	Alfreton 10-7
Jul 25	John Smith	w rtd 1	Dudley 10-8-8
Oct 31	Newton Barnett	w dis 2	Telford 10-10
Nov 28	Michael Oliver	w rsf 3	Liverpool 10-10
1992			
Feb 12	Paul Lynch	w rsf 4*	Wembley GH 11-2-12
Sep 30	Horace Fleary	w pts 8	Telford 11-1
Nov 2	Ensley Bingham	w rsf 10	Wolverhampton 10-13-8
	(eliminator, British light-middleweight title)		

Fights 13 Won 13

Spencer McCRACKEN

Welterweight
Birmingham born 8 August 1969
Birmingham City ABC
1990 Birmingham ABA welterweight semi-final (l S Handley)
1991 Birmingham ABA light-middleweight champion (w dis 3 P Davies, withdrew)

1991
Oct 15	Stuart Dunn	drew 6	Dudley 11-0
Dec 9	Seth Jones	w rsf 2	Brierley Hill 10-6

1992
Oct 27	Dave Lovell	w pts 4	Cradley Heath 10-6-8
Dec 7	Mark Antony	w ko 1	Birmingham 10-6-8

Fights 4 Won 3 Drawn 1

Mark McCREATH

Light-welterweight
Lincoln, born Bradford 30 May 1964
Springfield ABC, Keighley ABC, Triumph ABC, Bracebridge ABC
1983 NABC champion (w S Brantuo)
1987 Midlands ABA welterweight final (w rsf 2 A Din, w M Howell, w ko 2 P Allen, l M Elliot)
1988 ABA welterweight champion (w rsf 3 C Harrison, w M Elliot, w R Parker, w ko 1 G Logan, w J Hudd, w R Wileman)
1988 Silver medal at Finland multi-nations, Tampere (w M Stobak, Cze; w Aalto, Fin; l Haddad, Swe)
1988 Acropolis Cup (l R Antman, Swe)
1988 England (v Cze, w O Vohnout)

1989
May 11	Tom Heiskonen	w rsf 6	Tallin
Nov 1	Bianto Baekelandt	w ko 2	Izegem
Nov 29	Abdel Lahjar	w rtd 4	Paris
Dec 9	Pierre Conan	w rsf 4	France

1990
Feb 10	Josef Rajc	w pts 6	Roulers
Mar 26	Eric Capoen	w rsf 1	France
May 19	Mohammed Berrabah	w rsf 6	Montpelier
Aug 11	Mohamed Ouhmad	w rtd 5	Le Cap D'Agde
Sep 5	Mehmet Demir	w rsf 5	Belgrade
Oct 5	Patrick Vungbo (Belgian welterweight title)	l pts 10	Waregem

1991
Apr 17	Pat Barrett (European light-welterweight title)	l rsf 6	Albert Hall 9-13-8
Jun 21	Freddy Demeulenaere (Benelux welterweight title)	w rsf 5*	Waregem

1992
Apr 30	Gary Barron	w rsf 5	Mayfair 10-3-8
Oct 1	Chris Saunders	w rsf 4	Telford 10-4
Dec 7	Gary Barron	w rsf 5*	Mayfair 10-4-4

Fights 15 Won 13 Lost 2

Gary McCRORY

Heavyweight
Annfield Plain born Blackhill 22 October 1960
Consett ABC
1985 North-East England ABA super-heavyweight champion (w M Hallett,withdrew)
1986 ABA super-heavyweight final (w T Hallett, w rsf 1 C Mitchell, w R Nagle, l rsf 2 J Oyebola)
1987 Northern ABA super-heavyweight champion (w ko 1 W Harewood, w rsf 2 D Elrington, l rsf 2 J Oyebola)

1988
Sep 29	David Jules	w pts 6	Sunderland 14-12
Nov 22	David Jules	w pts 6	Middlesbrough 15-3-8

1989
Feb 28	Rocky Burton	l pts 6	Middlesbrough
Apr 28	Jimmy Di Stolfo	l rtd 4*	Milan 14-4
Oct 21	Doug McKay	w pts 6	Middlesbrough 13-7
Nov 5	Herbie Hide	l rtd 1*	Albert Hall 14-10

1990
Jan 24	Doug McKay	w pts 6	Sunderland 13-12-8
Feb 19	Mike Aubrey	l pts 8	NSC 13-13
Sep 18	Ian Bulloch	w pts 8	Stoke 14-2

1991
Feb 18	Pedro Van Raamsdonk	l pts 8	Valkenswaard 13-9
Apr 5	Markus Bott	l pts 8	Hamburg 14-0-8

1992
Mar 6	Axel Schulz	l rsf 2	Berlin
Apr 22	J.A. Bugner	l pts 4	Wembley 15-2
Dec 10	Wayne Llewellyn	l rsf 2	Glasgow 14-0

Fights 14 Won 5 Lost 9

Glenn McCRORY

Cruiserweight
Annfield Plain, born Stanley 23 September 1964
Consett ABC
1981 Junior ABA champion (w L Gent)
1983 Young England (v WGer, w C Honhold)

1984
Feb 6	Barry Ellis	w rsf 1	Mayfair 13-11-8
Feb 22	Denroy Bryan	w pts 6	Albert Hall 13-9
Mar 21	Steve Abadom	w pts 6	Mayfair 14-0-12
Apr 30	Frankie Robinson	w pts 6	Mayfair 14-5
May 9	Frankie Robinson	w rsf 4	Mayfair 14-5
Jun 13	Andy Gerrard	w pts 6	Port Talbot 14-5
Sep 6	Andy Gerrard	w pts 8	Gateshead 14-9
Oct 27	Tony Velasco	w pts 8	Gateshead 14-7
Nov 24	Mike Perkins	w pts 8	Gateshead 14-5

1985
Jan 19	Nate Robinson	w rsf 2*	NEC 14-3
Feb 20	Alex Williamson	w pts 8	Muswell Hill 14-7-8
Mar 27	Gipsy Carmen	w pts 8	Gateshead 14-5-8
May 28	Alfonso Forbes	w ko 1	Muswell Hill 14-4
Sep 3	John Westgarth	l ko 4	Gateshead 14-12
Dec 10	Roy Skeldon	w pts 8	Gateshead 14-6

1986
Apr 9	Rudi Pika	l pts 8	Albert Hall 15-5-8
Apr 18	Anders Eklund	l pts 8	Randers 14-13-8
Jun 17	Dave Garside	l rsf 7*	Blackpool 15-4

Oct 7	Hughroy Currie	l rsf 2	Oldham 15-8
Nov 25	Joe Adams	w pts 6	Louisville 14-8

1987

Jan 8	Calvin Sherman	w ko 1	Houston 13-12
Feb 5	Danny Lawford	w pts 8	Newcastle 13-5
Feb 18	Barry Ellis	w pts 8	Fulham 13-11
Mar 31	Andy Straughn	w rsf 10	Oldham 13-7-12
	(eliminator, British cruiserweight title)		
Sep 4	Chisanda Mutti	w pts 12	Gateshead 13-7-4
	(Commonwealth cruiserweight title)		

1988

Jan 21	Tee Jay	w pts 12	Battersea 13-7
	(British & Commonwealth cruiserweight titles)		
Apr 22	Lou Gent	w rtd 8*	Gateshead 13-8
	(British & Commonwealth cruiserweight titles)		
Nov 1	Ronnie Lee Warrior	w ko 4	Oklahoma City 13-7-12
Nov 15	Lorenzo Boyd	w ko 2	Metairie

1989

Feb 28	Steve Mormino	w pts 10	Middlesbrough
Jun 3	Patrick Lumumba	w pts 12	Stanley 13-8
	(vacant IBF cruiserweight title)		
Oct 21	Siza Makhathini	w ko 11	Middlesbrough 13-8
	(IBF cruiserweight title)		

1990

Mar 22	Jeff Lampkin	l ko 3	Gateshead 13-7-8
	(IBF cruiserweight title)		

1991

Feb 16	Terry Armstrong	w ko 2	Thornaby 15-7
Oct 1	Lennox Lewis	l ko 2	Albert Hall 15-11
	(British & European heavyweight titles)		

1992

Sep 26	Mohamed Bouchiche	drew 8	Paris

Fights 36 Won 28 Lost 7 Drawn 1

Shaun McCRORY

Super-middleweight
Annfield Plain born Shotley Bridge 13 June 1969
Consett ABC
1989 North-East Division ABA light-heavyweight final (w P Mason, l dis 3 I Meredith)

1989

Jun 3	Hugh Fury	w pts 6	Stanley 11-13-12
Oct 10	Mick Maw	l pts 4	Sunderland 12-2

1990

Feb 27	Ian Vokes	w pts 6	Middlesbrough 11-9
Mar 6	Benny Simmons	w rsf 6	North Shields 12-0
Mar 27	Mark Spencer	w rsf 2	Chester-le-Street 11-12
Apr 21	Sean Stringfellow	w pts 6	Sunderland 11-11-12
Jun 5	Alan Pennington	l pts 8	Liverpool 11-9
Sep 5	Tony Booth	w pts 6	Stoke 11-8
Oct 15	Richard Carter	l pts 8	Brierley Hill 12-0-8
Nov 19	Ian Henry	l pts 6	Manchester 12-2

1991

Jan 21	Ian Henry	l pts 6	Glasgow 11-11-8
Feb 6	Tony Booth	w pts 6	Liverpool 11-10
May 13	John Oxenham	w pts 6	Middlesbrough 12-4 /CTD..

(Shaun McCRORY ctd.)

Aug 3	Ron Collins	l pts 8	Selvino 11-11-8
1992			
Apr 13	Paul Wright	l pts 6	Manchester 11-12
Apr 28	David Johnson	drew 6	Houghton-le-Spring 11-12
Oct 5	Eddie Knight	w pts 6	Bristol 12-2

Fights 17 Won 9 Lost 7 Drawn 1

Errol McDONALD

Welterweight
Nottingham born 11 March 1964
Ruddington ABC

1985 ABA welterweight champion (w ko 2 R Golding, w L Ferrie, w R Lewis, w S Kyriakides, w P Nicholson, w B Teague, w T Kershaw)

1985

Oct 21	Dave Heaver	w ko 1	NSC 10-7-4
Nov 5	Robert Armstrong	w rsf 4	Wembley 10-8-12
1986			
Jan 20	Lennie Gloster	w pts 8	NSC 10-4
Feb 17	Kid Milo	drew 6	NSC 10-4-8
Feb 27	Gary Flear	w rsf 5*	Bethnal Green 10-1
Apr 9	Lennie Gloster	w pts 6	Albert Hall 10-3-12
Oct 29	Gerry Beard	w rsf 4	NSC 10-2
1987			
Jan 19	Mark Simpson	w ko 5	NSC 10-4-8
Aug 30	Jose Maria Castillo	w rsf 3	Marbella
Sep 30	Rory Callaghan	w rsf 4	NSC 10-7-8
Nov 18	Billy Cairns	w rtd 3	NSC 10-6
1988			
Feb 3	Mike English	w rsf 2	Wembley 10-4
Mar 29	Ramon Nunez	w rsf 3	Wembley 10-4
Apr 21	Nick Meloscia	w pts 8	Bethnal Green 10-2-8
Sep 26	Jimmy Thornton	w rsf 2*	NSC 10-9
Oct 5	Alfredo Reyes	w ko 2	Wembley GH
Nov 30	Sammy Floyd	w rsf 3	Southwark 10-11-8
1989			
Jan 18	Nick Meloscia	w rsf 1	Albert Hall 10-11
Dec 19	Mick Mulcahy	w rsf 3	Bethnal Green
1990			
Jan 27	Joe Hernandez	w pts 8	Sheffield 10-9
Mar 28	Robert Lewis	w rsf 4	Bethnal Green 10-8-10
Apr 25	Mario Lopez	w ko 1	Brighton 10-9-6
Jun 5	Steve Larrimore	w rsf 9	Nottingham 10-8-14
Nov 18	Ray Taylor	w rtd 3*	NEC 10-8-8
1991			
Feb 23	Juan Rondon	w rsf 7*	Brighton 10-8
Jun 8	Patrizio Oliva	l dis 12	La Spezia
	(European welterweight title)		
Dec 10	Jose Luis Saldivia	w pts 8	Sheffield 10-8-8
1992			
Mar 10	Robert Wright	l ko 3	Bury
Nov 24	Gordon Blair	w rsf 5*	Doncaster 10-8

Fights 29 Won 26 Lost 2 Drawn 1

Billy McDOUGALL

Light-middleweight
Birmingham born Moseley 11 October 1965
Amateur in South Africa

1992
Nov 2	Jimmy Reynolds	l pts 6	Wolverhampton 10-0
Nov 19	Dean Carr	w pts 6	Evesham 10-8
Dec 7	Dean Carr	w pts 6	Birmingham 10-12
Dec 14	Kevin Mabbutt	l rtd 4*	Northampton 11-0

Fights 4 Won 2 Lost 2

Simon McDOUGALL

Light-heavyweight
Blackpool, born Manchester 11 July 1968
Lytham St Anne's ABC
1988 East Lancs & Cheshire ABA light-heavyweight final (w J Henry, l M Coore)

1988
Nov 14	Andrew Braveo	w ko 4	Manchester 12-4-8

1989
Jan 16	Steve Osborne	l pts 6	Bradford 12-10
Jan 25	Steve Osborne	l pts 6	Stoke 12-12
Feb 20	Wayne Connell	w rsf 4*	Bradford 12-5-12
Apr 5	Lee Woolis	l pts 6	Manchester 12-4
Oct 12	George Ferrie	w pts 6	Glasgow 12-2
Nov 30	Jimmy Cropper	w pts 6	Oldham
Dec 7	Sean O'Phoenix	l pts 6	Manchester 12-5

1990
Apr 7	Eddy Smulders	l pts 6	Eindhoven 12-5-8
May 15	Terry French	w pts 4	South Shields 12-4
Oct 12	Ray Alberts	l pts 6	Cayenne
Oct 22	Glenn Campbell	l rsf 4	Manchester 12-4
Dec 10	Maurice Thomas	w rsf 2	Bradford 12-6

1991
Jan 28	Ian Henry	w pts 8	Bradford 12-5
Feb 28	Glenn Campbell	l pts 10	Bury 11-12-4
	(Central super-middleweight title)		
Apr 23	Paul Burton	l pts 8	Evesham 12-4
May 10	Ian Henry	l pts 6	Gateshead 12-11
Oct 1	Doug Calderwood	w rsf 4*	Liverpool 12-6
Oct 10	Terry French	l pts 6	Gateshead 12-5
Oct 19	Andrea Magi	l rsf 5	Terni

1992
Mar 3	Paul Hitch	l pts 6	Houghton-le-Spring 12-4
Mar 11	Ian Henry	l pts 8	Solihull 12-8
Mar 30	Nigel Rafferty	l pts 8	Coventry
Jun 8	Mark McBiane	w pts 6	Bradford 12-7
Oct 6	Gary Delaney	l pts 8	Antwerp
Dec 12	Gary Delaney	l pts 8	Muswell Hill 12-9-8

Fights 26 Won 9 Lost 17

Allan McDOWALL
Lightweight
Renfrew, born 29 September 1967
Gallowgate ABC
1991 Scottish ABA lightweight champion (w rsf 1 S McLevy, w rsf 1 G Hughes, w T Ahmed, l P Gallagher)

1991
Sep 24	John Patterson	w pts 4	Glasgow 9-6-6
Nov 28	John Patterson	w pts 6	Glasgow 9-7

1992
Jan 31	Charles Shepherd	w rsf 3*	Glasgow 9-9
Feb 24	Mark O'Callaghan	w pts 6	Glasgow 9-11
Mar 12	James Jiora	w ko 2	Glasgow 9-12
May 29	Karl Taylor	w pts 6	Glasgow 9-7-4
Oct 22	Robert Lloyd	w rtd 4	Glasgow 9-8

Fights 7 Won 7

James McGEE
Light-middleweight
Nuneaton born 9 May 1968
Bedworth Ex-Service ABC

1991
Mar 19	Adrian Din	w pts 6	Leicester 11-0
Apr 15	Marty Duke	l pts 6	Leicester 10-13
May 20	Cliff Churchward	w pts 6	Leicester 10-12
Jun 11	Julian Eavis	w pts 6	Leicester 11-1
Oct 1	Trevor Meikle	l pts 6	Bedworth 10-13-8
Oct 21	Crain Fisher	l rsf 4	Bury 11-0
Dec 11	Julian Eavis	drew 6	Leicester 11-1

1992
Feb 11	Chris Mulcahy	w pts 6	Wolverhampton 10-13
Mar 25	Darren Morris	drew 6	Hinckley 11-6
May 11	Julian Eavis	w rsf 3*	Coventry 11-2
Oct 5	Julian Eavis	l pts 6	Bardon 10-12
Nov 23	James Campbell	drew 6	Coventry 10-12

Fights 12 Won 5 Lost 4 Drawn 3

Ian McGIRR
Featherweight
Clydebank born 14 April 1968
Antonine ABC
1987 Young Scotland (v Ire, l R Daly)
1987 Scotland (v Wal, l rsf 1 R Edwards)
1988 Scottish ABA bantamweight prelim (l J Drummond)
1989 Scottish ABA featherweight semi-final (w S Wood, l D Anderson)

1989
Nov 23	Eddie Cook	w pts 6	Motherwell 9-1-8
Dec 18	James Milne	w pts 6	Glasgow 9-0

1990
Feb 19	Peter Buckley	w pts 6	Birmingham 9-0
Mar 26	Eddie Cook	l pts 6	Glasgow 9-2-12
Oct 9	Steve Walker	l rsf 4*	Glasgow 9-5
Nov 19	Eddie Cook	l pts 6	Glasgow 9-4-12

1991			
Feb 18	Colin Innes	w pts 6	Glasgow 9-6
Mar 1	Eddie Cook	l pts 6	Irvine 9-3
Mar 18	Noel Carroll	l pts 6	Manchester 9-2
Sep 24	Peter Judson	w pts 6	Glasgow 9-5-8
Oct 8	Tony Feliciello	l pts 8	Wolverhampton 9-5
Oct 21	Chris Clarkson	drew 6	Glasgow 9-4-8
Dec 12	Darren Elsdon	l ko 4	Hartlepool
1992			
Sep 21	Chip O'Neill	w pts 6	Glasgow 9-5
Oct 12	Chris Jickells	l rsf 3	Bradford 9-2-8
Nov 18	G.G. Goddard	w pts 6	Solihull 9-6-8

Fights 16 Won 7 Lost 8 Drawn 1

Brian McGLOIN
Super-middleweight
Doncaster born Glasgow 20 March 1964

1991			
Dec 11	Marc Rowley	w pts 6	Leicester 12-0
1992			
May 18	Chad Strong	drew 6	Bardon 11-7
Sep 8	Martin Jolley	l pts 6	Doncaster 12-6

Fights 3 Won 1 Lost 1 Drawn 1

Steve McGOVERN
Welterweight
Bembridge, Isle of Wight, born Newport, IOW 17 April 1969
Sandown & Shanklin ABC, Parade ABC
1988 Southern ABA light-welterweight prelim (l B Chambers)
1989 Southern ABA light-welterweight semi-final (w J Welling, l T Turner)

1989			
Sep 21	Mike Morrison	w pts 6	Southampton 10-2
1990			
Apr 17	Justin Graham	w pts 6	Millwall 10-5
1991			
Jan 21	Mark Dinnadge	w pts 6	Crystal Palace 10-7
Feb 23	Tim Harmey	w pts 6	Brighton 10-7
Apr 23	Frank Harrington	w pts 6	Evesham
May 8	Rocky Milton	w pts 6	Millwall 10-7
Dec 16	Chris Mylan	w pts 8	Southampton 10-8-8
1992			
Mar 3	Tony Swift	l rsf 4*	Cradley Heath 10-9
Oct 27	Ricky Mabbett	drew 6	Leicester 10-9

Fights 9 Won 7 Lost 1 Drawn 1

Graham McGRATH

Bantamweight
Warley born West Bromwich 31 July 1962
No amateur experience

1992

May 21	Paul Kelly	w rsf 2	Cradley Heath 8-7
Jun 1	Greg Upton	l pts 6	NEC 8-10
Jul 9	Wilson Docherty	l rsf 4	Glasgow 8-12-8
Sep 25	Paul Lloyd	l rsf 3	Liverpool 8-11
Nov 2	Dennis Oakes	l pts 4	Liverpool 8-7
Dec 1	Leo Beirne	w pts 6	Liverpool 8-8
Dec 10	Shaun Anderson	l pts 6	Glasgow 8-6

Fights 7 Won 2 Lost 5

Dominic McGUIGAN

Super-featherweight
Newcastle born Hexham 13 June 1963
West End ABC & West Denton ABC

1989

Oct 10	Dave Buxton	w pts 6	Sunderland 9-5

1990

Jan 24	John Milne	drew 6	Sunderland 9-9-8
Mar 20	Frankie Foster	drew 6	Hartlepool 9-6
Apr 21	Chris Bennett	w pts 6	Sunderland 9-5-12
May 22	Lester James	l pts 6	Thornaby 9-6-8

1991

Sep 16	Barrie Kelley	drew 6	AASC 9-4
Nov 28	John Milne	w rtd 3	Glasgow 9-4-8

1992

Apr 30	Kevin Lowe	w rsf 6	Mayfair 9-8
May 15	Rene Weller	l pts 8	Augsburg
Oct 7	Harry Escott	l rtd 5	Sunderland 9-5-8
Nov 12	Kevin Lowe	w rsf 2	Liverpool 9-5-12

Fights 11 Won 5 Lost 3 Drawn 3

Davey McHALE

Super-featherweight
Glasgow, born 29 April 1967
Bellahouston ABC, Renfrew ABC
1987 Scottish ABA featherweight semi-final (l C Kane)
1990 Scottish ABA lightweight prelim (l M Gowans)

1990

Oct 8	Sol Francis	w ko 2	Glasgow 9-4-8

1991

Nov 25	Eddie Gabbutt	w rsf 1	Liverpool 9-3-8

1992

Mar 30	Kevin Lowe	w rsf 5	Glasgow 9-8-4
Jun 1	Chris Jickells	w rsf 4	Glasgow 9-2-4
Jul 9	G.G.Goddard	w rtd 4	Glasgow 9-4-12
Oct 19	Lee Fox	w rsf 3	Glasgow 9-3-8
Nov 23	Karl Taylor	w pts 8	Glasgow 9-6

Fights 7 Won 7

Darren McINULTY
Welterweight
Bedworth, born Coventry 11 November 1970

1991
May 20	Dave Binsteed	drew 6	Leicester 11-0
Oct 1	Dean Carr	w pts 6	Bedworth 10-8
Nov 11	Ricky North	w pts 6	Stratford 10-7

1992
Jan 20	Chris Mulcahy	w pts 6	Coventry 10-8
Feb 4	Richard O'Brien	l pts 4	Alfreton 10-4-12
Mar 11	Eddie King	w rsf 1	Stoke
Mar 25	Robert Riley	l pts 6	Hinckley 10-9-8
Apr 28	Dean Bramhald	w pts 6	Wolverhampton 10-6
May 11	Dean Bramhald	w pts 6	Coventry 10-3
Sep 10	Hugh Davey	l pts 6	Sunderland 10-10
Nov 23	Mark Antony	w pts 6	Coventry 10-7
Dec 2	Dean Hiscox	drew 6	Bardon 10-10

Fights 12 Won 7 Lost 3 Drawn 2

Alan McKAY
Featherweight
Willesden born Watford 1 June 1967
Southpaw
All Stars ABC & West Hendon ABC
1986 NW London ABA lightweight prelims (l T Hobbs)
1987 NW London ABA featherweight champion (w dis 1 W Champagne, l rsf 2 C McMillan)
1988 London ABA featherweight final (w J O'Meara, w dis 2 S McNamara, w T Flook, l C McMillan)

1988
Sep 19	Mike Chapman	w pts 6	NSC 9-0-12
Nov 18	Mark Holt	w pts 6	NSC 9-0-8

1989
Jan 12	Jamie Hind	w rsf 3	Southwark 9-0-12
Jan 31	Colin McMillan	w rsf 3*	Bethnal Green 8-13-12
Mar 1	Jeff Dobson	w pts 6	Bethnal Green
Apr 27	Lance Williams	w pts 6	Southwark 9-1-12
May 26	Nico Lucas	w pts 6	Bethnal Green 9-2
Sep 4	Jari Gronroos	drew 6	Helsinki 9-1-4
Oct 24	Tim Driscoll	l pts 6	Bethnal Green 8-13
Nov 28	Steve Walker	drew 6	Battersea 9-0

1990
May 3	Gary Hickman	w pts 8	Marble Arch 8-13
Oct 22	Steve Robinson	w pts 6	NSC 9-1
Dec 14	Gary De Roux	l rsf 5	Peterborough 8-13-4
	(vacant Southern featherweight title)		

1991
Apr 9	Paul Harvey	l rsf 4	Mayfair 9-2
Nov 13	Gary De Roux	w rsf 8	Bethnal Green 9-0
	(vacant Southern featherweight title)		

1992
Jan 18	Peter Buckley	drew 8	Albert Hall 9-1
Oct 27	Kelton McKenzie	w pts 10	Cradley Heath 9-0
	(eliminator, British featherweight title)		

Fights 17 Won 11 Lost 3 Drawn 3

Darren McKENNA

Super-middleweight
Sheffield born 21 December 1962
Sheffield Boxing Centre ABC
Southpaw

1987
Nov 19	Tony Behan	w rsf 1	Ilkeston 12-7
Nov 24	Calvin Hart	l pts 4	Wisbech 12-7-8
Dec 2	Darren Jones	l rsf 3	Stoke 12-8

1988
Jan 20	Darren Jones	l pts 6	Stoke 12-9
Jan 27	Sean Stringfellow	l ko 3	Stoke
Mar 7	David Jono	w dis 3	Manchester 12-10
Mar 8	Peter Brown	l pts 6	Batley 12-7
Mar 29	Russell Barker	l rsf 4	Middlesbrough 12-7
May 17	Mark Watts	w rsf 2	Leicester 12-4
Jun 6	Carl Thompson	l rsf 2	Manchester 12-9
Sep 5	Russell Barker	l rsf 3	Manchester 12-8
Nov 2	Maurice Thomas	l ko 4	Bradford 12-6

1989
May 24	Peter Elliott	l pts 8	Hanley 12-3
Oct 5	Jimmy Cropper	l pts 4	Middleton 12-7
Oct 23	Sean Stringfellow	w rsf 8*	Hull

1990
Jan 29	Graham Burton	l pts 4	Hull 12-0
Mar 6	Peter Elliott	l pts 8	Stoke 12-0
Mar 12	Fidel Castro	l pts 6	Hull
Apr 5	Alan Millett	w rsf 2	Liverpool 12-7
Apr 17	Nicky Piper	l rtd 4	Millwall 12-10
Sep 12	Steve Aquilina	drew 8	Stafford 12-1
Oct 8	Dave Owens	l pts 6	Leicester 12-7

1991
May 9	Denzil Browne	l pts 6	Leeds 13-4
Jun 24	Johnny Held	l pts 8	Rotterdam 12-12-12

1992
Jan 23	Denzil Browne	l pts 6	York 12-13-12
Jun 4	Maurice Thomas	w rsf 2	Newcastle-under-Lyme 12-0
Oct 17	Terry Dixon	w rsf 3	Wembley 13-4

Fights 27 Won 7 Lost 19 Drawn 1

Duke McKENZIE

Super-bantamweight
Croydon born 5 May 1963
Battersea ABC & Sir Philip Game ABC
1980 NABC Class B final (l P Gabbitus)
1981 Young England (v Hun, l Kineses; w T Lakatos)
1981 ABA flyweight semi-final (w S Nolan, w I Winter, w T Kennard, w J Dawson, l D Williams)
1982 SE London ABA flyweight champion (l S Nolan)
1982 Young England (vFin, l J Lytikaeninen)

1982
Nov 23	Charlie Brown	w rsf 2	Wembley

1983
Jan 24	Andy King	w rsf 2	AASC
Feb 27	Dave Pearson	w rsf 1	Las Vegas
Mar 3	Gregorio Hernandez	w ko 3	Los Angeles

Mar 19	Lupe Sanchez	w rsf 2	Reno
Oct 18	Jerry Davis	w rsf 2	Atlantic City
Nov 22	Alain Limarola	w pts 6	Wembley

1984

Jan 15	David Capo	w pts 4	Atlantic City
May 23	Gary Roberts	w ko 1	NSC 8-1

1985

Mar 6	Julio Guerrero	w pts 8	Albert Hall 8-1
Jun 5	Danny Flynn (vacant British flyweight title)	w rsf 4	Albert Hall 7-13-12
Oct 16	Orlando Maestra	w pts 8	Albert Hall 8-2-12

1986

Feb 16	Sonny Long	w pts 10	Albert Hall 8-0-8
May 20	Charlie Magri (British & European flyweight titles)	w rtd 5	Wembley
Nov 19	Lee Cargle	w pts 10	Atlantic City 8-2-4
Dec 17	Giampiero Pinna (European flyweight title)	w pts 12 (m)	Acquiterme 7-13-4

1987

Mar 24	Jose Manuel Diaz	w pts 8	Wembley
Dec 2	Juan Herrera	w pts 10	Wembley 8-0-12

1988

Mar 9	Agapito Gomez (European flyweight title)	w ko 2	Wembley GH 8-0
May 4	Jose Gallegos	w pts 10	Wembley GH 8-4
Oct 5	Rolando Bohol (IBF flyweight title)	w ko 11	Wembley GH 8-0
Nov 30	Artemio Ruiz	w pts 10	Southwark 8-4

1989

Mar 8	Tony De Luca (IBF flyweight title)	w rsf 4*	Albert Hall 8-0
Jun 7	Dave McAuley (IBF flyweight title)	l pts 12	Wembley 8-0
Oct 12	David Moreno	w pts 10	Southwark 8-8
Nov 8	Memo Flores	w pts 8	Wembley GH 8-8

1990

Sep 30	Thierry Jacob (vacant European bantamweight title)	l pts 12	Calais 8-5-12

1991

Jan 10	Peter Buckley	w rsf 5	Battersea 8-5-8
Feb 7	Julio Blanco	w rsf 7	Watford 8-6
Apr 4	Chris Clarkson	w rsf 5	Watford 8-9
Jun 30	Gaby Canizales (WBO bantamweight title)	w pts 12	Southwark 8-5-12
Sep 12	Cesar Soto (WBO bantamweight title)	w pts 12	Battersea 8-6

1992

Mar 25	Wilfredo Vargas (WBO bantamweight title)	w rsf 8	Albert Hall
May 13	Rafael Del Valle (WBO bantamweight title)	l ko 1	Albert Hall 8-5
Sep 7	Peter Buckley	w rtd 3	Bethnal Green 8-11-8
Oct 15	Jesse Benavides (WBO super-bantamweight title)	w pts 12	Catford 8-8-8

Fights 36 Won 33 Lost 3

Kelton McKENZIE
Featherweight
Leicester born 18 September 1968
Belgrave ABC
1989 Midlands ABA featherweight final (w ko 2 A Williamson, l P Ramsey)

1990
Oct 18	Tony Silkstone	l pts 6	Dewsbury 8-13-8
Nov 29	Neil Leitch	drew 6	Marton 9-0
Dec 11	Sylvester Osuji	w pts 6	Evesham 8-13

1991
Jan 21	John Williams	drew 6	Crystal Palace 9-0
Mar 14	Craig Dermody	l rsf 3	Middleton 8-12
May 1	Tim Yeates	w pts 6	Bethnal Green 8-11
Jun 17	Derek Amory	w rsf 6	Edgbaston 9-2
Nov 5	Richard Woolgar	w rsf 5	Leicester 9-3-12

1992
Jan 22	Colin Lynch	w rsf 5	Solihull 9-1-8
Mar 26	Brian Robb	w rsf 4	Telford 9-2
Apr 29	Elvis Parsley	w rsf 5	Solihull 8-12

(vacant Midlands featherweight title)
Jul 18	Steve Walker	w ko 2	Manchester 9-2
Oct 27	Alan McKay	l pts 10	Cradley Heath 9-0

(eliminator, British featherweight title)

Fights 13 Won 8 Lost 3 Drawn 2

Kevin McKENZIE
Light-welterweight
Hartlepool born 18 October 1968
1988 Northern ABA lightweight final (w B Wright, w F Foster, w R Palmer, l N Boyd)

1992
Jun 8	Jason Brattley	w rtd 3*	Bradford 10-1
Sep 21	Alan Ingle	w pts 6	Glasgow 10-3
Oct 22	Dave Anderson	l rtd 3*	Glasgow 9-12
Dec 1	Seth Jones	l rsf 3*	Hartlepool 10-1

Fights 4 Won 2 Lost 2

Roger (R.F.) McKENZIE
Heavyweight
Croydon born 3 October 1965
St Monica's ABC
1988 NE London ABA light-heavyweight final (w rtd 1 P Lawson, l R Parkes)

1989
Jan 31	Gerry Storey	w pts 6	Bethnal Green 13-7

1990
Sep 24	Mark Bowen	l rsf 1*	AASC 13-9-8
Nov 29	Denzil Browne	w pts 6	Sunderland 13-12-12

1991
Feb 12	Noel Magee	l pts 6	Belfast 13-3
Mar 21	Denzil Browne	l pts 6	Dewsbury 13-11-12
May 28	Steve Yorath	l pts 6	Cardiff 13-11
Sep 7	Ray Kane	l pts 4	Belfast 13-11-8
Oct 9	Denzil Browne	w pts 6	Manchester

Oct 28	Pedro Van Raamsdonk	w ko 7	Arnhem 14-0-4
Dec 12	Norbert Ekassi	l rsf 3	Massy
1992			
Mar 14	Niels H. Madsen	l pts 6	Copenhagen 13-5
Apr 25	Noel Magee	l pts 8	Belfast 13-1
Oct 31	Warren Richards	drew 6	Earls Court 15-2

Fights 13 Won 4 Lost 8 Drawn 1

Tony McKENZIE
Light-welterweight
Leicester born 4 March 1963
Belgrave ABC
1979 National Schools champion
1981 Midlands ABA light-welterweight final (w rsf 2 L McIntosh, l C McIntosh)
1982 Midlands ABA light-welterweight final (w J Faulkner, w M Haywood, l C McIntosh)

1983			
Nov 22	Albert Buchanan	w ko 3	Wolverhampton 9-12
Dec 7	Peter Flanagan	w pts 6	Stoke 10-0-8
1984			
Jan 30	Vince Bailey	w rsf 1	Birmingham 10-0-8
Feb 27	David Irving	w rsf 3	Birmingham 9-13
Mar 5	Johnny Grant	w rsf 4*	Leicester
Apr 16	Danny Shinkwin	l rsf 1	Birmingham 10-0-8
May 9	Ray Price	w pts 8	Leicester 10-0
Oct 3	Michael Harris	l pts 8	Solihull
Oct 10	Manny Romain	w ko 5	Stoke 10-4
Oct 29	Peter Flanagan	w rsf 8	Nottingham 10-3
Nov 16	Lennie Gloster	w pts 8	Leicester 10-4-12
1985			
Mar 14	Tony Laing	l rsf 8*	Leicester 9-13
	(vacant Midlands light-welterweight title)		
Sep 7	Tony Adams	w pts 8	Douglas 10-2
Nov 20	Raffaele Feliciello	w rsf 6	Solihull 10-0
1986			
Mar 19	Simon Eubanks	w rsf 4	Solihull 10-2-8
May 7	Michael Harris	w pts 10	Solihull 9-13-12
	(eliminator, British light-welterweight title)		
Sep 20	Clinton McKenzie	w ko 3	Hemel Hempstead 9-13-12
	(vacant British light-welterweight title)		
Oct 25	Michael Harris	w ko 10	Stevenage
	(British light-welterweight title)		
Nov 29	Ford Jennings	w rsf 5*	Battersea 10-3-4
1987			
Jan 28	Lloyd Christie	l rsf 3	Croydon 9-13-8
	(British light-welterweight title)		
May 12	David Griffiths	w rsf 3	Alfreton 10-2-8
Nov 3	Kelvin Mortimer	w rsf 3	Bethnal Green 10-5
1988			
Feb 24	Jeff Decker	w rsf 2	Leicester 10-1-12
Nov 3	Lofti Ben Sayel	l rsf 2*	Leicester 10-0-8
1989			
inactive			
1990			
Jan 27	Benji Marquez	drew 8	Sheffield 10-2
Mar 20	Benji Marquez	w pts 8	Norwich 10-2-10
Jun 5	Art Blackmore	w rsf 4*	Nottingham 10-2 /CTD..

(Tony McKENZIE ctd.)
1991
Mar 19	King Zaka	w ko 1	Leicester 10-0
	(eliminator, Commonwealth light-welterweight title)		
Jun 11	Albert Machong	w ko 3	Leicester 9-13-8
	(eliminator, Commonwealth light-welterweight title)		
Nov 5	Marty Duke	w rsf 7	Leicester 10-2-8
Nov 20	Gordon Blair	w rsf 5	Norwich 10-4-8

1992
Feb 27	Andy Holligan	l rsf 3	Liverpool 9-13-9
	(British & Commonwealth light-welterweight titles)		

Fights 32 Won 25 Lost 6 Drawn 1

Kevin McKILLAN
Light-welterweight
Manchester, born Belfast 1 March 1969
Real name: Kevin Prendergast
West Wythenshawe ABC
1990 North-West Counties ABA lightweight final (w G Collins, w dis 2 J Williams, l G Thornhill)

1991
Oct 28	Michael Byrne	w pts 6	Leicester 10-1
Nov 13	Barry Glanister	w pts 6	Liverpool 9-10

1992
Jan 22	Sugarboy Wright	w pts 6	Solihull 9-12
Feb 10	Jamie Davidson	l pts 6	Liverpool 9-11
Mar 11	Jamie Davidson	drew 6	Stoke 9-10
Jun 1	Steve Howden	w rsf 2	Manchester 10-1
Jun 12	Floyd Churchill	w pts 6	Liverpool 9-12-12
Sep 25	John Smith	w pts 6	Liverpool 10-3-8
Oct 7	J.T.Williams	l pts 6	Barry 9-9-8
Nov 20	Steve Foran	l pts 6	Liverpool 9-13-8

Fights 10 Won 6 Lost 3 Drawn 1

Ian McLEOD
Featherweight
Kilmarnock born 11 June 1969
Croy Miners ABC, Springside ABC
1990 Scotland (v Eng, l J Irwin; v Wal, w J Cody)
1991 Scottish ABA featherweight final (w rsf 1 T McDonald, w w J Twycross, l B Carr)
1991 Scotland (v Ire, l P Ferris)
1992 Scottish ABA featherweight semi-final (l C Melucci)

1992
Nov 23	Robert Braddock	drew 6	Glasgow 9-2

Fights 1 Drawn 1

Colin McMILLAN
Featherweight
Barking born 12 February 1966
Barking ABC
1985 ABA featherweight semi-final (w R Deeble, w P Bell, w R McLean, w J Good, w C Day, l F Havard)
1986 London (v New York, l F Liberatore)
1986 London ABA featherweight champion (w rsf 3 L Abrahams, w rsf 1 R Deeble, w T Driscoll, w J Stephens, l P Hodkinson)
1986 England (v Ire, w B McCarthy)
1987 Finland Multi-nations (w V Salvatore, Can; l E Murin, Fra)
1987 ABA featherweight final (w M Biggs, w rsf 2 A McKay, w T Davis, w C Day, l P English)
1987 England (v Ire, l C Carlton)
1988 ABA featherweight final (w rtd 1 M Jones, w rsf 2 P Stephens, w A McKay, w M Smyth, w R Edwards, l D Anderson)
1988 Canada Cup (w rsf 1 S Dahlin, Swe; l R Garnett, USA)

1988
Nov 29	Mike Chapman	w pts 6	Battersea 9-1-12
Dec 10	Aldrich Johnson	w pts 6	Crystal Palace 9-0-8

1989
Jan 31	Alan McKay	l rsf 3*	Bethnal Green 9-0
Jun 12	Miguel Matthews	w rsf 3	Battersea 8-12-4
Sep 19	Graham O'Malley	w pts 8	Millwall 9-1
Oct 11	Marcel Herbert	w pts 6	Millwall 8-13
Nov 30	Sylvester Osuji	w rsf 4	Barking 9-0

1990
Feb 14	Vidal Tellez	w rsf 2	Millwall 8-13-8
Apr 17	Jesus Muniz	w pts 8	Millwall 9-3
May 3	Steve Walker	w pts 6	Marble Arch 9-1
Jul 5	Tyrone Miller	w ko 2	Greenville, Ms
Jul 17	Malcolm Rougeaux	w ko 1	Lake Charles, La. 9-2
Sep 25	Darren Weller	w rsf 2	Millwall 9-0-4
Oct 10	Graham O'Malley	w pts 6	Millwall 9-2
Nov 12	Mark Holt	w pts 8	Norwich 9-2

1991
Mar 5	Russell Davison	w pts 6	Millwall 9-2-4
Apr 26	Willie Richardson	w pts 8	Crystal Palace 9-0-4
May 22	Gary De Roux (British featherweight title)	w rsf 7	Millwall 8-12
Jul 3	Herbie Bivalacqua	w rsf 3	Reading 8-13-8
Sep 4	Kevin Pritchard (British featherweight title)	w rsf 7	Bethnal Green 9-0
Oct 29	Sean Murphy (British featherweight title)	w pts 12	Albert Hall 8-13

1992
Jan 18	Percy Commey (vacant Commonwealth featherweight title)	w pts 12	Albert Hall 9-0
Mar 25	Tommy Valdez	w rsf 6	Dagenham 9-3
May 16	Maurizio Stecca (WBO featherweight title)	w pts 12	Muswell Hill 8-13-4
Sep 26	Ruben Palacio (WBO featherweight title)	l rsf 8*	Olympia 9-0

Fights 25 Won 23 Lost 2

Con McMULLAN

Bantamweight
Acton, born Larne 21 June 1967
Old Actonians ABC & Carnlough ABC
1990 SW London ABA featherweight champion (w N Dickinson, l dis 2 K Middleton)

1990
Jun 6	Ceri Farrell	w rsf 5	Battersea 8-6
Dec 4	Neil Parry	w rsf 2	Southend 8-9

1991
Nov 12	Mark Loftus	w pts 6	Milton Keynes 9-0

1992
Oct 28	Barry Jones	l pts 6	Cardiff 8-7

Fights 4 Won 3 Lost 1

Jason McNEILL

Light-heavyweight
Swansea, born Bristol 12 August 1971
RAOB ABC
1991 Welsh ABA middleweight prelim (l G Boddy)

1991
Oct 3	Mark Paine	l pts 6	Burton 12-4
Oct 15	Tony Colclough	l pts 6	Dudley 12-1-4
Nov 28	Mark McBiane	w pts 6	Evesham 12-4-8

1992
Jan 21	Gipsy Johnny Price	l pts 4	Stockport 12-1
Mar 11	Paul McCarthy	w pts 6	Cardiff 12-5
Apr 23	Abel Asinamali	l ko 3	Eltham 12-3
Sep 7	Mark Baker	l rsf 2	Bethnal Green 12-6
Oct 23	Paul Wright	l rsf 1	Liverpool 12-4

Fights 8 Won 2 Lost 6

Steve McNESS

Light-middleweight
Bethnal Green born Bow 17 November 1969
Repton ABC
1988 NE London ABA welterweight prelim (l ko 1 R Bryan)
1989 NE London ABA welterweight champion (w A Jones, w R Bryan, withdrew)
1991 London ABA welterweight final (w N Thurbin, w D Gardiner, l V Rose)

1992
Apr 22	Rick North	w pts 6	Wembley 10-10-8
May 13	Mark Verikios	l rsf 5*	Albert Hall 10-12
Sep 3	Steve Goodwin	w pts 6	Dunstable 10-11
Oct 28	Mark Dawson	l rsf 2*	Albert Hall 10-12-4

Fights 4 Won 2 Lost 2

George NAYLOR

Lightweight
Liverpool born 4 July 1968
Southpaw
Transport ABC
1984 National Schools champion (w J Armour)
1991 Northern ABA lightweight final (w G Thornhill, w J Farrell, w dis 3 B Connolly, l rsf 2 A Green)
1992 West Lancs & Cheshire ABA light-welter prelim (l J Neary)

1992
Sep 25	Charles Shepherd	l rsf 4	Liverpool 9-11
Oct 30	Dean Martin	w pts 6	NEC 9-9
Nov 20	Emlyn Rees	w pts 6	Liverpool 9-9
Dec 15	Renny Edwards	l rtd 5*	Liverpool 9-8

Fights 4 Won 2 Lost 2

Shea NEARY

Light-welterweight
Liverpool born 18 May 1968
Real name: Jimmy Neary
Liverpool Golden Gloves ABC
1991 West Lancs & Cheshire ABA light-welterweight semi-final (w rsf 1 P Campbell, l L Rimmer)
1992 West Lancs/Cheshire ABA light-welterweight final (w G Naylor, w ko 1 J Vlasman, l L Rimmer)

1992
Sep 3	Simon Ford	w rsf 1	Liverpool
Oct 5	Sean Armstrong	w rsf 6	Liverpool 9-13
Nov 2	Jason Barker	w rsf 3	Liverpool 9-13
Dec 1	Chris Saunders	w pts 6	Liverpool 10-3

Fights 4 Won 4

Johnny NELSON

Cruiserweight
Sheffield born 4 January 1967
Unity ABC

1986
Mar 18	Peter Brown	l pts 6	Hull 11-10
May 15	Tommy Taylor	l pts 6	Dudley 12-5
Oct 3	Magne Havnaa	l pts 4	Copenhagen 13-1
Nov 20	Chris Little	w pts 6	Manchester

1987
Jan 19	Gipsy Carmen	w pts 6	NSC 13-0
Mar 2	Doug Young	w pts 6	Huddersfield 13-0
Mar 10	Sean Daly	w rsf 1*	Manchester 13-4
Apr 28	Brian Schumacher	l pts 8	Halifax 12-13
Jun 3	Byron Pullen	w rsf 3	Southwark 12-10
Dec 14	Jon McBean	w rsf 6	Edgbaston 13-2

1988
Feb 1	Dennis Bailey	l pts 8	Northampton 13-5
Feb 24	Cordwell Hylton	w rsf 1	Sheffield 13-4
Apr 25	Kenny Jones	w ko 1	Liverpool 13-2
May 4	Crawford Ashley	w pts 8	Solihull 13-4
Jun 6	Lennie Howard	w ko 2	Mayfair 13-7
Aug 31	Andy Gerrard	w pts 8	Stoke 13-9-12
Oct 26	Danny Lawford	w rsf 2	Sheffield 13-6-12
	(vacant Central cruiserweight title)		

/CTD..

(Johnny NELSON ctd.)
1989

Apr 4	Steve Mormino	w rsf 2	Sheffield 13-9-8
May 21	Andy Straughn	w ko 8	Finsbury Park 13-8
	(British cruiserweight title)		
Oct 2	Ian Bulloch	w ko 2	Hanley 13-8
	(British cruiserweight title)		

1990

Jan 27	Carlos De Leon	drew 12	Sheffield 13-8
	(WBC cruiserweight title)		
Feb 14	Dino Homsey	w rsf 7*	Brentwood 13-12
Mar 28	Lou Gent	w rsf 4	Bethnal Green 13-7-12
	(British cruiserweight title)		
Jun 27	Arthur Weathers	w rsf 2	Albert Hall 13-11
Sep 5	Andre Smith	w pts 8	Brighton 14-2
Dec 14	Markus Bott	w rsf 12	Karlsruhe
	(vacant European cruiserweight title)		

1991

Mar 12	Yves Monsieur	w rtd 8	Mansfield 13-7
	(European cruiserweight title)		

1992

May 16	James Warring	l pts 12	Fredericksburg 13-7-4
	(IBF cruiserweight title)		
Aug 15	Norbert Ekassi	l rsf 3	Ajaccio
Oct 29	Corrie Sanders	l pts 10	Morula Sun 13-13

Fights 30 Won 21 Lost 8 Drawn 1

Kenny NEVERS
Super-middleweight
Hackney born 10 August 1967
Islington Boys ABC
1991 London ABA light-heavyweight final (w rsf 3 S Miller, w rsf 1 A Brady, l C Okoh)
1992 NW London ABA light-heavyweight final (w rsf 1 G Walters, w rsf 2 F Yemofio, l rsf 3 M Prince)

1992

Dec 10	Hussain Shah	l pts 4	Bethnal Green 12-1-8

Fights 1 Lost 1

Ray NEWBY
Light-welterweight
Nottingham, born Sunderland 16 December 1963
Cotgrave ABC

1984

Sep 20	Rocky Lawlor	drew 6	Dudley 9-3
Oct 10	Jess Rundan	w rsf 3	Evesham
Oct 29	Dean Bramhald	w pts 6	Nottingham 9-9-8
Nov 7	Gary Flear	l pts 6	Evesham 9-4
Nov 21	Glenn Tweedie	w pts 6	Solihull 9-8
Dec 10	Wayne Trigg	w rsf 6	Nottingham 9-8-8

1985

Feb 4	Peter Bowen	w pts 8	Nottingham 9-7
Mar 7	Steve Cooke	l pts 8	Nottingham 9-10
Sep 25	Billy Laidman	w rsf 2	Stoke

Oct 3	John Faulkner	w pts 8	Nottingham 9-12
Nov 21	Michael Marsden	l pts 6	Huddersfield 9-9

1986

Jan 20	Steve Griffith	l rsf 3	NSC 9-12
Feb 24	Ian Harrison	w pts 6	Coventry 10-0
Mar 5	Mark Pearce	drew 6	Stoke 9-8
Mar 24	Paul Dawson	w rsf 3	Wandsworth 9-11
Apr 7	Wayne Cooper	w rsf 2	Nottingham 9-7-8
Apr 14	Les Remikie	l pts 6	NSC 9-11
Jun 3	Peter Till	w pts 10	Wolverhampton 9-7
	(vacant Midlands lightweight title)		
Sep 15	George Baigrie	w pts 8	Coventry 9-9-8
Oct 6	Muhammad Lovelock	w pts 8	Leicester 9-9
Oct 29	Andrew Williams	l pts 8	Ebbw Vale 9-9
Dec 1	George Baigrie	w dis 1	Nottingham 9-7
Dec 11	Ian McLeod	l pts 8	Livingstone 9-10

1987

Feb 16	Mervyn Bennett	w ko 8	Glasgow 9-10
Mar 24	Joey Joynson	l pts 8	Wembley 9-10-4
Apr 7	Mark Pearce	l pts 8	West Bromwich 9-10
Apr 14	Floyd Havard	l rsf 7	Cumbernauld 9-8
Oct 12	Brian Nickels	l pts 8	NSC
Oct 19	Tony Borg	l pts 8	Nottingham 9-8
Dec 11	Joey Dee	w pts 8	Coalville 9-8

1988

Feb 17	Wayne Weekes	w pts 8	Bethnal Green 9-10-8
Mar 8	Darren Connellan	w rsf 7	Batley 9-11
Apr 10	Aladin Stevens	l rsf 8	Eldorado Park 9-8
May 9	Ian Honeywood	w rsf 1	Nottingham 9-10-8
Jun 14	Peter Till	l pts 10	Dudley
	(Midlands lightweight title)		
Oct 31	Les Remikie	w pts 8	Leicester 9-9
Nov 11	Madjid Madjoub	l pts 8	Venissieux

1989
inactive

1990

Sep 25	Rocky Milton	l pts 6	Millwall 10-0-8
Nov 12	Brian Cullen	w pts 6	Stratford 10-0-8
Nov 30	Peter Till	l pts 8	Birmingham 9-11

1991

Apr 12	Henry Armstrong	l pts 8	Manchester 9-8

1992

Jan 22	Dean Bramhald	w pts 8	Solihull 10-5-8
Feb 11	Dean Bramhald	w rsf 7	Wolverhampton 10-3
Mar 24	Ronnie Shinkwin	w pts 8	Wolverhampton 10-2
May 18	Ronnie Shinkwin	w rsf 5	Bardon 10-2
Jul 2	Riki Burton	l pts 6	Middleton 10-0-8
Nov 10	Bernard Paul	drew 6	Dagenham 10-3

Fights 47 Won 25 Lost 19 Drawn 3

Shaun NORMAN

Flyweight
Leicester born 1 April 1970
Belgrave ABC
1989 Leics, Rutland & Northants ABA flyweight final (l I Baillie)
1990 Midlands ABA flyweight final (w rsf 3 I Baillie, l ko 3 R Williams)
1991 Leics, Rutland & Northants ABA flyweight final (l K Hassell)

1991
Nov 11	Louis Veitch	w rsf 5	Bradford 8-3
Nov 27	Dave Campbell	l pts 6	Marton
Dec 14	Micky Cantwell	l pts 8	Bexleyheath 8-2

1992
Feb 20	Dave Hardie	l pts 6	Glasgow 8-5
Apr 10	Neil Armstrong	drew 8	Glasgow 8-2-12
Apr 25	Naseem Hamed	l rsf 2	Manchester 8-2-8
Jun 16	Francis Ampofo	l rsf 4*	Dagenham 8-2
Oct 19	Alan Ley	l pts 6	Mayfair 8-3
Nov 23	Paul Weir	l pts 8	Glasgow 8-1-8

Fights 9 Won 1 Lost 7 Drawn 1

Ricky NORTH

Welterweight
Grimsby born 2 February 1968
Grimsby Exchange ABC
1990 Yorkshire & Humberside ABA welterweight semi-final (l rsf 2 P Waudby)
1991 Yorkshire & Humberside ABA welterweight final (l P Waudby)

1991
May 28	Michael Smyth	l rsf 1	Cardiff 10-8
Sep 16	Eddie King	w rsf 5*	Cleethorpes 10-5
Oct 21	Steve Bricknell	w pts 6	Cleethorpes 10-5
Nov 11	Darren McInulty	l pts 6	Stratford 10-7
Dec 9	Michael Byrne	w rsf 2	Cleethorpes 10-4

1992
Jan 23	Ron Hopley	l pts 6	York 10-4-8
Feb 19	Bernard Paul	l pts 6	Muswell Hill 10-2
Mar 11	Patrick Loughran	l pts 6	Stoke
Apr 22	Steve McNess	l pts 6	Wembley 10-8
Jun 3	Mark Dawson	l pts 6	Newcastle-under-Lyme 10-4
Sep 3	Andreas Panayi	drew 6	Liverpool
Sep 21	Hugh Davey	drew 6	Cleethorpes 10-8
Oct 5	Andrew Jervis	l pts 6	Liverpool 10-8
Oct 21	James Lawlor	w pts 6	Stoke 10-5
Oct 29	David Larkin	l pts 6	Leeds 11-0
Nov 20	Andreas Panayi	l pts 6	Liverpool 10-9
Dec 14	Lee Soar	w pts 6	Cleethorpes 10-6

Fights 17 Won 5 Lost 10 Drawn 2

Chris NURSE

Super-middleweight
Birmingham born 17 May 1968
No amateur experience

1992
Nov 24	Paul Hanlon	l pts 6	Wolverhampton 12-0

Fights 1 Lost 1

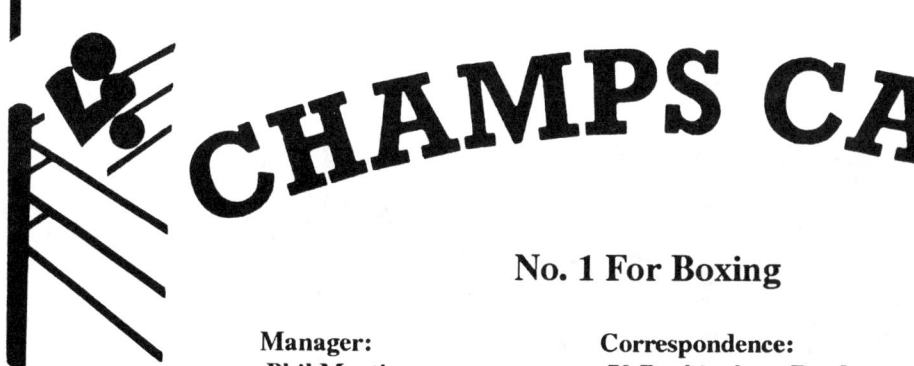

CHAMPS CAMP

No. 1 For Boxing

Manager:	Correspondence:	Gymnasium
Phil Martin	79 Buckingham Road	139 Princess Road
Tel: 061 881 7872 (Home)	Chorlton	Moss Side
061 226 4540 (Gym)	Manchester	Manchester
Fax: 061 226 3196	211QT	M14 4RE

BOXING TEAM

		Ranked
JOHN GREEN	Bantam	2
PETER JUDSON	Feather	16
HENRY ARMSTRONG	Feather	7
NICK BOYD	Super Feather	U/R
STEVE WALKER	Super Feather	10
PAUL BURKE	Light	2
TONY EKUBIA	Light Welter	Former British & Commonwealth Champ
DES ROBINSON	Welter	21
HUMPHREY HARRISON	Welter	11
CARL HARNEY	Light Middle	47
ENSLEY BINGHAM	Light Middle	7
QUINTON PAYNTER	Middle	11
ERIC NOI	Middle	U/R
FRANK GRANT	Middle	British Champion
FRANK EUBANKS	Super Middle	10
TREVOR DORE	Light Heavy	U/R
MAURICE "HARD" CORE	Light Heavy	British Champion
CARL THOMPSON	Cruiser	British Champion
STEVE GARBER	Heavy	9

TO ALL PROMOTERS

THESE VALUE-FOR-MONEY BOXERS ARE AVAILABLE FOR YOUR SHOWS

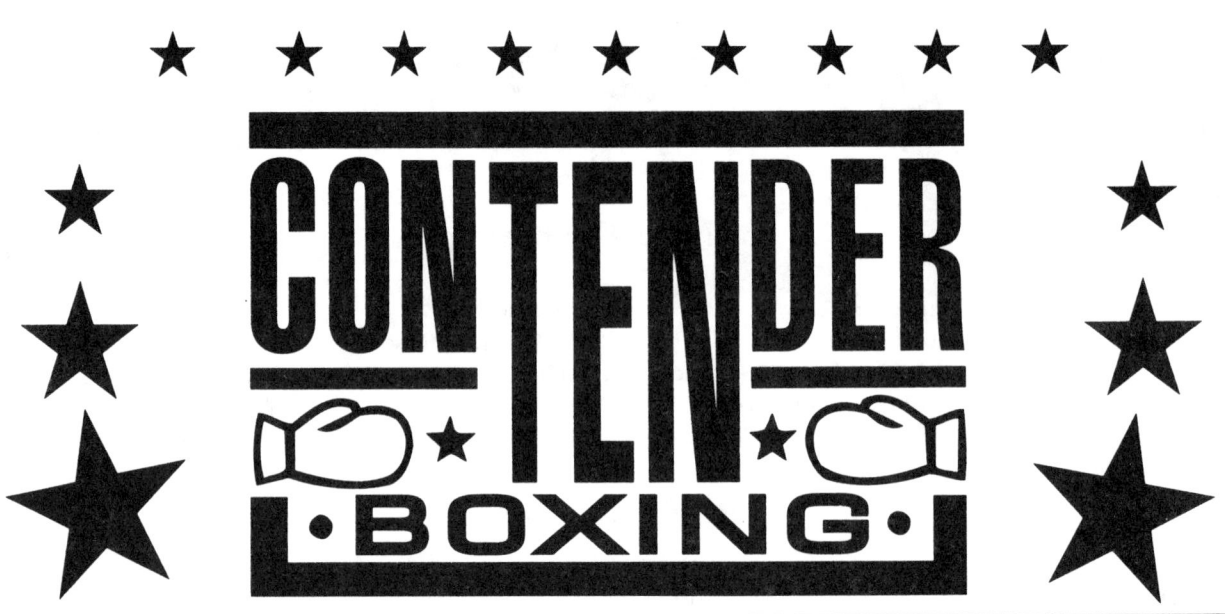

CONTENDER TEN BOXING

THE BEST BOXING SHOWROOM IN THE COUNTRY

AMATEUR OR PRO... IT'S THE PLACE TO GO!

Main stockist for:
LONSDALE, EVERLAST, TITLE
and our own **CONTENDER** range.

PENN SPORTS Unit 7 Sunbeam Studios, Sunbeam Street, Wolverhampton WV2 4PF.

Send S.A.E. for Price List.
24 hr Answerphone and Fax Service
Phone: 0902 715725   Fax: 0902 715726

Open: 9.30 - 5.00 Monday - Saturday
Closed: All day Wednesday

Prop: JOHN COYLE
(International Referee W.B.A.)

Dennis OAKES

Featherweight
St Helens, born Prescot 16 June 1966
Greenall St Helens ABC
1983 Junior ABA final
1985 NABC Class C champion
1985 West Lancs & Cheshire featherweight final (l rsf 1 P Hodkinson)
1987 West Lancs & Cheshire lightweight champion (w C Wright, l P Hampson)
1989 West Lancs & Cheshire featherweight prelims (l ko 1 J Sillitoe)

1992
Jan 22	Chris Lyons	w rsf 3	Stoke 8-10
Feb 10	Mark Hargreaves	w rsf 3	Liverpool 8-10
Mar 11	Des Gargano	w pts 6	Stoke 8-10
Sep 3	Colin Lynch	w rsf 1	Liverpool
Nov 2	Graham McGrath	w pts 4	Liverpool 8-9
Dec 1	Steve Robinson	l rtd 2*	Liverpool 8-13

Fights 6 Won 5 Lost 1

Marvin O'BRIAN

Middleweight
Leeds born 3 September 1966
Burmantofts ABC
Real name: David Powell

1990
Jan 31	Tony Hodge	l rsf 3*	Bethnal Green 12-0
Apr 4	Gary Osborne	l ko 2	Stafford 11-6-8
Sep 7	Mike Phillips	l rsf 1*	Liverpool 11-5
Nov 10	Mike Phillips	w pts 6	Liverpool 11-11

1991
Jan 17	Barry Messam	l pts 6	Alfreton 11-2
Feb 21	Russell Washer	drew 6	Walsall 11-8
Mar 1	Quinton Paynter	drew 6	Irvine 11-5
Mar 21	Nick Manners	l ko 2	Dewsbury 11-8
May 31	Carl Harney	w rsf 5	Manchester 11-10
Jun 24	Frank Eubanks	l pts 6	Liverpool 11-6
Sep 7	Cornelius Carr	l rsf 8	Salemi 11-9-4

1992
Mar 2	John Oxenham	l pts 6	Marton 12-7
Mar 26	John Ashton	l pts 8	Telford 11-12
Apr 5	Quinton Payntor	l pts 6	Bradford 11-10
May 17	Lester Jacobs	l pts 6	Harringay 11-10-12
Nov 20	Fran Harding	l rsf 4	Liverpool 11-12

Fights 16 Won 2 Lost 12 Drawn 2

Richard O'BRIEN

Welterweight
Alfreton, born Newton, Derbyshire 29 October 1971
No amateur experience

1990
May 14	Finn McCool	w rsf 3	Northampton 10-2	
May 21	Andy Rowbotham	w rsf 5	Bradford 10-4-8	
Jun 21	James Lawlor	drew 6	Alfreton 10-4	
Oct 16	Richard Swallow	w rtd 1*	Kettering	
Oct 22	Crain Fisher	l ko 3	Manchester 10-9	
Dec 13	Mickey Duncan	l pts 6	Dewsbury 10-11	/CTD..

(Richard O'BRIEN ctd.)

1991
Jan 17	Steve Hardman	l pts 6	Alfreton 10-9
Feb 11	Neil Porter	w rsf 4	Manchester 10-11-8
Feb 21	Darren Morris	w pts 6	Walsall 10-5
Mar 28	Trevor Ambrose	l rsf 1	Alfreton
Oct 21	Tony Connellan	l pts 8	Bury 10-7-8
Nov 21	Chris Mulcahy	w rsf 2	Ilkeston
Dec 2	Tony Britland	w rsf 2*	Birmingham 10-6

1992
Feb 4	Darren McInulty	w pts 4	Alfreton 10-8-8
Mar 3	Scott Doyle	l pts 4	Cradley Heath 10-9
May 21	Howard Clarke	l ko 1	Cradley Heath
Oct 23	Hugh Davey	l pts 6	Gateshead 10-10

Fights 17 Won 8 Lost 8 Drawn 1

Mark O'CALLAGHAN

Light-welterweight
Tunbridge Wells born 17 January 1969
Tunbridge Wells ABC
1990 Southern ABA light champ (w rsf 3 M Ghal, w ko 1 T Elcock, w rsf 2 A Ticehurst, l rsf 1 P Ramsey)
1991 Southern ABA light-welterweight semi-final (w J Bloomfield, l ko 1 T Turner)

1991
Oct 3	Chris Mylan	drew 6	Burton 9-9
Oct 24	Nico Lucas	w pts 6	Dunstable 9-13
Dec 11	Richie Joyce	l rsf 3	Stoke 9-11

1992
Feb 20	Allan McDowall	l pts 6	Glasgow 9-10
Nov 12	Erwin Edwards	l rsf 6*	Bayswater 9-13

Fights 5 Won 1 Lost 3 Drawn 1

John OGISTE

Middleweight
Islington born 16 July 1965
Colvestone ABC

1988
Dec 7	Robert Gomez	l rsf 4	NSC 11-11

1989
May 8	Dean Murray	w rsf 4	NSC 12-3-4
Sep 25	Jimmy McDonagh	w rsf 4	NSC 11-9
Nov 30	Stan King	drew 6	Marble Arch 11-8

1990
Apr 30	David Brown	drew 6	NSC 11-10-8
Jun 6	Martin Smith	l rsf 2*	Battersea 11-8

1991
Feb 18	Colin Manners	w pts 6	NSC 11-3
Mar 14	Colin Manners	w pts 8	Leeds
Jun 30	John Kaighin	w pts 6	Southwark 11-7-8
Oct 21	Darron Griffiths	l pts 6	AASC 11-5-12

1992
Feb 17	Darron Griffiths	l rsf 5	AASC 11-8-4
May 18	William Krijnen	l pts 8	Valkenswaard 11-7-12
Sep 15	Quinton Paynter	l pts 6	Liverpool 11-6

Fights 13 Won 5 Lost 6 Drawn 2

Richard OKUMU

Middleweight
Tottenham, born Uganda 18 December 1970
East African Games gold medal

1991
Feb 4	Benji Joseph	w pts 6	Leicester 10-10-8
Feb 18	Colin Pitters	l pts 6	Birmingham 11-3
Mar 5	Kevin Sheeran	w rsf 2	Millwall 10-13-8
Oct 24	Benji Good	w ko 6	Bayswater 11-10-12
Dec 5	Andy Flute	drew 8	Cannock 11-10

1992
Jan 22	Darron Griffiths	l pts 8	Solihull 11-10
Oct 22	Roberto Welin	w rsf 2	Bethnal Green 11-3-12
Nov 26	Ian Chantler	w rsf 2*	Mayfair 11-0-8

Fights 8 Won 5 Lost 2 Drawn 1

Michael OLIVER

Welterweight
Cefn Hengoed, born Caerphilly 1 December 1969
Fleur de Lys ABC
1984 National Schools final (l T Collins)
1987 Welsh ABA light-welterweight final (w dis 3 J Williams, w ko 3 J Hudd, l D Jenkins)
1988 Welsh ABA light-welter final (w rsf 3 K Hammond, w rsf 3 C Stevens, w rsf 3 T Harris, l rsf 1 M Smyth)

1988
Jun 6	Dave Pierre	w pts 6	Northampton 9-12
Jun 17	James Lawlor	drew 6	Edgbaston 9-13
Jul 10	Gary Baker	w rsf 2	Eastbourne 10-3
Aug 9	David Bacon	w pts 6	St Helier 10-8
Aug 30	Dom Barry	w rsf 2	Bristol 10-9-8
Sep 20	Darren Mount	l pts 6	Stoke 10-2
Oct 10	James Lawlor	w rsf 4	Edgbaston 10-3-12
Oct 31	Spencer Alton	l rsf 2	Leicester 10-4
Dec 7	Tony Britland	w rsf 2*	Port Talbot 10-8
Dec 20	Dave Worthington	l rsf 4	Swansea 10-9-8

1989
Apr 27	Simon Eubanks	l pts 6	Mayfair 10-3
May 8	Brian Cullen	w rsf 5*	Manchester
Jun 22	Richard Adams	l pts 6	Stevenage 9-12
Jul 21	Mauro Corrente	l rsf 4	Tarkunia 9-13

1990
inactive

1991
Oct 24	Adrian Riley	l pts 6	Dunstable 10-11
Nov 13	Jamie Robinson	l pts 6	Bethnal Green 10-13
Nov 28	Robert McCracken	l rsf 3	Liverpool 10-10-8

1992
Feb 1	Ernie Loveridge	l pts 8	Birmingham 10-9
Feb 9	Ossie Maddix	l rsf 3	Bradford 10-7

Fights 20 Won 8 Lost 11 Drawn 1

Graham O'MALLEY

Featherweight
Middlesbrough born 9 January 1963
Wellington ABC
1985 North-East Division ABA bantamweight final (l G Rushworth)

1987
Apr 23	Jimmy Lee	l rtd 5*	Newcastle 9-0
Nov 24	Carl Gaynor	w rsf 1	Middlesbrough 9-0
Nov 30	Paul Chedgzoy	w rsf 3	Manchester 9-0
Dec 2	Derek Amory	l pts 8	Birmingham 9-0

1988
Jan 26	Des Gargano	w pts 4	Hartlepool 8-8
Feb 1	Nigel Crook	w pts 8	Manchester 8-6
Feb 29	Dave Adam	l pts 6	Glasgow 9-1-8
Mar 29	Des Gargano	w pts 8	Middlesbrough 8-11
Jun 29	Glen Dainty	w ko 2	Basildon 8-6-12
Sep 10	Thierry Jacob	l pts 8	Grand-Synthe
Oct 25	Donnie Hood	l rsf 9*	Hartlepool 8-6
	(eliminator, British bantamweight title)		

1989
Jan 31	Joe Kelly	l pts 8	Glasgow 8-8
Apr 27	John Lowey	l pts 8	Mayfair 9-1-8
May 6	Fabrizio Cappai	l rsf 4*	Syracusa 8-10
Sep 19	Colin McMillan	l pts 8	Millwall 9-0-8
Oct 16	Henry Armstrong	l pts 8	Manchester 9-1
Oct 28	Herve Jacob	l pts 8	Lille

1990
Jan 31	Tim Driscoll	l pts 8	Bethnal Green 9-5
May 23	Richie Wenton	l pts 6	Belfast 8-13-8
Sep 15	Richie Wenton	l pts 6	Belfast 9-1
Sep 25	Mario Culpepper	l pts 6	Glasgow 8-13
Oct 10	Colin McMillan	l pts 6	Millwall 9-2
Nov 28	Hichem Dahmani	drew 8	Geneva

1991
Apr 26	Daniel Londas	l pts 10	Reims
Jul 5	Mehdi Labdouni	l pts 6	Autun
Nov 18	Noel Carroll	l pts 6	Manchester

1992
Jan 28	Mike Deveney	w rsf 1	Piccadilly 9-4
Mar 10	Carl Roberts	w pts 6	Bury 9-4
Mar 31	Richie Wenton	l pts 6	Stockport 9-2
May 14	Jimmy Owens	l pts 6	Liverpool 9-5

Fights 30 Won 8 Lost 21 Drawn 1

Chip O'NEILL

Featherweight
Sunderland born 10 December 1963
Full name: Michael O'Neill
Hylton Castle ABC & Sunderland ABC
1981 Northern ABA flyweight final (w rsf 2 S Black, l rsf 2 K Wallace)
1982 North-East Division ABA bantamweight final (l rsf 2 B Hardy)

1982
Jun 28	Charlie Brown	l pts 6	Bradford
Sep 20	Danny Flynn	l rsf 2	Glasgow

1983
Mar 7	Charlie Brown	l rsf 3	Glasgow

1984-91 inactive

1992
Apr 28	Robert Braddock	w pts 6	Houghton-le-Spring 9-2
Sep 10	Vince Wilson	w rsf 1	Sunderland 9-2
Sep 21	Ian McGirr	l pts 6	Glasgow 9-2-8
Oct 5	Phil Lashley	w pts 6	Manchester 9-1
Nov 9	Robert Braddock	l rsf 3	Bradford 9-1

Fights 8 Won 3 Lost 5

Sean O'PHOENIX

Light-heavyweight
Manchester born Glossop 16 September 1963
Real name: John Phoenix
CIE Dublin ABC
1982 Ireland (v USA, l R Burton)
1983 Ireland (v Sco, w G Watson; v Wal, w ko 3 S Morgan)
1984 Irish ABA middleweight champion (w T Corr)
1984 Ireland (v Sco, w G Ferrie; v Pol, l H Petrich)

1984
Nov 26	Alan Baptiste	drew 6	Sheffield 11-8-8
Dec 5	Mark Watts	w rsf 1*	Stoke 11-8-8

1985
Feb 5	Simon Harris	l pts 6	Battersea 11-12
Mar 11	Seamus Casey	w pts 6	Manchester 11-9
Mar 20	Seamus Casey	w pts 6	Stoke 11-6-8
Apr 15	Gary Tomlinson	w pts 6	Manchester 11-8
Apr 29	Mark Watts	w rsf 3*	Nottingham 11-8
May 14	Gary Tomlinson	drew 6	Mansfield 11-9-8
Jun 3	David Scere	w pts 6	Manchester 11-7-12
Oct 14	Sean West	w rtd 2	Leicester 11-8
Oct 21	Alan Baptiste	w pts 8	Nottingham 11-9
Dec 9	Sammy Brennan	l pts 6	Liverpool 11-9

1986
Feb 5	Sammy Storey	l pts 6	Sheffield 11-8-8
Mar 18	Mark Walker	drew 8	Hull 11-13
Apr 14	T.P.Jenkins	l pts 8	NSC 12-2
Jun 16	Mike Farghaly	w rsf 6	Manchester
Sep 15	Dave Mowbray	w dis 3	Manchester 12-7
Oct 27	Blaine Logsdon	l ko 3	Liverpool 12-6
Nov 26	Tommy Taylor	l rsf 3*	Wolverhampton 12-6

1987
Mar 18	Harry Cowap (Irish light-heavyweight title)	l rsf 8	Queensway 12-4

1988 inactive

1989
Mar 7	Carl Thompson	l rsf 4	Manchester 12-6
Oct 20	Tony Lawrence	w pts 6	Manchester 12-2
Dec 7	Simon McDougall	w pts 6	Manchester 12-2

1990
Feb 6	Steve Foster	l rsf 4*	Oldham 11-9-8
Apr 9	Terry French	drew 8	Manchester 12-0
May 1	Ahmet Canbakis	drew 4	Oldham 11-12 /CTD..

(Sean O'PHOENIX ctd.)

Sep 24	Dave Owens	w pts 8	Manchester 12-3
Nov 26	Glenn Campbell	l rsf 4	Bury 11-12-4
	(vacant Central super-middleweight title)		
1991			
Mar 18	Tony Lawrence	w pts 8	Manchester 12-2-4
Apr 3	Terry French	w pts 8	Manchester 12-2-12
1992			
Oct 29	Denzil Browne	l rsf 4	Leeds 13-0
Dec 9	Trevor Small	l pts 6	Stoke 12-7

Fights 32 Won 15 Lost 12 Drawn 5

Gary OSBORNE
Light-middleweight
Walsall born 24 August 1963
Birmingham City ABC
1988 Birmingham ABA light-middleweight final (l R Woodhall)

1989			
May 8	Peter Reid	w ko 5	Edgbaston 11-2-8
1990			
Mar 22	Peter Reid	w ko 1	Wolverhampton 10-13
Apr 4	Marvin O'Brian	w ko 2	Stafford 11-2
May 24	Julian Eavis	w pts 6	Dudley 10-9-8
Sep 18	Paul Hanlon	w rtd 2*	Wolverhampton 11-2
Oct 17	Chris Richards	w pts 8	Stoke 11-2
Dec 6	Darren Morris	w pts 8	Wolverhampton 10-8-8
1991			
Apr 10	Micky Lerwill	w pts 10	Wolverhampton 10-7
	(vacant Midlands welterweight title)		
Sep 10	Ernie Loveridge	l rsf 1	Wolverhampton 10-6-8
	(Midlands welterweight title)		
1992			
Mar 17	Seamus Casey	w rsf 5	Wolverhampton 10-13-12
	(vacant Midlands light-middleweight title)		
Apr 28	Gary Pemberton	w ko 3	Wolverhampton 11-2

Fights 11 Won 10 Lost 1

Steve OSBORNE
Light-heavyweight
Nottingham born 27 June 1965
Bulwell Red Lion ABC

1987			
May 29	Gary Railton	l pts 6	Jarrow 12-13
Jun 9	Ian Bulloch	l pts 6	Manchester 13-0
Sep 24	Bobby Frankham	l pts 6	Glasgow 13-6
Oct 5	Ray Thomas	l rsf 8	NSC 13-0
Dec 14	Branko Pavlovlic	l rsf 3	Bedford 13-0
1988			
inactive			
1989			
Jan 16	Simon McDougall	w pts 6	Bradford 12-10
Jan 25	Simon McDougall	w pts 6	Stoke 13-2
Feb 2	Dave Furneaux	w ko 4	Southwark 13-0-8

Feb 13	Carl Thompson	l pts 6	Manchester 12-12
Mar 6	Jim Cropper	w pts 6	Manchester 12-12
Apr 5	Jim Cropper	l pts 6	Halifax 12-12
May 16	Henry Brewer	w pts 6	Halifax 13-3
Jun 12	Carl Thompson	l pts 8	Manchester 12-10
Nov 16	Dave Lawrence	w pts 6	Ilkeston 12-10-8
Dec 19	Herbie Hide	l rsf 6	Bethnal Green
1990			
Feb 5	Dave Lawrence	w pts 8	NSC 13-2
Feb 20	Rob Albon	l pts 6	Brentford 13-9
Mar 3	Darren Westover	l rsf 6	Wembley 13-8
Nov 15	Michael Gale	l pts 6	Oldham 13-2
Dec 8	Niels H. Madsen	l rsf 5	Aalborg
1991			
Apr 16	Art Stacey	drew 6	Nottingham 12-10-8
May 9	Michael Gale	l rsf 2	Leeds 12-12
Nov 11	Art Stacey	l pts 6	Bradford 13-6
Nov 21	Bruce Scott	l pts 6	Burton
Nov 29	Maurice Core	l pts 6	Manchester 12-12
1992			
Feb 12	Phil Soundy	l pts 6	Wembley GH 13-2
Nov 12	Terry Dunstan	l pts 6	Bayswater 13-2
Dec 10	Ole Klemetsen	l rsf 1	Bethnal Green 13-0

Fights 28 Won 7 Lost 20 Drawn 1

Clay O'SHEA

Light-middleweight
Islington born 3 November 1966
St Pancras ABC, Repton ABC & Islington ABC
1983 London Junior ABA final (l D Dyer)

1990			
Feb 20	Calton Myers	w rsf 1	Brentford 10-12
Mar 14	Tony Grizzle	w rsf 1	Albert Hall 10-13
Oct 4	Benji Good	w ko 2	Bethnal Green 11-2-8
Oct 30	Remy Duverger	w pts 6	Wembley 11-1-8
1991			
Apr 4	Robert Peel	w pts 6	Watford 10-13
Sep 11	Seamus Casey	w pts 6	Hammersmith 11-1
Sep 26	Tony Wellington	w ko 1	Dunstable 11-2-4
1992			
Mar 25	Andrew Furlong	drew 6	Albert Hall 11-0-8
May 13	Andrew Furlong	drew 6	Albert Hall 11-1-8
Oct 15	Steve Thomas	w pts 6	Catford 11-5-8
Dec 17	Mark Jay	w ko 1	Wembley GH 11-1-8

Fights 10 Won 8 Drawn 2

Slugger O'TOOLE   See   Fidel CASTRO

Dave OWENS
Light-heavyweight
Castleford born 11 December 1954
Airedale ABC & Castleford ABC
1973 Northern ABA light-middleweight final (w rtd 1 B Gregory, w rsf 1 R Nairns, l ko 1 R Davies)
1974 Northern ABA light-heavyweight final (w ko 1 M Taylor, w W Holbrook, withdrew)
1975 North-East ABA middleweight final (l P Jackson)
1976 South-West Yorkshire ABA middleweight final (l D Bickerdyke)

1976
May 12	Steve Heavisides	w rsf 2	Bradford
Jun 8	Joe Jackson	w pts 4	Bradford
Sep 10	Carl McCarthy	w ko 2	Birmingham
Sep 21	Steve Fenton	w rsf 3	Bethnal Green
Sep 27	Neville Estaban	drew 6	NSC
Nov 30	Owen Robinson	w pts 6	Leeds

1977
Apr 20	Billy Hill	w rsf 2	Manchester
Apr 27	Jim Moore	w pts 8	Bradford
May 15	Howard Mills	w rsf 8	Manchester
Jul 10	Pat Brogan	w rsf 9	Birmingham
	(vacant Central middleweight title)		

1978
Mar 13	Paul Shutt	w rsf 2	Nottingham
May 8	Howard Mills	l rtd 4	Nottingham
Sep 4	Glen McEwan	l ko 1	Wakefield
Dec 7	Torben Andersen	l pts 6	Copenhagen

1979
Mar 12	Romal Ambrose	l pts 8	Manchester
Sep 20	Dave Davies	w ko 3	Liverpool
Oct 17	Jimmy Pickard	w rsf 4	NSC
	(Central middleweight title)		

1980
Apr 29	Eddie Smith	l ko 1	Stockport
Aug 12	Doug James	l pts 8	Gowerton
Oct 13	Earl Edwards	l rsf 3	Windsor

1981-84 inactive

1985
Sep 3	Barry Ahmed	drew 6	Gateshead 12-0-8
Sep 20	Simon Harris	w pts 6	Longford 12-2
Oct 25	Aneurin Williams	w pts 8	Fulham 12-7-8

1986
Jan 20	Tony Wilson	l rsf 2	NSC 12-10
Dec 1	Pedro van Raamsdonk	l ko 1	Arnhem 12-9-8

1987
Mar 2	Peter Brown	l pts 8	Huddersfield 12-7
May 5	Seamus Casey	w pts 6	Leeds 12-6
Nov 18	John Foreman	w rsf 5	Solihull 12-8-12
Dec 5	Darryl Ritchie	l dis 7	Doncaster 12-4-8

1988
Feb 7	Brian Schumacher	l ko 1	Stafford 12-4-8
Nov 28	John Foreman	l ko 1	Edgbaston 12-2-12

1989
Jan 31	Adam Cook	drew 6	Reading 12-4
Mar 13	James Wray Harkin	l pts 6	Glasgow 12-2
Apr 29	Jose Seys	l rsf 6	Waregem 12-5-8
Nov 20	Steve Williams	drew 6	Glasgow 12-6

Dec 19	Nicky Piper	l ko 1	Gorleston 12-6
1990			
Apr 6	Everton Blake	l rsf 6	Stevenage 12-9
May 14	Joe Frater	w pts 6	Cleethorpes 12-9
Sep 24	Sean O'Phoenix	l pts 8	Manchester 12-3
Oct 8	Darren McKenna	w pts 6	Leicester 12-8
Oct 29	Fidel Castro	l pts 6	Birmingham 12-7
Nov 18	Sean Heron	l pts 8	NEC 12-7
Dec 6	Gil Lewis	l ko 2	Wolverhampton 12-3
1991			
Feb 17	Anton Josipovic	l pts 8	Prijedor
Mar 24	Christophe Girard	l rsf 7	Vichy
Apr 23	Joe Frater	w pts 6	Evesham 12-7-8
May 27	Eddy Smulders	l rsf 1	Rotterdam 12-5-12
Nov 14	Ian Henry	l pts 8	Gateshead 12-4-4
1992			
Mar 3	Terry French	w ko 1	Houghton-le-Spring 12-8
Mar 26	Tony Booth	l pts 6	Hull 12-8
Apr 14	Martin Smith	l pts 6	Mansfield 11-12
Oct 26	Joe Frater	w pts 6	Cleethorpes 12-10
Nov 27	Bernard Bonzon	l rsf 5	Geneva

Fights 53 Won 21 Lost 28 Drawn 4

Jimmy OWENS

Super-featherweight
Liverpool born 15 February 1966
Army
Southpaw

1990			
Jan 29	Greg Egbuniwe	w pts 6	Hull 9-4
Mar 6	Steve Armstrong	w pts 4	Stoke 9-3
May 4	Martin Evans	w rsf 2	Liverpool 9-2
May 21	Kruga Hydes	w pts 6	Hanley 9-1
Sep 7	Nigel Senior	w pts 6	Liverpool 9-3
Nov 10	Martin Evans	w rsf 3	Liverpool 9-3
1991			
May 1	Peter Judson	w pts 6	Liverpool 8-13
May 16	Des Gargano	w rsf 2*	Liverpool 9-4-8
Jun 24	Miguel Matthews	w pts 6	Liverpool 9-1
Sep 9	Russell Davison	l pts 10	Liverpool 8-13
	(Central featherweight title)		
1992			
May 14	Graham O'Malley	w pts 6	Liverpool 9-5-4

Fights 11 Won 10 Lost 1

John OXENHAM

Light-heavyweight
Doncaster born 11 June 1968
Bentley ABC & Elmfield House ABC
1988 Humberside & Yorkshire ABA light-heavyweight final (w ko 1 M Brook, l rsf 2 M Gale)
1990 Yorkshire ABA light-heavyweight champion (w rsf 3 G Wassell, l I Meredith)

1990
Sep 4	Benji Good	w rsf 6	Southend 12-6

1991
May 13	Shaun McCrory	l pts 6	Middlesbrough 12-4
Oct 9	Dennis Afflick	w dis 4	Middlesbrough 12-10
Oct 24	Maurice Thomas	w rsf 6	Glasgow 12-7
Nov 27	Ian Henry	l pts 6	Marton

1992
Mar 2	Marvin O'Brian	w pts 6	Marton 12-8
Apr 27	Joe McCluskey	l pts 4	Glasgow 12-9
May 18	Andy Manning	w pts 6	Marton 12-7
Sep 3	Joey Peters	l pts 6	Dunstable 12-10
Nov 10	Gary Delaney	l ko 5	Dagenham 12-11

Fights 10 Won 5 Lost 5

Mark PAINE

Light-heavyweight
Wolverhampton born 7 April 1972
Real name: Mark Leslie

1991
Oct 3	Jason McNeill	w pts 6	Burton 12-7

1992
Feb 12	Vic Wright	w rsf 1	Watford 13-0
Jun 3	Kevin Morton	l pts 6	Newcastle-under-Lyme 12-8
Sep 9	Glyn Rhodes	l pts 6	Stoke 11-12
Dec 3	Bruce Scott	l rsf 5	Catford 13-5

Fights 5 Won 2 Lost 3

Andreas PANAYI

Welterweight
St Helens, born Cyprus 14 July 1969

1990
Nov 21	Trevor Ambrose	l rsf 5	Solihull 10-9

1991
Feb 4	Cliff Churchward	w pts 6	Leicester 10-8
Feb 12	Eddie King	w ko 2	Wolverhampton 10-8
Feb 27	Trevor Meikle	l pts 6	Wolverhampton
Apr 15	Mick Mulcahy	w rsf 2	Leicester 10-7
Apr 24	Darren Morris	drew 6	Stoke 10-7
Sep 11	Robert Riley	w pts 6	Stoke 10-3
Sep 30	Steve Hardman	w rsf 5	Liverpool 10-5
Oct 23	Darren Morris	w pts 6	Stoke 10-6
Nov 25	Marvin P. Gray	w pts 8	Liverpool 10-3
Dec 11	Mark Kelly	drew 8	Stoke 10-3

1992
Mar 11	Dean Bramhald	l pts 8	Stoke
May 14	Dave Maj	w ko 6	Liverpool 10-5
Sep 3	Ricky North	drew 6	Liverpool
Oct 5	John O. Johnson	w rtd 1*	Liverpool 10-7
Oct 23	Trevor Meikle	w pts 6	Liverpool 10-9
Nov 20	Ricky North	w pts 6	Liverpool 10-10
Dec 15	Mark Kelly	w pts 8	Liverpool 10-9

Fights 18 Won 12 Lost 3 Drawn 3

Delwyn PANAYIOTIOU

Welterweight
Llanelli born 26 September 1967
Gwent ABC

1992
Sep 7	Sean Baker	l rsf 2	Southend 10-5

Fights 1 Lost 1

Wayne PANAYIOTIOU
Light-middleweight
Llanelli born 19 October 1965
Gwent ABC
1988 Welsh ABA light-middleweight semi-final (l rsf 1 W Ellis)
1990 Welsh ABA light-middleweight prelim (l rsf 2 W Hughes)

1990
Oct 16	Russell Washer	l rsf 2*	Evesham 11-3

1991
Jan 24	Russell Washer	l rsf 4*	Gorseinon 11-11
Dec 9	Stuart Dunn	l ko 4	Brierley Hill 11-0

1992
Sep 8	Raziq Ali	l pts 6	Doncaster 10-10
Sep 15	Carl Wright	l rsf 2	Liverpool 10-7
Dec 1	Sean Baker	l rsf 3	Bristol 10-12

Fights 6 Lost 6

Neil PARRY
Bantamweight
Middlesbrough born 21 June 1969
Phil Thomas School of Boxing ABC & Lambton Street ABC
1988 North-East England ABA bantamweight semi-final (l J Davison)
1989 North East England ABA bantamweight final (w rsf 3 W Wastle, l M Gibbons)

1989
Jun 12	Des Gargano	l pts 6	Manchester 8-6
Dec 21	Kevin Jenkins	l pts 6	Kings Heath 8-8

1990
Jan 31	Francis Ampofo	l pts 6	Bethnal Green 8-5
Mar 12	Paul Dever	w pts 6	Hull
Mar 19	James Drummond	l rsf 4	Glasgow 8-6-4
Nov 27	Stevie Wood	w pts 6	Glasgow 8-6-8
Dec 4	Con McMullan	l rsf 2	Southend 8-7

1991
Jan 21	Stevie Wood	l pts 6	Glasgow 8-7
Feb 6	Paul Dever	w pts 6	Liverpool 8-6
Mar 5	Tony Smith	drew 6	Leicester 8-6
Apr 24	Paul Dever	drew 6	Stoke 8-4
May 17	Gary White	l pts 6	Bury 8-7
Jun 3	Stevie Wood	w rsf 2	Glasgow 8-7
Jun 20	Tony Smith	w pts 6	Liverpool
Sep 12	Mark Tierney	l pts 6	Battersea 8-3
Oct 21	Neil Johnston	l pts 8	Glasgow 8-3-8

1992
Jan 27	Drew Docherty	l rsf 4	Glasgow 8-7
Feb 28	Stevie Wood	w pts 6	Irvine 8-8
May 11	Tim Yeates	l pts 6	Piccadilly 8-11
Sep 21	Paul Weir	l rsf 4	Glasgow 8-4-8
Nov 27	Eyup Can	l pts 6	Randers 8-6

Fights 21 Won 6 Lost 13 Drawn 2

Elvis PARSLEY

Featherweight
Bloxwich, born Walsall 6 December 1962
Wednesbury ABC
1988 South Midlands ABA featherweight final (w rsf 1 G Marston, l K Kearney)
1990 South Midlands ABA featherweight final (l Y Vorajee)

1990
Jun 4	Phil Lashley	w rsf 3	Birmingham 9-0
Jun 20	Mark Bates	l ko 1	Basildon 9-3
Sep 27	Andrew Robinson	w rtd 3*	NEC 9-4
Dec 10	Karl Taylor	w pts 6	Birmingham 9-3

1991
Feb 18	Peter Campbell	w rsf 3	Derby 9-7
May 1	Neil Leitch	w ko 2	Solihull 9-3-8
May 20	Neil Smith	l rsf 5	Leicester 9-5
Oct 2	Muhammad Shaffique	w ko 1	Solihull 9-2

1992
Apr 29	Kelton McKenzie	l rsf 5	Solihull 8-12
	(vacant Midlands featherweight title)		

Fights 9 Won 6 Lost 3

Neil PATTERSON

Light-middleweight
Darlington, born Sedgefield 21 April 1962
Darlington ABC
1980 Young England (v EGer, l rsf 1 H Frehse)
1980 Northern ABA light-flyweight final (w M Priestly, l J Lyon)

1984
Mar 22	Gary Champion	l pts 6	Maidenhead 9-13
Apr 30	Alistair Laurie	l pts 6	Glasgow 10-0
Oct 11	Chris McReedy	w pts 6	Barnsley 10-3
Dec 4	John Faulkner	w pts 6	Southend 10-2

1985
Feb 2	Andy O'Rawe	w pts 6	Darlington 10-2
Feb 23	Gary Muire	l pts 6	Belfast 10-1
Apr 13	Nicky Day	w pts 6	Darlington 10-0-12
Oct 3	Young Tony Carroll	w pts 6	Liverpool 9-13-12
Nov 21	Ken Foreman	l pts 10	Hartlepool 10-3
	(vacant Northern welterweight title)		

1986
Feb 24	Billy Buchanan	l pts 6	Glasgow 10-4
Mar 20	Karl Ince	l pts 6	Blackpool 10-7

1987
Feb 5	Seamus Casey	w pts 6	Newcastle 11-2
Feb 26	Robert Armstrong	l ko 4	Hartlepool 11-2-8
Apr 30	John Mullen	w pts 6	Washington 10-10
May 22	Mike McKenzie	w rsf 5	Peterlee 10-12
Sep 23	Mark Holden	w rsf 4	Stoke 10-12
Oct 8	Johnny Andrews	w rsf 4	Bethnal Green 10-12
Nov 24	Ossie Maddix	l rsf 6	Middlesbrough 10-13

1988
Jan 26	Ken Foreman	l rsf 6	Hartlepool 10-11
	(vacant Northern light-middleweight title)		/CTD..

(Neil PATTERSON ctd.)
1989
Jan 27	Spencer Alton	l ko 1	Durham 11-0

1990-91 inactive

1992
Dec 10	Mark Jay	l pts 6	Hartlepool 11-1

Fights 21 Won 10 Lost 11

Steve PATTON
Super-featherweight
Wembley born Ballyshannon, Ireland, 3 August 1970

1992
Feb 12	Jasdeep Singh	w rsf 1*	Watford 9-4
Dec 7	Marco Fattore	l rsf 6*	Mayfair 9-7

Fights 2 Won 1 Lost 1

Bernard PAUL
Light-welterweight
Tottenham, born Mauritius 22 October 1965
Islington ABC, Finchley ABC, New Enterprise ABC
1988 London ABA lightweight final (w rsf 2 E Brown, w N Dickinson, l S Nolan)

1991
May 1	Trevor Royal	w ko 1	Bethnal Green 10-0-8
Jun 4	David Jenkins	w rsf 1	Bethnal Green 10-1-8
Sep 24	Patrick Delargy	w rsf 5	Basildon 10-2
Oct 26	Gordon Webster	w rsf 4	Brentwood 10-0
Nov 26	John O. Johnson	w pts 6	Bethnal Green 10-2

1992
Feb 19	Rick North	w pts 6	Muswell Hill 9-13-6
Mar 17	Mick Mulcahy	w pts 6	Mayfair 10-0-12
Jun 16	Brendan Ryan	w ko 6	Dagenham 10-1
Oct 13	Dean Bramhald	drew 6	Mayfair 9-13-14
Nov 10	Ray Newby	drew 6	Dagenham 10-0
Dec 12	Michael Driscoll	l rsf 2*	Muswell Hill 10-0-4

Fights 11 Won 8 Lost 1 Drawn 2

Quinton PAYNTER
Middleweight
Manchester, born Bermuda 19 August 1965
PYC Bermuda ABC 5ft 9in
1988 Seoul Olympics light-middleweight (l ko 2 V Nardiello, Ita)

1989
Oct 12	Willie Beattie	l pts 8	Glasgow 11-2
Oct 20	Paul Hendrick	w rsf 5*	Manchester

1990
Jan 11	Tommy McCallum	w ko 2	Dewsbury 11-3
Jan 15	Benji Good	w pts 6	NSC 11-3
Feb 23	Mike Paul	w rtd 4	Irvine 11-4

Mar 6	Graeme Watson	w pts 6	Glasgow 11-10
Mar 26	George Ferrie	w rsf 6	Glasgow 11-10
May 4	Fran Harding	l pts 6	Liverpool 11-4
Aug 17	Hector Rosario	l pts 8	Hamilton, Bermuda 11-8
Dec 10	Gordon Blair	l pts 6	Glasgow 11-4
1991			
Jan 21	W.O.Wilson	w pts 8	Crystal Palace 11-5
Mar 1	Marvin O'Brian	drew 6	Irvine 11-2
May 16	Ali Forbes	drew 6	Battersea 11-3
Nov 14	Terry French	w ko 6	Gateshead 12-1
1992			
Jan 18	Val Golding	w rsf 7	Albert Hall 11-11
Apr 5	Marvin O'Brian	w pts 6	Bradford 11-5-8
Jul 18	Chris Richards	w rsf 6	Manchester 11-10-12
Sep 15	John Ogiste	w pts 6	Liverpool 11-8
Sep 28	Stinger Mason	w ko 1	Manchester 11-11

Fights 19 Won 13 Lost 4 Lost 2

Glen PAYTON

Middleweight
Telford born Gateshead 15 May 1964
Real name: Glen Kennedy
Telford ABC & Wrekin School of Boxing ABC
1984 Birmingham ABA middleweight champion (w rsf 1* T Meszaros, withdrew)
1986 South Midlands ABA middleweight final (l G Baker)

1991			
Oct 31	Wilf McGee	w rsf 6*	Telford 11-5
Dec 5	John Baxter	w rsf 3	Telford 11-4
1992			
Feb 20	Paul Hanlon	w pts 6	Telford 11-8
Mar 26	Chris Richards	l pts 6	Telford

Fights 4 Won 3 Lost 1

Andy PEACH

Light-middleweight
Bloxwich
Pleck ABC
1989 Staffordshire ABA light-middleweight semi-final (l rsf 2 P Spencer)
1990 Staffordshire ABA light-middleweight semi-final (l rsf 2 K Reeves)
1991 Staffordshire ABA light-middleweight semi-final (l M Lee)
1992 South Staffs ABA light-middleweight final (w ko 3 P Lewis, l D Bain)

1992			
Oct 27	Stuart Dunn	l rsf 3	Leicester 11-2
Dec 9	Jason Fores	w pts 6	Stoke 11-0

Fights 2 Won 1 Lost 1

Alan PEACOCK

Light-welterweight
Cumbernauld, born Glasgow 17 February 1969
Condorrat ABC
1989 Scottish ABA light-welterweight prelims (l J Townsley)

1990
Feb 23	Gary Quigley	w pts 6	Irvine 9-13
Mar 6	Gary Quigley	w pts 6	Glasgow 10-4
May 29	John Ritchie	w pts 6	Glasgow
Jun 11	Chris Mulcahy	w rsf 3	Manchester 10-4-12
Sep 17	John Ritchie	w pts 6	Glasgow 10-1-8
Oct 9	Dave Anderson	l rsf 3*	Glasgow 10-1
Nov 27	Stuart Rimmer	w rsf 4	Glasgow 9-12

1991
Feb 11	Oliver Harrison	l rsf 6	Glasgow 10-0
Mar 18	Darren Mount	w pts 8	Glasgow 10-1-8
Mar 27	Giovanni Parisi	l pts 6	Venice 9-11-8
Apr 6	Allan Hall	l pts 6	Darlington 10-0
May 25	Giorgio Campanella	l ko 1	Trezzano Sul Naviglio
Sep 23	Trevor Meikle	l pts 6	Glasgow 10-5
Nov 27	Dave Whittle	l pts 6	Marton

1992
Jan 28	Trevor Meikle	w pts 8	Piccadilly 10-3-12
Feb 20	John O.Johnson	l pts 6	Glasgow 10-1-12
Mar 4	Rob Stewart	drew 8	Glasgow 10-2
Mar 12	Dave Whittle	drew 8	Glasgow 10-2
Mar 30	Peter Bradley	l pts 8	Glasgow 10-1-8
Oct 7	John Smith	tdraw 6*	Glasgow 10-2-8
Nov 18	Dave Lovell	w pts 6	Solihull 10-2

Fights 21 Won 9 Lost 9 Drawn 3

Robert PEEL

Light-middleweight
Llandovery, born Birmingham 11 January 1969
Towy ABC
1990 Welsh ABA middleweight prelims (l S Walters)

1991
Jan 24	John Kaighin	w pts 6	Gorseinon 11-5
Feb 12	John Kaighin	l pts 6	Cardiff 11-4-8
Mar 13	Andy Flute	l pts 6	Stoke 11-6
Apr 4	Clay O'Shea	l pts 6	Watford 11-2
Apr 11	Adrian Wright	l rsf 6	Willenhall 11-7
May 15	John Kaighin	w pts 8	Swansea 11-4
Oct 29	Jason Matthews	l rsf 6*	Cardiff 11-0-12

1992
Feb 3	Warren Stowe	l pts 6	Manchester 11-3-4
Mar 2	Steve Thomas	drew 6	Merthyr 11-2
May 11	Steve Thomas	l pts 6	Llanelli 11-2-12
Jun 4	Darren Pilling	l pts 6	Burnley 10-13
Oct 28	Barry Thorogood	l pts 6	Cardiff 11-2

Fights 12 Won 2 Lost 9 Drawn 1

Gary PEMBERTON

Middleweight
Cardiff born 15 May 1960
Roath Youth ABC

1986
Sep 10	Johnny Nanton	w rsf 4	Muswell Hill 11-0
Oct 20	Alex Mullen	l rsf 4	Glasgow 11-3-8
Nov 24	Shaun Cummins	l rsf 6*	Cardiff 11-0-8

1987
Jan 28	Tommy Shiels	l ko 1	Croydon 11-0
Apr 6	Paul McCarthy	w rsf 4	Southampton 11-1-12
Jun 23	Sean West	l rsf 2	Swansea 11-0-8
Sep 28	Simon Paul	w rsf 1	Dulwich 11-4
Oct 6	Danny Shinkwin	w rsf 2	Southend 11-1
Oct 28	Mark Howell	w pts 6	Swansea 11-3
Nov 19	Steve Huxtable	w rsf 4	Weston-super-Mare 11-5

1988
Mar 1	Alex Romeo	l rsf 4*	Southend 11-4
Apr 14	Tony Britton	drew 8	NSC 11-2
Jun 7	Winston Wray	l pts 6	Southend 11-7
Oct 4	Tony Cloak	w rsf 1	Southend
Oct 25	Kevin Hayde	l ko 4	Pontardawe 11-2
Dec 14	Crisanto Espana	l rsf 1	Liverpool 10-5

1989
Mar 1	Shaun Cummins	l ko 2	Cardiff 11-1
Aug 19	Alan Richards	w pts 6	Cardiff 11-2-8
Sep 19	Ray Close	l pts 6	Belfast 11-5
Sep 25	Steve Craggs	w ko 1	Leicester 11-0
Oct 11	Tony Collins	l ko 1	Millwall 11-9
Dec 6	Jimmy McDonagh	l ko 2	Wembley GH 11-2

1990
Jan 16	Jimmy Farrell	l rsf 2	Cardiff 11-5-8
Jun 15	Chris Richards	l rtd 1*	Telford 11-3
Sep 13	Barry Bennett	w rsf 4	Watford 11-7
Oct 4	Brian Robinson	l pts 6	Bethnal Green 11-2
Oct 29	Tony Kosova	w rsf 1	Nottingham 11-1
Nov 19	Carlo Colarusso	l rsf 3	Cardiff 11-3-12

1991
Jan 24	Carlo Colarusso	l rsf 8	Gorseinon 10-13-8
	(vacant Welsh light-middleweight title)		
Apr 10	Colin Pitters	l rsf 3	Newport 11-4-12
Oct 1	Adrian Strachan	l rsf 2	Sheffield 11-4

1992
Feb 12	Andy Furlong	l pts 6	Wembley GH 11-2
Apr 28	Gary Osborne	l ko 3	Wolverhampton 11-2
Oct 22	Jamie Robinson	l rsf 3	Bethnal Green 11-5

Fights 34 Won 11 Lost 22 Drawn 1

Jimmy PETERS

Light-heavyweight
Southampton born 24 October 1964
Titchfield ABC
1980 NABC champion
1981 Junior ABA champion (w T Hewitson)
1981 National Schools champion
1982 Young England (v Fin, w rsf 3 M Anttila)
1983 Young England (v WGer, w ko 1 S Macht)
1983 Southern ABA middleweight champion (w A Thomas, l A Baptiste)
1984 Southern ABA middleweight champion (w rsf 3 T Heron, w J Ashton, w V Wright, l rtd 2 B Schumacher)
1984 England (v Sco, w ko 3 M Sangster)

1987			
Apr 6	Tony Behan	w pts 4	Southampton 12-9
Sep 25	Alan Torrance	w rsf 1	Westcliff
Oct 28	Carlton Jackson	w rsf 1	Wembley GH 12-9-8
Dec 2	Cliff Curtis	w rsf 2	Wembley GH 12-8
1988			
Jan 28	Lee Woolis	w pts 8	Bethnal Green 12-7-8
Feb 25	Byron Pullen	w rsf 6	Bethnal Green 12-10-8
Apr 13	Andy Balfe	w ko 2	Bethnal Green 12-10
May 11	Dennis Banton	w pts 6	Wembley 12-9
Oct 5	Mike Aubrey	w pts 8	Wembley GH
Nov 2	Winston Burnett	w pts 8	Southwark 12-9-8
1989			
Feb 2	Derek Myers	w rsf 3	Southwark 12-8-8
Apr 27	Lee Woolis	w pts 8	Southwark 12-9
1990			
Feb 5	Cordwell Hylton	l rsf 4*	Southwark 12-13-8
May 9	John Ellis	w rsf 5	Wembley CC 12-9
Oct 10	Terry Duffus	w rsf 2	Albert Hall 12-10
Dec 12	Cliff Curtis	w rsf 1*	Albert Hall 12-8-12
1991			
Feb 14	Serg Fame (Southern light-heavyweight title)	w rsf 4	Southampton 12-4-8
May 23	Ed "Dino" Stewart	w rsf 6	Southampton 12-12-8
Sep 11	Tony Booth	w pts 8	Hammersmith 12-8
1992			
Jan 30	Crawford Ashley (British light-heavyweight title)	l rsf 1	Southampton 12-5-12

Fights 20 Won 18 Lost 2

Joey PETERS

Light-heavyweight
Southampton born 10 December 1971
Titchfield ABC
1986 National Schools champion
1987 Junior ABA Class A champion
1988 Junior ABA Class B champion
1988 NABC Class B champion
Gold medal in junior multi-nations, Italy
1989 World Junior Championships (l ko 2 M Garcia, PR)

1991			
Apr 25	Dennis Afflick	w pts 6	Basildon 12-8
May 23	Tony Behan	w pts 6	Southampton 12-10
Jul 4	Randy B. Powell	w pts 6	Alfreton 12-10-8
Oct 17	Lee Prudden	w pts 6	Southwark 12-9

1992

Mar 25	Terry Duffus	w rsf 1	Albert Hall 12-8
Apr 27	Paul Hanlon	w ko 2	AASC 12-9
Sep 3	John Oxenham	w pts 6	Dunstable 12-8-4
Oct 28	John Kaighin	drew 6	Albert Hall 12-9
Dec 3	Bobby Mack	w pts 6	Catford 12-8-4

Fights 9 Won 8 Drawn 1

Mike PHILLIPS

Light-middleweight
Warrington born 15 July 1964
Warrington ABC
1989 Welsh ABA light-middleweight final (w A Richards, w dis 3 S Law, l J Farrell)
1990 Welsh ABA middleweight prelims (l S Thomas)

1990

Sep 7	Marvin O'Brian	w rsf 1*	Liverpool 11-0
Sep 18	Paul Walters	drew 6	Stoke 11-0
Oct 8	Steve Welford	w rsf 2	Bradford 11-3
Oct 22	Tommy Warde	w rsf 5	Cleethorpes 11-2
Oct 29	Matt Mowatt	w pts 6	Birmingham 11-2
Nov 10	Marvin O'Brian	l pts 6	Liverpool 11-4
Nov 27	Darren Parker	w ko 5	Stoke 11-4
Dec 5	Paul Walters	l pts 6	Stafford 11-5
Dec 12	Paul Walters	w pts 6	Stoke 11-8

1991

Jan 23	Matt Mowatt	w rsf 6	Stoke 11-3
Feb 4	Dean Cooper	l pts 6	Leicester 11-3
Feb 22	Carl Harney	w rsf 5*	Manchester 11-7-8
Mar 13	Stinger Mason	drew 6	Stoke 11-6
Apr 30	Rocky McGran	w rsf 2	Stockport 11-4-8
May 17	Rob Pitters	w pts 8	Bury 11-2
Oct 1	Martin Smith	l pts 6	Sheffield 11-4
Oct 22	Rob Pitters	l pts 4	Hartlepool 11-3-8
Nov 25	David Johnson	w pts 6	Liverpool 11-4-8

1992

Mar 10	Steve Foster	l rsf 4*	Bury 11-5
Jul 14	Wayne Ellis (Welsh middleweight title)	l rsf 7	Mayfair 11-3-8
Sep 24	Warren Stowe	l rsf 1	Manchester 11-3-12

Fights 21 Won 11 Lost 8 Drawn 2

Dave PIERRE

Light-welterweight
Peterborough born 10 September 1964
Mid-Anglia ABC & Focus ABC
1983 Eastern ABA light-welterweight final (l E Payne)
1986 Eastern ABA light-welterweight champion (l A Bush)

1986

Nov 28	Steve Tempro	w rsf 5	Peterborough

1987

Feb 19	Tony Whitehouse	w rsf 1	Peterborough 9-13
May 1	Peter Bowen	w rsf 2	Peterborough 10-0

1988

Jun 6	Michael Oliver	l pts 6	Northampton 9-12 /CTD..

(Dave PIERRE ctd.)

Jun 16	Michael Driscoll	w pts 6	Croydon 9-13
Oct 2	George Jones	w dis 5	Peterborough 9-13
Oct 21	Crisanto Espana	l pts 6	Belfast 10-4-12
1989			
Jun 28	Patrick Delargy	w rtd 2*	Kenilworth 10-0
Sep 26	Jim Talbot	l pts 6	Oldham 10-1
Oct 5	Phil Nurse	l pts 6	Middleton 9-12
Nov 30	John Smith	w pts 6	Marble Arch 10-3
Dec 8	Mark Ramsey	w rsf 2	Doncaster 10-1
1990			
Feb 5	Dave Griffiths	w rsf 6	NSC 10-3-8
Mar 8	John Smith	w pts 6	Peterborough 10-1
May 29	Alex Dickson	l pts 8	Glasgow
Dec 14	Seamus O'Sullivan	w pts 10	Peterborough 9-13-12
	(vacant Southern light-welterweight title)		
1991			
Apr 19	Oliver Harrison	w pts 8	Peterborough 10-1-8
1992			
Feb 6	Marvin P. Gray	w rsf 7	Peterborough 10-2
Apr 30	Carlos Chase	w rsf 7	Watford 10-0
	(Southern light-welterweight title)		
Sep 17	Allan Hall	l pts 10	Watford 9-13
	(eliminator, British light-welterweight title)		
Nov 7	Valery Kayumba	l ko 9	Differdange
	(European light-welterweight title)		

Fights 21 Won 14 Lost 7

John PIERRE

Cruiserweight
Newcastle born 22 April 1966
Real name: Walter Pierre
Grainger Park ABC
1991 North-East Division heavyweight champion (w rsf 3 P Hindes, w l Laskey, w rsf 2 M Hopper, l A Nuttall)

1991			
Oct 10	Gary Charlton	w pts 6	Gateshead 14-10-8
1992			
Jan 20	Art Stacey	l pts 6	Bradford 13-9
Sep 21	Albert Call	l pts 6	Cleethorpes

Fights 3 Won 1 Lost 2

Darren PILLING

Light-middleweight
Burnley born 18 May 1967
Sandygate ABC

1988			
Sep 3	Glyn Davies	w rsf 5	Bristol 11-13-8
Oct 6	Paul Hendrick	l pts 6	Manchester 11-4
Oct 26	Mark Holden	l pts 6	Sheffield 11-1-8
Nov 14	Paul Burton	l rsf 2*	Manchester 11-10
1989			
Oct 10	Terry French	w pts 6	Sunderland 11-6
Nov 16	Carl Watson	w pts 6	Ilkeston 11-7-8
1990			
Jan 30	Spencer Alton	w pts 6	Manchester 11-6

| Mar 5 | Alan Richards | w pts 8 | Northampton 11-5 |
| Mar 22 | Paul Jones | l rtd 7 | Gateshead 11-8 |

1991
inactive

1992
Jun 4	Robert Peel	w pts 6	Burnley 11-1-8
Sep 24	Geoff Calder	w rsf 5	Manchester 11-2
Nov 12	Robert Riley	l pts 6	Burnley 11-2

Fights 12 Won 7 Lost 5

Johnny PINNOCK

Light-middleweight
High Wycombe, born Hornsey 21 August 1968
Hayes ABC

1991
| Apr 4 | Lee Crocker | l rsf 5 | Watford 11-0 |
| Jun 1 | Darren Murphy | l pts 6 | Bethnal Green 11-0 |

1992
| Oct 29 | Harry Dhami | l pts 6 | Hayes 10-10 |

Fights 3 Lost 3

Nicky PIPER

Super-middleweight
Cardiff born 5 May 1966
Penarth ABC & Victoria Park ABC
Won 5 Welsh Schools titles
1982 National Schools final (l P Passley)
1982 Welsh Youth final (l W Watkins)
1985 Welsh ABA light-middleweight champion (w C Jenkins, l G Phillips)
1985 Gold medal at Norway multi-nations (w D Milligan, Sco; w R Antman, Swe; w W Fuchsreiter, Aus)
1986 Welsh ABA middleweight semi-final (l P Lewis)
1987 Welsh ABA middleweight champion (w D Cronin, w ko 2 P Lewis, l R Douglas)
1987 Wales (v Ire, w H Byrne)
1988 ABA middle final (w ko 1 G Thomas, w rtd 3 A Richards, w rtd 1 P Evans, w P Busby, l M Edwards)
1988 Wales (v Ire, w R Close; v Sco, w rsf 1 J Garvie; v Nor, w R Hague)
1989 ABA light-heavyweight champion (w rsf 3 R Washer, w rsf 1 J Mitchell, w P Wright, w L Hudson)

1989
Sep 6	Kevin Roper	w ko 2	Port Talbot 12-5
Oct 17	Gus Mendes	w rsf 3	Cardiff 12-8-8
Dec 19	Dave Owens	w ko 1	Gorleston 12-7-4

1990
Apr 17	Darren McKenna	w rtd 4	Millwall 12-7
May 22	Maurice Core	drew 6	St Albans 12-4
Oct 23	Paul McCarthy	w rsf 3	Leicester 12-5
Nov 12	John Ellis	w ko 1	Norwich 12-7

1991
Mar 5	Johnny Held	w rsf 3	Millwall 12-8-8
May 8	Serge Bolivard	w rsf 1	Millwall 12-5
May 22	Martin Lopez	w ko 1	Millwall 12-10
Jul 3	Simon Harris	w rsf 1	Reading 12-8-8
Sep 4	Carl Thompson	l rsf 3	Bethnal Green 12-7-8
Oct 29	Franki Moro	w rsf 4	Albert Hall 12-2-8
Nov 20	Carlos Christie	w ko 6	Cardiff 12-2-8

1992
| Jan 22 | Frank Eubanks | w pts 10 | Cardiff 12-0 |
| | (eliminator, British super-middleweight title) | | /CTD.. |

(Nicky PIPER ctd.)

Mar 11	Ron Amundsen	w pts 10	Cardiff 12-0
May 16	Larry Prather	w pts 8	Muswell Hill 12-2
Jul 25	Johnny Melfah	w rsf 5*	Manchester 11-13-12
	(eliminator, British super-middleweight title)		
Dec 12	Nigel Benn	l rsf 11	Muswell Hill 11-13-10
	(WBC super-middleweight title)		

Fights 19 Won 16 Lost 2 Drawn 1

Rob PITTERS
Light-middleweight
Gateshead, born Handsworth 28 May 1960
Victoria ABC

1990

Sep 26	Neil Porter	drew 6	Manchester 10-8
Oct 8	Colin Sinnott	w pts 6	Bradford 10-5
Oct 15	Mick Costello	w rsf 4	Kettering 10-6
Nov 26	Mickey Duncan	drew 6	Bury 10-9
Dec 13	Karl Ince	w rsf 5	Hartlepool 10-10

1991

Feb 21	Martin Rosamond	w rsf 2	Walsall 10-13
Feb 28	Crain Fisher	w rsf 6	Bury 10-10
Apr 15	Gordon Blair	w pts 6	Glasgow 10-9-12
May 10	Mickey Duncan	w rsf 3	Gateshead 11-1
May 17	Mike Phillips	l pts 8	Bury 11-0
Oct 22	Mike Phillips	w pts 4	Hartlepool 10-13

1992

Mar 11	Julian Eavis	w pts 6	Solihull 10-11
Jun 4	Warren Stowe	l pts 8	Burnley 11-1-8

Fights 13 Won 9 Lost 2 Drawn 2

Steve POLLARD
Lightweight
Hull born 18 December 1957
Kingston ABC
1976 North-East ABA featherweight final (l J Decker)
1977 North-East ABA lightweight final (l G Feeney)
1978 Humberside ABA lightweight final (l rsf 2* J Hunter)
1980 North-East ABA lightweight final (w S Morrow, l dis 1 G Felvus)

1980

Apr 28	Brindley Jones	w pts 6	NSC
May 27	Pat Mallon	w pts 6	Glasgow 8-10
Jun 2	Andy Thomas	w pts 6	NSC 9-2-4
Oct 2	Eddie Glass	w pts 6	Hull 9-4
Nov 3	Rocky Bantleman	w ko 2	NSC 9-2
Dec 1	Chris McCallum	w pts 6	Hull

1981

Feb 17	Billy Laidman	w pts 6	Leeds
Mar 2	Brindley Jones	w rsf 5*	NSC 9-4
Mar 30	John Sharkey	l rsf 5*	Glasgow
Apr 27	Ian McLeod	l pts 8	NSC 9-3
Jun 1	Gary Lucas	l pts 8	NSC 9-3
Jun 11	John Sharkey	w pts 8	Hull 9-2

1982

Mar 8	Brian Hyslop	drew 8	Hamilton

Apr 22	Rocky Bantleman	w rsf 8	NSC
May 18	Lee Graham	drew 8	NSC
May 26	Alan Tombs	drew 8	NSC
Sep 23	Pat Doherty	l pts 8	Wimbledon
Oct 26	Lee Halford	l pts 8	Hull
Nov 25	Kevin Howard	l pts 8	Sunderland

1983

Feb 10	Keith Foreman	l pts 8	Sunderland 9-3
Mar 29	Steve Farnsworth (Central featherweight title)	w rsf 2	Hull 8-12-8
Jun 18	Andre Blanco	w pts 8	Izegem
Oct 4	Jim McDonnell	l rsf 5*	Bethnal Green
Nov 22	Joey Joynson	l pts 8	Wembley

1984

Jan 22	Jean-Marc Renard	l pts 8	Izegem
Nov 13	Jim McDonnell	l rsf 6	Bethnal Green 9-2-8
Dec 17	John Doherty (Central featherweight title)	l pts 10	Bradford 8-13

1985

Mar 12	Mike Whalley	l rsf 8	Manchester 9-3

1986

Jan 20	Alex Dickson	l rsf 7	Glasgow 9-10
Mar 10	Dave Savage	l pts 8	Glasgow 9-5
Mar 26	Peter Harris	l rsf 3*	Swansea 9-3
Nov 13	Dean Marsden	l ko 7	Huddersfield 9-6

1987

Apr 7	Darren Cunningham	w pts 8	Batley 9-5
Apr 15	Paul Gadney	l pts 8	Lewisham 9-4
Apr 30	Gary Nickels	l rsf 1*	Battersea 9-3-8
Sep 20	Kevin Taylor	l pts 8	Oldham 9-2
Nov 18	Gary De Roux	drew 8	Peterborough 9-3
Dec 11	Gary Maxwell	l pts 8	Coalville 9-4

1988

Jan 28	John Bennie	l pts 6	Bethnal Green 9-5-12
Feb 24	Craig Windsor	l pts 8	Glasgow 9-2-8
Mar 9	Peter Bradley	l pts 8	Wembley 9-5
Mar 30	Scott Durham	w pts 8	Bethnal Green 9-0-8
Apr 25	Colin Lynch	w pts 8	Birmingham 9-4
May 18	John Bennie	w pts 8	Lewisham 9-6-8
Aug 31	Mike Chapman	w pts 8	Holborn 9-10
Nov 15	Tony Foster	l rsf 3*	Hull 9-3-8

1989

Jan 17	Peter Bradley	l pts 8	Woodford 9-7
May 31	Carl Crook	l rsf 4*	Manchester 9-7
Sep 4	Michael Armstrong	l pts 8	Hull 9-2
Oct 10	Tony Foster	l rsf 3*	Hull 9-6-4

1990

Mar 22	Chris Bennett	w pts 4	Gateshead 9-7
Apr 7	Frank De Winter	l pts 6	St Eloois
May 20	Mark Ramsey	l pts 6	Sheffield 9-10
Nov 30	Shaun Cooper	l pts 6	Birmingham 9-12

1991

Feb 11	Dave Anderson	l pts 6	Glasgow 9-7
Mar 2	Allan Hall	l pts 6	Darlington 9-13
Dec 5	Shaun Cogan	l pts 6	Telford 10-0

1992

Jan 18	Ian Honeywood	l pts 6	Albert Hall 9-13
Mar 30	J.T.Williams	w pts 6	Eltham 9-9-8 /CTD...

(Steve POLLARD ctd.)
Apr 30	Jason Rowland	l rsf 2*	Albert Hall 10-2-8
Sep 10	Paul Charters	l rtd 5	Sunderland 10-1
Oct 19	Kevin Toomey	l rsf 7*	Hull 9-9-8

Fights 62 Won 19 Lost 39 Drawn 4

Danny PORTER
Flyweight
Hitchin, born Biggleswade 27 April 1964
1981 England (v Sco, w ko 2 K Grant)
1982 Young England (v Fin, w ko 3 V Vaelimaeki)
1982 England (v Fin, w ko 1 J Arola; v Ire, l rtd 1 G Hawkins)
1982 Home Counties ABA light-flyweight champion (w rsf 3 A Derry, w ko 1 P Gerring, l J Lyon)
1983 Great Britain (v USA, l T Merrill)
1983 ABA light-flyweight final (w P Maher, w rsf 2 P Shone, l J Lyon)
1984 England (v Sco, w ko 2 J Rae; v Can, w A Charlesbois)
1984 ABA light-flyweight semi-final (w D Thompson, l W Williams)
1985 England (v Hun, w rsf 1 R Isaszeg)
1985 Gold medal at Canada multi-nations (w ko 1 S D'Souza, w ko 3 C Burton)
1985 Home Counties ABA light-flyweight final (l M Smith)
1986 Home Counties ABA light-flyweight champion (w ko 1 M Davies, l rsf 3 M Epton)

1986
Nov 9	Antti Juntumaa	l pts 4	Vasa

1987
Feb 9	Donnie Hood	l rsf 4	Glasgow 8-0
Apr 8	Kerry Webber	w ko 5	Evesham 8-2

1988
Mar 7	David Jones	w rsf 4	NSC 8-1
May 10	Phil Dicks	w rsf 4	Southend
Sep 30	Gordon Shaw	w rsf 1	Gillingham 8-8
Nov 15	Mark Goult	l pts 6	Norwich 8-5-8
Dec 7	Paul Dever	w ko 1	Stoke 8-2

1989
Apr 6	Francisco Garcia	w pts 8	Stevenage 8-3
Jun 22	Amon Neequaye	w rsf 7	Stevenage 8-3-8
Oct 24	Pat Clinton (British flyweight title)	l rsf 5	Watford 7-13-8

1990
Feb 14	Des Gargano	w pts 6	Brentwood 8-7
Mar 20	Mark Goult (vacant Southern bantamweight title)	l pts 10	Norwich 8-5-2
Jul 6	Alfred Kotey (Commonwealth flyweight title)	l pts 12	Brentwood 8-0
Oct 31	Pablo Salazar	w rsf 7*	Crystal Palace 8-2-12

1991
Mar 19	Kevin Jenkins	w rsf 7	Leicester
Jun 12	Salvatore Fanni (European flyweight title)	l rsf 9*	Sassari 8-0
Nov 19	Kevin Jenkins	w rsf 2*	Norwich 8-5

1992
Feb 12	Salvatore Fanni (European flyweight title)	drew 12	Sarno 7-13-12
Jun 1	Miguel Matthews	w pts 6	Glasgow
Sep 19	Pat Clinton (WBO flyweight title)	l pts 12	Glasgow 7-13-12

Fights 21 Won 12 Lost 8 Drawn 1

Darren POWELL
Light-welterweight
Manchester born 13 June 1969

1992
Jun 4	Mark Antony	l ko 2	Burnley 10-2

Fights 1 Lost 1

Gipsy Johnny PRICE
Super-middleweight
Bolton born Wigan 10 April 1973
Bolton ABC, Bury ABC

1991
Oct 21	Graham Wassell	w rsf 5	Bury 12-0

1992
Jan 21	Jason McNeill	w pts 4	Stockport 12-2
Mar 10	Martin Jolley	l rsf 3	Bury 12-2
Nov 12	Seamus Casey	w pts 6	Burnley

Fights 4 Won 3 Lost 1

Kenley PRICE

Cruiserweight
Liverpool born 23 December 1966
Southpaw
Wavertree ABC
1988 West Lancs & Cheshire ABA light-heavy champ (w rsf 1 B Jones, l dis 3 M Coore)
1989 West Lancs & Cheshire ABA heavyweight final (l D Roberts)
1990 West Lancs & Cheshire ABA heavyweight champ (w.o. l dis 2 C Bowen-Price)

1992
Dec 15	Zak Goldman	w rtd 2	Liverpool 13-7

Fights 1 Won 1

Ray PRICE
Middleweight
Swansea Born 16 July 1961
Swansea RAOB

1979
Apr 30	Gerry Howland	drew 4	Portsmouth
Sep 17	Tim Moloney	l pts 4	WSC
Sep 24	Bonnet Bryant	w pts 4	AASC
Oct 16	Kid Curtis	w ko 2	West Bromwich
Oct 22	Bill Smith	drew 4	AASC
Oct 30	Philip Morris	drew 6	Caerphilly
Nov 6	Neil Brown	w pts 6	Stafford
Nov 21	Neil Brown	w pts 6	Evesham
Nov 28	Shaun Durkin	drew 6	Doncaster
Dec 3	Tim Moloney	l pts 6	Marylebone

1980
Mar 17	Terry Parkinson	w pts 6	WSC
May 19	Colin Wake	l pts 6	NSC /CTD..

(Ray PRICE ctd.)
1981

Mar 26	Billy Vivian	l pts 8	Ebbw Vale
Apr 7	Tyrell Wilson	w pts 6	Newport
May 11	Barry Price	w pts 8	Copthorne 10-0
Jun 8	John Lindo	w rsf 2	Bradford 9-12
Oct 13	Robbie Robinson	l rsf 1	Blackpool

1982

Mar 22	Geoff Pegler	w pts 10	Swansea
	(vacant Welsh light-welterweight title)		
Oct 25	Willie Booth	l pts 8	Airdrie
Nov 9	Tony Adams	l rsf 1	Albert Hall

1983

Mar 2	Lee Halford	w pts 6	Evesham
Mar 21	Gunter Roomes	l rsf 1	AASC
May 27	Geoff Pegler	nd 1	Swansea 9-12
	(Welsh light-welterweight title)		
Oct 4	Mo Hussein	l pts 8	Bethnal Green
Dec 19	Geoff Pegler	l rtd 8	Swansea 9-13-8
	(Welsh light-welterweight title)		

1984

Jan 30	Steve Tempro	w pts 8	Birmingham 10-6
Mar 14	Ken Foreman	l pts 6	NSC 10-3
May 9	Tony McKenzie	l pts 8	Leicester 10-2
Jun 13	Michael Harris	l pts 10	Port Talbot 10-0
	(vacant Welsh light-welterweight title)		
Jun 30	David Irving	l rsf 4	Belfast
Dec 8	Frank Moro	l pts 8	Swansea 10-12

1985

Feb 4	Claude Rosse	w rsf 6	Nottingham 10-7
Sep 18	George Collins	l pts 4	Muswell Hill 10-8-8
Dec 2	Steve Elwood	l rsf 5	Dulwich 10-9-8

1986-1991 inactive

1992

Oct 7	Steve Thomas	w pts 6	Barry 11-9-8

Fights 35 Won 13 Lost 17 Drawn 4 No decision 1

Lee PRUDDEN
Light-heavyweight
Redditch, born Birmingham 3 December 1968
Redditch ABC
1990 Birmingham ABA light-heavyweight final (l P Christie)

1991

Jan 28	Paul Murray	w pts 6	Birmingham 12-2
Feb 27	Barry Downes	w pts 6	Wolverhampton 12-5
Mar 13	Paul Murray	drew 6	Stoke 12-1
Mar 26	Nigel Rafferty	l pts 6	Wolverhampton
Apr 10	Paul Hanlon	w pts 6	Wolverhampton 11-13
May 13	Paul Hanlon	w pts 6	Birmingham 12-0
May 23	Paul Hanlon	l pts 6	Southampton 12-6
Jun 5	Nigel Rafferty	l pts 6	Wolverhampton 12-0
Jul 3	James Woolley	w pts 6	Brentwood 12-6
Sep 21	James Woolley	w pts 6	Tottenham 12-6-8
Oct 1	Gil Lewis	drew 8	Bedworth 12-12
Oct 17	Joey Peters	l pts 6	Southwark 12-9

1992

Jan 22	Paul Hanlon	l rsf 4*	Stoke 12-10
Apr 22	Phil Soundy	l rsf 5	Wembley 13-5
Jul 9	Joe McCluskey	l pts 6	Glasgow 12-6-12
Sep 7	Bruce Scott	l pts 6	Bethnal Green 13-0
Nov 23	Stephen Wilson	l pts 6	Glasgow 12-12-8
Dec 9	Steve Loftus	w pts 6	Stoke 12-9

Fights 18 Won 7 Lost 9 Drawn 2

Chris PYATT

Middleweight
Leicester born 3 July 1963
Belgrave ABC
1977 National Schools champion
1979 National Schools champion
1980 Junior ABA champion (w A Till)
1981 Young England (v Hun, w Nagy; v Blaogh; v Swe, w T Hasselstrom)
1981 ABA welterweight final (w D Stokes, w K Petrou, w L Gloster, w B Rudgewick, w J Andrews, w ko 2 J McIntosh, l T Marsh)
1982 Young England (v Fin, w ko 2 H Tuusa)
1982 England (v Swe, w S Blomqvist)
1982 ABA welterweight champion (w C Thomas, w rsf 2 A Marren, w rsf 1 F Lyons, w L Gloster, w S Watt, w J McAllister, w B McKenley)
1982 Commonwealth Games welterweight gold medal (w S Renwick, NZ; w J McAllister, Sco; w C Nwokolo, Nig; w L Mukdbe, Sam)

1983

Mar 1	Paul Murray	w rtd 2*	Albert Hall
Apr 5	Billy Waith	w rsf 8	Albert Hall 10-12-4
Apr 28	Lee Hartshorn	w rsf 3	Leicester 11-0
Sep 27	Darwin Brewster	w pts 8	Wembley 10-12
Oct 8	Tyrone Demby	w rtd 2	Atlantic City
Nov 22	Tony Britton	w rsf 4*	Wembley

1984

Feb 22	Judas Clottey	w pts 8	Albert Hall 10-8-4
Mar 15	Pat Thomas	w pts 10	Leicester 10-12-8
May 9	Franki Moro	w ko 4	Leicester 10-10
May 23	Alfonso Redondo	w rsf 3	NSC 11-0-8
Oct 16	John Ridgman	w rsf 1	Albert Hall 11-1-4
Nov 16	Brian Anderson	w pts 12	Leicester 10-13

(final eliminator, British light-middleweight title)

1985

Feb 12	Helier Custos	w rsf 5	Albert Hall 11-1
Jun 5	Graeme Ahmed	w rsf 3	Albert Hall 11-1-12
Jul 1	Mosimo Maeleke	w rsf 6	NSC 11-1-8
Sep 23	Sabiyala Diavilla	l rsf 4*	NSC 11-2-4

1986

Feb 19	Prince Rodney	w ko 9	Albert Hall 10-11-12

(British light-middleweight title)

May 20	Thomas Smith	w rsf 1	Wembley 11-1
Sep 17	John van Elteren	w rsf 1	Albert Hall 10-13

(vacant European light-middleweight title)

Oct 25	Renaldo Hernandez	w rsf 3	Paris

1987

Jan 28	Gianfranco Rosi	l pts 12	Perugia

(European light-middleweight title)

Apr 18	Dennis Johnson	w ko 2	Albert Hall 11-2
May 26	Sammy Floyd	w rsf 2	Wembley 11-2

Oct 28	Gilbert Josamu	w pts 8	Wembley GH 11-1-12
1988			
May 26	Jose Duarte	w rsf 4	Albert Hall 11-2
Nov 23	Eddie Hall	w rsf 2	Bethnal Green 11-2
Dec 1	Knox Brown	w rsf 2	Edmonton 11-1-8
Dec 14	Tyrone Moore	w ko 1	Bethnal Green 11-2
1989			
Feb 15	Russell Mitchell	w rsf 4*	Bethnal Green 11-2
May 17	Daniel Dominguez	w rsf 10	Millwall
Oct 11	Wayne Harris	w rsf 3	Millwall 11-2
1990			
Apr 25	Daniel Sclarandi	w rsf 2	Millwall 11-2
Oct 23	John David Jackson	l pts 12	Leicester 10-12-4
	(WBO light-middleweight title)		
1991			
Nov 5	Craig Trotter	w pts 12	Leicester 10-12-8
	(vacant Commonwealth light-middleweight title)		
1992			
Feb 1	Ambrose Mlilo	w rsf 3	Birmingham 11-0
	(Commonwealth light-middleweight title)		
Mar 31	Melvin Wynn	w ko 3	Norwich 11-5-8
Apr 28	James Tapisha	w rsf 1	Wolverhampton 10-13-12
	(Commonwealth light-middleweight title)		
May 23	Ian Strudwick	w pts 10	Birmingham 11-6
Oct 27	Adolfo Caballero	w ko 5	Leicester 11-5-8
	(vacant WBC International middleweight title)		

Fights 39 Won 36 Lost 3

Danny QUACOE

Welterweight
Crawley, born Hammersmith 3 December 1965
Horsham ABC
1991 Southern ABA welterweight final (w ko 2 R Purkis, l C Flanagan)
1992 Southern ABA light-middleweight final (w K Lamley, w rsf 3 R Blair, l rsf 1 D Francis)

1992			
Oct 22	Joel Ani	l ko 1	Bethnal Green 10-8

Fights 1 Lost 1

Willie QUINN

Middleweight
Tranent, East Lothian, born Edinburgh 17 February 1972
Haddington ABC
1990 Scotland (v Eng, l T Taylor)
1991 Scotland (v Eng, l ko 1 R Reid)
1991 Scottish ABA light-middleweight semi-final (w S Magee, l P Dolan)

1991			
Oct 9	Mark Jay	l pts 6	Glasgow 11-3
1992			
Jan 27	Hugh Fury	w rsf 3	Glasgow 11-8-12
Mar 18	Andy Manning	w pts 6	Glasgow 11-5
Mar 30	John Mackenzie	w rsf 4*	Glasgow 11-7
Sep 19	Martin Rosamond	w rsf 4	Glasgow 11-9-8

Fights 5 Won 4 Lost 1

Dave RADFORD

Light-middleweight
Hemsworth born 30 May 1969
Batley & Dewsbury ABC

1990
Mar 27	Tommy Warde	l ko 3	Leicester 11-2
May 9	Chris Micolazczyk	w pts 6	Solihull 11-2
May 21	Brian Keating	w pts 6	Bradford 11-2
Jun 28	Paul Hanlon	w rsf 2	Birmingham 10-12
Sep 3	Andre Wharton	l rsf 5	Dudley 11-3-12

1991
Jan 16	Tony Kosova	w pts 6	Stoke 11-4
Feb 21	Griff Jones	l pts 6	Leeds 11-8
Apr 15	Paul Burton	l rtd 1*	Birmingham 11-6
May 13	Pete Bowman	w ko 2	Manchester 11-2-8
Dec 2	Dave Binsteed	w rsf 6	Liverpool 11-5
Dec 14	Delroy Matthews	l ko 1	Bexleyheath 11-3

1992
Feb 24	Mark Jay	l pts 6	Bradford 11-3-8
Mar 9	Tyrone Eastmond	drew 6	Manchester 11-2
Apr 25	Warren Stowe	l rsf 3	Manchester 11-4-8

Fights 14 Won 6 Lost 7 Drawn 1

Nigel RAFFERTY

Light-heavyweight
Wolverhampton born 29 December 1967
Windmill ABC
1989 Staffordshire ABA middleweight semi-final (w P Addlington, l D Ashton)

1989
Jun 5	Carl Watson	l pts 6	Birmingham 11-7
Jun 28	Tony Hodge	l pts 6	Brentwood 12-0
Jul 6	Tony Hodge	w pts 6	Chigwell 12-1
Sep 4	Joe Frater	l pts 6	Cleethorpes 12-4
Oct 24	Paul Wesley	w pts 6	Wolverhampton 11-7-8
Nov 22	Paul Wesley	w pts 8	Stafford 11-7-8
Nov 28	Paul Wesley	w pts 6	Wolverhampton 11-7
Dec 4	Dean Murray	w pts 6	Cleethorpes 11-12
Dec 20	Paul Wright	drew 6	Liverpool 12-0

1990
Jan 17	Gil Lewis	l pts 6	Stoke 12-2-8
Jan 31	Antoine Tarver	l pts 4	Bethnal Green 12-4
Feb 19	Paul Wesley	w pts 8	Birmingham 11-9-8
Mar 19	Terry Gilbey	w pts 6	Cleethorpes 12-5
May 1	Sean Heron	l rsf 2	Oldham 12-8
Sep 13	Paul Murray	w pts 6	Watford 12-0
Sep 27	Paul Murray	drew 6	NEC 12-0
Oct 9	Paul Murray	w pts 6	Wolverhampton 12-0
Oct 24	Andy Flute	l ko 6	Dudley 11-10-8
Nov 27	Carlos Christie	l pts 8	Wolverhampton 11-12
Dec 6	Carlos Christie	l pts 6	Wolverhampton 11-13

1991
Jan 28	Alan Richards	drew 8	Birmingham 11-13
Mar 4	Carlos Christie	l pts 8	Birmingham 12-6
Mar 26	Lee Prudden	w pts 6	Wolverhampton
May 13	Tony Behan	w dis 7	Birmingham 12-3
Jun 5	Lee Prudden	w pts 6	Wolverhampton 11-13 /CTD..

(Nigel RAFFERTY ctd.)

Sep 10	Paul Busby	l rsf 2	Wolverhampton 11-10
Nov 20	Julian Johnson	drew 6	Cardiff 12-5-8
Dec 2	Kesem Clayton	w pts 8	Birmingham 11-13
1992			
Jan 21	Glenn Campbell	l rsf 6	Stockport 12-2
Mar 30	Simon McDougall	w pts 8	Coventry 12-6
Apr 25	Sammy Storey	l rsf 3	Belfast 12-5
Jun 16	Gary Delaney	l ko 5	Dagenham 13-0
Nov 24	Graham Burton	w pts 8	Wolverhampton 12-0
Dec 2	John J. Cooke	l pts 6	Bardon 12-10

Fights 34 Won 15 Lost 15 Drawn 4

Gary RAILTON
Heavyweight
Burnopfield, born Consett 15 July 1966

1987			
Apr 30	Mamdou N'didye	w rsf 2	Washington
May 28	Steve Osborne	w pts 6	Jarrow
Sep 4	Mick Cordon	w pts 6	Gateshead
Oct 11	Ian Bulloch	l pts 6	Batley
Dec 14	Eric Cardouza	l ko 2	NSC
1988-89 inactive			
1990			
Dec 13	Denzil Browne	l rsf 2	Dewsbury 14-7
1991			
Nov 11	Gary Charlton	w pts 6	Bradford 15-2
1992			
Feb 6	J.A. Bugner	l ko 3	Peterborough 15-7

Fights 8 Won 4 Lost 4

Kenny RAINFORD
Light-heavyweight
Liverpool born 28 July 1968. Based USA.

1992			
Nov 5	Aaron Nance	w rsf 3	Natchez, Ms. 12-6-4
Dec 10	Anthony Campbell	w pts 4	Oklahoma City 12-7

Fights 2 Won 2

David RAMSDEN
Featherweight
Bradford born 22 January 1970
1986 National Schools champion
1988 Yorkshire & Humberside ABA featherweight semi-final (l J Irwin)

1992			
Jan 20	Glyn Shepherd	w rsf 1	Bradford 8-12
Mar 30	Eunan Devenney	w rsf 2	Bradford 8-12
Apr 27	Des Gargano	w pts 6	Bradford 8-13
Jun 8	Des Gargano	w pts 6	Bradford 8-10
Sep 14	Mike Deveney	w pts 6	Bradford 9-0
Dec 14	Chris Clarkson	l pts 4	Bradford 9-0

Fights 6 Won 5 Lost 1

Calum RATTRAY

Welterweight
Aberdeen born 30 March 1963
Aberdeen ABC
1983 Scottish ABA lightweight final (l A Dickson)
1985 Scottish ABA welterweight prelims (l F Cummings)

1989
Mar 6	Willie Beattie	l rsf 3*	Glasgow 10-3
Apr 6	Paul Day	l pts 6	Stevenage 10-7
Apr 19	Dean Bramhald	l pts 6	Doncaster 10-6
May 29	Delroy Waul	l pts 6	Dundee 10-0
Jun 12	Delroy Waul	l pts 6	Glasgow 10-1
Jun 27	Willie Beattie	l rsf 2	Glasgow 10-4
Sep 10	Riki Burton	l rsf 4*	Glasgow 10-4

1990
Sep 25	Gordon Blair	l rsf 3	Glasgow 10-0

1991
inactive

1992
Feb 24	Allan Grainger	l rtd 5	Glasgow 10-11-8

Fights 9 Lost 9

Mark REEFER

Super-featherweight
Bethnal Green born 16 March 1964
Beacon Youth ABC
1979 National Schools champion

1983
Oct 4	Neville Fivey	w pts 6	Bethnal Green
Nov 8	Tony Rahman	w rsf 4	Bethnal Green 9-3
Dec 1	Mark Pearce	w pts 6	Basildon

1984
Mar 27	Muhammad Lovelock	w pts 6	Battersea 9-4-8
May 1	Alec Irvine	w pts 6	Bethnal Green 9-2
Sep 24	Joey Joynson	drew 8	NSC 9-3
Nov 13	Dave Pratt	w rsf 3	Bethnal Green 9-2

1985
Jan 18	Dean Bramhald	w rsf 8	Bethnal Green 9-1-4
May 8	Robert Dickie	l rsf 1	Solihull 9-2
Oct 21	John Feeney	l rsf 3	NSC 9-4

1986
Nov 26	Nigel Haddock	w rtd 3*	Lewisham 9-3-12

1987
Apr 7	George Jones	w rsf 5	Ilford 9-7-8
Apr 30	Peter Crook	w rsf 2	Bethnal Green 9-10-8
Oct 24	Wayne Weekes	w rsf 1	Tottenham 9-6-8
Dec 3	George Jones	w rsf 3	Southend 9-5-12

1988
Feb 24	Davey Robb	w ko 1	Southend
Mar 21	Abdul Kareem	w rsf 5	Bethnal Green 9-9
	(Southern lightweight title)		
May 26	Belaid Khaldi	l rsf 4	Bethnal Green 9-8-8
Sep 21	Fernando Blanco	w ko 1	Basildon 9-6-8
Oct 28	Mo Hussein	l rsf 10	Brentwood 9-8
	(Commonwealth lightweight title)		/CTD..

(Mark REEFER ctd.)

Dec 16	Kevin Pritchard	w rsf 6*	Brentwood	9-5-8
1989				
Jan 25	Guy Bellehigue	w rsf 3	Basildon	9-6
Apr 21	Les Walsh	w pts 8	Bethnal Green	9-5-8
May 26	Kid Sumaila	w pts 8	Bethnal Green	9-5-4
Sep 19	John Sichula	w pts 12	Bethnal Green	9-4
	(Commonwealth super-featherweight title)			
Dec 19	Sam Akromah	w rsf 5	Bethnal Green	
	(Commonwealth super-featherweight title)			
1990				
Feb 14	Daniel Londas	l rsf 8*	Brentwood	9-4
	(European super-featherweight title)			
May 1	Sugar Gibiliru	w rsf 5	Oldham	9-4
	(Commonwealth super-featherweight title)			
Jun 27	Pedro Gutierrez	l rsf 12	Albert Hall	9-4
	(vacant WBC International super-featherweight title)			
1991				
Feb 12	Andrew De Abreu	w pts 10	Cardiff	9-3-8
	(eliminator, British super-featherweight title)			
Apr 18	Thunder Ayeh	l rsf 2*	Olympia	9-3
	(Commonwealth super-featherweight title)			
1992				
Mar 17	Peter Till	l rsf 3	Mayfair	9-10

Fights 32 Won 23 Lost 8 Drawn 1

Emlyn REES

Lightweight
Tonypandy born 19 November 1965

1992
Nov 20	George Naylor	l pts 6	Liverpool	9-9-12

Fights 1 Lost 1

Fred REEVES

Super-featherweight
Hull born 14 April 1969

1992
Nov 9	Tim Hill	l ko 4	Bradford	9-5
Dec 14	Leo Turner	l rsf 2	Bradford	9-5

Fights 2 Lost 2

Robbie REGAN

Flyweight
Cfen Forest, born Caerphilly 30 August 1968
Fleur de Lys ABC
1986 Welsh ABA light-flyweight champion (l M Cantwell)
1986 Commonwealth Games, Edinburgh light-flyweight (l M Epton)
1986 Wales (v Sco, l W Docherty)
1987 Welsh ABA light-flyweight champion (l M Epton)
1987 Wales (v Ire, w P O'Halloran; v Sco, l W Docherty)
1988 Norway & Sweden multi-nations gold medals
1988 ABA light-flyweight final (w ko 1 W Jenkins, w I Lang, l M Cantwell)
1989 Welsh ABA flyweight final (l E George)

1989
Aug 19	Eric George	drew 6	Cardiff 8-3

1990
Mar 6	Francis Ampofo	w pts 6	Bethnal Green 8-3
Apr 26	Kevin Downer	w rsf 4	Merthyr 8-5
Jun 20	Dave McNally	drew 6	Basildon 8-4
Nov 19	Ricky Beard	w rsf 6	Cardiff 8-2
Dec 21	Michele Poddighe	drew 6	Sassari 8-1-8

1991
Feb 12	Kevin Jenkins (vacant Welsh flyweight title)	w pts 10	Cardiff 7-13-8
May 28	Joe Kelly (vacant British flyweight title)	w pts 12	Cardiff 7-13-12
Sep 3	Francis Ampofo (British flyweight title)	l rsf 11*	Cardiff 7-13
Dec 17	Francis Ampofo (British flyweight title)	w pts 12	Cardiff 8-0

1992
Feb 11	Juan Bautista	w rsf 1	Cardiff 8-0-12
May 19	James Drummond (British flyweight title)	w rsf 9	Cardiff 7-12-8
Nov 14	Salvatore Fanni (European flyweight title)	w pts 12	Cardiff 7-13-8

Fights 13 Won 9 Lost 1 Drawn 3

Mick REID

Light-middleweight
Rugby born 27 November 1964
Triumph ABC

1991
Apr 29	Dean Carr	w rsf 1	Cleethorpes 10-7
May 20	Chad Strong	l pts 6	Leicester 10-4
Sep 24	Paul Dyer	l pts 6	Basildon 10-8
Oct 16	Rafaelle Feliciello	w pts 6	Stoke 10-11-8
Oct 26	Ojay Abrahams	l rsf 5	Brentwood 10-13

1992
Mar 25	Lee Ferrie	l rsf 3	Hinckley 10-13

Fights 6 Won 2 Lost 4

Peter REID

Welterweight
Derby born 19 February 1966
Arboretum ABC
Formerly boxed as Peter Vance

1986
Sep 1	Andy Till	l rsf 6	Ealing 11-0
Oct 10	John Davies	l rsf 2	Gloucester 11-1

1987
inactive

1988
Dec 12	Mark Holden	l rsf 4	Manchester 11-3

1989
Jan 16	Steve Kiernan	w pts 6	Bradford 11-5
Jan 30	Frank Mobbs	w pts 6	Durham 11-1
Feb 20	Frank Mobbs	w pts 6	Bradford 11-2
Mar 1	Alfie Andrews	w rsf 2	Stoke 11-3
May 8	Gary Osborne	l ko 5	Edgbaston 11-4
Sep 26	Jim Beckett	l pts 8	Chigwell
Nov 13	Martin Robinson	l pts 6	Brierley Hill 11-3
Dec 20	Paul Lynch	l rsf 4	Swansea 11-1

1990
Mar 10	Martin Rosamond	w rsf 6	Bristol 11-3
Mar 22	Gary Osborne	l ko 1	Wolverhampton 11-1
Oct 18	Andrew Tucker	l pts 6	Hartlepool 11-1
Oct 25	Dean Cooper	l rsf 1	Nottingham 10-12

1991
Nov 21	Robert Riley	w pts 6	Ilkeston
Dec 4	Julian Eavis	l pts 6	Stoke 10-4

1992
Feb 20	James Campbell	l pts 6	Telford 10-9-8
Apr 6	Kevin Mabbutt	w pts 6	Northampton 10-12
Apr 13	Dave Maj	l ko 1	Manchester 10-9
Jun 4	Warren Bowers	w rsf 2	Cleethorpes 10-8
Nov 12	Dean Hiscox	w pts 6	Stafford 10-7

Fights 22 Won 9 Lost 13

Paddy REILLY

Heavyweight
Derby, born 29 October 1965
Real name: Clifton Mitchell
Askam ABC, Merlin Youth ABC

1986 Midlands ABA super-heavyweight champion (w ko 1 W Williams, w E McLean, l rsf 1 G McCrory)
1987 Midlands ABA super-heavyweight final (l ko 3 J Shakespeare)
1988 ABA super-heavyweight semi-final (w dis 3 M Richards, w E McLean, w ko 1 C Jackson, w ko 1 R Callus, l dis 3 K McCormack)
1989 Midlands ABA super-heavyweight champion (w ko 1 G Williams, w J Shakespeare, w ko 1 P Eugene, l P Passley)
1990 Midlands ABA super-heavyweight champion (w rsf 1 C Brown, l rsf 1* P Eugene)

1991
Apr 6	John Harewood	w rsf 2	Darlington 17-7
Aug 1	John Harewood	w ko 1	Dewsbury 17-0
Oct 3	Michael Richards	w pts 6	Burton 16-8
Nov 21	Michael Richards	w rsf 6	Burton 16-11

1992
Apr 14	Michael Murray	w rsf 8	Mansfield 16-7

Fights 5 Won 5

Jimmy REYNOLDS

Lightweight
Birmingham born 25 June 1970
Aston Villa ABC & Dudley ABC
1987 NABC Class B champion

1989
Sep 25	Delroy Waul	l rsf 4	NEC 9-10-8
Dec 11	David Jenkins	l pts 6	Birmingham 9-12

1990-91
inactive

1992
Oct 1	Steve Howden	w rtd 2	Telford 9-13-12
Nov 2	Billy McDougall	w pts 6	Wolverhampton 9-13-8

Fights 4 Won 2 Lost 2

Glyn RHODES

Light-middleweight
Sheffield born 22 October 1959
St Thomas ABC

1979
Nov 14	John Lindo	l pts 6	Liverpool
Nov 28	Mark Osbourne	w pts 4	Doncaster
Dec 10	Mike Clemow	l pts 6	Torquay

1980
Jan 9	Steve Sims	w rsf 6	Stoke
Jan 25	Shaun Durkin	w pts 6	Hull
Feb 5	John Cooper	w pts 6	Southend
Feb 12	Bill Smith	w pts 4	Sheffield
Mar 3	Kevin Sheehan	l ko 1	Nottingham
Mar 24	Derek Groarke	w rsf 4	Bradford
Apr 21	John Henry	w rsf 5	Bradford
Apr 29	Jackie Turner	l pts 8	AASC 9-7-8
Jul 28	Bill Hay	drew 6	Fivemiletown 9-5
Sep 4	Jarvis Greenidge	w rsf 8*	Morecambe 9-6
Sep 15	Gary Ball	drew 6	WSC 9-13
Oct 7	Ceri Collins	w rsf 8	NSC 9-12-12
Oct 30	Jimmy Bunclark	l rsf 7*	Liverpool 9-10
Dec 1	Bobby Welburn	l ko 1	Hull

1981
Jan 22	Brian Snagg	l pts 8	Liverpool
Mar 9	Jimmy Brown	w pts 8	AASC 9-12
Mar 24	Eric Wood	l pts 8	Sheffield 9-9
Apr 29	Doug Hill	w rtd 6*	Stoke 9-10
May 11	Jackie Turner	w rsf 2*	AASC 9-12
Jun 13	Paul Keers	w rsf 1	Sheffield 9-10
Oct 26	Lance Williams	drew 8	AASC

1982
Jan 12	Vernon Vanriel	l ko 2	Bethnal Green
May 5	Lance Williams	l rsf 7	Solihull
Jun 3	Brian Snagg	w rsf 4*	Liverpool
Nov 22	Kevin Pritchard (vacant Central lightweight title)	w ko 5	Liverpool

1983
Mar 11	Jimmy Bunclark (Central lightweight title)	l pts 10	Sheffield

/CTD..

(Glyn RHODES ctd.)

Nov 9	Robert Lloyd	w pts 8	Sheffield 9-12
1984			
Jan 13	Frederic Geoffroy	l rsf 5	Nemours
Apr 11	Mo Hussein	l rsf 1	Albert Hall 9-12
Oct 29	Willy Wilson	w rtd 3	Nottingham 9-9-8
1985			
Oct 13	Muhammad Lovelock (vacant Central lightweight title)	l ko 10	Sheffield 9-7-12
1986			
inactive			
1987			
Oct 19	Andy Holligan	l pts 6	Belfast 10-2
Dec 5	Sugar Gibiliru	w pts 8	Doncaster 10-2-8
1988			
Feb 24	Marvin P.Gray	w rsf 1*	Sheffield 9-13
Mar 23	Nigel Senior	w pts 8	Sheffield 9-12
Apr 22	Chris Blake	l pts 6	Lisbon 10-1
Sep 28	Sugar Gibiliru	drew 8	Solihull 10-1
Oct 26	George Baigrie	w rsf 2	Sheffield 9-13-12
Dec 22	Habib Hammani	l dis 5	Milan
1989			
Mar 9	George Baigrie	w rsf 5	Glasgow 10-2
Apr 4	Kid Silvester	l pts 6	Sheffield
Sep 25	Jeff Decker	w pts 6	NSC
Oct 5	Tony Connellan	l pts 6	Middleton 10-4
Nov 21	Louie Antuna	w pts 8	Glasgow 10-8
Dec 4	Barry Messam	w pts 6	Manchester 10-4-8
1990			
Jan 27	Billy Couzens	l pts 6	Sheffield 10-2
Mar 13	Paul Moylett	w rsf 4*	Bristol 10-2
May 1	Willie Beattie	l rsf 5*	Oldham 10-5-8
Jun 5	Steve Foran	drew 6	Nottingham 10-6
Sep 5	Tony Swift	w rsf 7*	Stoke 10-5
Nov 14	Julian Eavis	w rsf 5*	Sheffield 10-6
1991			
Jan 29	Simon Eubanks	w rsf 3	Wisbech 10-8
Feb 23	Neil Foran	w rsf 2	Brighton 10-6
May 18	Itoro Mkpanam	l rsf 5*	Verbania 10-11-8
Jun 29	Antoine Fernandez	l ko 2	Le Touquet
Sep 21	Eamonn Loughran	l pts 8	Tottenham 10-11
Dec 26	Jean-Charles Meuret	l ko 2	Berne 10-10
1992			
Sep 9	Mark Paine	w pts 6	Stoke 11-0

Fights 61 Won 31 Lost 25 Drawn 5

Alan RICHARDS

Middleweight
Barry, born Cardiff 9 April 1965
Colcot ABC & Rhoose ABC
1987 Welsh ABA middleweight prelim (l P Lewis)
1987 Wales (v Bavaria, l A Mellin)
1988 Welsh ABA middleweight semi-final (w S Phillips, l rtd 3 N Piper)
1988 Wales (v Ire, l C Thornton; v Sco, l D Young; v Nor, l A Bredahl)
1989 Welsh ABA middleweight prelim (l M Phillips)

1989			
May 22	Tony Grizzle	w pts 6	Cardiff 11-4
Jun 5	Ernie Loveridge	w pts 6	Birmingham 11-1
Aug 19	Gary Pemberton	l pts 6	Cardiff 11-1
Nov 22	Martin Robinson	w rsf 2	Stafford 11-0
Nov 28	Jim Beckett	w rsf 2	Wolverhampton 11-0
Dec 11	Tony Britland	w rsf 7	Birmingham 10-12
Dec 21	Colin Pitters	l pts 6	Kings Heath 11-2
1990			
Feb 26	Winston May	w pts 6	Crystal Palace 11-3-8
Mar 5	Darren Pilling	l pts 8	Northampton 11-2-8
Mar 27	Colin Pitters	w pts 8	Wolverhampton 11-2
May 9	Paul Wesley	l pts 8	Solihull 11-5
Jun 6	Trevor Smith	l rsf 7	Battersea 11-4
Sep 12	Andy Till	l pts 8	Battersea 11-1
Oct 24	Wayne Timmins	w ko 4	Dudley 11-2-8
Nov 21	Wally Swift	l pts 8	Solihull 11-2-12
1991			
Jan 28	Nigel Rafferty	drew 8	Birmingham 12-0
Feb 6	Andy Till	l pts 8	Battersea
Apr 12	Frank Grant	l rsf 5	Manchester 11-7
May 14	Andy Flute	l pts 8	Dudley 11-8
Nov 20	Russell Washer	w pts 6	Cardiff 11-11-8
1992			
Feb 11	Wayne Ellis	l pts 10	Cardiff 11-5-8
	(vacant Welsh middleweight title)		
Oct 29	Cornelius Carr	l pts 8	Bayswater 11-10

Fights 22 Won 9 Lost 12 Drawn 1

Chris RICHARDS
Middleweight
Nottingham born 4 April 1964
Nottingham School of Boxing ABC
1983 Midlands ABA welterweight champion (w P Rogers, l L Gloster)
1987 Notts & Lincs ABA light-middleweight final (l C Burton)

1987			
Sep 7	Darren Bowen	w rsf 1	NSC 10-10
Sep 23	Shaun Cummins	l pts 6	Loughborough 11-1
Oct 13	Damien Denny	l pts 6	Windsor 10-11
Nov 3	Brian Robinson	l pts 6	Bethnal Green 11-6
1988			
Jan 18	Stan King	w ko 5	NSC 11-2
Jan 29	Lou Ayres	w rsf 3	Holborn 11-4
Mar 26	Terry Magee	l pts 8	Belfast
May 26	Tony Collins	l rsf 3	Albert Hall 11-2
Oct 10	Antonio Fernandez	l pts 6	Edgbaston 11-2
Nov 23	Antonio Fernandez	l pts 8	Solihull 11-2
Dec 10	Terry Morrill	l pts 6	Crystal Palace 11-3
1989			
Jan 16	Mark Holden	l dis 3	Northampton 11-3
Jan 24	Ian Strudwick	l pts 6	Battersea 11-5
Feb 13	G.L.Booth	w rsf 8	Manchester 11-2-8
Mar 10	Theo Marius	l rsf 2	Brentwood 11-1
May 8	G.L.Booth	w ko 2	Manchester
May 22	Barry Bennett	l pts 8	NSC 11-4 /CTD..

(Chris RICHARDS ctd.)

1990

May 16	Mickey Duncan	l pts 6	Hull
Jun 4	Antonio Fernandez	l pts 8	Edgbaston 11-3
Jun 15	Gary Pemberton	w rtd 1*	Telford 11-1
Sep 14	Seamus Casey	w pts 6	Telford 11-0
Oct 17	Gary Osborne	l pts 8	Stoke 11-2
Nov 13	Andrew Tucker	w ko 2	Hartlepool 11-10-8
Dec 13	Neville Brown	l rsf 2	Dewsbury 11-4-8

1991

Feb 13	Delroy Waul	l pts 6	Wembley CC 11-2
Apr 16	Paul Smith	drew 6	Nottingham 11-5
Apr 24	Colin Pitters	l rsf 6	Stoke 11-2
Nov 26	Adrian Strachan	l pts 6	Bethnal Green 11-4-8

1992

Mar 26	Glen Payton	w pts 6	Telford 11-6
Jun 18	Stefan Wright	l pts 6	Peterborough 11-8
Jul 18	Quinton Paynter	l rsf 6	Manchester 11-7

Fights 31 Won 9 Lost 21 Drawn 1

Michael RICHARDS**

Heavyweight
Wolverhampton born 3 June 1967
Wolverhampton ABC
1988 Midlands ABA super-heavyweight final (w R Brown, w H Henlon, l dis 3 C Mitchell)
1989 Staffordshire ABA super-heavyweight final (l R Brown)

1990

Jan 29	Sean Hunter	w rsf 2	Hull 16-3
Mar 26	Wayne Buck	l ko 1	Nottingham 16-0
May 24	Vance Idiens	w rsf 5	Dudley 16-1
Oct 18	Al Malcolm	w ko 9	Birmingham 16-10
	(Midlands heavyweight title)		
Dec 6	Paul Neilson	w rsf 2	Wolverhampton 16-5

1991

Mar 13	Steve Gee	w pts 6	Stoke 16-3
Jul 3	Herbie Hide	l rsf 3	Brentwood 16-9
Oct 3	Clifton Mitchell	l pts 6	Burton 16-11
Nov 21	Clifton Mitchell	l rsf 6	Burton 16-7

1992

Mar 26	Henry Akinwande	l rsf 2	Telford 17-4

Fights 10 Won 5 Lost 5
** Michael Richards died of a heart attack at home, 27.5.92

Warren RICHARDS

Heavyweight
Eltham born 10 July 1964
Eltham ABC

1990

Apr 24	Mark Langley	w rsf 2	Eltham 15-8
May 26	Mick Cordon	w ko 1	Reading 16-0
Oct 24	Sean Hunter	l rsf 3	Stoke 15-12

1991

Mar 21	Joe Adams	w ko 4	Meridian, Ms 15-7
Apr 12	Johnny Wright	w ko 2	Greenville 15-5

1992
Mar 30	John Westgarth	drew 6	Eltham 16-8
Apr 23	Newbirth Mukosi	w rsf 1	Eltham 16-8
Oct 31	Roger McKenzie	drew 6	Earls Court 16-6

Fights 8 Won 5 Lost 1 Drawn 2

Wayne RIGBY

Super-featherweight
Manchester born 19 July 1973

1992
Feb 27	Lee Fox	l pts 6	Liverpool 9-3-8
Jun 8	Leo Turner	w pts 6	Bradford 9-4
Oct 5	Colin Innes	w pts 6	Manchester 9-6
Dec 1	John B. Kelly	l pts 6	Hartlepool 9-4-8

Fights 4 Won 2 Lost 2

Robert RILEY

Light-middleweight
Sheffield born 22 June 1965
St Vincents ABC

1985
Feb 4	Alan Williams	w pts 6	Liverpool
Oct 13	Wayne Hall	w pts 6	Sheffield

1986
Mar 10	Mick Kane	w pts 6	Manchester

1987
Mar 31	Ossie Maddix	l rsf 3	Oldham

1988-90 inactive

1991
Sep 11	Andreas Panayi	l pts 6	Stoke 10-10
Nov 21	Peter Reid	l pts 6	Ilkeston
Dec 19	Charlie Moore	l pts 6	Oldham 10-10-8

1992
Mar 25	Darren McInulty	w pts 6	Hinckley 11-0
Oct 13	Crain Fisher	w pts 4	Bury 11-2
Nov 12	Darren Pilling	w pts 6	Burnley 11-2

Fights 10 Won 6 Lost 4

Darryl RITCHIE

Light-heavyweight
Rhyl born 26 April 1963
Real name: Darryl Jones
Rhyl ABC

1986
Apr 8	Graham Jenner	l rsf 3	Southend 11-12

1987
Mar 4	Jim Cropper	w rsf 2	Stoke 12-8	
Mar 18	Paul Wesley	drew 4	Stoke 12-2	
Apr 7	Peter Brown	l pts 6	Batley	
Sep 23	Sean Stringfellow	w rsf 1	Stoke 12-6	/CTD..

(Darryl RITCHIE ctd.)

Sep 28	Terry Gilbey	w pts 6	Manchester 12-6
Nov 25	Terry Gilbey	w rsf 7	Cottingham 12-9
Dec 5	Dave Owens	w dis 7	Doncaster 12-7

1988
Apr 26	Adam Cook	l rsf 5	Bethnal Green 12-1

1989
Mar 1	Simon Collins	l rsf 1	Cardiff 12-4
Jun 8	Dario Deabreu	w rsf 6	Cardiff 11-6

1990
inactive

1991
Dec 2	Tony Behan	l rsf 1	Birmingham 12-7

1992
Mar 24	Lee Archer	l pts 6	Wolverhampton 12-6
Nov 14	Karl Mumford	l pts 6	Cardiff 12-7-8

Fights 14 Won 6 Lost 7 Drawn 1

Brian ROBB
Featherweight
Telford born Liverpool 5 April 1967
Shropshire Golden Gloves ABC
1986 Midlands ABA bantamweight champion (l S Murphy)
1987 Midlands ABA bantamweight champion (w rsf 2 Y Vorajee, w rsf 3 P Neale, w D Adams, withdrew)
1988 Birmingham ABA bantamweight final (l rsf 3 K Whistance)

1989
Feb 14	Miguel Matthews	l rsf 2*	Wolverhampton 8-12

1990
Mar 27	Neil Leitch	w pts 6	Wolverhampton 9-2
May 9	Peter Judson	l pts 6	Solihull 9-4
May 22	Nicky Lucas	w pts 6	Canvey Island 9-3
Jun 20	Paul Harvey	l pts 6	Basildon 9-3
Oct 9	Des Gargano	w pts 6	Wolverhampton 9-0
Oct 24	Paul Harvey	l rsf 2	Dudley 9-2

1991
Jan 23	Jason Primera	l rsf 7*	Solihull 9-4
Mar 4	Peter Buckley	l rsf 7*	Birmingham 9-4
Jun 5	Peter Buckley	l pts 10	Wolverhampton 9-3-8
	(vacant Midlands super-featherweight title)		
Aug 29	Renny Edwards	w pts 6	Telford 9-5-12
Oct 31	Miguel Matthews	drew 6	Telford 9-1
Dec 5	Neil Leitch	w ko 2	Telford 9-2

1992
Feb 20	Peter Buckley	l rsf 10	Telford 9-2-8
	(Midlands super-featherweight title)		
Mar 26	Kelton McKenzie	l rsf 4	Telford 9-2
Oct 13	Paul Harvey	l rtd 2	Mayfair 9-5-14
Dec 4	Kevin Middleton	l rsf 1	Telford 8-13

Fights 17 Won 5 Lost 11 Drawn 1

Davey ROBB

Light-welterweight
Telford, born Liverpool 14 August 1964
Royal Navy
1984 Combined Services ABA lightweight final (l ko 1 C Crook)
1985 Combined Services ABA lightweight final (l N Haddock)
1986 Scotland (v Wal, w H Thomas)
1987 Scottish ABA lightweight final (w M Cowans, w K Salmon, w M Logan, l D Anderson)
1987 Navy ABA final (l rsf 2 Q Shillingford)

1987
Nov 9	Steve Phillips	w pts 6	Birmingham 9-12
Nov 24	Andy Morgan	l pts 6	Wolverhampton 9-13
Dec 2	Peter Bowen	w pts 6	Stoke 10-0-8

1988
Jan 20	Dean Bramhald	w pts 8	Stoke 10-0
Feb 24	Mark Reefer	l ko 1	Southend
Apr 13	Dean Bramhald	l rsf 4*	Wolverhampton 10-1-8
Oct 6	Steve Phillips	w pts 8	Dudley 10-1
Nov 10	Oliver Henry	w pts 8	Wolverhampton 10-2
Dec 14	Frankie Lake	w rsf 3	Evesham 9-13

1989
Feb 2	Darren Mount	l rsf 5	Wolverhampton 10-1-8
May 26	Neil Foran	l rsf 4	Bethnal Green 9-12

1990
inactive

1991
Oct 31	Carl Hook	w pts 4	Telford 9-13
Dec 5	Tony Doyle	w pts 6	Telford 9-13

1992
Feb 20	Brian Coleman	w pts 6	Telford 10-2-4
Mar 26	John O. Johnson	w pts 6	Telford 10-2
Dec 10	Nigel Wenton	l rsf 3	Bethnal Green 10-1

Fights 16 Won 10 Lost 6

Carl ROBERTS

Super-featherweight
Blackburn born 19 March 1970
Blackburn & Darwen ABC, Blackburn YMCA
1989 East Lancs & Cheshire ABA featherweight semi-final (l C Breakwell)
1990 East Lancs & Cheshire ABA lightweight semi-final (l rsf 1 J Williams)

1990
Sep 26	Peter Judson	l pts 6	Manchester 9-5-8
Oct 22	Sean Hickey	w ko 4	Manchester 9-6
Nov 26	Colin Innes	w rsf 3	Bury 9-2-4
Dec 17	Trevor Royal	w pts 6	Manchester 9-5-8

1991
Jan 29	Derek Amory	l pts 4	Stockport 9-3
Feb 28	Des Gargano	l pts 6	Bury 8-13-8
Apr 3	Neil Leitch	l rsf 6	Manchester 9-2
Sep 19	Colin Innes	w pts 4	Stockport 9-3-12
Oct 14	Kevin Lowe	w pts 6	Manchester 9-3
Dec 16	Robert Braddock	w pts 6	Manchester 9-0

1992
Mar 10	Graham O'Malley	l pts 6	Bury 9-2
Dec 7	Mike Deveney	l pts 6	Manchester 9-4

Fights 12 Won 6 Lost 6

Dewi ROBERTS

Light-welterweight
Dolgellau, born Bangor 11 September 1968
Idris ABC
Southpaw

1991				
Nov 28	Gavin Lane	l pts 6	Evesham	9-13
1992				
Feb 11	Edward Lloyd	l rsf 1*	Cardiff	10-0
May 11	Nigel Burder	w ko 3	Llanelli	10-7-8

Fights 3 Won 1 Lost 2

Pete ROBERTS

Light-welterweight
Isle of Man & Hull, born Liverpool 15 July 1967

1988				
Oct 25	Mark Jackson	w ko 2	Hartlepool	9-13
Nov 7	Frankie Foster	l pts 6	Bradford	9-9
Nov 17	Tony Banks	l pts 6	Stockport	
1989				
Mar 20	Brendan Ryan	l pts 6	Nottingham	9-13
1990				
Apr 5	Michael Close	w ko 1	Liverpool	10-0
Apr 23	Brendan Ryan	l pts 6	Bradford	9-13
May 4	John Smith	w pts 6	Liverpool	9-11
Oct 9	John Smith	l pts 8	Liverpool	10-0
1991				
Feb 25	Peter Crook	w rsf 6*	Bradford	10-0
Jun 13	Wayne Windle	l rsf 7	Hull	9-7-12
	(vacant Central lightweight title)			
Oct 7	John Smith	w pts 8	Liverpool	10-2
Nov 28	Dave Anderson	l rsf 3	Glasgow	10-0
1992				
Jan 27	Kris McAdam	l ko 2	Glasgow	10-2
Apr 29	Joey Moffat	l rsf 3	Liverpool	9-13

Fights 14 Won 5 Lost 9

Mark ROBERTSON

Flyweight
Kilwinning, born Johnston 30 April 1965

1987				
Sep 21	Gordon Shaw	l pts 6	Glasgow	8-2-4
1988				
Jan 25	Tony Smith	w rsf 1	Glasgow	8-3
Apr 11	Kid Sumaila	drew 6	Glasgow	8-4
1989				
Jan 31	Gordon Shaw	l pts 6	Glasgow	8-3
Feb 17	Gordon Shaw	l pts 6	Irvine	
1990-91				
inactive				
1992				
Jan 31	Neil Armstrong	l rsf 6*	Glasgow	8-2
Apr 10	Louis Veitch	w pts 6	Glasgow	8-3

Fights 7 Won 2 Lost 4 Drawn 1

Andrew ROBINSON

Lightweight
Birmingham born 6 November 1965
Real name: Andrew White
Small Heath ABC
Southpaw

1988
Jun 14	Darrell Pettit	drew 6	Birmingham 9-5
Sep 29	Darrell Pettit	w pts 6	Stafford 9-1
Oct 17	Sean Hogg	l pts 6	Birmingham
Dec 1	Mark Antony	l pts 6	Stafford 9-8
Dec 12	Peter Bowen	l ko 4	Birmingham 9-8

1989
Mar 15	Phil Lashley	w pts 6	Stoke 9-1
Oct 10	Jamie Morris	w pts 6	Wolverhampton 9-6

1990
Mar 7	Dean Bramhald	w pts 6	Doncaster 9-12
Mar 19	Peter Judson	l pts 6	Cleethorpes 9-7
Apr 11	Tony Silkstone	l pts 6	Dewsbury 9-3
Apr 26	Tony Silkstone	l pts 6	Halifax 9-3
May 30	Kruga Hydes	l pts 6	Stoke 9-1
Jun 21	Mark Antony	l pts 6	Alfreton 9-12
Jul 10	Bradley Stone	l pts 6	Canvey Island 9-3
Sep 27	Elvis Parsley	l rtd 3*	NEC 9-3
Oct 24	Richard Woolgar	l rsf 3	Dudley 9-6
Nov 26	Sugar Free Somerville	w pts 6	Bethnal Green 9-12

1991
Apr 15	Finn McCool	drew 6	Leicester 9-7
May 13	Dean Bramhald	w rtd 1*	Birmingham 9-9
May 16	Craig Dermody	l pts 6	Liverpool 9-1-8

1992
Apr 29	Lee Fox	l pts 6	Stoke 9-9

Fights 21 Won 6 Lost 13 Drawn 2

Billy ROBINSON

Light-welterweight
Hinckley born Desford 3 October 1963
Venture ABC
1990 North Midlands ABA welterweight semi-final (l S Taylor)

1991
Oct 1	Steve Bricknell	w pts 6	Bedworth 10-2

1992
Feb 11	Mark Antony	w rsf 5	Wolverhampton 10-2
Mar 25	Dave Lovell	w pts 6	Hinckley 10-4

Fights 3 Won 3

Des ROBINSON

Welterweight
Manchester born 5 January 1965
Moss Side ABC & West Gorton ABC
1987 East Lancs ABA light-welterweight semi-final (w ko 1 D Lincoln, l N Boyd)

1989
Sep 26	Carl Watson	w rtd 2*	Oldham 10-10-12	
Oct 5	Tommy Warde	w rsf 2	Middleton 10-12	/CTD..

(Des ROBINSON ctd.)

Oct 20	Martin Smith	l pts 6	Manchester 10-12
Nov 10	Richard Adams	drew 6	Battersea 10-7
Nov 16	David Heath	w rsf 3	Manchester
Dec 3	Colin Pitters	w pts 6	Birmingham 10-11-8
1990			
Feb 27	Ricky Nelson	w rsf 6	Manchester 11-2
Mar 15	Jim Talbot	w pts 8	Manchester 10-7
Mar 26	Tony Baker	w pts 8	Bradford 10-12
Apr 26	Rocky Bryan	w pts 6	Battersea 10-9
May 22	Jimmy Harrison	w pts 6	St Albans 11-2-8
Jun 11	Tony Britland	w pts 8	Manchester 10-10
Oct 25	Razor Akwei Addo	l pts 8	Bayswater 10-9
1991			
Feb 11	Willie Beattie	l pts 8	Glasgow 10-8-12
Mar 19	Lindon Scarlett	l rsf 4	Birmingham 10-10-8
Oct 17	Gary Logan	l pts 8	Southwark 10-7-12
1992			
Sep 28	Darren Morris	w pts 6	Manchester 10-3-8
Nov 14	Michael Smyth	l pts 6	Cardiff 10-7-8

Fights 18 Won 11 Lost 6 Drawn 1

Jamie ROBINSON

Middleweight
West Ham born 12 September 1968
Repton ABC
1984 National Schools champion (w D Phillips)
1984 NABC Class A final (l K Whalley)
1985 Junior ABA Class B champion
1988 NE London ABA middleweight semi-final (w rtd 1 J Warren, l rtd 2 V Golding)
1989 NE London ABA light-middle quarter-final (l T Taylor)
1990 ABA middleweight semi-final (w T King, w rsf 3 J Matthews, w rsf 2 C Tsirtos, w rsf 2 S Kerr, w E Noi, l D Griffiths)

1990			
Aug 17	Deke DePalma	w pts 4 (m)	Las Vegas 11-7
Oct 4	Rodney Knox	l rsf 1	Atlantic City 11-4-8
1991			
Oct 23	Dave Whittle	w rsf 4	Bethnal Green 11-2
Nov 13	Michael Oliver	w pts 6	Bethnal Green 10-13
1992			
Feb 11	Julian Eavis	w pts 6	Barking 11-3-8
Apr 2	Mark Jay	w pts 6	Basildon 11-4
Oct 22	Gary Pemberton	w rsf 3*	Bethnal Green 11-6
Dec 17	Lee Crocker	w rtd 2	Barking 11-2

Fights 8 Won 7 Lost 1

Steve ROBINSON

Featherweight
Cardiff born 13 December 1968
Ely Star ABC

1989			
Mar 1	Alan Roberts	w pts 6	Cardiff 9-2
Mar 13	Terry Smith	w rsf 4	NSC 9-4
Apr 6	Nico Lucas	l pts 8	Cardiff 9-2

May 4	John Devine	w pts 6	Mayfair 9-0
Aug 19	Marcel Herbert	l pts 6	Cardiff 8-12
Nov 13	Shane Silvester	w rsf 2	Brierley Hill 9-0
1990			
Jul 10	Mark Bates	l pts 6	Canvey Island 9-3
Sep 12	Tim Driscoll	l pts 8	Bethnal Green 8-13
Sep 26	Russ Davison	w pts 8	Manchester 9-0
Oct 3	Drew Docherty	l pts 8	Solihull 8-11-4
Oct 22	Alan McKay	l pts 6	NSC 8-13
Nov 19	Neil Haddock	w rsf 9*	Cardiff 9-2-8
	(final eliminator, Welsh super-featherweight title)		
Dec 19	Brian Roche	drew 6	Preston 9-0
1991			
Apr 24	Russ Davison	w rtd 6	Preston 9-0
May 28	Colin Lynch	w rsf 6	Cardiff 9-1
Jul 18	Peter Harris	w pts 10	Cardiff 8-13-8
	(Welsh featherweight title)		
1992			
Jan 31	Henry Armstrong	l pts 6	Manchester 8-13
May 11	Neil Haddock	l pts 10	Llanelli 9-1
	(vacant Welsh super-featherweight title)		
Oct 7	Edward Lloyd	w rtd 8	Barry 9-3-8
Oct 30	Stephane Haccoun	w pts 8	Istres 8-12-8
Dec 1	Dennis Oakes	w rtd 2*	Liverpool 9-0

Fights 21 Won 12 Lost 8 Drawn 1

Tim ROBINSON

Middleweight
Grimsby born 28 June 1968
Grimsby Exchange ABC
1991 North-East Counties ABA middleweight final (w A Manning, l rsf 1 P Hitch)
1992 Yorkshire & Humberside ABA middleweight quarter-final (l rsf 3 G Dunbar)

1992			
Sep 21	Paul Hanlon	l pts 6	Cleethorpes 11-10
Oct 15	Griff Jones	l rsf 3*	Hull 11-8
Dec 14	Mohammed Malik	w rsf 3	Cleethorpes 11-6

Fights 3 Won 1 Lost 2

Martin ROSAMOND

Middleweight
Southampton born Cyprus 10 March 1969
Golden Ring ABC
1988 Southern ABA welterweight semi-final (w ko 1 M Philpott, l K Rayment)

1989				
Mar 2	Andy Tonks	w rsf 2	Southampton 10-13	
Apr 4	Barry Bennett	l pts 6	Southend	
Apr 26	Johnny Stone	l rsf 3	Southampton 11-0	
Sep 21	Tony Grizzle	w rsf 5	Southampton 11-0	
Sep 28	Max Wallace	l rsf 1	Battersea	
1990				
Feb 8	Darren Burford	l rsf 5	Southwark 11-0	
Mar 10	Peter Reid	l rsf 6	Bristol 11-0-8	
May 21	Tony Grizzle	w rsf 2	NSC 11-0	
Jun 22	Jimmy McDonagh	w rsf 6	Gillingham 11-2	/CTD..

(Martin ROSAMOND ctd.)

Oct 18	Matthew Jones	w pts 6	Birmingham 11-0
Nov 6	Kid Silvester	l rsf 3	Mayfair 11-0
Dec 8	Cliff Churchward	w pts 6	Bristol 11-0
1991			
Feb 21	Rob Pitters	l rsf 2	Walsall 10-10
Apr 11	Seamus Casey	l pts 6	Willenhall 11-2
Apr 23	Barry Messam	l pts 6	Evesham 11-1
May 8	Marty Duke	drew 8	Millwall 11-3
May 23	Mike Morrison	w pts 6	Southampton 11-5-8
Jun 4	Adrian Strachan	l pts 6	Bethnal Green 11-4
Jul 3	Kevin Sheeran	l ko 1	Reading 11-1-8
Sep 24	Adrian Strachan	l pts 6	Basildon 11-7
1992			
Jan 20	Lee Ferrie	l rsf 2	Coventry 11-4
Sep 19	Willie Quinn	l rsf 4	Glasgow 11-9-8

Fights 22 Won 7 Lost 14 Drawn 1

Vince ROSE
Light-middleweight
Tottenham
New Enterprise ABC
1992 NWLondon ABA welter champion (w A Katerega, w E Diedrick, w rsf 1 J Paul, l dis 3 S Prendergast)

1992

Oct 13	Ojay Abrahams	w rsf 3*	Mayfair 10-9
Nov 14	Marty Duke	w pts 6	Cardiff 11-1-8

Fights 2 Won 2

Jason ROWLAND
Light-welterweight
West Ham born 6 August 1970
Repton ABC
1984 National Schools final (l A Wright)
1986 NABC Class A champion
1986 Junior ABA champion
1987 NABC Class B champion
1989 London ABA light champ (w J Weatherman, w P Harvey, w M Moran, w T Franklin, l M Ramsey)

1989

Sep 19	Terry Smith	w rsf 1	Millwall 9-10
Nov 15	Mike Morrison	w pts 6	Reading 9-12-8
1990			
Feb 14	Eamonn Payne	w pts 6	Millwall 9-13
Apr 17	David Jenkins	w ko 1	Millwall 10-0
May 22	Mike Morrison	w pts 6	St Albans 10-0
1991			
Feb 12	Vaughan Carnegie	w pts 6	Basildon 10-1-8
Mar 7	Vaughan Carnegie	w ko 2	Basildon 10-1
Dec 11	Brian Cullen	w rsf 4*	Basildon 10-3-8
1992			
Apr 30	Steve Pollard	w rsf 2*	Albert Hall 10-2-8
Dec 17	Jimmy Vincent	w pts 6	Wembley GH 10-2-8

Fights 10 Won 10

Roy ROWLAND

Welterweight
West Ham born 19 May 1967
Repton ABC
1981 National Schools champion (w R Thomas)
1982 National Schools champion (w S Durham)
1982 Junior ABA champion (w N Stansfield)
1983 National Schools champion
1983 Junior ABA final (l A Steadman)
1983 NABC Class A champion (w A Banks)
1984 NABC Class B champion (w T Langton)
1985 Young England (v YEGer, l D Krouse, l ko 2 J Wolter)
1986 London ABA light-welter final (w rsf 3 D Hinds, w rsf 2 D Farquhar, w M Moran, l dis 3 R Bryan)

1986
Oct 29	Nicky Lucas	w pts 6	Muswell Hill 10-2
Dec 3	Nick Meloscia	w pts 6	Muswell Hill 10-3-4

1987
Jan 13	Ray Golding	w pts 6	Oldham 10-5
Mar 4	Andy Cox	w rsf 3	Oldham 10-7-8
Sep 20	Brian Wareing	w ko 1	Bethnal Green 10-7-4
Nov 3	Wilbert Halliday	w rsf 1	Bethnal Green 10-7
Dec 2	Roy Callaghan	w pts 6	Albert Hall 10-7

1988
Mar 9	Dave Haggarty	w rsf 1	Bethnal Green 10-7-8
Mar 29	Nick Meloscia	l rsf 1*	Bethnal Green 10-6-8
Sep 7	Kelvin Mortimer	w pts 6	Reading 10-8-8
Nov 1	Kevin Hayde	w pts 6	Reading 10-9

1989
Jan 25	Andy Tonks	w rtd 1*	Bethnal Green
Feb 15	Mike Russell	w rsf 2	Bethnal Green 10-6
Mar 28	Paul Seddon	w rsf 3	Bethnal Green
Sep 14	John Smith	w rsf 3*	Basildon 10-6
Nov 15	Lloyd Lee	w pts 8	Reading 10-8

1990
Apr 25	Peter Eubanks	w rsf 8*	Millwall 10-5-8

1991
Feb 12	Paul Lynch	l rtd 4*	Basildon 10-10
Jun 6	Mark Kelly	w rsf 4	Barking 10-7-8
Oct 2	Peter Eubanks	w pts 8	Barking 10-8-8

1992
Mar 25	Humphrey Harrison	w ko 7	Dagenham 10-9-12
Oct 28	Darren Morris	w rsf 2*	Albert Hall 10-10
Dec 17	Gary Logan	l rsf 4*	Wembley GH 10-6-8
	(vacant Southern welterweight title)		

Fights 23 Won 20 Lost 3

Marc ROWLEY

Super-middleweight
Hinckley, born Chatham 3 October 1972
Venture ABC

1991
Sep 16	Dave Hall	l pts 6	Cleethorpes 11-8	
Oct 8	Dave Hall	l pts 6	Wolverhampton 11-7-8	
Nov 7	Mark Hale	l pts 6	Peterborough 12-1-8	
Dec 2	Andy Manning	l pts 6	Liverpool 12-0	
Dec 11	Brian McGloin	l pts 6	Leicester 12-0	/CTD..

(Marc ROWLEY ctd.)
1992

Jan 15	Danny Walker	w ko 5	Stoke 11-7
Mar 25	Mark Hale	l pts 6	Hinckley 12-2-8
May 18	Lee Archer	l pts 6	Bardon 12-8

Fights 8 Won 1 Lost 7

Jess RUNDAN

Light-welterweight
Plymouth, born Redruth 17 October 1961
Devonport ABC

1984

Oct 10	Ray Newby	l rsf 3	Evesham

1985

Jan 18	Dave Smith	l ko 3	Bethnal Green
Mar 15	Dave Henderson	drew 6	Maidenhead
Apr 1	Paul McKenzie	l rsf 4	Dulwich
May 19	Jimmy Harrison	l rsf 2	Bayswater
Jul 31	Young Doherty	l rsf 3	Porthcawl

1986

May 19	Barry Bacon	w rsf 1	Plymouth
Sep 8	Mark Dinnadge	l rsf 3	Dulwich
Nov 17	Mickey Crawford	l rsf 3	Dulwich

1987

Jan 27	B.F.Williams	w pts 6	Plymouth
Feb 25	Paul Gadney	l pts 6	Lewisham
May 26	Ian Honeywood	l rtd 3	Plymouth

1988-90 inactive

1991

Nov 20	Seth Jones	l ko 4	Cardiff 10-2-8

1992

Apr 30	Ronnie Shinkwin	l rsf 1	Watford 9-13

Fights 14 Won 2 Lost 11 Drawn 1

Mike RUSSELL

Middleweight
Plymouth born 12 July 1967
Ford ABC

1986

May 19	Joey Dee	w pts 6	Plymouth 9-2
Jun 26	Paul Gadney	w ko 5	Chippenham 9-4
Sep 26	Davey Hughes	l pts 6	Swindon 9-5-8
Oct 22	Rudi Valentino	l pts 6	Greenwich 9-7
Nov 17	Tim Driscoll	l pts 6	Dulwich 9-3-8
Nov 26	Paul Gadney	w dis 1	Lewisham 9-8

1987

Jan 27	Mickey Crawford	w pts 6	Plymouth
Mar 2	Wayne Weekes	l pts 6	Lewisham 9-11
Mar 26	Andrew Prescod	l rsf 5	Wimbledon 9-10
Apr 30	Robert Smythe	l pts 6	Newport 9-9
Jun 25	Mark Bates	w pts 6	Bethnal Green 9-8
Aug 3	Pat Barrett	l pts 6	Stoke 10-0

Sep 18	B.F. Williams	l pts 8	Swindon 9-12
Sep 28	Tony Ekubia	l rsf 3	Manchester 9-12
Oct 28	Mark Pearce	drew 6	Swansea 9-11
Nov 5	John Dickson	l pts 6	Bethnal Green 10-1-8
Dec 8	Neil Haddock	l pts 8	Plymouth 9-5

1988

Feb 6	Ron Shinkwin	l pts 8	Newbury 10-3
Feb 25	Tony Gibbs	w pts 6	Bethnal Green 10-4-8
Mar 15	Mark Purcell	nc 1	Bournemouth 9-12

(final eliminator, Western light-welterweight title)

Apr 20	Chubby Martin	l pts 6	Muswell Hill 9-13
Apr 26	Tony Borg	l pts 6	Hove 10-0-8
May 3	Richie Joyce	l pts 4	Stoke 9-12
Jun 8	Nigel Bradley	l pts 6	Sheffield 9-12
Aug 31	Michael Driscoll	l ko 2	Holborn 10-3

1989

Jan 12	Gary Logan	l ko 1	Southwark 10-8-8
Feb 15	Roy Rowland	l rsf 2	Bethnal Green 10-12
Mar 22	Kid Silvester	l pts 6	Gloucester 11-2
Apr 20	G.W. Gully	l pts 6	Weston-super-Mare 10-12
Jun 20	Dennis Sullivan	l rsf 3	Plymouth 10-10-8
Sep 5	Dave Worthington	l ko 2	Southend
Dec 11	Robert Wright	l ko 1	Birmingham 10-7

1990

Oct 25	Darren Murphy	l pts 6	Battersea 11-0
Nov 15	Delroy Waul	l ko 1	Oldham 10-10-8

1991

Nov 20	Michael Smyth	l rsf 3	Cardiff 11-2

1992

Feb 12	Danny Shinkwin	l pts 6	Watford 11-0
Feb 25	Tony McCarthy	l pts 6	Crystal Palace 11-7
Apr 2	Kevin Sheeran	l rsf 2	Basildon 11-5

Fights 38 Won 6 Lost 30 Drawn 1 No Contest 1

Brendan RYAN

Light-welterweight
Nottingham born 2 November 1970
Clifton ABC & Ruddington ABC

1989

Mar 6	Andy Rowbotham	w rsf 2	Leicester 9-10
Mar 20	Pete Roberts	w pts 6	Nottingham 9-13
May 8	Andy Sweeney	w pts 6	Leicester 9-10
May 15	Andy Kent	w pts 6	Northampton 9-11
May 22	Andy Kent	w pts 6	Peterborough 9-9
Jun 5	John Ritchie	l pts 6	Glasgow 9-11
Sep 25	Lyn Davies	l rsf 2	Leicester 9-10
Nov 20	Mick Mulcahy	w pts 6	Leicester 9-13
Dec 4	Wayne Windle	drew 6	Manchester 9-9-8
Dec 11	Paul Bowen	w pts 6	Nottingham 9-10

1990

Jan 24	Brian Cullen	l pts 8	Stoke 9-13
Feb 5	Oliver Henry	drew 6	Leicester 9-13
Feb 19	Brian Cullen	w pts 8	Nottingham 9-11
Feb 26	James Jiora	l pts 6	Bradford 9-11
Mar 19	John Smith	w pts 6	Leicester 10-0
Apr 10	Mark Kelly	l pts 6	Doncaster 10-0-4 /CTD..

(Brendan RYAN ctd.)

Apr 23	Pete Roberts	w pts 6	Bradford
May 14	Vaughan Carnegie	l pts 6	Leicester 10-2
May 21	Dean Bramhald	drew 6	Cleethorpes 10-1-4
Jun 4	Malcolm Melvin	w rsf 7	Edgbaston 10-3
Sep 17	John Townsley	drew 8	Glasgow 10-3
Nov 13	Malcolm Melvin	l pts 10	Edgbaston 10-0
	(vacant Midlands light-welterweight title)		
1991			
Apr 24	Richie Joyce	l pts 8	Stoke 10-3
1992			
May 14	Carl Wright	l pts 4	Liverpool 10-3
Jun 16	Bernard Paul	l ko 6	Dagenham 10-4

Fights 25 Won 11 Lost 10 Drawn 4

Paul RYAN

Lightweight
Hackney born 2 February 1965
St Monicas ABC
1991 London ABA light-welter champ (w A Hennessey, w rsf 1 E Roseway, w rsf 1 M White, l ko 3 G Smith)

1991			
Sep 26	Chris Mylan	w pts 6	Dunstable 9-10
1992			
Jan 18	Alex Sterling	w rsf 4	Albert Hall 9-11-12
Mar 25	Michael Clynch	w rsf 4	Dagenham 9-13-8
May 16	Greg Egbuniwe	w rsf 4	Muswell Hill 9-12
Sep 26	Korso Aleain	w ko 4	Olympia 9-12
Dec 17	Rick Bushell	w rsf 1	Barking 9-13-8

Fights 6 Won 6

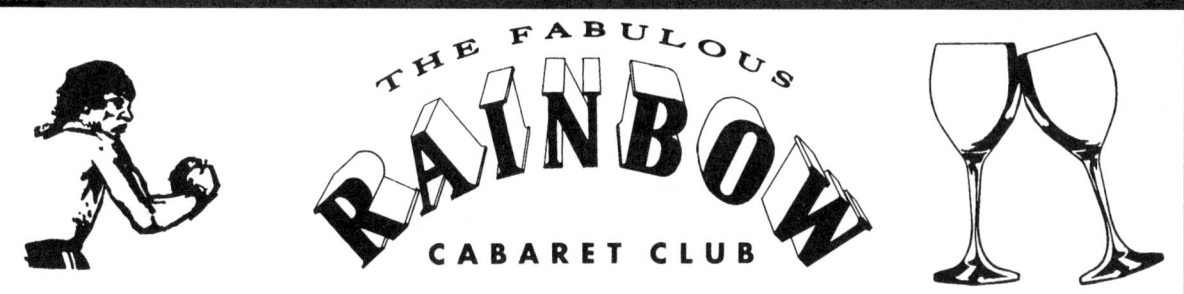

McMahon Promotions
CHRIS SANIGAR - General Manager
DEAN POWELL - Matchmaker

Tel: 0831 359978

60 Stapleton Road	3 Atlantic Avenue	35 Chapel Market
Easton	Belfast	Islington
Bristol BS5 0RB	BT15 2HN	London N1 9EN
Tel: 0272 411385	Tel: 0232 743535	Tel: 071 833 8656
Fax: 0272 559740	Fax: 0846 676935	Fax: 071 278 7389

Supported by

THE WINNING COMBINATION

144 High Street, Sunderland
Tyne & Wear SR1 2BL
Tel: 091 567 6871
Fax: 091 565 2581

TOMMY CONROY
Manager and trainer
ANNETTE CONROY
First North East lady promoter
Matchmaker: Graham Lockwood
Trainers: Tommy Tote, Micky Hitch,
Charlie Armstrong, Billy Melton, Barry Norman

JOHN DAVISON
RANKED WORLD No 8 BY WBO

SUNDERLAND BASED STABLE RECORD (To December 1992)

		C	W	L	D				C	W	L	D	
JOHN DAVISON	Newcastle	17	14	3	0	WBC Int. Super Bantamweight Champ. Undefeated ex. WBC Int. Featherweight Champ. No. 1 EBU Featherweight Cont. British Featherweight Champ	PAUL HITCH	Wingate	10	9	1	0	No. 1 Contender Northern Area Light Middleweight Title
							DAVE JOHNSON	Boldon	11	9	1	1	Middleweight
PAUL CHARTERS	North Shields	32	19	13	0	Northern Area Lightweight Champ. British EBU Commonwealth Lightweight Cont.	COLIN INNES	Newcastle	17	6	10	1	Super Featherweight
							MICKY HALL	Ludworth	6	3	2	1	Lightweight
FRANKIE FOSTER	Newcastle	25	11	11	3	Northern Area Super-Feather weight Champ. British EBU Commonwealth Super-Featherwt Cont.	CHIP O'NEILL	Sunderland	5	3	2	0	Featherweight
TERRY FRENCH	Dunston	27	14	12	1	Northern Area Light Heavyweiaght Champ	HUGH DAVEY	Wallsend	5	4	0	1	Welterweight
IAN HENRY	Gateshead	16	13	3	0	No. 1 Contender Northern Area Light Heavyweight Title	ALAN GRAHAM	Newcastle	2	1	1	0	Lightweight
ROB PITTERS	Gateshead	13	9	2	2	No. 1 Contender Northern Area Light Middleweight Title	TIM HILL	North Shields	1	1	0	0	Lightweight

---

THE 'STARDUST' SPORTING CLUB

Beveridge Lane, Bardon, Leicestershire LE6 2TB

JOHNNY GRIFFIN BOXING PROMOTIONS AND MANAGEMENT TAKES GREAT PLEASURE IN PRESENTING HIS ALL-ACTION TEAM LICENSED WITH THE B.B.B.C.

Lee Ferrie
Light-middleweight
(Coventry)

J. J. Cooke
Super-middleweight
(Coventry)

Ray Newby
Light-welterweight
(Nottingham)

Brendan Ryan
Light-welterweight
(Nottingham)

Chris Walker
Super-middleweight
(Nottingham)

Billy Robinson
Light-welterweight
(Hinckley)

Marc Rowley
Super-middleweight
(Hinckley)

Craig Hartwell
Welterweight
(Rugby)

James McGee
Light-middleweight
(Bedworth)

Wilf McGee
Middleweight
(Bedworth)

Mark Hale
Super-middleweight
(Nuneaton)

Darren McInulty
Welterweight
(Nuneaton)

Jamie Morris
Light-welterweight
(Nuneaton)

Colin Anderson
Welterweight
(Leicester)

Mark Brogan
Light-middleweight
(Leicester)

Michael Postesous
Cruiserweight
(Nottingham)

MORE NEW SIGNINGS TO BE ANNOUNCED LATER
All enquiries to Johnny Griffin (0533) 629287 any time,
98 Stonehill Avenue, Birstall, Leicester LE4 4JD

CHAMPS

FOR ALL OF YOUR BOXING REQUIREMENTS AND LEISURE WEAR

CHAMPS

52 HIGHTOWN ROAD, LUTON, BEDS. LU2 0DQ
Telephone: (0582) 482286

Ricky SACKFIELD
Welterweight
Salford, born Birmingham 11 April 1967

1991
Apr 30	Willie Yeardsley	w pts 4	Stockport 10-7
Sep 19	Seth Jones	w rsf 1*	Stockport 10-3
Oct 21	Rob Stewart	l pts 6	Bury 10-1-8

1992
Jan 21	Dave Thompson	w ko 1	Stockport 10-1-8
Feb 3	Scott Doyle	w pts 6	Manchester 10-4
Mar 9	John O. Johnson	l pts 6	Manchester 10-1
Mar 31	Carl Wright	l rsf 1	Stockport 10-3-12
Sep 24	Mark Legg	l pts 6	Manchester 10-1-8

Fights 8 Won 4 Lost 4

Kenny SANDISON
Heavyweight
Liverpool born 30 July 1966
Rose Heath ABC

1992
Dec 1	Gary Williams	l pts 6	Liverpool 14-5

Fights 1 Lost 1

Chris SAUNDERS
Light-welterweight
Barnsley born 15 August 1969
Southpaw
Wombwell ABC
1989 Yorkshire ABA light-welterweight champion (w W Nuttall, w P Sellers, l rsf 1 A Hall)

1990
Feb 22	Malcolm Melvin	w pts 4	Hull 10-1-8
Apr 10	Mike Morrison	w pts 6	Doncaster 9-11
May 20	Justin Graham	w rsf 3	Sheffield 10-1-8
Nov 29	Ross Hale	l pts 6	Bayswater 10-0

1991
Mar 5	Rocky Ferrari	l pts 4	Glasgow 9-10-8
Mar 19	Richard Woolgar	w rsf 3*	Leicester 9-10
Mar 26	Felix Kelly	l pts 6	Bethnal Green 9-11-8
Apr 17	Billy Schwer	l rsf 1*	Albert Hall 9-12
May 16	Riki Burton	l pts 6	Liverpool 10-4
Jun 6	Mark Tibbs	w rsf 6	Barking 10-0-8
Jun 30	Billy Schwer	l rsf 3	Southwark 9-10-12
Aug 1	James Jiora	w pts 6	Dewsbury 9-13
Oct 3	Gary Flear	l pts 6	Burton 10-7
Oct 24	Ronnie Shinkwin	w pts 6	Dunstable 10-2-12
Nov 21	Jason Matthews	l rsf 4*	Burton 10-3

1992
Jan 30	John O. Johnson	l pts 6	Southampton 10-0-4
Feb 11	Eddie King	w rsf 4	Wolverhampton 10-2
Feb 27	Riki Burton	l pts 10	Liverpool 9-13-9
	(vacant Central light-welterweight title)		
Sep 9	John O. Johnson	drew 6	Stoke 10-4
Sep 30	Mark McCreath	l rsf 4	Telford 10-3-8
Dec 1	Shea Neary	l pts 6	Liverpool 10-5

Fights 21 Won 8 Lost 12 Drawn 1

Lindon SCARLETT

Welterweight
Dudley born 11 January 1967
Dudley ABC

1987
Apr 22	Tommy Shiels	l pts 6	Albert Hall 10-10
May 7	Johnny Miller	w pts 6	Bayswater 10-11
Nov 9	Sean Heron	l pts 6	Glasgow 11-0

1988
Jan 20	Simon Paul	w pts 6	Solihull 10-12
Apr 12	Ted Kershaw	l rsf 7	Oldham 10-11

1989
Oct 11	Carlo Colarusso	w pts 8	Stoke 10-12
Nov 22	Carlo Colarusso	w pts 8	Solihull 10-12-8
Dec 6	Julian Eavis	w pts 8	Stoke 10-10

1990
Feb 14	Wayne Ellis	drew 6	Millwall 11-0-8
Mar 13	Romolo Casamonica	l pts 10 (s)	Milan 10-10
May 8	Mickey Lloyd	l rsf 2*	Brentford 10-7-12
Oct 18	Kevin Spratt	w rsf 2	Birmingham 10-6
Nov 16	Tony Gibbs	w pts 6	Telford 10-4-8

1991
Mar 19	Des Robinson	w rsf 4	Birmingham 10-7-8
Oct 24	Razor Akwei Addo	w pts 8	Bayswater 10-9-8

1992
Jan 22	Kelvin Mortimer	w rsf 1	Solihull 10-8-12
Feb 8	Javier Castillejos	l pts 8	Madrid
May 23	Chris Peters	drew 8	Birmingham 10-6-8

Fights 18 Won 10 Lost 6 Drawn 2

Billy SCHWER

Lightweight
Luton born 12 April 1969
Luton Irish ABC
1983 National Schools champion
1984 National Schools champion (w D Ashton)
1984 Junior ABA semi-final (l D Binch)
1987 NABC Class C final (l T Mock)

1987 Young England (v Yug, w rsf 2 Farizaj; v WGer, w D Schillinger; v Sco, w rsf 1 I Black; v EGer, l M Hulsmann)
1988 Home Counties ABA lightweight champion (w ko 1 T Saunders, w R Woolgar, l rsf 2 M Ramsey)
1989 Bronze in Multi-nations in Finland
1989 Home Counties ABA lightweight champion (w rsf 1 T Cromwell, l P Dyer)
1990 ABA lightweight final (w rsf 2 S Garner, w P Ramsey, w G Thornhill, w D Connolly, l P Gallagher)

1990
Oct 4	Pierre Conon	w rsf 1	Bethnal Green 9-10
Oct 30	Mark Antony	w rsf 2	Wembley 9-8-12
Dec 12	Sean Casey	w rsf 1	Albert Hall 9-8

1991
Jan 16	David Jenkins	w pts 6	Albert Hall 9-8-8
Feb 7	John Smith	w rsf 2*	Watford 9-8-8
Mar 6	Chubby Martin	w rsf 3*	Wembley 9-8-8
Apr 4	Andy Robins	w rsf 2	Watford 9-9-12
Apr 17	Chris Saunders	w rsf 1*	Albert Hall 9-8-8
May 2	Karl Taylor	w rsf 2*	Northampton 9-9
Jun 30	Chris Saunders	w rsf 3	Southwark 9-8-8

Sep 11	Tony Foster	w pts 8	Hammersmith 9-9
Sep 26	Felix Kelly	w rsf 2	Dunstable 9-8
Oct 24	Patrick Kamy	w ko 1	Dunstable 9-8
Nov 20	Marcel Herbert	w pts 8	Albert Hall 9-8
1992			
Feb 12	Tomas Quinones	w ko 8	Wembley GH 9-8-8
Mar 25	Bobby Brewer	w rsf 4*	Albert Hall 9-7-12
Sep 3	Wayne Windle	w ko 1	Dunstable 9-9-12
Oct 28	Carl Crook	w rtd 9	Albert Hall 9-8
	(British & Commonwealth lightweight titles)		
Dec 17	Mauricio Aceves	w rsf 3*	Wembley GH 9-9-8

Fights 19 Won 19

Bruce SCOTT

Cruiserweight
Hackney, born Jamaica 16 August 1969
St Monicas ABC
1990 NE London ABA light-heavyweight semi-final (l dis 3 G Delaney)

1991			
Apr 25	Mark Bowen	l pts 6	Mayfair 13-11
Sep 16	Randy B. Powell	w rsf 5	AASC 12-11-8
Nov 21	Steve Osborne	w pts 6	Burton
1992			
Apr 27	John Kaighin	w ko 4	AASC 12-12
Sep 7	Lee Prudden	w pts 6	Bethnal Green 13-0
Dec 3	Mark Paine	w rsf 5	Catford 13-7-8

Fights 6 Won 5 Lost 1

Steve SCOTT

Welterweight
Chorley, born Preston 20 January 1966

1992			
Mar 4	Allan Grainger	l pts 6	Glasgow 10-11
Mar 26	Rob Stevenson	l pts 6	Hull 10-8
Sep 14	Danny Harper	drew 6	Bradford 10-10
Oct 27	Steve Levene	w rsf 1	Cradley Heath 11-0
Oct 30	James Campbell	l pts 6	NEC 10-12
Nov 26	Rob Stevenson	w pts 6	Hull 10-10
Dec 14	Kevin Spratt	l pts 6	Bradford 10-8

Fights 7 Won 2 Lost 4 Drawn 1

Greg SCOTT-BRIGGS

Light-heavyweight
Chesterfield, born Manzine, Swaziland 6 February 1966
Chesterfield & Danesmore ABC

1992			
Feb 4	Mark McBiane	w pts 6	Alfreton 12-5
Mar 3	Tony Colclough	w rsf 2*	Cradley Heath 12-11
Mar 30	Carl Smallwood	l pts 6	Coventry 12-8
Apr 27	Richard Atkinson	l pts 6	Bradford 12-2
May 23	Steve Walton	w pts 6	Gosforth 12-9
Jun 4	Joe Frater	l pts 6	Cleethorpes 12-8-8
Sep 30	Carl Smallwood	l pts 6	Solihull 12-8

Fights 7 Won 3 Lost 4

Hussain SHAH

Light-heavyweight
Crayford, born Pakistan 1 June 1964
Real name: Hussain Syed Shah
1988 Olympic middleweight bronze medal (w pts Amarillas, Mx; w M Kabongo, Zre; w Z Fuezescy, Hn; l E Marcus, Can)
1990 Commonwealth Games middleweight prelim (l S Wilson, Sc)

1992
Apr 30	Paul McCarthy	w rtd 4	Albert Hall 12-6-8
Sep 26	Nicky Wadman	w rsf 4	Olympia 12-7-8
Dec 10	Kenny Nevers	w pts 4	Bethnal Green

Fights 3 Won 3

Kevin SHEERAN

Light-middleweight
Crawley, born Redhill 10 August 1971
Crawley ABC
1987 Junior ABA final
1987 National Schools final
1988 NABC Class B final
1989 Southern ABA welterweight final (w rsf 3 D Groves, l B Wisbey)
1990 Southern ABA light-middle champ (w P Tuckey, w S Barnett, w rsf 3 S Kenneth, w dis 3 C Demonte, l ko 1 A Arthur)

1991
Mar 5	Richard Okumu	l rsf 2	Millwall 11-2-4
May 8	Cliff Churchward	w pts 6	Millwall 10-13-8
May 22	Stuart Good	w pts 6	Millwall 11-3
Jul 3	Martin Rosamond	w ko 1	Reading 11-1
Sep 4	Clive Dixon	w rsf 4*	Bethnal Green 11-0
Oct 29	Dave Hall	w rsf 1	Albert Hall 11-2
Nov 20	Horace Fleary	w rsf 2	Cardiff 11-5

1992
Apr 2	Mike Russell	w rsf 2	Basildon 11-3
Apr 30	Tracy Jocelyn	w rsf 3	Albert Hall 11-0
Sep 26	Val Golding	w rsf 1	Olympia 11-3

Fights 10 Won 9 Lost 1

Steve SHELLEY

Cruiserweight
Mansfield, born Oldham 18 August 1970

1991
Dec 9	Stuart Fleet	w rsf 1	Cleethorpes 13-3
Dec 26	Issa "Keke" Moluh	l rsf 2	Berne

1992
Mar 6	Des Vaughan	l rsf 5	Battersea

Fights 3 Won 1 Lost 2

Charles SHEPHERD

Lightweight
Silloth, born Burnley 28 June 1970
Currick House ABC

1991
Oct 28	Chris Aston	w pts 6	Leicester 9-12

1992
Jan 31	Allan McDowall	l rsf 3*	Glasgow 9-9
May 18	Mark Legg	w pts 6	Marton 9-9
Sep 25	George Naylor	w rsf 4	Liverpool 9-13
Oct 22	Didier Hughes	l pts 4	Bethnal Green 9-11-14

Fights 5 Won 3 Lost 2

Glyn SHEPHERD

Bantamweight
Carlisle born Liverpool 30 May 1963

1991
Oct 7	Robert Braddock	drew 6	Bradford 8-12
Oct 28	Tony Smith	w pts 6	Leicester 8-9

1992
Jan 20	Dave Ramsden	l rsf 1	Bradford 8-9
May 18	Dave Campbell	l rsf 1	Marton 8-7
Oct 22	Darren Fifield	drew 4	Bethnal Green 8-5-8
Dec 15	Paul Lloyd	l rsf 1	Liverpool 8-9-8

Fights 6 Won 1 Lost 3 Drawn 2

Wayne SHEPHERD

Welterweight
Silloth, born Liverpool 3 June 1959
Bangor ABC
1987 Welsh ABA light-middleweight prelim (l N Pearce)

1991
Oct 7	Benji Joseph	w pts 6	Bradford 10-9
Oct 28	Noel Henry	w pts 6	Leicester 10-10
Dec 16	Dave Maj	drew 6	Manchester 10-8-8

1992
Feb 3	Dave Maj	l pts 6	Manchester 10-7-8
Mar 30	Hugh Davey	l pts 6	Bradford 10-8
May 18	Dave Whittle	w pts 6	Marton 10-6
Oct 14	Richard Swallow	l pts 8	Stoke 10-3
Oct 31	George Scott	l rsf 6	Earls Court 10-3

Fights 8 Won 3 Lost 4 Drawn 1

Shane SHERIDAN

Light-welterweight
Derby, born Reading 5 November 1968

1991
Mar 28	David Thompson	w ko 5	Alfreton 10-1
Jul 4	Dean Bramhald	w pts 6	Alfreton 10-3
Nov 21	Scott Doyle	l pts 6	Ilkeston

1992
Nov 12	Gary Hiscox	l pts 6	Stafford 10-0
Dec 9	Alex Moffat	w pts 6	Stoke 9-10

Fights 5 Won 3 Lost 2

Danny SHINKWIN

Welterweight
Boreham Wood, born Watford 25 November 1961
Brookside ABC
1981 Home Counties ABA welterweight final (l B Rudgewick)

1982
Apr 1	Mark Crouch	w pts 6	Walthamstow
Apr 19	Gary Petty	w pts 6	Bristol
Apr 27	Eric Purkis	l pts 6	Southend
Sep 4	Danny Myers	w pts 6	Marylebone

1983
inactive

1984
Apr 9	Elvis Morton	l pts 6	Watford 10-7
Apr 16	Tony McKenzie	w rsf 1	Birmingham 10-2
May 19	Colin Neagle	l pts 6	Bristol 10-8-4
Jun 5	David Irving	l ko 2	Albert Hall 10-1-8

1985-86
inactive

1987
Sep 25	Eddie Brooks	l pts 6	Tooting 11-2
Oct 6	Gary Pemberton	l rsf 2	Southend 11-1
Nov 11	Kevin Thompson	l ko 4	Stafford 10-12

1988
Jan 20	Martin Smith	l pts 6	Hornsey 10-8

1989-90
inactive

1991
May 16	Marty Duke	w pts 6	Battersea 11-1-8
Nov 12	Kevin Anderson	l rsf 4*	Milton Keynes 11-2

1992
Feb 12	Mike Russell	w pts 6	Watford 10-10
Apr 30	Cliff Churchward	l pts 6	Watford 10-8
Sep 17	Bozon Haule	drew 6	Watford 10-8-4

Fights 17 Won 6 Lost 10 Drawn 1

Ronnie SHINKWIN
Light-welterweight
Boreham Wood, born Watford 27 November 1964
Brookside ABC & Finchley ABC
1982 Home Counties ABA light-welterweight champion (w V Russell, w T Smith, l rsf 2 C McIntosh)

1982

May 6	Vince Vahey	l pts 4	WSC
Sep 13	Shaun Robinson	l pts 4	Brighton
Oct 11	Glyn Mitchell	l pts 4	Bristol
Nov 26	Jim Paton	l pts 4	Glasgow

1983

Feb 14	Michael Betts	w pts 4	Lewisham 9-8
Mar 16	Michael Betts	w pts 6	Cheltenham
Mar 21	Willy Wilson	drew 4	Nottingham
Apr 16	Graeme Griffin	w pts 4	Bristol 9-11-8
Apr 25	Chris Harvey	l pts 4	Southwark 9-13
May 10	Abdul Kareem	l pts 6	Southend 9-11
Sep 5	Ricky Andrews	w pts 6	Mayfair 9-11
Oct 6	T. Roy Smith	drew 6	Basildon 9-13
Nov 23	Carl Green	w pts 6	Solihull

1984

Feb 16	John Faulkner	w pts 6	Basildon 9-12
Mar 7	Steve Friel	l pts 6	Brighton 10-0
Apr 6	Mike Durvan	l pts 6	Watford 10-1
May 31	Gary Champion	w ko 6	Basildon 9-12
Oct 25	Wayne Poultney	w pts 6	Birmingham 9-11
Nov 26	Jimmy Thornton	l rsf 2	Sheffield 9-9

1985

Jan 31	Teddy Anderson	l pts 8	Basildon 9-11-4
Feb 11	Willy Wilson	w rsf 5	Dulwich 9-12
Mar 1	Tommy Cook	l pts 8	Glasgow 9-13-8
May 4	Abdul Kareem	l rsf 5	Queensway 10-0

1986
inactive

1987

Oct 12	Paul Seddon	drew 6	NSC
Nov 11	Dean Bramhald	l pts 8	Stafford 10-0
Nov 18	Dave Kettlewell	w pts 6	Peterborough 10-1
Dec 14	Dean Bramhald	w pts 8	Bedford 10-1-8

1988

Feb 6	Mike Russell	w pts 8	Newbury 10-1
Mar 16	Tony Swift	l pts 8	Solihull 10-0

1989-90
inactive

1991

Sep 26	Carl Hook	w pts 6	Dunstable 10-2
Oct 24	Chris Saunders	l pts 6	Dunstable 10-1-4
Dec 4	Dean Bramhald	l pts 8	Stoke 10-0
Dec 16	Danny Cooper	l pts 6	Southampton 10-4-8

1992

Jan 30	Dean Bramhald	w pts 6	Southampton 10-4-12
Mar 24	Ray Newby	l pts 8	Wolverhampton 10-2
Apr 30	Jess Rundan	w rsf 1	Watford 9-13
May 18	Ray Newby	l rsf 5	Bardon 10-0-8

Fights 37 Won 15 Lost 19 Drawn 3

Shaun SHINKWIN

Light-welterweight
Borehamwood born Watford 30 November 1962
Brookside ABC
1981 Home Counties ABA bantamweight champion (l K Ryan)

1982

Apr 1	Billy Ruzgar	l pts 4	Walthamstow
Apr 19	Vince Vahey	l pts 4	Bristol
May 10	Kevin Hay	w pts 6	Copthorne
Aug 6	Eugene Maloney	w pts 4	Southend
Jun 14	Eddie Morgan	l pts 6	Mayfair
Oct 13	Joe Donohoe	l pts 6	Walthamstow
Nov 22	Allen Terry	w pts 4	Lewisham
Nov 29	Carl Gaynor	w pts 6	Southwark
Dec 6	Eddie Morgan	drew 6	Bristol

1983

Jan 24	Steve King	w rsf 5	Mayfair
Jan 31	Carl Gaynor	l pts 6	Mayfair
Feb 21	Dave Pratt	w pts 6	Mayfair
Mar 9	Eddie Morgan	w pts 6	Solihull
Mar 17	Chris Harvey	w pts 6	Marylebone
Apr 16	Michael Harris	l pts 6	Bristol

1984-91 inactive

1992

Feb 12	Greg Egbuniwe	l dis 1	Watford 9-9
Oct 29	Steve Hearn	w pts 6	Hayes 9-13

Fights 17 Won 9 Lost 7 Drawn 1

Tony SILKSTONE

Featherweight
Leeds born 2 March 1968
Market District ABC
1984 National Schools champion (w S Willsher)
1985 NABC Class B final (l S Gander)
1986 Young England (v Hun, w Bognor; v Ausl, w Saunders)
1986 North-East ABA bantamweight final

1990

Apr 11	Andrew Robinson	w pts 6	Dewsbury 8-12
Apr 26	Andrew Robinson	w pts 6	Halifax 9-0
Oct 18	Kelton McKenzie	w pts 6	Dewsbury 8-12-8
Nov 15	Sean Casey	w pts 6	Oldham 8-13
Dec 13	Neil Smith	w pts 6	Dewsbury 9-2

1991

Mar 21	Tony Falcone	w pts 6	Dewsbury 8-13-12
May 9	Alan Smith	w pts 6	Leeds 9-3
Jun 13	Miguel Matthews	w pts 6	Hull 9-0
Aug 1	Dave Buxton	w pts 6	Dewsbury 9-1-8
Oct 30	Renny Edwards	w pts 6	Leeds 9-0-8

1992

Apr 8	Eddie Cook	w pts 8	Leeds 9-0
Sep 23	Dave Campbell	w rsf 4	Leeds 8-8-4

Fights 12 Won 12

Kevin SIMONS
Super-featherweight
Swansea born 8 November 1968

1992
Jan 22   Jason Lepre   l pts 6   Cardiff 9-5

Fights 1 Lost 1

Jasdeep SINGH
Super-featherweight
West Ham, born Romford 12 June 1965

1992
Feb 12   Steve Patton   l rsf 1*   Watford 9-4

Fights 1 Lost 1

Tiger SINGH
Flyweight
Peterborough, born Punjab, India 28 October 1970
Real name: Sukhdarshan Singh Mahal
Focus ABC & Aldermans ABC
1991 Eastern ABA bantamweight final (l rsf 1 D Dainty)
1992 Eastern ABA bantamweight final (l rsf 3 D Dainty)

1992
Dec 10   Ian Baillie   w pts 6   Corby 8-1

Fights 1 Won 1

Colin SINNOTT
Light-welterweight
Preston born 10 September 1965
Bamber Bridge ABC

1990
Mar 26   Barry North   w ko 6   Nottingham
Oct 8   Rob Pitters   l pts 6   Bradford 10-3
Oct 16   Andy Robins   w pts 6   Evesham 10-2-8
Nov 1   Dave Thompson   w pts 6   Hull 10-0
Dec 10   Dean Bramhald   l pts 6   Bradford 10-2
1991
Jan 28   Dave Kettlewell   w rsf 3   Bradford 10-2
Feb 21   Trevor Meikle   l pts 6   Leeds 10-4
Apr 22   Gary Chadwick   w ko 3   Bradford 10-3
May 30   Mark Ramsey   l pts 6   Birmingham 10-1
Oct 8   Dean Bramhald   w pts 8   Wolverhampton 10-2
Oct 21   Dean Bramhald   l pts 6   Cleethorpes 10-3
Nov 18   Kris McAdam   l pts 6   Glasgow 9-13-8
1992
Oct 23   Paul Charters   l rtd 4   Gateshead 10-1-4

Fights 13 Won 6 Lost 7

Trevor SMALL
Light-heavyweight
Birmingham born 26 February 1968
Kingshurst ABC
1990 Midlands ABA heavyweight final (w K Hitchins, w W McGreevy, w R Yates, missed scales)
1991 Midlands ABA heavyweight final (w K Taylor, w J Birbeck, w B Summers, l P Oko)
1992 Midlands ABA heavy champ (w K Hitchins, w S Murray, w F Woodrow, w M Langtree, l rsf 3 S Welch)

1992
Dec 9	Sean O'Phoenix	w pts 6	Stoke 12-7

Fights 1 Won 1

Carl SMALLWOOD
Light-heavyweight
Atherstone born Nuneaton 15 April 1973
Atherstone ABC
1991 Warwickshire ABA light-heavyweight semi-final (l rsf 1 J Cooke)

1992
Mar 30	Greg Scott-Briggs	w pts 6	Coventry 12-7
Apr 28	Lee Archer	w pts 6	Wolverhampton 12-8
Sep 30	Greg Scott-Briggs	w pts 6	Solihull 12-7-8
Oct 14	Martin Jolley	l pts 6	Stoke 12-4
Nov 12	Richard Atkinson	w pts 6	Stafford 12-5

Fights 5 Won 4 Lost 1

Alan SMITH
Super-featherweight
Pembroke Dock born 15 September 1964
Penner ABC

1991
Mar 13	Mitchell Barney	w pts 6	Stoke 9-6
Apr 22	Tony Falcone	w rsf 5*	AASC 9-2
May 9	Tony Silkstone	l pts 6	Leeds 9-1-8
May 30	Tony Falcone	l pts 6	Mayfair 8-11
Sep 4	Eunan Devenney	l ko 1	Bethnal Green 9-2-8

1992
Feb 27	John White	l rsf 1	Liverpool 9-1-8
Jul 2	Craig Dermody	l rsf 3	Middleton 9-2-8

Fights 7 Won 2 Lost 5

Jacob SMITH
Bantamweight
Darlington born 30 January 1974

1992
Apr 8	Andrew Bloomer	w pts 6	Leeds 8-7
Sep 28	Jason Morris	w pts 6	Manchester 8-9-8
Oct 7	Norman Dhalie	l pts 6	Sunderland 8-9

Fights 3 Won 2 Lost 1

John SMITH

Light-welterweight
Liverpool born 13 October 1959
Rotunda ABC
1983 West Lancs ABA light-welterweight final (l D Jennings)
1984 West Lancs ABA light-welterweight final (l D Jennings)
1984 Great Britain (v Ire, w B McClean)
1984 England (v Can, l D Lambert)
1985 West Lancs ABA light-welterweight prelim (l J Mudd)
1986 West Lancs ABA light-welterweight semi-final (l K Wall)

1986
Jun 26	Ray Golding	w pts 6	Edgbaston 10-4
Sep 22	John Townsley	w pts 6	Edgbaston 9-13-8
Nov 6	Robert Harkin	l pts 8	Glasgow 10-2
Nov 20	John Best	l pts 6	Bredbury 10-2-8
Dec 8	Gary Somerville	drew 8	Edgbaston 10-2

1987
Mar 18	John Best	l rsf 2	Solihull 10-1
Apr 24	Brian Wareing	l pts 8	Liverpool 10-1
Sep 24	John Dickson	l pts 6	Glasgow 9-13-8

1988
Feb 1	Peter Crook	l pts 6	Manchester 10-0
Mar 17	Mick Mason	drew 8	Sunderland
Mar 29	Paul Seddon	w rsf 4*	Middlesbrough 9-12
Jun 17	Gary Somerville	w rsf 5*	Edgbaston 10-4-8
Nov 28	Gary Somerville	l pts 8	Edgbaston 10-2-4

1989
Jan 24	Mark Kelly	l pts 8	Kings Heath 10-1-12
Mar 22	John Davies	l pts 8	Solihull 10-2
Jul 17	Richard Adams	w rsf 3*	Stanmore 10-3
Sep 9	Muhammad Lovelock	w pts 8	Liverpool
Sep 14	Roy Rowland	l rsf 3*	Basildon 10-2
Oct 17	Jim Talbot	l pts 6	Oldham 10-7-8
Oct 25	Kevin Plant	l pts 6	Doncaster 10-2
Nov 10	Seamus O'Sullivan	l pts 6	Battersea 10-1
Nov 30	Dave Pierre	l pts 6	Marble Arch 10-2-8
Dec 8	Allan Hall	l rsf 2	Doncaster 10-3

1990
Jan 29	Darren Mount	l pts 8	Liverpool 10-3
Mar 8	Dave Pierre	l pts 6	Peterborough 10-0
Mar 19	Brendan Ryan	l pts 6	Leicester 10-2
Apr 5	Darren Mount	l pts 8	Liverpool 10-0
May 4	Pete Roberts	l pts 6	Everton 10-2
Sep 24	Mark Dinnadge	w rtd 2*	Lewisham 10-2
Oct 9	Pete Roberts	w pts 8	Liverpool 10-0
Nov 13	Paul Charters	l rsf 4*	Hartlepool 10-1-8

1991
Jan 21	Kris McAdam	l pts 6	Glasgow 10-2-8
Feb 7	Billy Schwer	l rsf 2*	Watford 9-12-8
Mar 26	Andy Morgan	l rsf 4*	Wolverhampton
Apr 24	Andy Morgan	l pts 6	Port Talbot 10-2
May 16	Kevin Toomey	l pts 6	Liverpool 10-5-8
Jun 13	Kevin Toomey	l pts 6	Hull 10-4-8
Jul 25	Robert McCracken	l rtd 1	Dudley 10-6
Oct 7	Pete Roberts	l pts 8	Liverpool 10-1
Oct 23	Dean Hollington	l pts 6	Bethnal Green 10-3
Nov 12	Mark Elliot	l pts 6	Wolverhampton 10-3-8
Nov 21	Riki Burton	l pts 6	Burton 10-3 /CTD../

(John SMITH ctd.)

Dec 2	Mike Calderwood	drew 8	Liverpool 10-3
Dec 19	Riki Burton	l pts 6	Oldham 10-1-12
1992			
Feb 1	George Scott	l rsf 3*	Birmingham 10-4
Mar 3	Paul Charters	l pts 8	Houghton-le-Spring 10-5
May 12	Ross Hale	l ko 1	Crystal Palace 10-4-12
Sep 3	Chris Mulcahy	drew 6	Liverpool
Sep 25	Kevin McKillan	l pts 6	Liverpool 10-6
Oct 7	Alan Peacock	tdraw 6*	Glasgow 10-1
Nov 12	Mark Tibbs	l rsf 6*	Bayswater 10-4-8

Fights 51 Won 8 Lost 38 Drawn 5

Martin SMITH

Light-middleweight
Sheffield born London 16 August 1967
Holmfirth ABC
1983 National Schools champion
1987 Yorkshire ABA light-welterweight final (w dis 3 S Phillips, l J Iwenjiora)

1987

Sep 14	Tony Britland	drew 6	Crystal Palace 10-0-8
1988			
Jan 20	Danny Shinkwin	w pts 6	Hornsey 10-4-8
Mar 10	Cecil Branch	w pts 6	Croydon 10-3
Apr 13	Tony Britland	w rsf 2	Gravesend 10-5-8
May 11	Simon Paul	w rtd 5	Greenwich 10-7
May 26	Oliver Henry	w pts 6	Albert Hall 10-3-8
Jun 25	Damien Denny	nc 5	Luton 10-7
1989			
Feb 16	Winston May	drew 6	Battersea 10-12
Sep 14	Brian Robinson	l pts 6	Basildon 11-0
Oct 20	Des Robinson	w pts 6	Manchester 10-6
Nov 13	Joni Nyman	l pts 8 (s)	Helsinki 10-12
Nov 24	Andre Kimbu	l pts 8 (s)	Calais 10-12
1990			
Feb 22	Robert Harron	w pts 6	Hull 11-1
Mar 15	James Collins	w pts 6	Manchester 11-0
Jun 6	John Ogiste	w rsf 2*	Battersea 11-4
1991			
Feb 12	Rex Kortram	w pts 6	Rotterdam 11-2-8
Mar 19	Shaun Cummins	drew 8	Leicester 11-1
May 7	Danny Quigg	w pts 6	Glasgow 11-2
Oct 1	Mike Phillips	w pts 6	Sheffield 11-2-8
Oct 28	Gilbert Hallie	drew 8	Arnhem 11-3-12
1992			
Jan 10	Said Skouma	w pts 8	Marseilles
Apr 14	Dave Owens	w pts 6	Mansfield 11-4
May 8	Freddie Demeulenaere	drew 8	Waregem 10-13-8

Fights 23 Won 14 Lost 3 Drawn 5 No Contests 1

Neil SMITH
Super-featherweight
Leicester born 15 January 1972
Belgrave ABC
Southpaw
1990 North Midlands ABA featherweight champion (w rtd 2 A Williamson, w N Exton, missed scales)

1990
Dec 13	Tony Silkstone	l pts 6	Dewsbury 9-2

1991
Feb 6	Dennis Adams	l pts 6	Bethnal Green 9-4
Mar 14	John Naylor	w rsf 6	Middleton 9-2
May 20	Elvis Parsley	w rsf 5	Leicester 9-5
Jun 11	Lee Fox	w pts 6	Leicester 9-6
Nov 5	Neil Leitch	w rsf 1	Leicester 9-6-8

1992
Feb 4	Harry Escott	l pts 8	Alfreton 9-5

Fights 7 Won 4 Lost 3

Paul SMITH
Middleweight
Sheffield born 14 July 1960
Eckington ABC

1983
Oct 3	David Scere	l pts 6	Liverpool 11-4
Oct 17	David Scere	l pts 6	Manchester 11-4
Nov 9	Billy Ahearne	l pts 6	Sheffield 11-4
Dec 5	Billy Ahearne	drew 8	Manchester 11-3

1984
Jan 30	Billy Ahearne	w rsf 5*	Manchester 11-2
Mar 12	Mike Farghaly	l pts 8	Manchester 11-1
Apr 9	Mike Farghaly	l rsf 3*	Manchester 11-6-8
Jul 22	Malcolm Davies	w rtd 4*	Sheffield

1985
Feb 11	Seamus Casey	l pts 6	Manchester 11-6
Mar 1	Gary Tomlinson	l pts 6	Mansfield 11-8
Mar 15	Mark Watts	l rsf 4*	Leicester 11-9
Apr 17	Nigel Pearce	w pts 6	Nantwich 11-0
Apr 29	Robert Armstrong	w rsf 6	Nottingham 10-12
Oct 13	Seb Solomon	w rsf 3	Sheffield 11-2
Dec 3	Rocky McGran	l pts 6	Belfast 11-5

1986
Feb 5	Kevin Hughes	w rsf 5	Sheffield 11-2
Feb 15	Rocky McGran	l pts 6	Dublin 11-5-8
Apr 21	Simon Collins	drew 6	Birmingham 11-5
May 30	John Ashton	l pts 8	Stoke 11-6
Sep 10	Cliff Domville	w dis 2	Stoke 11-3
Sep 26	Johnny Williamson	l rsf 7*	Swindon 11-6-8

1987
Apr 6	Sean West	w pts 6	Leicester 11-7
Apr 30	Mickey Ould	w pts 6	Battersea 11-9
Jun 3	Dennis O'Brien	w rsf 2	Southwark 11-7-8
Oct 28	Ian Bayliss	l rsf 3	Sheffield 11-4-8
	(vacant Central middleweight title)		

1988
Mar 8	Dave Thomas	l pts 6	Batley 11-9 /CTD..

(Paul SMITH ctd.)

1989			
Apr 4	Paul Mundy	w rtd 1	Sheffield
1990			
inactive			
1991			
Jan 29	Marty Duke	w pts 6	Wisbech 11-8
Mar 6	Benji Good	l pts 6	Croydon 11-8
Mar 19	Paul Busby	l pts 6	Leicester 11-8
Apr 16	Chris Richards	drew 6	Nottingham 11-6-8
Aug 29	Neville Brown	l rsf 3*	Telford 11-6
1992			
Apr 28	Andy Flute	l rsf 5	Wolverhampton 11-10

Fights 33 Won 12 Lost 18 Drawn 3

Scott SMITH
Light-welterweight
Birmingham, born Kidderminster 11 July 1969
Worcester City ABC
Southpaw

1992			
Dec 9	Jonathan Thaxton	l pts 6	Stoke 10-0

Fights 1 Lost 1

Sean SMITH
Super-middleweight
Hull born 5 January 1967

1992			
Oct 15	Graham Wassell	l rsf 2	Hull 12-2

Fights 1 Lost 1

Terry SMITH
Lightweight
Kettering born 17 October 1967
No amateur experience

1992			
Apr 29	Floyd Churchill	l rsf 2	Liverpool 9-8
Dec 10	Alan Graham	l pts 6	Corby 9-10

Fights 2 Lost 2

Tommy SMITH
Super-featherweight
Darlington born 18 December 1970
Darlington ABC

1990			
Dec 10	Danny Connelly	l pts 6	Glasgow 9-6
1991			
Feb 16	John Patterson	w pts 6	Thornaby 9-4
Mar 2	Colin Innes	l pts 6	Darlington 9-3
Apr 6	Paul Wynn	w pts 6	Darlington 9-2-12 /CTD..

(Tommy SMITH ctd.)

Oct 22	Kevin Lowe	w rsf 4*	Hartlepool 9-2-8
Dec 12	Colin Innes	w pts 6	Hartlepool
1992			
May 28	Colin Innes	w pts 6	Gosforth 9-3

Fights 7 Won 5 Lost 2

Tony SMITH
Bantamweight
Burnley born 4 May 1969
Bacup Lads ABC

1987

May 18	Gordon Shaw	l pts 6	Glasgow 8-3-12
Sep 7	Gordon Shaw	w pts 6	Glasgow 8-5-8
Sep 14	Gordon Shaw	l pts 6	Glasgow 8-5-8
Oct 7	John Hales	w rsf 4	Burnley 8-6
Oct 26	Wull Strike	l rsf 5	Glasgow 8-5-8
Dec 7	Joe Mullen	l rsf 6	Glasgow 8-6
1988			
Jan 25	Mark Robertson	l rsf 1	Glasgow 8-5-8
Apr 25	John Hales	w rsf 5	Nottingham 8-3-4
Jun 8	Gordon Shaw	l pts 6	Glasgow 8-4
Jun 18	Mark Priestley	w rsf 6	Gateshead 8-7
Sep 5	Paul Dever	w pts 6	Manchester 8-10-8
Sep 12	Mick Markie	drew 6	Northampton 8-9-8
Oct 6	Gordon Stobie	w pts 6	Manchester 8-5
Oct 29	Salvatore Fanni	l ko 1	Milan 8-7-12
1989			
Jan 16	Mick Markie	l rsf 2	Northampton 8-12
Apr 5	George Bailey	w pts 6	Halifax 8-8
Apr 17	Seamus Tuohy	drew 6	Middleton 8-5
Sep 10	James Drummond	l rsf 1	Glasgow 8-9
Nov 30	Seamus Tuohy	l pts 6	Middleton
1990			
Jan 29	Billy Proud	w pts 6	Bradford 8-8-8
Feb 27	Billy Proud	l rsf 2	Middlesbrough 8-6
May 14	Stewart Fisher-Mack	l pts 6	Leicester 8-8
May 21	Stevie Wood	l rsf 6	Bradford 8-7
Oct 1	Des Gargano	l pts 6	Cleethorpes 8-8-8
Oct 17	Peter Buckley	l pts 6	Stoke 8-10
Oct 24	Paul Dever	w pts 8	Stoke 8-7-8
Nov 26	Des Gargano	l pts 8	Bury 8-8
Dec 3	Des Gargano	l pts 6	Cleethorpes
1991			
Jan 16	Des Gargano	l pts 6	Stoke 8-9
Mar 5	Neil Parry	drew 6	Leicester 8-8
Mar 18	Gary White	l pts 6	Manchester 8-10
May 7	Steve Wood	l rtd 2	Glasgow 8-8
Jun 10	Robert Braddock	drew 6	Manchester 8-9
Jun 20	Neil Parry	l pts 6	Liverpool 8-7
Oct 28	Glyn Shepherd	l pts 6	Leicester 8-10
Nov 18	Chris Jickells	l rsf 4	Manchester
1992			
Jun 1	Craig Murray	l rsf 2	Manchester 9-6

Fights 37 Won 9 Lost 24 Drawn 4

Michael SMYTH

Welterweight
Barry, born Caerphilly 22 February 1970
Rhose ABC
1988 Welsh ABA light-welterweight champion (w ko 1 G Jones, w rsf 3 J Alsop, w rsf 1 M Oliver, l A Hall)
1988 Wales (v Sco, w rsf 2 A Leekie; v Nor, w P Saue)
1989 Welsh ABA light-welterweight champion (w C Donovan, l A Hall)
1989 Wales (v Sco, l C Kane, w rsf 1 W Lechie; v Nor, w J Ness)
1990 Commonwealth Games light-welterweight (w rsf 1 N Wood, NZ; l ko 1 M James, Nig)
1990 Welsh ABA welterweight champion (w ko 1 M Owen, w rsf 3 J Hudd, w J Calzaghe, l rsf 2 A Carew)

1991
May 2	Carl Brasier	w rsf 2	Bayswater 10-5
May 28	Ricky North	w rsf 1	Cardiff 10-0
Jul 18	Mike Morrison	w rsf 2	Cardiff 10-7-8
Sep 3	Julian Eavis	w pts 6	Cardiff 10-9-4
Nov 20	Mike Russell	w rsf 3	Cardiff 10-9
Dec 17	Julian Eavis	w pts 6	Cardiff 10-9

1992
May 19	Ojay Abrahams	w pts 6	Cardiff 10-8-8
Oct 7	Dave Lake	w ko 2	Barry 10-9-8
Nov 14	Des Robinson	w pts 6	Cardiff 10-10

Fights 9 Won 9

Lee SOAR

Welterweight
Barnsley born 12 October 1970

1991
Nov 25	Mark Broome	w pts 6	Cleethorpes 10-3

1992
Jan 28	Steve Bricknell	w pts 6	Piccadilly 10-8
Sep 14	Blue Butterworth	l ko 4	Bradford 9-12
Dec 7	Mick Hoban	l pts 6	Manchester 10-2
Dec 14	Rick North	l pts 6	Cleethorpes 10-4

Fights 5 Won 2 Lost 3

Phil SOUNDY

Cruiserweight
Benfleet born 24 October 1966
Billericay ABC

1989
Oct 4	Coco Collins	w rsf 2	Basildon 13-4
Oct 24	Trevor Barry	w rsf 1*	Bethnal Green 13-1

1990
Feb 14	Andy Balfe	w rsf 3	Brentwood 13-12
Mar 28	Chris Coughlan	w pts 6	Bethnal Green 13-1-14
May 22	Cliff Curtis	w pts 6	Canvey Island 13-0
Jul 6	Steve Yorath	w ko 3	Brentwood 13-5
Sep 12	Rob Albon	w rsf 1	Bethnal Green 13-4
Oct 3	Steve Yorath	w pts 6	Basildon 13-5
Dec 12	David Haycock	w rsf 3	Albert Hall 13-3-8

1991
Jan 16	Chris Coughlan	w pts 6	Albert Hall
Feb 12	Gus Mendes	w rsf 3*	Basildon

Mar 7	Terry Duffus	w rsf 2	Basildon 13-4-8
Apr 25	Steve Yorath	l pts 6	Basildon 13-7-8
Sep 11	Gus Mendes	l rsf 3*	Hammersmith 13-6
1992			
Feb 12	Steve Osborne	w pts 6	Wembley GH 13-4
Apr 22	Lee Prudden	w rsf 5	Wembley 13-5-8
May 13	Tony Booth	l pts 6	Albert Hall 13-1
Sep 7	Dean Allen	w rtd 4	Bethnal Green 13-2
Oct 28	Des Vaughn	w rtd 4	Albert Hall 13-5-4

Fights 19 Won 16 Lost 3

Kevin SPRATT

Light-welterweight
Yeadon, born Leeds 22 March 1966
Southpaw
1985 North-East ABA lightweight semi-final (l M Stones)

1986

May 19	Wayne Goult	w rsf 5	Bradford 9-11
Jun 17	Barry Bacon	w pts 6	Blackpool 9-10-8
Sep 4	A.M.Milton	drew 6	Wimbledon 9-12
Sep 22	Kevin Plant	w pts 6	Bradford 9-9-8
Oct 6	Rocky Lester	w pts 6	Leicester 9-13
Oct 20	Kevin Plant	w rsf 4	Bradford
Nov 13	Tony Banks	drew 6	Huddersfield 9-11-8
1987			
Jan 26	Brian Murphy	w pts 6	Bradford 9-12
Feb 10	Darren Connellan	l pts 8	Batley 9-9-8
Apr 6	David Bacon	w pts 6	Nottingham 10-0
Apr 27	Dean Bramhald	w pts 8	Bradford 9-12
Jun 2	Marvin P.Gray	w pts 8	Bradford 9-12
Oct 16	David Maw	w pts 8	Gateshead 9-13-8
Dec 15	Marvin P.Gray	w rsf 6	Bradford 9-8-12
1988			
Feb 9	Darren Connellan	w pts 6	Bradford 9-13
Mar 10	Jim Moffat	l pts 8	Glasgow 9-10-8
Apr 26	Oliver Harrison	w rsf 7	Bradford 9-12
Oct 12	Steve Hogg	w pts 8	Stoke 10-0
1989			
Feb 27	Calvin Meeks	l rsf 3	Reseda, Ca.
May 22	David Bacon	l rsf 6*	Bradford 9-12
Oct 13	Peter Crook	w rsf 3*	Preston 9-13-8
	(vacant Central light-welterweight title)		
1990			
Jan 24	Mark Kelly	w rsf 9	Solihull 10-0
	(Central light-welterweight title)		
May 9	Kevin Plant	w pts 10	Solihull 10-0
	(Central light-welterweight title)		
Oct 18	Lindon Scarlett	l rsf 2	Birmingham 10-4-8
Dec 10	Trevor Meikle	w pts 6	Bradford 10-4
1991			
Mar 18	John Townsley	w rtd 6	Glasgow 10-3
May 10	Paul Charters	l rsf 2	Gateshead 10-2-8
1992			
Sep 14	Trevor Meikle	l rsf 4	Bradford 10-2
Dec 14	Steve Scott	w pts 6	Bradford 10-5

Fights 29 Won 20 Lost 7 Drawn 2

Art STACEY

Cruiserweight
Leeds, born 26 September 1964
Real name: Michael Stacey

1990
Oct 9	Trevor Barry	drew 6	Liverpool 13-1
Nov 6	Chris Coughlan	w rsf 4*	Southend
Nov 27	Alan Millett	w pts 6	Liverpool

1991
Feb 21	Tony Lawrence	w pts 6	Leeds 13-0
Mar 18	Paul Gearon	w rsf 1	Derby 13-6
Apr 16	Steve Osborne	drew 6	Nottingham 13-2
Jun 3	Dennis Afflick	w pts 6	Glasgow 13-3
Nov 11	Steve Osborne	w pts 6	Bradford 13-5
Nov 21	Gil Lewis	l rsf 4	Stafford 12-11

1992
Jan 20	John Pierre	w pts 6	Bradford 13-7
Oct 26	Ian Bulloch	l pts 6	Cleethorpes 13-2-8
Nov 27	Niels H. Madsen	l pts 8	Randers 13-6
Dec 14	Art Call	l pts 6	Cleethorpes 13-8

Fights 13 Won 7 Lost 4 Drawn 2

Warren STEPHENS

Light-middleweight
Birmingham born 18 May 1970

1992
Apr 4	John Duckworth	l rsf 5	Cleethorpes 11-2
May 21	Alfie Andrews	l pts 6	Cradley Heath 11-0
Oct 30	Alfie Andrews	l pts 6	NEC 11-0
Nov 23	Simon Fisher	w pts 6	Coventry 10-13
Dec 7	Steve Levene	l ko 2	Birmingham 11-1

Fights 5 Won 1 Lost 4

Ronnie STEPHENSON

Featherweight
Doncaster born 18 November 1960
No amateur experience

1986
Jan 22	Paddy Maguire	w pts 4	Stoke 8-12
Mar 10	Jamie McBride	l pts 4	Glasgow 8-10
Apr 27	Phil Lashley	w pts 4	Doncaster 8-10
Jun 3	Billy Cawley	l pts 6	Wolverhampton 8-13
Sep 15	Gerry McBride	w pts 6	Manchester 8-6
Sep 22	Bobby McDermott	drew 6	Glasgow 8-10
Nov 24	Gerry McBride	l pts 8	Leicester 8-8

1987
Mar 10	Gerry McBride	l rsf 7	Manchester 8-5-12
	(vacant Central bantamweight title)		
May 6	Joe Kelly	l pts 8	Livingstone 8-8
Jun 13	Chris Clarkson	l pts 8	Great Yarmouth 8-8-8
Aug 9	Sean Murphy	l rsf 1	Windsor 8-9

Sep 14	Bobby McDermott	l rsf 2	Glasgow 8-12
Nov 9	Phil Lashley	drew 4	Birmingham 8-8
Nov 24	Chris Cooper	w rsf 4	Wolverhampton 8-9
Dec 14	Nigel Crook	l pts 6	Bradford 8-8
1988			
Jan 29	Chris Cooper	w pts 4	Torquay
Feb 24	Chris Cooper	w pts 6	Southend
Mar 14	Mark Goult	l rsf 4	Norwich 8-11
Apr 11	Joe Mullen	l pts 8	Glasgow 8-9
Apr 25	Des Gargano	l pts 8	Bradford 8-10
May 14	Andre Hoeffler	l pts 6	Anderlecht
May 26	Glen Dainty	l rsf 6	Bethnal Green 8-6
Sep 8	Phil Lashley	l pts 6	Doncaster 8-9
Oct 19	Chris Cooper	w pts 6	Evesham 8-8
Nov 14	Michael Close	l pts 4	Stratford 8-13
Nov 21	Des Gargano	l pts 6	Leicester 8-9-8
Dec 7	Mark Walker	w rsf 6	Stoke 9-0
1989			
Feb 14	Alan Roberts	w pts 6	Wolverhampton 8-13
Mar 6	Mark Walker	w rsf 5*	Leicester 8-8
Mar 21	Miguel Matthews	drew 6	Wolverhampton 8-11
Apr 3	Robert Braddock	w ko 4	Manchester 8-13-8
Sep 4	Des Gargano	l pts 6	Hull 8-9-8
Oct 10	Peter Buckley	w pts 6	Wolverhampton 8-13
Nov 13	Dave Buxton	l rtd 2	Bradford 8-13
1990			
Mar 14	Peter Buckley	drew 6	Stoke 9-0
Mar 27	Phil Lashley	l pts 6	Wolverhampton 9-1
Apr 4	Peter Buckley	w pts 8	Stafford 8-12
Apr 23	Peter Buckley	l pts 6	Birmingham 8-12
May 21	Phil Lashley	w pts 6	Cleethorpes 9-0
Jun 4	Peter Buckley	l pts 8	Birmingham 8-11
Dec 3	Dave Annis	l pts 6	Cleethorpes 8-13
1991			
Oct 21	Phil Lashley	w pts 6	Cleethorpes 9-2
Nov 21	Phil Lashley	w pts 6	Stafford 9-2
Dec 2	Chris Lyons	w pts 6	Birmingham 9-0
Dec 9	Chris Lyons	w pts 6	Cleethorpes 9-0
1992			
Jan 15	Chris Jickells	w pts 6	Stoke 9-0
Mar 30	Mark Hargreaves	w pts 6	Coventry 9-0
Jul 25	John White	l pts 6	Manchester 9-0

Fights 48 Won 20 Lost 24 Drawn 4

Alex STERLING

Lightweight
Tottenham born 21 December 1969
New Enterprise ABC

1989			
Mar 13	John Ritchie	l pts 6	Glasgow
Mar 21	Richard Dimmock	w rsf 1	Battersea 9-10
Jul 6	Billy Couzens	l pts 6	Chigwell 9-6
Oct 28	Frank Dewinter	l rsf 5	Ghent
1990			
inactive			

/CTD..

(Alex STERLING ctd.)
1991
Nov 14	Chubby Martin	l rsf 5	Marble Arch 9-12-12

1992
Jan 18	Paul Ryan	l rsf 4	Albert Hall 9-12
Apr 7	Greg Egbuniwe	l rsf 4	Southend 9-11

Fights 7 Won 1 Lost 6

Rob STEVENSON

Welterweight
Hull born 16 March 1971
No amateur experience

1991
Nov 26	Matt Mowatt	l pts 6	Hull 11-2

1992
Mar 26	Steve Scott	w pts 6	Hull 10-10
Apr 4	Chris Mulcahy	l pts 8	Cleethorpes 10-11
Apr 29	Alan Williams	w pts 6	Liverpool 10-10
Jun 1	Chris Mulcahy	l pts 6	Manchester 10-11
Oct 13	Dean Hiscox	l pts 6	Wolverhampton 10-9
Nov 26	Steve Scott	l pts 6	Hull 10-9

Fights 7 Won 2 Lost 5

Rob STEWART

Light-welterweight
Darwen born 17 January 1965
Blackburn & Darwen ABC, Blackburn YMCA
1990 East Lancs & Cheshire ABA light-welterweight semi-final (l rsf 3 N Boyd)
1991 East Lancs & Cheshire ABA light-welterweight semi-final (l rsf 3 D McCarrick)

1991
Oct 14	Gary Pagden	w pts 6	Manchester 10-1
Oct 21	Ricky Sackfield	w pts 6	Bury 10-2
Dec 4	Dean Carr	w rtd 5	Stoke 10-0

1992
Jan 21	Chris Aston	w rsf 4	Stockport 10-2-8
Feb 24	Tony Banks	drew 6	Bradford 10-1-8
Mar 4	Alan Peacock	drew 8	Glasgow 10-2
Mar 31	Mike Calderwood	w pts 4	Stockport 10-1-12
Sep 24	Riki Burton	l pts 10	Manchester 9-12-8
	(Central light-welterweight title)		

Fights 8 Won 5 Lost 1 Drawn 2

Steve STEWART

Heavyweight
Clapham, born Luton 10 August 1967

1992
Feb 17	Damien Caesar	l rsf 5	AASC 16-7
Mar 30	Wayne Llewellyn	l rsf 4	Eltham
Sep 8	Graham Arnold	w rsf 3*	Norwich 15-7

Fights 3 Won 1 Lost 2

Bradley STONE

Featherweight
Canning Town born Mile End 27 May 1970
Repton ABC
1989 London ABA featherweight final (w rsf 1 P Savva, w rsf 2 W Maraj, l T Rossiter)

1990
Mar 6	Des Gargano	w pts 6	Bethnal Green 8-12-12
Mar 28	Steve Wood	w rsf 2	Bethnal Green 8-9-2
Apr 14	Kruga Hydes	w pts 6	Albert Hall 8-8-10
May 29	Gary Hickman	drew 6	Bethnal Green 8-12
Jul 10	Andrew Robinson	w pts 6	Canvey Island 9-2
Oct 10	Gary Jones	w rsf 3	Millwall 8-13-8

1991
Feb 12	Stewart Fisher-mack	w pts 6	Basildon 8-12-12
Mar 7	Miguel Matthews	w rsf 4	Basildon 9-0
Apr 25	Miguel Matthews	w pts 6	Basildon 8-12-8
Oct 2	Andrew Bloomer	w pts 6	Barking 9-0

1992
Apr 2	Colin Lynch	w rsf 3	Basildon 9-1
May 16	Andrew Bloomer	w pts 6	Muswell Hill 9-1-12
Oct 15	Kevin Middleton	w pts 6	Catford 9-1
Dec 3	Norman Dhalie	w ko 4	Catford 8-12

Fights 14 Won 13 Drawn 1

Sam STOREY

Super-middleweight
Belfast born 9 August 1963
Holy Family ABC
Southpaw
1982 Irish Junior ABA champion
1982 Ireland (v USA, w T Gaynor; v Wal, w T Price; v Eng, w M Esa)
1983 Irish ABA final (withdrew, ill)
1983 Ireland (v Sco, w D Milligan; v Wal, w T Price)
1983 Commonwealth Federation Championships light-middleweight silver medal (w R Omoruyi, Nig; w B Scott, Sco; w R Finch, Aus; l R Douglas, Eng)
1984 Irish ABA light-middleweight champion (w P Ruth)
1984 Ireland (v Sco, w A Mullen; v GB, w ko 2 M Esa)
1984 Los Angeles Olympics (l rsf 3 R Casamonica, It)
1985 Irish ABA middleweight champion (w S Collins)
1985 Ireland (v Den, w K Nielsen)
1985 Ulster (v Aus, w J Harding)
1985 European Championships (l Z Fuzcesy, EGer)

1985
Dec 3	Nigel Shingles	w rsf 6	Belfast 11-8-8

1986
Feb 5	Sean O'Phoenix	w pts 6	Sheffield 11-7-12
Apr 22	Karl Barwise	w pts 6	Belfast 11-9
Oct 29	Jimmy Ellis	w rsf 5	Belfast 11-9

1987
Apr 25	Rocky McGran (vacant Irish middleweight title)	w pts 10	Belfast 11-4-12
Oct 19	Seamus Casey	w pts 6	Belfast 11-9-8
Dec 5	Paul Mitchell	w pts 6	Doncaster 11-8

1988
Jan 27	Steve Foster	w rsf 4	Belfast 11-8-8
Mar 18	Steve Collins (Irish middleweight title)	l pts 10	Boston

/CTD..

(Sam STOREY ctd.)

Oct 21	Tony Lawrence	w rsf 3	Belfast 12-1
Dec 7	Darren Hobson	w rsf 6	Belfast 11-12
1989			
Jan 25	Abdul Umaru Sanda	w rsf 8	Belfast 11-8-4
Mar 8	Kevin Roper	w rsf 3*	Belfast 11-11
Sep 19	Tony Burke	w pts 12	Belfast 12-0
	(vacant British super-middleweight title)		
Nov 29	Noel Magee	w rsf 9	Belfast 11-13-8
	(British super-middleweight title)		
1990			
Mar 17	Simon Collins	w rsf 7	Belfast
Oct 30	James Cook	l rsf 10	Belfast 11-13-8
	(British super-middleweight title)		
1991			
May 31	Saidi Ali	l pts 8	Berlin 12-1-8
Sep 7	Johnny Melfah	w pts 8	Belfast 11-13-12
Nov 13	Karl Barwise	w pts 6	Belfast 12-0-12
1992			
Apr 25	Nigel Rafferty	w rsf 3	Belfast 12-2-12

Fights 21 Won 18 Lost 3

Warren STOWE

Light-middleweight
Burnley born 30 January 1965
Sandygate ABC
1989 East Lancs & Cheshire ABA super-heavyweight champion (w.o., l rtd 1 P Dickinson)

1991			
Oct 21	Matt Mowatt	w rsf 3	Bury 11-8
Dec 7	Griff Jones	w rsf 6	Manchester
1992			
Feb 3	Robert Peel	w pts 6	Manchester 11-5
Mar 10	Barry Bennett	w pts 6	Bury 11-2-8
Apr 25	David Radford	w rsf 3	Manchester 11-4
Jun 4	Rob Pitters	w pts 8	Burnley 11-0-4
Jul 25	Seamus Casey	w ko 2	Manchester 11-4-4
Sep 24	Mike Phillips	w rsf 1	Manchester 11-3-8
Nov 12	Steve Thomas	w rsf 1	Burnley 11-4
Nov 28	Julian Eavis	w rsf 6	Manchester 10-13-12

Fights 10 Won 10

Adrian STRACHAN

Light-middleweight
Richmond, born Bromley 8 April 1966
Southpaw

1991			
Jun 4	Martin Rosamond	w pts 6	Bethnal Green 11-2-4
Sep 24	Martin Rosamond	w pts 6	Basildon 11-2
Oct 1	Gary Pemberton	w rsf 2	Sheffield 11-3
Nov 19	Tracy Jocelyn	w pts 6	Norwich 11-2
Nov 26	Chris Richards	w pts 6	Bethnal Green 11-2
1992			
May 12	Horace Fleary	w pts 6	Crystal Palace 10-12-12

Fights 6 Won 6

Chad STRONG

Light-middleweight
Leicester born 26 September 1970
Belgrave ABC
1991 Leics, Rutland & Northants ABA light-middleweight semi-final (l rsf 3 N Hutcheon)

1991
May 20	Mick Reid	w pts 6	Leicester 11-0
Nov 5	Griff Jones	l pts 6	Leicester 11-4

1992
May 18	Brian McGloin	drew 6	Bardon 11-5

Fights 3 Won 1 Lost 1 Drawn 1

Ian STRUDWICK

Middleweight
Hockley, Essex. Born Orsett, Sussex 1 April 1964
Army & Rayleigh Mill ABC
1986 Combined Services ABA middleweight champion (w R Morley, l J Melfah)
1988 Combined Services ABA middleweight final (l M Edwards)

1988
Oct 26	Newton Barnett	w pts 6	Albert Hall 11-6
Nov 29	Mark Howell	w pts 6	Albert Hall

1989
Jan 24	Chris Richards	w pts 6	Battersea 11-8
Apr 5	Tony Behan	w pts 6	Albert Hall
May 16	Tony Behan	w pts 8	Battersea 11-9
Jun 28	Robert Armstrong	w ko 1	Brentwood 11-5
Jul 6	Spencer Alton	w pts 8	Chigwell 11-4
Dec 5	Paul Wesley	w pts 6	Catford 11-9-12

1990
Feb 14	Tom Covington	w pts 8	Brentwood 11-6
Apr 14	Val Golding	w pts 6	Albert Hall 11-7-14
Jun 20	Errol Christie	w pts 8	Basildon 11-7
Oct 25	Tony Burke	l pts 10	Bayswater 11-5-8
	(eliminator, British middleweight title)		
Nov 29	Stan King	l rsf 2*	Bayswater 11-7-8

1991
Apr 3	Stan King	w rsf 8*	Bethnal Green 11-10
Sep 24	Fidel Castro	l rsf 6*	Basildon 11-12
	(vacant British super-middleweight title)		
Dec 11	Ray Webb	w ko 8	Basildon 11-13
	(vacant Southern super-middleweight title)		

1992
Mar 11	Ali Forbes	w pts 10	Solihull 12-0
	(Southern super-middleweight title)		
May 23	Chris Pyatt	l pts 10	Birmingham 11-7-8
Oct 29	Paul Wesley	l rsf 1	Bayswater 11-9

Fights 19 Won 14 Lost 5

Richard SWALLOW

Light-welterweight
Northampton born 10 February 1970
Kingsley Park ABC
1989 NABC Class C champion (w A Adams)
1990 Midlands ABA light-welter final (w C Kerr, w D Clarke, w rsf 2 L Smythe, l P Nightingale) **/CTD..**

(Richard SWALLOW ctd.)

1990
Oct 15	Richard O'Brien	l rtd 1*	Kettering 10-3

1991
Feb 14	Dave Fallone	w rsf 4	Southampton 10-4
Mar 6	Carl Brasier	w pts 6	Croydon 10-1
May 2	Mike Morrison	w pts 6	Northampton 10-1

1992
Mar 24	Dean Bramhald	w pts 8	Wolverhampton 10-1
Apr 6	Dean Bramhald	w pts 6	Northampton 10-3
Apr 29	Chris Aston	w rsf 3*	Solihull 10-2
Oct 14	Wayne Shepherd	w pts 8	Stoke 10-2-8
Nov 24	Chris Mulcahy	w pts 6	Wolverhampton 10-5

Fights 9 Won 8 Lost 1

Tony SWIFT
Welterweight
Solihull born 29 June 1968
1984 Junior ABA champion (w P Riley, w C Wright)
1985 Junior ABA champion
1985 NABC Class B champion (w T Williams)

1986
Sep 25	Barry Bacon	w pts 6	Wolverhampton
Oct 6	Wilbert Halliday	w pts 6	Birmingham 9-12
Oct 23	Patrick Loftus	w pts 6	Birmingham 9-8-8
Nov 26	Adam Muir	w pts 6	Wolverhampton 9-9
Dec 8	George Baigrie	w pts 6	Birmingham 9-10

1987
Jan 26	Dean Bramhald	w pts 8	Birmingham 9-10
Mar 4	Dean Bramhald	w rsf 5*	Dudley 9-12
Mar 25	Peter Bowen	w pts 8	Stafford 9-12
Jun 22	Peter Bowen	w pts 8	Stafford 9-12
Oct 7	Dean Bramhald	w pts 8	Stoke 9-13
Oct 19	Kevin Plant	w pts 8	Birmingham 9-12
Dec 2	Dean Bramhald	w pts 8	Stoke 10-1

1988
Mar 16	Ronnie Shinkwin	w pts 8	Solihull 9-13
May 3	Kevin Plant	drew 8	Solihull 9-13
Sep 28	Kevin Plant	drew 8	Solihull 10-0
Nov 23	Lennie Gloster	l pts 8	Solihull 10-0

1989
Jun 12	Humphrey Harrison	w pts 8	Manchester 10-5
Nov 28	Seamus O'Sullivan	w rsf 1	Battersea 10-2

1990
Feb 16	Ramses Evelio	w pts 6	Bilbao 10-5-8
May 30	Darren Mount	w pts 8	Stoke 10-2
Sep 5	Glyn Rhodes	l rsf 7*	Stoke 10-1
Oct 25	Jimmy Harrison	l pts 6	Battersea 10-4

1991
Apr 19	Gary Barron	drew 8	Peterborough
Nov 12	Carlos Chase	w pts 6	Milton Keynes 10-4

1992
Mar 3	Steve McGovern	w rsf 4*	Cradley Heath 10-4-8
Apr 10	Willie Beattie	w pts 10	Glasgow 10-5-6
	(eliminator, British welterweight title)		
Sep 29	Nigel Bradley	w pts 8	Stoke 10-5-8

Fights 27 Won 21 Lost 3 Drawn 3

Wally SWIFT

Light-middleweight
Solihull, born Nottingham 17 February 1966
Birmingham City ABC
1983 Junior ABA champion
1983 NABC Class B champion (w D Morgan)

1985
Sep 25	John Conlan	w rtd 3	Stoke 10-4
Nov 11	Steve Craggs	w rtd 4*	Birmingham 10-9
Dec 9	Steve Tempro	w rsf 4	Birmingham 10-0

1986
Jan 22	Teddy Anderson	w rsf 6	Solihull 10-2
Feb 4	Frankie Lake	w pts 8	Birmingham 10-0
Mar 24	Paul Cook	w pts 8	NSC 10-1-8
Jun 2	Gerry Beard	w pts 8	NSC 10-4
Sep 8	Steve Elwood	w pts 8	Dulwich 10-11-12
Oct 13	Dean Barclay	drew 8	Dulwich 10-12
Nov 19	Franki Moro	w pts 8	Solihull 10-12
Dec 3	Ian Chantler	w pts 8	Stoke 10-12

1987
Jan 22	Dave Dent	l pts 8	Bethnal Green 10-11
Feb 10	Granville Allen	w rsf 4	Wolverhampton 10-9
Feb 24	Dave McCabe	l pts 8	Glasgow 10-8-8
Mar 30	John Ashton	w pts 8	Birmingham 10-11
Oct 20	John Ashton	l pts 8	Stoke 10-12

1988
Jan 20	Tommy McCallum	w pts 8	Solihull 10-12
Mar 28	Ossie Maddix	l pts 8	Stoke 10-11-8
May 3	Chris Blake	w pts 8	Solihull 10-9-8
Sep 28	Terry Magee	l pts 8	Solihull 11-1

1989
Jan 25	Kevin Hayde	w pts 8	Solihull 11-0-8
Mar 1	Andy Till	l pts 8	Bethnal Green 10-11-12
Mar 13	Tony Britton	w pts 8	NSC 11-0
Apr 8	Alfonso Redondo	w pts 8	Madrid
Aug 19	Anibal Miranda	w pts 6	Benidorm
Sep 26	Ensley Bingham	l pts 10	Oldham 10-11
	(eliminator, British light-middleweight title)		

1990
Apr 26	Shaun Cummins	w pts 10	Merthyr 10-12-8
	(vacant Midlands light-middleweight title)		
Sep 18	Mark Holden	w rsf 3	Stoke 10-13
Nov 21	Alan Richards	w pts 8	Solihull 11-2-4

1991
Jan 23	Paul Wesley	w pts 10	Solihull 10-12-8
	(Midlands light-middleweight title)		
Mar 19	Ensley Bingham	w rsf 4	Birmingham 10-10-8
	(vacant British light-middleweight title)		
Jul 3	Tony Collins	w pts 12	Reading 10-10
	(British light-middleweight title)		

1992
Jan 8	Randy Williams	w pts 10	Burton-on-Trent 11-1
Apr 18	Jean-Claude Fontana	l pts 12	Hyeres 10-8-8
	(European light-middleweight title)		
Sep 17	Andy Till	l pts 12	Watford 10-12
	(British light-middleweight title)		

Fights 35 Won 25 Lost 9 Drawn 1

THE
MANAGEMENT TEAM
THAT PRODUCES
CHAMPIONS

84 GREEN LANES, LONDON N16 9EJ TEL: 071 249 9400 FAX: 071 249 8948

Cliff TAYLOR

Super-middleweight
Wheatley Hill born 13 October 1961

1992
Dec 1   Graham Wassell   l pts 6   Hartlepool 12-1-8

Fights 1 Lost 1

Karl TAYLOR

Lightweight
Birmingham born 5 January 1966
Ladywood ABC

1987
Mar 18   Steve Brown   w pts 6   Stoke 9-3-8
Apr 6   Paul Taylor   l pts 6   Southampton 9-7-8
Jun 12   Mark Begley   w rsf 1   Leamington 9-6
Nov 18   Colin Lynch   w rsf 4   Solihull 9-1-8
1988
Feb 29   Peter Bradley   l pts 8   Birmingham 9-6
1989
Oct 4   Mark Antony   w ko 2   Stafford 9-10
Oct 30   Tony Feliciello   l pts 8   Birmingham 9-7
Dec 6   John Davison   l pts 8   Leicester 9-0
Dec 23   Regilio Tuur   l rtd 1   Hoogvliet 9-3-4
1990
Feb 22   Mark Ramsey   l rsf 4   Hull 9-7
Oct 29   Steve Walker   drew 6   Birmingham 9-4
Dec 10   Elvis Parsley   l pts 6   Birmingham 9-4
1991
Jan 16   Wayne Windle   w pts 8   Stoke 9-12
May 2   Billy Schwer   l rsf 2*   Northampton 9-13
Jul 25   Peter Till   l rsf 4*   Dudley 9-9
               (Midlands lightweight title)
1992
Feb 24   Charlie Kane   l pts 8   Glasgow 10-3
Apr 28   Richard Woolgar   w pts 6   Wolverhampton 9-8
May 29   Allan McDowall   l pts 6   Glasgow 9-7
Jul 25   Michael Armstrong   l rsf 3*   Manchester 9-6
Nov 2   Hugh Forde   l pts 6   Wolverhampton 9-9
Nov 23   Davy McHale   l pts 8   Glasgow 9-6-8
Dec 22   Patrick Gallagher   l rsf 3*   Mayfair 9-9

Fights 22 Won 6 Lost 15 Drawn 1

Lee TAYLOR

Light-welterweight
Cardiff, born Pembroke
Southpaw
Gilfach Goch ABC
1992 Welsh ABA welterweight semi-final (w rsf 3 B Ahmed, l B Thorogood)

1992
Dec 14   Vaughan Carnegie   l rsf 2*   Cardiff 10-0-3

Fights 1 Lost 1

Jonathan THAXTON

Light-welterweight
Norwich born 10 September 1974
Norwich Lads ABC
1992 Norfolk ABA light-welterweight champion (w rsf 1 M Green, 1 G Smith)

1992
Dec 9   Scott Smith   w pts 6   Stoke 10-0

Fights 1 Won 1

Maurice THOMAS

Light-heavyweight
Bradford born 11 September 1968

1987
Mar 23	Reuben Thurley	w pts 4	Bradford 11-9-8
Jun 2	Darren Hobson	l rsf 1	Bradford 11-12
Nov 2	Sean Stringfellow	w rsf 1	Bradford 12-8
Dec 15	Lee Woolis	drew 6	Bradford 12-5-8

1988
Feb 29	Terry Duffus	l rsf 1	Bradford 12-3
May 23	Tony Lawrence	w rsf 6	Bradford 12-5-8
Nov 7	Darren McKenna	w ko 4	Bradford 12-7

1989
Jan 16	Keith Halliwell	l rsf 1	Bradford 12-6

1990
Feb 26	Tony Lawrence	w rsf 1	Bradford 12-8
Oct 16	Jason Baxter	w ko 1	Evesham 12-9
Dec 10	Simon McDougall	l rsf 2	Bradford 12-7

1991
Oct 24	John Oxenham	l rsf 6	Glasgow 12-9

1992
Jun 3	Darren McKenna	l rsf 2	Newcastle-under-Lyme 12-5

Fights 13 Won 6 Lost 6 Drawn 1

Steve THOMAS

Light-middleweight
Troedyrhiw born 13 June 1970
Merthyr ABC
1989 Wales (v Nor, l K Aas)
1990 Welsh ABA middleweight semi-final (w M Phillips, l D Griffiths)
1991 Welsh ABA middleweight champion (w C Winstone, w P Matthews, w G Boddy, l rtd 1 M Edwards)

1991
Oct 21	Jerry Mortimer	w pts 6	AASC 11-2
Nov 4	Andrew Manning	w pts 6	Merthyr 11-7

1992
Mar 2	Robert Peel	drew 6	Merthyr 11-2-8
Apr 8	Charlie Moore	l rsf 3	Leeds 11-0
May 11	Robert Peel	w pts 6	Llanelli 11-3-4
Oct 15	Clay O'Shea	l pts 6	Catford 11-3
Nov 12	Warren Stowe	l rsf 1	Burnley 11-3

Fights 7 Won 3 Lost 3 Drawn 1

Tucker THOMAS
Bantamweight
Leeds born 21 June 1972
Real name: Jason Lee

1991
Oct 9	Louis Veitch	l rsf 4	Middlesbrough 8-8

1992
May 29	Shaun Anderson	l rsf 1	Glasgow 8-11

Fights 2 Lost 2

Carl THOMPSON
Cruiserweight
Manchester born 26 May 1964
Real name: Adrian Thompson
Southpaw
No amateur experience

1988
Jun 6	Darren McKenna	w rsf 2	Manchester 12-12
Oct 11	Paul Sheldon	w pts 6	Wolverhampton 13-0

1989
Feb 13	Steve Osborne	w pts 6	Manchester 12-8
Mar 7	Sean O'Phoenix	w rsf 4	Manchester 12-8
Apr 5	Keith Halliwell	w rsf 1*	Manchester 12-9
May 4	Tenko Ernie	w ko 4	Mayfair 12-10
Jun 12	Steve Osborne	w pts 8	Manchester
Jul 11	Peter Brown	w rsf 5	Batley 12-3-12
	(final eliminator, Central light-heavyweight title)		
Oct 31	Crawford Ashley	l rsf 6	Manchester 12-7
	(Central light-heavyweight title)		

1990
Apr 21	Franco Wanyama	l pts 6	St Amandsberg

1991
Mar 7	Terry Dixon	w pts 8	Basildon 13-3-4
Apr 1	Yawe Davis	l rsf 2	Monte Carlo 13-0-12
Sep 4	Nicky Piper	w rsf 3	Bethnal Green 13-3

1992
Jun 4	Steve Lewsam	w rsf 8	Cleethorpes
	(vacant British cruiserweight title)		

Fights 14 Won 11 Lost 3

Dave THOMPSON
Lightweight
Hull born 14 March 1969
North Hull ABC

1990
Mar 26	Mark Conley	w pts 4	Bradford 9-13
Apr 9	Andy Rowbotham	w pts 6	Manchester 9-13
Apr 26	Andy Rowbotham	drew 6	Manchester 9-11
May 21	Johnny Walker	l ko 1	Bradford 9-10
Nov 1	Colin Sinnott	l pts 6	Hull 10-0
Nov 16	Carl Tilley	l ko 1	Telford 9-10
Dec 17	Eddie King	w pts 6	Manchester 10-2

/CTD..

(Dave THOMPSON ctd)
1991
Feb 18	Barry North	w pts 6	Birmingham 9-9
Feb 25	Stephen Winstanley	w rtd 4*	Bradford 9-10
Mar 28	Shane Sheridan	l ko 5	Alfreton 10-3
May 17	Jason Brattley	drew 6	Bury 10-2-8
Jun 13	James Jiora	drew 6	Hull 10-0-12
Jun 30	Nico Lucas	w pts 6	Southwark 9-13
Jul 25	Shaun Cogan	l ko 1	Dudley 9-13
Nov 13	Mark Tibbs	l pts 6	Bethnal Green 9-12
Nov 28	Kevin Toomey	l pts 6	Hull 10-0
Dec 9	Chris Aston	l pts 6	Bradford 10-2

1992
Jan 21	Ricky Sackfield	l ko 1	Stockport 10-0
Mar 30	Jason Brattley	l pts 6	Bradford 10-4

Fights 19 Won 6 Lost 10 Drawn 3

Kevin THOMPSON

Welterweight
Dudley, born Wolverhampton 11 February 1967
Priory Park ABC
1986 South Midlands ABA light-middleweight final (l N Brown)

1987
Apr 9	Roy Horn	w pts 6	NSC 10-8-12
Oct 13	Eddie Collins	w ko 1	Wolverhampton 10-10
Oct 26	Johnny Miller	w pts 4	NSC 10-11
Nov 11	Wilbert Halliday	w ko 4	Stafford 10-10
Dec 9	Wilbert Halliday	w pts 6	Evesham 10-11

1988
Jan 12	Frank McCord	w rsf 6	Cardiff 10-10
Mar 9	Robert Armstrong	w rsf 6	Stoke 10-8

1989
Sep 15	Mickey Lloyd	l ko 7	High Wycombe 10-7
Dec 2	Patrick Vungbo	l pts 8	Anderlecht

1990
Feb 13	Julian Eavis	w pts 8	Wolverhampton 10-10

1991
Feb 14	Leigh Wicks	l pts 8	Southampton

1992
Dec 4	Micky Lerwill	w pts 6	Telford 10-7

Fights 12 Won 9 Lost 3

Jimmy THORNTON

Welterweight
Sheffield born 22 September 1964
Southpaw
Richmond ABC & West Gorton Youth ABC
1981 NABC Class B champion (w D Shiels)
1982 South/West Yorkshire ABA lightweight final (l rsf 3 G Felvus)

1982
Nov 25	Stuart Carmichael	w pts 6	Morley
Dec 14	Seamus McGuinness	l pts 6	Belfast

1983
May 9	Edward Lloyd	w rsf 1*	Manchester 9-9
May 13	Colin Roscoe	w rsf 2	Morley 9-9
May 23	Peter Flanagan	w rtd 3*	Sheffield

Jun 13	Gary Williams	w rtd 5*	Doncaster
Sep 12	Lee Halford	l pts 8	Leicester 9-9
1984			
Feb 29	Ray Murray	w pts 6	Sheffield 10-1
Mar 12	Lennie Gloster	l pts 6	Manchester 10-0
Apr 9	Dave Haggarty	l pts 8	Glasgow 9-11
Jun 6	Peter Bowen	w pts 6	Sheffield 9-10
Jul 22	Peter Bowen	w rsf 2	Sheffield 9-12
Oct 25	Danny Myers	w pts 6	Birmingham 10-2
Nov 26	Ronnie Shinkwin	w rsf 2	Sheffield 9-11
Dec 10	Ray Murray	w rsf 4	Nottingham 10-2
1985			
Feb 4	Steve Tempro	w rsf 4	Birmingham 10-1
Mar 20	Mickey Bird	w pts 6	Stoke 10-1
Apr 10	Ricky Richards	l pts 6	Leeds 10-4
May 31	Raffaele Feliciello	l pts 8	Liverpool 9-13
1986			
inactive			
1987			
Mar 24	Kelvin Mortimer	w pts 6	Nottingham 10-5-8
Apr 13	Peter Ashcroft	l pts 6	Manchester 10-6
May 12	Tony Ekubia	l pts 6	Alfreton 10-9
Aug 9	George Collins	l rsf 1	Windsor 10-10
Dec 7	Andy Holligan	l rtd 2*	Belfast 10-7
1988			
Mar 9	Damien Denny	l pts 8	Bethnal Green 10-13
Apr 12	Tony Ekubia	l rsf 5	Oldham 10-8
Aug 9	Del Bryan	l pts 6	St Helier
Sep 26	Errol McDonald	l rsf 2*	NSC 10-9-8
Dec 7	Paul Jones	l pts 6	Stoke 10-11
1989			
Mar 6	Dave Andrews	l pts 6	Northampton 10-11
Apr 21	Roy Callaghan	w rsf 3*	Bethnal Green 10-8
May 19	Ray Taylor	l pts 8	Gateshead 10-13
Jul 6	Jim Beckett	l pts 8	Chigwell 11-0
Oct 12	Gary Logan	l pts 6	Southwark 10-13-8
1990			
Jan 29	Tony Baker	w pts 8	Bradford 10-9
Nov 22	Seamus Casey	l pts 6	Ilkeston 11-4
1991			
Feb 13	Neville Brown	l rsf 1	Wembley CC 11-3
1992			
Mar 2	Dave Whittle	w pts 6	Marton 10-12
Jul 2	Delroy Waul	l rsf 6	Middleton 10-7

Fights 39 Won 17 Lost 22

Barry THOROGOOD

Light-middleweight
Cardiff born December 1972
Highfield ABC
1991 Wales (v Ire, w E Fisher)
1992 ABA welterweight finalist (w rsf 1 B Jones, w L Taylor, w P Chapell, w P Burns, l rsf 2 M Santini)

1992
Oct 28	Robert Peel	w pts 6	Cardiff 11-1
Dec 14	James Campbell	w rsf 4	Cardiff 10-11

Fights 2 Won 2

Mark TIBBS
Light-welterweight
West Ham born 7 May 1969
Repton ABC
1982 England Schools (v Wal, l S Jones)
1982 National Schools champion (w A Brown)
1983 England Schools (v Wal, w M Flowers)
1984 National Schools final (l J Green)
1985 NABC Class A champion (w P Buckley)
1985 Junior ABA final
1986 NABC Class B final (l C Kerr)
1988 NE London ABA lightweight semi-final (l rsf 2 P Harvey)

1988
Nov 15	Mark Chapman	w pts 6	Norwich 9-6
Nov 23	Shane Tonks	w pts 6	Bethnal Green 9-6
Dec 14	G.G.Corbett	w pts 6	Bethnal Green 9-5-8

1989
Jan 25	Mick Mulcahy	w ko 1	Bethnal Green 9-6-8
Feb 15	Jamie Hinds	w rsf 1	Bethnal Green 9-6-8
Apr 5	Steve Taggart	w ko 1	Albert Hall
May 17	Mark Antony	w pts 6	Millwall 9-11-4
Sep 19	Hugh Ruse	w rsf 3*	Millwall 9-8
Oct 11	Dave Croft	w rsf 5	Millwall 9-9

1990
Feb 20	Mark Fairman	w ko 2	Millwall 9-12-8
Apr 25	Eddie King	w ko 1	Millwall 9-9
Sep 25	Mike Morrison	w pts 6	Millwall 9-12-8

1991
Mar 6	Mike Morrison	w rsf 4*	Wembley 9-12
Jun 6	Chris Saunders	l rsf 6	Barking 9-10-8
Oct 23	Rick Bushell	w rsf 4*	Bethnal Green 9-11
Nov 13	Dave Thompson	w pts 6	Bethnal Green 9-10
Dec 11	Rick Bushell	w rsf 2*	Basildon 9-11-8

1992
Mar 25	Felix Kelly	drew 8	Dagenham 9-10
Nov 12	John Smith	w rsf 6*	Bayswater 10-4
Dec 12	Dean Bramhald	w pts 6	Muswell Hill 10-2

Fights 20 Won 18 Lost 1 Drawn 1

Andy TILL
Light-middleweight
Northolt born Perivale 22 August 1963
Northolt ABC
1979 Junior ABA final (l E Christie)
1980 Junior ABA final (l C Pyatt)
1981 NABC Class C final (l M Flynn)
1986 NW London ABA middleweight champion (w S Palmer, w dis 2 M Edwards, l rsf 3* T Taylor)

1986
Sep 1	Peter Reid	w rsf 6	Ealing 11-0
Sep 25	Graham Jenner	w pts 6	Crystal Palace 11-3-12
Nov 10	Randy Henderson	w pts 6	Longford 11-3

1987
Jan 11	Tony Lawrence	w rsf 4	Ealing 11-6
Feb 18	Ian Bayliss	w pts 6	Fulham 11-5-12
Apr 30	Dean Scarfe	l pts 8	Battersea 11-1
Sep 14	Andy Wright	w rsf 2	Crystal Palace 11-0

1988			
Feb 19	Geoff Sharpe	w rsf 5	Longford 11-3
Nov 29	W.O.Wilson	w pts 10	Battersea 10-11-4
	(eliminator, Southern light-middleweight title)		
1989			
Mar 1	Wally Swift	w pts 8	Bethnal Green 11-1-12
Jun 12	Tony Britton	w rtd 8	Battersea 10-12
	(vacant Southern light-middleweight title)		
Nov 10	Nigel Fairbairn	w rsf 8*	Battersea 11-3
1990			
Mar 14	Steve Foster	w rtd 5	Battersea 11-5
Jun 6	Ensley Bingham	l dis 3	Battersea 10-13-8
	(final eliminator, British light-middleweight title)		
Sep 12	Alan Richards	w pts 8	Battersea 11-2-8
1991			
Feb 6	Alan Richards	w pts 8	Battersea 11-1
Jun 1	Terry Magee	w rsf 4*	Bethnal Green 11-0-8
Oct 15	John Davies	w pts 12 (s)	Dudley 10-12
	(vacant WBC International light-middleweight title)		
1992			
Sep 17	Wally Swift	w pts 12	Watford 10-12-8
	(British light-middleweight title)		
Dec 10	Tony Collins	w rsf 3	Bethnal Green
	(British light-middleweight title)		

Fights 20 Won 18 Lost 2

Peter TILL

Lightweight
Walsall born 19 August 1963
Bloxwich ABC
1980 Junior ABA semi-final (l B Welham)
1981 Midlands ABA lightweight final (w J Merritt, l L Remikie)
1982 South Midlands ABA light-welterweight semi-final (l rsf 3 C McIntosh)
1984 ABA light-welterweight semi-final (w K Clayton, w rsf 2 E Williams, w A Bush, w M Milne, w D Barclay, l B Buchanan)
1985 South Midlands ABA light-welterweight semi-final (l rsf 3 M Elliot)

1985			
Apr 25	Clinton Campbell	w ko 1	Wolverhampton 9-9
May 23	J.J.Mudd	w pts 6	Dudley 9-10
Oct 17	Patrick Loftus	w pts 6	Leicester 9-8-12
Nov 14	Paul Wetter	w rsf 3	Dudley 9-11
1986			
Jan 27	George Jones	w pts 8	Dudley 9-9
Apr 17	Tyrell Wilson	w ko 5	Wolverhampton 9-10
May 15	Les Remikie	w pts 6	Dudley 9-11
Jun 3	Ray Newby	l pts 10	Wolverhampton 9-9
	(vacant Midlands lightweight title)		
Sep 25	Gerry Beard	drew 8	Wolverhampton 9-11-8
Nov 26	Gerry Beard	w ko 4	Wolverhampton 9-9
1987			
Jan 28	George Baigrie	w pts 8	Dudley 9-7
Mar 4	Carl Merritt	w pts 8	Dudley 9-12
Mar 30	Tony Richards	l pts 8	Birmingham 9-7
Jul 19	Aladin Stevens	l ko 4	Johannesburg
Oct 19	Dean Bramhald	w pts 8	Birmingham 9-12
Nov 24	Dean Bramhald	w pts 8	Wolverhampton 10-2

/CTD..

(Peter TILL ctd.)

1988
Feb 7	Michael Marsden	w ko 1	Stafford 9-12
Feb 24	Neil Haddock	w pts 8	Port Talbot 9-11
Apr 13	Sugar Gibiliru	w pts 8	Wolverhampton 9-11-12
Jun 14	Ray Newby	w pts 10	Dudley
	(Midlands lightweight title)		
Sep 22	Jim Moffat	w rsf 4	Wolverhampton 9-8-4
Nov 10	George Jones	w rsf 8	Wolverhampton 9-7
	(Midlands lightweight title)		

1989
Feb 2	Camel Touati	w rsf 3	Wolverhampton 9-8-8
Apr 13	Philippe Binante	w rsf 3	Wolverhampton 9-10
Dec 21	Tony Richards	l ko 8	Kings Heath 9-6

1990
Oct 18	Nick Hall	w pts 6	Birmingham 9-9
Nov 30	Ray Newby	w pts 8	Birmingham 9-10

1991
Feb 21	Paul Charters	l rsf 6	Walsall 9-8
	(eliminator, British lightweight title)		
May 31	Valery Kayumba	l rsf 3	Grenoble
Jul 25	Karl Taylor	w rsf 4*	Dudley 9-8-8
	(Midlands lightweight title)		
Sep 21	Michael Ayers	l rsf 5*	Tottenham 9-9
	(eliminator, British lightweight title)		
Dec 9	Scott Doyle	w ko 3	Brierley Hill 9-11-8

1992
Feb 1	Michael Driscoll	l rsf 3	Birmingham
Mar 17	Mark Reefer	w rsf 3	Mayfair 9-10
Jun 4	Racheed Lawal	l rsf 1	Randers
Aug 15	Dingaan Thobela	l rsf 9	Springs

Fights 36 Won 25 Lost 10 Drawn 1

Carl TILLEY

Lightweight
Doncaster born 4 October 1967
Elmfield House ABC
1990 Yorkshire & Humberside ABA light-welterweight semi-final (l M Barker)

1990
Sep 4	Stuart Good	w rsf 5	Southend 9-9
Nov 16	Dave Thompson	w ko 1	Telford 9-11

1991
May 13	Steve Winstanley	w rtd 4*	Middlesbrough 9-9
Oct 9	Bobby Beckles	w rsf 4*	Middlesbrough 9-10-8

1992
Mar 2	James Jiora	w pts 6	Marton 9-9
Apr 30	Greg Egbuniwe	l pts 6	Albert Hall 9-12
Sep 15	Joey Moffat	l pts 6	Liverpool 9-8

Fights 7 Won 5 Lost 2

Wayne TIMMINS
Welterweight
Dudley born 18 March 1966
Southpaw

1988
May 16	Marty Duke	w pts 6	Wolverhampton 10-8
Jun 14	Ricky Maxwell	w pts 6	Dudley 10-7
Oct 6	Noel Rafferty	w pts 6	Dudley 10-9

1989
Feb 2	Steve Hogg	w pts 6	Wolverhampton 10-6
Feb 28	Steve Hogg	w pts 6	Dudley 10-7
Apr 17	Tony Britland	drew 6	Birmingham 10-8
Sep 25	Julian Eavis	w pts 6	NEC 10-8-8
Oct 30	Julian Eavis	w pts 8	Birmingham 10-7

1990
Mar 22	Julian Eavis	w pts 8	Wolverhampton 10-9
Apr 23	Tony Britland	w pts 8	Birmingham 10-9
May 24	Tony Britland	w pts 8	Dudley 10-9-8
Sep 18	Graham Burton	l pts 6	Wolverhampton 11-1-8
Oct 24	Alan Richards	l ko 4	Dudley 10-13-8
Dec 10	Wayne Appleton	l ko 4	Birmingham 10-10

1991
Apr 10	Trevor Meikle	w pts 6	Wolverhampton 10-9
May 14	Tony Britland	w pts 6	Dudley 10-8-8
Jun 5	Julian Eavis	w pts 6	Wolverhampton 10-9

1992
Feb 20	James Lawlor	w pts 6	Telford 10-10
Mar 17	Darren Morris	drew 6	Wolverhampton 10-9

Fights 19 Won 14 Lost 3 Drawn 2

Lee TONKS
Light-welterweight
Camberley born 1970
Pinewood Starr ABC, Camberley ABC & All Stars ABC. Based Campo, California.
1990 Home Counties ABA lightweight prelim (l R Woolgar)

1992
Aug 27	Martin Ramales	w ko 1	San Diego 10-0
Sep 4	Tommy Barrett	w pts 4	Reseda 10-0-8
Sep 29	Damon Franklin	l pts 4	Reseda 10-1
Nov 4	Benny Barrientos	w pts 4	Reseda 10-3
Nov 24	Tyrone Mitchell	w pts 4	Reseda 10-3

Fights 5 Won 4 Lost 1

Nick TOOLEY
Flyweight
Teignmouth born 19 December 1970
Dawlish ABC & Torbay ABC
1988 Western Counties ABA light-flyweight champion (w.o. to E s/f, l I Lang)
1989 Western Counties ABA light-flyweight champion (w rtd 1 M Stuckey, l M Cantwell)
1990 ABA light-flyweight champion (w rsf 2 N Stephenson, w M Hughes, w P Weir)
1991 Western Counties ABA light-flyweight champion (w.o. to E s/f, then l rsf 2 P Culshaw)

1992
Oct 26	Louis Veitch	w pts 6	Cleethorpes 8-2
Nov 19	Anthony Hanna	w pts 6	Evesham 8-2

Fights 2 Won 2

Kevin TOOMEY

Lightweight
Hull born 19 September 1967
St Mary's ABC
Southpaw

1989
Apr 24	Chris Mulcahy	l pts 6	Bradford 10-6
Sep 4	Andy Rowbotham	w rsf 1	Cleethorpes 10-0
Oct 3	Mick Mulcahy	l ko 5	Cottingham 10-3

1990
Nov 1	Joel Forbes	w pts 6	Hull 10-1
Dec 12	Andy Kent	drew 6	Leicester 10-1

1991
Jan 24	Barry North	w pts 6	Brierley Hill 10-3
Feb 18	Andy Kent	l rsf 5	Derby 9-12
Apr 22	Trevor Royal	w pts 6	Bradford 10-2
May 16	John Smith	w pts 6	Liverpool 10-3-8
Jun 13	John Smith	w pts 6	Hull 10-5-12
Sep 30	Mike Calderwood	l rsf 2*	Liverpool 9-13
Nov 28	David Thompson	w pts 6	Hull 10-1
Dec 10	Wayne Windle	l pts 6	Sheffield 10-2

1992
Feb 4	G.G.Goddard	w pts 6	Alfreton 9-10
Mar 26	Wayne Windle (Central lightweight title)	w dis 8	Hull 9-9
Sep 11	Dave Anderson	l pts 8	Glasgow 9-12-8
Oct 15	Steve Pollard	w rsf 7*	Hull 9-12
Nov 26	Dean Bramhald (Central lightweight title)	l pts 10	Hull 9-7-8

Fights 18 Won 10 Lost 7 Drawn 1

Tony TRIMBLE

Light-middleweight
Middlesbrough born 20 March 1960

1992
Oct 19	Allan Grainger	l pts 6	Glasgow 11-1
Dec 1	Mark Chicocki	l pts 6	Hartlepool 11-3

Fights 2 Lost 2

Leo TURNER

Super-featherweight
Bradford born 17 September 1970

1992
Jun 8	Wayne Rigby	l pts 6	Bradford 9-5
Jul 2	Wayne Rigby	l ko 5	Middleton 9-7-12
Oct 12	Mickey Hall	l rsf 5	Bradford 9-8
Dec 14	Fred Reeves	w rsf 2	Bradford 9-4

Fights 3 Lost 3

THE MARTINDALE REFLEX BALL

* Will vastly improve your reflexes, timing and hand and eye co-ordination.
* It is a vital part of a boxer's training equipment.
* Only the best English leather is used.
* It is fully adjustable on the top and rear of the harness to ensure a perfect fit.
* Fitted with quality rubber band and ball.
* Also available, same as above, in black nylon webbing.

LEATHER ..... £14.99 (add £2.50 p&p)
NYLON .... £11.99 (add £2.50 p&p)

TO ORDER: Please state which harness you require, i.e. leather or nylon. Please print your name and address, enclose cheque/postal order made payable to Martindale and send to:
**Martindale,
207 Tiptree Crescent,
Clayhall, Ilford, Essex, IG5 0ST.**

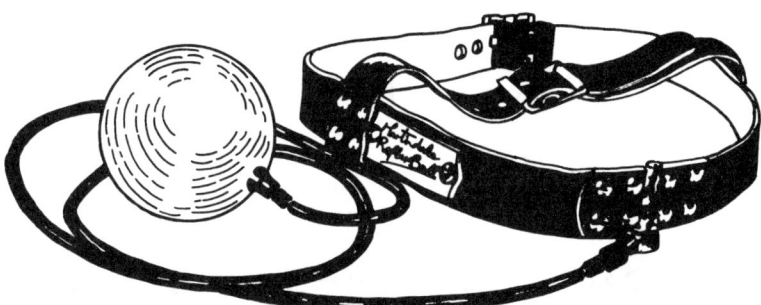

The new sensational Reflex Ball, as used by champions and top professional boxers.

Subscribe to *BOXING UPDATE* and *FLASH* ...

and the choice is yours: **Robinson, Marciano** or **Ali, Duran!!!**

Read America's *Boxing Update and Flash* every 10 days (3 per month) for the latest U.S. & worldwide boxing news, upcoming fights, plus action photos.

■ "The best"- Emanuel Steward.

■ "A great paper" -Bobby Czyz.

■ "A great job"- Gil Clancy

Mail bank draft in US$ payable at a US Bank to:

■ A *FREE* $18 T-shirt of your choice when you subscribe.

■ Choose the following sub rate, indicate your size under the shirt of your choice, and forward your payment to get the best in pro boxing coverage plus a great *FREE* T-shirt!

❑ 4-Mo. Flash/BU. . . **$45**
❑ 8-Mo. Flash/BU. . . **$90**
❑ 1-Yr. Flash/BU. . **$132**

❑ Large ❑ X-Large

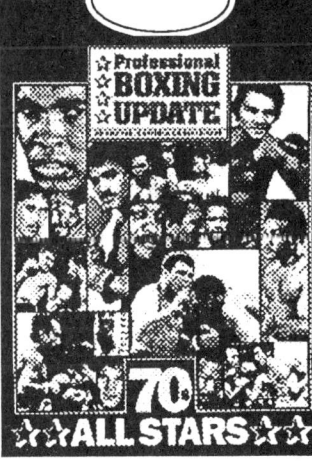

❑ Large ❑ X-Large

Name _____

Address _____

City, Country _____

Boxing Update/Flash - Post Office Box 789 - Capitola CA 95010-0789

THE WORLD FAMOUS

The Thomas A'Becket

PRO BOXING GYM

071-703 7334

NOW OPEN 7 DAYS A WEEK

The history, the atmosphere and the very best equipment.

Sauna, infra-red deep heat and electrical massage treatments.

Short/long term accommodation available and sponsorship contracts.

Main London stockists for JLC Sportswear and equipment.

Vintage boxing programmes/photos on sale.

General enquiries:
Chris Ashley T/as Thomas A'Becket
Thomas A'Becket House,
320 Old Kent Road
London SE1 5UE

Tel: 071-252 7605/5617

Johnny UPHILL

Light-heavyweight
Hastings, born Welling 27 January 1967
West Hill ABC

1988			
Mar 7	Keith Butler	w rsf 1	Hove 11-10
Apr 26	Tony Lawrence	l rsf 5	Hove 12-0-8
May 25	Benny Simmonds	w pts 6	Hastings 12-9
1989-90 inactive			
1991			
Apr 4	Kevin Morton	l ko 1	Watford 12-3
1992			
Mar 1	Julian Johnson	l ko 3	St Leonard's On Sea 12-9

Fights 5 Won 2 Lost 3

Greg UPTON

Featherweight
Teignmouth, born Oshawa, Ontario 11 June 1971
Dawlish ABC

1991			
Nov 28	Eunan Devenney	w pts 6	Evesham 9-2
1992			
Apr 29	Chris Morris	w rsf 2	Liverpool 9-0
Jun 1	Graham McGrath	w pts 6	NEC 9-0
Nov 19	Mark Hargreaves	l rsf 3	Evesham 9-0

Fights 4 Won 3 Lost 1

PADDY BYRNE
International Agent

<u>Office:</u>
70 Benfield Way
Portslade, Sussex
England, UK BN42DL

Tel: 0273 412498
Fax: 0273 430823

<u>MATCHMAKER FOR</u>
EASTWOOD PROMOTIONS
BELFAST
NORTHERN IRELAND

<u>MATCHMAKER FOR</u>
MOGENS PALLE
COPENHAGEN
DENMARK

Boxing equipment bought by novices to world champions.
Amateur club discounts available on request.
New Title leisure and sports clothing now selling in major High Street stores including River Island, Peter Brown, Champion Sports and Olympus.
For free boxing catalogue send S.A.E. to:

TITLE SPORTS
241 Southwark Park Road
London
SE16 3TS
Tel: 071 231 1519   Fax: 071 231 7094

VISA & ACCESS accepted over the 'phone

Opening times: Monday - Saturday 9am - 5.30pm

Paul VACHE
Light-middleweight
Bristol born 23 June 1967

1992
Oct 5   Mossa Azward   w rsf 2   Bristol 11-0

Fights 1 Won 1

Rudi VALENTINO
Lightweight
Hanwell born 6 July 1964
Real name: Rudolph Valentino Isaacs
Samuel Montagu ABC
1981 Junior ABA champion (w P Martin)
1983 SE London ABA featherweight final (l ko 3 P McKenzie)
1986 SE London ABA lightweight champion (w rsf 3 J Tossell, w rsf 2 G Andrews, l T Dwyer)

1986
| Oct 22 | Mike Russell | w pts 6 | Greenwich |
| Nov 26 | Tim O'Keefe | w pts 6 | Lewisham 9-7 |

1987
Mar 19	Neil Haddock	w pts 6	Bethnal Green 9-8-12
Apr 30	Marvin P.Gray	w pts 6	Washington 9-9
Sep 15	Peter Crook	l pts 6	Kensington 9-12
Nov 18	Paul Burke	l pts 6	Bethnal Green 9-10
Dec 2	Mark Pearce	w pts 6	NSC 9-10

1988
Jan 18	John Dickson	w pts 6	NSC 9-10
Mar 8	James Jiora	w pts 6	Batley 9-7
Apr 5	Hugh Forde	l rsf 2	Birmingham 9-7
May 18	Chubby Martin	l rsf 5	Lewisham 9-10-8

1989
Feb 8	Paul Moylett	w rsf 2	Albert Hall 9-8
Feb 15	Richie Joyce	l pts 6	Stoke 9-8-8
Apr 24	Steve Topliss	w pts 6	Nottingham 9-10
Jun 21	Sugar Gibiliru	w pts 6	Eltham 9-11-8
Sep 4	Jose Tuominen	l rsf 2*	Helsinki 9-8-4
Oct 20	Harry Escott	l rtd 4*	Manchester 9-6-8

1990
Mar 27	Peter Bradley	l pts 8	NSC 9-8
Apr 23	Lee Amass	w rsf 6	Crystal Palace 9-11-12
May 28	Pierre Lorcy	l pts 8	Paris 9-8-12
Oct 20	Gianni Di Napoli	drew 8	Lyon 9-9-4
Dec 15	Angel Mona	l pts 8	Vichy

1991
Apr 10   Marcel Herbert   w rsf 3   Newport 9-8-8
(eliminator, British lightweight title)
Jul 17   Giovanni Parisi   l pts 8   Abbiategrasso 9-11-8
Sep 13   Giorgio Campanella   l pts 8   Gaggiano

1992
Feb 19   Michael Ayers   l rsf 7   Muswell Hill 9-6-8
(Southern lightweight title; eliminator, British title)

Fights 26 Won 12 Lost 13 Drawn 1

Des VAUGHAN

Cruiserweight
Sydenham born 3 January 1965
St Monicas ABC
1990 NE London ABA heavyweight final (l P Lawson)

1990
Oct 25	Coco Collins	w ko 1	Battersea 13-7-12

1991
Feb 18	Rob Albon	l pts 6	Windsor 13-9

1992
Mar 6	Steve Shelley	w rsf 5	Battersea 13-8
Oct 28	Phil Soundy	l rtd 4	Albert Hall 13-3

Fights 4 Won 2 Lost 2

Louis VEITCH

Flyweight
Blackpool born Glasgow 9 March 1963
Barrhead ABC, Paisley ABC, St Anne's ABC

1991
Oct 9	Tucker Thomas	w rsf 4	Middlesbrough 8-0
Nov 11	Shaun Norman	l rsf 5	Bradford 8-0

1992
Mar 12	Neil Armstrong	l pts 6	Glasgow 8-3
Apr 10	Mark Robertson	l pts 6	Glasgow 8-2
May 16	Micky Cantwell	l pts 6	Muswell Hill 8-2
Jul 9	Paul Weir	l pts 6	Glasgow 8-0
Sep 11	Neil Armstrong	l pts 6	Glasgow 8-2
Oct 26	Nick Tooley	l pts 6	Cleethorpes 8-2-12
Dec 14	Lyndon Kershaw	drew 6	Bradford 8-3

Fights 9 Won 1 Lost 7 Drawn 1

Tony VELINOR

Light-middleweight
Stratford, London born 21 December 1964
West Ham ABC & Army ABC
1980 National Schools final (l J Davies)
1981 National Schools champion (w J Davies)
1985 Combined Services ABA welterweight final (l rsf 1 P Nicholson)
1986 ABA light-middle champion (w T Westwood, w S Pigott, w dis 2 N Brown, w rsf 1 G Thomas, S Butler)
1986 England (v Ire, w K Lynch)
1988 Combined Services ABA light-middleweight champion (w B Reid, w P Dyer, l rsf 2 N Brown)

1988
Oct 28	Robert Armstrong	w rsf 4	Brentwood 11-2
Nov 22	Andy Jones	w rtd 1*	Basildon 11-0
Dec 16	Kesem Clayton	l rsf 2	Brentwood 11-2

1989
Jan 25	Seamus Casey	w rtd 3*	Basildon 11-1
Mar 28	Ricky Nelson	w rsf 4	Chigwell 11-1-8
May 26	Skip Jackson	w rsf 2	Bethnal Green 11-4
Sep 19	Mark Howell	w pts 8	Bethnal Green 11-4

1990
Jan 31	Shaun Cummins	l pts 8	Bethnal Green 11-4

May 22	Trevor Grant	w pts 6	Canvey Island 11-2
Sep 12	Ian Chantler	l rsf 4*	Bethnal Green 11-2
1991			
Mar 12	Paul Jones	l pts 8	Mansfield 11-2-8
Jul 3	Jason Rowe	w rsf 1*	Brentwood 11-2
1992			
May 11	Stan King	l rsf 3	Piccadilly 11-4

Fights 13 Won 8 Lost 5

Mark VERIKIOS

Welterweight
Swansea born 31 October 1965
Premier ABC
1991 Welsh ABA light-middleweight prelim (l J Desforges)

1991			
May 15	Lee Farrell	w rsf 5*	Swansea 10-10
Jun 6	Tim Harmey	w ko 4	Barking 10-10
Sep 9	Dave Maj	w pts 6	Liverpool 10-8
1992			
May 13	Steve McNess	w rsf 5*	Albert Hall 10-10
Nov 12	Dave Maj	w pts 6	Liverpool 10-9

Fights 5 Won 5

Jimmy VINCENT

Light-welterweight
Doncaster born Barnet 5 June 1970
Coventry Boys ABC

1987			
Oct 19	Roy Williams	w pts 6	Birmingham 8-12
Nov 11	Mick Greenwood	w pts 6	Stafford 9-0
Nov 19	Darrel Pettit	w rsf 6	Ilkeston
Nov 24	Roy Williams	w pts 6	Wolverhampton 9-0
1988			
Feb 14	Neil Leggett	l pts 6	Peterborough 8-13
Feb 29	Billy Cawley	w ko 1	Birmingham 9-1
Apr 13	Dave Croft	w pts 6	Wolverhampton 9-8
May 16	Barry North	w pts 6	Wolverhampton 9-9
Jun 14	Dean Dickinson	w pts 6	Birmingham 9-6
Sep 20	Henry Armstrong	l pts 6	Stoke 9-6-4
Oct 10	Henry Armstrong	l pts 6	Manchester 9-5-8
Oct 17	Dean Dickinson	w pts 6	Birmingham
Nov 14	Peter Gabbitus	l pts 6	Stratford 9-8
Nov 22	Barry North	w rsf 4	Wolverhampton 9-10
Dec 12	Tony Feliciello	l pts 8	Birmingham 9-7
1989-91 inactive			
1992			
Sep 9	Mark Dawson	l pts 6	Stoke 10-4
Sep 23	Phil Epton	w rsf 6*	Leeds 10-6-8
Dec 17	Jason Rowland	l pts 6	Wembley GH 10-2-12

Fights 18 Won 11 Lost 7

Ian VOKES

Light-heavyweight
Hull born 27 March 1966
Hastings ABC

1989
Mar 13	Eugene Brown	l rsf 1	Leicester 12-7
Apr 24	Hugh Fury	l pts 6	Bradford 12-5
May 8	Tony Behan	l pts 6	Grimsby 12-5
May 22	Steve Davies	l pts 6	Bradford 12-6
Oct 3	Andrew Marlow	l pts 6	Cottingham
Oct 23	Andrew Braveo	w rsf 5	Cleethorpes
Oct 30	Tony Lawrence	l pts 6	NSC 12-5
Nov 13	Seamus Casey	l rsf 5*	Bradford 12-1

1990
Jan 27	Stinger Mason	l pts 6	Sheffield 12-2
Feb 13	David Maxwell	l pts 6	Wolverhampton 12-0
Feb 27	Shaun McCrory	l pts 6	Middlesbrough 12-1
Apr 19	Glenn Campbell	l ko 1	Oldham
Oct 8	Pete Bowman	w pts 6	Cleethorpes 12-7
Nov 1	Pete Bowman	w pts 6	Hull 12-4
Nov 12	Tony Lawrence	l pts 6	Bradford 12-5
Dec 12	Barry Downes	l pts 6	Leicester 12-6

1991
Feb 18	Barry Downes	w pts 6	Derby 12-6
Mar 19	Ian Henry	l rsf 2	Manchester 12-6
Apr 22	Joe Kilshaw	drew 6	Bradford 12-2-8
May 13	Steve Truepenny	l ko 2	Manchester 12-7
Nov 28	Seamus Casey	l pts 6	Hull 12-2

1992
Dec 14	Barry Downes	l pts 6	Northampton 12-12

Fights 22 Won 4 Lost 17 Drawn 1

Yusuf VORAJEE

Featherweight
Coventry born 21 August 1969
Southpaw
Triumph ABC & Nuneaton Boys ABC
1987 South Midlands ABA bantamweight final (l rsf 2 B Robb)
1988 Midlands ABA bantamweight final (w K Whistance, l rsf 2 P Neale)
1989 Warwickshire ABA bantamweight final (l R Heighton)
1990 Midlands ABA featherweight champion (w D Amory, w E Parsley, w L Reynolds, l rsf 1 M Bowers)
1991 South Midlands ABA featherweight final (l D Amory)
1992 Midlands ABA featherweight champion (w A Thomas, w R Brotherhood, w M Hermon, w M Walsh, w ko 2 J Gynn, l A Temple)

1992
Sep 30	Kid McAuley	l pts 6	Solihull 9-1
Oct 14	Mark Hargreaves	l rsf 4	Stoke 9-1

Fights 2 Lost 2

Peter VOSPER

Super-middleweight
Plymouth born 6 October 1966
Devonport ABC
Southpaw
1987 Western ABA middle champion (w S Stenson, w S McCarthy, w N Rodney, w K Greenwood, withdrew)
1988 Western ABA middleweight champion (w D McCarthy, w N Rodney, l M Edwards)

1989
Feb 15	Mark White	w pts 6	Bethnal Green
Mar 1	Lester Jacobs	l pts 6	Bethnal Green
Mar 29	George Moody	l pts 6	Bethnal Green 11-10
May 9	Tony Cloak	w rsf 2	Plymouth 11-10
Jun 20	Spencer Alton	w pts 6	Plymouth 11-11
Oct 17	Spencer Alton	drew 8	Plymouth 11-9-8
Nov 30	Ray Webb	l pts 6	Southwark 12-0

1990
Mar 3	Michael Gale	l rsf 2	Wembley 12-7-8
Apr 26	Mick Clarke	l pts 6	Battersea 12-0
May 21	Chris Walker	w rsf 2	NSC 12-3
Sep 26	Ali Forbes	l pts 6	AASC 12-0

1991
Apr 12	Frank Eubanks	l rsf 1	Manchester 11-10-12
May 30	Russell Washer	w pts 6	Mayfair 12-0-8
Jun 6	John Kaighin	drew 6	Barking
Jun 27	Nick Manners	l rsf 1	Leeds 12-1
Dec 16	Paul McCarthy	l pts 6	Southampton 12-2-12

1992
Feb 25	Roland Ericsson	l rsf 6	Crystal Palace 12-1
Dec 1	John Kaighin	l rsf 4	Bristol 12-0-12

Fights 18 Won 5 Lost 11 Drawn 2

BILLY AIRD PROMOTIONS

Triamond Construction Limited, Western House,
14 Western Road, Plaistow, London E13 9JF.
Tel: 081 552 3002/081 503 4616 Fax: 081 470 7057

Billy Aird Promotions would like to wish British Professional Boxers' Records 1993 every success in its first edition, and future publications.

Best Wishes from:
Billy Aird, Tom Burling, Pat Thomas, Jim Bennett and the future world champions.

TOMORROW'S CHAMPIONS

DARRON GRIFFITHS
MIDDLEWEIGHT

Future world champion

BARRY "ROCKY" THOROGOOD
LIGHT-MIDDLEWEIGHT

Ex ABA finalist and Welsh ABA champion

JERRY MORTIMER
LIGHT-MIDDLEWEIGHT

Always gives his best

LEE "TIGER" TAYLOR
LIGHT-WELTERWEIGHT

Young prospect, who needs experience.

MERVYN BENNETT
LIGHTWEIGHT

Strong fighter, who wants Welsh title.

BARRIE "THE GHOST" KELLEY
SUPER-FEATHERWEIGHT

Will challenge for the British title this season.

KEVIN MIDDLETON
FEATHERWEIGHT

Looking for the Southern area title this season.

BARRY "BABY BOY" JONES
FEATHERWEIGHT

The darling of Welsh boxing - another Howard Winstone.

MY WORD IS MY BOND

WE HAVE OUR OWN TRAINING FACILITIES IN LONDON AND CARDIFF.

Nicky WADMAN

Light-heavyweight
Brighton born 8 August 1965
Silver Ring ABC & Crawley ABC
1982 Junior ABA champion (w rsf 2 S Daly)
1984 NABC Class C champion (w ko 1 R Flanagan)
1986 Southern ABA light-heavyweight champion (w D Hutchins, w M Aubrey, l J Moran)
1987 Southern ABA light-heavyweight champion (w rsf 2 P Morris, l rsf 2 E Blake)

1992
Mar 11	Julian Johnson	w pts 6	Cardiff 12-9
Apr 23	Mark McBiane	w rsf 1	Eltham 12-10
Sep 26	Hussain Shah	l rsf 4	Olympia 12-13-8

Fights 3 Won 2 Lost 1

Chris WALKER

Super-middleweight
Nottingham born Trowbridge 25 December 1961
Real name: Chris Bonnick
Nottingham School of Boxing ABC

1987
Jan 22	Paul Murray	w pts 4	Bethnal Green
Feb 10	Paul Murray	l pts 4	Wolverhampton

1988 inactive

1989
Oct 23	Terry French	l pts 6	Nottingham 11-8

1990
Jan 24	Darren Parker	l pts 6	Stoke 11-10
Feb 5	Willie James	w ko 1	Leicester 11-10
Feb 19	Anthony Lawrence	l pts 6	Nottingham 11-10
Mar 10	Nigel Pearce	w rtd 3	Bristol 12-2
Mar 26	Tony Lawrence	w pts 6	Nottingham
Apr 11	Tony Lawrence	w rsf 5	Manchester 12-1
Apr 30	Andy Marlow	w pts 6	Nottingham 11-9
May 14	Alan Baptiste	w pts 6	Leicester 12-2
May 21	Peter Vosper	l rsf 2	NSC
Oct 29	Russell Washer	w rsf 2	Nottingham 12-0
Nov 13	Antonio Fernandez	l pts 6	Edgbaston 11-11-8
Dec 10	Paul Burton	w rsf 4*	Nottingham 11-12

1991
Mar 13	Adrian Wright	w pts 4	Stoke 11-11
Oct 10	Ian Henry	l pts 4	Gateshead 12-1
Oct 22	Paul Hitch	l pts 6	Hartlepool 12-1-4

1992
Mar 11	Doug Calderwood	w pts 6	Solihull 12-2
Apr 28	Paul Hitch	w rsf 2	Houghton-le-Spring 11-13
May 14	Paul Wright	l pts 6	Liverpool 11-11

Fights 21 Won 12 Lost 9

Danny WALKER
Super-middleweight
Port Talbot, born Neath 19 January 1967
Afan Lido ABC

1990
Nov 27	Tracy Jocelyn	w pts 6	Wolverhampton 11-10
Dec 10	Tracy Jocelyn	l pts 6	Birmingham 11-11-8

1991
Mar 15	Alan Gandy	w pts 6	Willenhall 11-9

1992
Jan 15	Marc Rowley	l ko 5	Stoke 11-12

Fights 4 Won 2 Lost 2

Steve WALKER
Super-featherweight
Manchester born 25 June 1962
Moss Side ABC
1987 East Lancs & Cheshire ABA featherweight semi-final (l P English)
1988 East Lancs & Cheshire ABA featherweight semi-final (l C Breakwell)

1989
Sep 14	Eddie Cook	l pts 6	Motherwell 9-3
Sep 28	Miguel Matthews	w pts 6	Cardiff 9-1-8
Oct 4	Paul Harvey	drew 6	Basildon 9-2
Oct 30	Jason Lepre	w ko 2	NSC 9-4
Nov 4	Eddie Cook	w pts 4	Eastbourne 9-4
Nov 28	Alan McKay	drew 6	Battersea 9-2-8
Dec 18	John Milne	drew 6	Glasgow 9-5-8

1990
Feb 23	Tommy Graham	w rsf 4	Irvine 9-4
Mar 6	John Milne	drew 8	Glasgow 9-6
Mar 28	Francisco Arroyo	w pts 6	Manchester 9-5-12
May 3	Colin McMillan	l pts 6	Marble Arch 9-4
Jun 4	Gary Peynado	w pts 6	Edgbaston 9-4
Oct 9	Ian McGirr	w rsf 4*	Glasgow 9-5
Oct 29	Karl Taylor	drew 6	Birmingham 9-3-8
Nov 12	Muhammad Shaffique	w pts 6	Stratford 9-4-8

1991
Jan 24	Richie Foster	w pts 8	Brierley Hill 9-5
Mar 2	Harry Escott	drew 6	Darlington 9-4
Mar 19	Mark Holt	w pts 8	Birmingham 9-3-8
Sep 20	Harry Escott	drew 6	Manchester 9-4
Nov 13	Ian Honeywood	l pts 6	Bethnal Green 9-11-8

1992
Jul 18	Kelton McKenzie	l ko 2	Manchester 9-2

Fights 21 Won 10 Lost 4 Drawn 7

Steve WALTON
Light-heavyweight
Whitley Bay, born Wallsend 3 December 1972

1992
May 28	Greg Scott-Briggs	l pts 6	Gosforth 12-7

Fights 1 Lost 1

Russell WASHER

Middleweight
Swansea born 21 January 1962
RAOB Swansea ABC
Welsh Schools champion
1988 Welsh ABA heavyweight final (l rsf 2 D Fearn)
1989 Welsh ABA light-heavyweight semi-final (l rsf 3 N Piper)

1990
Sep 15	Dean Cooper	l pts 6	Bristol 11-11
Oct 2	Nick Gyaamie	w rsf 4	Eltham 11-13
Oct 16	Wayne Panayiotiou	w rsf 2*	Evesham 11-7-8
Oct 29	Chris Walker	l rsf 2	Nottingham 11-8
Dec 11	Matt Mowatt	w rsf 6	Evesham 11-6-8

1991
Jan 24	Wayne Panayiotiou	w rsf 4*	Gorseinon 11-11-12
Feb 21	Marvin O'Brian	drew 6	Walsall 11-7
Mar 19	Tony Meszaros	l pts 6	Birmingham 11-12-8
Apr 10	Andy Flute	l pts 6	Wolverhampton 11-9
May 30	Peter Vosper	l pts 6	Mayfair 12-0
Sep 4	Val Golding	l rtd 5	Bethnal Green 11-8
Nov 11	Stinger Mason	l pts 4	Stratford 11-6
Nov 20	Alan Richards	l pts 6	Cardiff 11-11-8
Nov 29	Ensley Bingham	l rsf 4	Manchester 11-1

1992
Mar 11	Lee Crocker	l pts 6	Cardiff 11-7
Apr 22	Gilbert Jackson	l pts 6	Wembley 11-4
May 11	Carlo Colarusso	l rsf 5	Llanelli 10-9-4
	(Welsh light-middleweight title)		
Jun 18	Tony Collins	l rsf 2*	Peterborough 11-3
Sep 3	John Bosco	l rsf 2*	Dunstable 11-4
Oct 5	Sean Byrne	l pts 6	Northampton 11-8
Oct 15	Jerry Mortimer	l rsf 5*	Catford
Nov 28	Paul Wright	l pts 8	Manchester 12-2
Dec 10	Abel Asinamali	w pts 6	Bethnal Green 11-10

Fights 23 Won 5 Lost 17 Drawn 1

Graham WASSELL

Super-middleweight
Pontefract, born Wakefield 29 December 1966
Sharlston ABC
1990 Yorkshire & Humberside ABA light-heavyweight final (w A Call, l rsf 3 J Oxenham)

1990
Nov 13	Alan Gandy	drew 6	Edgbaston 11-13

1991
Oct 21	Gypsy Johnny Price	l rsf 5	Bury 12-0

1992
Oct 15	Sean Smith	w rsf 2	Hull 12-4
Dec 1	Cliff Taylor	w pts 6	Hartlepool 12-2

Fights 4 Won 2 Lost 1 Drawn 1

Peter WAUDBY

Light-middleweight
Hull born 18 November 1970
St Pauls ABC
1989 NABC Class C champion
1990 ABA welterweight final (w rsf 2 R North, w rsf 2 P Sellers, w rtd 2 C Moore, w P Burns, w L Innes, w A Craig, l rsf 2 A Carew)
1991 Northern ABA welterweight final (w R North, w J Pearse, l P Burns)
1991 England (v Den, l I Fidan)
1992 Northern ABA welterweight final (w M Stones, w rsf 3 J Herridge, w J Green, l P Burns)

1992
Sep 21	Simon Fisher	w rsf 2	Cleethorpes 11-2
Oct 15	Chris Mulcahy	w rsf 4	Hull 10-9
Dec 14	Seamus Casey	w pts 6	Cleethorpes 11-3

Fights 3 Won 3

Delroy WAUL

Welterweight
Manchester born 3 May 1970
Collyhurst & Moston ABC

1989
May 29	Calum Rattray	w pts 6	Dundee 10-0
Jun 12	Calum Rattray	w pts 6	Glasgow 9-13
Sep 25	Jimmy Reynolds	w rsf 4	NEC 9-9-8
Oct 10	Dave Maw	w pts 4	Sunderland 10-6
Dec 5	Richie Adams	w rsf 4	Dewsbury 10-3

1990
Jan 11	Richie Adams	w rsf 3	Dewsbury 10-4
Oct 22	Jim Talbot	w rtd 3*	NSC 10-9-8
Nov 15	Mike Russell	w ko 1	Oldham 10-8
Dec 13	Kid Silvester	w rsf 6	Dewsbury 10-8

1991
Jan 31	Kevin Hayde	w rsf 6	Stockport 10-10-8
Feb 13	Chris Richards	w pts 6	Wembley CC 10-8-8
Mar 14	Terry Morrill	drew 8	Middleton 10-9-12
May 2	Andy Furlong	w rsf 5	Northampton 11-1
May 16	Paul Wesley	w rsf 7*	Liverpool 10-9-8
Jun 20	Gordon Blair	l ko 2	Liverpool 10-9
Oct 9	Paul King	w rsf 6	Manchester
Dec 19	Jason Rowe	w rsf 4*	Oldham 10-8-8

1992
Jan 31	Patrick Vungbo	l dis 8	Waregem 10-7
Jul 2	Jimmy Thornton	w rsf 6	Middleton 10-6-8

Fights 19 Won 16 Lost 2 Drawn 1

Ray WEBB

Super-middleweight
Stepney born 10 March 1966
Southpaw
Gator ABC
1988 London ABA light-heavyweight final (l B Parkes, replaced Parkes, w ko 1 V Clarke, l rsf 1 T Dixon)

1988
Nov 2	Doug Calderwood	w rsf 6	Southwark 11-7-12

1989
Jan 12	Roberto Gomez	w rsf 1	Southwark 11-12
Nov 30	Peter Vosper	w pts 6	Southwark 11-9

1990
Apr 6	Carlo Colarusso	l pts 6	Telford 11-6
Sep 15	Ray Close	l pts 8	Belfast 11-11
Nov 6	Ahmet Canbakis	w pts 6	Mayfair 12-2
Dec 8	Franck Nicotra	l pts 8	Ferrara 12-0-4

1991
Jan 10	Carlos Christie	w pts 6	Battersea 11-12
Mar 27	Silvio Branco	l pts 8	Venice 11-13-12
May 30	Karl Barwise	w pts 8	Mayfair 12-1-12
Dec 11	Ian Strudwick	l ko 8	Basildon 11-13

(vacant Southern super-middleweight title)

1992
Mar 6	Oleg Volkov	l pts 8	Berlin

Fights 12 Won 6 Lost 6

Paul WEIR

Flyweight
Irvine, born Glasgow 16 September 1967
Springside ABC & Croy Miners ABC
1986 Scottish ABA light-flyweight final (l W Docherty)
1988 Scotland (v Ire, l C Notarantonio)
1989 Scotland (v Eng, w M Cantwell)
1989 Scottish ABA light-flyweight champion (w.o., then withdrew!)
1989 European Championships light-flyweight prelim (l I Hristov, Bul)
1989 Scotland (v EGer, l J Quast)
1990 Commonwealth Games light-flyweight (l A Ramadhani, Ken)
1990 ABA light-flyweight finalist (w rsf 1 J McCourt, w rsf 1 K Hassell, l N Tooley)
1990 Scotland (v USA, l O Malone)
1991 Scottish ABA light-flyweight champion (w A Mooney, withdrew)
1991 Scotland (v Ire, w M McQuillan; v Wal, w N Swain)
1991 European Championships light-flyweight bronze medal (w Y Ben Haim, Isr; l L Castiglione, It)
1991 Canada Cup bronze medal

1992
Apr 27	Eddie Vallejo	w ko 2	Glasgow 7-11
Jul 9	Louis Veitch	w pts 6	Glasgow 7-11-8
Sep 21	Neil Parry	w rsf 4	Glasgow 8-1
Nov 23	Shaun Norman	w pts 8	Glasgow 8-0

Fights 4 Won 4

Scott WELCH
Heavyweight
Brighton, born Great Yarmouth 21 April 1968
Hove ABC
1991 Southern ABA heavyweight semi-final (l E Knight)
1992 ABA heavyweight champion (w rsf 1 C Little, w rsf 3 T Small, w dis 3 G Cox, w rsf 3 M Levi, w A Caulfield, w ko 3 R Fenton)

1992
Sep 8	John Williams	w rsf 5	Norwich 14-12
Oct 6	Gary Williams	w pts 4	Antwerp 14-6

Fights 2 Won 2

Tony WELLINGTON
Middleweight
Deptford, born Nottingham 23 April 1965
St Anne's ABC
1990 SE London ABA middleweight semi-final (w rsf 2 G Oliver, l C Tsirtos)

1990
Sep 26	Gary Booker	l pts 6	AASC 11-10
Oct 25	Gary Booker	l pts 6	Battersea 11-7-8
Nov 6	Dean Cooper	l pts 6	Southend 11-5-12
Nov 15	John Kaighin	l pts 6	Oldham 11-5
Nov 26	Clayon Stewart	w pts 6	NSC 11-7-8
Dec 8	Clayon Stewart	w rsf 1	Bristol 11-1

1991
Jan 23	Paul Busby	l rsf 2	Brentwood
Sep 26	Clay O'Shea	l ko 1	Dunstable 11-6
Dec 5	John Mackenzie	l pts 6	Peterborough 11-8

1992
Mar 6	Gilbert Jackson	l ko 2	Battersea 11-5-8

Fights 10 Won 2 Lost 8

Nigel WENTON
Lightweight
Liverpool born 5 April 1969
Roseheath ABC & Window Lane ABC
1982 National Schools champion (w T Franklin)
1983 National Schools champion
1985 Junior ABA champion
1985 NABC Class A final (l S Tokeley)
1986 NABC Class B champion (w M Smyth)
1987 Young England (v YYug, w Vlahovic)
1987 NABC Class C champion (w J McMahon)

1988
Jun 8	Steve Taggart	w rsf 2	Sheffield 9-6-8
Jun 23	Rafael Saez	w rsf 3	Panama City
Oct 21	Neil Leggett	w rtd 2*	Belfast 9-7
Nov 2	Kid Sumaila	w rtd 3*	Southwark 9-7-8
Nov 15	Tony Graham	w rsf 3	NSC 9-8-12
Dec 7	John Bennie	w rsf 5	Belfast 9-7
Dec 14	John Rafiu King	w rsf 1	Liverpool 9-8

1989
Jan 18	Ian Honeywood	w rsf 3*	Albert Hall 9-9-8
Jan 25	Mark Pearce	w pts 6	Belfast
Mar 8	Juan Torres	w rtd 3*	Belfast 9-8

Apr 17	Edwin Murillo	w ko 2	Belfast 9-5
May 10	Nigel Senior	w rsf 2	Albert Hall 9-7-8
Jun 7	Eamonn Payne	w rsf 3	Wembley 9-9
Jul 28	Fabian Salazar	l pts 6 (s)	Isla Margarita, Venezuela
Sep 19	Sugar Gibiliru	w pts 8	Belfast 9-9
Oct 31	Tomas Arguelles	w pts 6	Belfast
Dec 13	Lance Williams	w pts 6	Liverpool 9-7
1990			
Feb 21	Luis Menditon	w rsf 3	Belfast 9-9-8
Mar 17	Scott De Pew	w rsf 2	Belfast 9-9-8
Apr 29	Sharmba Mitchell	l pts 8	Atlantic City 9-9
Jul 15	Bryant Paden	drew 10	Atlantic City
1991			
Sep 7	Oliver Harrison	w rtd 5	Belfast 9-12
Nov 13	Tony Richards	w rsf 5	Belfast 9-12
Dec 11	Jeff Roberts	w ko 2	Dublin 9-10-4
1992			
Apr 25	Ed Pollard	w rtd 6	Belfast 9-11-8
Dec 10	Davey Robb	w rsf 3	Bethnal Green 9-13

Fights 26 Won 23 Lost 2 Drawn 1

Richie WENTON

Featherweight
Liverpool born 28 October 1967
Roseheath ABC, South Liverpool ABC & Window Lane ABC
1983 National Schools champion
1984 National Schools champion (w M Ward)
1984 Junior ABA semi-final (l dis L Williams)
1985 West Lancs ABA bantamweight semi-final (l rsf 3 J Sillitoe)
1985 Young England (v YUSA, l rsf 2 N Skiles)
1986 West Lancs ABA prelims (l rsf 2 J Naylor)
1987 Northern ABA final (w S Mangan, w C Greer, w rsf 1 R Brindle, l rsf 2 J Davison)
1988 Northern ABA final (w rsf 3 C Wall, w J Gilberston, w P Wright, w rsf 1 R Brindle, l rsf 2 J Davison)

1988			
Dec 14	Miguel Matthews	w ko 2	Liverpool 8-12
1989			
Jan 25	Sean Casey	w pts 4	Belfast 8-12
Apr 10	Stuart Carmichael	w rsf 2	NSC 9-0
Dec 13	Joe Mullen	w rsf 5	Liverpool 8-8-8
1990			
Feb 21	Ariel Cordova	w pts 6	Belfast 8-9-8
Mar 17	Mark Johnson	w pts 4	Belfast 8-6
Mar 28	Jose Luis Vasquez	w pts 6	Manchester 8-7-4
May 23	Graham O'Malley	w pts 6	Belfast 8-9-8
Jul 9	Eugene Quincy Pratt	w ko 1	Miami Beach 8-9
Sep 15	Graham O'Malley	w pts 6	Belfast 8-10-8
Oct 30	Alejandro Armenta	w rsf 2	Belfast 8-9
1991			
Feb 12	Sean Casey	w pts 4	Belfast 8-13-8
1992			
Mar 31	Graham O'Malley	w pts 6	Stockport 8-13
Jul 25	Ramos Agare	w rsf 3	Manchester 9-0
Sep 26	Floyd Churchill	l rsf 2	Olympia 8-12

Fights 15 Won 14 Lost 1

Paul WESLEY
Middleweight
Erdington born 2 May 1962
Aston Villa ABC

1987
Feb 20	Barry Bennett	l pts 6	Maidenhead 11-6
Mar 18	Darryl Ritchie	drew 4	Stoke 12-0
Apr 8	Dean Murray	w pts 6	Evesham 11-8
Apr 29	John Wright	w pts 4	Loughborough 11-12
Jun 12	Leon Thomas	w rsf 2	Leamington 11-4
Nov 16	Steve McCarthy	l ko 8	Southampton 11-10

1988
Jan 25	Paul Murray	w pts 8	Birmingham 11-6
Feb 29	Paul Murray	drew 8	Birmingham 11-6
Mar 15	Johnny Williamson	w ko 2	Bournemouth 11-5-8
Apr 9	Joe McKenzie	w rsf 6	Bristol 11-6
May 10	Tony Meszaros	w pts 8	Edgbaston 11-6

1989
Mar 21	Carlton Warren	l ko 2	Battersea 11-6-8
May 10	Rod Douglas	l ko 1	Albert Hall 11-7-12
Oct 24	Nigel Rafferty	l pts 6	Wolverhampton 11-6
Nov 22	Nigel Rafferty	l pts 8	Stafford 11-4
Nov 28	Nigel Rafferty	l pts 6	Wolverhampton 11-6
Dec 5	Ian Strudwick	l pts 6	Catford 11-9

1990
Jan 24	Raffaele Feliciello	w pts 6	Solihull 11-5-8
Feb 19	Nigel Rafferty	l pts 8	Birmingham 11-7
Mar 22	John Ashton (Midlands middleweight title)	l pts 10	Wolverhampton 11-3
Apr 17	Winston May	drew 8	Millwall 11-4
May 9	Alan Richards	w pts 8	Solihull 11-5
Jun 4	Julian Eavis	w pts 8	Birmingham 11-0
Sep 18	Shaun Cummins	l rsf 1	Wolverhampton 11-2
Oct 17	Julian Eavis	w pts 6	Stoke 11-0

1991
Jan 23	Wally Swift (Midlands light-middleweight title)	l pts 10	Solihull 11-0
Mar 20	Horace Fleary	l rsf 5*	Solihull 11-4-12
May 16	Delroy Waul	l rsf 7*	Liverpool 11-4
Jul 4	Neville Brown	w rsf 1	Alfreton 11-3
Jul 31	Francesco Dell'Aquila	l pts 8	Casella 11-4-12
Oct 3	Neville Brown	l pts 8	Burton 11-4
Oct 29	Tony Collins	drew 8	Albert Hall 11-3

1992
Mar 3	Antonio Fernandez (vacant Midlands middleweight title)	l pts 10	Cradley Heath 11-4
Apr 10	Jean-Charles Meuret	l pts 8	Geneva
Jun 3	Sumbu Kalambay	l pts 10	Salice Terme 11-10
Oct 29	Ian Strudwick	w rsf 1	Bayswater 11-7
Nov 14	Paul Busby	l pts 8	Cardiff 11-4-8
Nov 24	Paul Jones	w rsf 2	Doncaster 11-2

Fights 38 Won 14 Lost 20 Drawn 4

John WESTGARTH

Heavyweight
Newcastle, born Malta 23 December 1959
West End Boys ABC
1982 Northern ABA super-heavyweight champion (w rsf 2 J White, w B Deasy, l K Ferdinand)

1982
Nov 29	Andy Gerrard	drew 6	Newquay
Dec 6	Frankie Robinson	w pts 6	Nottingham

1983
Feb 10	John Fallon	w pts 6	Walthamstow 15-8
Feb 23	Dave Garside	l rtd 6*	Mayfair

1984
Oct 22	Dave Russell	drew 8	South Shields 14-13
Dec 11	Dave Garside	w rsf 5*	South Shields 14-13

1985
Feb 12	Theo Josephs	w ko 2	South Shields 15-1
Apr 9	Rocky Burton	w ko 1	South Shields 15-3
Apr 26	Dominique Nato	l pts 8	Thionville
Sep 3	Glenn McCrory	w ko 4	Gateshead 14-13
Nov 14	Damien Marignan	w ko 3	Newcastle 15-3-8

1986
Feb 20	Anaclet Wamba	l pts 10	Newcastle 15-4
Apr 18	Steffan Tangstad	l pts 12	Randers 15-1
	(vacant European heavyweight title)		
May 28	Razor Ruddock	l ko 7	Muswell Hill 15-2
Oct 16	Dave Garside	l rsf 9	Newcastle 15-4
	(eliminator, British heavyweight title)		

1987
Sep 4	Tony Hallett	w rtd 3*	Gateshead 15-0
Oct 8	Derek Williams	l rsf 7	Bethnal Green 15-3-8

1988
Jan 26	Ian Priest	w rsf 1*	Hartlepool 16-0
Jun 29	Jess Harding	l rtd 5	Basildon 15-11-8
Aug 9	Andy Gerrard	w pts 8	St Helier 15-5-8
Oct 26	Derek Williams	l rsf 2	Albert Hall 16-2
Dec 8	Magne Havnaa	l pts 8	Copenhagen 15-8

1989
Jan 31	James Oyebola	l ko 3	Reading 15-12
Mar 7	James Oyebola	w rsf 5	Wisbech 15-11
Oct 17	Michael Murray	l rtd 4	Oldham 15-7

1990
Apr 26	Adam Fogerty	l rsf 4*	Halifax 15-8
Jul 6	Jess Harding	l rsf 5*	Brentwood 15-11

1991
May 14	Herbie Hide	l rtd 4	Dudley 17-1

1992
Mar 30	Warren Richards	drew 6	Eltham 16-6

Fights 29 Won 11 Lost 15 Drawn 3

Andre WHARTON

Light-middleweight
Brierley Hill, born Wordsley 16 June 1969
Merryhill ABC

1989
Nov 13	Alfie Andrews	w pts 6	Brierley Hill 11-1-8

1990
Feb 5	Alfie Andrews	w rsf 4	Brierley Hill 11-0
Mar 19	Gary Dyson	drew 6	Brierley Hill 11-2
Sep 3	Dave Radford	w rsf 5	Dudley 11-3-4
Oct 15	Mickey Duncan	w pts 6	Brierley Hill 11-2

1991
Jan 24	Stefan Wright	w rsf 5	Brierley Hill 11-3-12
Feb 18	Dean Cooper	l pts 8	Birmingham 11-2
Mar 15	Wayne Appleton	w rsf 7*	Willenhall 11-1

1992
Oct 27	Geoff Calder	w pts 4	Cradley Heath 11-0-12

Fights 9 Won 7 Lost 1 Drawn 1

Henry WHARTON

Super-middleweight
York born 23 November 1967
St Patricks ABC, Leeds
1985 Anglo-Scottish Select v USA select (l rtd 3 G Brown)
1987 Northern ABA middleweight finalist (w rtd 1 L Smith, l J Carr)
1987 England (v Ire, w ko 1 R Close; v Pol, w W Wieczorack; v Cze, l ko 1 M Franek)
1988 England (v Sco, w ko 2 J Mair; v Ire, w G Lawlor)
1988 Northern ABA middle final (w rsf 1 S McMahon, w ko 2 M Whitehouse, w ko 1 I Meredith, l E Noi)
1989 ABA middle finalist (w rsf 2 P Hitch, w E Noi, w L Woolcock, w rsf 1 J Farrell, l dis 2 S Johnson)

1989
Sep 21	Dean Murray	w rsf 1	Harrogate 11-12
Oct 25	Mike Aubrey	w pts 6	Wembley 12-0
Dec 5	Ron Malek	w rsf 1	Dewsbury 11-8

1990
Jan 11	Guillermo Chavez	w ko 1	Dewsbury 11-11
Mar 3	Joe Potts	w ko 4	Wembley 11-12
Apr 11	Juan Elizondo	w rsf 3	Dewsbury 11-10
Oct 18	Chuck Edwards	w rsf 1	Dewsbury 11-10
Oct 30	Ed "Dino" Stewart	w pts 8	Wembley 12-1

1991
Mar 21	Francisco Lara	w ko 1	Dewsbury 12-0-8
May 9	Frank Minton	w ko 7	Leeds 12-0-12
Jun 27	Rod Carr	w pts 12	Leeds 12-0
	(Commonwealth super-middleweight title)		
Oct 30	Lou Gent	drew 12	Leeds 11-13-12
	(Commonwealth super-middleweight title)		

1992
Jan 23	Nicky Walker	w pts 10	York 12-1-12
Mar 19	Kenny Schaefer	w ko 1	York 12-4
Apr 8	Rod Carr	w rsf 8	Leeds 12-0
	(Commonwealth super-middleweight title)		
Sep 23	Fidel Castro	w pts 12	Leeds 11-12-12
	(Commonwealth & British super-middleweight titles)		

Fights 16 Won 15 Drawn 1

Gary WHITE

Bantamweight
Rochdale born 13 April 1971
1987 Junior ABA final

1991
Feb 28	Steve Wood	w pts 6	Bury 8-8
Mar 19	Tony Smith	w pts 6	Manchester 8-9-8
May 17	Neil Parry	w pts 6	Bury 8-7-8

1992
Dec 7	Robert Braddock	w pts 6	Manchester 8-11-8

Fights 4 Won 4

Jason WHITE

Super-featherweight
Thame born 16 February 1970
Southpaw
Aylesbury ABC
1992 Home Counties ABA lightweight final (w M Leonard, l J Wilson)

1992
Sep 3	Marco Fattore	l rsf 1*	Dunstable 9-5-8
Oct 29	Jason Lepre	w pts 6	Hayes 9-7
Dec 4	Gareth Jordan	l rsf 2	Telford 9-7

Fights 3 Won 1 Lost 2

John WHITE

Featherweight
Salford born 6 November 1970
St Boniface ABC, Sale West ABC
1988 East Lancs & Cheshire ABA bantamweight final (l rsf 3 R Brindle)
1989 East Lancs & Cheshire ABA bantam champion (w rsf 2 J Burrows, w rsf 2 R McGahon, l rsf 1 P Lloyd)
1990 Northern ABA featherweight final (w ko 2 S Stewart, w rsf 1 J Hoole, w rsf 1 T Peacock, l rsf 2 A Green)
1991 Northern ABA bantamweight final (w rsf 1 C Rourke, w rsf 2 P Lloyd, l rsf 3 M Gibbons)

1992
Feb 27	Alan Smith	w rsf 1	Liverpool 8-13
Jul 2	Norman Dhalie	w rsf 6	Middleton 8-12-12
Jul 25	Ronnie Stephenson	w pts 6	Manchester 8-13
Oct 13	Kid McAuley	w pts 4	Bury 9-0
Nov 28	Mark Hargreaves	w pts 4	Manchester 8-12-12

Fights 5 Won 5

Robert WHITEHOUSE

Light-middleweight
Swansea, born Oxford 9 October 1965
Swansea City ABC, Premier ABC, Oxford YMCA, Blackbird Leys ABC

1992
Sep 7	Jerry Mortimer	l rsf 3	Southend 11-0
Oct 23	Steve Foran	l rsf 2	Liverpool 10-8
Dec 3	Jason Beard	l rsf 3	Catford 10-11

Fights 3 Lost 3

Dave WHITTLE

Welterweight
Newcastle, born North Shields 19 May 1966
Benfield ABC

1988			
Nov 22	Mark Jay	l pts 6	Middlesbrough 10-10
1989			
Feb 28	Tony Farrell	w pts 6	Middlesbrough
Mar 31	Seamus Sheridan	w rsf 2	Scarborough 10-7
May 19	Chris Mulcahy	l pts 6	Gateshead 10-4
Jun 3	Ian Thomas	w pts 6	Stanley 10-5-8
Dec 13	Ian Thomas	w pts 6	Liverpool
1990			
Feb 27	Trevor Meikle	drew 8	Middlesbrough 10-7
Jun 4	Alfie Andrews	w pts 6	Edgbaston 11-0
Nov 29	Trevor Meikle	w pts 6	Marton 10-11
1991			
May 13	Barry Messam	l pts 6	Middlesbrough 11-6
Oct 23	Jamie Robinson	l rsf 4	Bethnal Green 11-1
Nov 27	Alan Peacock	w pts 6	Marton
1992			
Mar 2	Jimmy Thornton	l pts 6	Marton 10-8
Mar 12	Alan Peacock	drew 8	Glasgow 10-6
Apr 14	Nigel Bradley	l ko 3	Mansfield 10-6
May 18	Wayne Shepherd	l pts 6	Marton

Fights 16 Won 7 Lost 7 Drawn 2

Leigh WICKS

Welterweight
Brighton, born Worthing 29 July 1965
Southpaw
Phoenix Silver Ring ABC
1987 Southern ABA light-middleweight final (w L Ransley, l S Smith)

1987			
Apr 29	Fidel Castro	w pts 6	Hastings 11-2
Sep 23	Jason Rowe	w pts 6	Hastings 11-2
Nov 18	Lou Ayres	w pts 6	Holborn 11-0-12
1988			
Jan 26	Theo Marius	l pts 8	Hove
Feb 15	Seamus Casey	w pts 6	Copthorne 11-2
Apr 26	Franki Moro	drew 6	Hove 11-0
May 4	Tony Britton	w pts 8	Wembley GH 11-2
May 18	Mark Howell	w rsf 8*	Portsmouth 11-0
May 25	Newton Barnett	drew 8	Hastings 11-5
Nov 22	Roy Callaghan	l pts 8	Basildon
1989			
Mar 16	Tony Britland	w pts 8	Southwark 10-4
Oct 12	Tony Gibbs	w ko 2	Southwark 10-9
1990			
Feb 8	Ernie Noble	w pts 8	Southwark 10-9-4
Apr 26	Julian Eavis	drew 8	Mayfair 10-8
Nov 6	Gordon Blair	w pts 8	Mayfair 10-8-4
1991			
Jan 10	Barry Messam	w pts 6	Battersea
Feb 14	Kevin Thompson	w pts 8	Southampton
Oct 21	Tony Britland	w rsf 3	AASC 10-10-12

1992

Feb 20	Mickey Duncan	l pts 8	Glasgow 10-9-12
Apr 30	Darren Morris	drew 6	Mayfair 10-8
Oct 19	Bozon Haule	w pts 8	Mayfair 10-10

Fights 21 Won 14 Lost 3 Drawn 4

Alan WILLIAMS

Middleweight
Liverpool, born 2 August 1962
Salisbury ABC
1983 West Lancs & Cheshire ABA welterweight final (l ko 3 T Culshaw)
1984 West Lancs & Cheshire ABA welterweight prelim (l D Ashcroft)

1984

Jun 11	Bobby McGowan	w dis 1	Manchester 11-1
Oct 24	Michael Justin	l rsf 6	Birmingham 10-10
Nov 30	Cliff Domville	l rsf 3	Liverpool 10-4

1985

Feb 4	Robert Riley	l pts 6	Liverpool 10-1
Mar 29	Bobby Welburn	l ko 2	Liverpool 10-3

1986-90 inactive

1991

Mar 18	Stephen Welford	l ko 1	Derby 11-9

1992

Apr 29	Rob Stephenson	l pts 6	Liverpool 10-7
Sep 28	Tony Massey	l rsf 3*	Manchester 11-4

Fights 8 Won 1 Lost 7

B.F.WILLIAMS

Light-welterweight
Watford born 14 December 1965
Real name: Robert Williams
Bushey ABC
1985 Home Counties ABA lightweight champion (w J Doran, l I Kemp)
1986 Home Counties ABA lightweight final (l A Carolan)

1986

May 28	Kenny Watson	w rsf 5*	Catford 9-8
Oct 1	Andrew Prescod	l rsf 4	Lewisham 9-9-8

1987

Jan 27	Jess Rundan	l pts 6	Plymouth 9-11-8
Feb 18	Dave Nash	w rsf 3	Fulham 9-12-4
Mar 19	Les Remikie	w pts 6	Bethnal Green 9-8
Apr 15	John Mullen	l pts 6	Lewisham 9-9
Apr 30	Paul Kennedy	w pts 6	Washington 9-9-8
Sep 18	Mike Russell	w pts 8	Swindon 9-12
Nov 19	Ian Hosten	w pts 6	Battersea 9-12-8
Dec 9	Chubby Martin	drew 8	Greenwich 9-8-8

1988

Feb 17	Neil Haddock	w pts 8	Bethnal Green 9-11-8
Sep 28	Tony Borg	l rsf 7	Edmonton 9-13-4
Nov 28	James Lawlor	l pts 6	Edgbaston 10-0-4

1989

Jan 31	Danny Ellis	w rsf 6	Bethnal Green 10-2 /CTD..

(B.F.WILLIAMS ctd.)

Mar 29	Paul Charters	w pts 6	Bethnal Green 9-13
Apr 26	Seamus O'Sullivan	l rsf 6	Battersea 10-1-4
Sep 15	Tony Gibbs	w pts 6	High Wycombe 9-13
Oct 25	Richie Joyce	w rsf 4	Stoke 10-0-8
Dec 12	Steve Taggart	w rsf 2	Brentford 10-1

1990

Jan 16	Mike Morrison	w pts 6	Cardiff 10-3
Feb 22	Michael Driscoll	l ko 2	Battersea 9-12
Oct 25	Danny Cooper	l pts 6	Battersea 10-1-12
Nov 14	Nigel Bradley	l ko 2	Sheffield 10-2

1991

| Feb 7 | Rick Bushell | l rtd 2 | Watford 10-0 |

1992

Feb 12	Cliff Churchward	w pts 6	Watford 10-3
Apr 7	Erwin Edwards	w pts 6	Southend 10-4-8
Apr 30	Trevor Meikle	w pts 6	Watford
Sep 17	James Campbell	w pts 6	Watford 10-3

Fights 28 Won 17 Lost 10 Drawn 1

Derek WILLIAMS

Heavyweight
Peckham born 11 March 1965
Wandsworth ABC
1984 SW London ABA heavyweight final (w P French, l dis 2 G Best)

1984

| Oct 24 | Tony Tricker | w rsf 6 | Mayfair 14-10-8 |

1985

Jan 24	Mike Creasy	w rsf 3	Streatham 15-6-8
Feb 11	Barry Ellis	w rsf 2	Dulwich 15-7-8
Mar 26	Alfonso Forbes	w rsf 2	Wimbledon 15-9-4
Sep 20	Ron Ellis	l pts 8	Longford 15-2-8

1986

| Jan 30 | Steve Gee | w pts 6 | Wimbledon 15-10 |

1987

Feb 22	Steve Gee	w pts 6	Wembley GH 16-1
Mar 24	Andy Gerrard	w pts 6	Wembley 16-1-8
Jun 25	Jess Harding	w pts 8	Bethnal Green 16-7
Oct 8	John Westgarth	w rsf 7	Bethnal Green 16-5

1988

Jan 28	Dave Garside	w pts 10	Bethnal Green 16-9
May 18	Mark Young	w ko 4	Portsmouth 16-10
Oct 26	John Westgarth	w rsf 2	Albert Hall 16-4-12
Nov 29	Young Haumona	w ko 4	Albert Hall 16-3

(vacant Commonwealth heavyweight title)

1989

Feb 14	Noel Quarless	w ko 1	Battersea 16-6-8
Apr 5	Al Evans	w rsf 2	Albert Hall
Aug 24	Mark Wills	l pts 8	New York 15-12
Dec 5	Hughroy Currie	w rsf 1	Catford 16-3-12

(Commonwealth & vacant European heavyweight title)

1990

| Feb 3 | Jean Chanet | l pts 12 | St Dizier 17-1 |

(European heavyweight title)

| May 28 | Jean Chanet | l pts 12 | Paris 16-7-12 |

(European heavyweight title)

1991			
May 1	Jimmy Thunder	w rsf 2	Bethnal Green 17-5
	(Commonwealth heavyweight title)		
Sep 30	David Bey	w rtd 6	Albert Hall 17-1
1992			
Jan 18	Tim Anderson	w rsf 1	Albert Hall 16-10-8
Apr 30	Lennox Lewis	l rsf 3	Albert Hall 16-9
	(British, Commonwealth & European heavyweight titles)		

Fights 24 Won 19 Lost 5

Everald WILLIAMS

Light-welterweight
Hornsey, born Jamaica 10 June 1969
St Pancras ABC, St Monicas ABC
1990 London North-East ABA light-welterweight champion (w G Loblack, w S Jean-Paul, l R Edwards)
1991 London North-West ABA light-welterweight semi-final (l A Brown)

1992			
Mar 6	Korso Aleain	w ko 6	Battersea 10-0-8

Fights 1 Won 1

Gary WILLIAMS

Heavyweight
Nottingham born 25 September 1965
Phoenix ABC
1989 North Midlands ABA super-heavyweight final (l ko 1 C Mitchell)
1990 Midlands ABA heavyweight champion (w.o. x 3, l rsf 3 K Inglis)
1991 North Midlands ABA heavyweight final (w S Truepenny, l P Oko)

1992			
Apr 27	Damien Caesar	l rsf 4	AASC 14-4
Sep 7	J.A. Bugner	l pts 4	Bethnal Green 14-7
Oct 6	Scott Welch	l pts 4	Antwerp 15-4
Dec 1	Kenny Sandison	w pts 6	Liverpool 13-13

Fights 4 Won 1 Lost 3

John WILLIAMS

Cruiserweight
Birmingham born 26 October 1963
Real name: Kirk Gibbon
Birmingham City ABC

1985			
Feb 12	Dougie Isles	w rsf 5	South Shields 13-0
Oct 14	Alex Romeo	w pts 6	Birmingham 12-8
Nov 11	Roy Smith	l rsf 2	Birmingham 13-0
1986			
Feb 27	Lou Gent	l rsf 4	Wimbledon 13-2-8
May 12	Blaine Logsdon	l rsf 3	Manchester 12-10
Sep 15	Steve Williams	l pts 6	Glasgow 12-6-12
Nov 10	Simon Harris	l pts 6	Longford 12-6
1987			
Jan 27	Sean Daly	l rsf 2	Manchester 13-5
1988			
Jan 19	Jon McBean	w ko 3	Kings Heath 13-1 /CTD..

(John WILLIAMS ctd.)

Feb 17	Lennie Howard	l rsf 5	Bethnal Green 13-0-8
May 26	Gerry Storey	w pts 6	Bethnal Green 13-5
Oct 28	Magne Havnaa	l rtd 4*	Copenhagen
1989			
Oct 23	Denroy Bryan	drew 6	NSC 13-8-12
1990			
Feb 21	Joe Egan	l pts 6	Belfast 13-12-8
Mar 3	Luigi Gaudiano	l rsf 1	Pagani
Sep 24	Steve Yorath	w pts 6	AASC 13-5-8
Nov 26	Crawford Ashley	l rsf 1	NSC 13-4
1991			
inactive			
1992			
May 12	Gary Delaney	l pts 6	Crystal Palace 13-13
Sep 8	Scott Welch	l rsf 5	Norwich 14-0

Fights 19 Won 5 Lost 13 Drawn 1

John (J.T.) WILLIAMS

Super-featherweight
Cwmbran, born Pontylottyn 22 May 1970
Pontypool & Panteg ABC
1982, 1984, 1985 Welsh Schools champion   1986, 1987, 1988 Welsh Youth champion
1988 Wales (v Nor, w rsf 1 F Thorsen)
1988 European Junior Championships bantamweight prelim (l Ivanov, Bul)
1989 NABC Class C champion (w ko 1 T McPhee)
1989 Wales (v Sco, l M Deveney; w rsf 3 J Stewart)
1989 ABA featherweight finalist (w S Sparey, w rsf 1 K Sheehan, w M Smyth, l P Richardson)
1990 Commonwealth Games featherweight prelim (l H Ally, Tan)
1990 ABA featherweight finalist (w.o., w K Hodkinson, l B Carr)
1990 Wales (v Sco, w rsf 1 G Ferrie)

1991			
Jan 21	Kelton McKenzie	drew 6	Crystal Palace 9-4
Apr 10	Dave Buxton	w pts 8	Newport 9-2
May 28	Frankie Ventura	w pts 6	Cardiff 9-0-8
Jul 18	Billy Barton	w pts 6	Cardiff 9-2-8
1992			
Jan 22	Derek Amory	w pts 6	Cardiff 9-5
Mar 30	Steve Pollard	l pts 6	Eltham 9-6
Oct 7	Kevin McKillan	w pts 6	Barry 9-8-8
Nov 14	Peter Judson	drew 6	Cardiff 9-6-8

Fights 8 Won 5 Lost 1 Drawn 2

Leigh WILLIAMS

Bantamweight
Chelsea born 23 July 1967
Battersea ABC
1984 Junior ABA final (w dis R Wenton, l M Hermon)
1985 ABA flyweight final (w.o. l J Green, replaced Green, w J Pardoe, l P Clinton)
1986 London ABA flyweight final (w M Ward, l M Fairman)

1991			
Jun 30	Andrew Bloomer	w pts 6	Southwark 8-6-12
Sep 12	Tony Rahman	w pts 6	Battersea 8-7-8
Oct 17	Andrew Bloomer	w pts 6	Southwark 8-9-8
1992			
Feb 17	Alan Ley	l pts 6	AASC 8-8

Fights 4 Won 3 Lost 1

George WILSON

Welterweight
Camberwell born 7 April 1966

1992
Jun 18	Sean Cave	l pts 6	Peterborough 10-7
Jul 7	Erwin Edwards	l rsf 4	Bristol 10-3-8
Sep 7	Erwin Edwards	l rsf 3*	Southend 10-3-8

Fights 3 Lost 3

L.C.WILSON

Bantamweight
Rotherham born 8 July 1972

1992
Dec 10	Neil Armstrong	l pts 6	Glasgow 8-8

Fights 1 Lost 1

Stephen WILSON

Light-heavyweight
Wallyford born 30 March 1971
Haddington ABC
1988 Scotland (v Ire, w D Galvin)
1989 Scottish ABA middle champ (w D Crawford, w rsf 2 C Black, w M McAllister, w J McCluskey, wthdrw)
1989 European Championships middleweight (w A Bredahl, Nor; l rsf 2 D Drumov, Bul)
1989 World Junior Championships middleweight silver medal (w rsf 2 J Matenstein, WG; w A Brito, Ven; l rsf 1 R Garbey, Cub)
1989 Scotland (v Wal, w S Thomas; v EG, w M Olesch)
1990 ABA middleweight champion (w rsf 2 K McCosh, w M McAllister, w S Johnson, w D Griffiths)
1990 Commonwealth Games (w H Shah, Pk; l rsf 2 C Johnson, Can)
1990 Scotland (v Eng, w E Noi; v US, l F Vassar)
1991 Scottish ABA middleweight champion (w rsf 1 I Crichton, w.o., withdrew)
1991 Scotland (v Ire, w D Galvin; w rsf 2 C Cullen)
1991 European Championships middleweight (w L Sayed, Swe; l S Ottke, Ger)
1991 World Championships middleweight prelim (l J Crawford, Aus)
1992 Scottish ABA light-heavyweight champion (w W Cane, withdrew)
1992 Scotland (v Ire, w rsf 3 D Curran)
1992 Olympic Games, Barcelona light-heavyweight (w M Masoe, Sam; l R Zaulitschny, Rus)

1992
Nov 23	Lee Prudden	w pts 6	Glasgow 12-10-8

Fights 1 Won 1

Stuart WILSON

Light-middleweight
Rochdale, born Derby 11 April 1969

1992
Jun 4	Willie Yeardsley	l pts 6	Burnley 11-2

Fights 1 Lost 1

Tony WILSON

Light-heavyweight
Wolverhampton born 25 April 1961
Wolverhampton ABC

1977 Junior ABA final (l dis 3 I Painter)   1978 NABC champion (w rsf 2 S Roberts)
1980 Midlands ABA middleweight final (w L Bird, l ko 2 M Christie)
1981 South Midlands ABA light-heavyweight final (l rsf 1 J Moran)
1981 England (v USA, l B Heard; v Sco, w R Barker)
1982 Midlands ABA light-heavyweight champion (w J Moran, w rsf 3 R Smith, l R Xavier)
1982 England (v USA, w E Cruz; v Ire, w rsf 2 G Lawlor)
1983 England (v Sco, w ko G Brown; v USA, l J Williams; v WGer, w T Spurgin)
1983 ABA light-heavyweight champion (w J Moran, w dis 2 J Ashton, w rsf 1 C Lee, w rsf 1 R Xavier, w dis 1 D Simmonds, w rsf 1* H Affleck, w C Edwards)
1984 England (v Can, w rtd 1 K Johnson)
1984 ABA light-heavyweight champion (w J Moran, w rsf 1 R Smith, w ko 1 G Donaldson, w K McGreath, w D Angol, w A Blackstock, w C Edwards)
1984 Los Angeles Olympics light-heavyweight (w rsf 1 R Oviedo, Arg; l M Moussa, Alg)

1985
Feb 12	Blaine Logsdon	w rsf 4	Albert Hall 12-4-8
Feb 28	Winston Burnett	w rsf 5	Wolverhampton 12-9
Jun 5	Cordwell Hylton	w ko 5	Albert Hall 12-8-4
Nov 14	Alex Romeo	w rsf 2	Dudley 12-8

1986
Jan 20	Dave Owens	w rsf 2	NSC 12-7-4
Mar 4	Jonjo Greene	w pts 8	Wembley 12-8-4
May 20	Dennis Bailey	w rsf 6	Wembley 12-6-8
Dec 3	Simon Harris	w rtd 6*	Muswell Hill 12-8-8
Dec 16	Pat Strachan	w rsf 3	Alfreton 12-11-4

1987
Mar 24	Keith Bristol	w ko 1	Nottingham 12-6-4
May 5	Jesse Shelby	l rsf 2	Leeds 12-8
Nov 11	Louis Coleman	w rsf 3	Usk 12-5
Dec 14	Blaine Logsdon	w rsf 6*	Cardiff 12-5-8

(vacant British light-heavyweight title)

1988
May 10	Brian Schumacher	w rsf 6	Tottenham 12-6-8

(British light-heavyweight title)

Nov 29	Randy Smith	w pts 10	Manchester 12-7
Dec 14	Tony Harrison	w pts 8	Bethnal Green 12-6

1989
Jan 25	Brian Schumacher	w rsf 3	Bethnal Green 12-5-12

(British light-heavyweight title)

Mar 22	Tom Collins	l rsf 2	Reading 12-6-8

(British light-heavyweight title)

Sep 21	Steve McCarthy	w rtd 3*	Southampton 12-6

(eliminator, British light-heavyweight title)

Dec 21	Dave Lawrence	w rtd 6	Kings Heath 12-9-8

1990
Aug 30	Steve Harvey	w rtd 8*	Boise, Indiana
Oct 30	James Flowers	l pts 10	Chicago 12-6

1991
Oct 2	Glazz Campbell	l pts 8	Solihull 12-7
Nov 28	Cordwell Hylton	w pts 8	Wolverhampton 12-13
Dec 11	Noel Magee	l rsf 3	Dublin 12-9

1992
Mar 21	Fabrice Tiozzo	l pts 8	Saint Denis 12-10-8
May 23	Ginger Tshabalala	l rsf 3	Birmingham 12-9
Nov 18	Tony Booth	drew 8	Solihull 12-7-12

Fights 28 Won 20 Lost 7 Drawn 1

Vince WILSON

Lightweight
South Shields born 1 December 1960
Gateshead Victoria ABC

1986
May 8	Carl Gaynor	drew 6	Newcastle 9-0-8
Jun 2	John Bennie	l rsf 4	Glasgow 9-3-8
Oct 16	Carl Gaynor	l rsf 1	Newcastle 9-2

1987
Feb 5	Alvin Finch	l rsf 4	Newcastle 9-7

1988
inactive

1989
Feb 28	Geoff Ward	w ko 1	Middlesbrough
Sep 19	Mick Markie	l rsf 1	Northampton

1990-91
inactive

1992
Sep 10	Chip O'Neill	l rsf 1	Sunderland 9-2

Fights 7 Won 1 Lost 5 Drawn 1

Wayne WINDLE

Lightweight
Sheffield born 18 October 1968
Unity ABC

1988
Oct 25	Mick Mulcahy	l pts 6	Cottingham 9-8-8
Nov 17	Dave Pratt	l pts 6	Ilkeston 9-5

1989
Feb 2	Jeff Dobson	l rsf 6	Croydon 9-1-8
Apr 4	John Ritchie	drew 4	Sheffield
Oct 5	Des Gargano	l pts 6	Middleton 9-1
Oct 16	Des Gargano	w pts 6	Manchester 9-2
Nov 16	Noel Carroll	l pts 6	Manchester 9-3
Dec 4	Brendan Ryan	drew 6	Manchester 9-5

1990
Jan 29	Mike Close	w pts 6	Liverpool 9-10
Feb 5	Mike Close	w pts 6	Brierley Hill 9-8-8
Mar 12	Barry North	w pts 6	Hull
Mar 21	Neil Foran	l pts 6	Preston 9-8
May 29	Terry Collins	l pts 6	Bethnal Green
Jun 5	Muhammad Lovelock	w pts 6	Manchester 9-8
Sep 12	Brian Cullen	w rsf 1	Stafford 10-0-4
Sep 22	Bernard McComiskey	w pts 6	Albert Hall 9-10
Oct 8	Johnny Walker	drew 6	Leicester 9-8
Oct 22	Mick Mulcahy	w pts 4	Cleethorpes 10-2
Nov 14	Andy Robins	w pts 6	Sheffield 10-1-8
Nov 26	Michael Driscoll	l rsf 3*	Bethnal Green 10-0

1991
Jan 16	Karl Taylor	l pts 8	Stoke 9-12
Feb 6	Felix Kelly	l pts 6	Bethnal Green
Mar 12	Mark Antony	w ko 1	Mansfield 9-12
Apr 24	Steve Foran	l ko 3	Preston
Jun 13	Pete Roberts	w rsf 7	Hull 9-9
	(vacant Central lightweight title)		
Aug 15	Suwanee Anukun	l pts 6	Marbella
Sep 21	George Scott	l ko 2	Tottenham 10-2 /CTD..

(Wayne WINDLE ctd.)

Dec 10	Kevin Toomey	w pts 6	Sheffield 10-0
1992			
Mar 26	Kevin Toomey	l dis 8	Hull 9-9
	(Central lightweight title)		
Sep 3	Billy Schwer	l ko 1	Dunstable 9-11

Fights 30 Won 12 Lost 15 Drawn 3

Stephen WINSTANLEY
Super-featherweight
Chorley, born Blackburn 19 August 1965
Chorley ABC

1987			
Feb 26	Carl Gaynor	l rsf 2*	Hartlepool 9-4-8
Apr 6	Jimmy Lee	w pts 6	Leicester 9-4
Sep 28	Tony Foster	w pts 6	Bradford 9-5-8
Oct 5	Thomas McCarthy	w pts 6	Manchester 9-7
Nov 26	Paul Kennedy	l rsf 3*	Horwich 9-9
1988			
Feb 29	Neil Leggett	w pts 6	Bradford 9-5
Apr 17	Neil Leggett	drew 6	Peterborough 9-5
May 23	Steve Pike	l rsf 2*	Bradford 9-6
Sep 8	Peter Gabbitus	l pts 6	Doncaster 9-7
1989			
Feb 20	Dave Pratt	w pts 6	Bradford 9-6
Oct 2	Mark Geraghty	w pts 6	Bradford 9-4
Oct 30	Lester James	w pts 6	Birmingham 9-6
Nov 13	Frankie Foster	w pts 6	Bradford 9-3-8
1990			
Jan 24	Alan Levene	drew 6	Preston 9-6
1991			
Feb 25	David Thompson	l rtd 4*	Bradford 9-6
Apr 24	Stuart Rimmer	w pts 6	Preston 9-8
May 13	Carl Tilley	l rtd 4*	Middlesbrough 9-9
1992			
May 5	Alan Levene	l rsf 2	Preston 9-8

Fights 18 Won 9 Lost 7 Drawn 2

Steve WOOD
Bantamweight
Kirkcaldy, born Manchester 3 September 1967
Kirkcaldy ABC
1988 Scottish ABA featherweight semi-final (w rsf 2 L Lenzi, w J McLeod, l A Ewen)
1989 Scottish ABA featherweight quarter-final (w rsf 3 J Carroll, l I McGirr)

1989			
Sep 10	Kevin James	w rsf 4	Glasgow 8-13-8
Oct 2	Peter Judson	w pts 6	Bradford 8-10
Oct 23	James Milne	l ko 1	Glasgow 8-11-8
Dec 11	Peter Buckley	l pts 6	Bradford 9-0
1990			
Feb 16	Cristobal Pascal	l ko 1	Bilbao
Mar 20	Billy Proud	w pts 6	Hartlepool 8-9-4
Mar 28	Bradley Stone	l rsf 2	Bethnal Green 8-8-10
May 21	Tony Smith	w rsf 6	Bradford 8-9
Nov 27	Neil Parry	l pts 6	Glasgow 8-5-12

1991			
Jan 21	Neil Parry	w pts 8	Glasgow 8-7-12
Feb 28	Gary White	l pts 6	Bury 8-6-8
May 7	Tony Smith	w rtd 2	Glasgow 8-5-8
Jun 3	Neil Parry	l rsf 2	Glasgow 8-4-8
Oct 9	Kevin Jenkins	drew 8	Glasgow 8-3-8
Nov 14	Drew Docherty	l rsf 1	Edinburgh 8-4-2
1992			
Feb 28	Neil Parry	l pts 6	Irvine 8-5
Oct 19	Lyndon Kershaw	l pts 6	Glasgow 8-5-8
Nov 9	Adey Benton	l pts 6	Bradford 8-6

Fights 18 Won 6 Lost 11 Drawn 1

Richie WOODHALL

Middleweight
Telford, born Polesworth 19 April 1968
1981 National Schools semi-final (l S Foran)
1984 National Schools semi-final (l S Foran)
1986 Young England (v Hun, w Kolomfar; v EGer, won twice;)
1987 East German TSC multi-nations, Berlin (l E Richter, EGer, 4-1)
1987 England (v Cze, w rsf 1 P Rigo)
1988 England (v Sco, w rsf 3 J Brannan)
1988 Midlands ABA light-middleweight final (w G Osborne, w rsf 3 E Wilkinson, l N Brown)
1988 Seoul Pre-Olympic tournament, silver medal
1988 Canada Cup light-middleweight silver medal (l D Sherry)
1988 Olympic Games light-middleweight bronze medal (w D Williams, SLe; w A Silvera, Ang; w R Rivera, PRic; l R Jones, USA)
1989 Cologne multi-nations (w J Cmokrak, Aus; l M Gusnick, WG)
1989 Canada Cup bronze medal (l R Downey)
1989 European Select v Bulgaria (w A Stoyanov)
1989 England (v Pol, w J Dydak; v Ire, w rsf 3 W Walsh)
1989 World Amateur Championships light-middleweight (w J L Hernandez, Cub; l R Obreja, Rum)
1990 Commonwealth Games light-middleweight gold medal (w A Cadeau, Sey; w S Figota, WSam; w R Downey, Can)
1990 Acropolis Cup silver medal (w Kourtidis, Gre; w C Petru, Rum; w Sust, Cze; l Delibas, Hol)

1990			
Oct 18	Kevin Hayde	w rsf 3	Birmingham 11-3
Nov 30	Robert Harron	w rsf 2*	Birmingham 11-3-4
1991			
Jan 16	Chris Haydon	w rsf 3	Albert Hall 11-1-12
Feb 21	Seamus Casey	w rsf 3	Walsall 11-4-8
May 30	Marty Duke	w rsf 4*	Birmingham 11-1
Aug 29	Nigel Moore	w rsf 1	Telford 11-1-4
Oct 31	Colin Pitters	w pts 8	Telford 11-2
1992			
Feb 4	Graham Burton	w rsf 2	Alfreton 11-4-8
Mar 26	Vito Gaudiosi	w ko 1	Telford 11-4-12
	(vacant Commonwealth middleweight title)		
Oct 1	John Ashton	w pts 12	Telford 11-4-12
	(Commonwealth middleweight title)		
Dec 4	Horace Fleary	w pts 8	Telford 11-6

Fights 11 Won 11

Richard WOOLGAR

Lightweight
Northampton, born Newport Pagnell 29 October 1967
Northampton ABC, Vauxhall Motors ABC, Hitchin Youth ABC
Southpaw
1983 Junior ABA champion (w R Woodhall, w rsf 2 D James, w M Moran)
1984 National Schools champion (w M Moran)
1986 Midlands ABA lightweight champion (w R Joyce, w rsf 3 A Carolan, l J Jacobs [eng sf])
1987 Midlands ABA lightweight final (w S Turley, w A Collier, withdrew)
1988 Home Counties ABA lightweight final (w J Doran, l B Schwer)
1989 Home Counties ABA light-welterweight champion (w rsf 1 A Saunders, w C Chase, l T Turner)
1990 Home Counties ABA light-welterweight semi-final (w L Tonks, l S Connolly)

1990
Oct 24	Andrew Robinson	w rsf 3	Dudley 9-7
Dec 12	Mark Antony	w rsf 5	Basildon 9-11

1991
Mar 19	Chris Saunders	l rsf 3*	Leicester 9-11
Nov 5	Kelton McKenzie	l rsf 5	Leicester 9-4-8
Dec 10	Kevin Lowe	w pts 6	Sheffield 9-3-8

1992
Jan 21	Lee Fox	w pts 6	Norwich 9-6
Apr 28	Karl Taylor	l pts 6	Wolverhampton 9-9
Oct 27	Joe Fannin	w pts 6	Leicester 9-7

Fights 8 Won 5 Lost 3

Jim WOOLLEY

Super-middleweight
Camden Town, born Epping 29 August 1964

1990
Sep 24	John Kaighin	w pts 6	Lewisham 12-0-8
Oct 15	John Smith	w rsf 6	Lewisham 12-8-8
Nov 26	Mark Spencer	w rsf 2	Lewisham 12-2-8

1991
Jun 4	Mark Spencer	w rsf 1	Bethnal Green 12-3
Jul 3	Lee Prudden	l pts 6	Brentwood 12-3
Sep 21	Lee Prudden	l pts 6	Tottenham 12-5

1992
Feb 19	Paul Murray	l ko 4	Muswell Hill 12-2

Fights 7 Won 4 Lost 3

Derek WORMALD

Light-middleweight
Rochdale born 24 May 1965
Southpaw
Fox ABC
1981 NABC Class A champion (w S Griffith)

1986
Apr 28	Dave Binsteed	w rsf 2	Liverpool 10-12
May 20	Taffy Morris	w pts 6	Huddersfield 11-1-8
Jun 16	Claude Rosse	w pts 6	Manchester 10-12
Sep 23	Seamus Casey	w pts 8	Batley 11-1
Oct 16	Nigel Moore	drew 6	Wimbledon 11-0-12
Nov 11	David Scere	w rsf 3*	Batley 11-0
Nov 25	Cliff Domville	w rsf 4	Manchester 11-2

Dec 8	Martin McGough	w rtd 4*	Edgbaston 11-0
1987			
Feb 10	Manny Romain	w ko 3	Batley 10-11
Apr 7	Tony Brown	w rsf 6	Batley 10-11-8
Apr 28	Johnny Stone	w rsf 1	Manchester 11-2
Sep 15	Sammy Sampson	w pts 10	Batley 10-13
	(final eliminator, Central light-middleweight title)		
1988			
Feb 9	Richard Wagstaff	w rsf 6	Bradford 11-1
Feb 23	Judas Clottey	w pts 10	Oldham 10-13
Apr 12	John Ashton	w rsf 4*	Oldham 11-0
	(eliminator, British light-middleweight title)		
1989			
Oct 11	Gary Stretch	l rsf 1	Millwall 10-13
	(British light-middleweight title)		
1990-91 inactive			
1992			
Sep 24	Mark Jay	w rsf 5	Manchester 11-2

Fights 17 Won 15 Lost 1 Drawn 1

Adrian WRIGHT

Light-heavyweight
Wolverhampton born 8 November 1967
Wolverhampton ABC
1986 Staffordshire ABA champion
1987 Staffordshire ABA middleweight champion (w M Pugh, w S Aquilina, withdrew)
1988 South Midlands ABA middleweight final (w P Walters, l P Busby)
1989 South Midlands ABA middleweight final (w rsf 2 P Donnelly, w A Flute, w G Lewis, l P Busby)
1990 Midlands ABA light-heavyweight champion (w J Cooke, w rsf 1 K Morton, l G Donaldson)

1990			
Sep 5	Roger Wilson	w pts 4	Stoke 12-0
Sep 18	Pele Lawrence	w ko 2	Stoke 12-0
Nov 12	Stinger Mason	w rsf 4	Stratford 12-0
Dec 12	Frank Eubanks	l pts 6	Stoke 12-0
1991			
Feb 6	Ali Forbes	l pts 6	Battersea 12-0
Mar 13	Chris Walker	l pts 4	Stoke 11-10
Apr 11	Robert Peel	w rsf 6	Willenhall 11-12
Aug 29	John Kaighin	l pts 6	Telford 12-2-12
Dec 2	Justin Clements	l pts 6	Birmingham 11-13
Dec 11	Darron Griffiths	l pts 6	Stoke 11-9
1992			
Apr 29	Andy Manning	l pts 6	Stoke 11-9
Sep 9	Kevin Morton	l pts 6	Stoke 11-13-8
Oct 29	Eddie Knight	w pts 6	Bayswater 12-6
Dec 3	Mark Baker	l rsf 1	Catford 12-5-4

Fights 14 Won 5 Lost 9

Andrew "Sugarboy" WRIGHT

Lightweight
Dudley born 13 December 1969
Dudley ABC
1984 National Schools champion
1985 Junior ABA champion
1987 Young England (v WGer, w rsf D Schillinger; v Ire, l rsf 3 E Bolger; v EGer, l rsf 3 L Kischel)

1991
Dec 4	Jamie Morris	w pts 6	Stoke 9-9

1992
Jan 22	Kevin McKillan	l pts 6	Solihull 9-11

Fights 2 Won 1 Lost 1

Andy WRIGHT

Super-middleweight
Tooting, born Aldershot 20 December 1963
Tooting ABC
1984 SW London ABA middleweight final (l rsf 3 D Howe)

1986
Mar 20	Seamus Casey	w rsf 4	Wimbledon 11-7
Apr 15	J.J. Smith	l pts 6	Wimbledon 11-9-12
May 28	Seamus Casey	w pts 6	Catford 11-6-8
Sep 4	Kevin Roper	w ko 2	Wimbledon 11-9
Nov 20	Winston Burnett	w pts 8	Wimbledon 12-0

1987
Feb 24	Nicky Vardy	w rsf 1	Battersea 11-10-8
Jun 3	Simon Collins	drew 6	Southwark 11-10-8
Sep 14	Andy Till	l rsf 2	Crystal Palace 11-5
Dec 1	Alex Romeo	w rsf 2	Southend 11-9
Dec 14	Paul McCarthy	w ko 3	NSC 11-9

1988
Feb 3	Steve McCarthy	l rsf 4	Wembley GH 11-12
Mar 30	Errol Christie	l ko 2	Bethnal Green 11-13-8
Nov 15	Darren Hobson	l rsf 3	Hull 12-0

1989
Mar 8	Ray Close	l rsf 4	Belfast 11-11

1990
inactive

1991
Mar 20	Paul McCarthy (Southern super-middleweight title)	w ko 5	Battersea 11-13-8
Oct 22	John Kaighin	drew 6	Battersea 12-4

1992
Feb 25	John Kaighin	w pts 6	Crystal Palace 12-4

Fights 17 Won 9 Lost 6 Drawn 2

Carl WRIGHT

Light-welterweight
Liverpool born 19 February 1969
Salisbury ABC
1984 Junior ABA final (w J Wellings, l T Swift)
1985 National Schools champion
1985 NABC Class A champion
1986 NABC Class B champion
1986 Young England (v EGer, w O Trenn, l O Trenn)
1987 Young England (v Sco, w rsf 1 A Grainger; v EGer, l O Trenn)
1987 England (v Sco, l M Gowans)
1987 West Lancs & Cheshire ABA lightweight semi-final (l D Oakes)
1987 World Junior Championships (l A Szasz, Hun)
1988 North-West ABA lightweight final (w dis 2 A Mock, l rsf 1 N Boyd)
1989 North-West ABA light-welterweight final (w A Mock, w D Thomas, w J Joynson, l D McCarrick)

1989
Oct 13	Mick Mulcahy	w pts 6	Preston
Oct 31	Mick Mulcahy	w pts 6	Manchester 10-4

1990
Jan 24	Mike Morrison	w pts 6	Preston 10-2
Dec 19	Julian Eavis	w pts 6	Preston 10-5-8

1991
inactive

1992
Mar 31	Ricky Sackfield	w rsf 1	Stockport 10-1-8
May 14	Brendan Ryan	w pts 4	Liverpool 10-1
Jun 12	Dean Bramhald	w pts 6	Liverpool 10-1-8
Sep 15	Wayne Panayiotiou	w rsf 2	Liverpool 10-5-4
Sep 25	Mick Mulcahy	w pts 8	Liverpool 10-4
Nov 12	James Lawlor	w rsf 3	Liverpool 10-0-12

Fights 10 Won 10

Paul WRIGHT

Super-middleweight
Liverpool born 24 February 1966
Salisbury ABC & Rotunda ABC
1984 Young England (v EGer, l W Schmidt; l H Rettig)
1987 Northern ABA middleweight final (w w rsf 2 P Harper, w G Jenkins, w M Khan, l J Carr)
1988 West Lancs & Cheshire ABA middleweight champion (w W Chisnall, w G Drew, l dis 3 E Noi)
1989 ABA light-heavy semi-final (w G Jenkins, w rsf 2 B Jones, w M Coore, w M Gale, w G Delaney, l N Piper)

1989
Oct 13	Andy Balfe	w rsf 1	Preston 12-1
Oct 31	John Tipping	w rsf 1	Manchester 12-0-8
Dec 20	Nigel Rafferty	drew 6	Liverpool 12-0

1990-91
inactive

1992
Apr 13	Shaun McCrory	w pts 8	Manchester 12-1-12
May 14	Chris Walker	w pts 6	Liverpool 11-13
Sep 15	John Kaighin	w dis 5	Liverpool 12-1
Oct 23	Jason McNeill	w rsf 1	Liverpool 12-2
Nov 28	Russell Washer	w pts 8	Manchester 11-12

Fights 8 Won 7 Drawn 1

Robert WRIGHT

Welterweight
Dudley born 25 August 1966
Dudley ABC
1985 NABC Class C final (l D Adams)
1988 Birmingham ABA welterweight final (w H Clarke, l M Elliot)

1988
May 16	Steve Hogg	w pts 6	Wolverhampton 10-2
Jun 14	Joff Pugh	w rsf 5	Dudley
Sep 22	Martin Campbell	w rsf 5	Wolverhampton 10-1-8

1989
Apr 17	Steve Hogg	w pts 6	Wolverhampton
Jun 5	Dean Dickinson	w rsf 4	Birmingham 10-4
Oct 10	Julian Eavis	w pts 8	Wolverhampton 10-6
Dec 11	Mike Russell	w ko 1	Birmingham 10-7-8

1990
Mar 20	Mickey Hughes	l rsf 7	Norwich 10-9-1
Nov 16	Tony Britland	w rsf 3	Telford 10-4

1991
Oct 2	Chris Mulcahy	w rsf 1	Solihull 10-8
Nov 20	Tony Gibbs	w rtd 2	Solihull 10-9
Nov 26	Darren Dyer	l rsf 3	Bethnal Green 10-9

1992
Jan 15	Julian Eavis	w pts 8	Stoke 10-10
Mar 10	Errol McDonald	w ko 3	Bury 10-8
Mar 17	Donovan Boucher (Commonwealth welterweight title)	l rsf 11	Mayfair 10-5-12
Jul 9	Gary Jacobs (British welterweight title)	l rsf 6	Glasgow 10-6-13

Fights 16 Won 12 Lost 4

Stefan WRIGHT

Light-heavyweight
Peterborough born 23 May 1970
Aldermans ABC
1989 Eastern ABA light-heavyweight semi-final (l K Cattermole)
1990 Eastern ABA light-heavyweight final (w C Black, w K Goodyear, l rsf 3 N Anderson)

1990
Oct 22	John Kaighin	w pts 6	Peterborough 11-0
Dec 14	Seamus Casey	w pts 6	Peterborough 11-3-8

1991
Jan 24	Andre Wharton	l rsf 5	Brierley Hill 11-2-12
Nov 7	Gary Brooker	w pts 6	Peterborough 11-9-8

1992
Apr 28	Jerry Mortimer	w rsf 4	Corby 11-10
Jun 18	Chris Richards	w pts 6	Peterborough 11-9-8
Dec 10	Paul McCarthy	w pts 6	Corby 12-6

Fights 7 Won 6 Lost 1

Vic WRIGHT

Cruiserweight
Newport Pagnell, born London 8 July 1966

1991
Nov 12	Randy B. Powell	w rtd 4	Milton Keynes 13-6

1992
Feb 12	Mark Paine	l rsf 1	Watford 13-0

Fights 2 Won 1 Lost 1

Willie YEARDSLEY

Light-middleweight
Isle of Man born 1 May 1962
Southpaw

1991
Feb 25	Pat Durkin	w pts 6	Bradford 11-2
Apr 3	Chris Mulcahy	w pts 6	Manchester
Apr 30	Ricky Sackfield	l pts 4	Stockport 10-9
Jun 13	Phil Epton	l rsf 3*	Hull 11-1
Sep 9	Allan Grainger	l pts 6	Glasgow 10-12-8
Oct 7	Dave Binsteed	w pts 6	Liverpool 11-2
Nov 25	Mickey Duncan	l pts 6	Liverpool 11-2

1992
Jan 20	Benji Joseph	w pts 6	Bradford 10-11
Feb 6	Benji Joseph	w rsf 4*	Peterborough 10-12
Feb 24	Matt Mowatt	w pts 6	Bradford 11-1
Mar 9	Dave Maj	l rsf 1	Manchester 10-10-4
Jun 4	Stuart Wilson	w pts 6	Burnley 11-1
Nov 26	Trevor Meikle	l pts 6	Hull 10-10

Fights 13 Won 7 Lost 6

Tim YEATES

Bantamweight
Southend, born Worcester 19 August 1966
Rochford ABC
1985 Eastern ABA featherweight champion (w G De Roux, l P Cooper)
1988 Eastern ABA featherweight champion (w.o., w dis 3 E Small, withdrew)

1990
Oct 3	Ceri Farrell	w pts 6	Basildon 8-8
Oct 17	Kevin Jenkins	w pts 6	Bethnal Green
Dec 12	Ceri Farrell	w pts 6	Basildon 8-8

1991
Jan 23	Eric George	w rsf 6*	Brentwood 8-10
May 1	Kelton McKenzie	l pts 6	Bethnal Green 9-0

1992
May 11	Neil Parry	w pts 6	Piccadilly 8-10-8

Fights 6 Won 5 Lost 1

Steve YORATH

Cruiserweight
Cardiff born 8 August 1965
St Josephs ABC

1985
Nov 21	Dai Davies	l rsf 5	Blaenavon

1986
Mar 13	John Ashton	l ko 3	Alfreton

1987-89
inactive

1990
May 8	Rob Albon	l pts 6	Brentford 13-8
Jul 6	Phil Soundy	l ko 3	Brentwood 13-5
Sep 17	Chris Coughlan	w pts 6	Cardiff 13-9
Sep 24	John Williams	l pts 6	AASC 13-8
Oct 3	Phil Soundy	l pts 6	Basildon 13-8
Oct 19	Niels H. Madsen	l pts 6	Skive /CTD..

1991
Apr 15	Tony Colclough	w pts 6	Birmingham 14-0
Apr 25	Phil Soundy	w pts 6	Basildon 14-0-8
May 28	Roger McKenzie	w pts 6	Cardiff 13-9
Jun 27	Denzil Browne	l pts 6	Leeds 13-9

1992
Jan 21	Graham Arnold	w pts 6	Norwich 14-7
Mar 31	Graham Arnold	l pts 6	Norwich 13-13-8
May 18	Marco Van Spaendonck	l pts 4	Valkenswaard 14-1-4
Sep 23	Denzil Browne	l pts 8	Leeds 13-6-8
Nov 26	Terry Dunstan	l pts 8	Mayfair 13-5

Fights 17 Won 5 Lost 12

Ty ZUBAIR

Lightweight
Bury, born Pakistan 22 July 1969
Real name: Tahir Zubair
Lancs Constabulary ABC

1986
Nov 24	Mark Millington	l pts 4	Marton 9-0-8

1987
Apr 23	J.B.Chadwick	l rsf 4	Newcastle 8-12

1988-90 inactive

1991
Nov 18	Jamie Davidson	l pts 6	Manchester 9-12

1992
Jun 1	Paul Hughes	l pts 6	Manchester 9-11

Fights 4 Lost 4

BOXING NEWS

The Grandaddy of them all -
the world's oldest fight newspaper -
continuous weekly publication
since September 1909 -
welcomes the newest addition
to the boxing family,
and wishes

British Professional Boxers' Records

an equally long and successful life.

....

Boxing News - the greatest fight publication
in the world.

£1.00 every Friday.

Place a regular order with your newsagent
or
write or fax for current subscription details to

**30-34 Langham Street
London W1N 5LB**

Fax no: 071 436 8268.

ALPHABETICAL INDEX OF BOXERS

Ojay ABRAHAMS	5
Kevin ADAMSON	5
Tanveer AHMED	5
Henry AKINWANDE	6
Korso ALEAIN	6
Raziq ALI	7
Michael ALLDIS	7
Dean ALLEN	7
Mark ALLEN	7
Jimmy ALSTON	8
Spencer ALTON	8
Trevor AMBROSE	9
Dean AMORY	9
Derek AMORY	9
Francis AMPOFO	10
Colin ANDERSON	11
David ANDERSON	11
Shaun ANDERSON	12
Alfie ANDREWS	12
Dave ANDREWS	12
Dennis ANDRIES	13
Derek ANGOL	15
Joel ANI	16
Mark ANTONY	16
Nick APPIAH	17
Wayne APPLETON	17
Lee ARCHER	17
John ARMOUR	17
Henry ARMSTRONG	18
Michael ARMSTRONG	19
Neil ARMSTRONG	19
Sean ARMSTRONG	20
Graham ARNOLD	20
Crawford ASHLEY	20
John ASHTON	21
Abel ASINAMALI	22
Chris ASTON	22
Richard ATKINSON	23
Michael AYERS	23
Mossa AZWARD	23
Ian BAILLIE	25
Mark BAKER	25
Sean BAKER	25
Phil BALL	25
Tony BANKS	26
Nicky BARDLE	26
Jason BARKER	26
Newton BARNETT	27
Pat BARRETT	28
Gary BARRON	29
Karl BARWISE	30
Mark BATES	31
Jason BEARD	31
Ricky BEARD	31
Willie BEATTIE	32
Chris BECK	32
John BECKLES	32
Tony BEHAN	33
Leo BEIRNE	34
Nigel BENN	34
Barry BENNETT	35
Mervyn BENNETT	36
Adey BENTON	36
Ensley BINGHAM	37
Dave BINSTEED	37
Gordon BLAIR	38
Chris BLAKE	38
Everton BLAKE	39
Andrew BLOOMER	40
Gareth BODDY	40
Tony BOOTH	41
Tony BORG	41
John BOSCO	42
Mark BOWEN	43
Mark BOWERS	43
Warren BOWERS	43
Steve BOYLE	44
Robert BRADDOCK	45
Nigel BRADLEY	45
Peter BRADLEY	46
Dean BRAMHALD	47
Jason BRATTLEY	49
Steve BRICKNELL	50
Mark BROOME	50
Dave BROSNAN	50
Neville BROWN	51
Denzil BROWNE	51
Frank BRUNO	52
Del BRYAN	53
Denroy BRYAN	54
Wayne BUCK	55
Peter BUCKLEY	55
J.A.BUGNER	56
Ian BULLOCH	57
Nigel BURDER	57
Paul BURKE	58
Winston BURNETT	58
Gary BURRELL	61
Graham BURTON	61
Paul BURTON	62
Riki BURTON	62
Rocky BURTON	63
Paul BUSBY	64
Rick BUSHELL	65
Blue BUTTERWORTH	66
Michael BYRNE	66
Sean BYRNE	66
Damien CAESAR	69
Geoff CALDER	69
Doug CALDERWOOD	70
Mike CALDERWOOD	70
Albert CALL	71
Dave CAMPBELL	71
Glazz CAMPBELL	71
Glenn CAMPBELL	72
James CAMPBELL	73
Razza CAMPBELL	73
Micky CANTWELL	73
George CARMEN	74
Ian CARMICHAEL	75
Vaughan CARNEGIE	75
Cornelius CARR	75
Dean CARR	76
Noel CARROLL	76
Ronnie CARROLL	77
Richard CARTER	78
Seamus CASEY	78
Fidel CASTRO	81
Sean CAVE	81
Ian CHANTLER	82
Gary CHARLTON	83
Paul CHARTERS	84
Carlos CHASE	85
Zak CHELLI	85
Mark CHICOCKI	85
Carlos CHRISTIE	86
Floyd CHURCHILL	86
Cliff CHURCHWARD	86
Jimmy CLARK	87
Howard CLARKE	88

Index of Boxers 2/

Chris CLARKSON	 88
Kesem CLAYTON	 89
Justin CLEMENTS	 90
Pat CLINTON	 90
Ray CLOSE	 91
Judas CLOTTEY	 92
Michael CLYNCH	 93
Shaun COGAN	 93
Carlo COLARUSSO	 94
Tony COLCLOUGH	 94
Brian COLEMAN	 95
Eddie COLLINS	 95
Simon COLLINS	 96
Steve COLLINS	 97
Tom COLLINS	 98
Tony COLLINS	 99
Danny CONNELLY	... 100
Eddie COOK	... 101
James COOK	... 101
John J. COOKE	... 102
Maurice CORE	... 103
John CORCORAN	... 103
Chris COUGHLAN	... 104
Lee CROCKER	... 104
Con CRONIN	... 104
Carl CROOK	... 105
Phil CULLEN	... 106
Shaun CUMMINS	... 106
Derrick DANIEL	... 109
Hugh DAVEY	... 109
Jamie DAVIDSON	... 109
John DAVIES	... 110
John DAVISON	... 110
Russell DAVISON	... 111
Mark DAWSON	... 112
Gary DELANEY	... 112
Patrick DELARGY	... 113
Carlos DEMONIKOS	... 113
Damien DENNY	... 113
Craig DERMODY	... 114
Mike DEVENEY	... 115
Eunan DEVENNEY	... 115
Norman DHALIE	... 115
Harry DHAMI	... 116
Michael DICK	... 116
Clive DIXON	... 116
Terry DIXON	... 116
Alex DOCHERTY	... 117
Drew DOCHERTY	... 117
Wilson DOCHERTY	... 118
John DOHERTY	... 118
Paul DONAGHEY	... 119
Darrit DOUGLAS	... 120
Barry DOWNES	... 120
Scott DOYLE	... 120
Tony DOYLE	... 120
Michael DRISCOLL	... 121
Tim DRISCOLL	... 122
James DRUMMOND	... 123
John DUCKWORTH	... 123
Terry DUFFUS	... 123
Marty DUKE	... 124
Marcus DUNCAN	... 125
Mickey DUNCAN	... 125
Stuart DUNN	... 126
Terry DUNSTAN	... 126
Darren DYER	... 126
Tyrone EASTMOND	... 129
Julian EAVIS	... 129
Bobbi Joe EDWARDS	... 130
Erwin EDWARDS	... 131
Renny EDWARDS	... 131
Steve EDWARDS	... 132
Greg EGBUNIWE	... 132
Tony EKUBIA	... 132
Mark ELLIOT	... 133
Barry ELLIS	... 134
Wayne ELLIS	... 135
Darren ELSDON	... 135
Phil EPTON	... 136
Roland ERICSSON	... 136
Tenko ERNIE	... 137
Harry ESCOTT	... 137
Crisanto ESPANA	... 138
Chris EUBANK	... 139
Frank EUBANKS	... 140
Simon EUBANKS	... 141
Tony FALCONE	... 143
Serg FAME	... 143
Joe FANNIN	... 144
Ceri FARRELL	... 144
Lee FARRELL	... 145
Marco FATTORE	... 145
Vince FEENEY	... 145
Antonio FERNANDEZ	... 146
Rocky FERRARI	... 146
Lee FERRIE	... 147
Darren FIFIELD	... 147
Crain FISHER	... 147
Simon FISHER	... 148
Horace FLEARY	... 148
Andy FLUTE	... 149
Steve FORAN	... 149
Ali FORBES	... 150
Simon FORD	... 150
Hugh FORDE	... 151
John FOREMAN	... 152
Jason FORES	... 152
Paul FORREST	... 152
Frankie FOSTER	... 153
Steve FOSTER	... 154
Tony FOSTER	... 154
Lee FOX	... 155
Phil FOXON	... 156
Chris FRANCIS	... 156
Joe FRATER	... 156
Terry FRENCH	... 157
Andrew FURLONG	... 158
Hugh FURY	... 159
Carl GAFFNEY	... 161
Michael GALE	... 161
Patrick GALLAGHER	... 162
Paul GAMBLE	... 162
Steve GARBER	... 163
Des GARGANO	... 164
Al GARRETT	... 166
Dermot GASCOIGNE	... 166
Steve GEE	... 166
Lou GENT	... 167
Mark GERAGHTY	... 168
Tony GIBBS	... 169
Sugar GIBILIRU	... 170
Barry GLANISTER	... 171
G.G.GODDARD	... 171
Val GOLDING	... 172
Zak GOLDMAN	... 172
Steve GOODWIN	... 172
Alan GRAHAM	... 173
Herol GRAHAM	... 173
Johnny GRAHAM	... 175

Index of Boxers 3/

Name	Page	Name	Page
Allan GRAINGER	176	Graham JENNER	218
Derek GRAINGER	176	Andrew JERVIS	218
Frank GRANT	177	Chris JICKELLS	219
Marvin P. GRAY	177	James JIORA	219
John GREEN	179	Tracy JOCELYN	220
Wayne GREEN	179	Ian JOHN-LEWIS	220
Darron GRIFFITHS	180	David JOHNSON	221
Bobby GUYNAN	180	John O. JOHNSON	221
Neil HADDOCK	183	Julian JOHNSON	221
Mark HALE	183	Martin JOLLEY	222
Ross HALE	184	Barry JONES	222
Allan HALL	184	Griff JONES	222
Dave HALL	185	Matthew JONES	223
Micky HALL	185	Paul JONES	223
Simon HAMBLETT	186	Seth JONES	224
Naseem HAMED	186	Gareth JORDAN	224
Paul HANLON	186	Benji JOSEPH	224
Anthony HANNA	187	Dean JOSHAM	225
Dave HARDIE	187	Peter JUDSON	225
Fran HARDING	187	David JULES	226
Billy HARDY	188	John KAIGHIN	227
John HAREWOOD	189	Charlie KANE	227
Mark HARGREAVES	190	Barrie KELLEY	228
Carl HARNEY	190	Felix KELLY	228
Danny HARPER	190	Joe KELLY	229
Frank HARRINGTON	191	John B. KELLY	230
Peter HARRIS	191	Mark KELLY	230
Simon HARRIS	192	Paul KELLY	231
Humphrey HARRISON	193	Andy KENT	231
Craig HARTWELL	193	Lyndon KERSHAW	231
Paul HARVEY	194	Danny KETT	232
Adrian HAUGHTON	194	Eddie KING	232
Bozon HAULE	194	Paul KING	233
Floyd HAVARD	195	Stan KING	233
Steve HEARN	196	Nigel KITCHING	234
Darren HENDERSON	196	Eddie KNIGHT	234
Ian HENRY	197	Paul KNIGHTS	234
Marcel HERBERT	197	Dave LAKE	235
Brian HICKEY	198	Gavin LANE	235
Gary HICKMAN	198	David LARKIN	235
Herbie HIDE	198	Phil LASHLEY	236
Tim HILL	199	James LAWLOR	237
Dean HISCOX	199	Dave LAWRENCE	237
Gary HISCOX	200	Mark LEGG	238
Paul HITCH	200	Jason LEPRE	238
Mick HOBAN	200	Micky LERWILL	239
Paul HODKINSON	201	Alan LEVENE	239
Andy HOLLIGAN	202	Steve LEVENE	240
Dean HOLLINGTON	202	Gil LEWIS	240
Mick HOLMES	203	Lennox LEWIS	241
Mark HOLT	203	Steve LEWSAM	242
Lloyd HONEYGHAN	204	Alan LEY	242
Ian HONEYWOOD	205	Earl LING	243
Donnie HOOD	206	Wayne LLEWELLYN	243
Carl HOOK	207	Edward LLOYD	243
Ron HOPLEY	207	Paul LLOYD	244
Steve HOWDEN	208	Robert LLOYD	244
Mickey HUGHES	208	Steve LOFTUS	245
Paul HUGHES	209	Gary LOGAN	245
Roger HUNTE	209	Eamonn LOUGHRAN	246
Cordwell HYLTON	209	Patrick LOUGHRAN	246
Vance IDIENS	211	Dave LOVELL	247
Alan INGLE	211	Ernie LOVERIDGE	247
Colin INNES	211	Kevin LOWE	248
John IRWIN	212	Nicky LUCAS	248
Cyril JACKSON	215	Kevin LUESHING	249
Gilbert JACKSON	215	Colin LYNCH	249
Gary JACOBS	215	Dean LYNCH	250
Mark JAY	217	Paul LYNCH	251
Kevin JENKINS	217	Chris LYONS	251

Index of Boxers 4/

Ricky MABBETT	... 253	Errol McDONALD	... 292
Kevin MABBUTT	... 253	Billy McDOUGALL	... 293
Bobby MACK	... 253	Allan McDOWALL	... 294
John MACKENZIE	... 253	James McGEE	... 294
Dave MADDEN	... 254	Ian McGIRR	... 294
Ossie MADDIX	... 254	Brian McGLOIN	... 295
Noel MAGEE	... 254	Steve McGOVERN	... 295
Terry MAGEE	... 255	Graham McGRATH	... 296
Pat MAHER	... 256	Dominic McGUIGAN	... 296
Dave MAJ	... 257	Davey McHALE	... 296
Mohammed MALIK	... 257	Darren McINULTY	... 297
Colin MANNERS	... 257	Alan McKAY	... 297
Nick MANNERS	... 258	Darren McKENNA	... 298
Andy MANNING	... 258	Duke McKENZIE	... 298
Gary MARSTON	... 258	Kelton McKENZIE	... 300
Chubby MARTIN	... 259	Kevin McKENZIE	... 300
Dave MARTIN	... 259	Roger McKENZIE	... 300
Dean MARTIN	... 260	Tony McKENZIE	... 301
Sean MARTIN	... 260	Kevin McKILLAN	... 302
Stinger MASON	... 260	Ian McLEOD	... 302
Tony MASSEY	... 260	Colin McMILLAN	... 303
Jason MATTHEWS	... 261	Con McMULLAN	... 304
Miguel MATTHEWS	... 261	Jason McNEILL	... 304
Winston MAY	... 262	Steve McNESS	... 304
Trevor MEIKLE	... 263	George NAYLOR	... 305
Johnny MELFAH	... 264	Shea NEARY	... 305
Malcolm MELVIN	... 265	Johnny NELSON	... 305
Sean METHERELL	... 265	Kenny NEVERS	... 306
Kevin MIDDLETON	... 266	Ray NEWBY	... 306
Rocky MILTON	... 266	Shaun NORMAN	... 308
Alex MOFFAT	... 267	Ricky NORTH	... 308
Joey MOFFAT	... 267	Chris NURSE	... 308
Charlie MOORE	... 267	Dennis OAKES	... 311
Andy MORGAN	... 268	Marvin O'BRIAN	... 311
Karl MORLING	... 268	Richard O'BRIEN	... 311
Terry MORRILL	... 269	Mark O'CALLAGHAN	... 312
Chris MORRIS	... 269	John OGISTE	... 312
Darrren MORRIS	... 269	Richard OKUMU	... 313
Jamie MORRIS	... 270	Michael OLIVER	... 313
Jason MORRIS	... 271	Graham O'MALLEY	... 314
Mike MORRISON	... 271	Chip O'NEILL	... 314
Jerry MORTIMER	... 272	Sean O'PHOENIX	... 315
Kelvin MORTIMER	... 272	Gary OSBORNE	... 316
Kevin MORTON	... 273	Steve OSBORNE	... 316
Hamid MOULAY	... 273	Clay O'SHEA	... 317
Matt MOWATT	... 273	Dave OWENS	... 318
Dave MUHAMMED	... 274	Jimmy OWENS	... 319
Chris MULCAHY	... 274	John OXENHAM	... 320
Mick MULCAHY	... 275	Mark PAINE	... 321
Karl MUMFORD	... 276	Andreas PANAYI	... 321
Darren MURPHY	... 276	Del PANAYIOTIOU	... 321
Sean MURPHY	... 276	Wayne PANAYIOTIOU	... 322
Craig MURRAY	... 277	Neil PARRY	... 322
Michael MURRAY	... 278	Elvis PARSLEY	... 323
Paul MURRAY	... 278	Neil PATTERSON	... 323
Kris McADAM	... 283	Steve PATTON	... 324
Dave McAULEY	... 283	Bernard PAUL	... 324
Kid McAULEY	... 284	Quinton PAYNTER	... 324
Mark McBIANE	... 285	Glen PAYTON	... 325
Jamie McBRIDE	... 285	Andy PEACH	... 325
Kevin McBRIDE	... 286	Alan PEACOCK	... 326
Paul McCARTHY	... 286	Robert PEEL	... 326
Steve McCARTHY	... 287	Gary PEMBERTON	... 327
Tony McCARTHY	... 287	Jimmy PETERS	... 328
Joe McCLUSKEY	... 288	Joey PETERS	... 328
Robert McCRACKEN	... 288	Mike PHILLIPS	... 329
Spencer McCRACKEN	... 289	Dave PIERRE	... 329
Gary McCRORY	... 290	John PIERRE	... 330
Glenn McCRORY	... 290	Darren PILLING	... 330
Shaun McCRORY	... 291	Johnny PINNOCK	... 331

Index of Boxers 5/

Nicky PIPER	... 331		Danny SHINKWIN	... 368
Rob PITTERS	... 332		Ronnie SHINKWIN	... 369
Steve POLLARD	... 332		Shaun SHINKWIN	... 370
Danny PORTER	... 334		Tony SILKSTONE	... 370
Darren POWELL	... 335		Kevin SIMONS	... 371
Gipsy Johnny PRICE	... 335		Jasdeep SINGH	... 371
Kenley PRICE	... 335		Tiger SINGH	... 371
Ray PRICE	... 335		Colin SINNOTT	... 371
Lee PRUDDEN	... 336		Trevor SMALL	... 372
Chris PYATT	... 337		Carl SMALLWOOD	... 372
Danny QUACOE	... 338		Alan SMITH	... 372
Willie QUINN	... 338		Jacob SMITH	... 372
Dave RADFORD	... 339		John SMITH	... 373
Nigel RAFFERTY	... 339		Martin SMITH	... 374
Gary RAILTON	... 340		Neil SMITH	... 375
Kenny RAINFORD	... 340		Paul SMITH	... 375
David RAMSDEN	... 340		Scott SMITH	... 376
Calum RATTRAY	... 341		Sean SMITH	... 376
Mark REEFER	... 341		Terry SMITH	... 376
Emlyn REES	... 342		Tommy SMITH	... 376
Fred REEVES	... 342		Tony SMITH	... 377
Robbie REGAN	... 343		Michael SMYTH	... 378
Mick REID	... 343		Lee SOAR	... 378
Peter REID	... 344		Phil SOUNDY	... 378
Paddy REILLY	... 344		Kevin SPRATT	... 379
Jimmy REYNOLDS	... 345		Art STACEY	... 380
Glyn RHODES	... 345		Warren STEPHENS	... 380
Alan RICHARDS	... 346		Ronnie STEPHENSON	... 380
Chris RICHARDS	... 347		Alex STERLING	... 381
Michael RICHARDS	... 348		Rob STEVENSON	... 382
Warren RICHARDS	... 348		Rob STEWART	... 382
Wayne RIGBY	... 349		Steve STEWART	... 382
Robert RILEY	... 349		Bradley STONE	... 383
Darryl RITCHIE	... 349		Sam STOREY	... 383
Brian ROBB	... 350		Warren STOWE	... 384
Davey ROBB	... 351		Adrian STRACHAN	... 384
Carl ROBERTS	... 351		Chad STRONG	... 385
Dewi ROBERTS	... 352		Ian STRUDWICK	... 385
Pete ROBERTS	... 352		Richard SWALLOW	... 385
Mark ROBERTSON	... 352		Tony SWIFT	... 386
Andrew ROBINSON	... 353		Wally SWIFT	... 387
Billy ROBINSON	... 353		Cliff TAYLOR	... 389
Des ROBINSON	... 353		Karl TAYLOR	... 389
Jamie ROBINSON	... 354		Lee TAYLOR	... 389
Steve ROBINSON	... 354		Jonathan THAXTON	... 390
Tim ROBINSON	... 355		Maurice THOMAS	... 390
Martin ROSAMOND	... 355		Steve THOMAS	... 390
Vince ROSE	... 356		Tucker THOMAS	... 391
Jason ROWLAND	... 356		Carl THOMPSON	... 391
Roy ROWLAND	... 357		Dave THOMPSON	... 391
Marc ROWLEY	... 357		Kevin THOMPSON	... 392
Jess RUNDAN	... 358		Jimmy THORNTON	... 392
Mike RUSSELL	... 358		Barry THOROGOOD	... 393
Brendan RYAN	... 359		Mark TIBBS	... 394
Paul RYAN	... 360		Andy TILL	... 394
Ricky SACKFIELD	... 363		Peter TILL	... 395
Kenny SANDISON	... 363		Carl TILLEY	... 396
Chris SAUNDERS	... 363		Wayne TIMMINS	... 397
Lindon SCARLETT	... 364		Lee TONKS	... 397
Billy SCHWER	... 364		Nick TOOLEY	... 397
Bruce SCOTT	... 365		Kevin TOOMEY	... 398
Steve SCOTT	... 365		Tony TRIMBLE	... 398
Greg SCOTT-BRIGGS	... 365		Leo TURNER	... 398
Hussain SHAH	... 366		Johnny UPHILL	... 401
Kevin SHEERAN	... 366		Greg UPTON	... 401
Steve SHELLEY	... 366		Paul VACHE	... 403
Charles SHEPHERD	... 367		Rudi VALENTINO	... 403
Glyn SHEPHERD	... 367		Des VAUGHAN	... 404
Wayne SHEPHERD	... 367		Louis VEITCH	... 404
Shane SHERIDAN	... 368		Tony VELINOR	... 404

Index of Boxers 6/

Mark VERIKIOS	... 405
Jimmy VINCENT	... 405
Ian VOKES	... 406
Yusuf VORAJEE	... 406
Peter VOSPER	... 407
Nicky WADMAN	... 409
Chris WALKER	... 409
Danny WALKER	... 410
Steve WALKER	... 410
Steve WALTON	... 410
Russell WASHER	... 411
Graham WASSELL	... 411
Peter WAUDBY	... 412
Delroy WAUL	... 412
Ray WEBB	... 413
Paul WEIR	... 413
Scott WELCH	... 414
Tony WELLINGTON	... 414
Nigel WENTON	... 414
Richie WENTON	... 415
Paul WESLEY	... 416
John WESTGARTH	... 417
Andre WHARTON	... 418
Henry WHARTON	... 418
Gary WHITE	... 419
Jason WHITE	... 419
John WHITE	... 419
Robert WHITEHOUSE	... 419
Dave WHITTLE	... 420
Leigh WICKS	... 420
Alan WILLIAMS	... 421
B.F.WILLIAMS	... 421
Derek WILLIAMS	... 422
Everald WILLIAMS	... 423
Gary WILLIAMS	... 423
John WILLIAMS	... 423
John (J.T.) WILLIAMS	... 424
Leigh WILLIAMS	... 424
George WILSON	... 425
L.C.WILSON	... 425
Stephen WILSON	... 425
Stuart WILSON	... 425
Tony WILSON	... 426
Vince WILSON	... 427
Wayne WINDLE	... 427
Stephen WINSTANLEY	... 428
Steve WOOD	... 428
Richie WOODHALL	... 429
Richard WOOLGAR	... 430
Jim WOOLLEY	... 430
Derek WORMALD	... 430
Adrian WRIGHT	... 431
Andrew WRIGHT	... 432
Andy WRIGHT	... 432
Carl WRIGHT	... 433
Paul WRIGHT	... 433
Robert WRIGHT	... 434
Stefan WRIGHT	... 434
Vic WRIGHT	... 434
Willie YEARDSLEY	... 435
Tim YEATES	... 435
Steve YORATH	... 435
Ty ZUBAIR	... 436

frank warren productions

CENTURION HOUSE • BIRCHERLEY GREEN
HERTFORD • HERTS. SG14 1HP • ENGLAND

TELEPHONE: 0992 505550
FACSIMILE: 0992 505552

MATCHMAKER: ERNIE FOSSEY

WORKING IN ASSOCIATION WITH

EASTWOOD PROMOTIONS

EASTWOOD HOUSE
2 - 4 CHAPEL LANE • BELFAST 1
NORTHERN IRELAND

Watch out for these fighters

PAUL HODKINSON
CHRISANTO ESPANA
PAT BARRETT
COLIN MCMILLAN
NICKY PIPER
DAVE MCAULEY
CRAWFORD ASHLEY
DEREK WILLIAMS
SHAUN CUMMINS
SEAN MURPHY
NIGEL WENTON
RITCHIE WENTON
JAMIE ROBINSON
DEREK GRAINGER
PAUL RYAN
KEVIN SHEERAN
TONY COLLINS
DERMOT GASCOYNE
KEVIN MCBRIDE
BERNARDO CHEKA

On Frank Warren Promotions in 1993

INDEX TO ADVERTISERS

Advertiser	Page
Billy Aird Promotions	408
Anglo-Swedish Promotions	142
Boxing News	437
Boxing Update/Flash	399
Pat Brogan	24
Paddy Byrne	402
Champion Enterprises Ltd.	388
Champs	362
Champs Camp	309
Tommy Conroy	362
Pat Cowdell	213
Mickey Duff & National Promotions	128
Joe Frater Snr.	281
Gardiner & Hayde	281
Tommy Gilmour Jnr.	67
Johnny Griffin	362
Terry Lawless/National Promotions	160
London Weekend Television	252
Lonsdale International Sporting Club	181
Dennie Mancini	142
Martindale	399
Matchroom Boxing Ltd.	68
McMahon Promotions	361
Katherine Morrison	282
Penn Sports	310
Ringcraft	182
Gus Robinson Promotions	108
Sport Art	214
The Thomas A'Becket	400
Title Sports	402
Frank Warren Productions	444/5